D0065635

NOBEL
THE MAN AND HIS PRIZES

THE PORTRAIT OF NOBEL

BY PROFESSOR E. ÖSTERMAN

NOBEL
The Man & His Prizes

Third Edition

EDITED BY THE NOBEL FOUNDATION
and
W. Odelberg, Coordinating Editor

Individual sections written by

H. SCHÜCK—R. SOHLMAN—A. ÖSTERLING
—C.G. BERNHARD—A. WESTGREN
—M. SIEGBAHN and K. SIEGBAHN—
A. SCHOU—N. K. STÅHLE

American Elsevier
Publishing Company, Inc.

New York • London • Amsterdam

FIRST EDITION 1950 BY SOHLMANS FORLAG, STOCKHOLM, AND UNIVERSITY OF OKLAHOMA PRESS, NORMAN, OKLAHOMA

SECOND EDITION 1962

By ELSEVIER PUBLISHING COMPANY, Amsterdam

THIRD REVISED AND ENLARGED EDITION 1972

By AMERICAN ELSEVIER PUBLISHING COMPANY, INC., New York

International Standard Book Number 0-444-00117-4

Library of Congress Catalog Card Number 77-169840

Printed in the United States of America

CONTENTS

INTRODUCTION ix

ALFRED NOBEL'S WILL x

Henrik Schück
ALFRED NOBEL – A BIOGRAPHICAL SKETCH 1

Ragnar Sohlman
ALFRED NOBEL AND THE NOBEL FOUNDATION 15
Introduction 17
The closing years of Alfred Nobel's life 19
Personal impressions of Alfred Nobel 27
The settlement of Alfred Nobel's estate 37
The negotiations with the heirs and the prize-awarding institutions 49
The Nobel Foundation 68

Anders Österling
THE LITERARY PRIZE 73
Alfred Nobel and literature 75
The Swedish Academy and the Nobel Prize in Literature 80
The Literary Prize-winners 90

Göran Liljestrand
THE PRIZE IN PHYSIOLOGY OR MEDICINE 139
The background 141
How the Medical Prize-winners are selected 147
A statistical survey of the Nobel Prizes in Physiology or Medicine 151
The Nobel Prizes in wartime 155
The first award 159
Insect-borne infections – Insecticides 161
Microbiology – Immunology 166
Chemotherapy 181
Phototherapy – Fever treatment 186
Tumours 188
Classical genetics 191

Developmental mechanics 194
From classical genetics to Molecular Biology and the deciphering of the genetic code 197
Intermediary metabolism 208
Hormones 223
Vitamins 228
Culmination of classical Neuroanatomy and Neurophysiology 242
Autonomic nervous functions – Chemical transmittors 247
Transmission in nerve fibres and synaptic junctions 253
Neuropharmacology 259
Neurosurgery 261
Sensory Physiology 263
In retrospect 269
The Nobel Medical Institute – The special fund of the prize-jury 272
Conclusion 276

Arne Westgren
THE CHEMISTRY PRIZE 279
Introduction 281
The Chemistry Prizes during the first few years 285
Radioactivity and atomic chemistry 305
Chemical thermodynamics and its technical applications 324
Colloids, chromatography and surface chemistry 330
X-ray and electron interference by gases and vapours – Dipole moments – Valence forces 336
Chemical change 341
Inorganic chemistry 344
Microchemistry 346
Preparative organic chemistry 349
The constitution of organic compounds and biochemistry 353
Agricultural chemistry 383

Manne Siegbahn and Kai Siegbahn
THE PHYSICS PRIZE 387
The state of physics in 1901 389
The first award 393
Radioactivity 398
The electron, its charge and its mass 402
Effects of electric and magnetic fields on optical spectra – Relativity 406

Electrons from metals 411
Radio waves, solidstate electronics and quantum electronics 412
Magneto-hydrodynamics 419
Atomic theory applied to gases and liquids – Low temperatures and high pressures 420
The quantum nature of energy 427
The quantized atomic model 430
X-rays in atomic research 432
Physics and technology 441
Waves as quanta – Particles as waves 443
The new quantum theories 446
Magnetic quantum effects – Quantum electrodynamics 450
Cosmic radiation – Elementary particles 454
Nuclear reactions and nuclear structure 464
Experimental methods in nuclear physics 468
Magnetism 473
Conclusion 475

Arne Westgren
THE NOBEL INSTITUTE OF THE ACADEMY OF SCIENCES 477

August Schou
THE PEACE PRIZE 483
Introduction 485
Pioneer peace workers 490
The development of international law 507
Mediation and the policy of arbitration 514
The international idea during the First World War 519
The League of Nations and its leading men 523
Easing of international tension 1925–1930 535
The church and peace 547
Women and peace 551
Acts of aggression in the 1930's and resistance to them 555
The Second World War and after 569
In the service of the United Nations 574

Problems of disarmament 585
Struggle for human rights 589
Humanitarian activities 596

Nils K. Ståhle
ADMINISTRATION AND FINANCES OF THE NOBEL FOUNDATION 609

THE STATUTES OF THE NOBEL FOUNDATION 617

LIST OF THE NOBEL PRIZE WINNERS 638

INDEX 647

INTRODUCTION

In 1950 the Nobel Foundation could look back on fifty years of activity. The stock-taking resulted in a book 'Nobel, the Man and his Prizes', which appeared simultaneously both in Swedish and in English on Sohlmans Förlag, Stockholm [1950] and in an American edition on Oklahoma University Press [1951].

This book gave the history of the first fifty years of prize-giving written by prominent Swedish connaisseurs and of the prize-awarding activities of the five Nobel domains

PHYSICS – Professor Manne Siegbahn, Royal Academy of Sciences, Nobel Laureate in Physics 1924,

CHEMISTRY – Professor Arne Westgren, Royal Academy of Sciences,

PHYSIOLOGY OR MEDICINE – Professor Göran Liljestrand, Royal Caroline Medico-Chirurgical Institute,

LITERATURE – Doctor Anders Österling, Swedish Academy,

PEACE – August Schou, M.A., Norwegian Nobel Institute.

The story of the achievements which had been honoured with Nobel Prizes was at the same time to a very large degree a review of the remarkable progress made in the five Nobel domains.

In the book was also incorporated a short biography of Alfred Nobel by the late professor Henrik Schück, Swedish Academy, and once Chairman of the Board of Directors of the Nobel Foundation; further an account of the birth of the Foundation given by one of its principal architects the late Ragnar Sohlman, collaborator and friend of Alfred Nobel and later executor of his will; finally the Executive Director of the Foundation since 1948, Nils K. Ståhle, summarized its functions and activities.

In 1962 a revised edition was published by the Elsevier Publishing Company, Amsterdam. Now, a new issue is appearing at the American Elsevier Publishing Company, New York. The issue is brought up to date by the same authors with the exception that Professor Carl Gustaf Bernhard, Royal Caroline Medico-Chirurgical Institute, has revised the domain Physiology or Medicine. The domain Physics is a result of cooperation between Professor Manne Siegbahn and his son Professor Kai Siegbahn, University of Uppsala.

Stockholm in July 1971

ALFRED NOBEL'S WILL

The whole of my remaining realizable estate shall be dealt with in the following way:

The capital shall be invested by my executors in safe securities and shall constitute a fund, the interest on which shall be annually distributed in the form of prizes to those who, during the preceding year, shall have conferred the greatest benefit on mankind. The said interest shall be divided into five equal parts, which shall be apportioned as follows: one part to the person who shall have made the most important discovery or invention within the field of physics; one part to the person who shall have made the most important chemical discovery or improvement; one part to the person who shall have made the most important discovery within the domain of physiolcgy or medicine; one part to the person who shall have produced in the field of literature the most outstanding work of an idealistic tendency; and one part to the person who shall have done the most or the best work for fraternity among nations, for the abolition or reduction of standing armies and for the holding and promotion of peace congresses.

The prizes for physics and chemistry shall be awarded by the Swedish Academy of Sciences; that for physiological or medical works by the Caroline Institute in Stockholm; that for literature by the Academy in Stockholm; and that for champions of peace by a committee of five persons to be elected by the Norwegian Storting. It is my express wish that in awarding the prizes no consideration whatever shall be given to the nationality of the candidates, so that the most worthy shall receive the prize, whether he be a Scandinavian or not.

Paris, November 27, 1895 ALFRED BERNHARD NOBEL

Testament

Jag undertecknad Alfred Bernhard Nobel förklarar härmed efter moget betänkande min yttersta vilja i afseende å den egendom jag vid min död kan efterlemna vara följande:

Öfver hela min återstående realiserbara förmögenhet förfogas på följande sätt: Kapitalet, af utredningsmännen realiseradt till säkra värdepapper, skall utgöra en fond hvars ränta årligen utdelas som prisbelöning åt dem som under det förlupne året hafva gjort menskligheten den största nytta. Räntan delas i fem lika delar som tillfalla: en del den som inom fysikens område har gjort den vigtigaste upptäckt eller uppfinning; en del den som har gjort den vigtigaste kemiska upptäckt eller förbättring; en del den som har gjort den vigtigaste upptäckt inom fysiologiens eller medicinens domän; en del den som inom literaturen har producerat det utmärktaste i idealisk rigtning; och en del åt den som har verkat mest eller bäst för folkens förbrödrande och afskaffande eller minskning af stående armeer samt bildande och spridande af fredskongresser. Prisen för fysik och kemi utdelas af Svenska Vetenskapsakademien; för fysiologiska eller medicinska arbeten af Carolinska Institutet i Stockholm; för literatur af Akademien i Stockholm samt för fredsförfäktare af ett utskott af fem personer som väljas af Norska Stortinget. Det är min uttryckliga vilja att vid prisutdelningarne intet afseende fästes vid någon slags nationalitetstillhörighet sålunda att den värdigaste erhåller priset antingen han är Skandinav eller ej.

Detta testamente är hittils det enda gilltiga och upphäfver alla mina föregående testamentariska bestämmelser om sådane skulle förefinnas efter min död.

Slutligen anordnar jag såsom varande min uttryckliga önskan och vilja att efter min död pulsådrorna uppskäras och att sedan detta skett och tydliga dödstecken af kompetenta läkare intygats liket förbrännes i så kalladt crematorium.

Paris den 27 November 1895

Alfred Bernhard Nobel

ALFRED NOBEL

A BIOGRAPHICAL SKETCH

BY HENRIK SCHÜCK

ALFRED NOBEL

A BIOGRAPHICAL SKETCH

Probably few Swedish names are better known throughout the world than that of Alfred Nobel, and yet the general public knows very little about him. It recalls that he was a great inventor, but exactly of what, besides dynamite, remains vague; it also knows that he was a great prize donor. But of his personal character hardly anyone has much of a notion, and if certain people have visualized him in their minds, the picture is not, as a rule, flattering. At times, some have imagined him to have been an uneducated man, somewhat vain and fond of both publicity and personal attention. But this picture is just the opposite of the true one. The real Alfred Nobel was a retiring, considerate person who detested all forms of publicity, a highly educated man and a thorough-going idealist.

From the name one might conclude that his family was of foreign origin, descended perhaps from one of the many strangers who have come to Sweden to stay. Even Alfred Nobel's own father seems to have believed that the founder of the family was an English clergyman who, for some reason or other, had happened to settle in our country. That, however, is a complete mistake. The Nobels are descendants of Scanian farmers from the southern tip of Sweden, and the name, which was originally Nobelius, was assumed, in the usual seventeenth-century manner, by the first member of the family who was able to get a university education. The reason why he chose Nobelius was that he had been born in the parish of Nöbbelöv.

This Petrus Olavi Nobelius, who happened to attend the University of Uppsala, was especially gifted in music, and this talent brought him into touch with the great Olof Rudbeck, the intellectual leader of the university, who may also be regarded as the founder of musical life in Uppsala. After Nobelius had completed his studies and had become a judge in the province of Uppland, he asked for the hand of his patron's daughter, Vendela Rudbeck, and it is from this union that the family is descended. By one of their grandsons, who in his youth was in military service, the name was shortened to Nobel.

This origin has a certain significance, because the qualities of Olof Rudbeck recur, more or less, in his descendants – their interest in art and, particularly, the inventive ability which was so marked in our first natural scientist, whose multifarious scientific interests always had a practical aim. This Rudbeckian trait can be recognized with special clarity in Alfred Nobel and his brothers, as well as in their father, Immanuel Nobel.

The last-named was an unusual personality – a natural genius without any education to speak of. He had had hardly any formal schooling, knew no foreign languages, could barely write, and practically everything he knew he had learned by himself. But he was full of ideas and schemes, some of them quite fantastic, while others indicated an unusual degree of intelligence. When he was only fourteen he had to leave school and was sent to sea as a cabin-boy on a ship from Gävle, the port in northern Sweden where he was born in 1801. It was bound for the Mediterranean, and the trip lasted three years. After his return, he seems to have been apprenticed to a builder, at first to one in Gävle and then to another in Stockholm. During his free time in the latter city he attended, for a few hours each week, the only trade-schools then to be found in the capital, the School of Architecture of the Academy of Art, and the so-called Mechanical School. At the age of twenty-four or twenty-five he set up as an architect and builder himself. His ventures were quite ambitious, but he had bad luck – among other things, one building he had bought burned down – and in 1833 he had to go into bankruptcy.

After that he found it rather hard to make his way in Stockholm, and in 1837 he moved to Russia, hoping to make a new career in that country. At first he was successful beyond expectations. He was able to start a machineshop which he expanded rapidly, especially after the outbreak of the Crimean War. From the Russian Government he then received commissions to improve the defence of the Russian coast-line by means of submarine mines, to build steamboats and other things. But after the war was over the Russians went back on their promises to Nobel. His factory, which he had enlarged to meet the many expected orders, stayed idle, and once more he became bankrupt.

Depressed and disappointed, he returned to his native country. By this time he was already an old man, and to start all over again was not so easy as before. But his energy was still considerable, his wealth of ideas undiminished, and once more he was to make a contribution to technical industry. This time, however, he did it thanks to the aid he received from his son Alfred.

When the older Nobel left Sweden in 1837, his wife and three sons remained in Stockholm and did not move to St. Petersburg until 1842. All three sons became important men. The eldest, Robert, developed the great petroleum industry at Baku, the second, Ludvig, founded a world-famous arms factory in St. Petersburg, and also had charge of the finances of the Baku organization. The third son was Alfred, who was born on October 21, 1833.

Strangely enough, he never attended any school, with the exception that at the age of eight he was admitted to the first grade of the elementary school in Jacob's parish. But he remained there only one year; after that the family moved to St. Petersburg. There all three sons received instruction from a private tutor, and Alfred never attended any university. Nor did he ever obtain any degree, and, like his father, he may therefore be called a practically self-educated man, because the tutorial instruction, too, came to an end as early as 1850 when he was only sixteen.

It is, however, apparent that even at that age Alfred Nobel stood head and shoulders above his contemporaries of the same age, both as regards knowledge and intellectual maturity. He was then a scientifically trained chemist and a remarkable linguist who knew German, English and French, besides Swedish and Russian; he took a serious interest in literature, especially the English, and, in general, had the main lines of his personal philosophy of life clearly laid out. The letters he wrote at this time give the impression of a prematurely developed, unusually intelligent, but sickly, dreamy and introspective youth who preferred to be alone.

At that time his father's financial situation was good, and to improve his education further, Alfred Nobel was allowed to make a trip abroad, which lasted two years and included America. Most of the time he appears to have lived in Paris, where at some laboratory or other he continued his chemical studies. After his return, he was employed in his father's factory and there he remained until the bankruptcy in 1859. How he managed to support himself immediately after that is not clear, but enough is known to make it certain that as early as this he began to experiment with nitroglycerine, which Ascanio Sobrero, an Italian scientist, had discovered in 1847 and to which Professor Zinin of St. Petersburg had called his attention. The first explosion that Nobel managed to bring about took place in May or June, 1862, and in October of the following year he obtained in Sweden a patent on his invention of a percussion detonator, called the 'Nobel lighter'.

The reason why he made his first application in Sweden was that his father believed he had discovered a new and more powerful gunpowder and had asked Alfred to come home and help him to develop it further. He came but found the discovery worthless and then set up, instead, a small plant at Heleneborg near Stockholm, for the manufacture of nitroglycerine. Production had hardly begun, when, in September, 1864, the little factory blew up. Several lives were lost, and among the dead was Alfred Nobel's youngest brother Emil. This disaster crushed the aged father. A few weeks later he suffered a stroke and though he recovered somewhat, he never regained either his mental or his physical powers, and in 1872 he died.

During the gloomy period after the explosion, Alfred Nobel himself never lost his courage, and within a month he had organized a Swedish company for the manufacture of nitroglycerine of a less dangerous kind and immediately after that a Norwegian one; then he went abroad to get more patents on his discovery and to form stock companies for the production. The obstacles he had to overcome were enormous, but within a few years the manufacture of nitroglycerine had developed into a world industry. In addition to this organization work, which forced him to spend his time in constant travel – in France, England, and America – he continued his scientific experiments and then invented the new, improved explosive, dynamite, on which he obtained a patent in 1867. After that, one new discovery followed the other.

Having started with a pair of empty hands, Nobel thus became rapidly a very wealthy man. But he never gained happiness, and his experiences with other men were often disappointing. 'You refer', he wrote in a letter, 'to my many friends. Where are they? On the muddy bottom of lost illusions, or busy listening to the rattle of saved pennies? Believe me, numerous friends one gains only among dogs which one feeds with the flesh of others, or worms which one feeds with one's own. Grateful stomachs and grateful hearts are twins.' By nature he was a melancholic, a dreamer and something of a recluse. During protracted periods, his close associates relate, he would disappear, and no one knew where he was. That was when, to use his own words, the 'spirits of Niflheim' pursued him and he felt the need of being alone. 'I want to live', he wrote, 'among trees and bushes, silent friends who respect the state of my nerves, and I escape when I can from both large cities and deserts.' He was never a social success, though he had every quality required to be one: he was highly educated, was endowed, as his letters show, with genuine *esprit*, was naturally witty, and spoke German, English and French just as fluently as Swedish.

But even in Paris he had few acquaintances; the greater part of his time he spent in his laboratory, where he became so absorbed in his research work that he often forgot his meals. On the other hand, he was in no sense a helpless slave to his work, and when he met some congenial soul he could reveal himself to be a courteous, witty, experienced man of the world. Bertha von Suttner, the Austrian writer, has described her first meeting with him. He had advertised for a private secretary, she had replied and had been engaged. 'Alfred Nobel', she writes, 'made a very favourable impression. In his advertisement he had called himself 'an elderly gentleman' and we had imagined him to be grey-haired and full of quirks and pains. But that was not the case. He was then only forty-three, was somewhat below average height, wore a dark full beard; his features were neither ugly nor handsome; his expression was somewhat gloomy, but was relieved by his kindly blue eyes; his voice alternated between a melancholy and a satirical tone. He met me at the hotel where I was staying and, thanks to the letters we had exchanged, we did not feel like strangers. Our conversation soon became lively and absorbing.'

To some extent the life of a recluse which he led was due to the dislike, almost horror, he felt for all kinds of pretence and show. He was, of course, a famous man and was therefore often asked for his biography and his photograph. To such requests he replied vigorously in the negative and asked to be left in peace. 'I am not aware', he once wrote in reply to such a request, 'that I have deserved any notoriety and I have no taste for its buzz.' Another time he replied: 'In these days of conspicuous and unashamed publicity, only those who are specially adapted to the purpose ought to let their photographs appear in a newspaper.' He did not even have his portrait painted, and the only one of him that exists was painted after his death. The public honours he received were extremely few and in a letter he gives an amusing, though perhaps not wholly truthful, account of the reasons for the decorations he had obtained. 'My decorations have no explosive basis', he wrote. 'For my Swedish North Star I am indebted to my cook whose art appealed to an extremely aristocratic stomach. My French order I received because of my close personal acquaintance with a member of the cabinet, the Brazilian Order of the Rose because I had happened to be introduced to the Emperor, Dom Pedro, and, finally, as far as the famous Order of Bolivar is concerned, I received that because Max Philipp* had seen *Niniche* and wanted to demonstrate how true to

* Director of the German Dynamite Company.

life was the way decorations were handed out in the play.' Obviously, he was not vainglorious.

He was a lonely man, and with his sensitive nature he suffered keenly from the misfortune of being without a home. He was born a Swede and always regarded himself as one, but at the early age of nine he had left his native country and after that returned to it only on temporary visits. He was never established anywhere. His parents' home in St. Petersburg was broken up in 1859, when the old people moved back to Sweden. When he began his world-wide industrial activities, he first settled at Krümmel, near Hamburg, but what he had there was more of a laboratory than a home, and most of his time was spent in railway carriages, steamship cabins and hotels. In 1875, he acquired a house in the Avenue Malakoff in Paris, but when the laboratory there turned out to be too small, he built a new one at Sévran, on the outskirts of the French capital. But he did not take root there either, and in 1890 he moved to Italy where he bought a villa at San Remo, *Mio Nido*. Towards the end it was clear that he intended to establish a home in Sweden where he could spend the milder season each year and where he presumably hoped to finish his days. At Bofors he therefore had a house prepared for himself. But this plan was forestalled by his death, and it was in *Mio Nido* that, on December 10, 1896, he closed his eyes for ever.

This homelessness Nobel felt keenly, and he always regarded himself as a foreigner in the countries in which he lived more or less temporarily. In theory he was a cosmopolitan, as were so many members of his generation, but at heart he remained attached to the country in which his cradle had stood, and this feeling found expression in his will. It is closely connected with his highly developed family loyalty. Presumably, there have been few as dutiful and devoted sons as Alfred Nobel. He worshipped his mother and almost every year he returned to Stockholm on her birthday to make the old lady happy. By letters he arranged for Christmas gifts, not only for her, but for all those he knew she wanted to remember. Thanks to his generosity, she was a wealthy woman when she died; without worry she had been able to follow her impulses to help and do good. He renounced the inheritance she had left him in her will and had it distributed, instead, in the form of donations bearing her name or in gifts to her relatives and friends.

There have been few people as generous as Alfred Nobel, and his charities often exceeded the limits of his income. To Alarik Liedbeck, a

Swedish industrialist, who was probably his closest friend, he wrote in 1886 that though his income was large, he had spent for such purposes during the previous two years an additional million francs taken from his capital, and, he adds, 'such a system can be followed for a while, of course, but not in the long run.' If printed, the begging letters and letters of thanks found among his papers would fill volumes. Naturally, these constant appeals forced him to be circumspect, and in many instances he had to deny them. When it was a case of real need or a scientific project, he seldom said no, but if the requests were for statues, or memorial celebrations, he was indifferent. 'As a rule', he wrote, 'I'd rather take care of the stomachs of the living than the glory of the departed in the form of monuments', and another time: 'My natural inclination is less to honour the dead who have no feelings and who must be insensible to our marble tributes than to help the living who suffer want.'

Nobel's helpfulness was inspired by his religious views. To him religion had value only in so far as it expressed itself in love for mankind. On the basis of a few remarks, made in a hasty mood, he was regarded by many as being an out-and-out atheist, an enemy of all religious faith. But his so-called atheism was of a special kind. While still a youth he had been deeply impressed by Shelley and, on the whole, his own view of the world and Shelley's were closely similar. From a philosophical standpoint, it may have been somewhat confused, but its main content was a highly developed idealism. Nobel certainly rejected the concept of God in all the predominant religious faiths of the day, because to him their God seemed a cruel, unjust world-ruler, who was to blame for all the religious wars and persecutions. But behind this denial may be dimly seen the image of a Being free from all the defects of the accepted one, a God of peace and universal love of man, so that, in reality, the atheism of Shelley and Nobel came very close to both Christianity and Platonism. This philosophy of life is revealed most clearly in the poems Nobel wrote in his youth. They are all inspired by a deep religious feeling. But it also appears in his letters, one of which is so characteristic of him that I must cite its contents in full.

The pastor of the Swedish Church in Paris had turned to him with a request for aid on behalf of a needy fellow-countryman. To this Nobel replied as follows:

'Though often called on too much, I always feel happy to be able to help honest and industrious people in difficulties against which they struggle in vain. Mr. B. felt he could get along with 600 francs, but since I know very well that inadequate help and no help at all are not very far apart, I increased the amount of my own accord to 1,000 francs. I hope the money will be of real use to him. He had, moreover, what seemed to me a good pleader, for whom, though – to my own loss – we seldom meet, I feel the greatest esteem. Our religious views differ, perhaps, more in form than in substance, since we agree that we should treat others as we want to be treated by them. Personally, I go still further since I feel a dislike of myself, which I in no wise feel for my fellow-man. As regards my theoretical religious views, I admit that they depart considerably from the beaten path. Precisely because these problems are so far beyond us, I refuse to accept solutions made by the human intellect. To know in religious matters what one *should* believe is just as impossible as to square the circle. But to know what one *cannot* believe, by no means lies beyond the realm of possibility. And this border I do not cross. Any thinking person must, of course, realize that we are surrounded by an eternal mystery, and on that is based all true religion. What we *can* see through the veil of the All-Father is nil. What we *believe* we see depends on our individual imagination and should, therefore, be regarded as only our own personal view.'

It may be added that among those who most consistently supported the Swedish Church in Paris was the supposed enemy of Christianity, Alfred Nobel, and that one of the last friends he won was the future Archbishop of Sweden, Nathan Söderblom. In reality, Nobel was so little an enemy of religion that probably few people have had a higher appreciation than he of the spiritual values in life.

Neither were his political convictions so radical as has been supposed. No doubt, he had received certain impressions of Russian nihilism, which was much in the air during his youth, and of the absolute dictatorship of the Czar he was naturally a pronounced enemy. But an anarchist he was least of all – rather the contrary. Among his papers have been found the beginnings of a novel in which one of the characters with the significant name of M. Avenir [Mr. Future] expounds Nobel's own political programme.

As a matter of fact, declares Avenir, there are in the world only three forms of government: hereditary autocracy, constitutional monarchy, and the republican type of government. All three are equally bad. Attacks against autocracy are easy to make and common. But Avenir also condemns the constitutional monarchies, and his reason is that the king has no power. In his place it is the parliament, or as Avenir calls it, the 'House of Bluster', which rules. 'The main occupation in it is to talk and, in some countries, to take bribes. Its members are therefore recruited chiefly from lawyers and other red-tape parasites.' 'Consequently,' he says, 'this many-headed form of government lacks the power which every executive ought to have, and the same defect is inherent in the republican form in which the President, as a rule, is impotent.' But the remedy proposed by Avenir is probably not so effective as he imagines. In this case he has in mind, first of all, France and divides the country into fifty different provinces. At the head of each province is to be placed a governor, elected by 'the public, or by the educated part of it,' for 'giving the same suffrage rights to the educated and the uneducated inevitably leads to corruption and all kinds of other abuses. It can be taken for granted, of course, that an educated person has better judgment than an uneducated one, and since that is true, why depart in political life from an order that elsewhere is a matter of course?' I may add that while Avenir does give women, that is the educated ones, the right to vote, he regards it as inadvisable to elect one as governor or president. 'It is best', he says, 'to avoid, in this respect, the competition of women. To command is, so to speak, a masculine function.'

In this way, there would be fifty provincial governors, and from their number the country's president would be chosen by the parliament, whose sole function this would be. Everything else would be attended to by the president, who would, consequently, be a full-fledged dictator. That he would use his autocratic powers in a wise way, Avenir feels sure, because the parliament would, of course, elect as president the governor who in the exercise of his official duties had already proved himself to be the most efficient.

As to the practicality of this programme there can, of course, be different opinions, but it can hardly be called radical; as a matter of fact, it is undeniably closer to fascism than to communism.

Neither was Nobel the dogmatic advocate of peace many people believe him to have been and which one may be tempted to assume from the wording of his will that he was. Like Shelley, he was a complete pacifist, but in regard to the proposed methods of making war impossible he was rather sceptical. When he was asked to aid a periodical to support disarmament and peace work, he declared that it would do just as much good to throw the money out of the window. Neither did he believe, according to his letters, in the possibility of a general disarmament in the near future, and on this point he argued with Bertha von Suttner. He never attended any peace congress, and to Bertha von Suttner he remarked, when she tried to induce him to take part in one: 'My factories may make an end of war sooner than your congresses. The day when two army corps can annihilate each other in one second, all civilized nations, it is to be hoped, will recoil from war and discharge their troops.'

He was, however, sincerely interested in the efforts to establish permanent peace, and in 1893, that is two years before he made his final will, he wrote a letter to Bertha von Suttner on the subject. It is a noteworthy letter since in it he set forth his own peace programme. According to that, the only effective way to prevent war would be to make an agreement among all countries to take up arms together against the nation which first violated peace and began a war. He writes as follows: 'I am prepared to set aside a part of my estate for a prize to be awarded every fifth year – let us say six times, because, if in thirty years it has not been possible to reform the present system, we shall unavoidably fall back into barbarism. This prize would be awarded to the man or woman who had induced Europe to take the first step toward the general idea of peace. I do not mean disarmament, which can be brought about only very slowly. Neither do I mean compulsory arbitration among the nations. But it ought to be possible to reach rather soon the goal that all countries loyally pledge themselves to turn against the initial aggressor. That would make wars impossible. Even the most quarrelsome nation would then be forced, either to appeal to a court or to keep quiet. If the Triple Alliance, instead of including only three countries, included all, peace would be assured for centuries.'

I do not venture to judge whether this programme should be called Utopian, but if so, it is a Utopia in which the world's statesmen of to-day believe or at least pretend to believe.

Nobel's leading interests were, however, literary and scientific. He had, in fact, to a marked degree the gifts of a poet – deep feeling and considerable powers of imagination. His early poems, which he wrote before he was twenty, rank, in my opinion, quite high. They are, it is true, influenced in style by Shelley and written in English, but at the same time they are decidedly personal, giving expression, as they do, to his melancholia, his sensitive temperament and his religious brooding. A highly educated, elderly English clergyman who had had the opportunity to read one of them, regretted, to be sure, that Nobel's conception of Christianity was not such that he could approve of it but added that the ideas expressed were so valid and so brilliant that every reader must be carried away by his presentation of them. 'I should have regarded this poem', he wrote, 'as a superior product of an Englishman, but the wonder becomes hundredfold when one bears in mind that the author is a foreigner. If you can write a poem like that in English, what couldn't you produce in your own language?'

Precisely herein lay one of the reasons why Nobel never did become an author. No one can really master more than one language, and while Nobel wrote excellent letters in Swedish, he had lived abroad so long that he had lost the feeling for the finer shades required in a Swedish literary work. His English was better, but this language too was a foreign one, and he was conscious of this. Thus as a writer, too, he was without a home.

To this should be added another circumstance: he had written his poems while still young. After that came his extensive business enterprises and his scientific experiments, and these naturally took him away from literary work. When a few years before his death he wanted to return to it, it was too late. His imagination was not so strong as it had been when he was twenty, and his use of words had become vague and uncertain. But what he always retained was his love for the art of writing, and despite his heavy burden of work he took time to keep abreast of current literary developments, including those in Scandinavia. Most important to him were the ideas conveyed, and literature he regarded, first of all, as a source of health for humanity in its progress towards the future about which he dreamt. To this concept, his will also bears witness.

Another source of health was science, above all natural science, and, according to his belief, it was the conquests of the latter that were to create happiness for coming generations. 'To spread knowledge', he wrote, 'is to spread well-being. I mean general well-being, not individual prosperity, and with the arrival of such well-being will disappear the greater part of the evil which is an inheritance from the dark ages. The advance in scientific research and its ever-widening sphere stirs the hope in us that the microbes, those of the soul as well as the body, will gradually disappear, and that the only war humanity will wage in the future will be the one against these microbes.'

It was, in fact, to this battle that he assigned the greater part of the fortune he had built up. It had been won through victories of science and it was to be devoted to a continuation of them. For, in spite of the bitterness that is sometimes revealed in his letters, he was at heart a pronounced optimist and believed in a happier and healthier humanity in the future.

ALFRED NOBEL

AND THE NOBEL FOUNDATION

BY RAGNAR SOHLMAN

INTRODUCTION

Alfred Bernhard Nobel was born in Stockholm on October 21, 1833, and his eventful life came to an end at San Remo, Italy, on December 10, 1896. Early in January the following year both the Swedish and the foreign publics were surprised to learn that in his will he had provided that the major part of his large estate should be converted into a fund the income from which should 'be distributed annually in the form of prizes to those who during the preceding year had conferred the greatest benefit on mankind.'

The unusual terms of the will as well as its partially defective form at once produced a great sensation, but soon also led to doubts and criticism, some of which was directed against the donor himself for his 'unpatriotic' attitude. Not until after four years of negotiations and conflicts, which, at times, were quite bitter, and after obstacles of various kinds had either been overcome or circumvented, was it possible to put into legal form the fundamental ideas Nobel had expressed in his will, and to organize the Nobel Foundation which was to put them into effect. By a decree of the Swedish Government, issued on June 20, 1900, the charter and by-laws of the Foundation were officially sanctioned, including special instructions for the Swedish prize-distributors regarding the performance of their duties.

Now that five decades have passed* since the first Nobel Prizes were awarded, the original criticism of the main idea behind these prizes and their founder has, of course, long since died down. In Sweden the annual prize distribution on December 10 is rather looked upon as an event of national importance, and the right to select the winners in physics, chemistry, medicine and literature as well as the administration of the endowment are held to be a national asset calculated to enhance Sweden's reputation as a civilized country. Similar benefits are derived by Norway from its right to award the Nobel Peace Prize. As a result, public interest in and respect for the personality of the donor have increased considerably, both in Sweden and elsewhere.

All members of Alfred Nobel's own generation, or those born during the first half of the nineteenth century who were his intimates, are now dead, and of those born later who had the opportunity to come into personal contact with the great inventor and idealist and who could therefore help

* Written in 1947.

to draw a more life-like picture of his personality, only a few are still living.

As Alfred Nobel's private assistant during the last three years of his life, I came into almost daily contact with him, partly by direct personal association, and partly through a most extensive correspondence, which chiefly concerned the experimental development of his ideas. By a provision in his will, about which I was not informed until after his death, I was appointed one of the executors to whom he entrusted the settlement of his estate and the realization of his last wishes. Since I was the executor who had known him most intimately, it was taken for granted that I should have charge of the principal work in this connection – an assignment for which, in view of my youth and lack of practical experience, particularly in financial and legal matters, I must have been considered, in all frankness, to have been but poorly qualified. In any event, it fell upon me to take an active part, both in winding up Alfred Nobel's business interests in various countries, including all the legal complications and financial dissensions involved in that work, as well as in settling the dispute over the validity of his will which arose when certain relatives decided to contest it. Finally, I had to take part in the protracted discussions with representatives of the various institutions he had designated to select the winners of his prizes and in the committee work to prepare a charter and by-laws for the Nobel Foundation, which had to be created out of hand to become the residuary legatee.

In connection with this work it became my duty and privilege to go through Nobel's voluminous business correspondence which had been preserved in his numerous letter-copy books, as well as to acquaint myself with the contents of his extensive private papers. In recent years I have also had occasion to examine a certain part of his strictly personal correspondence into which, for various reasons and out of regard for persons still living, it had not previously seemed proper to delve. In this way I obtained a better understanding of the circumstances that led Alfred Nobel to make the disposition of his property that was stipulated in his will. I also feel I have obtained a more thorough insight into his mind and his emotions. In any case, as an act of gratitude to the men now dead who in different ways helped to put into effect as satisfactorily as possible the aims of Alfred Nobel and who served as advisers and supporters of a young and inexperienced executor in the performance of his often difficult task, I have felt it to be my duty to put into writing a summary account of the settlement of his estate and the events connected with it.

While, in the main, and in all its really important details, this account is supported by letters and other documents preserved in the archives of the Nobel Foundation in Stockholm, certain parts of it are based on purely personal impressions and recollections.

THE CLOSING YEARS OF ALFRED NOBEL'S LIFE

During the last fifteen years of his life, or from about 1880 to 1896, Alfred Nobel was subjected to many both physical and mental tribulations. His private letters show touchingly how deeply depressed, lonely and afflicted he often felt in the midst of all his intense activities and impressive accomplishments, whether in chemistry, industrial organization or financial management. The reasons for this were of various kinds. In the first place, his increasingly poor health affected his mental state. Ever since childhood he had been frail and sickly, as he several times recalled with bitter irony, for instance, in a letter to his brother Ludvig in which, instead of an autobiographical sketch that had been requested, he sent the following satirical description of himself: 'Alfred Nobel, a miserable half-life, ought to have been choked to death by a philanthropic physician as soon as, with a howl, he entered life.' During his years of adolescence, his health seems to have worried his parents. In the summer of 1854, for instance, he was sent to take the water cure at Franzensbad in Bohemia – a treatment he often had to repeat in his later years in spite of his extreme dislike of spa-life and the relative inactivity it enforced. Of his first 'bath- and bibbing cure' he wrote quite contemptuously in his letters home. He felt, he insisted, that his health had benefited more from his stay in Stockholm and at Dalarö, near the capital, with friends and relatives than from his whole season at Franzensbad with its 'chance acquaintances, with whom one can, of course, spend a few pleasant hours, but from whom one later parts with as much regret as from an old, worn-out coat.' This remark by a youth of twenty-one expressed the same feeling of emptiness and boredom that persons casually encountered in society often inspired in him as a man of fifty or sixty.

Throughout the 1860's and 1870's, however, Nobel's preoccupation with his inventions, as well as his native energy, will-power and capacity for action seem to have enabled him to overcome, at least partially, his physical handicaps. It was during those years that he made his great inventions, and, while constantly travelling or living abroad, he founded the various industrial enterprises that soon became the sources of his constantly increasing wealth. He then gives the impression of a restlessly active man in his best years who, without faltering, or yielding to despondency, could bear the heaviest material reverses and the most acute emotional strains, such as those caused by the premature death of his younger brother Emil as a result of an accidental explosion, which also led to his father's collapse from a stroke, and after that by a long series of similar disasters in various parts of the world, involving heavy losses of life and property, as well as by unscrupulous attempts of business rivals, some of whom were of the international swindler type, to deprive him of the honour and benefit of his inventions, etc. Even as late as the first half of the 1870's, when his invention of dynamite had become an established success, he continued to devote himself with his customary energy and undiminished vitality to the completion and improvement of his inventions, as well as to the development of better methods of production and to the organization and promotion of stock companies formed for the manufacture and sale of his explosives. In addition to that, he had strength and interest left for comparatively active personal contacts and frequent correspondence with intellectual or artistic acquaintances in Paris. In 1875 he made his third important invention, namely that of blasting gelatine [that is to say, if his mercury percussion cap, or the 'Nobel lighter', may be regarded as his first, and the kieselguhr dynamite as his second]. During the next few years he was intensely preoccupied with the technical perfection and practical use of his most recent invention. But towards the end of the 1870's, signs of gradual exhaustion began to appear. Its causes are perhaps to be sought, first of all, in his increasingly delicate health. Easily subject to ailments due to colds, he suffered from changes in climate and was particularly sensitive to chilly weather.

As the years passed, he showed new and more serious symptoms indicating heart trouble, an affliction that on April 12, 1888, caused the death of his elder brother, Ludvig. About that time Alfred, too, began to complain in his private letters of attacks of angina pectoris, which gradually struck him more and more frequently and became increasingly alarming, especially during his frequent travels.

His feeling of loneliness and his longing for a really close friend are most movingly expressed in letters dating from this period. In October, 1887, he writes, for instance: 'For the past nine days I have been ill and have had to stay indoors with no other company than a paid valet; no one inquires about me. It seems to me that this time I am much worse than Bouté [his physician] believes, for the pain is so persistent; it does not let up at all. And, besides, my heart has become as heavy as lead. When at the age of fifty-four one is left so alone in the world, and a paid servant is the only person who has so far showed one the most kindness, then come heavy thoughts, heavier than most people can imagine. I can see in my valet's eyes how much he pities me, but I cannot, of course, let him notice that.'

The cause of this isolation, which perhaps was only felt by himself, may probably be ascribed, in the first place, to certain conflicts in his intimate relationships which were of a strictly private nature. But he undoubtedly suffered also from abuses of his confidence and from his discoveries of character defects, which sometimes went as far as downright fraudulent acts, in certain persons with whom he had worked closely for a number of years. This was particularly true of his experience with his old-time associate Paul Barbe and the men who had been placed by Barbe at the head of the French companies, *La Société Générale pour la Fabrication de la Dynamite* and *La Société Centrale de Dynamite.*

As a result of a dispute in the Chamber of Deputies between Barbe and the French Premier and Minister of War, de Freycinet, a violent newspaper campaign was launched against the two partners, Barbe and Nobel, who were attacked because, to the detriment of France, they had sold Nobel's recent discovery of ballistite, or smokeless powder, to the Italian Government. Nobel was furthermore accused of having conducted at his laboratory in Sévran-Livry, near Paris, military espionage on the work at a nearby experimental station belonging to the official *Administration des Poudres et Salpètres,* where the development of a smokeless powder for the French armed forces, discovered by Sarrau and Vieille, was under way. Nobel's laboratory as well as his private proving grounds for rifle and artillery ammunition were closed by the police, and he personally was threatened with imprisonment if he continued his experiments on French soil. Consequently, he felt compelled to leave France and transfer his experimental activities, first to Italy, where he bought a villa surrounded by rather extensive grounds at San Remo, and then to Bofors, in Sweden. In 1890 and 1892 the French dynamite companies, *La Société Centrale* and *La Société Générale,* suffered heavy losses, partly as a result of improper speculations and partly from pure frauds committed by the officers most directly in charge of the management, men who were close intimates of Paul Barbe. On behalf of the *Société Centrale* large speculative purchases of glycerine had been made, though that was not one of the company's normal activities. To save it from bankruptcy, Nobel had to grant it, at once, a considerable credit. Shortly after that it was found that outright frauds and actually criminal manipulations had also been committed in the *Société Générale* by its managing director, a former French senator. In this work the latter had been associated with another close friend of Barbe, who had been employed by him as his *alter ego* in the most delicate negotiations, and who was later found guilty and sentenced to jail for forgeries and various other crimes.

The losses involved were so considerable that when Nobel was informed of them during a visit to Hamburg he believed himself to have been completely ruined, and, according to what a director of the German Dynamite Company later told me, he asked for a position as a chemist with his German concern. As a member of the board of directors of the French companies, although he had not taken a personal part in their administration, he could be held financially responsible for the losses they had sustained. After he had obtained more detailed information by telegraph, he calmed down, however, and then decided on a battle to clear up the concern, both financially and administratively. On his return to Paris he was able to have the previous board of directors discharged; the company was then saved from the threatened catastrophe by a bond issue of which Nobel himself took over a considerable share.

This satisfactory outcome may be attributed to a veritable *tour de force* by a sixty-year-old man who was already exhausted by illness and other reverses. But the worries and conflicts it involved weakened his health still further. On this point he wrote to his nephew, Emanuel Nobel, on October 10, 1892, as follows: 'My position here [in Paris] is no longer what it once was; I am at daggers drawn with all the directors I had to get rid of. The result is that I have had to acquire and keep a majority of the stock, which means 20,000 shares, at 450 to 500 francs. Even if a few friends help me, it is, nevertheless, a tremendous parcel which I must be prepared to carry. If I don't, both I and my co-directors may get into a sticky mess, for we are dealing with a pack of crooked lawyers and bloodsuckers. Nothing in the world is more dangerous than to be a director in a French stock company.'

In another letter, dated November 1, 1892, and addressed to an English business associate, he writes: 'A few days ago a demand was made on me for the tidy little sum of 4,600,000 francs on the pretext that I was responsible for the recent embezzlements. French law is peculiar, and directors who act in perfectly good faith can be held responsible, if it can be shown that there has been a lack of adequate supervision. The other members of the board and their lawyers are, it is true, of the opinion that there has been no such laxity, but when it comes to a lawsuit, Wisdom herself is blind, and a judge's affliction with constipation, or the opposite, can often influence his views as to what is right or wrong...'

Another disappointment which at this time touched Nobel on a very tender spot was his conflict with Sir Frederick Abel and Professor James Dewar in connection with the so-called cordite case. The point at issue here – quite apart from the great financial interests that were at stake – was Nobel's priority rights as the inventor of smokeless, nitroglycerine gunpowder. It may be recalled that while in 1887 to 1889 Nobel was working most intensely on his development of ballistite, the British Government had appointed a committee with Sir Frederick Abel and Professor Dewar as its leading and most representative members to determine which would be the best type of smokeless powder to use – a problem that was then an urgent one for all the Great Powers. For this purpose Abel and Dewar got into touch with Nobel and in the course of a year obtained from him detailed, confidential information about his discovery and the efforts he was making to improve it. But simultaneously, they also started experiments on their own account with nitroglycerine gunpowder, using a slightly different kind of gun-cotton than the one he had employed, and then, without informing Nobel, took out a patent on the smokeless powder they had thus produced, which they called 'cordite'.

Naturally Nobel protested, and after all efforts at arriving at an amicable settlement had failed, it was decided that the matter should be disposed of by a 'friendly suit' in the British courts. This 'friendly contest', which gradually became enormously complicated – the printed record alone fills several yards of shelves in the Nobel Foundation's archives – was finally decided against the plaintiff, the British Nobel Company, which also had to defray litigation costs amounting to about £30,000. The only satisfaction Alfred Nobel received was a verbal statement by Lord Justice Kay during the proceedings before the Court of Appeal in which the latter said that while on purely technical grounds he had to agree with his two colleagues in favour of the defendant, he recognized Nobel's claims as a pioneer in the field. 'It is obvious', he observed, 'that a dwarf who has been allowed to climb up on the back of a giant can see farther than the giant himself... In this case I cannot but sympathize with the holder of the original patent. Mr. Nobel made a great invention, which in theory was something extraordinary, a really great innovation – and then two clever chemists got hold of his specifications for the patent, read them carefully and, after that, with the aid of their own thorough knowledge of chemistry, discovered that they could use practically the same materials, though with a slight difference in regard to one of them, and thereby obtain exactly the same result. If possible, one should like to come to the conclusion that this could not be done in such a way that it deprived Mr. Nobel of the benefit of an extraordinarily important patent.'

A more severe condemnation of the methods used by Nobel's opponents can hardly be imagined – and yet it did not mention what was probably the most delicate point of all – the confidential relationship that had obtained between Nobel and Messrs. Abel and Dewar in their study of the gunpowder problem. Nobel's resentment at having been cheated and unjustly treated can well be understood. When he returned to Paris he tried to relieve his feelings by writing a play, *The Patent Bacillus,* in which he burlesqued the British court system [see p.77].

Nobel's state of gloom and depression was further aggravated at this time by the death of two members of his family to whom he had been particularly attached. On April 12, 1888, as already stated, his elder brother Ludvig had died at Cannes, and on December 7, 1889, came the death in Stockholm of his mother with whom he had remained on the closest terms up to the very end.

The need of sympathy and tenderness which, in spite of his occasional outbursts of misanthropy and contempt for his fellow-men, Alfred Nobel always felt at the bottom of his heart, had never been wholly satisfied, of course, by his devotion to his mother. He probably also wanted to know and form mutual ties of devotion with some younger woman – if possible one of the same high intellectual stature as himself.

On several occasions, even during his final years, he tried to find a suitable secretary, preferably a lady, without ever being able to find one who quite satisfied his requirements. A French housekeeper whom he had once employed appears to have helped him with some of his simplest filing and cataloguing work, without being able to assist him with his correspondence. A certain partiality which he always felt for Vienna and the old Austria may have been the reason why, in the spring of 1876, he placed an advertisement in a Vienna newspaper, according to which 'a wealthy, highly educated elderly gentleman, living in Paris,' was looking for 'a lady of mature years with a knowledge of languages to act as his secretary and housekeeper'.

This advertisement was answered by Countess Bertha Kinsky von Chinic und Tettau, who was then thirty-three years old and a member of an impoverished family belonging to the Austrian aristocracy. While employed as a governess to young daughters of a wealthy, baronial family named von Suttner, she had fallen in love with and become secretly engaged to the son of the house, Arthur von Suttner, who was seven years her junior. When his parents found out about the situation, they firmly opposed the very idea of a marriage, partly because of the difference in age and partly on account of the poverty of the Kinsky family. This was the reason why Bertha Kinsky applied for the position offered by Alfred Nobel in Paris.

In her memoirs she describes her first meeting with her new employer [see p.7]. He had met her at the station and escorted her to a hotel, where she was to live until the rooms he was having prepared for her in a part of his elegant private house in Avenue Malakoff were ready. With his secretarial work, however, the young countess never had a chance to occupy herself. How their acquaintanceship developed during the short time they were together – only a week – can only be surmised.

To judge from her photographs, Bertha von Suttner was then a radiant beauty. According to her own statements, she had a complete command of French, English, and Italian, besides her native German; she was musically gifted, had literary abilities and interests, and possessed high intelligence, great conversational ability, and good social manners – all qualities which must have impressed Nobel deeply. Beyond doubt, he was fascinated by her personality – it is also possible that he felt drawn to her by even deeper feelings. Because of Nobel's preoccupation with business, however, their association was limited to a couple of hours daily, at luncheon in the winter garden of his home or during drives in his elegant carriage through the Bois de Boulogne, then in its full spring glory. According to her own account, Nobel asked her one day, when he had observed her depressed mood, whether her heart was free and unattached. She answered in the negative and then told him about her secret engagement to von

Suttner and her resolve to break off the connection out of consideration for his family and to make a career for herself. 'You have acted very bravely,' she reports Nobel remarked, 'now continue to be courageous, give up all correspondence – let some time pass – a new mode of life – fresh impressions – and both of you will soon forget – he, perhaps, before you.'

After a week, Nobel informed her that urgent business matters forced him to make a trip, and he then left her alone in Paris. In the meantime she had been bombarded daily with despairing letters from Arthur von Suttner and also from his younger sisters, her former pupils, who described in vivid terms their brother's state of despair after she had left and, like him, implored her to return. According to her own account, she was seized with a homesickness she could not conquer and left Paris, after explaining in a letter to Nobel that she must give up the position he had offered her and adding the reason for her decision. Her departure and what then ensued had a definitely dramatic and romantic aspect: to get money for the hotel bill and the ticket back to Vienna she had to sell a valuable diamond ornament she had inherited; once she arrived in Vienna she visited her future husband, who declared that he could never bear to be parted from her. After having been married, without the knowledge of their families, in a little church outside of Vienna, the newly married couple set out on their wedding trip to the Caucasus, where they had relatives and friends and where they remained for nine years before Arthur's parents became reconciled to their marriage, and the new Baroness von Suttner was received back at the family estate.

To Alfred Nobel the sudden departure of his intended secretary must have been a bitter experience – if not a painful one. Perhaps he had thought that in her he had found not only a much-needed assistant for his work, but also a congenial companion to give him a little of the home atmosphere he had always lacked in his daily life. Not until eleven years later was he to meet Bertha von Suttner again; with her husband she then visited him in Paris. In the meantime, however, they had kept up a steady contact by letters, and he still retained a feeling of warm sympathy and respect for her. During the last ten years of his life, when he had become keenly interested in the peace movement she had launched, their correspondence became increasingly frequent, and she undoubtedly had a strong influence on the final shaping of his will and, particularly, the founding of the Peace Prize.

In August 1892, Nobel again met Bertha von Suttner and her husband, this time in Zurich, where he had invited them as his guests for a few days after they had participated in a world peace congress and inter-parliamentary conference at Berne. It was this encounter and the subsequent correspondence which for the first time made Alfred Nobel think of remembering the peace movement in his will by instituting a prize for work to promote peace.

PERSONAL IMPRESSIONS OF ALFRED NOBEL

Towards the end of his life Alfred Nobel seemed able to overcome almost entirely the acute mental depression from which he had suffered during the 1880's and the first years of the 1890's. In spite of the aggravation of his heart trouble, he was then once more full of energy and plans for the future. Th is improvement is also attested by his photographs, some of which had been taken in his youth, others when he was about forty-five, some at the age of fifty-eight, and, finally, one taken in his last year. It was clearly connected with his renewal of contacts with Sweden and Swedish people. As already explained, these relations had never been wholly broken. Besides his mother and brothers, he had kept up a fairly regular correspondence with several other persons living in that country.

In the autumn of 1893 I was engaged as his personal assistant. One summer while I was still a student at the Stockholm Institute of Technology, I had had the opportunity to travel on a tanker built in Sweden for the Nobel Brothers Naphtha Company at Baku, to be used for the transport of petroleum on the Caspian Sea. Taking advantage of the spring floods it took the canal and river route across Russia – approximately the same as that once followed by the Swedish vikings – and then crossed the Caspian Sea to Baku. There I had a chance to visit both the Nobel oil refineries and the drilling fields; in *Villa Petrola,* a club house for employees, I met Robert Nobel, Alfred's eldest brother, and Robert's eldest son Hjalmar, whose acquaintance I had already made in Stockholm, where I was a schoolfellow of his younger brother Ludvig.

After passing my final examinations at the Institute of Technology, I worked, in 1890-93, as an engineer in the United States, where for a while I was employed as a chemist at a dynamite factory belonging to the Hercules Powder Company, now a subsidiary of the famous Du Pont organization. During the summer of 1893, I was employed in the Swedish section of the Columbian Exposition in Chicago.

And then in September, 1893, while still in Chicago, I received, to my great surprise and joy, a telegram from home informing me that I had been offered a position as personal assistant to Alfred Nobel, to start immediately. As I learned later, the offer had been made on the strength of a letter of recommendation to Nobel from J. V. Smitt, a Swedish capitalist who had been Alfred Nobel's first financial backer and who until the end of his life served as head of the Nobel Dynamite Company in Sweden. According to what I heard many years later, my schoolmate, Ludvig Nobel, had also recommended me to his uncle in Paris.

Naturally I accepted the attractive offer immediately and with the greatest gratitude, especially as the United States was then in the throes of a severe depression. In October, 1893, only a few weeks later, I presented myself with some trepidation at the private house of the great inventor in Avenue Malokoff in Paris, and was at once escorted by his *maître d'hôtel* to the owner's study, where I was cordially received by my future employer.

At that time Nobel was sixty years old. He was rather less than medium height, had strongly marked features, a high forehead, bushy eyebrows, and somewhat deep-set eyes whose glance was both keen and changeable, as was his whole temperament, for that matter.

After I had finished my first assignment, which was to arrange his library and letter files, I was ordered to proceed to San Remo and begin work in his private laboratory. The latter was housed in a long, one-story building situated in the extensive garden and park that surrounded Nobel's villa. It contained three rooms: a large machine-room with a gas motor and electrical generators for various voltages and tensions for lighting, electrolysis and other experiments, an equally large workroom for special chemical tests and other experimental work, and a somewhat smaller room which contained a reference library, scales and diverse instruments, as well as rifles for ballistic tests. The firing was done towards the sea along a steel pier that projected from the shore; a chronograph to measure the velocities was mounted inside the laboratory.

A few weeks after my arrival Nobel himself came to San Remo from Paris where he had been delayed, and after that he began to spend a few hours every day in the laboratory, where he checked up on the work in progress and gave further instructions on how to proceed.

What especially interested him during the following winter of 1893-94 was, partly, tests with various new types of gunpowder that were almost smokeless, including experiments with a new type of safety fuse for civilian blasting operations, and, partly, attempts to find a substitute for rubber, with which it fell to my lot to occupy myself. Nobel's idea, on which he had applied for a preliminary patent, was to produce substitutes for both rubber and leather from a low-nitrated cellulose which was transformed into an elastic or quite solidly gelatinated substance by being treated with suitable, non-evaporating, gelatinizing agents. My assignment was to find and test new or not previously known agents of that kind, as a rule by the synthetic production of the appropriate chemical compounds – which to a young chemist was most fascinating work. The results obtained were very promising, and Nobel believed he would soon be able to found a new important industry, which, in addition, would be a strictly civilian enterprise on which he placed high hopes. The latter, it is true, were not fulfilled during his own lifetime; as substitutes for rubber the materials produced turned out to be unfit, despite their promising appearance, and the factory to make artificial leather which, as late as the last year of his life, Nobel planned to build at Gullspång in Sweden was never erected. The results obtained, however, were afterwards of use in connection with the production of certain kinds of artificial leather, the so-called pegamoid and other types, as well as of ingredients in some of the modern cellulose lacquers.

Besides the laboratory work, which intensely absorbed him, Nobel was much preoccupied during the winter of 1893-94 with negotiations, by correspondence, for the purchase of Bofors, a Swedish steelworks in the province of Värmland, about which more will be told later, as well as with writing letters and drawing up memoranda regarding the cordite lawsuit, which irritated him greatly. As a result, he often suffered from such severe headaches that he had to write with his head wrapped in wet towels that had to be changed quite often. When his headache and nervous depression became unbearable, he dropped all such work and, for relief, devoted himself to his literary experiments – *Nemesis* and *The Patent Bacillus*, a parody on the cordite case [see pp. 77-78].

To get diversion and mental rest, Nobel often drove about in his carriage. He liked to drive, and at San Remo, as earlier in Paris and later on at Björkborn in Sweden, he kept a stable of thoroughbreds. Sometimes he invited both his assistants and once in a while only myself to accompany him. On these latter occasions he would talk Swedish to me; otherwise, when Beckett, his English assistant, was present, we always spoke English. It seemed to amuse Nobel to return to his mother-tongue for a change.

About the middle of January 1894, Nobel informed me that he intended to go away for a few weeks, first to London in connection with his appeal to the House of Lords in the cordite case, and then to Sweden, where he planned to visit Bofors, having just bought a majority of the shares in the Bofors-Gullspång Company, owner of the steelworks.

His plan had been to acquire a factory in Sweden for the manufacture of guns and other war materials which would enable him to carry on his experiments on a larger scale and without such interference from the authorities as that to which he had been subjected in France, and also to be relieved of the limitations of the laboratory in San Remo as well as of his neighbour's complaints about his use of explosives. Undoubtedly, the new attraction he felt for his native land and his desire to acquire a permanent foothold there also played a part. His first negotiations were for the purchase of Finspång, an ancient brassworks in central Sweden, which had been offered for sale, but when Nobel visited the place he found the contrast between the magnificent castle, dating from the seventeenth century, and the antiquated workshops too discouraging. Shortly afterwards his attention was called to Bofors, which was also for sale.

To list the multifarious experiments conducted by us during the next few years at Björkborn and Bofors to test Nobel's ideas would be out of place here. But to give some idea of the great variety of subjects covered by these experiments it may be permissible to mention, in addition to those already listed: new kinds of gunpowder, for instance, the so-called progressive powder, explosives and fuses for artillery shells, hot and cold drilling of gun barrels, propulsion charges for rocket projectiles, tightening bands for artillery shells, topographical map-making by means of cameras carried aloft by rockets and then suspended by parachutes, light metal alloys, electrolytic production of potassium and sodium, etc.

Many of these projects seemed, of course, quite fantastic or even whimsical to the industrialists and technicians of those days, who, as a rule, were inclined to be critical of everything new, and by them Nobel's judgment in technical matters was often questioned. But it should not be forgotten that some of the ideas that were derided by contemporary industrialists were put into practice by Nobel and have later proved to be of the greatest value. Neither should it be forgotten that other ideas of his have since been applied in other ways or in entirely different fields from those he had originally had in mind.

As already mentioned, Nobel's fresh contacts with his native country during the final three years of his life and probably also his decision as to what to do with his estate seemed to give greater balance and satisfaction to his life. The depressed state of mind which, to judge from his letters, had been so persistent during the latter half of the 1880's and the first three years of the 1890's appeared to be a thing of the past, in spite of his increasingly frequent heart attacks. He had found a new aim in life which interested him keenly; he had been able to realize his dream of finding a home, or rather two of them, in beautiful surroundings and far from the bustle of large cities; he had found a new circle of friends with whom he was in full sympathy. His earlier, oppressive sense of being isolated had apparently been eased. In my personal association with him during his closing years I never observed any of the attacks of nervous depression which he used to call 'visits from the spirits of Niflheim' and which I had witnessed so often in San Remo during the winter of 1893-94.

In the late autumn of 1895, Nobel spent about two months in Paris, staying as late as the middle of December. He then formulated the terms of his final will on which the Nobel Foundation and its activities are based. The will is dated November 27, 1895, and was drawn up by Nobel himself in his own handwriting, evidently in his Paris house, and without the aid of any lawyer. The final signature was appended one of the first days of December at the Swedish Club in Paris in the presence of four witnesses he had brought together. They were Thorsten Nordenfelt, a Swedish-born munitions manufacturer then living in Paris, Sigurd Ehrenborg, a retired Swedish army officer, R. V. Strehlenert and Leonard Hvass, two young Swedish engineers.

By this will Nobel expressly cancelled 'all previous testamentary provisions', in case any such should be found after his death. No such provisions have been preserved, except the earlier will that was dated March 14, 1893, and by which the Royal Swedish Academy of Sciences was designated as the principal residuary legatee as well as distributor of prizes. The fundamental idea of both wills, however, was that the main part of the estate was to be devoted to the support of scientific research and pioneering work 'in the wide sphere of knowledge and human progress', including the peace movement, and that the responsibility for the realization of the testator's aims was entrusted to Swedish institutions – according to the final will, in co-operation with a special committee appointed by the Norwegian Storting to select winners of the Peace Prize.

Nobel's very last letter addressed to me in Sweden was dated December 7, 1896; it was still lying on his desk when I arrived in San Remo after his death. It closed with these words: 'Unfortunately my health is again so poor that I write these lines with difficulty but will return as soon as I am able to the subjects that interest us. Your devoted friend, A. Nobel.'

The handwriting was the same as usual, perfectly clear and readable; it gave no signs of the imminent collapse. But immediately after writing these words he seems to have felt symptoms of the cerebral haemorrhage that ended his life on December 10, 1896, at two o'clock in the morning.

Alfred Nobel's final hours were deeply tragic. The fears he had expressed in several of his letters turned out to be justified: he ended his days surrounded only by his French servants and without having, as he had dreaded, near him any 'close friend or relation whose kind hand would some day close one's eyes and whisper in one's ear a gentle and sincere word of comfort.'

From his study he was carried by his house staff to his bedroom on the second floor of the villa; they then summoned his Italian doctor, who at once understood the seriousness of the situation and prescribed absolute rest with confinement to bed. This order was difficult to enforce as the patient had strong attacks of restlessness and had to be prevented from getting up. He seems to have lost some of his power of speech and all memory of other languages than that of his childhood; his oldest servant and butler, Auguste, said later that Nobel had used a number of words that were unintelligible to the staff. They believed they understood, however, that he wanted them to telegraph, and Auguste did get off telegrams to Nobel's two nephews, Emanuel and Hjalmar, as well as to me, asking me to inform the family.

At Bofors I received the telegram about his illness on the morning of December 8, and after communicating with Hjalmar and Ludvig Nobel I decided to set out for San Remo at once in order to be of some service, if possible, during my employer's illness. Hjalmar Nobel too decided to go; we met on the way and arrived at San Remo together on the evening of December 10, but too late to find Alfred Nobel alive. While on our way we had, in fact, received a telegram announcing his death. Emanuel Nobel, who like us had set out immediately after receiving the first telegram and who had arrived ahead of us on December 10, was also too late. Alfred Nobel had ended his days just as alone as he had lived.

In a recently published biographical account of his life and personality, which is partly imaginative, Alfred Nobel is called 'a man nobody knew'. Though exaggerated, this characterization is, after all, justified to some degree. In the higher industrial and financial circles of Paris, London, Berlin, and Vienna, Nobel's activities were certainly well known and highly respected. But his dislike of every kind of public appearance as well as of all forms of publicity and self-advertising had the effect of leaving his own personality wholly unknown to the public, especially to that of his native land, so that, compared with two other contemporary Swedish geniuses, Captain John Ericsson, inventor of the Monitor, and Gustaf Patrik de Laval, inventor of the steam turbine and the cream separator, Nobel was truly 'a man nobody knew'. To this was added his strong disinclination to allow anyone to become too close to him.

At the same time, and particularly after his mother's death in 1889 and his own decline in health, he felt quite often a strong need for some intimate friend on whose devotion he could rely under all circumstances. This inner contradiction in his mental and emotional life was not the only one.

In fact, his character presented a number of other contrasts which in several cases led to discrepancies between his theoretical views and his actions.

Politically, for instance, Nobel considered himself to be a Social Democrat, or at least he so described himself – though one of the 'moderate' kind. In practice, it must be admitted that both in his principles and in his actions he was quite far removed from the social-democratic tenets. At least he was no democrat in the proper sense of the term. Personally, he kept strictly aloof from the workmen in the industries he controlled, in sharp contrast to the policy of his brother Ludvig, who took a keen interest in the living conditions of all employees and thus became a pioneer in social welfare for both salaried staff and wage-earners. To his personal servants, however, Alfred Nobel was a generous master, though insisting on the strict observance of etiquette and never permitting any familiarity, even when he was ill and felt the need of it.

As an industrial magnate – if such a term can be applied to a man who was so modest and retiring as Alfred Nobel – and as a 'capitalist', he protected his own financial interests with both skill and energy, and because of his always telling remarks and the personal respect he enjoyed he was able, as a rule, to carry his point. His desire for gain and additional riches was, however, hardly prompted by a craving for further power and increased influence or by a wish to satisfy any personal vanity. His native talents included a rare combination of inventive genius and financial skill. In addition to the organization of his world-wide industrial enterprises, he employed the latter talent in stock market operations, as shown by the fact, for instance, that among the assets found after his death were not a few shares in gold mines and other purely speculative enterprises. In regard to these stock market operations he stated in his letters that he had engaged in them as a pastime and to get relief from his melancholia. Such speculations involved, however, only straight purchases of stocks and bonds, never any marginal transactions, and they were always kept within narrow limits in relation to his total assets. By means of his simplified, conveniently arranged system of bookkeeping, which he kept in his own hand, Nobel was always aware of his exact financial position, and for a number of years he even drew up, as often as quarterly, a kind of trial balance to show the successive changes in his fortune. One almost gets the impression that he devoted himself to this work as a sort of hobby, comparable, in a sense, to that of a collector of coins or stamps.

Numerous bitter experiences in his later years made Alfred Nobel a sceptic who was rather suspicious of his fellow-men, and the constantly increasing, almost overwhelming number of persons who asked for his help or who wanted his financial support for various more or less dubious enterprises, helped to keep this feeling alive. But when he felt convinced that a gift of money would be of real value to a deserving person who had inspired his confidence, or when he became interested in some new scientific project, such as S.A. Andrée's trip to the North Pole in a balloon, he took great satisfaction in being generous.

It was especially in his dealings with young people with whom he had become acquainted and in whom he felt interested that he enjoyed helping and showing himself open-handed. Perhaps his recollections of his own youth and the difficulties and obstacles he had had to overcome also influenced him; his suspicions may also have been lulled when he was dealing with youngsters who had had little experience with life.

Another apparent contradiction between Nobel's theories and his practical work that has been regarded as especially striking and hard to explain was the interest he showed in the peace movement, while at the same time he tried to improve various kinds of war materials. In this respect there has been an almost universal misunderstanding of Nobel's most important achievements as an inventor and the truly pioneering contributions he made to the development of better communications, namely, his invention of modern explosives, such as dynamite, that were essential in the construction of highways, railways and canals as well as in mining. This misconception of a public not familiar with technical matters is revealed in the idea that nitroglycerine and dynamite are primarily war materials and not industrial products which under normal circumstances are used almost entirely for civilian purposes.

As a result of this mistaken idea, many people have been inclined to regard Nobel's fortune as based principally on his invention and production of war supplies, which is fundamentally wrong. As a matter of fact, the major part of his fortune was derived from his inventions in the field of purely civilian explosives, that is to say, first of all, his discovery of how to make nitroglycerine of practical use and then his invention of dynamite with the successive improvements he made later, especially his explosive gelatine [dating from 1875]. Nobel's only invention of any real military significance was his smokeless powder. But when that product was developed in 1887-89, Nobel had already become exceedingly wealthy from his earlier patents and the companies he had organized for the production of his new explosives. His patent on ballistite did, of course, bring him some revenue in the form of royalties and licence fees, but the total amount that accrued to him from this source up to his death in 1896 most probably did not exceed one-tenth of his estate when he died. At the same time he expended during those years rather large sums on further experiments. His financial interest in Bofors during the last three years of his life, in so far as it had anything to do with the production of war materials, did not bring him any profit whatever, rather the contrary.

When, in his *Tal till den svenska nationen* [Talks to the Swedish People], August Strindberg, perhaps in his disappointment at not having been included among the recipients of the literary Nobel Prize, refers in a derogatory way to 'Nobel money – some say dynamite money' as something morally tainted, he was obviously influenced by the above-mentioned misconception as to the real use of dynamite, though he may also have associated, as others have often done, the use of dynamite with the outrages committed by anarchists. But even if the relative importance of Nobel's preoccupation with munitions has been misjudged or exaggerated, there remains a certain inconsistency between his activities in that field and his interest in the peace movement. He certainly was aware of this seeming lack of logic himself, and in his letters to Bertha von Suttner and probably in his own mind he tried to justify it by the claim that his improvements in the means of destruction were more likely to make an end of war than the Baroness's peace congresses, which he also hailed with approval. Since the advent of the atomic age, technical developments have seemed to give fresh supports to this thesis, but actually it was hardly a premonition of this turn of events that inspired Nobel's work as an inventor of war implements, but rather his natural impulse to invent and improve. Once, when he discussed with me some of his ideas for improvements in this field, he suddenly remarked: 'Well, you know, it is rather fiendish things we are working on, but they are so interesting as purely theoretical problems and so completely technical as well as so clear of all financial and commercial considerations that they are doubly fascinating.'

In his outward appearance Nobel gave the impression of being rather nervous. His movements were lively, his gait somewhat mincing, his facial expression very changeable, as was his conversational style, which was often spiced with odd remarks and strange ideas. At times these remarks seemed almost absurd and appeared to be deliberately intended to shock old fogies. To his Swedish fellow-countrymen, who were unaccustomed to his light, French-inspired way of talking, he often seemed a bit bewildering, to say the least. An example of this is to be found in the memoirs of the late Count Hugo Hamilton, Speaker of the First Chamber of the Swedish Riksdag, in which he describes his meetings with Nobel, first at a dinner in a Stockholm restaurant together with A. E. Nordenskiöld, the famous explorer, at which Nobel was the host, and later during discussions in the presence of King Oscar II with S. A. Andrée regarding the latter's projected flight in a balloon to the North Pole.

On the former occasion Nobel had explained his plan for a kind of luxurious home in Paris for prospective suicides in which they could depart from this life with dignity and without pain, instead of having to drown themselves in the dirty waters of the Seine. To Nobel this was a form of intellectual sport, no matter how grim, in which I, too, heard him indulge on several occasions. The chief difference, compared with Hamilton's versions, was that the projected 'suicide institute' should be set up on the Riviera and provide a beautiful view of the Mediterranean and be equipped with a first-class orchestra, which would play only the most beautiful music.

In the presence of King Oscar and other people Nobel is reported to have developed a theory according to which the earth's crust ought to have deep cavities at the two Poles as a result of the rotation of the earth – obviously another *jeu d'esprit* which was not to be taken too seriously. I can recall a number of similar ideas and whimsies with which he liked to amuse himself and which he often used on purpose to confuse his associates, frequently with complete success. As for myself, I soon became accustomed to taking them for what they were intended to be, namely, a change of conversation and a form of mental relaxation after a busy day.

As another indication of Nobel's nervous temperament must also be considered his frequent travels and changes of residence. During the last three years of his life he owned, of course, three 'homes', those in San Remo, Paris and Bofors, which he visited alternately, as a rule, a couple of times annually. But each time his stays were usually limited to, at most, two or three months, and sometimes less. During an earlier period of his life, especially in the 1870's and 1880's, his travelling had no doubt been necessary in connection with his widespread activities and interests as an organizer and technician, but later on it had become a habit and a necessity even after his business activities no longer required it. However, during the last year of his life when in spite of his increasingly frequent heart attacks he felt inspired both by an undiminished urge to be active and a renewed desire to live, he seems to have planned to cut down his travels and to divide his time between his villa at San Remo during the winter season and his renovated manor house at Björkborn, near Bofors, during the summer months. But all such plans were terminated by his death.

THE SETTLEMENT OF ALFRED NOBEL'S ESTATE

On December 11, 1896, the day after Alfred Nobel's death, there were present at San Remo, two of his nephews, Hjalmar Nobel, the eldest son of his elder brother, Robert, and Emanuel, the eldest son of his next eldest brother, Ludvig, who as successor to his father was then manager of the Nobel Brothers Naphtha Company in Baku, as well as myself, who for the previous three years had been Alfred Nobel's personal assistant. As the eldest of the relatives and the one who had been in closest touch with the deceased, Emanuel Nobel naturally took charge of the arrangements for the funeral. It was decided that after a simple ceremony in the villa the remains should be sent to Stockholm for a public funeral and interment. For the service in the house Emanuel asked the pastor of the Swedish church in Paris, the Rev. Nathan Söderblom, who had known Nobel personally and been highly regarded by him, to come to San Remo, which is situated on the Italian Riviera just across the French border. On his way from Paris, he left the train at Nice and then walked over the high coastal road, *La Corniche*, with its magnificent views of the Mediterranean, as far as Menton, while he prepared in his mind the eloquent and dignified memorial address which he delivered on December 17 at the bier of Alfred Nobel in the villa at San Remo.

After the simple but moving ceremony in the house, the flower-decked coffin was taken in procession to the local railway station to be sent to Stockholm. There the more formal funeral rites were conducted on the afternoon of December 29, in the old Stockholm cathedral, *Storkyrkan*, which for the occasion had been profusely decorated with flowers.

After the service the coffin was escorted in solemn procession, preceded by mounted torchbearers, to the *New Cemetery* [Nya Kyrkogården], where in accordance with a wish expressed by the deceased in his will, cremation took place in the rather primitive establishment then available for the purpose.

Until the funeral was over, the Nobel relatives had been completely ignorant as to what provisions the will contained, even as to whether any will existed at all. As for myself, I was in a state of deep depression; I had lost a highly respected and beloved benefactor and friend whom I sorely missed, and the circumstances of his death, as described to me by his staff – all alone except for an Italian physician and a few French servants, who could not understand his final words – pained me deeply.

On top of that came the uncertainty as to what would happen to the experimental work on which I was busy in Sweden and in which I was keenly interested. It affected my own future as well as that of my friends and comrades in the laboratory. In the evening of December 15, when I was still on the Riviera and had already gone to bed in my hotel room, I was visited by Emanuel and Hjalmar Nobel, who informed me that they had received a telegram from Stockholm telling them that their uncle's will, which had been deposited in the Enskilda Bank of Stockholm, had been opened and that I, together with Rudolf Lilljeqvist, a Swedish industrialist, had been appointed executor of the estate. No other information as to the contents of the will had been given in the telegram, except that it directed that after the testator's death his veins should be opened and that not until that had been done and clear signs of death had been attested by qualified physicians, was the body to be cremated.

The request for the opening of his veins was prompted by a fear of being buried alive which had haunted Alfred Nobel as it had his father, Immanuel Nobel. When I conveyed this direction to the Italian physician who had attended him and who had already signed the death certificate, the latter appeared to be somewhat shocked. He pointed out, however, that the operation in question had already been performed as part of the embalming.

The information about my appointment as an executor caused me, at the outset, a completely sleepless night. I was confronted with a task that was wholly strange to me and for the accomplishment of which I lacked the essential qualifications. I had never met Rudolf Lilljeqvist, and how my association with him would turn out I did not know. As far as I could see, the only reason why Nobel had entrusted to me the duty of carrying out his last wishes in spite of my lack of the proper training, which must have been apparent to him, was that he had felt he could be sure that, to the best of my ability, I would try to follow his directions. The outcome of my meditations was, in fact, a firm resolve to make that my constant guide.

A day or so after the funeral service in San Remo, a letter arrived from Stockholm containing the full text of the will. I must admit that its contents, which affected those of us who were present in such different ways, at first made a discouraging impression on all of us. This was particularly true, of course, of Emanuel Nobel. While making a preliminary examination of the papers his uncle had left behind him in the house at San Remo, we had come across the older will dated March 14, 1893, on which the testator had made the notation that it had been cancelled and was replaced by another drawn up November 27, 1895.

Emanuel Nobel could not refrain from comparing the provisions in the two wills and observing the changes made in the later one by which the bequests to him and other members of the family had been considerably reduced, while he, personally, was no longer designated as one of the executors. The purely formal defects of the second will were, of course, also obvious, even when compared with the first one. The principal legatee, the future Nobel Foundation, did not exist as yet, and had, therefore, to be organized, and it seemed uncertain as to when and how this was to be done, and what would happen in the meantime, for instance, to the great Russian corporation, the Nobel Brothers Naphtha Company of Baku, in which Emanuel Nobel was especially interested and in which the stock owned by Alfred Nobel amounted, in effect, to a controlling interest.

At the same time, it seemed distasteful to him from the very start to oppose his uncle's expressed wishes.

These reflections and fears he confided to me, and I could very well sympathize with him. To this day I cannot recall without emotion the high-mindedness and courtesy he displayed towards me, though I had been appointed to represent interests which might be regarded as running counter to those he represented himself. As a matter of fact, he was to become my best supporter and guide in my future work as an executor to the will. A remark he once made left a deep impression on me. 'You must always remember,' he said, 'the obligation implied in the Russian word for the executor of a will – *Dushe Prikashshik* – which means "the spokesman for the soul". You must try to act accordingly.'

In retrospect, I must confess that the first reading of Nobel's will caused me genuine disappointment and worry. I had become deeply absorbed in the experiments I had performed for Nobel and under his supervision, and from his remarks I had concluded that, in some form or other, they were to be continued after his death. I also felt concerned about the future of Bofors after Nobel's strong financial support and technical experience were no longer available, and the idea of having to sell off or otherwise break up his large share in the Bofors Company [in Sweden], as well as in the Nobel Dynamite Trust Company [in Britain] and the Naphtha Company [in Russia] did not appeal to me at all.

At first these minor considerations somewhat overshadowed in my mind the main provisions of the will, i.e., Nobel's plans for the prizes. Only gradually did these become clear to me, and after that I was able to devote myself more wholeheartedly to their accomplishment. Fortunately, my fellow-executor, Rudolf Lilljeqvist, who was older and more experienced, had a more realistic outlook and was less inclined than I to be influenced by personal considerations. Throughout, he was, therefore, able to exert a wholesome influence on our decisions and our common actions.

After making temporary arrangements about the Nobel villa at San Remo, Emanuel Nobel and myself left for Sweden together. Having spent the Christmas holidays in my home at Bofors, I went to Stockholm, and there I had my first meeting with Mr. Lilljeqvist, which was the beginning of a close association that was to last for some years. He was about fourteen years older than I, considerably more experienced, especially in business matters, and, on the whole, perhaps of a more critical disposition. Though there were, of course, differences of opinion at various times, we were able to work together on the best of terms, and now, twenty years after his death, I still recall him with affection and respect.

We were both rather inexperienced in the court formalities and legal procedures that confronted us as executors and our most urgent need was, therefore, for a suitable Swedish lawyer who could guide our actions in such matters. On the advice of my brother Harald, we turned to Carl Lindhagen, the future Lord Mayor of Stockholm, who was then a Deputy Justice of the Svea Court of Appeal.

This choice turned out to be highly fortunate for the final realization of Nobel's ideas as expressed in his will. Lindhagen took a broad and not too formalistic view of the legal problems connected with our work; he became personally much interested in carrying out the testator's ideas, and he had special qualifications for dealing with both the Swedish institutions appointed to select the prize-winners and the Swedish authorities officially concerned with the proving of the will. He became, in effect, an associate executor.

On January 2, 1897, four days after the funeral, a Stockholm newspaper published the text of the most important part of Nobel's will, which was, of course, his direction that the main part of his estate should be set aside for a fund, the income from which should be distributed annually in the form of prizes in five different fields of human endeavour. This provision was declared by the paper itself, and with the endorsement of various prominent persons it had consulted, to be 'a gift to mankind, intended to further its development and promote its welfare, as well as to serve purely idealistic purposes – probably the most magnificent one of its kind that a private person has ever had both the desire and the ability to make.'

As a matter of fact, the publication was made earlier than seemed desirable from the point of view of the executors, for they had hoped that somewhere among Nobel's papers, whether in Paris or San Remo, they would be able to find some additional directives or instructions as to how the testator wanted certain provisions of the will to be applied. It was, of course, clear from the start that in this respect some kind of supplementary clarifications were necessary, and that in other respects too, the will was seriously defective in a formal sense. As already stated, the main legatee was a fund or endowment which did not yet exist and which therefore had to be created, while the institutions appointed to select the prize-winners had had imposed on them heavy duties involving great responsibilities without any provisions being made for their compensation and without any directions as to what should be done in case no suitable candidates could be found or agreed upon.

Furthermore, there was another difficulty of a purely legal nature: it was uncertain as to where the testator had had his legal residence, and, consequently, what judicial tribunal would be competent to decide on the validity of his will, as well as on the inventory of his estate and the administration of the property.

From several quarters, bitter attacks that gradually increased in virulence soon began to be directed against the fundamental idea of the will, while at the same time the formal defects in the terms were stressed more and more as reasons for declaring the whole endowment invalid. A rather sharp press campaign was also started, obviously with the support of some of Alfred Nobel's closest relatives in Sweden, who were openly urged by the newspapers in question to contest the will and to try to bring about a compromise by which the assets would be divided between the nearest relatives and the Swedish institutions designated as prize-juries.

The principal charges against the will were: the outright lack of patriotism shown by a Swede who, while neglecting Swedish national interests, had wanted to support, instead, certain international activities; the incapacity of the institutions designated as prize-awarders to perform satisfactorily the duties entrusted to them, which would, furthermore, interfere with their normal activities and expose their members to attempts at bribery and corruption; and, finally, the provision that the Peace Prize was to be awarded by a committee appointed by the parliament of Norway, which was held to involve the greatest dangers to Swedish interests, particularly in view of Sweden's strained relations with Norway over the union that was then in force.

Gradually, more and more newspapers, especially the conservative ones, became increasingly dubious about both the possibility and the wisdom of approving and applying the will. From the left, too, came severe criticism, which, in retrospect, may seem rather surprising. In a signed article of four columns, entitled: 'Alfred Nobel's Will – Magnificent Intentions – Magnificent Blunder', the late Hjalmar Branting, the Social-Democratic leader, criticized sharply the testator's provisions, partly from a practical and partly from a theoretical point of view.

The practical objections were of several kinds: the testator had not shown any interest in social welfare problems, or 'how these assets, which are the products of both nature and labour, may benefit everybody', and these tremendous prizes had been offered, he wrote, so far ahead along the course of human endeavour that those who received them would in any case obtain all the fame and wealth our civilization could offer. As regards the literary prize, which was to be awarded to the writer who had produced the best work of an idealistic character, it was held by Branting 'that the whole donation is blemished, in fact bungled, by Nobel's unfortunate choice of the Swedish Academy as the prize-jury', considering the interpretation which the Academy could be expected to place on the words 'an idealistic tendency'.

The Peace Prize too was criticized – by a future winner. After paying tribute to the Norwegian Storting as the prospective distributor, Mr. Branting wrote: 'The only way to peace, however, is through an international organization of the working classes in all countries, both in a political and an economic sense. From that it follows that really effective work for peace can never be performed by a single individual; that being so, the masses ought certainly to have a share in the sums which the Nobel Foundation may be able to disburse for this purpose and then use them to promote a steady and increasingly intensive peace propaganda.' In conclusion, Branting voiced his opposition, from the theoretical Marxist point of view, to the donation as a whole and the economic system that had made it possible. 'A millionaire who makes a donation may personally be worth every respect,' he declared, 'but it would be better to be rid of both millionaires and donations.'

On one point, however, the will was perfectly explicit, and that was the appointment of Lilljeqvist and myself as executors and what our duties were. It was, therefore, incumbent on us to make the most of this provision and to try to uphold our prerogatives. A definite obstacle was the fact that the rights and duties of executors had not by that time been definitely established in Swedish law, so that they were based entirely on what was accepted as current practice. In these matters we had to rely on Lindhagen for information and advice.

The problems we faced could be summarized as follows:

1. Legal formalities and contentious matters.
2. Economic transactions connected with the liquidation of the property and the reinvestment of all proceeds in 'first-class securities', as specified in the will.
3. The organization of a proper administrative body for the permanent management of the endowment fund and the formulation of rules for the annual distribution of the prizes.

In many respects these problems and projects were so intimately connected that they had to be taken up simultaneously. The legal aspects, to begin with, included, on the one hand, certain necessary, purely formal steps in different countries where the testator had owned property, and, on the other, a number of rather involved problems in regard to which differences of opinion or disputes could be expected to arise. The first category included, [a] the filing and proving of the will, and [b] legal authority for the executors to take charge of the assets, whether real or personal, of the deceased, including the right to make inventories in all countries, or wherever assets could be located, to collect whatever income might accrue, and, finally, put through the prescribed liquidation of the estate.

Among the contentious matters about which there might be differences of opinion was, first of all, the problem of the right court or judicial tribunal to which the will could be submitted for probate and whose approval should be sought for the solution of other legal questions connected with it – including possible lawsuits over the validity of the will and various other claims that might be made against the estate.

The problem of jurisdiction was, of course, intimately connected with that of the testator's legal residence or factual domicile, which, as already stated, was quite unsettled. At his death he owned two rather magnificent houses: those in Paris and San Remo, as well as the right to occupy the manor house at Björkborn, which had been recently renovated and partly rebuilt for the purpose, being, in fact, formally owned by the Swedish Bofors-Gullspång Company in which Nobel had a controlling interest. But since his ninth year, when he left Sweden with his mother and brothers to settle in Russia, he had never been a legal resident of any country – he was, in fact, what has been humorously described as 'Europe's wealthiest tramp'. In a strictly formal sense, jurisdiction over matters concerning his will and the estate would be exercised by the court authorities in the community of which he had last been a legal resident, which, in this case, was

Stockholm. On that theory Lindhagen took steps, on behalf of the executors, to have the will proved in the City Court of the Swedish capital.

In 1897 and 1898 Rudolf Lilljeqvist was intensely preoccupied with the construction of a new electro-chemical factory at Bengtsfors, which was remote from Stockholm. It therefore devolved on me to travel around and take whatever steps were necessary for the administration of the estate outside of Sweden, that is, in France, Italy and Germany. My first foreign visit, however, was made to Christiania, now Oslo, the capital of Norway, where I went early in 1897 to make contact as early as possible with representatives of the Norwegian Storting and make sure of their co-operation in the proving and application of the will. I first called on Sievert Nielsen, the President of the Storting, whom I had to see in his home, as he was slightly indisposed. Through Professor Brögger I also met a few more of the leading parliamentarians of Norway, and they all expressed themselves as favourably disposed toward the assignment given in the will to the Storting, namely, the selection of the Peace Prize winners.

About the middle of January I left for Paris, accompanied by my wife. We established ourselves in a small hotel of the old-French family-type near Nobel's former residence in the Avenue Malakoff, and there I often stayed during the next two years. My first call was made on the joint Swedish-Norwegian Minister in Paris, Frederik G. K. Due, who was a Norwegian and a distinguished composer of music as well as a diplomat. Personally, he had been well acquainted with Alfred Nobel. To get the proper help with whatever steps were immediately necessary in France, he advised me to get into touch with the Swedish Consul General in Paris, Gustaf Nordling, who had also known Nobel. Due also advised me to try to obtain Nordling's assistance on a more permanent basis.

When I called on the Consul General, I was received with the utmost cordiality, and he promised to do all he could to help us carry out our duties. The first step, he said, was to find a suitable French lawyer for consultation concerning the validity of the will in France and as to what legal formalities would be required. On the Consul General's advice, I turned to Maître Paul Coulet, a lawyer who was accredited before the Court of Appeal in Paris and who had been consulted on various occasions by the Swedish Legation and the Consulate General. To make the inventory, the assistance of a French notary was likewise required, and for this purpose Maître M. Labitte, owner of an old reputable notary's office in Paris, was selected.

From my very first discussions with Coulet and Nordling two things became clear to me: first, that from the French point of view it would be possible to maintain that Alfred Nobel's real home, or *domicile de fait*, was Paris, and, second, that under French civil law, the *Code Civil*, the validity of the will was more than doubtful because of its serious formal defects which were especially conspicuous when compared with the detailed and strict requirements of French law. But if Nobel's legal residence was determined to be in Paris, the will could also be contested before a French court, whose decision would be final, at least with regard to all property in France and possibly also in a few other countries, particularly Germany. In addition, there was the fact that if Paris was established as Nobel's legal residence, all property belonging to his estate in France, including all foreign securities deposited there, would be subject to French death duties, whereas if his legal residence was found to have been, for instance, in Sweden, only strictly French securities could be so taxed. That being the case, the official French taxation authority, the dreaded *Fisc*, could be expected to make every effort to have Paris declared Nobel's *domicile de fait*.

From every point of view it was therefore extremely urgent to have it established that Nobel's legal residence and, consequently, the jurisdiction over his estate was in Sweden. But to try to maintain before the French authorities that his factual domicile had been in Stockholm, where he had had no permanent home since he was nine years old [i.e., with his mother before she moved to Russia], would obviously be hopeless as being contrary to French law. The only hope of having a Swedish *domicile de fait* recognized thus lay in a claim that the house at Björkborn, near Bofors, had been his legal residence for a number of years just prior to his death, and that the local Karlskoga County Court consequently had jurisdiction over all matters affecting both the will and the estate.

After threshing this out in Paris, I summarized the above conclusion in a letter to Lindhagen, explaining the arguments in favour of abandoning the City Court in Stockholm as the proper tribunal and substituting the County Court of Karlskoga, whose jurisdiction covered Bofors and Björkborn, and recommending that the will should be filed in the latter court for probate, which was actually done.

But in order to obtain for the executors the right to dispose of Nobel's property in France, whether real or personal, an official act or document was required, in addition to the will itself. It would have to certify the executors' authority under existing Swedish law and practice. But to get such a certificate from the Swedish authorities before the will had been proved would obviously take a great deal of time, to say the least. It was found, in fact, when Lindhagen somewhat later tried to get such a document formulated in a way that would be acceptable in France, that the obstacles were really insurmountable. In Paris, the problem was solved in a practical way by having the Consul General issue, by virtue of his position as a representative of Swedish authorities and interests, a so-called *certificat de coutume,* setting forth Swedish legal practice in regard to the rights and privileges of executors of wills.

By that time it appeared that the publication of Nobel's will had begun to cause great inconveniences and complications to the Nobel Brothers Naphtha Company in Baku and that as a result his nephew, Emanuel Nobel, had been placed in a very difficult dilemma. The value of the company's shares had shrunk considerably on account of the rumours that had been circulated, partly by rival business concerns, to the effect that a forced sale of Alfred Nobel's stock was imminent; certain business transactions that had been planned in consultation with Alfred Nobel himself had to be called off, and Emanuel Nobel was bombarded from various quarters with pleas to contest the will. Personally, he did not know what to do. I tried to induce him to await developments and promised him I would insist that there should be no forced sale of the oil stock and that we would try to come to a satisfactory agreement on that point.

While Emanuel Nobel was still in Paris, we had a meeting arranged by the Swedish Consul General with a prominent French journalist, Adolphe Brisson, at which Nordling himself and Per Lamm, a Swedish businessman living in Paris, were also present. On the basis of the information then given him about Alfred Nobel and his will, Brisson wrote a couple of prominently displayed articles in the leading Paris afternoon newspaper, *Le Temps,* in which he rectified a few rather unfavourable statements about Nobel that had appeared in the French press. Emanuel Nobel expressed his satisfaction with this move and during the interview made weighty contributions himself to explain his uncle's general attitude and the fundamental ideas in his will. Thereby he clearly committed himself to a certain degree in favour of the will. On the other hand, I learned from my conversations with him that we could expect a contest from some of the relatives living in Sweden.

From the very first it had seemed to me extremely desirable to avoid a dispute with the Nobel heirs over the validity of the will, provided it was in any way possible to do so by mutual agreement and without defeating the testator's fundamental purposes. On this point I exchanged letters with his nephew, Ludvig Nobel, and later with the latter's elder brother, Hjalmar Nobel, both sons of Alfred's eldest brother, Robert. In view of the way matters threatened to develop, it was considered urgent at the discussions with Nordling and Coulet to speed up in every way possible the settlement of matters connected with the estate in France and the disposal of its assets in that country so as to forestall the risk of a lawsuit in a French court over the question of legal residence and the validity of the will. By myself, I neither wished to nor could assume the entire responsibility for that and therefore asked Lilljeqvist to give his power of attorney to Nordling as his legal representative, in case he could not come to Paris himself. I furthermore wrote to Lindhagen, asking him to come to Paris, which he did, arriving on February 16, 1897.

We then agreed to take possession of all valuable documents and securities that had been deposited by Alfred Nobel in different French banks or with private banking firms in Paris or elsewhere, so as to forestall a possible legal attachment on behalf of the relatives. The securities were kept in a number of places, at the Comptoir National d'Escompte, the Crédit Lyonnais, Messein, Weille & Cie. and the private banking firm of Le Guay, while in Nobel's private safe in the house in Avenue Malakoff only a few worthless stock certificates were found.

On the strength of the certificate signed by Nordling, all of the securities owned by Alfred Nobel were gradually withdrawn from the various open deposit accounts and placed in three large *coffres forts* or cash boxes at the Comptoir d'Escompte to await an opportunity to send them out of France to a safer storing place. The withdrawal and re-deposit took about three weeks, and was continued by Nordling after I had left Paris for a short visit to England, where I engaged Timothy Warren as our lawyer. He had known Alfred Nobel since the days of the cordite suit and later rendered us invaluable services in the settling of the estate in Great Britain. I also made arrangements with the head of the Union Bank of Scotland, which Nobel himself had used for many years, for the deposit of the securities he had kept in Paris as well as for their ultimate sale. After my return to Paris and after the securities which had been kept in open deposit at the Comptoir National d'Escompte and which represented the bulk of Nobel's estate in France, had been transferred to vaults engaged in the name of the executors and Nordling, I returned to Sweden.

In Sweden the will had been submitted for probate on behalf of the executors at the Stockholm Court on February 5, 1897, and also at the County Court of Karlskoga on the 9th of the same month. In connection with the hearing in the City Court, two of the witnesses to the signature of the will were heard, the engineers R. V. Strehlenert and Leonard Hvass, who, after acknowledging their own signatures under oath, gave sworn testimony as to remarks made by the testator in their presence about his motives for the provisions in the will. Charles Waern, who had been in touch with the donor on various occasions during the later years of Nobel's life, also recounted under oath some of the remarks made to him by Nobel a few months before his death.

The publication of these testimonies in full in the newspapers caused a fresh sensation and started another press debate as to the possibility of carrying out the provisions of the will. At the same time, some of the evidence provoked redoubled irritation among the relatives living in Sweden. With some justification they felt they had been unnecessarily humiliated by the repetition by one of the witnesses of a remark by Alfred Nobel in which he criticized his brother Robert's disposal of his own estate. The executors' relations with the members of Robert Nobel's family were thereby made even more strained and, to some extent perhaps, unnecessarily so.

THE NEGOTIATIONS WITH THE HEIRS AND THE PRIZE-AWARDING INSTITUTIONS

After a conference in Stockholm with Lindhagen the executors decided to address identical letters to the Swedish institutions appointed in Alfred Nobel's will to select winners of his prizes, asking them to assume that responsibility. The text of the letter sent to the Academy of Sciences, for instance, was as follows:

'Stockholm, March 24, 1897.

Gentlemen,

We, the undersigned, who have been designated by the late Dr. Alfred Nobel as executors of his last will and testament, have the honour to transmit herewith a certified copy of the will in question with a respectful request that the Academy will accept the appointment to award the prizes in physics and chemistry and inform us of its decision.

It is, however, obvious that with regard to the conditions and procedure connected with the award of the prizes established by Dr. Nobel, more detailed regulations are required than the general terms contained in the will. In so far as it affects the prizes to be presented in Sweden, it seems to us that this can best be arranged by having the Swedish prize-adjudicating institutions appoint special representatives: for instance, two from the Academy of Science, and one each from the Caroline Institute and the Swedish Academy, respectively, who will then confer with us on this subject.

Subsequently, a definitive proposal, approved by the said institutions and by the undersigned, ought to be submitted to His Majesty the King through the Ministry of Education and Ecclesiastical Affairs with a humble request for His Majesty's sanction. It is also our intention to submit at the same time to His Majesty our suggestions for the necessary rules regarding the management of the endowment fund.

On the above grounds, and assuming that the Academy accepts the responsibility in question, we further request that you will appoint two delegates who, together with one from the Caroline Institute and another from the Swedish Academy, will consult with us about detailed regulations concerning the terms and methods of awarding the prizes.

[Signed] Ragnar Sohlman Rudolf Lilljeqvist.'

On the same day the executors also sent to the Norwegian Storting a copy of the will with a respectful request that the Storting would accept the responsibility entrusted to it under the will, namely, the selection of the Peace Prize winners. Only a month later, on April 26, 1897, that body adopted a formal resolution assuming the task. The reactions of the Swedish institutions will be described later.

In compliance with suggestions from various influential quarters to the effect that it would be appropriate to present a copy of the will to His Majesty King Oscar II, Lilljeqvist and myself attended for that purpose one of the King's general audience hours. We were cordially received, but on that occasion the King did not engage in any conversation regarding either the will or its execution. In the press, of course, fears had been expressed that the provision giving the Norwegian Storting the right to select winners of the Peace Prize might have a disturbing effect on the relations between Norway and Sweden [see p. 42].

My immediate return to Paris was necessitated by telegrams and letters from Consul General Nordling, informing us that Hjalmar and Ludvig Nobel, the sons of Alfred Nobel's elder brother Robert, together with their brother-in-law, Count Carl Gustaf Ridderstolpe, husband of their sister Ingeborg, had arrived in Paris to investigate the situation with a view to a possible court action against the will.

Immediately after my arrival we therefore began to transfer the Nobel securities from the bank in Paris [see p.48], partly to London and partly to Stockholm. The stocks and bonds which we thought should be sold were sent to the London headquarters of the Union Bank of Scotland and the Government bonds and other securities which we felt ought to be kept by the estate to the Enskilda Bank in Stockholm.

The securities were sent in insured postal packages, which had to be presented at a special *Expédition des Finances* at the Gare du Nord. At first it had been proposed that I should personally make a few trips to London and then to Stockholm with the valuables, but since that seemed a little risky and also too slow, an agreement was made, instead, with the Rothschild banking firm to insure the consignments, since the French post office could not insure any packages for more than 20,000 francs. In the Rothschild policy it was stipulated that the shipments on any single day should not exceed two and a half million francs in value and that the insurance should take effect only after the French postal insurance receipts for the first 20,000 francs in each package had been presented to the banking firm.

Securities to the value of not more than the above sum of two and a half million francs were then withdrawn daily for a week from the vaults of the Comptoir National d'Escompte and taken to the Consulate General's office in Rue de la Pépinière, where they were listed, tied up in bundles, wrapped up and sealed. In the afternoon they were taken to the *Expédition des Finances* at the Gare du Nord to be sent to London or Stockholm, as the case might be. Since the actual transfers to and from the Consulate General involved certain risks of hold-ups and robberies, special precautions were taken and care was exercised to avoid attention. From the bank vaults the papers were fetched by Nordling and myself, assisted by a clerk named Jacob Seligmann, who had been sent from Stockholm, and after they had been packed in a suitcase we took an ordinary horse-cab to the Consulate General. With a loaded revolver in my hand I sat in the cab prepared to defend the suitcase in case a collision with another carriage had been arranged by robbers – at that time a not unusual occurrence in Paris. The transfer to the Gare du Nord was made in the same style.

In retrospect it may seem rather odd that we proceeded that way instead of simply instructing the bank to make the transfers itself in the usual manner. But we feared that under the circumstances such an order would attract undue attention and lead to objections from, for example, the French tax authorities – *Le Fisc* – particularly in view of the still unsettled question as to whether death duties were to be paid in France on all the securities stored there or only on those of French origin – a problem connected with the question of Alfred Nobel's legal residence.

One day while we were engaged in these activities, the Consul General was visited in his office by Hjalmar and Ludvig Nobel and Count Ridderstolpe, who had come to discuss with him the matter of Alfred Nobel's legal residence and the validity of his will, etc. In the meantime Seligmann and myself were occupied in another room with the listing and packaging of the Nobel securities, but the visitors remained unaware of our presence. As an official representative of Sweden, Nordling felt, however, that he had been placed in an uncomfortable position, and after the last consignment had left – this was on a Saturday – he proposed that we should inform the relatives about what we had done. For this purpose he suggested that the next day we should invite them to a 'peace and reconciliation' dinner at which I was to tell them what had happened. Obviously, I could not object, and a choice dinner was arranged by Nordling, who, as an old Parisian, had had plenty of experience in such matters.

The dinner was held at the famous Noël Peter restaurant in the Passage des Princes. The atmosphere, which at first was somewhat heavy, gradually became brighter. When the coffee was served we began to discuss the situation in France with regard to Alfred Nobel's legal residence and the proving of his will. Hjalmar Nobel tried to make me admit that the claim as to a legal residence at Bofors was pure pretence and that we ought to be able to agree that his uncle's real domicile had been in Paris, or possibly at San Remo, but that the strongest arguments favoured Paris, where he had lived for seventeen years and where his house and his servants were still to be found. The proper tribunal to determine his legal rights should therefore be a French court, which should also decide on the validity of his will.

To this I replied that, naturally, the matter was open to discussion, but that it was of only theoretical interest, anyway, since all his important securities had been removed from Paris and were no longer under French jurisdiction. I, therefore, advised him to give up every thought of a contest in France and turn, instead, to a Swedish court, if he still insisted on making objections. This information naturally caused a great sensation, and at first Hjalmar refused to believe my statement, which was, however, confirmed by the Consul General. Hjalmar then proposed that we should submit our differences to arbitration, but he did not explain his plan in detail, and I found it hard to understand.

A French court decision to the effect that Alfred Nobel's *domicile de fait* had been in Paris would not only have meant that all his assets would have been taxable in France, no matter where located, but that his will might also have been declared invalid, particularly in view of its formal defects, which from the point of view of French law were especially glaring, and that, in turn, would have meant that his whole bequest would have been nullified. That he himself had never imagined such an outcome was perfectly clear to me. When he wrote his will in Swedish and selected Swedish fellow-countrymen as both witnesses and executors as well as Swedish or Norwegian institutions to choose the winners of his prizes, he must have considered himself a Swede, even if one of an international type, and, having absolute faith in the integrity of the Swedish courts, he obviously took it for granted that a Swedish judicial authority would ultimately decide on the validity of his final testamentary provisions. If he had foreseen any difficulties because Paris might be found to have been his legal residence, he certainly would have had his securities transferred exactly as we had done. While alive, he was in the habit of constantly changing his places of deposit.

The immediate result of our announcement was an increase in the activities of Hjalmar Nobel and the other Nobel relatives associated with him. It was rumoured that the prominent French lawyers they had already consulted in Paris were extremely annoyed at the new situation, especially – according to what M. Coulet told me – because they felt they were to blame for not having taken action earlier to sequester the securities. On their advice, Hjalmar Nobel now asked for a court attachment on whatever property was left in Paris, both on his own account and on behalf of the other relatives in Sweden. This affected, first of all, the house in the Avenue Malakoff, the sale of which was thereby prevented, causing the estate a considerable loss. [The furniture and other personal property had already been sold by auction.] Moreover, Hjalmar Nobel went to Germany and there applied through his lawyer for an attachment on all the Nobel property in that country. A similar action was also begun in Britain, though without success. In Germany I had long before engaged a Dr. Scharlach, a prominent German jurist, as our lawyer. He had been recommended by the directors of the German Dynamite Company, which was a successor to Alfred Nobel & Company in Hamburg. His duties were to protect the interests of the executors and the estate as to assets of more than six million kronor which were deposited with German banks and other concerns.

As a preparation for a possible French court action against the will by the disappointed Swedish relatives, for which we would need a better known and more widely recognized lawyer than Maître Coulet, I had instructed Nordling to visit, together with Coulet, the famous French jurist and statesman, Pierre Waldeck-Rousseau, and provisionally engage him as our chief legal adviser in a possible contest. Nordling then told me that he and M. Coulet had met Waldeck-Rousseau and that Coulet had explained to him the whole problem affecting the will in France and also informed him of our actions so far. In general, I was told, Waldeck-Rousseau had shared Coulet's views as to the proper legal tribunal and the limitation of French tax rights to purely French securities.

While I was in Paris, I too had an opportunity to visit Waldeck-Rousseau in his home and was greatly impressed by his personality. He explained his own view as to the question of domicile and said he was of the opinion that according to French law Bofors could be the only alternative to Paris as Alfred Nobel's *domicile de fait.* He also discussed the prospects of getting the will proved in a French court, which he considered possible, while at the same time he shared our apprehensions as to the difficulties and uncertainties that might be encountered.

In Sweden preliminary court skirmishes between the two opposing parties had taken place during the spring of 1897. They had been formally started by test-suits, in Stockholm and Bofors, respectively, to determine which court had jurisdiction over the estate. The decisions in both cases favoured the County Court of Karlskoga, under whose jurisdiction Bofors fell, while at the same time the objections raised by the relatives to the right of the executors to intervene as parties to the action were overruled. Successive appeals by the plaintiffs to the higher courts had the same result, and before the matter was finally settled by a decree of the Swedish Government to the same effect on April 6, 1898, or a year later, it could also be announced on behalf of the executors that in a suit in Paris against the estate involving a considerable sum, the French Court had likewise declared itself incompetent to decide on the matter, because at the time of his death Alfred Nobel had not been a resident of Paris but of Bofors, in Sweden.

In Paris, as already stated, Consul General Nordling had worried about his assistance to the executors, although, as Lindhagen had certified, 'he had not been guilty of anything except of aiding, as a conscientious Swedish official should, in the accomplishment of Nobel's commendable purposes.' His concern was, however, much allayed by a decision of the Swedish Government, on May 21, 1897, to instruct the Attorney General of Sweden to institute on behalf of the Government whatever legal actions were necessary to have the will declared valid. This decision had been preceded by a letter from the executors, dated April 21, 1897, in which they had enclosed a copy of the will 'for the information of His Majesty's Government in connection with whatever measures the Government might consider appropriate'.

In his comment on this letter the Attorney General had then stated that while no direct interests of the Crown required him to intervene on the side of the executors in their petition to have the will admitted to probate, the donation had been made by a Swedish subject for a public purpose, supervision over which would ultimately devolve on the Swedish authorities, and that also, since the Swedish institutions designated as distributors of the prizes established by the will would, thereby, not only assume certain responsibilities but also acquire certain rights, the Government ought to do what it could to help to put the testator's noble intentions into effect by taking the proper measures on behalf of the State to have the will legally proved.

In connection with its instructions to the Attorney General to take such measures, the Government also directed the Swedish Academy, the Academy of Sciences, and the Chancellor of the Swedish State Universities, as the representative of the Caroline Institute, to take the appropriate legal steps for the same purpose, in which they would be entitled to assistance from the Attorney General.

Consequently, the will was submitted for probate at the Karlskoga County Court not only by the executors, but also on behalf of the Swedish Government, as well as the Swedish Academy, the Royal Academy of Sciences, and the Caroline Institute. At the request of the executors, the

Norwegian Storting likewise petitioned the Court for probate, being represented in this action, at the suggestion of the executors, by one of the latter's own legal advisers, Judge Henrik Santesson, who after that continued to represent the Storting in matters affecting the will in Sweden as well in the discussions of the charter and by-laws of the prospective Nobel Foundation. The above recommendation of the Swedish Attorney General and the Government's decision based on it must unquestionably have been a disappointment to the Swedish relatives who wanted to contest the will. While awaiting the final outcome of a possible appeal by these relatives to the higher courts, there was nothing to do but to renew our attempts to enlist the co-operation of the prospective prize-juries in clarifying the sketchy provisions in the will regarding the future prize awards. A special opportunity for this was offered in connection with the discussions that took place within those bodies concerning the previously cited letter of the executors [see p. 49].

In the most influential circles within the institutions designated as prize-juries there had appeared from the beginning, as already stated, a certain difference of opinion as to whether the new duties should be assumed, and strong fears were expressed that the proposed endowment would only cause harm to scientific research in Sweden as well as to the prize-judges themselves. The debate on this point was especially lively in the Swedish Academy and the Royal Academy of Sciences. At the Caroline Institute, too, certain members, led by Professor Axel Key, agitated for a remodelling of the whole plan so that each institution named as a prize-adjudicator would have the widest possible opportunities to use its share in the Nobel estate as it saw fit – a desire that could, of course, be attained only with the assistance of the relatives and by supporting their efforts to have the will declared invalid. In the Swedish Academy, the final vote in favour of accepting the responsibility was twelve to two.

On my return to Stockholm from France in May, 1897, I therefore called, as Lindhagen had suggested, on some of the most influential members of the above institutions, first of all on those I had known personally since my early youth. Besides Carl David af Wirsén, who was then Permanent Secretary of the Swedish Academy, I saw its President, Hans Forssell, a prominent historian, publicist, and politician, as well as a member also of the Academy of Sciences, Professor Magnus Gustaf Retzius of the Caroline Institute and Fredrik Adam Smitt, Professor of Zoology at the University of Stockholm, both members of the Academy of Sciences, and finally Professor Axel Key, the Rector of the Caroline Institute.

Forssell told me that, in theory, he was opposed to having the academies of which he was a member accept the new assignments but felt that in both institutions he was alone in this respect. However, he would now try, he explained, to have the academies assume their new responsibilities but only on the condition that all doubtful points could be cleared up in a satisfactory manner. He did not go into details as to what he meant by that. To formulate specific conditions, he said, would only give the heirs an opportunity to complain that the conditions did not harmonize with the terms of the will.

The others took a favourable attitude and declared themselves prepared to support the executors' request. Professor Key let me read an answer he had drafted for the approval of the Caroline Institute, which was later secured. In the draft the faculty declared itself ready to assume the new duties, provided that official sanction could be obtained for certain amplifications of the will and more detailed instructions for its application. Furthermore, in Key's draft the Institute declared itself prepared to appoint a delegate to represent it at future conferences with the executors and delegates from the other prize-awarding institutions. As such a delegate the Institute later selected Professor Key himself, who after his retirement was succeeded by Count K. A. H. Mörner, another professor at the Institute.

For its part, the Academy of Sciences appointed a special committee to report on the will in so far as its bequests for public purposes were concerned. In its report dated May 7, 1897, the committee recommended acceptance of the commission, provided that sufficient clarifications were legally approved so as to obviate as far as possible all obstacles to the practical application of the will. The additions to its terms which the committee regarded as necessary were listed in an attached memorandum. In principle, they contained nothing beyond what was subsequently incorporated in the statutes of the Nobel Foundation. They were also in accord on all essential points with what was later stated in a letter of May 29, 1897, from the Caroline Institute to the executors.

When the subject came up before the Academy of Sciences, however, Hans Forssell, who had already been defeated in the Swedish Academy [see p. 56], succeeded in having the committee's report rejected and in persuading the Academy of Sciences not to commit itself as to whether it would accept the appointment to act as a prize-jury until the will had been legally proved. He also induced the Academy to table the executors' request for the appointment of two delegates to confer with them and the other delegates regarding the proposed amplifications of the will. Surprisingly enough, Forssell's argument against such participation was that this would only encourage the relatives to start a court action against the will on the grounds of the proposed additions and clarifications.

Owing to the negative attitude of the Academy of Sciences, which had been designated as distributor of prizes in both physics and chemistry, the whole problem of getting the will approved thus reached a deadlock – a situation which must have been anticipated by the shrewd Forssell, whose expressed desire it had been from the very beginning to thwart the whole project.

In order to get the will proved it was necessary, of course, that the prize-adjudicating institutions should accept in advance their respective assignments, as otherwise the will would be null and void, in one respect or another. And when one of the prospective prize-juries refused even to appoint delegates to discuss the terms on which it would accept such a responsibility, no binding negotiations on the subject were possible. No progress could therefore be made in the matter.

This situation forced the executors to try to reach some sort of compromise with the relatives, who were represented by a prominent lawyer from Gothenburg, Dr. Philip Leman. The latter had already let it be known that he would be willing to do what he could to bring about an amicable settlement. Personally, I was also strongly inclined to favour one, while Lilljeqvist remained sceptical both as to the possibility of arriving at an acceptable solution of that kind and as to our power as executors to commit the estate, and ultimately the future Nobel Foundation, to economic concessions which would affect unfavourably the interests of future Nobel Prize winners. As a matter of fact, his attitude strengthened our position considerably during the final negotiations.

In order to get a clearer view of the whole situation and the prospects abroad in case we became involved in a contest over the will, we decided to invite the foreign legal advisers of the estate to meet with Lindhagen and ourselves in Stockholm early in July, 1897. On July 2-3 we met at the Hotel Rydberg in that city with Maître Coulet from Paris and Mr. Timothy Warren from Glasgow, but in place of Dr. Scharlach from Hamburg came his younger associate, a Dr. Westphal. The outcome of the conference was that Coulet and Warren considered the respective situations in France and Britain favourable to the extent that there was no danger of any further legal action against the validity of the will in those countries, while Westphal recommended an immediate compromise with the relatives. In this he had undoubtedly been influenced by Max A. Philipp, President of the German Dynamite Company, who earlier in the year had tried, at Hjalmar Nobel's request, to induce me to agree to arbitration.

This conference with three prominent jurists from different countries, each one quite typical of his own nation, was extremely interesting and also had amusing moments. The most talkative was Coulet, who made long and eloquent addresses in the grand manner in which he discussed the arguments for and prospects of a realization of Alfred Nobel's high-minded ideas without any compromise, as if he had been pleading in some important suit before the Court of Appeal in Paris. When he was through we applauded him, too. Even the dryly humorous Scotchman, Mr. Warren, remarked afterwards: 'The little chap speaks quite nicely, doesn't he?' In addition to these, as it were, formal debates on theories, we naturally availed ourselves of the opportunity to discuss thoroughly with each one of the foreign lawyers the special problems that had come up in their respective countries.

The size of Alfred Nobel's estate and its wide distribution over a number of different countries, as well as the often complicated conditions in those countries, which affected the appraisal of the assets, had delayed our performance of the duty which first of all devolved upon us as executors, namely, making a consolidated inventory of the estate. For that reason we had to ask, on two separate occasions, for the permission of the County Court at Karlskoga to postpone our report.

The work progressed, however, so that, finally, the heirs could be invited to be present at the formal proceedings on October 30, 1897, at Bofors. Judge E. Hagelin attended as representative of Mrs. Pauline Nobel, widow of Robert Nobel, as well as of her sons, Hjalmar and Ludvig Nobel, and Count Ridderstolpe and his wife. Hjalmar Nobel was also present. Nothing was heard from the other heirs. Lindhagen appeared for the executors, assisted by Jacob Seligmann, who had aided us in Paris, while Lilljeqvist and myself formally reported on the assets we had taken over.

Before we began, the representative of the Swedish heirs presented a written protest against the legality of the proceedings on the following grounds:

That it had not yet been finally determined which court had jurisdiction over the estate;

that in case a Swedish tribunal was designated, the heirs were of the opinion that it ought to be the City Court of Stockholm;

that the selection of a proper person to make the inventory would in that case be the duty of the Mayor and City Council of Stockholm, and, if a country district court was designated, of the heirs and not the executors; and finally,

that while, according to hearsay, inventories had been made of the property of the decedent in France and other foreign countries, the heirs had not been notified to attend.

This protest had no particular effect; the inventory was completed and was finally submitted in due form to the County Court at Karlskoga on November 9, 1897, or about eleven months after Nobel's death.

In the consolidated inventory, we had divided the assets, on Lindhagen's advice, into two groups:

A. Assets on which no foreign death duties were payable	18,123,043.42 Kr.
B. Foreign assets on which such duties were payable	15,110,748.78 Kr.
Total	33,233,792.20 Kr.
The liabilities were estimated at	1,646,589.92 Kr.
Net	31,587,202.28 Kr.

The geographical distribution of Nobel's assets at the time of his death, according to the countries in which they were either situated or deposited, was as follows:

Sweden	5,796,140.00	Austria	228,754.20	England	3,904,235.32
Norway	94,472.28	France	7,280,817.23	Italy	630,410.10
Germany	6,152,250.95*	Scotland	3,913,938.67	Russia	5,232,773.45
				Total	33,233,792.20 Kr.

The executors maintained that in Sweden death duties should be paid only on the securities listed under A, minus the debts, but the courts did

* Among the securities deposited with the Disconto Gesellschaft in Berlin were the following Russian stocks and bonds:
Russian Government Bonds 511,589.25 Kr.
Shares in the Nobel Brothers Naphtha Co. 169,000.00 Kr.

not sustain their claim, which was rejected by the Government too. The total death duties on all assets which the estate thus had to pay in Sweden amounted to 1,843,692.25 Kr., while those paid in foreign countries totalled 1,325,949.96 Kr., or altogether 3,169,642.21 Kr., i.e. close on ten per cent.

After the inventory had been filed in November, 1897, we began to dispose of such assets as should be sold at once as well as to clear up whatever commitments the deceased had made. This work forced me to make another trip abroad, and after visiting, first England and then Hamburg, I accepted, in December 1897, an invitation from Emanuel Nobel to visit him in St. Petersburg, where we had a few quiet days together during which we discussed, in detail, both the problem of the will in general, and the disposal of Alfred Nobel's Russian assets in particular. Informally, we took up the possibility of transferring, on behalf of the family, his shares in the Naphtha Company to Emanuel Nobel.

When I got back to Stockholm for Christmas, we tried to find a way to break the deadlock caused by the refusal of the Academy of Sciences to appoint delegates to consult with us. We decided to invite the delegates of the Swedish Academy and the Caroline Institute, Dr. Wirsén and Count Mörner, respectively, to confer informally with us and our lawyer, Carl Lindhagen, about the will and its application without waiting for the Academy of Sciences to make up its mind. At six protracted meetings during the months of January and February, 1898, the minutes of which were subsequently printed, we discussed, on the basis of a memorandum that had been prepared by Lindhagen in consultation with the executors, certain elaborations of and additions to the will which we felt should be incorporated in the statutes of the Nobel Foundation. As voluntary and non-official representatives of the Academy of Sciences, Professors L. F. Nilson and Otto Pettersson also took part. [Professor Nilson had been a member of the committee appointed the year before by the Academy to study and report on our original letter.] Wirsén was elected chairman and Lindhagen secretary of these informal meetings. The latter was also authorized to act as spokesman for the executors.

In the course of these discussions an agreement was reached as to what general principles should be followed in drawing up the future statutes. The establishment of a scientific institution, to be called *The Nobel Institute,* to aid the prize-juries in their choice of laureates, was proposed by Nilson,

Pettersson and Sohlman. In the discussion of this subject, which greatly interested the two members of the Academy of Science, Lindhagen's close friend, Professor Svante Arrhenius, the well-known physicist, also took part, but his name does not appear in the minutes since he was not then a member of the Academy of Sciences.

In the last two meetings Emanuel Nobel was invited by the executors to take part as a representative of the Nobel relatives living in Russia. In that capacity he made a statement at the meeting on February 11, 1898, which was to be decisive for the acceptance of the will and, consequently, also for the establishment of the Nobel Foundation. On this subject the second paragraph in the minutes for that day reads as follows:

'Mr. Nobel explained that he wished to respect his late uncle's aims and desires as expressed in his will. Consequently, he did not intend to dispute its terms. To achieve his uncle's wishes it was, however, necessary to make certain alterations in and additions to the will, and this could not be done without the consent of all the heirs.

'Mr. Nobel, therefore, asked to be informed about all such proposed changes or supplementary provisions in order to be able to decide, after comparing them with the wishes and plans of his late uncle, whether he and his nearest relatives could approve of them.

'In deference to this request all those present declared that they took it for granted that the opinions of all of Alfred Nobel's immediate heirs would be asked for, and, on behalf of the executors, Mr. Sohlman added that the latter had always wished to perform their tasks in close contact with the heirs and that, in view of Emanuel Nobel's expressed attitude towards his uncle's will, they would in the future, as they had in the past, regard it as their right and duty to make use of his advice and assistance in settling the estate, particularly in trying to reach a happy solution of the problems connected with the application of the will.'

Only ten days earlier the relatives living in Sweden had taken the definite step of starting a legal action to contest the will. Their complaint had been signed on February 1, 1898, and was submitted to the County Court of Karlskoga whose jurisdiction had by then been established. It was directed against the executors of the will, the Swedish Government, the Norwegian Storting, and the three Swedish institutions designated as prize-juries. The plaintiffs represented twelve of the twenty relatives entitled to a share in the estate, if the will was declared invalid. Their complaint was based on its alleged technical defects, such as its failure to designate a residuary legatee pending the organization of a definite Foundation, as well as the uncertainty as to where the testator had had his legal residence. The property should, therefore, it was claimed, be turned over to the relatives, and the executors be made accountable, first of all, to them. If any of the institutions designated as prize-juries should declare themselves willing to distribute the income in the form of prizes, the relatives should at least have charge of the management of the capital fund. To prevent possible misunderstandings the plaintiffs finally declared themselves prepared, in case they won the suit, to do what they could to carry out the testator's main purposes.

Because of the long delay in answering to which the Norwegian Storting was entitled as a foreign defendant, the first hearing of the suit could not take place until September 29, 1898, and when the case was called on that day, it was announced in two documents submitted to the court, dated respectively May 29, and June 5, 1898, that the dispute had been settled out of court. Since all parties had agreed to the compromise, the court had no choice but give its formal approval, and the case was closed.

Before the compromise was reached, however, Emanuel Nobel, as spokesman for the branch of the family living in Russia, including his younger brothers and sisters, had continued to be subjected to strong pressure and attempts to make him join cause with the relatives in Sweden in their opposition to the will. This pressure came not only from the relatives themselves, but also from the highest and most influential circles in Stockholm.

Personally, Emanuel Nobel was in a very odd and difficult situation as the guardian of his younger brothers and sisters and as such obliged to look after their interests as well as he could. One of them has since described how he called them together and, after explaining to them the situation, asked for their approval of the attitude he intended to take in regard to the will and any agreements he might sign in order to protect the honour of the Nobel family as well as the financial interests of the relatives. They were all deeply moved and readily consented to his proposal.

As has already been related, Emanuel had felt repelled from the very beginning by the idea of trying to interfere with his uncle's disposition of his property, or of participating in radical changes such as the proposed division of the estate between the relatives and the institutions designated to award the prizes. His whole financial interest in the settlement of the estate was limited to a wish to acquire for his family the controlling interest in the Nobel Brothers Naphtha Company in Baku which his uncle had owned, so as to keep the management of that concern in the hands of the Nobel relatives.

On this score there probably was a certain feeling of rivalry between Emanuel and his cousins, the children of Robert Nobel. After all, Robert had been the first to propose that the brothers should enter the oil business in Baku, and for a number of years he had been the local manager of the company until his failing health and possibly also his lack of persistence caused him to retire and live in Sweden as a *rentier*. After that the management of the great enterprise had been left in the competent hands of his younger brother Ludvig, and, after the latter's death in 1888, in those of his eldest son Emanuel. In the meantime, Robert Nobel resided at his country estate in Sweden and there he died on August 4, 1896, only four months before his younger brother, Alfred, who had supported the enterprise financially, but without taking part in the management.

From the first, I had been well aware of the dilemma facing Emanuel Nobel and at the same time I keenly felt the need of his continued support in carrying out the terms of his uncle's will. The various verbal negotiations we had had now led to a preliminary agreement to sell to Emanuel Nobel, as the representative of the heirs of Ludvig Nobel, living in Russia, all the stock that had been held by Alfred Nobel in the Nobel Brothers Naphtha Company – 4,000 shares with a par value of 250 roubles, and 200 so-called *pajer* shares, worth, at par, 5,000 roubles each – at their par value, or 2,000,000 roubles, which equalled 3,840,000 Swedish kronor at the prevailing rate of exchange. This was the value at which, on the recommendation of stockbrokers in Stockholm, these securities had been listed in the inventory of the estate, but it was certainly less than their value according to the current quotations on the stock exchange.

Since the price thus agreed upon was lower than the one indicated by the stock market, the agreement had, to a certain extent, the character of a compromise. For reasons that have been explained above, the executors felt entitled to make such an agreement in order to settle the estate without awaiting the formal approval of either the Swedish Government or the prospective distributors of the prizes, as that would have complicated matters very much. As far as Emanuel Nobel was concerned, he seemed to feel that by acquiring the stock in this way he would adequately safeguard the interests of his family.

The pressure on Emanuel Nobel to make common cause with his relatives in Sweden did not cease, however. One day while he was in Stockholm in February, 1898, he was summoned to King Oscar, who wanted to discuss the matter with him. Immediately after his return from this interview I met him at the Hotel Rydberg, and while still somewhat excited he repeated in vivid terms his conversation with the King. Since this conversation has already been referred to in the memoirs of Carl Lindhagen [on the basis of my report to him], I feel free to reproduce it from my memoranda made at the time.

The King began by urging Emanuel Nobel, as the foremost representative of the family, to bring about a change in his uncle's will, especially with reference to the Peace Prize which would only lead, he feared, to controversies and diverse complications. 'Your uncle has been influenced by peace fanatics,' he declared, 'and particularly by women.'

Emanuel: 'Your Majesty perhaps agrees with General Moltke: "Eternal peace – that is only a dream, and not a beautiful one either".'

The King: 'Did he say that, "A dream, and not a beautiful one either"?' [Which he repeated twice.]

The King then went on to say that the will was also defective in form and hard to implement, and this had caused the prize-awarding institutions to feel doubtful. The Royal Academy of Sciences, in particular, had declined to have anything to do with the matter until changes had been made. To this Emanuel replied that he had just participated in discussions with representatives of the prize-juries and that an agreement had been reached as to the future statutes.

The King: 'Well, of course, one cannot prevent people from getting together and talking, but they are not able to make any binding agreements. In any case, it is your duty to your sisters and brothers, who are your wards, to see to it that their interests are not neglected in favour of some fantastic ideas of your uncle.'

Emanuel: 'Your Majesty, I would not care to expose my sisters and brothers to the risk of being reproached, in the future, by distinguished scientists for having appropriated funds which properly belong to them.'

Emanuel thus stuck to his point, and the conversation came to no conclusion. But when he repeated it to his Russian lawyer, the latter became terrified and insisted on his leaving Stockholm immediately and returning to St. Petersburg, so as to avoid being arrested. By being so frank, hadn't he been guilty of *lèse majesté?*

In this connection it should be recalled that, once the Nobel Foundation had been organized and had begun its activities, the King consistently showed his appreciation of its high aims and, as long as he lived, added to the dignity of the prize distributions by personally presenting the prizes on the anniversary of Nobel's death.

Emanuel Nobel's decision to support his uncle's will gave us another opportunity to renew our attempts to come to terms with the other relatives and greatly facilitated the settlement of the lawsuit they had begun. On May 29, 1898, an agreement was reached with two of the legatees, and on June 5, 1898, the other relatives signed a document before a notary public in Stockholm, declaring that they accepted Alfred Nobel's will, both on their own behalf and that of their descendants. They, furthermore, agreed to abstain from any future claims on the estate beyond what was stipulated in the agreement and also to surrender every right to share in the management of the residuary fund or to make any objections to any future interpretations of the will, additions to it or instructions to the administrators or the prize-distributors which had been approved by the Swedish authorities. In return for these concessions, the heirs were to receive the interest on the assets for 1897.

Concurrently with these negotiations with the relatives, the discussions with the prospective distributors of the prizes were also renewed. Our first step in this direction was to send identical letters to the various institutions, dated March 27, 1898, to which were attached the minutes of the informal meetings held in February and attended, on two occasions, by Emanuel Nobel. In the letter to the Royal Academy of Sciences, which alone had refused to appoint any delegates until the will had been proved but which had been represented informally at the above discussions by two of its members, it was added that since Emanuel Nobel had committed himself to the support of his uncle's will, there could be no doubt that it would ultimately take effect, at least as far as the part of the family he represented was concerned. In view of this change in the situation, the Academy was once more asked to appoint official delegates to take part in drawing up the statutes of a future Nobel Foundation. As an additional reason for the Academy to take such a step, it was pointed out that, since the other relatives had by then begun their formal action against the will and the Academy of Sciences was included among the defendants, it would be necessary, if the suit came to trial, for all the defendants to confer about their common interests.

About six weeks later, on May 11, 1898, the Academy replied that it had appointed Professors L. F. Nilson and B. Hasselberg as its official representatives in all matters concerning the will and the future rules for the prize distributions.

In the compromise agreement with the Nobel relatives were also included certain stipulations as to the prize awards which were later incorporated in the statutes of the Nobel Foundation. These provisions were as follows:

a. The basic statutes common to the prize-awarding bodies, dealing with the manner of, and the conditions for, the award of prizes, as prescribed in the will, shall be drawn up in consultations with a representative of the family of Robert Nobel and submitted to the approval of the Crown.

b. There shall be no departure from the following main principles, viz., that each of the future prizes established by the will shall be awarded at least once during each five-year period, from and including the year immediately following that in which the Nobel Foundation commences it activities; and that the amount of a prize thus awarded shall under no circumstances be less than sixty per cent of the part of the annual yield of the fund available for each prize, nor shall it be divided into more than three shares at most. [Statutes of the Nobel Foundation, Art. 1].

The discussion of these so-called 'moral' conditions did not begin, however, until towards the end of the compromise negotiations. One of the reasons for including them in the final agreement was probably a desire to save it from appearing to be a purely economic bargain or business deal.

To the agreement was attached the general condition that it had to be approved by the Swedish Government and by all the prize-adjudicating institutions which had been made defendants in the contest. Such approval was granted by the Caroline Institute on June 7, the Swedish Academy on June 9, and the Royal Academy of Sciences on June 11, 1898. Through Lindhagen, representatives of these bodies had been kept continuously informed about the progress of the negotiations, which explains the promptness of the formal approvals.

As regards the Norwegian Storting, the situation was a little different, and special discussions turned out to be necessary to inform the delegates it had selected about what had been done to settle the various disputes over the will. After having accepted, on April 26, 1897, the assignment to select winners of the Peace Prize, the Storting appointed on August 7, the same year, a committee of three to confer with the executors of the estate.

This committee consisted of three former Prime Ministers, Schweigaard, Steen and Blehr. After the dispute with the Nobel relatives had been settled and the approval of the Storting requested, the latter appointed on June 19, 1898, a new committee consisting of the President of the Storting, V. Ullman, and two of its members, Jacob Lindboe and Emil Stang, to study and, if they saw fit, approve the compromise agreement with the Nobel relatives. The executors of the will, their counsel Carl Lindhagen, and Judge Santesson, who had already represented the Storting in the questions concerning the Nobel-will in Sweden, were then invited to come to Christiania [Oslo] early in July, 1898, to discuss the situation with the Norwegian committee. After a conference lasting a couple of days, the Norwegian delegates decided on July 4, 1898, to accept the agreement and to become parties to it. On September 9, the same year, the Swedish Government gave its formal approval after having had all the pertinent documents submitted to it.

THE NOBEL FOUNDATION

When the will of Alfred Nobel had been admitted to probate, the work of putting it into effect was resumed. Since February 11, 1898, when Emanuel Nobel had announced his support of his uncle's will, no meeting had been held, and a new conference with the delegates of the prize-awarding institutions was called for November 19, 1898. The Royal Academy of Sciences was then to be officially represented by the two professors already named.

Knotty problems were at once encountered in the proposed special regulations as to how winners were to be selected and the projected Nobel Institutes organized, as well as concerning the use of the income from the special funds of the prize-juries. According to the proposed statutes, each Swedish prize-awarding body was to formulate its own directives, which, however, in order to be valid, had to be approved by the Swedish Government. The rules regarding the Peace Prize were to be drawn up by the Norwegian Storting.

This plan caused hesitation in certain Swedish circles, and it was then decided that all the special statutes were to be submitted to the Swedish Government for approval, including the one relating to the Peace Prize. It was also added that 'in order to be valid, none of the special statutes may contain any provisions that conflict with the basic statutes'. To this the Norwegians objected, as it would place the Norwegian Nobel Committee under the jurisdiction of the Swedish authorities. [Though still in a personal union with Sweden, Norway had then been a self-governing country for nearly a century.] It was then decided not to mention the special statutes in the main charter, and the Norwegian Nobel Committee was allowed to draw up its own regulations, which were formally adopted on April 10, 1905. There has never been any conflict on this matter since.

Another difference of opinion came up in connection with the efforts of the Caroline Institute to retain the greatest possible freedom of action, both in the selection of prize-winners and in the organization of a Nobel Medical Institute. Emanuel Nobel and the executors, on the other hand, had favoured the strictest possible uniformity in the rules. The original idea had also been that the projected Nobel Institutes, which were to assist in the work of selecting the winners, were to be closely connected with each other, but to this there was strong opposition from medical quarters. The final text of paragraphs 11 and 12 in the statutes is, therefore, to some extent the result of a compromise. While they provide that each institute is to be under the supervision of the respective prize-awarding body, it remains the property of the Nobel Foundation, and in both its financial management and its formal organization it is independent. Its resources cannot, therefore, be used for the benefit of other establishments, whether owned by the prize-adjudicators in question or by other organizations or institutions.

The definitive text of the proposed 'Statutes of the Nobel Foundation,' as agreed on by the committee members, was finally approved on April 27 and 28 and was then submitted by the executors to the Swedish Government for examination and formal sanction. It contained certain clarifications of the will and various additions, including regulations concerning procedure in case a strict adherence to the will was either impossible or in obvious conflict with the testator's intentions. Finally, there were certain directives of a financial or administrative nature.

The clarifications covered the following points:

a. 'The Academy in Stockholm' was held to mean the Swedish Academy.

b. The term 'literature' was to comprise not only belles-lettres but also other works which by virtue of their contents and style had literary value.

c. The implication that the awards were to be made for works produced 'during the preceding year' was to be understood to mean that in awarding the prizes consideration should be given to the latest works in the cultural fields mentioned in the will, and to older works only in case their significance had not been established until recently.
d. To be considered for a prize a written work must have been printed.

The additions to the will covered mainly the following points:
a. A prize might be divided between two works, each of which had been judged worthy of a prize. It could also be awarded to two or more persons who had performed a piece of work together.
b. Prize-money which it had not been found possible to distribute might be returned to the main fund or placed in special funds to be used to further the testator's ultimate purposes in other ways than by prize-awards.
c. To help them in the preliminary investigations of works proposed for prize-awards, the Swedish prize-adjudicating institutions were to appoint Nobel Committees of from three to five members, while the preliminary investigations required for the award of the Peace Prize were to be made by a special Nobel Committee of the Norwegian Storting.
d. To assist them in investigations connected with the selection of prize-winners, the prize-adjudicators should have the right to organize scientific institutions and other establishments. These institutions, which were to belong to the Nobel Foundation, were to be known as 'Nobel Institutes'.

On the financial side, it was decided that from the share of the annual income from the main fund which was placed at its disposal, each prize-jury should have the right to deduct one-fourth to cover its expenses in connection with the selection of the winners and the expenses of its Nobel Institute.

It was further stipulated that the Foundation should be governed by a Board of five persons, with deputies, who should have charge of the financial management of the funds and other property of the Foundation, as well as its administration generally. The Chairman of this Board and his deputy were to be appointed by the Swedish Government, and the other four members with two deputies selected by special trustees chosen by the prize-awarding institutions. After each year's audit, the trustees should also have the right to absolve the members of the Board from financial responsibility.

In special provisional statutes it was finally provided, among other things, to set aside the necessary amounts for a building fund to make possible the acquisition of special premises for administrative purposes, as well as the sum of 300,000 kronor for each one of the prize-juries, or altogether 1,500,000 kronor, as special organization funds for their respective Nobel Institutes.

After the comments of the prize-adjudicating institutions and of the Attorney General of Sweden had been obtained and a few minor changes of a formal nature had been made, the Government approved, on June 29, 1900, the statutes as proposed by the committee, and the same day they were officially promulgated as a Government decree. Simultaneously, the special regulations for the Swedish prize-juries were sanctioned by the Crown.

On September 25, 1900, the trustees of the Nobel Foundation met for the first time at the invitation of the oldest member elected by the Academy of Sciences, R. Törnebladh, a Director of the Bank of Sweden. The full list of the first trustees, all of whom are now dead, was as follows:

For the Swedish Academy: Hans Forssell, its President, Carl David af Wirsén, its Permanent Secretary, and P. J. von Ehrenheim, former Cabinet Minister.

For the Royal Swedish Academy of Sciences: A. R. Åkerman, President of the Board of Trade, A. E. Törnebohm, Director of the Geological Survey, R. Törnebladh, Director of the Bank of Sweden, E. Sidenbladh, Director of the Statistical Office, Chr. Aurivillius, Curator of the Museum of Natural History, and J. E. Cederblom, Professor at the Royal Institute of Technology.

For the Caroline Medico-Chirurgical Institute: Count K. A. H. Mörner, its Rector, Jonas Waern, Professor of Pediatrics, and Ernst Almqvist, Professor of Hygiene.

The Nobel Committee of the Norwegian Storting: His Excellency, O. A. Blehr, Prime Minister of Norway, B. Getz, Attorney General of Norway, and H. J. Horst, Member of the Storting, as deputy for C. Berner, President of the Storting.

P. J. von Ehrenheim was elected Chairman of the Trustees, whereupon the meeting was adjourned for two days to consider privately the selection of the Board. The following were chosen as the first members of the Board of the Nobel Foundation: Hans Forssell, R. Törnebladh, Henrik Santesson and Ragnar Sohlman.

As the first President, the Government at once appointed a former Prime

Minister, E. G. Boström. [As recently as September 12, 1900, he had retired from his post as Premier, but returned to it on July 7, 1902, while still serving as President of the Nobel Foundation.] The Board met for the first time on October 3, 1900, and as its Executive Director it appointed Henrik Santesson.

The long battle over Alfred Nobel's will and the realization of its provisions was thus ended. In the light of our experience during the past fifty years* the result may well be called satisfactory and the task of distributing the Nobel Prizes, as well as the management of the Nobel endowment fund, a privilege and an asset of the highest value to our country. At all events, the predictions of great dangers and risks involved in the fulfilment of the duty entrusted to Sweden and Norway by Alfred Nobel have proved unfounded. Rather has the discharge of this task contributed to an increased knowledge of and respect for both countries and for northern civilization in general. As for myself, I feel it is an unforgettable experience to have taken part, from the very first, in the organization of the Nobel Foundation.

* Written in 1947.

THE LITERARY PRIZE

BY ANDERS ÖSTERLING

In Alfred Nobel's earlier will, the one made in Paris in 1893, and then cancelled, there was no specific bequest in regard to literature. Mention was made only in general terms of rewards for the most important and original discoveries or the most striking advances in the wide sphere of knowledge or on the path of human progress. Even though under these terms the presumptive legatee, in this case the Swedish Academy of Sciences, could have awarded prizes for literary achievements too, it is evident that the donor wished to aid, first of all, the exact sciences.

It was not until he drew up his final will, in November 1895, that he made the stipulation that one of the five annual awards should be given to 'the person who shall have produced in the field of literature the most outstanding work of an idealistic tendency', and that it should be distributed by 'the Academy in Stockholm' by which the Swedish Academy was obviously meant.

The assumption has been made that this significant change should be associated with the testator's newly reawakened interest in writing. It is a fact that during 1895 the sixty-two-year-old inventor was seriously occupied with the composition of dramas, partly to offset a justified feeling of bitterness over financial setbacks and partly to find mental relief during a period of inactivity due to illness. These dramatic attempts are, no doubt, amateurish and awkward, but if they developed in the donor a better understanding of the difficulties involved in creative writing, they were not, in any event, fruitless.

Nobel's commendable desire to help and promote the cause of letters was inspired, first and last, by his own interest in literature, which had been developed in his earliest youth and was later stimulated by his continued language studies. He not only read but mastered five languages, including Russian; his poems in English, written in his late teens and still preserved, show an astonishing mastery of poetic diction and an unmistakably poetic instinct. In the depth of his peculiarly complicated personality, requiring solitude and suffering from melancholy despair in the midst of a whirl of pressing business and industrial activities, there lay hidden a poetic nature. It is revealing that the poet who gave him in his first youth his richest spiritual experience was Shelley, whose philosophy of life he absorbed both as regards its Utopian idealism and its religiously coloured spirit of revolt.

As a matter of fact, it was only natural that Nobel should feel attracted by Shelley, whose inspirations so often show a kinship to inventive imagination. Shelley's dramatic poem about the unbound Prometheus contains images which, like flashes of lightning, seem to foreshadow the scientific and technical progress of the nineteenth century, and appropriately it has been pointed out that only a few years after Shelley's death in 1822, there came, one after another, a succession of technical developments which were to inaugurate a new epoch in human history: the first English railway was opened in 1825, electrical telegraphy was perfected in 1838, and in 1831 Faraday made his discovery of magnetic induction – all advances which may be said to have been foreshadowed in the poetic imagination of Nobel's favourite author.

There cannot be any doubt that Shelley's philosophy exercised a considerable influence on the practical idealism of the great Swedish donor; there are numerous indications of this, even apart from the fact that Nobel, as late as 1895, wrote his play *Nemesis* on the same theme as Shelley's Renaissance tragedy, *Beatrice Cenci.* The tersely expressed feeling of pity in a Shelley passage like the one below accords well with the personal philosophy of a misanthropic philantropist like Alfred Nobel.

> The good want power, but to weep barren tears.
> The powerful goodness want: worse need for them.
> The wise want love; and those who love want wisdom;
> and all best things are so confused to ill.
> Many are strong and rich, and would be just
> but live among their suffering fellow-men,
> as if none felt: they know not what they do.

Among the above-mentioned poems of his own youth, Nobel seems to have expended his most serious efforts on *A Riddle,* which has an autobiographical tone, expatiating as it does on disappointment in early love. There are many versions. Even after he had settled in the Avenue Malakoff in Paris, he had had prepared a handsomely bound, typewritten copy, which he sent to an English woman-friend, accompanied by a few apologetic and belittling comments: 'Rhyming gives good polish to metrical nonsense, and to rhyme I should have resorted. As it is, I have probably mixed blank meaning with blank verse until I have achieved the utmost in dullness. I do not pretend in the least to call my verses poetry; I only write now and then to ease my despondency, or to improve my English.'

In the same letter he asks whether Mrs. Granny has duly received, and in good condition, the caviar he had sent her from Hamburg. What stirs us, or at least touches us, in *A Riddle* is the wounded feelings of a dreamer or brooder who has been disappointed in his first opportunity to achieve happiness. Nobel also made an attempt to translate this little versified narrative into Swedish, which, in any event, reveals that he had had some purpose in his choice of motif even if he was not able to make the most of it.

But self-pity in verse was something the busy man soon outgrew. After that he stuck to prose, and even if he always had to struggle with obvious difficulties in his use of Swedish and never became a finished stylist, he was able at times to develop a certain logical effectiveness such as that found in his personal letters. Humour was not his gift, but he did not lack a satirical vein, and his world-wide experiences gave it an outlet. *The Sisters* is the title of a tendentious novel dealing with social reform which he once began to write. *In Lightest Africa* is another. As narrative art they are unquestionably rather crude, but in the argumentative passages can be found certain touches which prove that it is a man of ability who presides over the discussion.

The reader may, for instance, be reminded, at least momentarily, of the rebellious Strindberg of the eighties, when he is confronted with a chapter about Paris which begins in this lively fashion:

'In the capital everything went on as usual. The poor sighed for bread, the rich for appetite, mothers and daughters for new gowns, husbands and fathers for money to pay for them. The clergy sinned against the eleventh commandment [Thou shalt not be a hypocrite]; the common people against the twelfth [Thou shalt not endure tyrants]; the ragamuffins against the thirteenth [Thou shalt not beget children thou canst not feed]. But all these sins were expiated by diligent attendance at Holy Communion. Furthermore, the Lord was unusually well pleased with his people, because they had just built him a church which cost three millions, not counting the wax candles for his favourite saints.'

Even as late as 1895, when he had lost the complicated patent suit in England over smokeless powder, he gave vent to his just indignation by writing a comedy about the British legal system. The play is called *The Patent Bacillus* and may seem to echo faintly the arrogantly mocking tone in the contemporary dramatic satires of George Bernard Shaw. It is, however, improbable that Nobel was acquainted with them. At one time he called himself 'an untalented Rydberg'* and in reference to the comedy about patents, he might have described himself as a kind of 'untalented Shaw'. In the piece, Miss Lux is the both beautiful and crushingly witty counsel for the plaintiff, while the eminent judge bears the slightly foggy name of Haze. Throughout, the humour is rather forced. When, for example, one of the witnesses is about to kiss the Bible, he says, 'I don't kiss every book, but I book every kiss', which, of course, causes loud laughter in the court-room.

Only a single one of his works did Nobel have printed himself, the tragedy *Nemesis,* which had originally been called *The Death of Cenci.* He busied himself with this shortly before his death, in 1896, that is, at the same time as he drew up his famous will. After his death the privately printed edition was, however, burned at the request of his relatives; it was feared that the book might reflect on the late departed's new fame as a prize-giver. Only three copies have been preserved. In this play he borrowed the same gloomy motif from the criminal annals of the Renaissance as Shelley had already used in *Beatrice Cenci.* It is hard to imagine what could have attracted Nobel to this tale of horror, which had already been registered, so to speak, in the patent office of the world's great literature. One of the effective scenes is Beatrice's vision of the Madonna and the Devil, which is supposed to represent the heroine's inner struggle over the revenge she has to take. The language is otherwise more rhetorical than dramatic. Like a strange anachronism, Nobel's deep-seated anticlericalism suddenly flares up, as when Guerra, who himself wears the robes of the church, declares in the middle of the play: 'It is true that royal power is also horribly abused, so that the whole so-called Christian world still resembles a shambles, but compared to the horrors of a clerical dictatorship, this is but a trifle', and so forth. After the gruesome torture scene in the last act, during which Beatrice's stepfather is put to death under the supervision of the avenging woman herself, the same Guerra declares solemnly: 'Silence, Beatrice! You stand before the altar of death. Life on earth and life after death are both eternal mysteries. But the dying spark moves us to solemn awe and stills every voice except that of religion. Only eternity speaks.'

At the memorial service in San Remo that day in December, 1896, when Nobel's remains were to be carried to his native land, the youthful Nathan Söderblom, who was later to become Archbishop of Uppsala

* Viktor Rydberg [1828-1895] was Nobel's favourite contemporary Swedish author.

and who had known Nobel personally in Paris, borrowed for his farewell address at the bier these words from the Cenci tragedy. Inevitably, one makes the reflection that the phrase must be completely divorced from its context in the play to be appropriate at a funeral service as a dignified interpretation of the dead man's inmost thoughts about life and death.

As a sentimental exaggeration must likewise be regarded the words of the Austrian author, Bertha von Suttner, when in an obituary appraisal of Nobel she wrote: 'Had not this gifted man become a great inventor, he surely would have become, instead, a writer of high rank, and in that case would most likely have himself produced such literary works of an idealistic tendency as the bequest in his will has now stimulated future authors to create.'

Throughout his life, Alfred Nobel gave serious attention to literature and, as far as his absorbing and hectic existence permitted it, kept in touch with the literary developments of his time. In regard to his tastes, it is also known that he preferred works of an idealistic tendency and consequently strongly disapproved of the contemporary naturalism represented, for example, by Zola. Among Scandinavian writers he admired Björnson, Ibsen, Rydberg, and Lagerlöf. As a reader of literature, he looked for the living core; the ideas expressed interested him more than the forms.

Consequently, it was not by chance that he expressly stipulated that 'an idealistic tendency' was an essential qualification of literary works to be judged for the prize, even though the expression was vague and has caused endless arguments. What he really meant by this term was probably works of a humanitarian and constructive character, which, like scientific discoveries, could be regarded as of benefit to mankind.

Nobel called himself a super-idealist, and in spite of all his heavy disappointments, in spite of the great sum-total of his personal experiences, in spite of a rich man's misanthropy – inevitable in his situation – he seems to have clung to the faith, as a final *quand-même,* that men and nations would permit themselves to be taught a slight degree of unselfishness, fraternal amity, and tolerance by the influence of a great, idealistic, and ennobling literature. Under such circumstances, an idealistic tendency became for him a self-evident requirement, and he could not very well foresee that during the next half-century this term would receive a wider interpretation.

In literature the fundamental human values can be presented in so many different ways and in such varied forms – by indirection or argument, ironically or satirically – that the bare term *idealistic* becomes an altogether too rigid definition. In actual practice, it has also been shown that only the loosest possible interpretation of the word can be applied with profit. In the subsequent sections of this chapter I shall take the opportunity to survey the problems that have come up in connection with the concrete application of this particular testamentary stipulation.

THE SWEDISH ACADEMY AND THE NOBEL PRIZE IN LITERATURE

When within a month of Nobel's death in December, 1896, the Swedish Academy received the first information about the illustrious but delicate role that had been entrusted to it by his will, much hesitation was felt as to the wisdom of shouldering the new responsibility. Two of its members, Hans Forssell and Carl Gustaf Malmström,* stood out from the first as firm opponents of accepting the difficult task. Both insisted that by assuming world-wide responsibility for the awards, the academy of Gustavus III would inevitably be forced to neglect the duties imposed on it by its royal founder, and that the organization could not stand such an enormous increase in its burden of work. This opposition was, however, overcome by the Academy's Permanent Secretary, Carl David af Wirsén, who during the negotiations, both inside and outside the Academy, showed a highly commendable breadth of vision and sympathy for Nobel's purpose – an attitude which was far from typical of the circles that were then the most influential in Stockholm.

From the record of Wirsén's remarks during the discussion within the Academy it may be appropriate to quote the following, since it was probably these very arguments which finally convinced the members and gained the required majority for his proposal that Nobel's testamentary offer should be accepted. 'If the Swedish Academy refuses to assume this responsibility,' he said, 'the whole donation will be forfeited as far as literary awards are concerned, and by that very act the leading men of letters throughout Europe will be deprived of the opportunity to enjoy the financial rewards and the exceptional recognition for their long and brilliant

* Hans Forssell [1843-1901], historian and politician; Carl Gustaf Malmström [1822-1912], historian.

literary careers which Nobel had in mind. A storm will blow up, a storm of indignation. The Academy's responsibility is great; if it definitely rejects the task, it will suffer sharp reproaches; in these reproaches may join future generations of our eighteen members who are to succeed us and who may find it strange that for reasons of personal convenience the members of to-day deliberately declined an influential role in the world of letters. The task is said to be foreign to the true purposes of the Academy. The work will, no doubt, be both new and arduous, but it can hardly be called foreign since it is of a literary character. A body that is to judge the literature of its own country cannot afford to be ignorant of the very best produced abroad; the projected prizes are to be given to the best living writers anywhere, and, consequently, as a rule, to the very men whose work ought to be familiar to the Academy members anyway.'

In the spring of 1900, the Swedish Academy submitted to the Swedish Government its proposal for a special statute to govern the distribution of the prizes in literature. In the document was stressed the need of specific rules regarding the right to nominate candidates for these prizes. Such regulations could hardly be the same for all the different prize-juries. In the case of the Swedish Academy the problem was all the more complicated as there were no other institutions of the same type anywhere in the world, except the French and Spanish academies. It would obviously have been unfair to limit the nominating rights to these two bodies, and it would have been equally inappropriate to grant such rights to any institution as a body, since the Academy's freedom of action might thereby be hampered by overwhelming external pressure. It was therefore proposed that the right to nominate candidates should be granted to the individual members of such institutions and not to the institutions themselves. The Academy felt, it was further stated, that by distributing the nomination rights so widely, it had tried to make sure that proposals could be made by duly qualified persons in all parts of the world and that no domestic or foreign literary organization of any importance should have cause to complain that the rights and privileges of its members had been slighted.

The proposed text for the special statute was formulated as follows: 'The right to nominate candidates for the Prize in Literature is granted to members of the Swedish Academy; and of the French and Spanish Academies which are similar to it in character and objectives; to members of the humanistic sections of other academies, as well as to members of such humanistic institutions and societies as enjoy the same rank as academies, and to university professors of aesthetics, literature, and history.'

Since in the course of time the text of this statute proved unsatisfactory by being difficult to apply in some respects, besides excluding certain important groups which must be regarded as highly competent to make nominations, the Swedish Academy presented, in the autumn of 1948, a proposal for a modification, which in March, 1949, the Swedish Government approved.

The paragraph in question now reads in this way: 'The right to nominate candidates for the Prize shall be enjoyed by members of the Swedish Academy and of other academies, institutions and societies similar to it in membership and aims; by professors of the history of literature or of languages at universities and university colleges; by previous winners of the Nobel Prize in Literature, and by presidents of authors' organizations which are representative of the literary activities in their respective countries.'

On June 29, 1900, the Swedish Government sanctioned the original charter and by-laws of the Nobel Foundation. Here mention will be made only of the sections that deal with the literary prizes. Nominations must be received before February 1, each year, and consideration of those received even a few days later has to be postponed until the year following. It was further provided that 'under the term "literature" shall be comprised, not only belles-lettres, but also other writings which, by virtue of their form and method of presentation possess literary value.'

The stipulation in the will that prize-winners must have rendered mankind the greatest service 'during the preceding year' is interpreted to mean that 'the awards shall be made for the most recent achievements in the fields of culture referred to in the will, and for older works only if their significance has not become apparent until recently.' The purpose of the new phrasing was, obviously, to clarify in a legally proper way the testamentary requirement which, in most instances, it would have been impossible to interpret in any other way.

An injunction common to all the statutory regulations is that the prizes are to be given for a *work* or a *writing*. This rule was clearly phrased with reference to the Academy of Sciences and the Caroline Medico-Chirurgical Institute [which award, respectively, the prizes in science and medicine], but for the Swedish Academy it has been more difficult to observe. Usually the literary awards have been given for an author's entire production, without specifying any particular work. At times it has been done, however, 'with special reference' to a particular book, as in the case of Mommsen's *Roman History,* Spitteler's *Olympian Spring,* Hamsun's *Growth of the Soil,* Reymont's *The Peasants,* Mann's *Buddenbrooks,* Galsworthy's *Forsyte Saga,* and Martin du Gard's *Les Thibault.*

A permissive provision which, so far, has not been taken advantage of, or in any case has had no importance, is the one defining the requirements for election to membership in one of the Nobel Committees. According to the statutes, it is not necessary to be a Swedish subject or to be a member of one of the institutions making the awards. At least the Swedish Academy has never utilized this permission; its Nobel Committee has always been made up, naturally enough, of Academy members.

In consultation with the executors of the will, the Academy began at once to organize the institute and the library required for its new activity. A Nobel Committee was formed, made up of five members of the Academy, whose duty it was to present a full report on the nominations received, after they had been examined by qualified experts in the various languages. The first Nobel Committee was composed of Carl David af Wirsén, Esaias Tegnér, Carl Snoilsky, Carl Theodor Odhner, and Carl Rupert Nyblom.*

The Nobel Library, which was founded in 1900, has since grown into a very important institution whose collection of modern belles-lettres is now in a class by itself, at least in Europe, its shelves containing about 130,000 volumes. The library is also open to the public, and from being originally conceived merely as an aid in preparing decisions on the Nobel Prizes in Literature it has thus become an indispensable centre of literary studies and research, a development which is certainly in close harmony with the desire of the donor to establish something useful.

How the Academy appraised the situation officially in 1900 and in what mood its members assumed their delicate duty, is shown in the clearest possible way by an address which Esaias Tegnér delivered in his capacity as Director in December the same year; it was, in fact, intended to be a kind of programme declaration in regard to the Nobel assignment in its increasingly evident *servitude et grandeur.* At the outset, Tegnér emphasized

* Carl David af Wirsén [1842-1912], poet and critic; Esaias Tegnér [1843-1928], Orientalist; Carl Snoilsky [1841-1903], poet; Carl Theodor Odhner [1836-1904], historian; Carl Rupert Nyblom [1832-1907], professor of literature at Uppsala University.

that it was by no means in a light spirit that the Academy had shouldered its new duty, but that it could not shirk it, since, after all, the Nobel millions had not been given to the Academy, but to all humanity as represented by its foremost literary geniuses. He further voiced the hope that such a large prize would, at any rate, have the effect of making a good piece of work known in much wider circles than would otherwise have been the case – and that it would be an excellent piece of work, if not in every instance the best available for a prize, he felt could be taken for granted.

'The Swedish Academy', he proceeded, 'certainly does not cherish the illusion that even once it may be able to award a prize in such a way as to escape criticism. Nay, it anticipates with certainty that such criticism will often be merited. But it consoles itself with the assurance that in the whole world there is no other institution which would not meet the same fate... If there are drawbacks to being a small nation situated on the outskirts of the civilized world, there are also certain advantages. And when it is a question of a responsibility like this, a few of them become clearly evident. A person living on the border of a province is better able to decide which peaks inside it are the highest than an observer standing amidst the mountains themselves. In a different sense, this is also true of us. And in the fact that we are a small nation we have, in a way, a safeguard against partiality which the big nations lack: we shall less often be able to appear as contenders for the prize ourselves.'

How, on the other hand, the most influential Swedish opinion outside the Academy regarded the situation is best shown by the articles of the poet and critic Oscar Levertin on 'Art and Literature Academies', written during the summer of 1899. 'Under all circumstances,' he foresaw, 'the permanent contact with the European world of letters which the Swedish Academy will now have to maintain will be wholesome. For the first time foreign specialists in literature will direct their attention to the distant academy in Stockholm, and everywhere in different countries people with literary interests will eagerly wait to see which muse will be the Danaë on whom the Swedish Academy will pour its golden shower. Should her charms be dubious, there will be no lack of aspersions, and this international criticism will probably be more effective than the Swedish. Every mistake will be blamed, however, not only on the Academy, but on all the intellectuals in the country, and it is unthinkable that, faced by such prospects, the institution in question will not feel doubly obligated to incorporate in its ranks the truly creative literary people in the country, who alone can enable it to meet its obligations.'

Levertin thus hoped that the Nobel assignment would force a rejuvenation of the Academy's own membership so as to make it more equal to its new task. In a series of polemical articles under the general title of 'Conscription for Ideals,' the Swedish novelist Axel Lundegård broached the same idea by sarcastically proposing a double gold medal for the best answer to the question: 'How can the Swedish Academy be so reconstituted as to be able to serve better the purposes of its exalted founder?'

In regard to the competency of the Academy in those days to perform its new function, some doubt could, indeed, be legitimate when the composition of the body in 1897 was considered. Thanks to his sound literary education, Carl David af Wirsén himself undoubtedly had decided qualifications as a prize-judge, but otherwise there were at that time extremely few Academy members who could be regarded as literary experts; there were prominent historians and philologists, gentlemen with famous names in other spheres, and ecclesiastical dignitaries, but, with the exception of Wirsén, only a single poet, namely Carl Snoilsky.

The group was a stronghold of conservatism in defence of the national ideals and was usually regarded as having no relation to contemporary literature, either at home or abroad. It is not, therefore, surprising that in several instances the country's press expressed serious doubts – most definitely in an article by Hjalmar Branting, the Socialist leader, who declared that the whole purpose of the donation was defeated by the unhappy choice of the Swedish Academy as a distributor of prizes, especially in view of the interpretation the Academy could be expected to place on the stipulation regarding an 'idealistic tendency'.

The Academy at that time was, however, accustomed to storms, and its strength lay in its moral integrity which would not fail under pressure. Gradually, new men were seated in the Areopagus, literature's own men who could give to the Nobel assignment more of a personal interest, and, from then on, when new members were to be elected, it became natural to take into some consideration the candidates' qualifications in regard to the prize awards. At this point, one member should be singled out for special mention. Per Hallström was elected in 1907 and during the next four decades, thanks to his outstanding knowledge of modern literature, he was able to do a considerable part of the work involved in the selection of prize-winners.

Nobel's intention was, evidently, that the Prize in Literature should be a reward for some special work and at the same time serve as an encouragement for continued performance. It is obvious that in this respect the prize must be particularly hard to distribute. A good or even excellent work by a youngish author implies no guarantee that his future work will be kept up to the same level. The literary records of the past sixty years contain several instances of very promising books which have been followed by less successful ones, and have therefore turned out to be only temporary flashes of light in otherwise obscure or forgotten careers.

In order to obtain a somewhat sounder basis for the prize awards, it is therefore natural to take into consideration an author's entire works after they have had time to show their influence on the contemporary world and reveal their literary worth from different points of view. A regrettable consequence of this procedure is that young authors, as a rule, have to await their turn for consideration, and under no circumstances can they expect to occupy at once the centre of attention. When fault is found because the prizes have so often been given to authors already quite aged, it can be pointed out in defence that during the first decade of the century there were in Europe so many important writers who had become venerable and yet were too prominent to be ignored. Conversely, this does not mean that all worthy veterans have been rewarded; many good opportunities have unfortunately been missed and here no attempt will be made to cover them up.

On the other hand, it cannot be truthfully said that the winners of the literary Nobel Prizes have in general been old enough to be pensioned. A statistical study of the fifty-six prizes so far distributed shows that eighteen of the recipients were between fifty and sixty; sixteen were in their sixties, and thirteen in their seventies. Only seven were in their forties – the youngest of all being Rudyard Kipling – and of the remaining two exceptions, one was Theodor Mommsen, who received the award at the age of eighty-five, the oldest in the whole galaxy. The average age of the literary prize-winners can be figured at sixty-one, which is, of course, rather high. It now remains to be seen whether in the future it can be brought down.

A study of the Committee reports on candidates during the first years reveals at once the main difficulty which, after all, was unavoidable in this branch of the prize awards with its wide and inadequately defined divisions of literature that are to be considered. If it is difficult enough to judge the relative merits of literary creations which come under the classification of belles-lettres and which sometimes can be fairly equal, it is obviously even harder to make a choice between a leading writer on humanistic subjects and a prominent poet. We are here concerned with truly incommensurable quantities. A playwright, a novelist, and a lyric poet cannot be judged by the same standards; even less is it possible to subject the work of an historian and that of a philosopher to a comparative test. In one of his official letters as Permanent Secretary of the Academy to Bishop G. Billing in 1902, Wirsén correctly observes: 'It is absolutely impossible to decide whether a dramatist, an epicist or a lyric poet – whether a ballad writer or a man of ideas, ranks the highest. It is like deciding on the relative merits of the elm, the linden, the oak, the rose, the lily, or the violet. The main requirement is that everything should be genuine, clean-cut, and substantial.'

Under such circumstances it was inevitable that differences of opinion should develop; and that rather sharp ones did arise, both in the Committee and in the Academy itself, can be clearly seen from the Committee reports, especially those submitted during the Wirsén era. In Henrik Schück's still unpublished notes for a history of the Swedish Academy from 1883 to 1912, these debates are reported as fully as possible on the basis of the correspondence of the Academy members. The Academy's minutes relating to the Nobel Prizes, on the other hand, have always been purposely kept meagre and do not even contain the voting records.

Although secrecy requirements still preclude a frank treatment of this material for literary history, it may be permissible to cite at least a few examples of the conflicts that did occur during the earlier years. That in certain instances the clashes of opinion became much sharper than was necessary was largely due, of course, to Wirsén's despotic disposition and insistent demands to have his own way at any cost, even though it must be admitted that in such matters he was entitled to considerable authority.

In 1902, the Academy had to strike a balance between two such outstanding but incommensurable literary works as those of Herbert Spencer and the German historian, Theodor Mommsen, the outcome being that the latter was finally selected because of his superior literary artistry. In 1904, the Committee warmly recommended Frederi Mistral, but before the final decision was made, his narrative in verse, *Mireio,* happened to be published in a decidedly inferior Swedish translation which, unfortunately, had been made by a member of the Academy, and the final voting resulted in an unhappy compromise which split the prize between Mistral and an author of another nationality, the Spanish dramatist, José Echegaray. The following year the Polish writer, Henryk Sienkiewicz, was awarded the prize, but within the Committee the opinion was expressed that he should have shared it with his fellow-countrywoman, Eliza Orzeszko. In 1908, the Committee favoured Swinburne, whose candidature Wirsén energetically supported, but the name of Selma Lagerlöf had by then been advanced with equal energy by other members and the consequence of this difference of opinion was that the prize was finally awarded to the idealistic German philosopher, Eucken – unquestionably one of the Academy's weakest selections.

Selma Lagerlöf did receive the prize for 1909, but only after bitter opposition from the ever belligerent Wirsén, who strongly deplored that in the meantime his own candidate, Swinburne, had passed away without having had the opportunity to receive the honour. The English poet was by no means the only candidate of a high order to be deprived by death of a presumptive award. The Spaniard, Pérez Galdós, belongs to this group, as does Paul Valéry of a later period.

On a much more recent occasion when circumstances had brought about a situation requiring a decision between another Spaniard, Benavente, and the Irish poet, William Butler Yeats, the former a winner in 1922 and the latter the following year, the author of the Committee report made a declaration of principle which may deserve to be quoted in this connection. 'It is constantly necessary,' he wrote, 'to argue with oneself in order to maintain full objectivity in judgment, and such objectivity is ever required. There is a danger close at hand, namely that the Nobel Prize, which is intended to be an award for the whole world's richly varied production, distributed by Nobel's own countrymen, may gradually be restricted to a rather small, or limited circle, that is, if our greater or lesser ability to understand the mental peculiarities of different nationalities is allowed to influence our decisions. We must always be careful to judge literary works that are to us more or less strange, not according to our own standards, but against their proper background and according to what we may infer that they mean to the people of the country where they were produced and whose local traditions and national culture make it easier for them to appraise both the content and the form of such works.' This admonition is especially apposite in reference to the difficulty experienced by Northerners in properly judging the products of southern Romance literature, not to mention those of more distant regions.

Altogether, works in about thirty different languages have been proposed for the literary Nobel awards. It is self-evident that to make a systematic survey of this enormous production would have required an organization of forbidding size and cost. To a certain extent, when confronted by such an exacting assignment, the Academy has to depend on its enlightened intuition. The submission of suitable proposals from abroad must often be left to chance, even if it has to be admitted that, throughout, foreign nominations have come in at a rather steady rate. The first year, twenty-five such nominations were received in due form from different countries, and the next year the number rose to thirty-four. During the First World War the yearly nomination lists shrank considerably, causing the Academy members themselves to add, from then on, such names as seemed appropriate. In general, about thirty nominations are now given close examination each year, among them being many which may have been repeated from year to year, according to the important but not always observed rule that a nomination must be renewed each year in order to qualify for consideration. The invalid nominations, as, for instance, those made by writers all over the world who nominate themselves, or by wives of authors who propose their own husbands, make a somewhat bizarre and tragi-comic collection stored in the Academy's files and are there left to kind oblivion. Insome instances it has looked as if some ambitious candidates had had their own propaganda organizations to collect signatures and endorsements.

The list of nominations received during the first five years, classified according to nationalities, is as follows [see table p. 90].

These statistics have at least the value that they prove unfounded the fears that the adjudicators would be completely swamped by nominations, especially at first when the distribution was a novel experiment, sensationally announced all over the world. In one Swedish newspaper a mathematician went so far as to calculate that each year the Academy could expect to receive 19,000 different books for consideration, the mere storing of which would require twenty-three warehouses and 292 employees, who for three months of each year would be kept busy seventeen hours a day merely in sorting them. Fortunately, the actual experience has turned out to be less fantastic.

	Nominees					*Proposers*				
	1901	*1902*	*1903*	*1904*	*1905*	*1901*	*1902*	*1903*	*1904*	*1905*
Sweden	—	—	—	1	1	6	10	6	3	5
Norway	—	3	2	1	—	3	3	3	1	2
Denmark	—	—	1	1	1	—	—	18	1	1
Finland	1	1	—	—	—	1	—	1	—	19
Germany	3	6	2	1	—	14	22	21	—	1
Austria-Hungary	2	2	—	1	1	8	2	11	26	4
England	—	8	5	6	5	—	60	44	51	55
Switzerland	3	—	—	—	—	5	—	—	—	1
France	11	6	7	5	1	37	5	10	6	31
Belgium	—	—	1	1	—	—	—	4	15	—
Italy	1	2	1	—	1	—	2	—	—	—
Spain	1	3	3	1	1	1	16	20	1	24
Portugal	1	—	—	—	—	1	—	—	—	—
Roumania	1	—	—	—	—	1	—	—	—	—
Russia	—	2	1	1	1	—	1	7	—	3
Poland	1	1	1	1	2	1	—	—	—	6
Greece	—	—	—	1	1	—	—	—	1	1
Total	25	34	24	21	15	78	121	145	105	153

THE LITERARY PRIZE-WINNERS

If, on the basis of the list of winners of the Nobel Prize in Literature, one were to try to trace a pattern of development in world literature during the past half-century, the attempt would show that a continuous line can hardly be discerned. This is due, not merely to the unfortunate absence of a few individual names of outstanding importance – Tolstoy, Ibsen, Strindberg, Hardy, Valéry, Rilke, to mention only the most prominent – but also to the well-known fact that in the various branches of literary production there is no continuous development in the same sense as in scientific research, where a logical connection can be established between the different links in the chain. If, however, it is assumed that the end of naturalism had been reached before the turn of the century, and that the search for a new literary orientation, with greater scope for poetic imagination, became the most significant characteristic of the early years of the twentieth century, it can at least be said that in several instances the Nobel Prizes register this change of atmosphere and thus prove that the signs of the times were observed.

The fact that the first name on the Nobel Committee's initial list was Émile Zola may seem like an ironical challenge; it had been submitted by the famous French chemist, Pierre Berthelot. When seen in a more recent perspective, Zola could, presumably, be classified as a novelist with an idealistic tendency, but to his contemporaries he stood out, of course, as the standard-bearer of the crudest kind of naturalism and could, therefore, not be considered; it was known, moreover, that Nobel himself sincerely detested his works.

The choice of SULLY PRUDHOMME [1839-1907] as the first recipient of a Nobel Prize in Literature was, on the other hand, undeniably symptomatic. This philosophic dreamer, who in his well-polished poetical works interpreted the conflict between emotion and reason, or analysed the fundamental problems of human existence, certainly met in many ways the express requirements of the donor. But when in this way he was suddenly exposed to the spotlights, he did not measure up to expectations and was unjustly undervalued.

World opinion protested against the neglect of Tolstoy, and forty-two Swedish authors and artists signed a tribute to the slighted celebrity. Nor can there be any doubt as to the justification for this reproach. A deplorable consequence of the criticism which the Academy had thus brought on itself at the very start of the distribution was that it threw a shadow over its prize activities for many years to come. The only thing that can now be said in explanation is that the Russian author had not, as a matter of record, been duly nominated, and that the Nobel Committee itself had not then adopted the practice of making additions to the list of names. Even if bureaucratic, this was a respectable reason, since the real objective was complete impartiality in regard to nominations coming from outside.

Sully Prudhomme had been proposed by a large number of prominent members of the French Academy and to follow their advice was apparently regarded as a necessary gesture of courtesy from the Swedish daughter institution, especially as the proposed candidate was well qualified in his own right. On the other hand, the Academy could, of course, have repaired the damage the next year by honouring Tolstoy, who by that time had been nominated in due form. But it would not have been like Wirsén to yield to the pressure of public opinion, and in any case, it must be admitted that his critical estimate of Tolstoy in the 1902 Committee report correctly assessed both his merits and faults, though with greater emphasis on the latter.

In the interest of justice and historical knowledge, it may be appropriate to quote at least the climax of Wirsén's verdict on Tolstoy: 'If one were permitted to bear in mind only such immortal creations as *War and Peace* and *Anna Karenina,* it would be comparatively easy to award the palm of this literary contest to the great Russian author. But a decision is rendered difficult in view of many of Tolstoy's other works which have caused great sensation and cannot be ignored. He has condemned all forms of civilization and urged instead a primitive mode of life divorced from all forms of higher culture; he has denounced the right of a government to enforce laws against criminals; nay, even the government's own right to exist, recommending instead a theoretical anarchism; though completely inexperienced in Biblical criticism, he has arbitrarily rewritten the New Testament in a half-rationalistic, half-mystical spirit; he has firmly denied the right of both individuals and nations to self-defence. Confronted by such expressions of narrow-minded hostility to all forms of civilization, one feels dubious. One does not like to bestow recognition; and, in view of Tolstoy's own opinion about the lack of worth, nay, the harm in money prizes, which he has recently expressed, one is bound to conclude that it would be wrong to force on the great writer such a reward, at the presentation of which it must, perchance, be specified that it was given exclusively for his purely literary works, while his religious, sociological and political writings were regarded as both immature and misleading.'

When the Committee had undertaken, the year before, to select the world's most important contemporary writer, and its choice fell on Sully Prudhomme, this selection indicated a far-reaching limitation of scope and a lowering of the literary standard. The subtle, grey-shaded harmonies of the French lyric poet have probably by now faded out of our consciousness, as they have lost their hold on even the educated French public. But in the history of literature, Prudhomme retains his place of honour: he was one of the last writers of philosophical poetry of the classic type with traditions dating from Lucretius, and he did his utmost to reconcile idealistic needs with the discoveries of natural science. Even if his creative power cannot be compared to that of Viktor Rydberg, he is, nevertheless, in his aspirations and mentality, somewhat akin to him. It may be recalled that in one of his lectures on aesthetics, when referring to the relation between art and science, Rydberg called special attention to Prudhomme as a poet who in 'the natural sciences had found inspiration for beautiful poems in which his imagination soars with unrestrained freedom.' To that extent there is nothing to be said against the Academy's explanation of its award of the literary Nobel Prize to Sully Prudhomme, 'in special recognition of his poetic compositions, which give evidence of lofty idealism, artistic perfection and a rare combination of the qualities of both heart and intellect'.

The prize for *1902* was awarded to THEODOR MOMMSEN [1817-1903] as 'the greatest living master of the art of historical writing, with special reference to his monumental work, *A History of Rome*'. The peculiar significance of this award was that it indicated the range of the Academy's conception of literature, proving that the prize could also be given for important works in the humanities, provided the presentation was of the required literary and artistic quality. Mommsen remains the only historian who has ever been crowned with this laurel, nor has this exceptional honour been questioned by later generations. As a matter of fact, the special work rewarded belonged to a past era; its first three volumes had been completed in 1854-56, the fourth in 1885. But the tribute to the venerable scholar, who in his youth had been a comrade of the poet Theodor Storm and like him had intimate contacts with the golden age of German humanism, must be regarded as fully justified. What Gibbon with his *Decline and Fall* had done for his own century had found a modern counterpart in Mommsen's even more impressive and, in respect to all-round research, still unsurpassed achievement, which has enriched human knowledge as extremely few learned works of our own time have done. The critical old historian was no enthusiastic visionary, but in his gruff way he could express an idealistic faith in words like these, taken from the introductory chapter: 'The most magnificent system of civilization has its own circumscribing limits which it can reach, but not so the human race, for whenever it appears to have attained a certain goal, it is confronted anew with the old challenge to aim for more distant and ever higher objectives.'

When the *1903* prize was given to BJÖRNSTJERNE BJÖRNSON [1832-1910], it can be surmised that, in view of the political tension then existing between Norway and Sweden, the decision had been preceded by a thorough-going debate, and that special emphasis had been laid on the testamentary directive that no consideration should be given to a candidate's national origin. Ibsen too had been on the list, but had been sternly opposed by Wirsén. That it was Björnson who obtained a majority was due, as the Committee report indicates, to the fact that he appeared to have retained his creative powers, while the genius of Ibsen had unquestionably burnt out. A division of the prize between the two Norwegians had also been suggested but was rejected because their literary prestige required a whole prize for each one of them.

The proposal to divide the prize had won the support of Bishop Gottfrid Billing, who, in July 1902, set forth his arguments in a letter to Wirsén, in which he also took political considerations into account. 'It is true', he wrote, 'that a prize award must not become an official political act. But it is just as incontestable as it is inevitable that it has had, and will have, a political aspect. This is an unavoidable consequence of its international character. The Academy may disregard all political considerations as much as it pleases – the award will nevertheless become an international act which will be commented on by the international press from its own national point of view. As a by-product of the proposed division, which must not become a decisive factor, but which, nevertheless, should not be scorned, I regard the courtesy to Norway which would be implied in the award, and the good effect it would have in that country especially at this time when we, so to speak, have begun to tack among the Friendly Islands.'

When the existing relations between Norway and Sweden and Björnson's prominent role as a Norwegian nationalist are considered, the prize award may well be described as the result of a genuinely objective judgment and as a truly broad-minded act. The cordial wording of the citation is also remarkable: 'as a tribute to his noble, magnificent and versatile work as a poet, which has always been distinguished both for the freshness of its inspiration and its rare purity of spirit'.

Björnson was the first Scandinavian to receive the prize and he was not to be the last, but it is obvious that for a long time a certain reserve had to be maintained in regard to Scandinavian writers so as to forestall charges of partiality. This laudable restraint could also have unfortunate consequences. One of these was that Henrik Ibsen, who died in 1906, never received the well-deserved distinction, and that Nobel's roll of honour will for ever lack the name of one of the very greatest figures in the world's dramatic literature.

The fact that the prize for *1904* happened to be divided between two poets of different nationalities, FRÉDÉRI MISTRAL [1830-1914] and JOSÉ ECHEGARAY [1833-1914], has already been cited as an example of a compromise, when sufficient unity was not obtainable at the final moment. With due respect for the well-constructed and effective dramas of the Spanish author, it can hardly be disputed that Mistral deserved in a much higher degree to be honoured with a whole prize. *Mireio,* the beautiful poem which, above all, has been associated with Mistral's name, was, it is true, of a much earlier date; it had been published in 1859 and had been hailed with approval by the master of French Neo-Romanticism, Lamartine. But Mistral had subsequently twined many new garlands of song in honour of Provençal nature, and when he received the prize he was, in truth, one of the most gracious figures in the world of contemporary poetry, encircled by the Homeric brilliance of the Mediterranean culture which had given him birth, and the creator not only of an original, myth-laden poetry, but also of the musical, olive-scented language in which it was written. The prize citation properly stressed the 'fresh originality and true inspiration of his poetic production, which faithfully reflects the natural scenery and native spirit of his people, and, in addition, his significant work as a Provençal philologist'.

It seems almost inevitable that the plays of Echegaray should lose their freshness more quickly than the flowers that bloom in Mistral's poetry, and that the mixture of subtle wit and fiery spirit in his dramatic works should not in the same way survive the generation of which they had been a satisfactory reflection. But that does not mean that the general terms of eulogy used in the citation were exaggerated when they spoke of the Spaniard's 'numerous and brilliant compositions which, in an individual and original manner, have revived the great traditions of the Spanish drama'.

When the prize for *1905* was awarded to HENRYK SIENKIEWICZ [1846-1916] 'because of his outstanding merits as an epic writer', the desire to honour a representative of the Slavic nations was obviously influential. It is true that Tolstoy was still alive, but as he had not been able to obtain a majority earlier, the opportunity was seized to crown the Polish author, who was so highly esteemed by his own people, and whose magnificent novel about the Rome of the Emperor Nero, *Quo Vadis,* was in those years making its triumphant world progress, translated into most European languages. As already stated, a minority in the Committee held that Sienkiewicz ought to share the prize with his fellow-countrywoman,

Elisa Orzeszko, but a division of the prize for two successive years was regarded as inappropriate, apart from the fact that she was not considered the equal of the leading candidate. To this outcome an expert in Slavic literature such as Professor Harald Hjärne contributed greatly. Sienkiewicz' other works were naturally also placed in the scales, but the serious tone, the historical knowledge and skilful composition which distinguish his story of the battle between classical antiquity and Christianity turned the balance, and quite properly so, since the work in question remains fresh and is still read with undiminished interest.

In *1906* came the turn of Italy, whose foremost poet, the septuagenarian GIOSUÈ CARDUCCI [1835-1907], was then given the prize. This seems to have been one of the least debatable awards, 'not only in consideration of his deep learning and critical research, but above all as a tribute to the creative energy, freshness of style, and lyrical force which characterize his poetic masterpieces'. This conviction seems to have been shared by all the members of the Academy, because Carducci is one of the few prize-winners who have been chosen unanimously. The flaming passion in his indignation and love had culminated in a poetic production which even in its imitations of classical forms sparkles with southern vitality. He was born in Pietra Santa, where the marble quarries from the time of Michelangelo glow like snow on the mountains of Maremma; his verse is sculptured in the same hard, aristocratic material. When Carducci received the honour his strength was spent, and the annals of the Nobel Prize awards record the touching scene in Bologna, when the crippled old man was visited in his home by a member of the Academy, Baron Carl Bildt, who was the Swedish minister in Rome, and from him received the insignia of the prize while all Italy applauded. In his proud passion for liberty he had remained true to his youth; his first poems had been published the same year that Italy was unified, and until the end the spirit of the *Risorgimento* continued to animate his vision of the future. He could not foresee that a few years later the political developments would so cruelly contradict his exultant cry of an earlier period: 'Il mondo è bello e santo è l'avenir.'

For the choice in *1907* several weighty names had been submitted, such as those of Swinburne, Holger Drachmann, Georg Brandes, John Morley, Selma Lagerlöf, Antonio Fogazzarro, Paul Bourget, and RUDYARD KIPLING [1865-1936]. That the last-named was the one to carry off the laurel wreath may have been the result of a compromise, but this time the outcome was a happy one. Kipling's most notable work as a poet and story-teller then bore a relatively recent date, and his world-wide fame still retained the lustre of his quick, fascinating success, which was then at its peak, just like the British Empire, whose incomparable glorifier he was. Before his admiring contemporaries the wizard had spread the marvellous animal tales of the *Jungle Book,* the motley Indian scenes of Kim's childhood, and the grandiose lyrics of *The Seven Seas.* With good reason his diploma could refer to the 'power of observation, originality of imagination, virility of ideas and remarkable talent for narration which characterize the creations of this world-famous author'.

Kipling came to Stockholm to receive his prize just as King Oscar had died and in his memoirs he has described his impressions of the Swedish capital draped in mourning. The Nobel festival was cancelled and the Nobel Prizes for that year were distributed at a modest, private ceremony. It has been told that, during a visit to a school in Stockholm, Kipling promised to send his *Jungle Book* to one of the boys. The book arrived in due time with this genuinely Kiplingesque inscription, 'A promise to a boy should be kept'.

Far less approval met the award in *1908* to the idealistic German philosopher RUDOLF EUCKEN [1846-1926]. The clash of opinions which this time rent the Academy has already been mentioned. Its outcome was that the worthy, but none too original thinker was preferred, not only to a German scholar of Adolf Harnack's unquestionably high rank, but also to such truly inspired writers as Swinburne and Lagerlöf, who were the leading contenders. Eucken's *Grundlinien einer neuen Lebensanschauung,* published in 1907, had just then been translated by a pupil of the Swedish philosopher Boström and had been favourably received at Uppsala University. Consequently, he gained strong supporters in Vitalis Norström and Harald Hjärne,* whose high opinion of his scholarly worth was probably reflected in the prize-diploma's eulogy, 'in recognition of his earnest search for truth, his penetrating power of thought, his wide range of vision, and the warmth and strength in presentation with which in his numerous works he has vindicated and developed an idealistic philosophy of life'.

By the award in *1909* the literature of Sweden became for the first time a winner in the international competition, as then SELMA LAGERLÖF [1858-1940] finally received the honour which a vigorous public opinion

* Vitalis Norström [1856-1916], professor of philosophy at Gothenburg; Harald Hjärne [1848-1922], professor of history at Uppsala.

had long demanded on her behalf. It would be futile to try to hide what had been the main obstacle to such a distinction. From the beginning, Wirsén had misjudged her gifts and by stubbornly adhering to his opinion he had successfully opposed her candidature, which each year had been supported with increasing vigour and zeal inside the Academy itself. In his final, decidedly peppery pronouncement about Selma Lagerlöf, he permitted himself, for instance, to say: 'Since in the works of an author who is to be honoured with the Nobel Prize, I wish to discover fidelity to nature and not unnaturalness, real art and not artificiality, genuine fantasy and not unreality, and since Selma Lagerlöf in most of her works does not seem to me to meet these requirements, I cannot vote for her. While I am well aware that in these days one is almost regarded as an outcast if one does not unreservedly admire the writings of Miss Lagerlöf, I must nevertheless pay more attention to the inner biddings of my own convictions than to a passing public whim which pretends to have the supreme authority and which will hardly tolerate an opinion which goes against the fads of the day'.

But the opposition defied Wirsén's power, and in that respect Selma Lagerlöf's Nobel Prize marks an important turning-point in the history of the Academy. Wirsén's position became tragic for, despite his pre-eminent expert knowledge, he no longer enjoyed the confidence needed by a leader of the literary tribunal, and during his few remaining years he felt he had been ill requited for his unsparing efforts as Chairman of the Nobel Committee. It is safe to assume that he had not formulated the citation on the diploma presented to the author of *Gösta Berling's Saga* and *Jerusalem:* 'in appreciation of the lofty idealism, vivid imagination and spiritual perception that characterize her writings'. Five years later, Selma Lagerlöf was herself elected a member of the Academy and after that participated for twenty-five years in making the Nobel awards in literature.

The prize-winner in *1910* was PAUL HEYSE [1830-1914]. Oddly enough, he had never before been nominated by his own fellow-countrymen, but this time his candidature was supported by a large number of German professors from Berlin, Breslau, Halle, Leipzig, Munich, and Vienna. Heyse had just celebrated his eightieth birthday and on that occasion had been made an honorary citizen of Munich and had received other distinctions; it was then thought appropriate that Sweden should glorify this veteran with a prize of world-wide significance. In a certain sense the honour could, of course, be regarded as an anachronism, since Heyse's prestige belonged to a past era, but the members of the Committee regarded his writings as a pleasant reminder of their own youth. This was especially true of Wirsén, who wrote in his report: 'Germany has not had a greater literary genius since Goethe; Heyse's short stories are perfect masterpieces.' There were no acrimonious debates over this nomination, and Heyse's advanced age does not seem to have caused any scruples, since the prize was expressly awarded as 'a tribute to the consummate artistry, permeated with idealism, which he has demonstrated during his long productive career as a lyric poet, dramatist, novelist and writer of world-renowned short stories'. The severe storms of later years have inevitably diminished Heyse's prominence, but within his own period he still holds his place as a minor classic.

The list of candidates for 1911 contained several names of special interest, including that of the Swedish poet Gustaf Fröding, who, however, died in February of the same year and was therefore never the subject of a formal report. This was also the only occasion on which Strindberg came near being officially considered. He was, in fact, proposed by the future Archbishop of Sweden, Nathan Söderblom, later on a member of the Academy, but the nomination came a few weeks too late, and instead of being laid aside for consideration the next year, as was by then the custom, it was returned at the sponsor's own request and was never submitted by him again. It is indeed remarkable that Strindberg was never actually nominated for the prize, either by Swedes or foreigners, and that, in consequence, his great name was to remain for ever conspicuous by its absence from the Nobel Prize deliberations. It is true that Strindberg's fame shows a constantly fluctuating curve in which one of the down-waves happened to coincide with the first ten-year period of the Nobel Prizes. But the most obvious explanation is, of course, that it seemed futile to submit Strindberg's name to a panel made up as the Academy was in those years. He died, moreover, only a month before Wirsén, who had been his sworn opponent ever since he had been bitterly satirized in Strindberg's book *The New Kingdom*.

For several years MAURICE MAETERLINCK [1862-1949] had been a leading contender, when the prize was finally awarded to him practically without dissent in *1911*, 'in appreciation of his many-sided literary activities, and especially of his dramatic works, which are distinguished by a wealth of imagination and by a poetic fancy, which reveals, sometimes in the guise of a fairy tale, a deep inspiration, while in a mysterious way they appeal to the readers' own feelings and stimulate their imaginations'. In this unusually detailed citation the chief emphasis is thus put explicitly on Maeterlinck's dramatic compositions, which by their tremendous power of suggestion affected the contemporary mind as a new form of metaphysical, transcendental poetry. In some of the earlier Committee reports the question had been raised as to whether Maeterlinck should not be considered, rather, 'as an interesting oddity with supersensitive nerves', and regret had likewise been voiced that so far 'in his philosophy he has not arrived at a definite theism'. But it had also been admitted that 'in the beauty of his poetry he surpasses many of his rivals whose philosophy may, perchance, be more convincing'. In the final report, at least Wirsén was wholly favourable, declaring that Maeterlinck's pictures of life are remarkably precise, no matter how dream-like they may seem. 'They are not artificial,' he insisted, 'however veiled they appear; through the veil can always be discerned the outlines of something substantial, something that springs from the very source of human existence and is not merely ephemeral.' In these words there is also a hint of the tribute to symbolism which Maeterlinck's Nobel Prize implied and in which one of the significant literary movements of the period received well-merited recognition.

Germany was again honoured in *1912* when the fifty-year-old GERHART HAUPTMANN [1862-1946] received the prize 'primarily in recognition of his fruitful, varied and outstanding production in the realm of dramatic art'. Nothing was said about where the emphasis was laid, on the realistic or the romantic plays. Hauptmann's output is, on the whole, decidedly unsystematic; it shows no organic development, but breaks down into a number of impulsive, sometimes successful and sometimes unsuccessful efforts in different directions, indicating a strong urge to create. There can be no doubt, however, that at the time he was well qualified to be honoured as the leading German writer of modern problem plays, just as, thanks to his long life and continued activities, he gradually became a venerable and representative figure in his own country.

Up to that time the prizes had been awarded exclusively to European writers, but in *1913*, when RABINDRANATH TAGORE [1861-1941] became the winner, the horizon was suddenly widened and in a most satisfactory way. Tagore's renown in the English-speaking world itself was then quite new, but he had been sponsored by an Englishman, Thomas Sturge Moore, in his capacity as a member of the Royal Society in London, and the Committee report, written by Harald Hjärne, the new

Chairman, reveals that to its members his candidature came as a pleasant surprise. It is true that Hjärne assumed the attitude of an interested observer, expressing the opinion that in Tagore's fascinating poetry it was difficult to distinguish between what was original and what should be credited to the classical, pietistic element in Hindu religion. 'Not until there has been time to identify a little more clearly these historical links, will it be possible to differentiate, for the purpose of an independent estimate, between what is original and what is traditional in Tagore's religious mysticism and poetry, which remind an occidental reader of corresponding phenomena ranging from Plato's ideal love system and the allegorical interpretations in the Song of Solomon, to St. Bernard, St. Francis, and Count Zinzendorf with his Herrnhut.'

As a matter of fact, the Committee had decided to recommend another candidate, the French literary historian and moralist, Émile Faguet. But among the other members of the Academy, Tagore's name had by that time won enthusiastic supporters. To the final outcome a written statement by Verner von Heidenstam no doubt contributed a great deal. Regarding *Gitanjali,* a collection of poems which Tagore had published in his own English version, Heidenstam said: 'I read them with deep emotion and I cannot recall having seen for decades anything comparable in lyric poetry. It was a rare experience which I can compare only to the pleasure of drinking from a fresh, clear spring. The tender and sincere religious feeling which pervades all his thoughts and emotions, the purity of heart, the nobility and natural dignity of his style – all these qualities blend into a whole of deep and rare spiritual beauty. His poetry contains nothing debatable or disturbing, nothing that is vain, worldly or petty, and if ever a poet may be said to possess the qualities which entitle him to a Nobel Prize, he is precisely the man... Now that we have finally discovered an idealistic writer of really great stature, we should not pass him by. For the first and probably the last time for a number of years to come, the privilege has been granted us to discover a great name before it has time to be paraded for years up and down the columns of the daily newspapers. If this discovery is to be utilized, we must not delay and lose our chance by waiting another year.'

Among the members of the Academy there was, incidentally, only a single one who could read Tagore in the original. The writer of this chronicle recalls that when he was a young student of literature at the University of Lund, he sought out the venerable Professor Esaias Tegnér, the

Younger, and asked him how one could most easily get some idea of Tagore's writings. In answer, the veteran Orientalist handed me a Bengali grammar and assured me that by studying it for a couple of weeks I certainly ought to be able to enjoy Tagore in the original. During the immediately succeeding years, however, Tagore's most important works appeared in translations into many different languages, and the first impression as to the propriety of the award was then confirmed.

The prize was hailed, of course, with great acclaim in India, and it also had the result that ever since the people of India have been most persistent in honouring the Academy with new suggestions. The Tagore citation speaks of 'his profoundly sensitive, fresh and beautiful verse, by which, with consummate skill, he has made his poetic thought, expressed in his own English words, a part of the literature of the West'.

The list of candidates in 1914 likewise contained a rich variety of impressive names, but the sudden change in the world situation which came just as their works were being examined, naturally forced a serious consideration as to whether the Nobel Prizes should be awarded at all that year. As a matter of fact, the Nobel Committee of the Swedish Academy had already agreed to recommend the Swiss writer, Carl Spitteler, but the Academy itself decided, like the other prize-juries, to omit the distribution in 1914.

In the Committee report Professor Hjärne included a significant statement concerning the purpose of the prize as an aid to humanitarian causes in general which undeniably implied a certain censure, whether secret or open, of the national rivalries for world renown. 'In so far as nationalistic tendencies or contests for international power are stimulated by contemporary literature, it is the duty of the Academy', the statement said, 'to act in the spirit of Nobel and to do what it can to exert a soothing and moderating influence on whatever excesses are committed. Every effort should be made not to aggravate, even involuntarily, such clashes, precisely because the purpose of the prize is so closely associated, especially in foreign countries, with the founder's ideal of world peace, and it would surely be regarded as unfortunate if a prize which is intended to encourage the finest efforts of the human race as a whole should be misinterpreted as favouring any special nation. Such considerations have now become terrifyingly urgent, since we find ourselves in the midst of a great and widespread war, even though, as far as Sweden is concerned, only as spectators, but confronted, nevertheless, by all the consequent confusion in thought which now extends even to the higher levels of modern civilization.'

'We are witnessing', continued Hjärne, 'how the most eminent representatives of science, literature and art are suddenly carried away by the overpowering patriotic fervour which surrounds them, even in cases where this might be least expected, and how, at the same time, many of them in their zeal seem to lose their balance, break away from all contacts with the cultural work of their political enemies and publicly stoop to virulent attacks on this work, which only proves that they have weakened under the pressure of national hatred, and have lost the power to form and maintain objective opinions. Even a number of our living Nobel Prize winners, especially Maeterlinck and Hauptmann, Eucken and Kipling, have permitted themselves to be mixed up in such pen-feuds, which, as far as the progress of the epochal crisis is concerned, are quite futile, and in so doing they have taken occasion to make violent attacks on each other... In such a situation, the Academy must regard it as an especially heavy responsibility not to provide, by its choice of new prize-winners, a possible occasion for new outbursts of the prevailing bitterness, which, by some easily foreseeable misunderstanding of the Academy's duties and position, may be directed against our whole country.'

The prizes for 1914 were therefore turned over to the special funds of the prize-awarding institutions, but the *1915* prize was given in 1916 to ROMAIN ROLLAND [1866-1944] 'as a tribute to the lofty idealism of his literary production and to the sympathy and love of truth with which he has described different types of human beings'. In the Committee, opinions had been divided. The Spanish author, Pérez Galdós, was there supported by a majority, while Rolland, as a rival candidate, finally proved that he enjoyed greater favour in the Academy itself. It may be recalled that by his pacifist statements during the war, Rolland had incurred public anger, not only in Germany, but also in his own country, France, where for political reasons efforts had been made to condemn his whole literary production. Under these circumstances, the prize had the effect of a merited rehabilitation. Even though his fiction series, *Jean Christophe,* shows signs of artistic weakness and has failed to prove itself the perfect work of imaginative art of which Rolland had dreamt, there have been few epic efforts in our own times which in their humane purposes could be said to correspond better to Nobel's ideals. From this point of view and in a wider perspective, too, Romain Rolland has become one of the most appropriate and illustrious names on the list of prize-winners.

The prize for *1916* was awarded to VERNER VON HEIDENSTAM [1859-1940] 'in recognition of his significance as the leading representative of a new era in our literature'. This was the second time a Swedish author was honoured, and in this case he was also a member of the Academy. The members of the Committee had not thought it suitable to file a report on Heidenstam's qualifications, and had therefore limited themselves to making provisionally another proposal – the division of the prize between two Danish authors, Karl Gjellerup and Henrik Pontoppidan – while awaiting the Academy's attitude in regard to the Swedish candidature which turned out to be winning one. The year before, Heidenstam had presented to the nation his *Nya Dikter* ['New Poems'], which proved to be the monumental climax of his literary career. In these poems, full of rare beauty and mature wisdom, he glorified good will, peaceful social improvement and the gentle guardian spirits of the race. It was not really possible to raise any objections to this award, which elevated an author, already highly esteemed in his own country, to a world position and made him the object of international attention.

The proposed division of a prize between the two Danish authors was approved, instead, in *1917*, when KARL GJELLERUP [1857-1919] and HENRIK PONTOPPIDAN [1857-1943] were both chosen as prize-winners. In regard to the former, tribute was paid to 'his varied and rich poetry, which is inspired by lofty ideals', while the latter was said to have been rewarded 'for his authentic descriptions of present-day life in Denmark'. Inside the Committee, opinions had clashed; there was one which gave preference to Gjellerup, supported, among others, by a recommendation from the Danish literary historian, Vilhelm Andersen, in which Gjellerup's idealistic efforts were cited as especially praiseworthy in a period so much influenced by other tendencies. In the opinion of posterity, however, Pontoppidan's sound qualities as a story-teller will probably rank above the high-sounding, all-embracing aspirations of Gjellerup. The fact that such a comparison becomes inevitable is one of the drawbacks of a divided prize; in subsequent years the Academy has, in fact, avoided this procedure which in the public mind may often have the effect of reducing to one-half, not only the monetary value of the prize, but also the honour of receiving it.

The prize for 1918 was withheld, and the one for *1919* was awarded in 1920 to CARL SPITTELER [1845-1924] 'in special appreciation of his epic, *Olympian Spring*'. On several previous occasions this author had been nominated for a prize and now the Academy was practically unanimous in recognizing the significance of this imaginative, mythological epic in which German geniality was combined with classical Greek grandeur. Henrik Schück expressed a divergent opinion, describing Spitteler's epic as a kind of professorial poetry, involved and incomprehensible to the general public. Instead he supported the candidature of Georg Brandes, less in the latter's capacity as a scholar than as an author, insisting that the term 'idealistic' must not be interpreted too narrowly: a man like Brandes who throughout his whole life had been engaged in so many battles for ideas could hardly be denied the title of 'idealist'. This was probably the last time the candidature of Brandes was debated; he died in 1927. A poet like Spitteler cannot be one of the popular prize-winners; his original and ingenious creations do not invite translations. Yet the prize given him was fully justified as a tribute to a representative of the proud Swiss tradition in culture, as well as to a pupil and heir of Jacob Burckhardt.

When, in *1920,* the prize was awarded to KNUT HAMSUN [1859-1952], the Academy once more had the satisfaction of being able to refer to a specific book, which was also a recent one, 'his monumental work, *Growth of the Soil*'. In this powerful novel about the successful strivings of a Norwegian pioneer, there certainly was a clear-cut, idealistic strain of the kind that had previously been sought for in vain in his admirable production. Per Hallström had earlier voiced his hesitation: 'For the most part he has exerted an anarchic influence, and the idealistic tendency which the Nobel Prize is intended to encourage he has probably never recognized as even legitimate'. Hamsun's reward was, nevertheless, greeted with great applause by all those who clearly recognized him as one of the greatest contemporary interpreters of the interplay between the mysteries of nature and the tragicomedies of the human race. In the long run, the political disaster of his old age cannot have an effect on the appreciation of his rich literary merits.

For the prize in *1921* the Committee had recommended John Galsworthy, but a change of opinion in the Academy led to the choice of ANATOLE FRANCE [1844-1924]; not, however, without reservations as to whether his brilliant work could be said to exhibit an idealistic tendency. The most serious criticism was voiced by Hjärne, who said, among other things: 'With a few dashes of Aristophanic humour, or the more elementary forms of Socratic irony, mixed with the scepticism of the younger academic school, he has now and then tried to relax in the pleasure garden of Epicurus. In its immediate vicinity he has staked out for his own personal refinement and flower-cultivation a special little patch which, in view of the gifts bestowed on him and his own temperamental impulses, he has found best suited for development, under his supervision, into a productive site for a dainty hothouse built in his own Hellenizing style... But for that kind of cult and that sort of achievement the *idealistic* literature prize of Alfred Nobel was not intended. If I may be permitted to use a parable, I would say that as a contender Anatole France should be turned out of the arena, but gladly, if possible, with all honour, approximately in accordance with Plato's directions in regard to Homer, whom he wanted to have crowned with the most elegant wreath obtainable, and then, with manifestations of high respect, escorted out of his republic.'

Against this severe judgment, Henrik Schück maintained, in his dissenting opinion, that Anatole France both could and should be rewarded under the statutes. 'It is true', he wrote, 'that he is a sceptic, and those who are fortunate enough to have found a solution to the riddle of life may of course regard this as a fault, as something that conflicts with the Nobel Foundation's duty to protect idealism. But Anatole France has never been an idle doubter who with indifference has watched justice and humanitarianism trampled underfoot.' And then Schück continued: 'When seen as a whole, Anatole France's literary production, too, must be described as idealistic, provided we do not hedge the meaning of the word behind some sort of religious barrier. It expresses a reaction to Zola's naturalism; against the latter's earth-bound analysis of reality, Anatole France sets up the historical tradition, and injects, once more, romanticism into literature, not the old one, certainly, but a new and probably more genuine one. In any case, he tries to understand the different periods and, therefore, also to forgive. This may not be the highest form of idealism, but I hope I may be pardoned if I do not underestimate it, since it is also my own.'

These extracts from the arguments advanced by each side are cited to illustrate, once more, the constantly recurring difficulties in deciding to what extent an author's work meets the requirements specified in Nobel's will. In this case the Academy's doubts were finally resolved and, with every flourish, the prize was awarded to the witty creator of Abbé Coignard, 'in recognition of his brilliant literary achievements, which are characterized by nobility and vigour of style, great-hearted human sympathy, genuine charm and a true French temper'.

In *1922* another Spanish dramatist, JACINTO BENAVENTE [1866-1954], was selected, being warmly supported by Per Hallström, who, at that time, after the death of Hjärne, became Chairman of the Committee. Two-thirds of the members of the Spanish Academy had signed the nomination papers, so there could be no doubt as to the high esteem his plays enjoyed in his own country. Elegance and vivacity are the outstanding characteristics of this present-day successor to Lope de Vega, whom he equals in his mastery of stage technique and in his facility of invention. With some outstanding exceptions, such as *La Malquerida* and *Los Interesos Creados,* it is, however, only in the Spanish-speaking world that the dramatic production of Benavente has enjoyed an appreciation that does full justice to the richness and vitality of his artistry. He received the award 'for the happy manner in which he has continued the illustrious traditions of the Spanish drama'.

In regard to the prize for *1923*, which was given to WILLIAM BUTLER YEATS [1865-1939], it can surely be asserted that this was one of the happiest selections during this whole period, not merely because it meant welcome material support for the Irish dreamer, but also because during the succeeding years he was stimulated by it to score a new and surprising success in his already notable career as a lyric poet. His poems and plays had given the initial impulse to the Celtic movement, and his own symbolic language had been one of the great aesthetic stimulants of the period. No literary reward could have been better earned than the one now given him 'for his always inspired poetry, which in a highly artistic form gives expression to the spirit of a whole nation'.

From the statements in the Committee report for that year it appears, however, that a few of the members preferred Thomas Hardy as the leading candidate. Thus the Secretary of the Academy, Erik Axel Karlfeldt, wrote: 'Since for my own part I wish to acknowledge Thomas Hardy's monumental achievements in describing the English countryside and analysing the English temperament, and being, furthermore, convinced that continued neglect of him would cause a feeling of discontent and disappointment in England which I would not presume to call unjustified, and, finally, in view of the fact that Yeats, who is much younger, may be considered later, I urge the Academy to award this year's prize to Hardy.' The present writer, who had been a member of the Committee since 1921, had likewise been active in support of Hardy's candidature, one of the reasons being his feeling that special value should be set on his later lyric productions, which were an almost unprecedented achievement for a writer who had already reached such an advanced age. Among the members of the Academy, however, the conviction had long since taken firm root that Hardy's deep pessimism and inexorable fatalism were not to be reconciled with the spirit of the Nobel Prize. The feeling could not, unfortunately, be shaken by the persistent nominations that were annually renewed until Hardy's death. As time went on, his great age too became a definite obstacle; the honour would have come much too late and would thereby have lost its purpose.

In the case of the prize for *1924,* which was awarded to WLADYSLAW REYMONT [1868-1925], the Academy was confronted by the delicate problem of choosing justly between him and another Polish author, Stefan Zeromski, who was supported with much greater fervour by public opinion in Poland. Zeromski's vivid imagination and strong feelings stood out in striking contrast to Reymont's calm and matter-of-fact way of writing, especially in the work that was the mainstay of his claim. By honouring Reymont exclusively for 'his great national epic, *The Peasants*', the Academy returned to the same practice as that applied in the case of Hamsun. The four parts of the work form an epopee of the year in which winter, spring, summer, and autumn are merged harmoniously, in symphonically balanced proportions and with rich variations, into a hymn to the life of the people on their ancestral Polish soil. Unfortunately, Reymont passed away the following year and thus had no opportunity to show any further proof of his epic powers.

A prominent candidate who on this occasion was much in the minds of a couple of the Committee members ought to be mentioned here. In 1923 Guglielmo Ferrero had been nominated by several highly qualified sponsors, but had been opposed by Henrik Schück, who considered that the professional objections to Ferrero's *Roman History* precluded an award based solely on its literary merits. Hallström and the present writer expressed 'their deep-felt regret over this outcome and also raised the question as to whether the historical experts in their objections to Ferrero's works were not to some extent influenced by the prejudice of exact scholarship against the boldness required in a writer who tries to present to a wide public in a graphic and stimulating manner the often fragmentary and sometimes ambiguous results of strict scientific research'. Three years later the candidature of Ferrero was renewed through a proposal to divide the prize between him and Eduard Meyer, the German historian, but again without success.

The prize for *1925* was awarded in 1926 to GEORGE BERNARD SHAW [1856-1950] 'for his literary work which is marked by both idealism and humanity, and whose sharp satire is often infused with a singular poetic beauty'. As Shaw's main supporter, Per Hallström was particularly active, and his recommendation reveals a clear-sighted and detailed familiarity with Shaw's literary output. On the Academy's final decision the ageing author's most recent feat, his new play, *Saint Joan,* likewise had a strong effect. This time it could be taken for granted that the award would meet with world-wide approval; one of the most independent and brilliant writers of our age had in this case received his just tribute of honour, certainly a little late, but not, after all, too late. Hallström stressed that despite all his rationalistic rummages in human psychology, which at times looked like a merely provocative sport, Shaw had preserved a fundamentally idealistic attitude and in every kind of weather had mustered his moral courage for spirited fights against the superior forces of pharisaical prejudice.

Shaw accepted the prize with some hesitation but expressed gratitude for the honour and finally decided to use the prize money to create a fund for the promotion of better literary relations between Sweden and England. The resulting Anglo-Swedish Literary Foundation was able, during a number of years, to finance the publication of a series of good translations of modern and classical Swedish literature, including a selection of Strindberg's plays, in which for a long time Shaw had taken a personal interest.

The next name on the list of prize-winners was that of the Italian novelist GRAZIA DELEDDA [1875-1936], who in 1927 received the prize for *1926.* Her candidature had several times before been taken up for discussion and each time had been strongly supported inside the Academy by some particular admirers of Italy. Deledda's fame was based, primarily, on her genuine, colourful descriptions of life in Sardinia, and throughout her writings runs a vein of melancholy meditation with something of the insistent, monotonous rhythm of a solitary mountain spring. It may be true that her narratives seldom offer any surprises in the way of bold methods of treatment or choice of subjects, but within her limited field she shows a definite authenticity of feeling and style which should not be underestimated, as has sometimes been done. Quite properly, the award could be made 'for her idealistically inspired writings which with plastic clarity picture the life on her native island and with depth and sympathy deal with human problems in general'.

During the discussions of the 1927 and 1928 awards, when two prizes had to be decided upon, there was a sharp cleavage of opinion, especially in regard to two candidates who from different points of view were both prominent, the Russian, Maxim Gorki, and the Greek, Costis Palamas. In the case of the former, the Academy found it difficult to arrive at a wholly objective judgment both as to the intellectual part he had played during the revolution and as to his later production, which was politically coloured, while a work like his famous autobiography could, without hesitation, be placed in the front rank. The modern Greek poet, on the other hand, presented the problem that his language was unintelligible to the judges, and the Academy could not very well make up its mind solely on the basis of scattered translations and the opinions of foreign experts, as to whether he was really an author of the required stature about whom the members could agree on the basis of personal convictions.

The nomination which in the end gained the strongest support came, however, from France; it concerned the philosopher HENRI BERGSON [1859-1941], who received the prize for *1927* 'in recognition of his rich and vitalizing ideas and the brilliant skill with which they have been presented'. Although this was one of the rare occasions when the purely literary line was abandoned, it was obvious that Bergson's inspiring influence on modern literature was one of the main motives behind the decision. When his investigations into human psychology, including the functions of memory, as well as his theory of intuition, had influenced the general thinking of his time, this was most likely due just as much to indirect communication through the most important literature of the day as to a direct study of his works. The great vogue of Bergsonianism at the beginning of the twentieth century was a heartening counterbalance to materialism, and it has been compared to the influence of Schelling's philosophy a hundred years earlier. Unmistakably, it was in harmony with the spirit of Alfred Nobel.

On the same occasion the prize for *1928* was awarded to the Norwegian author SIGRID UNDSET [1882-1949], 'principally for her powerful descriptions of Northern life during the Middle Ages'. Using the Icelandic sagas as models, she had by that time completed her most impressive work, *Kristin Lavransdatter,* as well as its subsequent counterpart, *Olav Audunsson.* In modern Norwegian epic literature the first novel, in particular, stands out by virtue of its construction, which is both firm and full of character, its psychological insight and its expert historical knowledge.

Because of these solid qualities the book has been able to hold a place on the international level, too, and the earlier impression of the writer's strong, forthright personality was further enhanced during the war-time occupation of her country.

By the award of the prize for *1929* to THOMAS MANN [1875-1955], another already established world-celebrity was honoured. From German sources a nomination had been received five years earlier, and the delay is to be partly explained by the half-dusk which had descended on Germany after the disaster of the First World War, during which so much of what was worth-while in German literature before the war had sunk into a sort of semi-oblivion. In the citation this circumstance was, in fact, stressed when it was specified that the award had been made 'principally for his great novel, *Buddenbrooks,* which has won steadily increased recognition as one of the classic works of contemporary literature'.

As a matter of fact, the novel in question had been published as early as 1901, and since then twenty-eight years had passed – years that had been filled, as far as Mann was concerned, with intense work. It would therefore hardly be surprising if the German author observed with some discouragement that such an important work as *The Magic Mountain,* published in 1924, had been ignored in the Academy's decision. With the passing of time, however, the worth of this cyclopaedic novel of ideas has steadily increased; in its own class it is undoubtedly fully equal to the bourgeois family chronicle written in Mann's youth. But to-day there is again available for comparison some even more important material. Mann is one of the extremely few winners of a Nobel Prize who has afterwards built up a series of increasingly impressive new works, which, in addition, have been written in exile and under circumstances which must have required the highest power of resistance and an almost super-human energy.

The *1930* prize was awarded to SINCLAIR LEWIS [1885-1951] 'for his vigorous and graphic art of description and his ability to create, with wit and humour, new types of people'. On the final phrase special emphasis should be laid, because when the Academy agreed in favour of his nomination, it was influenced, among other things, by a desire to recognize a vigorous trend in modern literature – high-class American humour, the best traditions of which had been continued with such marked success by Sinclair Lewis.

Against him was weighed another wholly different painter of American reality, the ponderous and solemn Theodore Dreiser, the pioneer American writer of novels criticizing social conditions. Against Lewis's gay virtuosity and flashing satire could be set Dreiser's all-embracing sympathies and his affection for the productive chaos of existence, but the future alone can decide which is the more significant. From the Committee's report, which was prepared by Per Hallström, only a few lines can be cited here to clarify the comparison. 'Each of these authors', he wrote, 'has perhaps only once, if the word "only" may be used, reached real heights. This is just as true of Dreiser's *American Tragedy* as it is of Sinclair Lewis's *Babbitt*. Dreiser has fused the hard, dark phases of American life into a drama whose strict logical development and magnificent climax are truly impressive. Conversely, out of the lack of independent individuality and the spiritual shallowness of undeveloped youth, but at the same time retaining what is youthfully refreshing and attractive, Lewis has created a figure, the significance of which as a type has not been surpassed in contemporary literature, and in which his nation has recognized, with more or less satisfaction, its own image.'

The award in *1931* marked a departure from usual procedure in so far as, in this single instance, it was bestowed posthumously on ERIK AXEL KARLFELDT [1864-1931], who had been nominated in the prescribed way, but who died while his candidature was under formal consideration. According to the statutes this need not bar a final verdict in his favour. Special circumstances and considerations were also present. Karlfeldt had been chosen as a winner as early as 1919, but at that time he had declined because, as an official of the Academy, he felt he ought not to accept the honour. When he was again proposed in 1931, it was known that, having reached the statutory age-limit, he had decided to resign as Permanent Secretary, and after that he would obviously feel free to accept the prize. This special case has not, however, affected the Academy's general attitude in regard to the propriety of posthumous awards. The step can be judged in different ways. However, it was not sentimental reasons that prompted the decision, but a sincere conviction that Karlfeldt's poetry merited the distinction, even if death had prevented the laureate from receiving his wreath. In an address at the Nobel festival that year it was said in this respect: 'It is the self-elected fate and limitation of lyric poets that what is most deeply typical and freshly creative in their work is inextricably tied up with the roots and rhythm of the original language – with the exact shade and significance of every word. Karlfeldt's originality can possibly be inferred from a translation, but can be fully understood only in Swedish. Nevertheless, anyone who tries to judge for himself must in all fairness admit that even the treasures of the so-called great literatures are seldom enriched with gems as choice as those our Swedish poet has produced through the medium of our little-known language.'

On a couple of previous occasions JOHN GALSWORTHY [1867-1933] had already been a prominent candidate when in *1932* he was awarded the prize 'for his distinguished art of narration which takes its highest form in *The Forsyte Saga*'. By means of this lifelike gallery of skilfully drawn characters, representing several generations of the upper middle class, Galsworthy had been able to delineate the gradual disintegration and final decay of the Victorian era. It was above all thanks to the realistic artistry of this work that he rose above his contemporary rivals in English literature, even though H. G. Wells surpassed him both in strength of intellect and fertility of imagination. In the Committee, which this time filed a unanimous report, it was not, however, Wells who was scrutinized as the leading rival candidate. Instead, Professor Fredrik Böök had warmly recommended a German poet, Paul Ernst, calling him a neglected but highly gifted writer of the uncommercial type, to whom the Nobel Prize would obviously be of far greater benefit than to a popular and already world-famed celebrity like Galsworthy.

A sharp difference of opinion arose in *1933*, and the Committee could not unanimously recommend any candidate. In the course of the discussion, a sufficient majority was found, however, for the Russian *émigré* author IVAN BUNIN [1870-1953] who was then rewarded 'for the strict artistry with which he has carried on the classical Russian traditions in prose writing'. Bunin's work is by no means voluminous, but it does contain a number of short stories of rare quality, which attain the high literary standard developed by the foremost of his predecessors, Tolstoy, Chekhov, Turgenev, and Goncharov. The objection could, of course, be raised against Bunin's work that, for all its artistic merits of style, it was not richly or powerfully creative, but merely followed, in a slightly diluted form, the great traditions of Russian narrative art. At the time, however, the award was greeted with sympathy; the wind-driven Bunin had preserved at least an authentic touch of the past.

On the recommendation of the entire literary section of the Italian Academy, LUIGI PIRANDELLO [1867-1936] was selected as the prizewinner in *1934*, 'for his bold and ingenious revival of Italian dramatic and scenic art'. When Pirandello's plays began to dominate the theatre programmes, a first impression might have been that the interest they aroused was only a temporary fad. But it soon became evident that his dramatic art, which was always preoccupied with the identity of one's personality, was, in reality, a remarkable and cleverly reiterated presentation of philosophical and psychological problems which had never before been posed on the stage with such clarity and force, nor with the same striking ability to create endless variations. The Italian wizard was, in fact, something more than a virtuoso. In him were to be found a deep sense of the tragic complications of human existence and a painful seriousness which appeared even in his comedies of the lighter and faster-moving type. Pirandello's work proved to be a truly original contribution to modern drama, and it was now rewarded with a literary prize at an appropriate time.

Another dramatist of international significance was selected in *1936,* when the American playwright EUGENE O'NEILL [1888-1953] received the prize 'for the power, honesty and deep-felt emotions of his dramatic works, which embody an original concept of tragedy'. O'Neill's plays had been staged in Stockholm earlier than in most European cities; his foremost tragedy, *Mourning Becomes Electra,* was magnificently produced in 1933, and just as he had scored an early success on the Swedish stage, so he now received the supreme accolade from the Academy at a time when his fame was still fresh and his creative powers at their peak.

It has been remarked that the first two parts of his Electra tragedy are more effective than the third, but the same criticism could be levelled at his classical prototype, Aeschylus, whose *Oresteia* likewise becomes weaker in the concluding part. His boldly experimental and emotionally tense plays are America's most important contribution to modern dramatic art; no one has utilized the ideas borrowed from Europe with the same independence and imagination. As a typical sign of the times it may be mentioned that the name of Sigmund Freud, proposed by Romain Rolland, appeared the same year on the list of candidates. The famous creator of psychoanalysis had, however, to step aside for one of his many literary disciples.

In regard to the prize-winner in *1937* the Frenchman ROGER MARTIN DU GARD [1881-1958], it may be noted that, oddly enough, he had never been nominated by anyone in his own country, although he had reached a prominent position as soon as the first volumes of his cycle of novels had been published. It took a long time before *Les Thibault* reached completion; the work had begun to appear in 1922, but the final instalment was not ready until 1940. It is true that the novelist has not been able to solve all the extremely complicated problems he had set for himself, but his narrative offers the greatest interest, both as a description of an environment and as a psychological analysis of certain individuals; this is especially true of the two brothers Thibault in their contrast to each other. France has an abundance of similar fiction series, but its contemporary literature has hardly any counterpart to what Roger Martin du Gard has here achieved; nor has French opinion denied the justice of the honour that was bestowed on him 'for the artistic vigour and truthfulness with which he has pictured human contrasts as well as some fundamental aspects of contemporary life'.

An American writer, PEARL BUCK [b.1892], received the prize in *1938* 'for her rich and truly epic descriptions of peasant life in China and for her biographical masterpieces'. In this case there has been no lack of voices which have raised the question as to whether the prize-winner really possessed the required qualifications for a distinction of this importance. The decisive factor in the Academy's judgment was, above all, the admirable biographies of her parents, the missionary pair in China – two volumes which seemed to deserve classic rank and to possess the required prospects for permanent interest. In addition, her novels of Chinese peasant life have properly made a place for themselves by virtue of the authenticity, wealth of detail and rare insight with which they describe a region that is little known and rarely accessible to Western readers. But as literary works of art, the two biographies remain incomparable with anything else in Pearl Buck's both earlier or later production.

When the prize for *1939* was awarded to FRANS EEMIL SILLANPÄÄ [b.1888], Sweden's old sister nation, Finland, won for the first time a place in the world-wide literary contest. It should not be surprising if in its decision the Academy was somewhat influenced, whether consciously or unconsciously, by the contemporary situation, i.e. Finland's heroic fight against an overwhelmingly superior power. Sillanpää's books are remarkable for their gently shaded interpretations of the Finnish people's soul and of the Finnish landscape in all its austerity and tenderness, especially in the story of Silja with its soft atmosphere of summer night and resignation. Against the background of the political events of the day, his work naturally gained an increased symbolic value, even though the author's honest and attractive personality had long before been recognized and appreciated.

The Sillanpää prize was the last awarded before the new world tumult once more closed the portals of culture and disrupted the intellectual contacts among nations. Under the terms of a new royal decree, the prize distribution was suspended during the years 1940-43, inclusive, whereby, as allowed by the statutes, two-thirds of the prize money was turned over to the special funds of the respective prize-distributing institutions and one-third to the main fund. The work of selecting prize-winners went on, however, as before, despite the uncertainty as to whether it would ever have any visible results. No secret should be made of the fact that towards the end of the period some impatience was felt within the Academy at the annually repeated instructions to omit the prize awards on account of the war situation.

Finally the Nobel Foundation itself applied to the Government for instructions, but before this request was made in September, 1943, the Academy had been asked by the Foundation to give its opinion as to whether any representation should be made that year to the Government regarding the omission or postponement of the prize distribution. In its reply, the Academy declared itself ready both to adjudicate and to distribute prizes. On the same occasion it stressed the importance of a resumption of the Nobel activities as soon as possible as a natural step towards peace. In the sphere of literature the Academy considered it possible both to make a survey and to select winners, since, after all, the wartime break in the international relations had probably caused less hindrance to the Academy's work than to that of the other prize-juries. As far as the literary prize was concerned, duly formulated proposals were available, but in view of the omission of the prize awards for three consecutive years, these nominations had been shelved. Four members, however, filed objections to the Academy's statement, one of them being Henrik Schück, who correctly pointed out that one Nobel jury was still unable to function, namely the Norwegian, and that in Germany it was forbidden to accept Nobel Prizes, while nothing was known as to the situation in this respect in the countries occupied by the German armies. In the end, it turned out that the literary prize-jury was the only one to recommend awards in 1943, so that the distribution was once more omitted.

In *1944* the ice was finally broken and the literary prize could be awarded to the Danish writer, JOHANNES V. JENSEN [1873-1950], who had been proposed several times. Because of the German occupation of his country, however, he could not come to Stockholm to receive his prize until the following year. In him was honoured a great writer who had stood in the forefront since the beginning of the century. For a long time, to be sure, his merits had been debated, but he had always been admired for his exuberant vitality. This son of Jutland's rugged, wind-swept stretches seemed to have wanted, as if in pretended defiance, to surprise his contemporaries with a literary crop of rare luxuriance. His writings include the most varied kinds of epics and lyrics, realism and sagas, discussions of current events, theoretical expositions, and scientific forays in all directions. Being a man of both a nervous temperament and primitive traits, he has developed, through the use of exciting contrasts, a style of his own, which has pace, spice and vigour. In his highly imaginative narrative series, *The Long Journey,* he has glorified the fundamental characteristics of the Nordic people and their historic will to survive. The citation read: 'for the rare strength and fertility of his poetic imagination with which is combined an intellectual curiosity of wide scope and a bold, freshly creative style'.

By the side of Johannes V. Jensen at the Nobel festival in *1945* stood a stranger from afar with a half-Indian appearance, the Chilean poet, GABRIELA MISTRAL [1889-1957], who received the prize 'for her lyric poetry, which is inspired by powerful emotions and which has made her name a symbol of the idealistic aspirations of the entire Latin-American world'. For the prize-distributors it was a long-awaited pleasure to be able, at last, to reach Spanish-speaking America with this tribute to its leading poet.

Gabriela Mistral's poems, which had previously been wholly unknown in Sweden, had had the good fortune of being translated into Swedish by the poet Hjalmar Gullberg, whose rendering gave a thoroughly convincing impression of the vigour, tenderness and passion of the original. Her writings are not very extensive, but they include a number of poems which express the whole scale of emotions emanating from a warm heart and establish contact with a strong, artless personality. They make you believe you hear the authentic voice of the unknown, distant country, free from the European overtones and imitative resonances which can so often be detected in the numerous poets of South America.

The prize for *1946* was given to HERMANN HESSE [1877-1962] 'for his inspired writings which, while growing in boldness and penetration, exemplify the classical humanitarian ideals and high qualities of style'. Of all German authors, Hesse was the first to escape from the political tyranny over ideas and, even during the First World War, he settled in Switzerland where he became a citizen. The right to reside in a country which remained neutral before and during the Second World War permitted him to pursue his writing in relative peace. The course of events made him and Thomas Mann practically the only German authors who, with unimpaired dignity and independence, took over in trust the German cultural inheritance during the war period. As a novelist he became a highly sensitive interpreter of the world's anguish and the interplay of the demoniacal forces of the day. In spite of his wholly modern literary technique, he has remained in constant touch with the most distinguished German traditions, an heir to Mörike, Hoffmann, and Stifter.

As a lyric poet he combines a choice purity of tone with ardent feeling, and his nobly musical style is unexcelled in present-day writing. The distinction bestowed on Hesse in his sixty-ninth year was further justified by the fact that it called world-wide attention to an inquiring and courageous spirit who with rare integrity had pursued his calling and who, throughout a tragic era, had carried high the noble emblem of true humanism.

When the prize for *1947* was awarded to ANDRÉ GIDE [1869-1951], he had for a long time been regarded as a leader in French literary circles, where he had exercised great influence for several generations. It is therefore tempting to ask why his importance could not have been correctly diagnosed long before, but Gide unquestionably is the kind of writer who must be seen in a long perspective to be fully appreciated and who requires adequate time to pass through all three of the classical dialectic stages. Probably to a higher degree than any other writer of our times, he has been a man of contradictions, a Proteus experimenting with various points of view. His writings have the character of a continuous dialogue in which faith always contends with doubt, asceticism with the lust for life, discipline with the cry for freedom. But behind the steadily shifting scenes, the same keen intelligence and incisive psychology are always at work. In his fight against Pharisaism it was unavoidable that some accepted human standards of a rather delicate nature should be endangered. But throughout all stages of his development, Gide stands out as a courageous defender of literary integrity, based on the right and duty of the writer to formulate his own problems, independently and completely. In this respect, his long activity may certainly be said to represent an idealistic tendency. His citation read: 'for his comprehensive and artistically significant writings, in which human problems and conditions have been presented with a fearless love of truth and keen psychological insight'.

The winner in *1948*, THOMAS STEARNS ELIOT [b.1888], marks a departure from the type of writers usually selected as recipients of a Nobel Prize. A majority of them had been spokesmen for a literature which seeks its natural contacts in the popular mind and which uses more or less readily available means to establish such contacts. Eliot has chosen another approach, and his career is unusual to the extent that from an extremely exclusive and deliberately isolated position he has been able to exert an increasingly widespread influence. In both his verse and prose there is to be found a strong individual accent, which has commanded attention by its appeal to the modern mind – an ability to cut into the consciousness of our own generation with the sharpness of a diamond. In his poetic rhapsody, *The Waste Land,* dating from 1922, he drew an unforgettable picture of the aridity and impotence of modern civilization, and in his latest work, *Four Quartets,* he interprets his personal philosophy in a meditative mood, crowning it with a still more clearly defined, transcendental superstructure. In Eliot's case it may seem especially difficult to predict how future generations will appraise his work, but it cannot possibly be denied that in his own times he has played the role of a leading poser of questions or that he is a master of literary style, both in his verse and in his philosophical essays. The prize was given him 'for his outstanding, pioneer contribution to present-day poetry'.

The *1949* Literature Prize was withheld until the following year, when it was awarded to WILLIAM FAULKNER [1897-1962] 'for his vigorous and independently artistic contribution to America's new fiction'. Faulkner has drawn his narrative themes from the state of Mississippi, the southern *milieu* where his family has its roots and where he himself lived. There is something fraught with destiny in his relationship to this morbid and luxuriant river landscape with its scenes of social decay and its memories of vanished splendour. The indomitable individualism and thirst for revenge of those who have sunk in the social scale, the conflict between white and coloured, the irreparable aftermath of the Civil War and the bitter personal experiences of the First World War, are only some of the ingredients that go to make up the sultry, louring atmosphere in Faulkner's novels. The tragic sense of life does not exclude a grim humour, which makes itself heard even in the darkest scenes, or, rather, in them above all. *The Sound and the Fury, Light in August* and *Collected Short Stories* may be regarded as peaks in his production.

Within the new epic writing of America, Faulkner stood out on his own as a master with an experimentally varying technique and a brilliant command of language, faithful to his calling and uncompromising in his portrayal of human suffering and need.

Simultaneously, the English philosopher BERTRAND RUSSELL [b. 1872] was awarded the *1950* prize 'in recognition of his versatile and significant writings, which have shown him to be a champion of humanity and the freedom of thought'. Although Russell's works in the fields of philosophy and mathematical logic are considered epoch-making, it was not these scientific feats which the Literature Prize primarily wished to honour. What is important in this connection is that Russell has addressed himself at large to a world-wide audience of laymen and has succeeded to a rare degree in keeping the general interest in philosophy alive. His entire life's work comprises a stimulating vindication of the reality of common sense. He is a modern philosopher of enlightenment who carries on the line from the classic English empiricism of Locke and Hume. With his free and healthy good sense, his admirably clear style and his wit in the midst of gravity, he has, in so doing, developed qualities as an author which are to be found only in the very élite. It suffices to mention such works as *History of Western Thought, Human Knowledge, Sceptical Essays* and *My Mental Development.*

There is much in Russell to incite controversy. In this, he himself – unlike so many other philosophers – sees one of the most vital and natural purposes of authorship. His rationalism does not solve all irritating questions and is most unsuitable as a panacea. None the less, one must admire the rebellious courage of his plain speaking, a kind of dry, fiery strength and blithe resilience. In the best sense, his way of thinking can also be said to fulfil the very wishes and principles which guided Alfred Nobel when he founded his Prizes. There is quite a remarkable resemblance in their outlook on life. Both are at once sceptics and Utopians, both take a dark view of the contemporary world but believe staunchly in the possibility of bringing about logical norms for human behaviour. The Swedish Academy considers that it acted in the spirit of Nobel in wishing to honour Bertrand Russell on the 50th anniversary of the Foundation.

The Swedish writer PÄR LAGERKVIST [b.1891] was chosen as recipient of the *1951* prize. By this time he had, with his novel *Barabbas,* won esteem and response far beyond his own country for his moving portrayal of the heart-searchings and anguished conscience of the man for whom Jesus literally gave his life on the cross. Lagerkvist's candidature had also for the greater part been strongly preferred by those entitled to nominate in other countries, and thus had not emanated solely from the Academy's own circle.

As a writer, Lagerkvist has alternated between poetry, epic prose and the drama, and in each of these spheres he has created important works, in which his burning sincerity and breadth of perspective are always apparent. Unquestionably, he is one of the contemporary writers who have fearlessly and directly concerned themselves with the vital questions of humanity and who, time and again, have grappled with the basic problems of existence. If he does not always attain the heights at which he aims, this is of little importance in his case – what *is* important is that each work forms a part of the whole that he has conceived, and consummates his doctrine, which is ever one and the same: the poverty and greatness of all that is human, the fetters of the earthbound thrall and the heroic struggle of the spirit for its liberation. This theme runs through all the works whose titles here come to mind: *Gäst hos verkligheten* [Guest of Reality], *Onda sagor* [Evil Tales], *Hjärtats sånger* [Songs of the Heart], *Han som fick leva om sitt liv* [He who was allowed his life over again], *Dvärgen* [The Dwarf] and *Barabbas,* to mention only a few. Lagerkvist's Nobel Prize was awarded 'for the artistic power and deep integrity with which he seeks an answer in his writings to Man's eternal problems'.

1952's prizewinner FRANÇOIS MAURIAC [b.1885] has long since established his position as one of the finest contemporary authors. Moreover, he represents a religiously inspired trend which, in France particularly, has comprised, and still comprises, an extremely important spiritual formation. Of Mauriac it can be said that he uses the medium of the novel to present a definite aspect of human existence with Catholicism's system of thought and feeling as a background or superstructure. While this may, up to a point, make him a stranger to non-Catholic readers, through his psychological intensity he often attains so far that the confessional limits lose their significance, as also intimated in the wording in support of the award: 'the penetrating spiritual insight and artistic intensity with which, in the form of the novel, he has interpreted the human drama of life'. The scene of his novels is nearly always Gironde with its capital Bordeaux, the old wine-growing district with its châteaux and farms, together with

Les Landes with its pine woods and sheep pastures, where the cicadas sing in solitude and the Atlantic rumbles like thunder in the distance. The thematic repetition in his novels may tend to be monotonous, but the sharp focus calls forth the same admiration every time one re-encounters it. In the matter of linguistic terseness and expressiveness Mauriac is unexcelled: in a few vivid lines his prose can throw a glaring light on the most complex and undefinable things.

The smouldering unrest of youth, the treacherous chasms of evil, the sham temptations of the flesh, the grip of avarice on all that is material, the injurious effects of smugness and Pharisaism – these are constantly recurring themes in Mauriac's writings. But for all his analytical ruthlessness, he counts ultimately on a compassion that passeth understanding. His novels may be likened to narrow but deep wells, at the bottom of which can be glimpsed the mystic stream.

A great stir was caused by the Academy's decision to award the *1953* Literature Prize to SIR WINSTON CHURCHILL [b.1874] 'for his mastery in the presentation of history and biography and for the brilliant oratory with which he has stepped forward to the defence of our civilization'. This distinction in itself makes every closer presentation superfluous; no contemporary figure can display a more familiar physiognomy. Let it suffice here to recall the illustrious example of an author's career which runs parallel with a political life under the weight of the highest responsibility. This tradition, which in England has been upheld by such classical names as Burke, Disraeli and Morley, has, with rare authority and success, had new life infused into it by Churchill. His first books, a war correspondent's reports from India and the Sudan, had already appeared before the turn of the century, and his latest work, *The Second World War,* had not yet been completed: his energetic achievements as a writer thus extended over half a century. If a literary production of this character in English eyes belongs in a high degree to literature, this also is in full accord with the prescripts of the Nobel Prize, which expressly state that 'the term literature includes not only works of fiction but also other writings which, through their form and manner of presentation, possess literary worth'.

Churchill's public speeches, his monumental biography of Marlborough, his essays on notable contemporaries and his delightful account of his own youthful adventures, *My Early Life,* can certainly be counted among the world literature that one dares to predict will endure as a source of inspiration to future generations as well. This is true not least of the stately series of Churchill's political speeches, a slice of history that has been deeply experienced, epic in the word's oldest and most real meaning. How many flashing phrases, how many expressions of civilized broad-mindedness and heroic trust have been imprinted in our consciousness through these speeches, forged during one of humanity's direst and darkest periods! They indeed represent a literary genre all on its own and a noble one at that, with a lineage from Greece and Rome.

The *1954* prize was awarded to an American author who had already achieved a maximum of fame–ERNEST HEMINGWAY [1898-1961] is one of his country's pioneers in literature, and his ambition has been to reflect, honestly and fearlessly, the hard features of the age. His importance as one of the epoch's real creators of style is apparent time and again in the American and European fiction of the last generation, above all in the living give and take of dialogue, in which he has become a model which is easy to imitate but difficult to match. He reproduces with supreme skill all the variations of speech, and even the pauses in which the train of thought is lost and the nervous mechanism breaks down. The work of psychological reflection he prefers to leave to his readers, and this freedom gives him an enormous advantage in spontaneous observation.

Hemingway made his name as a writer in 1929 with the novel *A Farewell to Arms,* in which he mustered his forces for an artistically genuine account of his painfully confused impressions from the Piave front in 1918. Later, too, he was drawn with instinctive partiality to bloodstained scenes of battle and cruel spectacle, to the Africa of the big-game hunters and Spain torn by civil war; but one of his latest works is the famous short novel *The Old Man and the Sea,* which, within the framework of a sporting short story, grows into a tribute to the fighting spirit, and allows the robust details to accumulate into an impassioned and pregnant utterance: 'A human being can be annihilated but not vanquished.' The reason given for the prize award also mentions this very work when it stresses 'his vigorous mastery with its influence on style in contemporary story-telling, most recently manifest in *The Old Man and the Sea*'.

The honour of the *1955* prize fell to the Icelandic writer HALLDÓR KILJAN LAXNESS [b.1902]. Early aware of his literary calling, he left Iceland in his youth to roam the world as a restless seeker, but in 1930 he settled down on his native island where, in quick succession, he completed the works that laid the foundation of his now undisputed position as Iceland's leading author. The chief titles in his very extensive production are *Salka Valka,* which, with fresh, realistic strokes, depicts life in a poor Icelandic fishing-village with the tragic destiny of a woman in the foreground; *Free Men,* which is a moving epic of the Icelandic small-holder's struggle against overwhelming forces, and the trilogy *The Bell of Iceland,* which deals with a dark phase of the island's history under Danish rule. *Gerpla,* his latest work, is a tilt at Iceland's classical tradition of heroic feats and minstrel lays, and may largely be regarded as an ironic pastiche in the style of the Icelandic sagas.

Laxness' story-telling is impressive mainly because of its teeming breadth and wealth of invention, its natural stream gushing forth from national founts. At the same time he has achieved great things as a reformer of language by restoring his native Icelandic tongue to a sensitive instrument for artistic creation. This purely linguistic achievement ensures his position as a pioneer in a literature whose illustrious lineage goes back into the grey mists of time. The distinction was conferred on him 'for his vivid epic writing which has renewed the great narrative art of Iceland'.

When the *1956* prize was awarded to the Spanish poet JUAN RAMÓN JIMÉNEZ [1881-1958], long regarded as a pre-eminent master in his country's literature, the honour reached him in tragic circumstances, at the deathbed of his wife in Puerto Rico. His long career was characterized by a homogeneity – unusual in our disjointed age – in the aims of thought and feeling, by an indefatigable striving to pursue the poet's calling on an ever higher plane. Jiménez was a mystic dreamer, whose consciousness reflected inner realities. Through the methodical purification of form he seeked a beauty which is crystal-clear in its conciseness and naked as the rose. For him, this search was also a way of seeking God and of fashioning the divine concept as a final religious symbol of the very essence of poetry.

Even if his extremely refined and almost esoteric medium of expression must naturally restrict the number of his readers and place him among the recluses of literature, his delightful prose elegy about the donkey Platero has become a book of popular appeal in many Spanish-speaking countries – a song in praise of sunny Andalusia, his native countryside, full of Franciscan tenderness and the joy of nature. In type an idealistic dreamer, Jiménez seems in high degree to represent the category of writers that Alfred Nobel wished to support and reward. The Swedish Academy's substantiation for Jiménez' prize reads: 'for his lyric writing which, in the Spanish language, sets an example of lofty spirituality and artistic purity'.

The prize for *1957* was given to ALBERT CAMUS [1913-1960], 'for his important literary production, which with clear-sighted earnestness illuminates the problems of the human conscience in our times'. This French author, born in a small town in Algeria, moved at the age of 25 to France as a journalist, and in the mother country he was soon recognized as a writer in the front rank, quickly matured in the bitter and feverish atmosphere of the war years. With a purely classical mastery of language and intensive concentration he has fashioned his problems in philosophical essays and symbolic tales of high interest. Chiefly in the novels *L'étranger*, 1942, *La peste*, 1947 and *La chute*, 1956 his thoughts are brought to life in such a way that characters and story speak to us quite of themselves without any comment from the author. In all its calm, precise objectivity, utterly convincing as a realistic description, his work is also inspired by the experiences of the French resistance movement, and lauds the revolt against overwhelming evil of those with deep resignation and no illusions. There is in him a genuine moral fervour which inspires him, in a daring personal way, to grapple with the great fundamental problems of life, and this striving can undoubtedly be said to accord with idealistic aims on which the Nobel Prize is based.

The literary prize for *1958* gave rise to a controversial situation when the prize-winner, the Soviet-Russian writer BORIS PASTERNAK [1890-1960], having first expressed his thanks, subsequently announced that he did not wish to accept the award. This refusal, however, does not affect the validity of the prize, and even though it could not be presented, Pasternak retains his position in the line of prize-winners. He is one of the new Russia's most remarkable writers, famed as a poet even during the first Soviet epoch, when he emerged as a pioneer inspired by modern ideas. He made his name with the collection of poems *My Sister, Life,* which was followed by other works in both verse and prose. By reason of his imaginative and vivid language, his daring images and analogies, he was soon to be acknowledged, outside Russia too, as one of the most important contemporary poets.

In fact, Pasternak remained an individualist who went his own way without ever playing any part in public life. But after a long silence there appeared his great novel *Doctor Zhivago,* which deals with the fateful period in Russia's history between 1903 and 1929, such as it is experienced by a cultured doctor from Moscow, who from the outset welcomes the revolution but is gradually struck down by its pitiless tragedy. The past lives again and is brought close to us in the scenes of the novel, which are lit as though by flashes of lightning. It should be noted here that the author does not tell his story in order to accuse or to protest, but merely to create a fearless and true document of the age. It is indeed a feat to have been able, under difficult conditions, to complete a work of this magnitude, raised above all political trends – rather, it is anti-political in all its humane purpose. By reason of its pure and mighty spirit it can also, in rare degree, be said to fulfil the conditions originally laid down for the Nobel Prize for Literature. The Swedish Academy states its reasons for the award briefly as follows: 'For his important contribution to both contemporary poetry and the field of the great Russian narrative tradition'.

The prize for the year *1959* was awarded to the Italian poet SALVATORE QUASIMODO [1901-1968]. Born in the vicinity of Syracuse, in Sicily, he has acquired from this unique and historical landscape a valuable heritage of visions and myths which, with vigour and originality, he has interpreted in the five books of poetry that comprise – together with numerous outstanding translations of ancient verse – the bulk of his production up to now.

Quasimodo's first poems appeared in 1930, but it was only during the 1940's and 1950's that he established his reputation as one of Italy's foremost modern poets. His range of subjects was to widen with the years, at the same time as his warmth of human feeling broke irresistibly through the hermetic mould in which at first he was bound. It was above all the bitter experiences of the war which finally brought about this change of attitude and made him the interpreter of the entire nation's moral life in its daily confrontation with death. In any case, in this way he has become a living voice of the present age, passionately concerned with reality, and in his highest moments he is of universal scope.

The prize was awarded on the following grounds: 'For his poetic writing, which with classic fire expresses the tragic sense of life of the present age'.

The prize for *1960* was awarded to the French poet SAINT-JOHN PERSE [b.1887] 'for the soaring flight and the evocative imagery of his poetry, which in a visionary fashion reflects the conditions of our time'. For a literary man his biography is in several respects a remarkable one. He was born on the island of Guadeloupe in the Antilles with the real name Alexis Léger, began his career as a diplomat and held finally a very vital and responsible position at the Foreign Office. After the defeat of France in 1940 he went into exile and found refuge in Washington, where he continued his poetical activity. His first famous work was an epic called *Anabase,* which in a suggestive and adamantine form tells of a distant and enigmatic venture through the deserts of Asia. Later works are *Exil, Vents* and *Amers*. His metaphors are drawn from many domains of knowledge, from all epochs, mythologies and climes; his poetic cycles resemble those large sea-shells in which one seems to hear a cosmic music. This supremely expansive imagination is his strength. In his theme of the power and impotence of man can also be discerned a heroic call, not least in the last published *Chronique,* which contains many allusions to the conditions in the world to-day.

In his way Saint-John Perse follows a grandiose tradition in French poetry, above all the rhetorical tradition from its classics.

The *1961* Nobel Prize for literature was awarded to the Yugoslavian writer IVO ANDRIĆ [b.1892] who is acknowledged in his own country as a master of narrative art and whose fame of recent years has spread farther and farther afield in translations to different languages. For the Swedish Academy it was of course particularly gratifying to honour, in him, a spokesman, worthy in all respects, of a group of languages which has not previously been represented in the list of prize-winners. Andrić is a native of Bosnia, which during his childhood was occupied by Austria-Hungary. As a student he took part in the national revolutionary movement and, upon the outbreak of war in 1914, was imprisoned; as a grown man he served his country as a diplomat and when the Second World War broke out he was the Yugoslavian envoy in Berlin. During the occupation he managed to survive and in forced retirement wrote the three remarkable novels that are usually called his Bosnian trilogy, though the only thing they have in common is the historical and provincial background.

The first is *The Bridge on the Drina,* the splendid story of a famous bridge which a Turkish vizier built at the town of Visegrad in the middle of the 16th century. In the next, *The Chronicle of Travnik,* the story, from the time of the Napoleonic wars, deals with the struggle for power between the Austrian and French consuls in an isolated and backward little Bosnian town. The third volume, *The Spinster,* set in Sarajevo, is a study in avarice as a disease and obsession. Important, apart from these works, is *Town of the Doomed,* an unusually moving story of a Turkish remand prison in Istanbul.

In Andrić a modern psychological insight is combined with a fatalism from the Arabian Nights. He has great tenderness for human beings, but does not shrink from violence and horror. As a writer he is master of a subject matter that is entirely his own, he opens the world chronicle for us at a hitherto unknown page, appealing to us from the depths of a tortured national soul. The prize citation stresses 'the epic strength with which he depicts themes and destinies from his country's history'.

The *1962* prize was awarded to the American writer JOHN STEINBECK [1902-1968]. Born in the little Californian town of Salinas, some twelve miles from the Pacific coast and near the fertile Salinas Valley, which is the scene of many of the events in the lives of the people he has described, Steinbeck already had a number of books to his credit when, in 1935, he first captured the attention of the public with the publication of his narrative, *Tortilla Flat*. It is made up of tales, comic, vigorous and racy, about a band of paisanos – asocial individuals whose outbursts are comparable in a parodic way with those of the knights of *King Arthur's Round Table*.

But for Steinbeck the notion of being an entertainer, offering inoffensive consolation, held few charms. On the contrary, he now began to tackle themes heavy with indictment, notably the grave strikes in the fruit orchards and cotton fields of California. Those were the years of his literary crescendo. To the little masterpiece *Of Mice and Men*, in which we watch the great hands of the half-witted giant Lennie in pure tenderness crushing the life out of everything he touches, succeeded the remarkable collection of short stories entitled *The Long Valley*. From there onwards Steinbeck's path was clear, the path leading up to the great work on which, more than on any other, Steinbeck's name rests. In his epic chronicle, *The Grapes of Wrath*, are described the unemployment and abuses of power which provoked the exodus of oppressed Oklahomans to California. By concentrating on events experienced by one particular family of farmers who have set out on the endless and desperate road of all who seek an asylum and an abiding-place, this tragic episode in the history of American society expresses the very poignancy of human existence.

Among all those successive laureates who represent the narrative art as developed in modern America, from Sinclair Lewis to Ernest Hemingway, John Steinbeck is the one who can most justly claim a place of his own. In him runs a strain of raw humour which to some extent reconciles the reader to his often cruel and primitive themes. Always, his sympathies are with the underdog, with those who suffer and have not known how to adapt; always, he is inclined to contrast the simple joy of living with the brutality and cynicism of those who hunger and thirst after dollars. But in him, too, the American temperament manifests itself in a profound love of nature, of the great open spaces, of the wilds, of mountains and coasts; an inexhaustible spring which Steinbeck finds at the very heart both of the world of man and of the world beyond it.

The Swedish Academy motivated its decision to give him the prize, as follows: 'for his story-telling art, at once realistic and imaginative and characterized by a humour compounded of sympathy and deep social perception'.

The *1963* Nobel Prize for Literature went to a Greek poet, GIORGOS SEFERIS [1900-1971], a native of Smyrna.

The greatness of Seferis' poetic output does not lie in its abundance, but in its singularity of thought and style and in the beauty of its language, which have made it an uncontestible symbol of all that is changeless in the Hellenic sensibility and response to life. Today, after the disappearance of Palamas and Sikelianos, Seferis appears as the very incarnation of a Hellenic poet; a modern poet who has known how to take upon himself the mantle of the classical heritage, a great national figure who has also been acclaimed in such other countries as have been reached by his poetry in translation.

To read Seferis is to remember with peculiar intensity a fact sometimes forgotten: that Greece, geographically, is more than a peninsula. It is at least as much a universe of briny water, sown with myriads of islands, the immemorial realm of Poseidon, the haunt of the navigator, fraught with perils and compounded of storms. This aspect of Greece is ever-present behind Seferis' poetic *œuvre*, and the vision of it which he evokes possesses a grandeur at once rude and tender. This beauty is born of an uncommon refinement of rhythmic and metaphorical expression. One could also say of him that, better than any other, he has succeeded in interpreting the mystery of the very stones of Greece, of the inanimate marble fragments and its silently smiling statues.

But Seferis animates this background, tinged with melancholy resignation, by the joy, of which he is always so eloquant, inspired in him by the mountainous islands of his country and their whitewashed houses where they lie terraced above the azure sea – that perfect harmony of two pure tones which we fancy we discern in the Greek flag.

It remains to add the motivation of the Academy's award of the Prize to Seferis: 'For his remarkable lyric *œuvre*, which so deeply inspires a sense of the culture of the Hellenic world'.

The Prize for *1964* was awarded to the French writer JEAN-PAUL SARTRE [b. 1905]. In a few phrases it is impossible to characterize here the philosophical concepts involved in the word 'existentialism'. Thanks to Sartre they were to dominate a whole period in intellectual circles the world over. Briefly, according to this philosophy, man is himself the arbiter of whether an action is good or evil; and, further, must wholly take upon himself the consequences of this freedom. A doctrine in no way indulgent, in the prevalent atmosphere of determinism after the war, existentialism indubitably represented for that generation a germinal idea and provided both a refuge and an instrument of spiritual defense.

As a writer, Sartre has unceasingly discussed the human problems raised by these ideas. In his imposing series of dramatic work, he incisively presents their proofs. A few titles are particularly worthy of mention: *Les Mouches*, which revives the Orestes motif; *Huis-clos*, which introduces us to the hell of those who torture themselves with their own consciences; two wry comedies, *Les Mains Sales* and *La Putain Respectueuse*; and, the most recent of his plays, *Les Sequestrés d'Altona*, in whose plot the guilt theme is so subtly entwined. All these plays, one might say, treat of problems of loyalty and conscience, liberty and discipline, in conflicts ever more acute and anguished.

In the first volume of his autobiography, *Les Mots*, Sartre describes a childhood which forever made of him an anti-bourgeois rebel. He is characterized by incessant activity; and his literary works remain for us the most precious manifestation of his philosophy of action. Aggressive, consciously seeking controversy, he inscribes himself, on the level of our modern age, in a great French historical tradition: the tradition of those writers who moralize critically upon society. In motivating its choice the Academy invokes 'his works which, teeming with ideas, by virtue of their spirit of liberty and the search for truth to which they bear witness, have exercised an enormous influence upon our age.'

The laureate let it be known that he did not wish to accept the prize, but the fact of his declining this distinction naturally in no way modifies the validity of the award.

The *1965* Nobel Prize for Literature went to a Russian author MIKHAIL SHOLOKHOV [b. 1905]. His childhood was spent in the country of the Don Cossacks; and it is to the indomitable character of that people and their country he owes his feeling for tribal solidarity. A striking instance of the precociousness of that war generation, Sholokhov, while still only twenty-one, embarked on the first episodes of his great epic entitled *Quiet*

Flows the Don. But forty years had to pass before Sholokhov was able to bring his enterprise to fruition. Its accomplishment, from any point of view, is an amazing achievement. The work extends from the First World War to the Revolution and Civil War in Russia, and its principal theme is the tragic revolt of the Cossacks.

Convinced communist though he is, Sholokhov abstains from all political comment. His narrative is full of the breath of life and through its veins runs a blood so rich that it neutralizes the bloody sacrifices demanded by those fields of battle. The Cossack Grigorij, who changes sides between Reds and Whites and is trapped into carrying on the struggle to the bitter end, is at once hero and victim. He is only conquered by historical necessity, which here plays the same role as Nemesis did in antiquity. Behind the procession of human and military personages the enormous panorama of the Ukrainian countryside unfolds, the steppe at every season of the year, redolent of the smell of horses and the windblown grasses of those immense grazing grounds and of the banks of the great river whose sound rolls on forever.

One might say that Sholokhov uses an ancient, realistic and – by comparison with many of our recipes for novel-writing, which have so abounded in recent years – in no way innovatory technique, of a seemingly naïve simplicity. But his subject could doubtless never have been treated in any other fashion, and the epic, vigorous and regular flow which characterizes *Quiet Flows the Don* makes of it a novel doubly evocative of the river that is its theme.

Sholokhov's later writings, for instance *The Virgin Soil Upturned*, in which he tells of the introduction of the kolchoses, bear witness to an unabating vigour and a predilection for sturdy and droll popular types. But of course *Quiet Flows the Don* in itself suffices to justify this distinction which, even if it came to him a trifle late in the day, was nevertheless not too late to add to the list of Nobel Prizewinners one of the most eminent names of our epoch.

Motivating its choice, the Academy invoked 'the vigour and artistic integrity with which this author has expressed a historic phase in the life of the Russian people'.

The *1966* literary prize was awarded to two eminent Jewish writers, each of whom is representative of Israel's message to our time: namely, SAMUEL AGNON [1888-1970] and NELLY SACHS [1891-1970], of whom the former was living in Jerusalem and the latter, having emigrated to Sweden in 1940 and become a Swedish citizen, in Stockholm.

Samuel Agnon's reputation as the greatest name in modern Hebrew literature had to break through a language barrier, which in this case was particularly obstructive. In his youth Agnon had begun by writing in Yiddish, but soon abandoned it for Hebrew, a tongue which, according to those in a position to judge, he handles to perfection, writing with real mastery in a prose style of remarkable expressiveness. His peculiar qualities as a writer were above all embodied in his great cycles of novels from his home-town of Baczaca, once a flourishing centre of Jewish piety, today in ruins. Within the framework of a local chronicle he opens out a marvellous perspective of individual destinies, figures, attitudes to life and meditations. Agnon was a realist, but always with a certain strain of mysticism such as imbues even the greyest and most everyday scenes with a golden lustre of poetic fairy-story, often reminiscent of Chagall's Old Testament motifs. Agnon revealed himself as a deeply original writer, notably gifted with humour and wisdom and a sharp-witted intelligence allied to naïve concreteness of vision.

In the German-speaking part of the world Nelly Sachs has been acclaimed a poetess of impressive genuineness and burning devotion. With gripping insight she has interpreted the world-wide tragedy of the Jewish race, partly in the form of lyrical laments of an anguished beauty, and partly in dramatic legend-plays whose symbolic language combines modern boldness of expression with echoes of Jewish poetry going back to the dawn of her people's history. Her poetry has become the most intensive artistic expression of the Jewish spirit's way of reacting to suffering and thus, under this aspect, can in high degree be said to correspond to the humane ideals which dictated Alfred Nobel's will.

The *1967* prize was awarded to MIGUEL ANGEL ASTURIAS [b. 1899], from Guatemala, an eminent representative of the richly developed modern literature of Latin America. His early years founded in him a great love of his native country's nature and mythic world, and of its wild, primitive and freedom-loving popular tradition – a tradition which was later to dominate his writings, with their remarkable echoes of the past of the Maya peoples. His real début came with his novel *El Senor Presidente*, a grandiose and tragic satire on the Latin-American dictator-type, as he has been and still is. With powerful suggestivity, such as makes of his story an artistic call to action, Asturias evokes the atmosphere of a society poisoned by terror and suspicion. A trilogy, which followed, is constructed of interwoven mythological and political motifs from this tropical country where man is simultaneously obliged to do battle with a beautiful but hostile nature and with intolerable social conditions, oppression and caprice. In a later trilogy Asturias has taken up afresh one of his epic's urgent themes: namely, the struggle against the North American trust empires, and their economic consequences for the contemporary history of the banana republic. Here again we are confronted with tremendously colourful visions springing from Asturias' intense involvement in his own nation's predicament.

Asturias has completely freed himself from old-fashioned conventional story-telling technique. Obviously, he has been influenced by the breakthrough of modernism in Europe and his explosive style often reveals points of similarity with French surrealism. Yet his raw materials, it should be noted, are invariably drawn from his own experience. In his impressive cycle of poems *Claravigilia Primaveral* he treats of the genesis of the arts and of the creative act in a guise which seems to be borrowed directly from the magnificent plumage of the quetzal bird.

The *1968* Literature Prize was awarded to YASUNARI KAWABATA [1899-1972] for his 'narrative art which expresses with refined feeling the special qualities of the Japanese soul'. Although influenced by modern western realism, Kawabata is an author who has remained rooted in classical Japanese poetry and thus represents a definite tendency to care for and preserve a genuinely national stylistic tradition. More especially, he has been praised for his fine insights into feminine psychology, of which he has shown his mastery in two novels, *The Kingdom of the Snows* and *A Thousand Cranes*. Here he shows a virtuosic ability to throw light on the erotic episode, and an exquisitely sharp sense of detail, a subtle network of little secret values, such as often puts European narrative technique in the shade. But in a time of transition between the old order and the new he is also an acute social observer, of somewhat pessimistic sympathies. Motifs of this sort are developed in his later novel *Kyoto*, the action of which takes place in the capital of the old Japanese kingdom, whose poetry Kawabata has interpreted in a tender courtly manner and which is also expressive of an imploring appeal on the part of the author. In the violent post-war wave of Americanization his novel is a gentle reminder of how necessary it is to try to rescue something of the beauty and character of old Japan and to incorporate it in the new.

Crucial to the Academy's assessment was Kawabata's voicing of a moral-aesthetic awareness, imbued with an artistic quality all its own; thus, in his own way, throwing a bridge between East and West.

The *1969* Prize was awarded to SAMUEL BECKETT [b. 1906], an Irishman by birth who grew up in Dublin but whom the years have transformed into an acclimatized Parisian, and who has written both in English and in French. His first piece of writing was an essay entitled *Dante-Bruno-Vico-Joyce*, an essay which in an early stage of his authorship indicates in all essentials the main directions and influences later discernible in Beckett's own writings. One might call Beckett's philosophy purgatorial, a philosophy acquired as a result of a religious struggle, and constituting the sombre backdrop to all he has written. From beginning to end these writings have tended toward a disillusioned assessment of the basic human condition. In his narratives, formulated in abrupt and expressive prose (the trilogy *Molloy*, *Malone*, *The Unnamable*) and above all in his scenically suggestive dramas – among which *Waiting for Godot*, more especially, has won international acclaim – Beckett stands out as the creator of a contemporary literary genre all his own. Its message is a radical pessimism, and it constitutes a drastic deflation of many accepted values. But it can also be seen as searing invocation of man's ability to bear his earthly fate.

The motivation of the award reads: 'For his writing, which – in new forms for the novel and drama – in the destitution of modern man acquires its elevation'.

The *1970* Prize was awarded to the Russian author ALEXANDER SOLZHENITSYN [b. 1918] 'for the ethical force with which he has pursued the indispensable traditions of Russian literature.' The award was primarily motivated by the three remarkable narratives in which he has depicted destinies and circumstances which, as can be seen from his autobiography, he has himself experienced. During the Stalin epoch, a time when he had distinguished himself as an officer at the front, he was suddenly accused of political crimes and condemned to many years imprisonment, subsequently extended by his being sent to a special concentration camp. It is these bitter experiences which he has depicted, with great artistic force and truth, partly in his short novel *A Day in the Life of Ivan Denisovitch* (1962), partly in his larger scale works *The Cancer Clinic* and *The First Circle*, neither of which latter works, however, have so far been allowed to be published in the Soviet Union. If these stories as a whole are intensely gripping it is because they unite an unsentimental realism with psychological acumen, enabling him to bring to life an enormous gallery of human types and by his so-called polyphonic novel technique create an unforgettable overall picture of life in the Soviet Union during the historical period in question. His grasp on these things is that of a disappointed but spiritually indomitable idealist. In this way, this author has boldly wished to make a radical attack on the entire power-system, with all its paralysing effects, which, by terror and bureaucracy, has in his opinion betrayed the revolution.

It was perhaps inevitable that the award to Solzhenitsyn, obviously intended as act of pure literary justice, should have become controversial, and have been adjudged politically. One can only hope that his authorship will one day rank in his own fatherland, too, as one of the most important achievements of contemporary Russian literature.

At this point all the winners of the Nobel Prize in Literature have been surveyed and it is unavoidable that such a chronological review should look like a descriptive catalogue; but, at any rate, biographical data and descriptions of physical appearances have been left out as superfluous, partly because, as a rule, only exceedingly well-known persons have been mentioned, and partly because such information is readily available in the year-book *Les Prix Nobel*. For obvious reasons, no reports of the preliminary discussions have been included with regard to the more recent winners, who in most instances are still alive.

Only the geographical distribution remains to be mentioned. Of the literary prizes, France has, so far, won 11 – Great Britain, Germany, and the United States, 6 each – Italy, Russia, and Sweden, 4 each – Denmark, Norway, and Spain, 3 each – Ireland, Poland, and Switzerland, 2 each – while Belgium, Chile, Finland, Greece, Guatemala, Iceland, India, Israel, Japan, and Yugoslavia have received 1 each. These figures indicate an effort to do justice to the different linguistic areas, but obviously they cannot serve as a representative picture of the literary standards in each country. Conspicuous gaps still remain.

In retrospect, the question that first of all arises is to what extent the list of prize-winners reflects the world's literary development during the past seventy years. When this question is asked it must be recognized that the situation as regards literature is quite different from that in the scientific fields in which a clear and continuous line of advance can be traced. In scientific research and discovery there is a more or less logical development, to which there is nothing to correspond in the literary sphere. An author's personal work does not necessarily have any connection with contemporary literary styles or trends; often it constitutes a protest against them.

The most extreme forms of modernism, whatever their date, whether yesterday's or to-day's, seldom rise to the competitive level here required. And it is easily possible to harmonize the purpose of the Nobel Prizes with rewards for work which may not reach the highest contemporary level of literary development, but which instinctively and unaffectedly expresses the idealism that is such an important element in the very nature of poetry.

In addition to awards for such literary creations stressing the fundamental human values, the list of winners contains at least some leading figures of their day, who have introduced new literary styles and new ideas, such as Rudyard Kipling, Maurice Maeterlinck, Gerhart Hauptmann, Knut Hamsun, Anatole France, William Butler Yeats, George Bernard Shaw, Henri Bergson, Thomas Mann, Luigi Pirandello, Eugene O'Neill, Hermann Hesse, André Gide, T. S. Eliot – to name only the most prominent.

At the same time it could be objected that a number of equally significant names are conspicuous by their absence; a few have already been mentioned, and it is not to be denied that the history of the Nobel Prizes in Literature is also a history of inexpiable sins of omission. But even so, it may perhaps be said that the mistakes have been comparatively few, that no truly unworthy candidate has been crowned, and that, if allowances are made for legitimate criticism, the results have reasonably matched the requirements and difficulties of an almost paradoxical assignment.

Just as there are older prize-winners in whom a younger generation can take only slight interest, so there are recent winners who, to the older people, would have seemed unthinkable. The coming of new generations, with inevitable changes in literary tastes, must obviously be reflected in the history of the Nobel Prizes, and all the more clearly as time goes on. But under any circumstances it would be presumptuous to expect the Nobel Prizes to exercise any kind of guiding influence on the direction of literary progress. This has so far followed its own course, independently of the prizes, and will continue to do so in the future.

Another question which cannot be ignored in this connection concerns the purely practical benefit of the prizes. Truth demands the admission that only in a few instances could economic help have been really needed. To a majority of the winners the money has no doubt meant less than the honour. To-day an internationally known writer enjoys such financial opportunities that even this monetary award, which is still the highest given for literary work, has become smaller than the fees paid, for example, in the United States for the film rights alone. It would be a justified reaction to this commercialization, if in the future the Nobel Prize awards were to favour writers who do not enjoy the benefit of such a market and who, for the sake of it, do not compromise their literary standards. Only in that way would it be possible to come a little closer to Nobel's own wishes and to aid dreamers who are handicapped in their careers as writers by their struggle for daily bread. In the long run it would be better if the prizes were thereby to lose some of their present character of decorations, even though public opinion, both at home and abroad, seems to demand to a surprising degree that in the prize awards the honour should be principally stressed – for the general public naturally does not like to be surprised by names it has never heard of before.

Literature should be an experimental field for the spirit, giving ample room for all trends and movements. Once in a while such freedom is questioned, and particularly in our own day there is no lack of attempts to prescribe both what is suitable to write about and what is proper for the citizen to read. Literature too can be conscripted in the service of barbarism by being made to conform to official decrees which stifle all natural manifestations of life.

When seen in perspective, seventy years cover but a brief period in the development of the world, even though to those of us who have lived through the two World Wars with all their human and cultural loss of blood, it seems a memorable and eventful epoch, and in many respects a grim negation of Alfred Nobel's hopes. The role of literature in this short period of history can just as easily be overestimated as minimized.

Its power and impotence seem to alternate before our eyes, but even in periods of darkness and despair a spark of heroism illumines the gloomy horizon whenever a really fine and inspired work appears. Though in its origin Nobel's prize foundation was the creation of a bourgeois capitalist age, it can, despite every uncertainty as to the future, still continue to promote the cause of international tolerance and good will, and to the achievement of this ideal, literature too can make a real contribution.

THE PRIZE IN PHYSIOLOGY OR MEDICINE

BY GÖRAN LILJESTRAND

REVISED BY CARL GUSTAF BERNHARD

In his remarkable will of November 27, 1895, Alfred Nobel directed that the interest on his fortune should be 'annually distributed in the form of prizes to those who, during the preceding year, shall have conferred the greatest benefit on mankind'. He also specified that one of the five shares of the interest should be given 'to the person who shall have made the most important discovery within the domain of physiology or medicine', and the task of selecting the winners of this award he entrusted to the Caroline Institute in Stockholm.

The Caroline Medico-Chirurgical Institute [Karolinska Medico-kirurgiska Institutet] was founded in 1810, when it absorbed some older institutions for medical teaching. Not until 1906, however, when it was authorized to confer M.D. degrees, did it finally achieve fully equal status with the university schools of medicine. But long before that it had already become Sweden's largest medical school. The idea of rewarding discoveries in physiology and medicine was inspired by Nobel's own deep interest in the medical sciences. Alfred Nobel was born in Stockholm and had lived there for many years, so it was quite natural he should select the Caroline Institute to award the prizes in physiology and medicine. He had also personal contacts among representatives of the Institute.

In 1890 Dr. S. von Hofsten, assistant professor at the Caroline Institute, had a conversation with Alfred Nobel in Paris, which had important consequences. In a letter to his colleague, Dr. J. E. Johansson, at that time lecturer in physiology and later professor of the same subject at the Caroline Institute, Hofsten wrote that he had visited Nobel in Paris and had had with him 'a decidedly refreshing conversation that lasted one and one-half hours. I cannot recall ever having met such an intelligent and interesting person. On this occasion we also discussed some physiological and biological ideas which appealed strongly to his inventive and inquiring mind. In that connection he expressed his sincere wish to become acquainted with some young, well-trained Swedish physiologist with whom he could work, or rather, who might be able to carry out some of the many original and ingenious ideas on the subject of physiology that were germinating in his highly inventive brain. I then referred him to you and he asked me urgently to write you, and if you approve of his proposal in principle, to advise you to get into direct communication with him at once'.

Johansson did communicate with Nobel at once. The meeting took place early in October, 1890. Johansson stayed in Paris for five months and in his report on his relations with Nobel he wrote: 'In the talks I had with Nobel during this period I found him extremely interested in medical research by experiments. He himself developed ideas and plans for an experimental study of the progress of various physical ailments in the body and above all how to find, through experiments, methods of curing such diseases. At his request I carried out, in his laboratory at Sévran, a certain number of tests connected with blood transfusion, in which he took a special interest. On several occasions he declared himself ready to organize an institute of his own for medical research by experiments. Many times he hinted that he thought medical doctrines might be a hindrance and that anyone uninfluenced by them would find it easier "to approach the problems from a fresh angle"'.

In regard to the proposed institute, Johansson was not willing to give up his position at the Caroline Institute in Stockholm and went back to Sweden. On several occasions, he heard from Nobel, however, and also met him in person. At such times Nobel would express his regret that his many preoccupations with business had prevented him from giving more of his time to the solution of the medical problems that interested him so much.

Additional evidence of Nobel's interest in experimental medical research was furnished by the Russian physiologist I. P. Pavlov, winner of the Nobel Prize in Physiology or Medicine in 1904. In his Nobel lecture that year he related that about ten years earlier he and his colleague, M. Nencki, professor of medical chemistry at St. Petersburg, had received from Nobel a considerable sum for the benefit of their respective laboratories. In his letter accompanying the gift, the donor had described his deep interest in physiological experiments and had also discussed the problem of ageing and dying.

From all this it is clear that the donation of one of the five shares of his estate as prizes in physiology or medicine was by no means the result of a sudden whim, but rather the climax of a long-continued, personal interest in these subjects. The fact that medical science was at that time on the verge of a vast and fruitful expansion and had already given some promise of the development to be expected probably strengthened Nobel's belief in its future and stimulated his desire to help.

The Nobel awards in physiology or medicine are to be made to those 'who shall have conferred the greatest benefit on mankind'. Different interpretations of this phrase are possible; but our knowledge of the testator's general attitude and his cultural interests makes it reasonable to assume that what he had in view was achievements likely to further both the intellectual and the physical improvement of mankind: in other words, not only discoveries of a purely scientific character, but also those having an immediate, practical value. The phrase 'physiology or medicine' may well be interpreted in the same sense, especially in view of the fact that his own experiments in the field dealt both with the theoretical phase, i.e. the nature of pathological processes in the body, and the practical one, or the methods of healing.

The significance of the term 'the domain of physiology or medicine' was thoroughly discussed at the deliberations about Alfred Nobel's will which were attended both by representatives of the various institutions designated in the will as prize-juries and of the Nobel family, and by the executors. At first, the delegates of the Caroline Institute proposed that the following definition be inserted in the statutes: 'By "the domain of physiology or medicine" the donor is considered to have meant all the theoretical as well as the practical aspects of the physiological and medical sciences'. During a discussion at a later date, a memorandum made by Professor Johansson on January 29, 1899, was submitted to the delegates. It had been prepared at the request of the secretary to the delegates after they had been informed of Johansson's personal knowledge, arising from his close contacts with Nobel. In this memorandum Johansson wrote that in his opinion the domain of medicine meant experimental medicine as a whole, an interpretation which seemed, moreover, to be in harmony with what had become known through Johansson about the donor's personal interests.

Since physiology was also explicitly mentioned, it was obvious that Nobel had had that in mind, too. On the other hand, it was equally obvious from his own phrasing of the will that he had not intended to give any preference to that science over what he termed medicine. Probably Nobel regarded physiology as experimental medicine *par préférence*, an explanation that would furnish a reasonable interpretation of the combination used. Finally, however, it was decided not to insert in the statutes any definition of 'physiology or medicine', nor of 'physics' or 'chemistry', as had been intended at one stage of the discussions, but to leave the prize-awarding institutions free to make their own interpretations.

The discussion illustrates some of the most important points of view as to the meaning of the will. In practice, all branches of the medical sciences have been taken into consideration, and prizes have been awarded in several of them, as will be shown in a subsequent chapter. On the other hand, such aspects of physiology as fall entirely outside the medical sphere have not been taken into account. The interpretation placed by the Caroline Institute on the term 'the domain of physiology or medicine' has however, always been a liberal one, as is evidenced by many of the prizes, the decisive question being whether a work falls within the natural competence of the Institute or not. As a matter of fact, the prize has several times been given to scientists who were not medical men nor members of medical faculties, but whose work was considered to be of outstanding importance to the medical sciences. Conversely, on several occasions the Prize in Chemistry has been awarded by the Royal Academy of Sciences to men who have done their work in the medical field with results that have been of great value to medicine as well as to biochemistry. In several other instances, the work rewarded by prizes in chemistry has been of considerable value to medicine, illustrating how the borderlands of different sciences overlap.

It can safely be assumed that it was not by chance that in his will Nobel should have directed that the Prize in Physiology or Medicine be given for a *discovery* [in the earlier will, 'discovery or invention']. Being himself an inventor who during his lifetime had taken out more than 350 patents, he understood the special value of discovery and how widespread its influence can be. A scientific discovery has usually been interpreted as a contribution leading to new methods of procedure whereby ignorance is dispelled, misinterpretations corrected, wholly new fields opened up to research or new techniques developed – the kind of work which, in his earlier will, Nobel called pioneering.

Quite often, however, the development of a scientific process may occur only gradually and slowly, being built up out of a number of contributions from the same or different sources. In such cases, it is often difficult to point to a definite discovery or discoverer. And yet, taken together, a series of contributions, though each may only be of apparently moderate scope and importance, may lead to great progress and have a truly revolutionary effect. In such cases a Nobel Prize may be justified, even though it is often difficult to assign the credit to a single person. On the other hand, several contributions by the same person but in different fields, no one of which under the terms of the will is in itself important enough to qualify for a

Nobel Prize, have not been regarded as justifying consideration. The prizes, that is to say, are given for specific scientific achievements, rather than for general merit in medical research.

During the preliminary discussions of Nobel's intentions it was realized, of course, that if the high standard obviously required was to be maintained, the stipulation that the prize should be awarded for work done during the year immediately preceding could not be observed in practice. Only in rare instances would it be possible, the delegates agreed, to interpret the will strictly. In order to get round this difficulty, the following rule was inserted in the statutes: 'The provision in the will that the annual award of prizes shall refer to works "during the preceding year" shall be understood in the sense that the awards shall be made for the most recent achievements in the fields of culture referred to in the will, and for older works only if their significance has not become apparent until recently'.

In this connection it may be pointed out that the will does not require that the work to be rewarded shall itself necessarily have been done during the preceding year; merely that the person who is to receive the prize shall have contributed most to the welfare of mankind during that period. This may well have been done through work carried out or published several years earlier. The discovery of penicillin, for instance, took place in 1928; but nobody would have dreamt of proposing it for a Nobel Prize before its value as a 'benefit to mankind' had been established by its practical use in therapy, more than ten years later.

Similar situations are often likely to arise when new facts sometimes quite unexpectedly, enormously enhance the value of some earlier observation or discovery. On the other hand, accumulating experience may provide more statistically convincing evidence as to the value of some discovery made, perhaps, years earlier; but in such cases it is usually difficult to claim that the importance of the discovery has only recently been demonstrated. Certain differences of opinion among the members of the prize-jury are therefore unavoidable. It should always be borne in mind, however, that Nobel clearly intended to reward the most recent advances. Only rarely can a scientist's entire life-work, even if as a whole it covers some special aspect of the same problem, fulfill the requirements of the will; and still less can it do so if his or her work has been done on a number of unconnected problems in different fields.

This point has often given rise to misunderstandings, and doubtless such a life-work may sometimes be of greater value to mankind than some of the discoveries which have been rewarded with a prize. But this is a natural and inevitable consequence of the definite restrictions on the awards imposed by the testator himself. That the Nobel Prizes, in spite of these restrictions, have come to be regarded as the highest scientific distinctions in the whole world, can therefore only mean that certain well-defined discoveries have in fact been of paramount importance to the general progress of science.

On several occasions the Caroline Institute has availed itself of the permission to split the prize. Each time this has been done, the two halves have been awarded for relatively independent discoveries in closely related fields. The prize, or half of the prize, may also be awarded jointly to two or more persons who have done their work together, or in close conjunction. Usually, in cases where a prize has been divided, there has been a very close connection between its two halves. In no case has an award been given to more than three persons. Each winner has, therefore, always received a fairly substantial sum of money.

In view of Nobel's own attitude, the rule in the statutes to the effect that 'work produced by a person since deceased cannot be rewarded with a prize', seems quite clear and justified. The paragraph in question then continues as follows: 'If, however, his death occurred subsequently to a proposal having been submitted, in the stipulated manner, that the work should be rewarded, then a prize may be awarded'.

Several times it has happened that the Nobel Committee of the Caroline Institute has received suggestions from duly qualified persons that a prize be given to the survivors of men who had done outstanding work, but who had never received a Nobel Prize. In view of the regulations and the interpretation already applied, it is obviously impossible to consider such proposals.

The international character of the Nobel Prizes was clearly defined in the will and it has always been kept up, even in difficult political situations. The international scope of the prizes has been a source of much satisfaction to the members of the prize-awarding institutions. It has also enhanced the prestige and significance of the awards.

The axiom that knowledge of the man behind an institution makes it easier to understand his work and to carry out his intentions, applies with special cogency to Alfred Nobel. To the members of the prize-juries who have been entrusted with the task of putting his basic ideas into practice, the light shed by an understanding of his personality on the often obscure terms both of the will and the statutes has often provided extremely helpful guidance. It is regrettable that perhaps a majority of those who have been invited to nominate candidates for the honour have been unacquainted with the facts cited above, and have, therefore, often made inappropriate use of their opportunities. This lack of information has given rise to numerous misunderstandings and a certain amount of criticism.

HOW THE MEDICAL PRIZE-WINNERS ARE SELECTED

The work of prize-distribution is begun by a more or less detailed examination of the works duly proposed for the awards. This is done by the respective Nobel Committees, one for each of the adjudicating organizations, and whenever necessary they are aided by properly qualified experts. Each of the three Swedish Committees finally presents to its parent body a full report, containing its recommendations as to the award for the year and the reasons for its choice. After a discussion, if any is needed, the members of the prize-awarding institutions make the final decisions. These are not subject to confirmation by any higher authority and there is no appeal.

From the first it was clear to the adjudicators that choosing the most worthy recipient of such a prize would be a matter of great difficulty and heavy responsibility. Self-nominations had to be ruled out at once; in the majority of cases the work entailed in examining contributions so proposed would have been wasted. In the statutes the following sentence was, therefore, inserted: 'Personal applications for the award of a prize shall not be considered'.

It was felt to be desirable to obtain properly documented proposals from qualified scientists representing all branches of medicine in different countries, especially as this would emphasize the international character of the awards. This has been achieved in the following way.

In order to be taken into consideration, a candidate for a prize must be proposed in writing by some duly qualified person. Those qualified to make such proposals receive confidential invitations, sent out each year sometime in September, from the Nobel Committee of the Medical Faculty of the Caroline Institute. The recipients are asked to submit their proposals before February 1 the following year, and to include a description of the recommended discovery and a detailed argument in favour of an award, supported by publications and other relevant documents.

A permanent right to nominate candidates for the Nobel Prize in Physiology or Medicine is enjoyed by members of the professorial staff of the Medical Faculty of the Caroline Institute, by members of the medical section of the Royal Swedish Academy of Sciences, by previous winners of the same prize, and by members of the medical faculties at the universities in Denmark, Finland, Iceland, and Norway. In addition, the statutory regulations for the medical award direct that invitations to submit nominations shall be sent each year to the members of at least six other medical faculties, to be selected by the Caroline Institute in such a way that each year a number of different countries shall be represented. The Caroline Institute also has the right to invite individual scientists, of its own choice, to make nominations.

In view of the great value placed on the collaboration of medical colleagues throughout the world, the number of invitations regularly sent out is large. In fact, it has been found advantageous to include, over a certain number of years, representatives of virtually every medical faculty in existence. Consequently, in some large countries which have many universities, two or three different faculties have been chosen annually; while, in several of the smaller countries, only a single faculty can be selected each year; and to certain countries, possessing only one or two universities, it has only been possible to send a single invitation over a longer period of time. At present the members of about 35 academic bodies [faculties, research institutes, and academies] outside Scandinavia, representing 25 different countries, are included in each mailing list. Often, heads of departments in medical research institutes not connected with any university are also invited, so that in 1970, 1361 persons were offered an opportunity.

Several times since 1939, special difficulties have arisen. For a long time it was impossible to obtain the names of our Russian colleagues. This was the more regrettable, inasmuch as the faculty was thereby denied satisfactory information about work done in U.S.S.R. This is no longer the case. Neither were any invitations sent to Germany between 1938 and 1947, except to scientists who already enjoyed a permanent right to make nominations. This omission was due to Hitler's edict forbidding Germans to accept Nobel Prizes, and indeed it might well have been dangerous for them even to submit names of candidates. For some years after the war the lists of German faculty members were unobtainable, but this too has since been remedied.

All invitations are personal and confidential; and so are the nominations, which are always presumed to have been submitted without the aid, or even the knowledge, of the candidates themselves. Neither are the names of those invited to make suggestions usually revealed; obviously, it is desirable to protect them from any undue pressure by ambitious candidates. This preservation of the sponsors' anonymity seems to harmonize with the confidential nature of the invitations. Since the right to nominate candidates is strictly defined by the special statutes governing the medical prize awards, proposals from other than duly qualified sources cannot be entertained. This applies even to nominations by well-known medical societies, international congresses and to suggestions put forward through diplomatic channels, such as have sometimes been attempted, but always without success. It has even happened that a medical faculty, whose members have received the usual personal invitations to submit nominations, has sent a joint recommendation from the faculty as a whole. Naturally, such proposals have to be rejected as being contrary to the rules.

All nominations received before February 1 by the Nobel Committee of the Caroline Institute in Stockholm are examined, but only those conforming to the statutory regulations receive any further consideration. The Secretary of the Committee then prepares a memorandum containing the names and their respective sponsors, as well as brief summaries of the facts cited in the nominations.

In March a memorandum is sent to the Medical Faculty. When necessary by reason of the number and character of the nominations, the Nobel Committee, which formerly had only three, or, from 1961, five permanent members, can request a temporary reinforcement of one or more additional members, specialists in one or the other of the subjects involved. Such temporary members, usually professors at the Caroline Institute, are appointed by the faculty and their commissions generally expire at the end of September, by which time the Committee's work on the award for that year has normally been completed. At present, ten temporary members are regularly appointed.

The critical examination of the proposals is begun as soon as possible. This examination is made in two stages, the first being more or less preliminary. Many of the candidates have been proposed before; in some instances their work, though worthy of a prize, has for some reason or other not been rewarded; in which case the Committee can decide to consider them anew and submit them to another 'special investigation'. In other cases, the work may have been investigated before, but is not deemed of sufficient importance to justify a new special investigation.

In April, having received the experts' written opinions, the Committee makes its final decision as to which works shall be subjected to special investigations. In May the decision is submitted to the faculty, which has the right to add other names from the list of properly nominated candidates.

A kind of sifting has thus taken place; works held to correspond most closely to the stipulations in the will have been selected for a second, more detailed, examination. In Fig. 1 the number of candidates whose candidatures have survived as far as this test – the only ones that can be considered in the final judging – can be seen. Naturally, the number of special investigations [Curve C] varies from year to year, according to the total number of nominations received [curve A] and other circumstances.

The final investigations are intrusted to experts. These, in many cases, are not members of the Committee. Though they may be members of the faculty, it is by no means rare for the investigations to be made by outsiders. During the summer the detailed reports of these experts are prepared. They contain a critical study of the work in question, due emphasis being laid on the priority of the discovery and the fundamental question whether it is of sufficient importance to merit a Nobel Prize. An expert is required to give valid reasons for his opinion and to call attention to whatever special aspect of the discovery he regards as decisive.

By September 1 all the experts' reports must have been filed with the Committee, after which its members have an opportunity to compare and discuss them, in order to be in a position to make their final recommendations to the faculty before the end of the month. If, as is often the case, the Committee is unanimous, hardly any opposition is likely to be encountered within the faculty. If it is divided, the ultimate outcome is less certain. Before reaching its final decision, however, the faculty always has an opportunity to discuss the Committee's recommendations.

From this survey of the procedure it will be seen that the award of a Nobel Prize in Physiology or Medicine is the result of detailed careful investigations, examinations and discussions, extending over a period of at least eight months each year. The Caroline Institute has always had a deep feeling of responsibility toward the testator, and it has tried to carry out his instructions in strict accordance with the terms of his will, believing this to be the best way of maintaining the high level and prestige of the prizes. The difficulties inherent in the work are obvious; certainly no one could have expected them to be completely overcome, or that no mistakes would ever be made.

Winners of the Nobel Prize in Physiology or Medicine are chosen in October. At first the decisions were not made public until December 10, the anniversary of the donor's death, when the four prizes awarded in Sweden are personally presented to the winners at a solemn festival in Stockholm. Since 1910, however, the public announcement of the winner and the official description of his achievement have been sent out immediately after the decisive vote is taken.

For obvious reasons, all deliberations about the prize awards are confidential, and, under the statutes, no protests may be lodged against the decisions of the adjudicating bodies. As a rule, neither the members of the Nobel Committee nor the professors at the Caroline Institute are willing to enter into discussions about the prizes, either with the candidates or their sponsors, as this would only lead to endless complications. Such discussions could easily cause distress to those fortunate enough to have received Nobel Prizes, as well as spread ill will in wider circles. Those who have charge of the practical details of the prize distributions are, of course, fully aware of the difficulties inherent in the task and of the inevitability of errors. The attitude just described is not due, therefore, to any feeling of infallibility or superiority. Rather, it is based on the belief that public discussion of such personal matters as a candidate's qualifications would not only be to the detriment of all parties concerned, but also conflict with one of the main purposes of the Nobel donation: namely, the promotion of greater international understanding and good will.

A STATISTICAL SURVEY OF THE NOBEL PRIZES IN PHYSIOLOGY OR MEDICINE

The number of nominations received during the past seventy years from duly authorized sources is shown in Fig. 1. In this diagram are included not only the nominations received before February 1 each year, but also those that have arrived too late for consideration. The latter have been included as an index of the degree of interest shown by the medical scientists invited to make nominations and also of the general interest taken in medical research in their respective countries.

Figure 1 shows that, from the very beginning, considerable interest was taken in the Nobel Prizes in Physiology or Medicine. The number of pro-

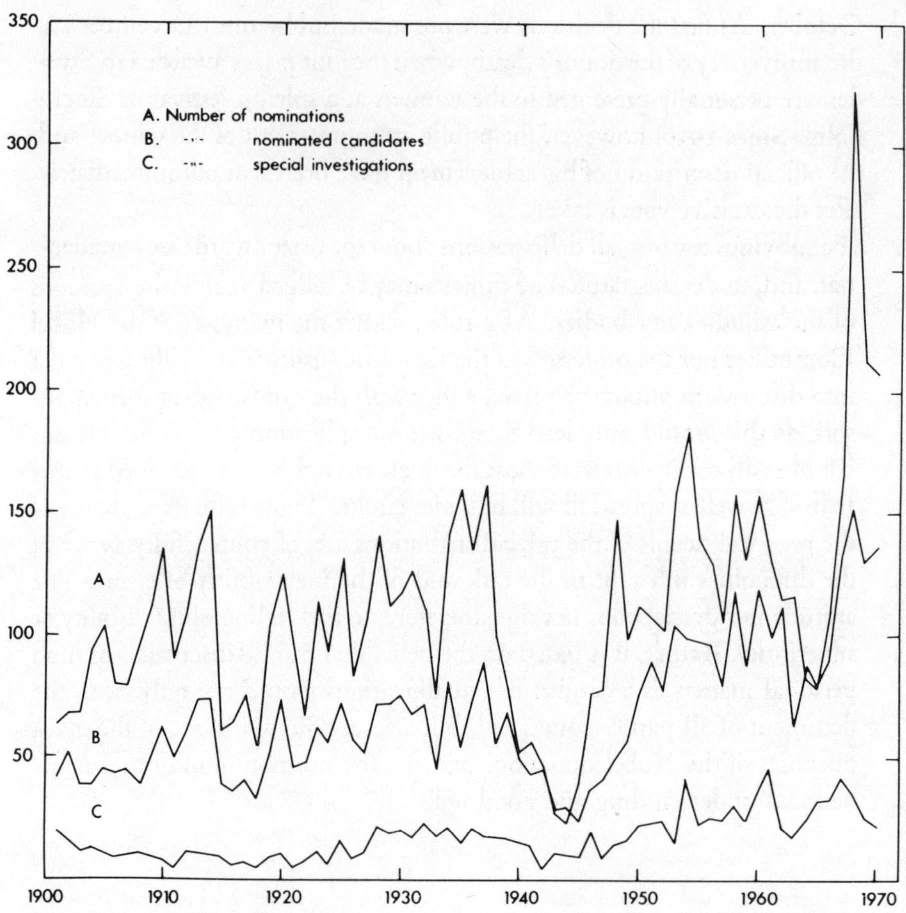

posals was large. Until about 1914, with certain fluctuations, the numbers, both of nominations received and of candidates proposed [Curve B], went on growing. A maximum was reached in 1914, when 151 proposals, mentioning 74 candidates, were received from fifteen different countries. After the First World War had broken out in the autumn of that year there was, naturally, a considerable drop. During the next years [1916–18] the number of candidates remained about the same as in 1915, but no medical prizes were awarded for the years 1915–18. That relatively few new names were suggested during these years is hardly surprising. In 1919, however, there was a decided increase, the number of proposals being about twice as large as in 1918, and the number of candidates about 50 per cent higher.

Many new candidates were also nominated. One reason for this was that some of the many important discoveries in the field of physiology or medicine made during the war years had not become known until the war was over.

After the war, the number of names suggested grew at a fairly regular rate from year to year, the maximum being reached in 1937 with 161 proposals, mentioning 89 candidates. In 1938, however, partly because no nominations were then permitted in Germany, another shrinkage began. The number of names proposed for the first time then reached 29. During the Second World War there was a further falling off. The new names during that period came chiefly from the United States, or from such European countries as were not directly involved in the war. An all-time low was reached in 1944, with only 23 proposals, and in 1945 only 24 names were suggested. These are the lowest figures on record.

If nominations were even fewer during the Second World War than during the first, this was undoubtedly due to the greater intensity of the struggle, to decreased interest in cultural achievements, to the greater isolation of the various countries and to other political circumstances. After 1946, the number both of proposals and of candidates suggested again began to rise. So did the number of new candidates.

The most striking features of the 1926–50 period were a drop in the number of nominations received from Germany and an increase in those from the United States. In 1937, Hitler forbade Germans to accept any further Nobel Prizes, and thereafter only a few names were proposed from that quarter or from Austria. This was no doubt due partly to the discontinuance of invitations to Germans – other than to those persons permanently enjoying that right – to submit nominations; but it is also not improbable that the reduced numbers of candidates reflected a reduction in scientific activity during the Hitler régime.

Many of the most eminent German scientists had, in fact, emigrated elsewhere, and those who remained behind were largely deprived of the stimulating atmosphere of freedom, so crucial to the best work. This supposition is further supported by the fact that even before Hitler had issued his decree, during the years 1935 and 1936, the numbers of new candidates from Germany were, respectively, 1 and 0.

The enormous increase in the number of candidates from the United States, on the other hand, is but one more indication among many that, ever since the turn of the century, medical research and discovery have en-

TABLE I
NATIONALITIES OF LAUREATES

	Number of Laureates			
	1901–25	1926–50	1951–70	Total
Argentine	—	1	—	1
Austria	1	3	—	4
Belgium	1	1	—	2
British Commonwealth of Nations				
Australia	—	—	2	2
Canada	2	—	—	2
Great Britain	2	7	7	16
Denmark	2	2	—	4
France	2	1	3	6
Germany	5	3	2	10
Hungary	—	1	1	2
Italy	1	—	1	2
The Netherlands	1	1	—	2
Portugal	—	1	—	1
Russia	2	—	—	2
Spain	1	—	—	1
Sweden	1	—	3	4
Switzerland	1	3	—	4
U.S.A.	1	12	26	39

joyed great facilities and been ever more vigorously promoted in the great republic.

During the 1951–1970 period the number of new candidates from the United States has continually risen, and the renewed scientific activity in Germany, too, is reflected in the great number of new names proposed. Great Britain and Ireland, as well as France and Italy, show relative increases. From Sweden the number is much higher than before; probably a result of much improved research facilities.

The total number of laureates in physiology or medicine for the years 1901–1970 was 104. Table I shows their distribution by countries. The United States is far in the lead; whereas, in the first period [1901–1925], there was only one American prize-winner, during the next period [1926–1950] the number rapidly rose to 12, and, during the next twenty years [1951–1970] to no fewer than 26. This confirms what has already been said about the swift growth of medical research in the United States during recent decades: in part, however, the increase is also due to ever commoner teamwork, as shown by the number of joint or divided awards to two or three scientists. This also holds true for the British Commonwealth of Nations, with a total of 20 laureates. The respective number of German laureates during the three periods were 5, 3, and 2. The low figure for Russia is, of course, due to the fact, already mentioned, that contacts have been difficult to arrange. Among the smaller nations, Austria, Denmark and Switzerland have been able to boast of 4 apiece: Belgium, the Netherlands and Sweden 2 and 4, respectively – a sign of the high standard maintained in those countries.

THE NOBEL PRIZES IN WARTIME

Crucial to a fair distribution of the Nobel Prizes is the maintenance of unbroken international contacts. Such contacts of course, are, best maintained by reading scientific monographs and periodicals, especially as the statutes prescribe that 'to be eligible for consideration for the award of a prize, a written work must have appeared in print'. Another effective source of contacts has been the invitations to properly qualified scientists, residing in all parts of the world, to nominate the best candidates available, giving specific reasons. All international contacts, however, are greatly affected by political disturbances, which must necessarily cast their shadow on the prize awards. Two World Wars, for instance, have made such contacts difficult to keep up.

At the outbreak of the First World War there was a sharp drop both in nominations and in the number of candidates proposed. Even so, a suitable laureate could perhaps have been selected without much difficulty each year. But in view of the extreme confusion prevailing throughout

Europe when the awards were to be made in the autumn of 1914, a suspension seemed to be in order. After the various prize-awarding institutions had submitted a joint petition to the Swedish Government, it was decreed that the prizes be postponed until 1915.

In view of the international situation, no awards were made in physiology or medicine for the years 1915–18. Under a provision in the statutes, the money was paid into the special fund of the prize-jury. The interruption of the awards inevitably led to an accumulation of very prominant candidates; and as these men had to be taken into account during the years immediately after the war, it became difficult to observe the rule that only recent discoveries should be considered.

The selection of the prize-winner for 1919 was consequently postponed until 1920. By that time a majority of the faculty had come to the conclusion that the best way to carry out Nobel's wishes, as expressed in his will, would be to award the prize annually, however difficult the political circumstances. In 1920, therefore, both the available prizes were presented, after which the awards have been made as regularly as possible.

That the new war clouds gathering on the European horizon at the end of the 1930's should again have interfered with the distribution of the Nobel Prizes was hardly surprising. Almost daily the international situation was becoming more complicated. In September and October, 1938 – shortly after the Munich crisis – the Nobel Committee and the professional staff of the Caroline Institute were preparing to make their customary selection. For reasons which will be explained later, however, it was decided to postpone the final choice until the following year, by which time there was a slight chance that the situation might have improved.

In 1939, therefore, the Institute once more had two prizes to allocate. The prize for 1938 was awarded. Under the statutes, however, the 1939 award had to be decided on 'before a decision is taken as to the amount reserved from the preceding year'. And here a difficulty arose.

As early as September, 1938, Professor Gerhard Domagk of Germany, who had been nominated from France and the United States, had been a strong contender for the Prize in Physiology or Medicine by virtue of his revolutionary work on the sulphonamides [prontosil]. The grave international situation raised the question as to whether, in view of its somewhat strained relations with Germany, such an award would embarrass the Swedish Government. The Chairman of the Nobel Committee of the Caroline Institute, who at that time was also Rector of the Institute, discussed the problem on his committee's behalf with the Prime Minister. The latter would make no official declaration; he merely gave it as his private opinion that if the Germans did not want any Nobel Prizes, the most natural course would be not to give them any. In this situation the members of the Committee felt they were free to use their own judgment; a majority voted against the proposed award to Domagk. It was their opinion, they declared, that practical experience of sulphonamides, particularly in Sweden, was still insufficient.

The following year Domagk was again nominated, this time from Britain and this time the Committee was of the unanimous opinion that prontosil was a discovery well worthy of a prize. The Caroline Institute discussed the matter on October 19, 1939, that is to say, more than a month and a half after the outbreak of the Second World War.

A large majority of the professors at the Institute were in favour of giving the prize to Domagk. Through an unfortunate indiscretion, however, the situation became known to the German Legation in Stockholm; and the result was a telegram to the Swedish Foreign Office from the Kulturministerium in Berlin, stating that the award of a Nobel Prize to a German was 'completely unwanted' (*durchaus unerwünscht*). The text of this telegram was conveyed by telephone to the Secretary of the Nobel Committee, who then asked the Swedish Foreign Office whether it had any comments to make. Since it had none, the Secretary remarked that the Caroline Institute would feel free to act in accordance with the statutes. The same conclusion was reached after a telephone conversation between the Rector of the Institute and the Swedish Minister for Foreign Affairs, on October 26, *1939*, about an hour before the final meeting to decide on the prize. The Caroline Institute decided by a large majority to give the prize for that year to GERHARD DOMAGK 'for his discovery of the antibacterial effects of prontosil'.

Domagk, who received the news of his award the same day, at once informed the Chancellor of Münster University and asked him how, in view of Hitler's interdict on any German accepting the prize, he should act. Since no reply to the Chancellor's repeated and urgent enquiries at the *Kulturministerium* was forthcoming, Domagk wrote to the Caroline Institute, thanking it for the great distinction conferred upon him, but adding that he must await his government's decision as to whether he could accept it. Shortly afterwards he was asked to send a copy of his letter of thanks to the Ministry for Foreign Affairs in Berlin, and on November 14, he was arrested, taken at pistol-point by the Gestapo to police headquarters, rudely handled, and interrogated about the prize by an SS-officer. Released after a week, he was again arrested by the Gestapo just as he was going to lecture on his own research to an international gathering of doctors in Berlin, and prevented from giving his lecture. The waiting audience were told it had been cancelled because of illness. Later, Domagk was compelled by the Kulturministerium to sign a letter, prepared in advance and addressed to the Caroline Institute, to the effect that he declined the prize.

The news that the Institute had decided to give the prize to Domagk was applauded in many countries. The entire situation shows how little value Hitler and his associates placed on cultural achievements or personal freedom.

On November 23, the Caroline Institute received Domagk's second letter, and was faced for the first time with a situation where a prize-winner declined the prize. This made necessary an addition to the statutes governing the Nobel Prize awards. This codicil stipulated that, in the event of a prize-winner declining the prize or failing to collect the monetary award before October 1 of the following year, the sum should be allocated to the funds. Only later were the circumstances under which Domagk had declined the prize clarified; and after the war and the fall of the Nazis an enquiry was received, from the Nordwestdeutscher Arztekammer in Hamburg as to whether he could now accept it, retroactively. Unfortunately the statutes, which now contained the new regulation, made it impossible for the Caroline Institute to accede to this request, the prize money having long ago been refunded. Nevertheless, Domagk was invited to the 1947 Nobel Festival, at which his achievements were acclaimed and where he received the diploma and gold medal that always accompany the prize, which the Institute had prepared for him after his first letter in 1939.

In view of the international situation, no prizes in physiology or medicine were awarded for the years 1940–43. The prize money of the first three years was allocated to the funds, and the 1943 prize was reserved and postponed until 1944.

Compared to the stupendous events of the war years, it may perhaps seem to be of little consequence whether the Nobel Prizes were distributed or not. But not only were the prize-juries under a moral obligation to resume their duties as soon as possible, they also felt that the awards could draw valuable attention to mankind's cultural progress, which is still among its great common assets. For the individual recipients the appreciation and encouragement of their colleagues abroad, symbolized by the Nobel Prize, was certainly not unwelcome.

THE FIRST AWARD

In the history of man, the infectious diseases occupy a special position. Their ravages have been widespread, and in times of peace as well as of war their effects have often been disastrous. Not until bacteriology had been sufficiently developed, during the latter half of the nineteenth century, did it become possible to obtain exact information as to the character of these diseases, to diagnose them accurately and successfully combat at least some of them. This development is still going on and is partly reflected in several of the Nobel Prizes.

When, in 1901, the first prizes were to be distributed there were several eminent achievements in bacteriology that could be rewarded. Among the proposals received were several urging that the prize should be given to the German physician, EMIL VON BEHRING [1854–1917]. In 1887, another German bacteriologist, F. A. Löffler, had assumed that the diphtheria bacillus, discovered by himself and others a few years earlier, produces a toxic substance which is the cause of the principal symptoms of the disease; and in 1888, thanks to the work of E. Roux and A. Yersin in France, the existence of such a toxin was confirmed. Similarly, the tetanus bacillus had been found to produce another toxin. Behring then assumed that if the poison could be neutralized in the body, it should be possible to some extent to alleviate the illness. The damage caused by the bacteria, which in diphtheria are to be found both in the throat and upper respiratory tract, and in tetanus in infected wounds, would then be limited to the immediately affected area, while diphtheria's dangerous repercussions, more particularly, on the heart and from tetanus, on the central nervous system, would be wholly averted. By advance injections of dead or weakened diphtheria germs, Behring was able to obtain in guinea-pigs a certain degree of immunity or reduced susceptibility to the virulent bacilli with which they were subsequently inoculated. In 1890, he proved that this was due to the appearance in the blood plasma of a counter-poison or antitoxin, which neutralized the toxin. Since a surplus of antitoxin was produced, it seemed possible to obtain a certain degree of protection against diphtheria bacilli by injecting an antitoxic serum obtained from pre-treated healthy animals. For technical reasons it was easier to produce this result with tetanus bacilli, on which the Japanese, S. Kitasato, was working in the same laboratory as Behring. The two scientists showed that a strong protection could be obtained against tetanus in animals, and Behring achieved a corresponding result with experimental diphtheria. From that point the step to the practical use of both sera on human beings was a not long one. Considerable experience was soon gained, proving the efficacy of the anti-diphtheria serum, especially when injected at an early stage. Although the anti-tetanus serum was of little value after tetanus had already set in, experience in both World Wars was to show it afforded virtually sure protection if injected immediately after the infection had taken place or in advance, i.e. as a prophylactic. Behring's discovery was both new in principle and a valuable asset in therapeutics.

It was obviously of prime importance that Nobel's will should be correctly implemented from the outset. That this was clearly understood by the Nobel Committee of those days is shown by its attitude towards Behring's candidature. According to the examiners, 'both the fundamental discovery and the proof of its practical value are so old, that, while admitting that in other respects they fully deserve a prize, we cannot now recommend them for the honour'. The same attitude was taken by the Nobel Committee, which proposed that the prize for *1901* be divided between Ross and Finsen. A minority preferred Pavlov to the latter. The faculty, however, did not accept the Committee's conclusions. Like the original sponsors, it was evidently of the opinion that the value of Behring's discovery had only recently been generally recognized – D. von Hansemann had disputed it as late as in 1895. After once more referring the matter back to the Committee, the faculty decided to award the prize to BEHRING 'for his work on serum therapy, especially its application against diphtheria, by which he has opened a new road in the domain of medical science and thereby placed in the hands of the physician a victorious weapon against illness and deaths', as the official announcement somewhat grandiloquently read.

Since antitoxin is produced in surplus quantities after a previous treatment with weakened bacteria, it seemed possible to use them to obtain directly an active immunity against infections. This method had already been employed successfully by Pasteur in his famous experiments with chicken cholera, anthrax, erysipelas in swine, and rabies. Thereafter, it had further been developed for use against a variety of other diseases. Thus W. Haffkine employed dead bacteria with good results in vaccination against cholera [1894] and plague [1896]. Later, A. Wright, R. Pfeiffer and W. Kolle adopted a similar procedure to prevent typhoid; while H. Vincent proved that vaccination against typhoid in the French army at the beginning of the First World War greatly reduced the mortality rate from this disease and made its control possible. Despite their great practical value, however, these advances did not bring any new principles to light.

INSECT-BORNE INFECTIONS – INSECTICIDES

Two of the early Nobel Prizes were awarded for important discoveries concerning malaria. Surely the most destructive disease on earth, malaria still takes an annual toll of millions of human lives. The cause of this illness had been sought in vain until the French scientist, ALPHONSE LAVERAN [1845–1922] found the explanation. While studying the dark brown grains usually found in the blood of malaria patients, he observed [1878–82] a number of other bodies of various shapes. Unlike bacteria, they could not be cultivated outside the living organism. They also differed from bacteria in other respects, especially in changing their appearance as the disease progressed. As a matter of fact, they belong to the unicellular animals called protozoa. The regular occurrence of these bodies [malaria plasmodia] in the blood of malaria patients, their disappearance after treatment with quinine, and their absence in healthy persons, all made it seem most probable that the actual cause of the disease was here involved. Further support of this assumption was furnished a few years later [1885–86] by the Italian physician, Camillo Golgi [see also p. 243], who discovered that the afebrile intervals identifying the various kinds of malaria [tertian and quartan fever] could be explained by the fact that the plasmodia require various periods to develop to the stage where the blood corpuscles disintegrate and the parasites are released into the blood plasma, thus transforming the red pigment in the blood corpuscles into the above-mentioned brown granules. By his discoveries Laveran laid the foundation of our knowledge regarding the origin of malaria. He was the first to prove that diseases in man may be caused by the presence in the blood of parasites belonging to the animal kingdom. In regard to these minute organisms he also made many other new and valuable observations and described several additional kinds of trypanosomes found in a variety of animals.

Laveran tried in vain to prove the existence of the malaria parasite outside the diseased organism. From his failure he drew the conclusion [1884] that the parasite in question is first developed in mosquitoes which by their stings transfer them to human beings. A similar conclusion had already been drawn by a British physician, P. Manson. In 1887, while working in China, Manson had discovered that the larvae of a roundworm, *Filaria bancrofti*, which occurs as a parasite in the lymphatic vessels of human beings and causes elephantiasis, unquestionably pass one stage of their development in the body of a certain type of mosquito, which serves as an intermediary host, or carrier. In 1894, Manson began to suspect that the parasites causing malaria also pass one stage of their development inside mosquitoes. Although Manson was himself unable to clear up the problem, he succeeded in arousing the interest of a young military surgeon, RONALD ROSS [1857–1932], who had already made a thorough study of malaria in India and had come to London to visit Manson in order to learn his view of the parasites discovered by Laveran.

On his return to India, Ross, in 1897, was able to show that a few days after a certain type of mosquito, which later turned out to be a species of *Anopheles*, had drawn blood from a malaria-infected person, new cells with a typical pigment, appeared in its intestinal walls. Owing to native opposition to compulsory anti-plague vaccination, just introduced, Ross abstained from further experiments with human beings and turned instead to the study of malaria in birds, the parasites of which showed striking similarities to those causing malaria in man. In 1898, he was able to trace the growth of the parasites in the body of a mosquito (a species of *Culex*). During the first days after the infecting sting, he obtained formations similar to those he had previously observed in *Anopheles*. He soon discovered that the parasites developed into so-called spore and sporozoite forms, and that the latter accumulated in the insect's salivary glands, after which the mosquito was able to transmit the infection by stinging healthy animals. Ross had thereby given proof of the transmission of bird malaria via a *Culex* mosquito and had made it seem extremely probable that the infection was transmitted in a corresponding manner from one person to another by *Anopheles*. The whole process was subsequently completely verified by the additional experiments of three Italian scientists, the zoologist, G. B. Grassi, and two physicians, A. Bignami and G. Bastianelli.

The Caroline Institute decided to award the *1902* Nobel Prize to Ross 'for his work on malaria, by which he has shown how it enters the organism and thereby has laid the foundation for successful research on this disease and methods of combating it'.

A certain similarity to malaria is displayed by the so-called Texas fever, an animal disease, often fatal, which causes a distintegration of the red blood corpuscles. In 1886, an American pathologist, Theobald Smith, discovered in the red corpuscles a protozoon in the shape of small, rounded formations [*Piroplasma bigeminum*]. Evidently this was the parasite that caused the illness, and togehter with F. L. Kilbourne he showed that the disease was spread by a cattle-tick [*Ixodes bovis*]. In this way it was demonstrated for the first time that arthropods can transmit a protozoan infection to mammals.

It was only natural that on several occasions the Nobel Committee of the Caroline Institute should have to make appraisals of Smith's work, particularly in view of his other valuable investigations, among them his studies of infectious hog diseases and tuberculosis, by which he was able to show that the human and bovine types of tubercle bacillus differ in many important respects. Although the Nobel Committee examiner found that his work on the Texas fever deserved a prize, the Committee objected, possibly because Kilbourne had not been included in the nomination.

The work on the transmission of trypanosomes had also been under consideration by the Nobel Committee. As early as 1880, G. H. Evans had discovered that a trypanosome [T. *evansi*] is the cause of a severe horse disease in India, called *surra*, as well as of *nagana*, which attacks horses, donkeys, dogs and cattle, and D. Bruce had demonstrated [1895–97] that the disease was transferred by the tsetse fly [*Glossina morsitans*]. In 1903, Bruce continued the work of A. Castellani who had found trypanosomes in the blood and spinal fluid of sleeping-sickness patients. Bruce was able to demonstrate that sleeping-sickness is caused by an infection with *Trypanosoma gambiense*, and that the latter is carried by a variety of the tsetse fly [*Glossina palpalis*].

The Nobel Committee's examiner reported that Bruce's work on sleeping-sickness merited a prize, but, again, the Committee did not agree with its investigator; presumably it was of the opinion that no new principle had been disclosed beyond what Ross had already revealed in regard to malaria.

As has been related above, the forerunner of the whole series of investigations into the transmission of infectious diseases by carriers, of course, had been Laveran's discovery of the role of protozoa in causing illness. No one doubted that his contribution deserved a prize, but its age seemed at first to be a definite obstacle. In *1907* the faculty finally awarded the prize to LAVERAN 'in recognition of his work regarding the role played by protozoa in causing diseases'. The phrasing indicates an attempt to meet the testamentary stipulation as to novelty by including Laveran's more recent works, though thereby his main contribution was unavoidably obscured.

Against this background and the fact that the transmission of an infectious disease like yellow fever by mosquitoes [see p. 178] had been demonstrated, it certainly seems remarkable that the *1928* Nobel Prize should have been awarded to CHARLES NICOLLE [1866–1936] 'for his work on typhus'. Nicolle had been able to transmit this disease to monkeys, guinea-pigs, rats and mice and had demonstrated that if clotheslice were allowed to suck blood from infected animals and then bite a healthy one, the latter caught the disease; the lice, however, did not spread the contagion until four or five days after they had absorbed the blood. Here was a parallel, therefore, to the investigations already described. Even if one bears in mind that Nicolle had shown that in certain animals [guinea-pigs, rats] the disease sometimes takes a so-called *inapparent* form, i.e. one free from symptoms, and that this fact may throw some light on the mystery of how the contagion survives between epidemics, it is understandable that the Nobel Committee felt hesitant. Admittedly it conceded in its report that Nicolle's contribution had been of fundamental importance in combating typhus during the First World War; but since it had not introduced any new ideas nor opened up any new roads of outstanding value to humanity, the members advised against an award. The faculty, however, decided to honour Nicolle with a prize, albeit far from unanimously.

Our knowledge of the role played by various insects and other arthropods as carriers of contagion has provided new opportunities for preventive measures. Among these is the use of chemical means to destroy the carriers. Such *insecticides* have been found to have great value outside the medical field, particularly in agriculture, since they attack the lower types of animals which act as parasites on useful plants. The lethal effect can be brought about in different ways, as by inhaling or consumption; sometimes mere contact is sufficient [contact poison], since the poison penetrates the skin of the parasites and then causes general effects, such as paralysis of the nervous system. For a number of years, P. Läuger and his associates had done research work in the laboratories of the Swiss firm of Geigy on moth-proofing textiles, and one of the latter, PAUL MÜLLER [1899–1965], while continuing this work, was led to investigate the properties of dichloro-diphenyl-trichoro-ethane, now known as DDT, a substance which had been described as early as 1874. While experimenting with the Colorado beetle, which had attacked some potato plants, he made the accidental discovery that certain larvae which had not consumed any of the poison were, nevertheless, paralyzed. DDT was therefore a contact poison, and subsequently Müller could show that, as such, it was in a class by itself. Its efficacy is extraordinary; one billionth part of a gramme is enough to kill a fly. Experience proved that DDT was an extremely effective means against many different kinds of arthropods. Its most crucial test came during a typhus epidemic which broke out in Naples in October, 1943. In January, 1944, when DDT was first used, sixty persons were falling ill each day; but after 1,300,000 inhabitants had been deloused with DDT, the outbreak was put under perfect control in three weeks – the first time in history that it had been possible to check such an epidemic in winter time. Similarly, in the work of preventing malaria and other diseases spread by arthropods, the use of DDT has shown its great value. In *1948* the Caroline Institute awarded MÜLLER the Nobel Prize 'for his discovery of the high efficiency of DDT as a contact poison against several arthropods'.

In recent years the use of DDT and other chlorinated hydrocarbons as insecticides has become highly controversial. DDT has been widely used against various pathogenic insects as well as in agriculture against plant parasites. While DDT has been instrumental in saving millions of lives by controlling insect vectors and increasing food production, its extreme use leads to ecological imbalances, with severe consequences for life on earth. The substance is volatile, and may thus be carried far and wide from the point of application. Further, since it is only very slowly degraded, nature at large becomes infected with this substance, until, today, DDT can be found in varying amounts in all animals and humans on earth. Through the food-chains in nature, the substance becomes more highly concentrated in some species, where it may cause functional disturbances, e.g. in their fertility. This can even lead to the disappearance of a whole species, the resulting ecological imbalance having the most serious consequences. One serious effect is the way in which DDT blocks the ability of green maritime algae to deliver oxygen. When one considers that about 70 per cent of all oxygen in the atmosphere is provided by the green algae, and that a concentration of 1 mg of DDT per 1,000 litres of water is sufficient to inhibit the algae's oxygen production, the danger of the extreme use of these types of substances, which could not be foreseen twenty years ago, becomes apparent. The trend is now to declare a ban on the use of these types of substances and to find alternatives which do not disturb the sensitive ecological systems.

MICROBIOLOGY – IMMUNOLOGY

The branch of research today known as microbiology grew out of Louis Pasteur's demonstration that the alcohol fermentation is caused by micro-organisms. In 1867, Joseph Lister, inspired by Pasteur's results concerning the transmission of micro-organisms by the air, introduced antiseptics, treating the operating theatre and its equipment with carbolic to prevent infection of the surgical wound. Antiseptics opened the way to aseptics, which from the moment when sterilization began to be introduced to prevent infection by micro-organisms, have made possible all our later advances in surgery. During the 1870's, 1880's and 1890's, Robert Koch made a number of brilliant discoveries of such far-reaching importance. Chief among these should be mentioned his demonstration of spore formation in anthrax bacilli; his development of bacteriological cultivating techniques; and his discoveries of the cholera and tubercle bacilli. Around him Koch assembled a great number of disciples. One of these was Paul Ehrlich, who made fundamental immunological discoveries, developed staining techniques for tissue cells and bacteria and founded chemotherapeutic research [see p. 181]. The discoveries by Pasteur, Koch and Ehrlich showed the way to later developments.

By the time the Nobel Prize had been instituted in 1901, Pasteur was already dead. Lister was proposed for a prize, but since his introduction of antiseptics had been made as long before as 1867, it was regarded as being of too antique a date to be rewarded. In view of the foregoing it is not surprising that, among the proposals submitted, many referred to discoveries of various specific carriers of infection. Nor is it surprising that many of the proposals included the name of ROBERT KOCH [1843–1910], citing the extraordinary importance that his discoveries had for 'the benefit of mankind'.

Usually his sponsors thought it sufficient to mention his magnificant lifework; occasionally there were specific references to such contributions as his work on infections in wounds, his discoveries of the tubercle bacillus and the cholera bacillus. 'There is so much to reward in Koch's works', one report declared, 'that the very abundance causes difficulties'. It could hardly be maintained, however, that the significance of the discoveries just enumerated had only recently been recognized. On the other hand, the opinion expressed in one investigation reports to the effect that 'in awarding the Nobel Prize it is impossible to ignore such a record in medical research' seemed to be shared by practically everyone. In the face of this dilemma, the possibility was discussed [1904] of awarding the prize to Koch for his contributions to the campaign against epidemics, which had shown their practical value in such comparatively recent instances as the cholera outbreak in Germany in 1892–93, and the fight against tuberculosis, malaria, and typhoid fever. While the Committee regarded his biological discoveries, which had made possible the campaigns against epidemics, as unquestionably entitled to an award by themselves, their practical application did not seem to involve any fresh discoveries or novel principles.

In 1905, however, Koch's works on tuberculosis were taken up as a unit. It was pointed out that the identification of the tubercle bacillus – described in 1882 in a report of two pages – was probably the most significant and also the most difficult of all of Koch's achievements, and that it had had a stimulating effect in wide areas of medical research because it showed that a large number of diseases which had previously been placed in different sections of the pathological system could now be grouped under the common head of tuberculosis, all being caused by one and the same bacillus, capable of producing a wide variety of effects. In the Committee's opinion, two recent developments gave renewed timeliness to Koch's discovery of the tubercle bacillus. One was the introduction of tuberculin, whose diagnostic value, especially in the campaign against tuberculosis in cattle, was incontestable, though its therapeutic importance was seriously questioned. Furthermore, it was possible to regard his work on tuberculin as a step towards the discovery of the antidiphtheria serum. The other recent development was his investigation of the bovine and human types of the tubercle bacillus with their different degrees of infectivity, by which Koch had confirmed or elaborated on the earlier findings of Smith [see p. 163]. On the basis of these facts, the faculty decided to award the prize for *1905* to KOCH 'for his investigations and discoveries in relation to tuberculosis'.

In 1921, Calmette's famous vaccination against tuberculosis was introduced. By cultivating tubercle bacilli on a bile medium, Calmette and C. Guérin after 230 transfers during 13 years obtained a non-virulent strain [BCG, *Bacille Calmette-Guérin*], which provokes in animals such a mild reaction that the body always overcomes it, and a certain immunity is thus built up. After being tested on calves, the method was tried on human beings, and it has become widely used in the vaccination of infants. In a number of proposals from different countries, Calmette was nominated for a Nobel Prize, sometimes together with Guérin; but in 1929 the examiner, in a very thorough report, listed a number of objections which had been raised in medical literature against the statistical evaluation of Calmette's results. He found that, while the Calmette vaccination raised high hopes, it would not be possible to reach any definite conclusion as to its worth until after several years of careful checking. Since the importance of Calmette's work obviously depended wholly on its practical value, and since it did not bring to light any new principle, the Committee was repeatedly of the opinion that no prize should be awarded.

While the discovery of the tubercle bacillus was thus found to merit a Nobel Prize because of its outstanding practical value and other developments of a later date, this line of argument has not been considered valid in a number of other instances in which the identification of a definite microbe as the cause of a certain disease had been proposed for an award, as in the case of the micro-organisms that cause leprosy [A. Hansen, 1874], diphtheria [F. Löffler, 1884], Malta fever [Bruce, 1886], and plague [A. Yersin, 1894]. The momentous discovery of the syphilis microbe by F. Schaudinn and E. Hoffmann [1905] could not be considered in time, since Schaudinn died the following year.

In reality, the road from the discoveries rewarded in 1901 to the prophylactic treatment of diphtheria which we have today was a long one. Behring tried to improve the immunization method by using mixtures of toxin and antitoxin. Crucial to developments on this front was the brilliant contribution made by PAUL EHRLICH [1854–1915] in reference to the quantitative treatment and standardization of toxins and antitoxins. In 1891, he succeeded in making test animals immune to certain vegetable poisons [abrin and ricin] and defined the degree of immunity as the ratio between the largest amount of poison an immunized animal can stand and the dose that would kill an untreated one. To develop fully the power of resistance to a poison a latent period is required, as is shown by a sudden increase in the resistance power of the test animals on the sixth day after the injection, the degree of resistance depending on the amount of poison injected. When the doses were gradually augmented, a correspondingly greater quantity of antitoxin was produced, until there was a tolerance to several hundred times the amount of poison that would originally have been fatal. While the active immunity thus obtained was not hereditary, it could be transmitted to the offspring by the mother's milk. The application of these results to the production of effective sera has been of outstanding practical value. The same is true of the method devised by Ehrlich to determine biologically the strength of a diphtheria serum.

Valuable results were gradually achieved, and, after later contributions by G. Löwenstein [1909] and G. Ramon [1923], weakened toxins [toxoids], or so-called anatoxins, came into use for prophylactic treatment of diphtheria and tetanus.

The introduction of quantitative methods in immunology caused Ehrlich to attempt an explanation of the immunization process. His conclusions were embodied in his celebrated 'side-chain' theory. Since the antitoxin has a much larger molecule than the toxin, it cannot be a derivative of it, he argued, but must be produced by the living organism's reaction. He supposed the toxin to contain special, so-called haptophorous groups, by which it can be bound to certain cell elements which Ehrlich called *receptors*, corresponding to the 'side-chains' attached to a benzene ring. These elements are consequently neutralized and made useless for their ordinary metabolic porposes. In the toxin, furthermore, there are so-called toxophorous groups, and with their aid the absorbed agent can attack the cell directly. If the cell survives the attack, new receptors are formed, and, as often happens under extreme strain, the reaction creates a surplus of them; some of the superfluous receptors are then discharged into the blood and into the tissue fluid in which they are able to absorb and neutralize the toxin. In certain cases [bacteriolysis, haemolysis] this does not happen until after the immune bodies have become fused with yet another element [complement]. Between the toxin and the antitoxin Ehrlich assumed the existence of a relatively stable chemical relationship.

A certain amount of criticism has been directed at some aspects of Ehrlich's 'side-chain' theory, especially by S. Arrhenius and T. Madsen, more particularly in reference to the relationship between the toxins and the antitoxins; but as a working hypothesis it has had considerable value. Within the Nobel Committee, too, doubts were expressed; but a majority was of the opinion that Ehrlich's contributions to immunity research were so outstanding that they deserved a prize. While some of his sponsors had cited such achievements as his creation of modern clinical haematology and his discovery that the tubercle bacillus is acid-fast, as arguments for an award, a majority of the nominations were based on his works on immunology. 'Whatever one may think of his side-chain theory, there can be no doubt that, since the death of Pasteur, Ehrlich has been the foremost within the entire domain of immunology'. Being in accord with that opinion, the Institute awarded one-half of the prize for *1908* to EHRLICH 'in recognition of his works on immunity'.

This meant that the prize went to a scientist whose later activities were to lead to epoch-making contributions. Together with S. Hata, Ehrlich did the painstaking work which led to the discovery of salvarsan [arsphenamine] and neo-salvarsan as remedies for syphilis [1910], and it is not surprising that on repeated occasions he should again have been discussed as a candidate for a second Nobel Prize [see p. 182].

The other half of the 1908 Prize was given to ÉLIE METCHNIKOFF [1845–1916], who had proved not only that the nature of the blood-serum itself is of importance to immunity, but that certain cells belonging to the category of the white blood corpuscles, or leucocytes, also play an important part. As early as 1882, he had observed that if bacteria or other foreign bodies are injected into the tissues of starfish larvae, the white blood corpuscles seek out the infecting bodies, gather round, absorb, and finally dissolve them [phagocytosis]. Later he found similar reactions in the higher animals. The cure and prevention of infection in the inflamed parts depends evidently to a great extent on the fact that phagocytes destroy the bacteria, whereas previously it had been assumed that, on the contrary, microbes find it easier to multiply and spread when pus cells are present. Metchnikoff showed that in many cases natural immunity is coincident with the appearance of phagocytes, while the latter are always absent when there is no such protection. When rabbits were made immune to hog cholera bacilli, leucocytes appeared in greater numbers than in the untreated animals. The immune serum, therefore, stimulated the growth of phagocytes. Actually, the division of the prize between him and Ehrlich stressed two different but equally fundamental aspects of immunology.

In treatments with anti-diphtheria serum the toxin produced by the bacteria is neutralized, while the bacteria themselves are not affected – they are offset by the body's own protective powers. In a few other infectious diseases an opposite effect was observed by R. Pfeiffer and A. von Wasserman. Filtrates of cholera brothcultures did not have a toxic effect until after a few weeks or months; that is to say, after numerous cholera vibrios had died and had been dissolved in the liquid of the medium. When the germs were injected into the abdominal cavity of guineapigs which had been immunized against cholera, it was found [1893] that the vibrios were killed much faster than normally, while the animal's resistance power to cholera toxin remained unchanged. Thus a new kind of immunity had been obtained, which was called *bacteriolytic*, since the bacteria were dissolved without any antitoxic immunity being developed. As regards typhoid bacteria, the situation was similar. In both cases the immunity was limited to the specific bacteria in question. Pfeiffer was able to utilize the new experience to determine whether a suspected bacterium was a cholera vibrio or not.

Of particular importance was JULES BORDET's [1870–1961] discovery, in 1896, that bacteriolysis of the cholera vibrio could also be achieved outside the body either by using absolutely fresh cholera immune serum or by adding a small amount of fresh serum taken from a healthy animal to the immune serum. Bacteriolysis is a complicated process resulting from the combined action of two substances, one of which is fairly heat stable, while the other [alexin or complement] breaks down when heated to a temperature of 55 – 60°C. The former substance [the immune body or amboceptor] is found in immune serum; the latter in ordinary serum, or in the fluid of the abdominal cavity. In 1885, Bordet had also observed that the cholera vibrios form lumps or become agglutinated when cholera immune serum is added. This observation was used in 1896 by M. Gruber and E. Durham to diagnose cholera or typhoid bacteria by a method that was much simpler than the one devised by Pfeiffer. When the specific immune serum is added to a broth culture of the bacteria, an easily observable agglutination takes place. This method had become highly important. By using it, Bordet, together with O. Gengou, was himself able, in 1906, to identify the whooping-cough bacillus. An ingenious variation of the method was introduced by F. Widal [1896]. By adding blood-serum from a patient suspected of having typhoid to typhoid bacilli, he could determine whether the suspicion was justified or not. If the peculiar agglutination took place, the presence of typhoid immune bodies in the serum was proved; consequently, the patient must either be suffering from typhoid or have been cured of it.

While scientists had previously worked chiefly on immunity against bacteria or toxins derived from them, Bordet, following up experiments by P. Ehrlich and J. Morgenroth, discovered that injection of rabbit's blood into guinea-pigs produced immune bodies which, together with the above-mentioned complement, could destroy the blood corpuscles in rabbits. The formation of immune bodies is actually caused by a general protective biological mechanism and produces, for example, a specific precipitation of any foreign protein with which the animal has already been treated or to which it has been made sensitive. On this extremely specific reaction is based an important method, worked out chiefly by P. Uhlenhuth, to determine, for instance, the presence of protein in samples containing traces of blood or flesh of various kinds of animals.

Bordet was also able to show [1900] that the substance used to obtain immunity, the antigen, together with its special immune body, binds the complement. In this way it is possible to remove the complement from the mixture, and by using this so-called complement fixation reaction, Bordet and Gengou were able to prove the presence of immune bodies in the serum in certain instances when no distinct bacteriolysis took place, as for example in the case of the bacteria of plague, anthrax and tuberculosis. This method has since been widely used. A special illustration is the well-known Wassermann test for syphilis, the theoretical interpretation of which remained uncertain, while the practical value became obvious through its extensive use.

Several of the discoveries in bacteriology and serology referred to have been found to deserve a prize by the Committee. When weighed against contributions in other less amply recognized fields, however, they had to be passed over. Those discoveries which have later been taken up for reconsideration have by that time often been found to be too old. Such was the Committee's opinion for some time in regard to Bordet's candidature; but when the prize distribution was resumed after the First World War, BORDET was found to have several strong supporters. In 1920, the faculty decided to award him the *1919* prize 'for his discoveries relating to immunity'.

After previous treatment with the blood of a different species, a serum can affect the red blood corpuscles of another kind of animal and thus produce flocculation [haemagglutination] and dissolution [haemolysis]. In 1900, however, Ehrlich and Morgenroth observed that a dissolution of red corpuscles can also be caused by serum from the same species of animal [isoagglutination].

Exceedingly fruitful studies of these problems were made by KARL LANDSTEINER [1868–1943], who in 1901 identified in human beings three blood groups of different characters; to these A. von Decastello and A. Sturli were able to add, the following year, yet another. Two different groups of blood corpuscle structures occur, A and B, either separately, or together [AB]. Conversely, both may be absent at the same time [the O group]. Under physiological conditions, serum cannot agglutinate an individual's own blood corpuscles, nor those of another having the same type of blood. Thus serum from a person belonging to the A group cannot agglutinate the red blood corpuscles of persons belonging to either the A or the AB groups, but does so in members of the B group; while serum from a member of the O group agglutinates those in all the others. On the other hand, blood corpuscles of the latter type are not affected by any of the four kinds of serum [A, B, AB, O]. An absence of the A or the B element means, therefore, that the corresponding antibodies are present. The full import of these findings by Landsteiner was only gradually recognized. One step was the discovery, by E. von Dungern and L. Hirszfeld in 1910, that the various types of blood are inherited according to Mendel's law, and that the A and B qualities are strongly dominant.

Landsteiner's discovery was the starting-point of modern blood-group research. It has been of basic medical significance, both for blood transfusion and other forms of transplants [where other tissues are transferred], for our understanding of complex sickness in new-born babies whose antigenes deviate in a particular manner from those of the mother, and for individual characterization by biological means, with applications in medical jurisprudence and fatherhood determination.

Landsteiner himself emphasized the fact that his observations explain the often uncertain results of blood transfusions from one person to another for therapeutic purposes. By taking care that the serum of the recipients does not contain antibodies to the blood corpuscles to be injected, it is possible to avoid agglutination and haemolysis, while the antibodies transferred with the serum, because of their dilution, do not seem to have any ill effect. Clearly, LANDSTEINER's discovery revolutionized the art of blood transfusion. When the Nobel Prize for *1930* was awarded to him 'for his discovery of the human blood groups', the examiner was, therefore, able to justify his recommendation by calling attention to recent experiences regarding the practical value of the contribution.

In this way the prize went to a scientist whose contributions have wielded a decisive influence on developments in serology and immuno-chemistry. At that time Landsteiner was about 62, surrounded by a number of disciples, fully active at the Rockefeller Institute, and during the next decade, as it turned out, was to make further observations of basic medical importance. Such is the case with his and A. S. Weiner's discovery of the blood-group system known as the Rh system. In 1941 its clinical significance was elucidated by Landsteiner's disciple, P. Levine. The discovery of the Rh system yielded the explanation of a serious haemolytic blood illness in new-born infants. In such cases the foetus has inherited the so-called Rh-positive characteristics from its father. The mother is Rh-negative. By transmission of blood corpuscles from the foetus via the placenta to the mother, she is stimulated to form Rh antibodies. These pass via the placenta to the foetus, with consequent damage to its Rh-positive blood corpuscles, thus causing the illness in question. The discovery that nature can immunize a person in this way, and that the immunization can cause such damage to the blood-corpuscles of the foetus, makes it possible to treat the new-born infant by exchanging its blood for Rh-negative blood.

As a matter of fact, all the body's cells and tissues carry a certain immunological pattern. This is illustrated by the well-known observation, that transplantation of tissues gives quite different results if performed from one part of the same object to another compared to those made between different individuals. In the former case the graft usually heals easily and permanently; in the second, an immunity reaction is elicited and after about two weeks the graft, which may have healed, is demarcated and rejected, the exception being that tissues or organs can be permanently exchanged between genetically identical individuals, such as identical twins.

In 1949, MACFARLANE BURNET [b. 1899], well-known for his numerous contributions to virology [cf. pp. 178, 206], with his collaborator F. Fenner, attempted to formulate a general theory on the mechanism of immunity. Apparently it is of vital importance that the body's own tissues do not induce reactions, and equally important that the defence mechanisms are promptly alerted by the intrusion of foreign substances. In Burnet's opinion, the capacity of 'self-'recognition occupies a central position among immunological phenomena. The 'self' pattern is already genetically determined and fully developed in the primordial cell. On the other hand, the faculty of developing full immunological immunity is reached only some time after birth. Burnet concludes that the 'self' recognition capacity is not inherited, but gradually acquired during embryonic life. Being constantly exposed to 'self' substances, the developing immunity-producing system learns to recognize the pattern and stores a 'memory' of it for the duration of life. Burnet predicted that in similar fashion a foreign pattern, introduced during the formative period, would leave its impression and, if reintroduced later, be accepted as 'self' and tolerated by the immunity-producing system.

Burnet's thesis was experimentally tested and confirmed by PETER MEDAWAR [b. 1915] and his co-workers, among whom R. E. Billingham and L. Brent should be especially mentioned. Mouse embryos, in the womb, were inoculated with tissue from a different breed of mice. Animals thus treated appeared healthy at birth and developed normally. When tissue from the same breed as the original donors was afterwards grafted, the majority of the treated mice accepted the grafts, whereas nontreated animals regularly rejected them. The prenatal treatment had produced 'acquired immunological tolerance'. Tissues from other breeds than the original donors were rejected in the usual way; as expected, tolerance proved to be as strictly specific a phenomenon as immunity.

The discovery of the tolerance phenomenon represents a major breakthrough in the field of immunology and has, indeed, opened a new chapter in experimental biology. Since 1953, when the first report was published, the technique has been highly developed. The new tools have laid several problems of great practical medical importance open to attack. New aspects are emerging on the causes and treatment of the large group of disorders in which normal immunity reactions represent an obstacle rather than a help, or where abnormal reactions are at the root of troubles. Thus, the new knowledge obtained has opened possibilities for the exchange of damaged or defective organs as well as for the treatment of radiation injuries, leukemia and certain allergic conditions. The Caroline Institute decided to award the prize for *1960* jointly to BURNET and MEDAWAR 'for their discovery of acquired immunological tolerance'.

Attempts to create immunities have sometimes resulted in an increased susceptibility to certain substances instead of the anticipated decrease in sensitivity. Thus, for example, Behring observed an increase in the toxic effect of diphtheria toxin if the animal had been treated with it in advance.

Such reactions were, however, regarded as exceptional, until CHARLES RICHET [1850–1935], who in *1913* received the Nobel Prize 'in recognition of his work on anaphylaxis', was able to show that this reaction was a normal one, the details of which he fully identified. As early as 1898, while studying the effect of eel serum on dogs, Richet had observed that a condition of hypersensitivity could develop after the second or third injection, and that it could even cause the animal's death. When, together with P. Portier, he later made experiments [1902] on the poisonous substance found in the tentacles of certain types of sea anemones, a glycerol extract of these was injected in dogs. When the corresponding amount was injected a few weeks later in the same test animals, a number of severe symptoms appeared, which in some cases caused death. It was typical of this state of increased susceptibility to the toxin, which Richet called anaphylaxis [the reverse of phylaxis or protection], that it did not develop until after some time had elapsed or, as a rule, from two to three weeks after the first injection, and that the acute symptoms did not at all resemble those caused by a single large dose injected at the outset.

On the other hand, regardless of the character of the poison injected, the anaphylactic reaction was the same. The following year M. Arthus, who had been encouraged by Calmette to make the tests after the latter had observed in himself severe symptoms from a second injection of diphtheria serum, showed that anaphylaxis can also be produced by the use of normal blood serum. Shortly after that it was found that extremely small quantities of a foreign protein are sufficient to cause anaphylaxis when introduced into the blood-plasma. The effect was produced, for instance, by milk, eggs or a muscle extract. By injecting the blood of an animal that had been made anaphylactic into one that had not been treated in advance, Richet was able to bring about a similar condition in the latter. The cause, consequently, is to be sought in some element in the blood, and strong reasons have appeared for identifying one such substance with histamine. While the anaphylactic effect is the same regardless of what substance has been used to cause it, there is a high degree of specificity, so that in order to bring about the result in question it is necessary to use the same material as that employed in the original sensitizing process. The effect of anaphylaxis lasts, as a rule, quite long, perhaps throughout life.

In a number of pathological conditions the anaphylactic reaction is of great interest. It explains, for instance, the so-called serum sickness, which often develops after repeated injections of serum, occasionally even after the first injection, though then usually in a mild and retarded form. The serious risks that may be connected with a serum treatment can be avoided by a careful desensitization effected by injecting, at first extremely small, and then gradually increased doses of serum. Many persons also exhibit symptoms which may be anaphylactic after eating certain foods [crabs, milk, eggs, oysters] or taking some medicines, and a number of diseases, such as hay fever and asthma, are connected with anaphylaxis. To describe the lowered power of resistance after recovery from an illness or after a preliminary treatment with certain alien substances, C. von Pirquet has coined the term *allergy* and has thereby called attention to the close relationship that exists between these phenomena.

In microbiology, as in bacteriology, new and outstanding gains have been made through *virus research* in connection with a number of serious afflictions such as poliomyelitis, influenza, yellow fever, measles, mumps, etc., which are caused by particles so small that they even pass through the pores of a filter of unglazed porcelain or infusorial earth. They are, therefore, invisible in the microscope; only by the use of the electron microscope has it become possible to observe them directly. In recent times, intensive research has been made on viruses and their reproduction, the eminent results of which have lead to new and important concepts in genetics [see p. 206].

In this context reference should only be made to the study of a virus which attacks the tobacco plant, the tobacco mosaic virus. Just before the turn of the century [1898], the Dutch microbiologist, M. Beijerinck, found that the infective substance causing this disease in the tobacco plant will pass through the fine pores of a porcelain filter, impassable to bacteria, and thus demonstrated that the disease can be transmitted by a filtrate which was bacteria-free. Beijerinck assumed that he here had to do with an infectious liquid 'contagium vivum fluidum', which he called virus [poison]. The same year Löffler and P. Frosch believed they had been able to prove that foot-and-mouth disease is caused by an ultra-visible virus; and in 1924, in co-operation with F. Dahmen, Frosch reported that it could be cultivated on solid nutrient media, but in 1925 a special investigating committee was severely critical of these experiments. That the Nobel Committee, under such circumstances, adopted an attitude of reserve was only natural.

On the other hand, in 1934, the Nobel Committee recommended for consideration the proof by E. Paschen [1906] that the virus of smallpox and of the specific vaccine consists of extremely small grains, which can be cultivated outside the body in tissue cultures. Of considerable importance, also, was the successful attempt of V. Ellermann and O. Bang [1908] to transmit a blood disease known as 'chicken leukaemia' by a cell-free filtrate, and likewise the discovery of P. Rous [1911] that a malignant tumour found in fowl, the so-called Rous sarcoma, must be caused by a virus [see also p. 189]. An important advance in virus research was the discovery by W. M. Stanley [1937] that the 'tobacco mosaic virus' can be produced in crystalline form and that it has the nature of a protein in which nucleic acid forms an important part [see p. 207].. Other forward steps have been the development of a method to cultivate viruses as well as the production in pure form and characterization of an additional number of viruses. That we are here concerned with a borderland between living and dead matter is shown by the fact that W. M. STANLEY, together with J. H. NORTHROP was awarded one-half of the *1946* Nobel Prize in Chemistry 'for their preparation of enzymes and virus proteins in a pure form'.

The progress made within virology also includes the demonstration by E. R. Shope [1930] of the swine influenza virus. Subsequently and independently, C. H. Andrewes, P. P. Laidlaw and W. Smith [1935] discovered the etiology of human influenza by making use of the ferret as an experimental animal. The viruses causing influenza in swine or in man, though not immunologically identical, seem to be closely related. The great value of these findings was acknowledged, but the death of Laidlaw made it impossible to consider these scientists for a prize. Further studies of the influenza virus were facilitated by the adaptation of the virus on the allantois sac of the chicken, a method that had been developed by several investigators and improved by Burnet. With this method G. K. Hirst observed that red blood corpuscles added to virus-containing allantois fluid became agglutinated, and that the process could be applied to quantitative determinations of the virus as well as its antibody. Burnet and his collaborators were then able to show that if different variations of the influenza virus were brought together in the chick embryo, new types might result from 'recombination'. According to Burnet, groups of viruses that are specifically adapted to different host organisms but biologically related occur.

During the first year of the Nobel Foundation's existence, a group of scientists were nominated for their work on the transmission of yellow fever. As early as 1881, a Cuban-American physician, C. J. Finlay, had reached the conclusion that yellow fever was transmitted from infected to healthy persons by a species of mosquito, later identified as *Stegomyia fasciata* or *Aedes aegypti.* In 1900, during an outbreak of yellow fever, an American Government commission arrived in Havana, where Finlay was working, to study yellow fever; it consisted of Walter Reed, as chairman, A. Agramonte, J. Carroll, and J. Lazear. Finlay called their attention to the rôle of the *Stegomyia* mosquito, and Reed gradually formed the hypothesis that the virus of the illness is transmitted by an intermediate host or carrier, inside of which its development requires a few weeks. By means of tests on themselves and other volunteers, the members of the Commission were able to establish the fact that *Stegomyia* was the responsible carrier. In the course of his work, Lazear himself died of yellow fever. Since Reed succumbed in 1902, it is understandable that the Nobel Committee could not recommend an award, especially as the problem involved was quite analogous to that of malaria, even if the actual cause of yellow fever had not been identified. The practical importance of the new observations was strikingly illustrated, however, by the work of General W. C. Gorgas. By exterminating the mosquitoes in the Panama region he was able to control both malaria and yellow fever, and in consequence the great canal project could be completed under remarkably improved sanitary conditions. Gorgas was repeatedly proposed for a prize, but could not be considered since his contribution was directly based on the work of his predecessors and did not include any independent or new discovery.

The discovery that this disease is transmitted by a mosquito made it possible greatly to limit its distribution. But in spite of all efforts it sometimes reappeared in places that had been free from it for a long time and, as far as could be ascertained, without having been introduced by diseased persons. In 1928 it was found by A. Stokes, J. H. Bauer and N. P. Hudson that yellow fever could be transmitted to the monkey *Macacus rhesus* by the injection of blood taken early in the disease; and some years later [1930], MAX THEILER [b. 1899] was able to inoculate it into the central nervous system of the albino mouse. After numerous passages from mouse to mouse it still killed these animals in a few days, whereas monkeys inoculated with it hardly even became ill. Blood from such pre-treated monkeys, injected into infected mice, gave a definite protection. It was concluded that antibodies against the virus had been formed in the monkey. These observations opened new aspects. Since a lifelong immunity against yellow fever usually persists after recovery from the infection, the demonstration of the specific antibodies in the blood made it possible to decide whether a person had had the disease or not. It turned out that in vast areas in Africa and South America immunity was widespread within the stationary population, but only seldom observed outside these regions. The explanation was given when it was found that the disease also attacks the free-living monkeys. It is transmitted by other mosquitoes than the *Aedes aegypti*, and some of these species may also attack man in the neighbourhood of the uncut forests or jungles, giving rise to a special form of the disease ['jungle yellow fever']. The monkeys thus form a kind of reservoir for the virus [just as the wild game in Africa does with regard to the trypanosome causing sleeping sickness].

These circumstances demonstrated the practical impossibility of eradicating yellow fever and emphasized the desirability of a method of immunizing large populations. In carrying out this program the observations on mice were also of fundamental importance. Since the virus had been altered so that no severe symptoms appeared in the monkey after the inoculation, even though antibodies were still induced, it was tempting to try it out in man, at first with simultaneous introduction of serum from patients who had recovered from the disease, and later with the virus alone. In this way Theiler succeeded in producing an active vaccine that gave good results, though serious reactions sometimes occurred. Later, he obtained a still better preparation, after having cultivated the virus in a suspension of living cells and its gradual attenuation. The investigations mentioned have provided new and powerful weapons against a disease which has long been a scourge in certain tropical and subtropical regions. The Nobel Prize for *1951* was awarded to THEILER 'for his discoveries concerning yellow fever and how to combat it'.

Great progress has also been made in the fight against poliomyelitis, that dreaded disease which causes numerous deaths, or often cripples for life. Of fundamental importance in the study of a virus disease is always the cultivation of the virus, but in the case of polio this had met with considerable difficulties. It was generally assumed that the only substrate that could be used successfully must contain nervous tissue, since the virus was considered to be 'neurotropic' [having a specific affinity only to the nervous system]. A. B. Sabin and P. K. Olitzky had shown it to be probable that a positive result might be obtained by such a method [1936], but for several reasons it could not be of practical use. The question was taken up as a team-project by JOHN ENDERS [b. 1897], FREDERICK ROBBINS [b. 1916] and THOMAS WELLER [b. 1915]. The fact that the polio virus sometimes is found in great amounts in the intestinal canal led them to the assumption that it must also be able to multiply independently of nervous tissue. They found it possible to cultivate the virus in suspension of skin, muscle, intestine or brain tissue from human foetus as well as of skin, muscle, kidney or uterus from fullgrown individuals, as demonstrated after inoculation in animals. Of decisive importance for their success was an apparently trivial alteration of the earlier technique already introduced by Enders and Weller [1948] when they succeeded for the first time in cultivating the virus of parotitis epidemica [mumps]. Enders, Robbins and Weller also made the important discovery that signs of cell damage in the infected cultures appeared earlier than in the non-infected controls; by observing the cells under the microscope and measuring the decrease in metabolism, they were able to elaborate a convenient method – without the necessity of infecting animals – for the determination of the presence and the amount of the virus. The addition of blood serum from patients who had recovered from polio prevented the multiplication of the virus. This effect was specific for the different strains of polio virus and thus could be used to determine the polio type as well as the degree of immunization in patients. The great diagnostic and epidemiological significance of these findings is obvious. It also made possible the production of virus on a large scale, necessary for the manufacture of a vaccine. The new method has also proved its value with regard to several other virus diseases and has made possible the isolation of the viruses in chicken-pox, herpes zoster and measles. The Caroline Institute decided to award the *1954* Nobel Prize to ENDERS, ROBBINS and WELLER jointly 'for their discovery of the ability of poliomyelitis viruses to grow in cultures of various types of tissue'.

CHEMOTHERAPY

The pioneer in chemotherapeutic research was Paul Ehrlich. In a speech made in 1906 he stated his view of the goals of chemotherapeutic research. 'Here we shall still be concerned with the problem of curing organisms infected by certain parasites in such a way that the parasites are exterminated within the living organism, so that the organism is disinfected, but in this case, not by the use of protective substances produced by the organism itself through a process of immunization, but by the use of substances which have had their origin in the chemist's retort'.

That is to say, it was a question of synthesizing substances which, without harm to the patient, should have the strongest possible effect on the pathogenic micro-organisms. One year after Ehrlich had received the prize, in 1909 for his immunological discoveries, the Japanese scientist S. Hata joined Ehrlich's institute. After Schaudinn and Hoffman's discovery of the syphilis microbe, in 1905, Hata had begun experimenting with syphilis on rats. Together with A. Bertheim, Ehrlich was just on the brink of synthesizing a large number of arsenic compounds on the basis of atoxyl, which, according to P. Uhlenhuth's observations, and although its high toxicity made its use impracticable, had a beneficial effect on syphilis. Careful work began, and when the various compounds were tested, it was found that preparation No. 606 [arsphenamine] was efficacious against syphilis. The medicine, which was given the name salvarsan, gained favour. While it was being tried out clinically, Ehrlich went on with his work and two years later [1912], found that his preparation No. 914, neosalvarsan, had a good effect and moreover offered the advantage of being more soluble in water than salvarsan. The salvarsan treatment, which also turned out to be effective in other microbe infections and against diseases caused by trypanozomes, was subsequently complemented with a bismuth preparation thanks to contributions from the Pasteur Institute, first by A. E. Robert and B. Sauton, and later by C. Levaditi and R. Sazerac. Although Ehrlich had already received a Nobel Prize in 1908 [see p. 170], he was again nominated in 1912 and 1913. Practical experience, however, was still too limited to determine the value of the remedy in the treatment of syphilis, which, of course, was the most important consideration. Because of Ehrlich's death in 1915, the subject was not again taken up; it is now generally admitted, however, that this contribution must be regarded as a landmark in the development of chemotherapy.

This first era within chemotherapy which lasted up to the 1930's, was chiefly characterized by the achievement of efficacious weapons against illnesses caused by amoebae, trypanozomes and spirochaetes. On the other hand the production of chemical substances which, in non-toxic doses, are efficacious against diseases caused by bacteria – for example, pneumo-staphylo-strepto and gonococci and tubercle bacilli – took some time. In an epidemiological monograph, written as late as 1935, we can read, concerning methods of combating streptococcal diseases: 'As each aspect of the streptococcal infections is examined, we become increasingly resigned in our attitude towards them. Neither our knowledge of the biology of the streptococci nor our weapons for the specific treatment of the streptococcal infections have made any notable advance in recent years. Only intensive work, in which all the faculties co-operate, holds any hope of progress – progress which is urgently desired, since the streptococcal infections are among the gravest problems of public health'.

This was written in the very year when the whole situation was to change radically. Chemotherapy entered its second epoch when GERHARD DOMAGK [1895–1964] introduced prontosil. Thanks to Ehrlich's early work on aniline dyes in a biological context, German industry had begun production in this field. This activity can be said to have followed a path staked out by Ehrlich, and Domagk made his important discovery when working for I. G. Farben Industrie, where he and his colleagues F. Mietzsch and J. Klarer were busy synthesizing various organic compounds and testing them on mice infected with virulent haemolytic streptococci. Mietzsch and Klarer had found that certain dyes, so-called azo-compounds, were active against bacteria in test-tube experiments [*in vitro*], but ineffective in experiments on living animals [*in vivo*]. As the experiments continued, a sulphanomide group was coupled in a particualr way to a certain azo-compound, yielding a preparation to which the name prontosil was given, and which Domagk found to be highly efficacious against bacterial infections in living animals. Thus he showed that, if treated with prontosil, mice infected with ten times the lethal dose of streptococci survived and that a favourable effect was also obtained on staphylococcic infections. The report on his results was published in 1935, and the very next year various clinics were able to report dramatic results from treatment of erisypelas of the face, staphylococcic angina and puerperal fever, all of them infectious conditions which had previously proved highly intransigeant. When the Caroline Institute, in 1939, decided to award the Nobel Prize to DOMAGK 'for his discovery of the antibacterial effects of prontosil', there was thus already a great deal of unanimous experience witnessing to the fact that a new era had opened in chemotherapy.

Closely allied to Domagk's publication was a work by the head of the Pasteur Institute, J. Trefouël and his wife [in collaboration with J. Nitti and D. Bovet] on the mechanism of substances of the kind that Domagk had shown to be effective. Prontosil is split within the body, in such a way that sulphanilamide is formed, and it was shown that this substance, in itself, was effective against streptococcal infections. Later works from other quarters indicated that the effect on the bacteria is due to the fact that this substance 'suppresses' enzymes necessary for their growth. In this way the sulphonamide preparations soon came into use as effective agents, not only against a number of different streptococcal infections, but against gonorrhoea, epidemic meningitis and pneumonia, later, also, against leprosy.

Thus, the sulpha treatment led to a revolutionary improvement in the treatment of a number of infectious diseases which previously had constituted a threat to life. As is the case with most discoveries, certain shortcomings were afterwards found in the sulpha drug treatment. A number of pathogenic micro-organisms turned out to be impervious to the sulpha preparations, e.g. the diphtheria, typhus and tubercle bacilli. Likewise viruses. Further, it turned out that infectious diseases which were initially sensitive to sulpha became, in the course of time, resistant to the treatment. When using sulpha preparations, one must also take note of the side effects, e.g. digestive disturbances, skin reactions, and changes in the blood picture.

Seven years before the publication of Domagk's discovery of prontosil, a work by the British bacteriologist ALEXANDER FLEMING [1881–1955] had come out, in which penicillin – today a household word – first appeared. Fleming had found that the staphylococcus colonies around a mould spot on one of his culture plates were killed and dissolved. A pure culture of the mould grown on nutrient broth was found to give off into the liquid a substance which, while it had a strongly inhibitory effect on the growth of many types of bacteria, particularly the cocci or ball-shaped kinds, was almost non-toxic to higher animals. After the mould genus *Penicillium*, the substance was called penicillin. Fleming supposed that it might be valuable in the treatment of diseases caused by micro-organisms that are sensitive to it. He began with experiments on infected wounds, in which he was moderately successful. However, ten years passed after Fleming's first observation before the next step was taken. ERNST CHAIN [b. 1906] and HOWARD FLOREY [1898–1968] had decided to extend their earlier joint studies of antibiotic substances to include penicillin. By proceeding carefully, they were able, with the assistance of a number of associates, to enrich penicillin to a high degree. They confirmed its relatively non-toxic character and by extensive tests on animals were able to establish definitely its remarkable curative properties in otherwise fatal infections from pus or gas gangrene bacteria. The quantities of the remedy available were at first extremely limited, being sufficient only for the treatment of a small number of serious cases. The results, however, were highly encouraging, and soon it became possible to draw freely on large English and American industrial resources. In this way, penicillin could be produced in pure and crystalline form, whereupon rigid clinical tests were made. By these it was definitely established that penicillin had an extraordinary effect on human beings suffering from serious infectious diseases, such as general blood poisoning, meningitis, gas gangrene, pneumonia, syphilis, infections of the urinary tract, endocarditis, etc. It is of special importance that many cases in which sulphonamides are ineffective can be treated successfully with penicillin. In fact, the introduction of the latter furnished the physician with a new remedy which has proved to be of the highest value. In view of this experience, the Caroline Institute decided in *1945* to award the Nobel Prize for that year jointly to FLEMING, CHAIN and FLOREY 'for the discovery of penicillin and its curative effect in various infectious diseases'.

The antagonism between different soil micro-organisms had for many years been the object of comprehensive investigations by SELMAN ABRAHAM WAKSMAN [b. 1888] and his numerous collaborators. It was hoped in this way to find substances capable of destroying microbes which cause diseases in man. Among the substances thus obtained, some, like thyrothricin and streptothricin, had powerful effects against certain bacteria, but owing to their general toxicity could only be used for external application. The excellent results with penicillin spurred scientists on to further efforts, and in 1944, A. Schatz, E. Bugie and Waksman announced the discovery of a new antibiotic with great efficiency against several bacteria, but only moderate toxicity for higher animals. The substance had been obtained from a fungus, *Streptomyces griseus*, described by Waksman 28 years earlier, and was called streptomycin. It acted powerfully against several disease-producing bacteria that were hardly influenced by penicillin or sulpha drugs. Of special importance was the effect on the tubercle bacillus. Because of its wax-like coating, it is unusually resistant, but it turned out that streptomycin had a fairly strong effect on cultures of this microbe.

Animal experiments by W. H. Feldman and H. C. Hinshaw gave such very encouraging results, that comprehensive studies on patients were started. The production of streptomycin in pure state has facilitated the administration of suitable doses and decreased side reactions, and the unraveling of its chemical constitution has led to the manufacture of dihydrostreptomycin, which in some respects seemed to be superior to the mother substance. Also a great material of treated cases became available and streptomycin was found to be valuable in several infectious diseases. Above all, it was found to be a most valuable therapeutic against tuberculosis. Under the new treatment, sufferers from acute forms of this disease, like miliary tuberculosis and tuberculous meningitis, earlier considered absolutely hopeless, recovered dramatically, and bone tuberculosis improved to a point where surgical intervention became facilitated. Chronic tuberculosis of the lungs also seems to be favourably influenced, though the treatment must be continued for a long time. It has been found useful to combine streptomycin with other substances having a certain action on the tubercle bacillus, such as para-aminosalicylic acid [PAS], introduced by J. Lehmann [1946], or isonicotinic acid hydrazide, which Domagk proved to be efficient in animal experiments.

Even if streptomycin is not the ideal remedy, it is still a milestone on the way to a definite control of one of the scourges of mankind. Its special value in this respect is emphasized in the decision to award the *1952* Nobel Prize to WAKSMAN 'for his discovery of streptomycin, the first antibiotic effective against tuberculosis'.

PHOTOTHERAPY – FEVER TREATMENT

Before the chemotherapeutic era, certain improvements in the treatment of tuberculosis of the lungs had been achieved by hygienic-dietetic methods in sanatoria, combined in certain cases with surgery to immobilize the affected lung or parts thereof.

It was assumed that sunshine had a healing effect when treating patients at sanatoria. But the efficacy of light therapy in certain tuberculous diseases was not definitely proved until 1896 by NIELS RYBERG FINSEN [1860–1904]. Being himself from early youth a sufferer from a chronic disease, he believed he had obtained a certain relief from sunlight, and thus became interested in problems of this nature. Thanks to the investigations of J. Widmark [1889] on sunburn and snowblindness, it was already known that the most refractive sun-rays, especially the ultraviolet rays, have strong biological effects which differ in character from those produced by the less refractive heat rays. By using highly concentrated radiation from the sun or an arc light, with the heat eliminated, Finsen was able to obtain a remarkably improved bactericidal effect. He then proceeded, in the same way, to treat patients suffering from *lupus vulgaris*, a chronically progressive type of tuberculosis of the skin or mucous membranes which usually affects the face and had previously been relatively inaccessible to treatment. Finsen's treatment of *lupus* with light proved to be revolutionary. In a majority of cases the affected parts healed completely; in others, a decided improvement was brought about. These successful results depend, at least partially, on the destructive effect of the sun-rays on the tubercle bacilli. A few other types of skin disease were also successfully treated by Finsen's method. Widmark, who was one of Finsen's sponsors for a prize, declared that he had been 'the first to devise a rational therapy based on the discovery of the effect exerted by certain light-rays on the living organism'. FINSEN received the *1903* Nobel Prize 'in recognition of his contribution to the treatment of diseases, especially lupus vulgaris, with concentrated light radiation whereby he has opened a new avenue for medical science'.

Infections are often accompanied by a higher body temperature. To a certain extent this is probably a symptom of the body's struggle against the disease, so that moderate amounts of fever may be beneficial. Evidence of this is furnished by, among other things, both older and more recent experiences with temporary infections that have a good effect on the course of already existing and especially chronic ailments, whether physical or mental. It was observations of this kind which led JULIUS WAGNER-JAUREGG [1857–1940] to conceive [1887] the idea that by deliberately causing a fever it ought to be possible to bring about improvements in certain mental cases. For this purpose he tried a variety of means, including Koch's tuberculin [1907], and found the results so encouraging that he decided to attack *paralysie générale* [general paralysis]. It was known to be of syphilitic origin, but had defied anti-syphilitic therapy as well as all other kinds of treatment. Since his experiments with tuberculin were only moderately successful against paralysis, Wagner-Jauregg became more and more convinced that a test should be made with infections caused by living organisms. For this purpose he selected a form of malaria [tertiana], which under suitable conditions could be checked with quinine, and with it, in 1917, he inoculated nine patients suffering from general paralysis. This time the results were good: three of the patients showed a moderate, though temporary, improvement, while three were completely cured and able to work again. Numerous subsequent tests in different places confirmed that in certain cases the treatment was effective – actually about 30 per cent, or the same proportion as in the first test. The Caroline Institute awarded the *1927* Nobel Prize to WAGNER-JAUREGG 'for his discovery of the therapeutic value of malaria inoculation in the treatment of dementia paralytica'.

TUMOURS

In the field of cancer research two prizes have been given for contributions made in the early years of this century. In one case the award was made in 1927 [the *1926* prize] for observations against which rightly enough, serious objections have subsequently been raised; in the other, the prize [*1966*] was given in recognition of a discovery whose importance was not fully realized until recently.

It certainly seems strange that the 1926 Nobel Prize should have been awarded to JOHANNES FIBIGER [1867–1928] 'for his discovery of the Spiroptera Carcinoma', according to the phrasing of the announcement. Clinical observations had suggested that there might be some connection between cancer and chronic irritation of a chemical or a mechanical nature or one caused by X-rays. Obviously, Fibiger's approach in producing artificial cancer in animals [1913] was regarded as a definite advance, since a necessary condition for experimental cancer research was the cancer cells.

In the stomachs of certain rats Fibiger accidentally observed a tumour in which he found an unknown parsitic worm [*Spiroptera neoplastica*]. He did not succeed, however, in producing tumours by feeding the rats with these worms or their eggs. What he did succeed in doing was to demonstrate that, during its development, the worm changes carriers – a process in which cockroaches play a part. In the latters' intestines the eggs produce larvae which, like trichinae, enter the muscles, wherein they become encysted. When cockroaches infected with this worm were eaten by the rats, sexually mature specimens of the worm developed in the latters' stomachs. In the so-called forepart of many of the rats' stomachs a new tumour formation then appeared. In several cases this had the morphological characteristics of a cancer tumour: it produced metastases and, in some instances, could be transplanted in other rats. This seemed to afford experimental proof that cancer can be caused by chronic irritation, in this case probably mechanical as well as chemical, being caused by the worm's metabolic by-products. It was believed that a dependable method had at last been devised for producing cancerous growths in animals. As has been said, serious objections were raised to Fibiger's findings. By feeding rats on a diet deficient in vitamin A, Y. Fujimaki was able to produce stomach tumours, some of which were benign [papillomas], while others were distinctly cancerous, and it is possible that this vitamin deficiency had largely been responsible for the results obtained by Fibiger.

Encouraged by Fibiger's success, K. Yamagiwa and K. Ichikawa began investigations along other lines. By repeatedly painting the ears of rabbits with coal tar, they were able, in 1915, to produce skin cancer in the animals; later on, the same effect could be obtained in the mammary glands of rabbits, by the use of coal tar injections. In 1918, H. Tsutsui found that repeated coal tar paintings on the backs of mice produced a cancer which promptly developed secondary growths. This meant that much simpler methods of producing experimental cancer in animals were found.

It took forty years before an award was made in this field [*1966*], and the prize honoured a discovery which had been made in 1911, but whose importance only became obvious much later. In 1908. V. Ellerman and O. Bang made successful attempts to transmit chicken leukaemia by a cell-free filtrate. Fowl leukaemias were, however, regarded as specific infectious diseases, without any significance for the problem of leukaemia in general. Then, in 1910, PEYTON ROUS [1879–1969] showed that a malignant connective tissue tumour which occurs spontaneously in hens could be transferred to healthy chickens by a cell-free filtrate and that the recipients developed the same type of tumour: a sarcoma. Positive inoculation results were also obtained on hens of different races as well as with other hen tumours, and each filtrate was found to reproduce its own original type of tumour. Since, apart from being filtrable, the pathogenic agent evoked specific antibodies, multiplied and, when exposed to various chemical and physical influences, exhibited virus-like characteristics, Rous concluded that this agent must be a virus – known today as Rous' sarcoma virus, or RSV. Since subsequent efforts by several research workers to transmit rat and mouse tumours in a similar way gave negative results, Rous' discovery was met with downright disbelief. Further, his observations were made at a time when little was known about viruses and when the very idea of an infectious tumour-producing agent seemed alien. When, about twenty years later, E. R. Shope demonstrated the virus background of a benign skin tumour in rabbits, Rous, who in the meantime had temporarily been devoting himself to other problems, again took up his tumour research. Working with the effect of chemical carcinogenes on this skin tumour, he obtained results leading to the conception of carcinogenesis as a two-stage mechanism; in the first phase normal cells change into latent cancer cells, which, in a second phase and under certain conditions, particularly after exposure to small and in themselves inefficient doses of chemical agents, may develop into independent anarchistic cancer cells. In the initial stage, which Rous designated as 'tumour initiation', the potential cancer cells are thus in a 'dormant' state. While Rous' findings concerning the tumour progression were confirmed, his virus theory was still met with scepticism even as late as the 1950's, when several viruses capable of inducing malignant tumours in mammals were discovered and there was a re-interpretation of the virus concept itself [see p. 207] More than a dozen viruses causing tumours of different types have been isolated. It has also been shown that the tumour viruses can change normal cells into cancer cells in the test tube, and that under certain conditions the Rous virus may induce cancer in mammalian species. It is not known how the virus induces cancer; but since it has been demonstrated that viruses can introduce part of their genetic material into a cell, to be integrated with its gene material, the genetic material of the virus may be responsible for the malignant behaviour of the virus-transformed tumour cells. In *1966*, PEYTON ROUS was awarded half the Prize 'for his discovery of tumour-inducing viruses'.

The prize was divided equally between him and CHARLES HUGGINS [b. 1901]. Huggins was rewarded 'for his discoveries concerning hormonal treatment of prostatic cancer'. Although there ware many cases of prostatic cancer which, because of insignificant symptoms, are not discovered, it is nevertheless known that this form of cancer is relatively common. Manifest prostatic cancer belongs to the diseases which occur in later life, and histological studies on section materials from men who died from various causes after reaching the age of sixty indicate that suspect cellular changes in the prostate gland may appear in about 25 per cent. Prostatic cancer is unquestionably the commonest form of malignant tumour in men, as common as breast cancer in women. As early as the end of the last century it was known that in cases of mammary cancer surgical elimination of the ovaries, i.e. a change in the hormonal regulation, could be followed by an improvement. Knowledge of the influence of male hormones on the prostate gland was taken up by Huggings in the 1940's, and in experiments on dogs he found that its growth and function could be enhanced by male, and inhibited by female, sex hormones. Assuming that the cancer cells of the prostate gland also respond to sex hormones, Hugging introduced the hormone therapy of prostate cancer. The treatment consists either in eliminating the source of the male sex hormones, by castration; or in antagonizing them by the administration of female sex hormones; or in a combination of the surgical and the medical treatments. In this way reamarkbly good results have been obtained in more than 50 per cent of cases of advanced prostatic cancer. Even substantial cancerous invasions of neighbouring tissues and distant metastasis may disappear. In this way Huggins had discovered a hormone-dependent tumour. On the basis of experimental work, he introduced a new type of cancer therapy, whose successful results were demonstrated in his clinical studies.

CLASSICAL GENETICS

The advances made in our time in our knowledge of heredity are to a great extent based on the famous laws of J. G. Mendel [1866]. According to the first of these laws, two different hereditary characters, after being combined in one generation, will be segregated again in the next; that is to say, in the new sex cells. When the latter, in turn, are fused with others, new combinations which are independent of each other can be formed [Mendel's second law]. After having remained unnoticed for a third of a century, these laws were rediscovered in 1900 by H. de Vries, K. Correns and E. von Tschermak, of whom the first two were nominated for Nobel Prizes. The contribution was declared to be worthy of a prize but had to yield to others, and when the names came up again in 1929 and 1930, it was in a completely changed situation [see p. 193].

Correns' work on the heredity and distribution of sex in the higher plants was also cited, but was considered too remotely related to the subject of medicine. In 1920, the Nobel Committee came to the same conclusion about W. Johannsen, who had been nominated for his introduction of the concepts of genotype and phenotype, based on his work on 'pure lines'. Having begun with a single plant, Johannsen was able to evolve, by means of self-fertilization in the first and succeeding generations, a fixed and constant type which could not be changed by further selection. Only by a regrouping of the herediatary factors, the genes, or by their elimination, or by the addition of new factors, as in mutation, was it possible to develop a new type.

The material basis of heredity had early been traced to the nuclei of the sex cells; and, at the beginning of the 1900's, W. Sutton and T. Bovery suggested that the actual carriers of hereditary characters were the chromosomes: thread-like formations, which stain easily. When the cells are about to divide, each chromosome splits longitudinally into two daughter chromosomes, which are separated at the actual division, so that each cell receives the same combination of chromosomes as that of the original cell. When the sex cells mature, on the other hand, new divisions, called maturation divisions, arise, by which the number of chromosomes is reduced by one-half. By the subsequent fusion of the male and the female sex cells, a double set of chromosomes is again produced; but one-half of each pair is now derived from the male and the other half from the female sex cell. In this process the mechanism imagined by Mendel was therefore supposed to be contained. Definite proof that this is so was supplied by THOMAS MORGAN [1866–1945], who found the fruit-fly [*Drosophila melanogaster*] an exceptionally suitable material for his studies, partly because it produces new generations in rapid succession [ten days from egg to egg], and partly because its cell nucleus contains only four chromosomes, thus greatly facilitating an exact analysis. With the aid of a number of co-workers, of whom C. G. Bridges, H. J. Muller and A. H. Sturtevant deserve special mention, Morgan evolved from his findings the modern doctrine of heredity.

Mendel's second law is subject to certain exceptions; heredity factors are sometimes found, which are not distributed among the offspring by chance, but are linked to each other in such a way that they are transmitted together. Morgan explained this phenomenon by assuming that the corresponding genes are lodged in the same chromosome. In the fruit-fly he thus observed four linkage groups, or the same number as the reduced number of chromosomes. One linkage group has only a few genes, and it corresponds to a much smaller chromosome than the others. Another linkage group is always sex-fixed. This can be identified as the sex or X-chromosome, which contains the female-determining factor. It has also been possible to identify linkage groups closely answering to the remaining two chromosomes. The linkage is not constant, however; at times a separation can take place, to a greater or smaller extent, even between factors which are usually found together. According to Morgan, this is due to an exchange of genes which occurs immediately before the maturation division between chromosomes belonging to the same pair. It has been assumed that there are one or more breaks in each chromosome and that the parts are then reunited crosswise ['crossing over'], so that the chromosomes that are separated by the maturation division are really new combinations, each one consisting of parts of the two original ones. The further from each other two genes lie in a chromosome, the greater is the probability that a break will take place between them, and the more often the factors involved are likely to be re-combined.

This rule can hold good only if the genes are arranged in a line. On the other hand, it is possible, by determining the rate at which such re-combinations occur, to measure the relative distance between different genes in a chromosome. In this way the Morgan school of scientists has been able to draw up charts for the various chromosomes, on which the genes wear something of the appearance of beads on a string.

The conclusions reached by Morgan and his co-workers have been confirmed by experiments with other animals and plants. In human beings too, it has been possible to identify linkage groups. These discoveries were of fundamental importance to biology as a whole and, therefore, also to medicine. In *1933*, the Caroline Institute decided to award the Nobel Prize in Physiology and Medicine to MORGAN 'for his discoveries concerning the rôle played by the chromosome in heredity'.

The term 'mutation' was introduced by de Vries for the sudden appearance of variations in the inherited characters. While the great majority of cases cited by him have since been explained as due to a re-linking of certain genes. there is no doubt that spontaneous mutations do occur. For various reasons it has seemed desirable to be able to increase the frequency of mutations artificially. In this respect, HERMANN MULLER [1890–1967] has shown the way. Exactly as with all other chromosomes, the above-mentioned sex or X-chromosomes are present in pairs in the cells of the female, while in the male only one X-chromosome is found. The latter, however, has a partner, the Y-chromosome, which differs from it both in form and in the number of genes it contains. When the male sex cells are developed, one-half of them get an X and the other half a Y-chromosome, while the female cells obtain only a single X-chromosome. On fertilization, two combinations are produced: X + X, or female, and X + Y, or male cells.

It has long been known that certain mutations result in the appearance of genes which sooner or later cause the death of the individual. These so-called lethal genes are generally recessive; that is to say, they are ineffective if present in only one member of a pair of chromosomes, the lethal effect being counteracted by the normal, non-mutated gene. Since, however, the males of the fruit-fly have only one X-chromosome, the presence in it of a lethal gene ought to cause a change in the proportion of males to females, of such a sort that the latter would number more than half the total. In fact it was found that, in certain strains of this fly, some percentages of lethal mutations did occur, whereas previously such mutations had been observed only about once in every 50,000 specimens.

After developing methods to record the occurrence of mutations, Muller, in 1927, made his great discovery that an extraordinary increase in the frequency of mutations could be obtained by X-ray irradiation. The mutations obtained in this way were stable, had the same characteristics as those appearing spontaneously, and could be produced in different chromosomes. By stronger irradiation it proved possible to cause the chromosomes to split in one or several places, only to unite again in varying combinations. Thanks to this method, it has been possible to make the above-mentioned charts more accurate. In most cases, individual specimens with mutated genes are less viable than the original ones; at times, however, mutations can result in increased adaptability. From the evidence so far adduced, it seems as if mutations of the latter type, which confer an increased survival value on the organism contain the clue to evolution. In extreme circumstances they can probably take place fairly rapidly. The study of mutations and the search for methods of accelerating or preventing them are of direct significance for medicine. Mutations, for instance, play a role in the development of new properties in bacteria, such as resistance to certain drugs. The appearance of hereditary diseases in human beings is, likewise, ultimately due to mutations. In *1946*, MULLER received the Nobel Prize 'for the discovery of the production of mutations by means of X-ray irradiation'. Since Morgan had already given parts of his prize to the families of Bridges and Sturtevant, four of the leading figures in classical genetics have had a share in the honour.

DEVELOPMENTAL MECHANICS

Fertilization is not only of fundamental importance to heredity because of the fusion which takes place between genes from male and female sex cells; it also initiates the division process and then stimulates the egg's continued development. The factors playing a part in this process have been the subject of extensive investigations.

In reference to the mechanism which brings about the division of the egg cell, J. Loeb made many important observations. While studying fertilized eggs of sea-urchins, he noticed that, if they were exposed to the action of certain salt solutions whose osmotic pressure was higher than that of seawater, the cell division ceased, only to start again when the eggs were returned to seawater. Morgan found that, by a similar treatment, unfertilized eggs could also be made to divide, although the process ceased at an early stage. Loeb then subjected the problem to a systematic investigation and in 1900 was able to carry the development of the fundament of the unfertilized eggs as far as larvae capable of swimming about. This was a case of genuine *parthenogenesis* [virgin birth, or reproduction with unfertilized eggs]. The unfertilized eggs lacked, it is true, the membrane usually found on the surface of the fertilized ones, but by preliminary treatment with monobasic fatty acids Loeb was able to initiate the formation of a fertilization membrane as soon as he placed the eggs in seawater. Another method of producing artificial parthenogenesis, which conformed to earlier observations on invertebrate animals, was introduced in 1910 by O. Bataillon, who punctured frogs' eggs with extremely fine needles. In this way he was able to bring about a division of the egg, and in some cases the development proceeded as far as free-moving tadpoles, especially if, at the puncture, white blood corpuscles had been injected into the egg. Loeb subsequently took up the same method, and at times was able to make the eggs develop into sexually mature frogs closely resembling those raised in the normal manner. The study of the 'form-creating forces' which are responsible for the repeated cell divisions until they culminate in the finished organism, is called developmental mechanics, a term proposed by W. Roux, the main founder of this branch of biology. Roux discovered, among other things, that the first cleavage furrow passes through the point where the spermatozöon penetrates, and that the surrounding area is then developed into the ventral side. After destroying one of the cleavage cells in the frog's egg, Roux obtained from the other a half-embryo, corresponding to one-half of the body, and by destroying two cells at the four-cell stage, he was able to develop either the forward or the rear part of half-formation, etc. [1888]. In certain animals the individual cleavage cells develop into definite parts of the embryo ['mosaic eggs'], and in others into complete formations ['regulation eggs']. According to Roux, there is a period of induction of the organs, when the future development is determined by an automatic differentiation which depends on something inside each part of the embryo. There follows a period during which 'functional adjustment' plays a leading role, since cells then appear and grow whenever the demands on them are increased, whereas they decay and disintegrate when inactive.

Through the years 1901–1924, both Loeb and Roux were nominated several times. In the case of Loeb, however, the examiners remained unconvinced as to the general significance of parthenogenesis, and Roux's discoveries – although worthy of a prize – were found too old for consideration.

Roux's experiments stimulated much subsequent research, and by improving his rather primitive methods HANS SPEMANN [1869–1941] made several important contributions to embryology. While the retina grows out of the rudimentary brain in the form of a vesicle, which is subsequently transformed into an eyecup, the eye-lens is derived from the epidermis close to the eyecup. Spemann showed that the eyeball can induce the formation of lenses even in areas of the epidermis which in normal embryonic development are not concerned with lens production. After the lens has been formed, the eyecup starts clearing up the covering epidermis area, a process connected with the genesis of the cornea. These investigations revealed the existence of the inductive effect which one area can exert on another.

Spemann was able to induce a number of different transformations in the eggs of the newt at various stages of their development. By constriction with fine hair loops during the earliest formation period, he was able, for instance, to bring about a partial or total halving of the egg. The continued division of a normal egg leads to the formation of a blastula, in which the cells are arranged inside a fluid-filled, spherical cavity. By a complicated invagination of a part of the blastula cover, a gastrula – a kind of double-bottomed sac with a wide opening [the blastopore] – is obtained. During both of these two stages, Spemann experimented with twists and transplantation which showed how the principal parts of the *Triton* embryo are determined. When, in his constriction experiments on the eggs, Spemann separated the left and right halves from each other, the result was two embryos, each one-half the normal size, and, in the case of imperfect constriction, partial duplication – namely, one embryo with a more or less completely duplicated forepart. If, on the other hand, the future dorsal side was separated from the ventral, the former grew into a normal embryo of half size, while the latter only developed to a very slight extent. The dorsal part of the embryo must, therefore, have special development tendencies.

These observations Spemann then confirmed and elaborated in a momentous investigation in 1918. He showed that if a piece of presumptive medullary plate, i.e. a piece of epidermis which would normally develop into medullary plate [from which the brain and the spinal cord are derived], was cut out and inserted into the epidermis of another embryo, it became a piece of skin, while a presumptive bit of skin grafted on a medullary plate became medullary tissue. The rearranged cells thus developed according to their new local environment. In addition, Spemann discovered that material from the dorsal blastopore lip, when implanted into the presumptive skin of another embryo, was able to induce the development of a secondary embryo. Further experiments showed that determination and differentiation, especially those of the medullary plate, are the result of organizing influences emanating from the upper blastopore lip. Spemann described the latter as an 'organization centre'. By subsequent investigations, a number of additional secondary organizers have been revealed. As already explained, the eyecup may also be regarded as a secondary organizer. SPEMANN received the *1935* Nobel Prize for 'his discovery of the organizer effect in embryonic development'.

For the study of growth during embryonic development, the method of cultivating animal tisssues outside of the body, introduced in 1907 by R. G. Harrison, has been of great value. From frog embryos, Harrison took fragments of the tissue of different parts of the body and placed them in a drop of clotted frog's lymph. The tissue remained alive and even continued to grow. Harrison found that shoots grew from the edges of pieces taken from the medullary tube and that, in certain cases, they were outgrowths of nerve cells. They grew rapidly, branched out, and in the end had the typical growth-cones. Harrison had also made a number of valuable observations on other tissues. His method, since improved, has been widely used by experimental biologists. In 1917, a majority of the Nobel Committee recommended that the prize be given to him. The faculty, however, decided not to award the prize for that year. When Harrison's work was again submitted to a special investigation in 1933, opinions diverged, and in view of the rather limited value of the method and the age of the discovery, no award was recommended.

FROM CLASSICAL GENETICS TO MOLECULAR BIOLOGY AND THE DECIPHERING OF THE GENETIC CODE

Fundamental knowledge about the nature of the gene, and the manner in which the information is stored in the genes, has been obtained in the last two centuries through research based on classical genetics, modern bacteriology and virology, as well as on chemistry and physics, all these disciplines contributing to a field called molecular biology. The genes exert an influence, not only on the form-creating processes, but also on biological developments in general. This is shown by certain hereditary metabolic disturbances, for example alkaptonuria and phenylketonuria, and it has also been demonstrated experimentally by GEORGE BEADLE [b. 1903] and EDWARD TATUM [b. 1909]. They brought about mutations in an ascomycete fungus, the bread mould *Neurospora crassa*, by irradiation with *X*-rays or ultra-violet rays. *Neurospora* can be grown on a simple culture medium consisting of sugar, salts and a growth factor, biotin. From these simple components it builds up its body constituents. Some of the *Neurospora* 'mutants' obtained by irradiation had lost the ability to grow on the simple culture medium, but thrived if certain substances were added. For example, in one case it was necessary to supplement the medium with vitamin B_1, in others with certain other substances, in order to obtain growth. In this way it was possible to unravel the detailed steps involved in the biosynthesis of vital cellular components. It could be demonstrated that the induced nutritional deficiencies were the result of mutations in single genes. The results obtained gave support to the hypothesis that each individual gene acts through the formation of a special enzyme. The work of Beadle and Tatum has not only led to a better understanding of genetics and intermediary metabolism, it has also thrown light on such problems as the origin and nature of the change in certain cells when they become malignant. The Caroline Institute decided to award one-half of the Nobel Prize for *1958* to BEADLE and TATUM, jointly, 'for their discovery that genes act by regulating definite chemical events'.

Meanwhile, mutation experiments of the type mentioned were started on bacterial strains of *Escherichia coli* by Tatum and JOSHUA LEDERBERG [b. 1925]. They were able to cross different mutants with each other, so that nutritionally self-sufficient 'recombinations' arose in a mixed culture of two nutritionally dependent mutants [1946]. Thus an exchange of genetic material had taken place.

Sexual recombination is not the only way leading to a recombination of characters in bacteria. Lederberg and his group observed that bits of genetic material, if introduced into the body of *Salmonella* bacteria, could be accepted by them and combined with their own, which accordingly became differently constituted; the new characters were stable and hereditary. The process has been called transduction. The bits of genetic material were introduced with the aid of bacteriophages. The process in partly analogous to the bacterial transformation, in which latter case the genetic material [DNA] is introduced directly without the use of bacteriophages.

The whole process of genetic transduction has been analysed by Lederberg and his school, as well as by others. It has a special interest with regard to the infection of a bacterium by a phage [see p. 206] of low virulence and the development of a 'lysogenic' bacterium, i.e. one that carries the genetic potentiality for producing identical phage particles in a future generation. Lederberg and his collaborators have shown that the so-called prophage is a part of the bacterial chromosome.

Lederberg's researches not only throw light on the nature of bacteria and viruses, they have also made it possible to study genetic problems in bacteria, and are of importance for the study of malignant tumours. The faculty decided to award one-half of the Prize for *1958* to LEDERBERG 'for his discoveries concerning genetic recombination and the organization of the genetic material of bacteria'.

The living cells contain a great amount of proteins, of which again most are enzymes. The large enzyme molecules are built up of sub-units, the amino-acids, linked together in a sequence. There are twenty different amino-acids and the biological specificity of the enzymes depends on the order in which the various amino-acids follow upon each other in the chain. A protein chain may contain between less than 50 and more than 500 amino-acids. From a biochemical point of view, the genetic characteristics of a cell or of an organism are due to specific chemical reactions, and these in turn are dependent on the presence of the various specific enzymes. The cell carries the genetic information for various enzymes, each gene controlling the formation of one single enzyme. The principle 'one gene, one enzyme', as expressed by Beadle and Tatum, represented a link between genetics and the study of metabolic processes, and it was assumed that the genes act as templates on which enzymes are formed.

One of the most important discoveries in modern biology was made in 1944 by O. T. Avery, who presented evidence that the heredity characters are carried by deoxyribonucleic acid, or DNA, one of a category of substances which had been known for a century.

Thus, we have to go back to 1869, when F. Mischer tried to separate different chemical constituents in cell nuclei – first in pus, and later in salmon sperm – and isolated a substance which he found to be rich in organic bound phosphoric acid, and which had characteristics indicating a high molecular weight. Since, as Mischer pointed out, this nucleoprotein, which he called nuclein, or nucleic acid, might have vital functions, it became essential to know more about its structure. ALBRECHT KOSSEL

[1853–1927], basing his research on Mischer's results, took up this question, and showed that by fairly simple operations a protein free from phosphorus can be obtained from nucleic acid. From this Kossel was able to isolate a number of substances belonging to the so-called purine bases. The interest in these compounds was further heightened by the fact that the group includes uric acid, a normal product of the metabolism and regularly excreted by the kidneys. Kossel also obtained from nucleic acids certain substances which, like the purine bases, have a sextuple ring of four carbon and two nitrogen atoms, separated by a carbon atom [pyrimidine ring], but which, on the other hand, lack the quintuple ring [imidazole ring], which in the purine group is combined with the former. Further, he showed that a sugar also enters into the composition of nucleic acid. Since, in this case, the phosphorus appears in a chemically bound form as phosphoric acid, all the component parts of the nucleic acids had therefore been identified. KOSSEL received the prize for *1910*, 'in recognition of the contributions to our knowledge of cell chemistry made through his work on proteins, including the nucleic substances'.

On the foundations laid by Miescher and Kossel, the study of nucleic acids has been successfully continued by several workers. P. A. Levene, for instance, identified the sugar constituents as pentoses. Further, A. Todd, who received the Nobel Prize for Chemistry in 1957 'for his work on nucleotides and nucleotide co-enzymes', was able to build up, from the above-mentioned components, so-called nucleotides, where molecules of sugar and phosphoric acid alternate and the nitrogenous bases are attached to each sugar molecule. The nucleotides, in their turn, are coupled to each other in smaller or larger chains, thus forming di-, tri-, and polynucleotides.

It turned out that there are two types of nucleic acids: deoxyribonucleic acid [DNA], containing four different nucleotide units, namely the purine bases adenine [A] and guanine [G] and the pyrimidine bases thymine [T] and cytosine [C]; and ribonucleic acid [RNA], in which the sugar deoxiribose is replaced by ribose and thymine is replaced by uracil [U].

Using the specific absorption of ultra-violet light for the localization and quantitative estimation of DNA and RNA in the cells, T. Caspersson and his school came to the conclusion [1938–1939] that DNA mainly occurs in the chromosomes and is closely connected with the reproduction of the hereditary genes, whereas RNA is of importance for the synthesis of protein. J. Brachet used a specific colour reaction in his studies of the distribution of nucleic acids and combined this with the application of the enzyme ribonuclease which splits RNA. He confirmed [1940] the view that RNA plays a role in the protein synthesis.

Avery, in collaboration with M. McCarty and C. M. McLeod, extracted and transferred nucleic acid [DNA] from one strain of bacteria to another, and showed that the latter thereby acquired the hereditary characteristics of the former, thus showing that DNA may provide the chemical and physical basis of heredity. The discovery, because of its far-reaching implications, aroused much interest, and Avery was proposed for a Nobel Prize. But doubts were also expressed, and the Nobel Committee found it desirable to postpone an award. Actually, Avery's finding was not accepted in all quarters until A. D. Hershey [see p. 208] and M. Chase, in 1952, demonstrated that bacteriophage-DNA carries the viral genetic information from parent to progeny.

Important knowledge was also obtained in experiments on other viruses. In general, the virus particle consists of a capsule of regularly arranged protein molecules surrounding a nucleus containing DNA [in larger animal viruses and bacteriophages] or RNA [in plant viruses and small animal viruses]. In work on the tobacco mosaic virus, TMV [see p. 178], it was shown by H. Fraenkel-Conrat and by A. Cierer and G. Schramm [1956–1957] that the RNA separated from the protein capsule contains the whole information for the biosynthesis of TMV in the infected cell, i.e. RNA is able to carry the genetic information. This nucleic acid thus serves the same function as DNA in bacteria.

Thus, Avery's discovery in 1944 of DNA as carrier of heredity represents one of the most important achievements in genetics, and it is to be regretted that he did not receive the Nobel Prize. By the time dissident voices were silenced, he had passed away.

The discovery that DNA carries the genetic information stimulated interest in the details of its structural characteristics, and, in 1953, FRANCIS CRICK [b. 1916] and JAMES WATSON [b. 1928] by interpreting the X-ray diffraction data of MAURICE WILKINS [b. 1916], presented a fruitful model for the three-dimensional structure of DNA. For the achievements in this field, both the use of X-ray crystallography introduced by W. H. and W. L. Bragg [Nobel Prize in Physics, 1915] and partition chromatography, invented by A. J. P. Martin and R. L. M. Synge [Nobel Prize in Chemistry, 1952], played an important role. Using the latter method, E. Chargaff had found [1950] that the numbers of adenine [A] and thymine [T] groups were always equal, and so, in any one species, were the numbers of guanine [G] in proportion to cytosine [C], whereas the relation between adenine [A] and guanine [G] showed species differences, indicating an important regularity, and that the biological specificity of DNA is dependent on the bases in the molecular chain. Further, with the aid of X-ray crystallography L. Pauling [Nobel Prize in Chemistry, 1954] had shown the helical structure of certain proteins and the importance of the hydrogen bonds as a stabilizing factor. On the basis of the X-ray diffraction patterns obtained by Wilkins in his eminent crystallographic studies, and taking into account Chargaff's findings, Crick and Watson came to the conclusion that the DNA molecule consists of a double helix, where the two sugar-phosphate chains represent the backbones, held together by a sequence of pairs of nucleotide bases [A.G.T.C.], joined by hydrogen bonds. There is a specific pairing [A-T; G-C], and each half of the helix forms its own complement. The genetic information is expressed by the nucleotide sequence, whose essential characteristics are that A is complementory to T and C to G. Because of this complementarity, DNA is able to replicate itself. The two helical structures are related like lock and key, and, when separated, each is able to make its own complement, thus reconstructing the whole double-strand DNA molecule. The principle for reproduction – in connection with cell division, when each of the daughter cells obtains a copy of the mother cell's gene – is indicated by the DNA structure.

The other principal function of the gene, i.e. to regulate the production of enzymes and other proteins by dictating their amino-acid sequences, could also be referred to the specific DNA structure. Because of the great significance of their achievements, CRICK, WATSON and WILKINS were awarded the *1962* Nobel Prize 'for their discoveries concerning the molecular structure of nuclear acids and its significance for information transfer in living material'.

Important discoveries concerning the synthesis of RNA and DNA through the action of enzymes were made by SEVERO OCHOA [b. 1905] and ARTHUR KORNBERG [b. 1918].

As already mentioned, RNA is present in the cytoplasm. One kind of RNA, of relatively small molecular size, is found in the protoplasm, the other, of much higher molecular weight, in the cell nucleus. In 1955, Ochoa isolated from the micro-organism *Azotobacter vinelandii* an enzyme capable not only of breaking down RNA but also, under suitable conditions, of catalyzing the synthesis of high molecular-weight RNA from simple naturally occurring precursors. The enzyme activated nucleotides with one extra group of phosphoric acid (diphosphates) in such a way that the extra phosphoric acid was liberated in connection with the binding of the remaining phosphoric acid to the sugar in another nucleotide-diphosphate molecule, which in the same way was linked to a third, etc. In all respects the synthetic product conformed to natural RNA, as shown, for example, by degradation with alkali or with different enzymes. If highly purified enzyme was used for the synthesis, this started very late and proceeded much more slowly than if a small amount of RNA had been added. This functioned as a 'primer'. Kornberg took up the problem of synthesizing DNA, obtaining the necessary synthetizing enzyme from the common intestinal bacterium, *Escherichia coli*. With its aid, the mononucleotides which occur in DNA were synthetized from the corresponding triphosphates and condensed to long chains of DNA-type by the splitting off of two of the phosphae groups. For this reaction the presence of magnesium salts, but also of some preformed DNA, was necessary. The enzyme is therefore taking directions from a primer or template. Kornberg also showed that, if small variations occurred in the configuration of the primers when they were obtained from different sources [such as *Mycobacterium phlei* or calf thymus], these variations were faithfully reproduced in the enzymatic synthesis. It is obvious that the helical structure, mentioned above, must be well suited for replication. For if the two chains separate and a new chain is formed to each of them, the result will be two pairs of strands, each pair identical to the original duplex and to each other.

OCHOA and KORNBERG were awarded the Nobel Prize for *1959* 'for their discovery of the mechanisms in the biologic synthesis of ribonucleic and deoxyribonucleic acids'.

In order to answer the question how the gene controls the building up – in the cell – of a specific protein in which the 20 amino-acids represent the units, the mechanisms had to be found through which DNA directs the amino-acid sequencies that define the specific structures and biological functions of the different proteins. The facts that, on the one hand, DNA is localized in the nucleus and, on the other, that that the ribosomes in the cytoplasm are rich in RNA and have to do with the protein synthesis, favoured the view that the RNA transfers the information from DNA in the nucleus to the system whic builds up the proteins.

In *1965*, FRANÇOIS JACOB [b. 1920], ANDRÉ LWOFF [b. 1902], and JAQUES MONOD [b. 1910] received the Nobel Prize 'for their discoveries concerning genetic control of enzyme and virus synthesis'. Their discoveries contributed in a highly significant way to our knowledge of the 'transscription' mechanism in the cell nucleus. In the nucleus, an RNA, called messenger RNA or mRNA, is formed. The DNA serves as a template, so that the sequence of the nucleotides in the mRNA is determined by the sequence in the DNA molecule. When mRNA is synthetized – that is, when the so-called transcription has been made – it moves out of the nucleus to the cytoplasm, thus carrying the code for the building up of the proteins. On the basis of studies on bacteria – preferably *Enscherichia coli* – three kinds of genes were recognized, and a model was presented of how the protein-synthesis is quantitatively controlled at the transcription level. The mRNA's – appearing in many short-living copies – are made by 'structural' genes. Parts of the DNA molecules are to be regarded as 'regulator genes', producing the 'repressor' substances. These substances can become attached specifically to the 'operator' genes, and each operator gene regualates the activity of a group of neighbouring genes, which may contain the information for a series of enzymes. The repression may block the transcription of a whole group of structural genes and thus also the building up of the corresponding proteins. The segment of the DNA molecule containing the operator gene and the subordinated structural genes forms a functional unit, called the 'operon'. The ability of the repressor to block the transcription of an operon can be eliminated by the influence of so-called 'inducers'. Jacob, Lwoff and Monod have thus made fundamental contributions to our knowledge of important feed-back mechanisms involved in the regulation of the enzyme synthesis.

In the attempts to decipher the genetic code, one is confronted with the question how the sequence of four nucleotides in a DNA molecule is translated into the sequence of 20 amino-acids in a protein. As mentioned, the mRNA – a single helical strand containing uracil [U] in place of thymine [T] in DNA – carries the code from DNA in the nucleus to the ribosomes where the proteins are built up, the 20 amino-acids serving as bricks. It seemed obvious that the genetic code for an amino-acid must contain more than one nucleotide, and Crick came to the conclusion that with three-letter combinations it would be possible to obtain 20 alternatives. Since there seemed to be no simple way in which a small sequence of nucleotides could directly specify an amino-acid sequence, Crick, in 1956, put forward the adaptor hypothesis, according to which each amino-acid would recognize a sequence of nucleotides through the mediation of a specific 'adaptor'. Experimental support for the adaptor theory very soon appeared when M. Hoagland, in 1957, discovered a type of RNA that could bind the amino-acids specifically – the binding requiring an enzyme and ATP – and also found that the bound amino-acids could be transferred into proteins. Contributions from several research workers led to the conception of transfer RNA or tRNA [referred to as 'soluble' RNA by Hoagland, also 'adaptor' RNA and 'acceptor' RNA]. In the ribosomes, mRNA serves as a template, along which the relatively small tRNA's line up according to their complementary nucleotide sequences. There are at least 20 tRNA's, and each reacts with a specific type of the 20 amino-acids. Thus the tRNA's carry the amino-acids to the mRNA, and the nucleotide sequence of mRNA determines the order according to which the amino acids are lined up by the tRNA's.

Most important discoveries elucidating the deciphering of the genetic code were made by ROBERT HOLLEY [b. 1922], HAR GOBIND KHORANA [b. 1922], and MARSHALL NIRENBERG [b. 1927]. Of great significance for the following development were the results that Nirenberg, together with J. H. Matthei, obtained when they succeeded in breaking the genetic code using synthetic RNA's which contained only one or two nucleotides instead of four, and which were shown to have specific effects in binding together amino-acids. An 'RNA' containing only uracil [U; polyuracil] specified a protein containing only one amino-acid, namely phenylalanine. Thus, the code word, or codon, for phenylalanine is UUU. The results were extremely promising in showing a principle according to which the question concerning the codons for the amino-acids could be solved. However, the experiments with the synthetic RNA's used did not give any answer concerning the sequence of the different nucleotides in the triplet code. These difficulties were solved thanks to the contribution of Khorana, who by systematic and painstaking work succeeded in building up synthetic nucleic acids in which the nucleotides were placed in certain sequences. In his products, the localization of all A, C, G, and U in the molecule were known. These nucleic acids could now be used as mRNA's. Khorana and his group managed to synthesize molecules containing all 64 possible triplets of the four nucleic bases, and it was shown how 61 out of the 64 possible triplet codes are used for the coding of the 20 amino-acids, whose codons are now known.

For the understanding of the principle by which the adaptors, i.e. the tRNA's, take part in the coding mechanism, it is necessary to understand their structural organization. In 1965, Holley, who had contributed to the discovery of tRNA, succeeded in determining the complete sequence of sub-units in a tRNA molecule. First he isolated the tRNA which functions as an adaptor for the amino-acid alanin, and then showed the sequence of all its 76 nucleotides; thus he was the first to make a complete structural description of a biologically active nucleic acid. By doing this, he also identified the 'anticode' which, in alanin-tRNA, binds this nucleic acid to the triplet code of alanin in mRNA. Thus, he managed to demonstrate the principle according to which, with the aid of tRNA, the amino-acids are placed in the protein in the sequence determined by the order of the triplet codes in mRNA. The discoveries of HOLLEY, NIRENBERG and KHORANA played the key role in the deciphering of the genetic code, and they were awarded the *1968* Nobel Prize 'for their interpretation of the genetic code and its function in protein synthesis'.

For the development of modern genetics during the last thirty years, fundamental results obtained in bacteriophage research have been instrumental. Already, at the beginning of this century, F. W. Twort [1915] and F. d'Herelle [1917] observed a peculiar disintegration of bacteria colonies, occurring in spots. This effect was caused by a filterable element which could be transferred indefinitely from one culture to another. On the other hand, it could not be made to grow by itself. The agent, therefore, was either a living virus, requiring for its growth the presence of bacteria, or a substance like an enzyme, produced by the bacteria themselves. The latter assumption was contradicted by the fact that it was possible to transmit the effect like a contagion. D'Herelle therefore surmised that the agent was a special 'bacteriophage', a kind of parasite on bacteria, which must be exceedingly small. Later, he tried to use the bacteriophages to combat various kinds of infectious diseases; but the results were not conclusive and the interest in bacteriophages faded. For a long time they were regarded as laboratory curiosities. A new era began towards the end of the 1920's, and important discoveries, which placed phage research in the centre of virology and genetics, were made during the following decades, especially in the works of F. M. Burnet in Australia, S. S. Cohen, MAX DELBRÜCK [b. 1906], ALFRED HERSHEY [b. 1908] and SALVADOR LURIA [b. 1912] in the United States, and A. Lwoff, in France, and their collaborators.

We know now that there are a great many 'phages', or bacterial viruses, which infect host cells of various bacterial strains, and that each phage type has its specific 'host range', while each bacterium has its own phage spectrum. Like other viruses, the phage consists of a proteineous bag containing one chromosome, represented by a nucleic acid molecule [DNA or RNA; see p. 200], most phages being of the DNA type. The majority of the phages studied [e.g. the so-called T phages], look like tadpoles, with head and tail. The hexagonal head contains the genome, i.e. the DNA molecule, and, with the aid of the tube-shaped tail equipped with long extensions of spider leg type, the phage attaches itself to the bacterium and 'injects' the DNA into the host cell. As a result, the bacterium's genome, i.e. its own DNA, breaks down. The production of its specific enzymes stops, and instead the synthesis of new phage material starts, directed by the genetic information carried by the phage DNA. The replication of phage DNA, as well as the formation of mRNA, now begins, followed by the production of the specific enzymes and structural proteins. Thus a great number of new generation phages are formed, which are dispelled when the bacterial host call disintegrates under the influence of lytic enzymes [lysozymes]. Clearly, the investigations which led to the elucidation of the processes, here briefly described, have in a most significant way increased our knowledge of the multiplication mechanisms of viruses and of molecular genetics in general. When the virus infects the cell, in this case a bacterium, the 'cell-virus complex' appears as a new individual; the chemical activity of the cell changes radically, while the virus enters into an eclipse or 'dark phase', loses its individuality, and triggers the chemical activity which, within some minutes, results in the formation of hundreds of new virus particles. The work, in 1939, of the physicist M. Delbrück, in collaboration with E. Ellis, showing the latent period during which the parental phage multiplies to yield an issue of several hundred progeny, represents the beginning of molecular phage research. It was demonstrated that the phage-infected bacterium offers an ideal experimental system for the study of self-replication, and exact experimental methods were introduced. In 1940, Luria, microbiologist and geneticist, came into contact with Delbrück and their joint work [1943], showing that the appearance of phage-resistant variants in cultures of phage-sensitive bacteria represents the selection of spontaneous bacterial mutants, was a break-through in bacterial genetics. In their following co-operative investigations during the years 1940–45, they demonstrated the main characteristics of the phage replication mechanisms. During this period the biochemist Hershey, who had been using bacteriophages in immunological studies, came into contact with Delbrück and Luria. Subsequently, both Hershey and Luria [1945] demonstrated the occurrence of spontaneous phage mutants, and, following studies by Delbrück and Hershey, brought about the discovery of genetic recombination in phage. The fact that two virus particles which simultaneously infect a cell can exchange parts of the genetic chain made it experimentally possible to map the virus' genetic constitution, experiments greatly facilitated by the shortness of the time needed for the production of new phage generations. Such a map shows the nucleic acid of the phage along which the positions of the genes responsible for various characteristics are marked; and it has been shown that about 75 various components are necessary for the building up of a virus with head and tail. The above-mentioned demonstration of the construction of the phage with its DNA content and its attachment to the bacterium, led Hershey and M. Chase [1952] to perform the important experiment, showing that the phage DNA is the principle component to enter the host cell. Their discovery that DNA is the genetic material of the phage was in harmony with Avery's conclusion, in 1944, that DNA carries the genetic information in bacteria. The discovery by Hershey and Chase focussed attention on DNA as carrier of the hereditary characteristics, and provided an important impetus for the study of the DNA structure carried out by Crick and Watson. It is now generally accepted that the replication mechanism shown in bacteriophages applies to all viruses, and DELBRÜCK, HERSHEY and LURIA were awarded the *1969* Nobel Prize 'for their discoveries concerning the replication mechanism and the genetic structure of viruses'.

INTERMEDIARY METABOLISM

As mentioned, enzymes or ferments which accelerate or catalyze chemical transformations are needed for the gradual breakdown of the constituents of the body as well as for their synthesis. Little was known about the exact nature of these substances until 1914, when OTTO WARBURG [1883–1970] was able to make clear the main structural aspects of an important enzyme that occurs in all cells. Since this is closely connected with the actual supply and consumption of oxygen in the individual elements of the cell, it has been called the respiratory enzyme.

While experimenting with a suspension of crushed sea-urchin eggs, Warburg noticed that the absorption of oxygen was greatly increased when quite small quantities of ferro-salts were added, and in 1921 he found that the oxidation of some substances, e.g. certain aminoacids, which at ordinary temperatures can be brought about by the addition of powdered charcoal, shows striking similarities to the oxidation phenomena in living tissue. It was, for instance, reduced by substances having a narcotic effect, as well as by hydrocyanic acid. The latter was effective even when highly diluted, and Warburg showed that this was due to the fact that it combined with and absorbed the small quantities of iron that were present. In this way his attention was called to the question whether the iron in the tissue enzymes had a corresponding function. That it did had been indicated by tests made in the 1880's by C. A. MacMunn, who by spectroscopic methods had shown the presence in certain tissues of a previously unknown component which, after being reduced by a lack of oxygen, showed absorption bands like those found in haemoglobin, the red pigment of the blood containing iron. MacMunn's experiments were severely criticized and his findings were not accepted. Strong evidence for the assumption that the respiratory enzyme contains iron was obtained, however, by Warburg when he found [1926] that intracellular respiration could be retarded by carbon monoxide. As is well known, this substance acts on haemoglobin by expelling the oxygen from its union with the iron, and here was a clear analogy, although much stronger concentrations of carbon monoxide were required to render the respiratory enzyme inactive.

In his subsequent studies, Warburg could utilize an observation by Haldane and J. L. Smith [1896] to the effect that light upsets the equilibrium between haemoglobin, carbon monoxide, and oxygen in favour of the oxygen compound. The same result Warburg found to ensue in the case of the respiratory enzyme, and by determining to what extent the retardation of the intracellular respiration was affected by light from different parts of the spectrum he was able to show that the effect was similar to that observed in the case of haemoglobin. From these findings he concluded that the respiratory enzyme contains the same nucleus as haemoglobin, namely, iron linked to a porphyrin ring consisting of four pyrrole groups. A physical analysis had thus led to the goal, regardless of the fact that the low concentration of iron in the enzyme [corresponding to one part in ten millions] made it seem extremely unlikely that a verification would be possible by the use of ordinary chemical methods. It is quite likely that Warburg's respiratory enzyme absorbs molecular oxygen from the blood and then binds it chemically in the same way as haemoglobin, that is to say, in a dissociable union with bivalent iron. In the combustion process an additional series of ferrous enzymes participates, and the iron they contain fluctuates between the bivalent and the trivalent states. The respiratory enzyme is thus followed by 'cytochromes' [*a*, *b* and *c*] which correspond to the pigment described by MacMunn. These processes have been explained in great detail by D. Keilin.

WARBURG received the *1931* prize 'for his discovery of the nature and mode of action of the respiratory enzyme'. Since then he has still further increased our knowledge of the combustion processes. Together with W. Christian he discovered, for example, a respiratory enzyme that does not contain iron, the so-called yellow enzyme, out of which the active [prosthetic] group could be split off in the form of a greenish yellow pigment. Since then a number of different yellow enzymes have been shown to exist in nature, and in this respect Warburg has made conclusive contributions, particularly by proving that some of these contain active groups of a slightly more complicated kind than the riboflavinphosphoric acid, namely, a combination of the latter with adenylic acid, a so-called dinucleotide.

To be effective, certain enzymes sometimes require the presence of so-called 'coenzymes' which usually consist of thermostable substances of a less complicated structure than the enzyme itself. Warburg and Christian have shown [1935] that the coenzyme which acts together with the yellow enzyme contains nicotinic acid amide as its active constituent. These discoveries by Warburg of two groups of great importance to intermediary metabolism, namely, flavine [in the yellow enzymes] and nicotinic acid amide, as well as his other important achievements, caused him to be nominated for a prize a second time in 1944, when he was again found to deserve the honour, but he had to make place for others.

At one time Warburg had assumed that the whole cellular oxidation process is caused by ferrous respiratory enzymes which convey the oxygen to the substrate that is to be oxidized. But in 1912 H. Wieland advanced a theory according to which the biological combustion process begins when two hydrogen atoms in the substrate are activated by the influence of an enzyme in such a way that they can directly combine with molecular oxygen and thus form a hydrogen peroxide. This theory was then taken up by T. Thunberg. In minced, uncleansed, and especially in cleansed muscle he found that the consumption of oxygen greatly increased after certain organic acids had been added. Particularly effective were the 'vegetable acids' – succinic acid, fumaric acid, malic acid, and citric acid – and Thunberg therefore regarded them as normal products of intermediary metabolism. Through experiments by F. Battelli, L. Stern and H. Einbeck it was then revealed that under the influence of enzymes the succinic acid is first converted into fumaric acid which then turns into malic acid. According to Thunberg, these findings could easily be reconciled with Wielands' theory; Thunberg was able to identify the active enzymes which make it possible to split off hydrogen and are therefore called dehydrogenases by using methylene blue, which absorbed the liberated hydrogen and thereby lost its own colour. In this way a number of enzymes could be detected. The supposed formation of hydrogen peroxide could not, however, be verified under normal circumstances, while, on the other hand, the reduction in respiration that took place after the ferrous enzymes had been inactivated by the use of carbon monoxide or hydrocyanic acid clearly proved the important role played by the latter in the transfer of oxygen. Various circumstances indicated, nevertheless, that non-ferrous enzymes likewise play a part. Warburg then succeeded in explaining the functions of all the components involved in the biological oxidation process of hexose-monophosphoric acid. In this process there is participation by the yellow enzyme as well as by the dehydrogenase, which, however, requires the presence of the above-mentioned coenzyme containing the amide of nicotinic acid. The hydrogen is transferred from the substrate to the dehydrogenase coenzyme, whereupon it is further catalyzed by the ferrous enzymes.

In 1933, the nature of the 'first' yellow enzyme was once again investigated, this time by HUGO THEORELL [b. 1903]. He came to the task well prepared, having been able, shortly before, to crystallize the coloured principle of the muscles, myoglobin. This had been possible by a skilful combination of several methods such as precipitation with salts at different acidities and separation of substances through their varying capacity of penetrating certain membranes [dialysis] and their varying transport by the electric current [electrophoresis]. He obtained the enzyme in a pure crystalline state and could then take a further highly important step: after splitting off from the enzyme a yellow pigment and a colourless protein component, each of which was inactive, he succeeded in recombining them in definite proportions with the return of the original effect. The pigment group was known to consist partly of riboflavin or vitamin B_1. Theorell proved that it also contains phosphoric acid [thus forming a riboflavin-phosphoric acid], and this acid has later been found to play a special role in attaching the pigment to protein in other yellow enzymes as well. The discovery of the reversible separation of the prosthetic group and the protein part has been characterized as the first definite production of a pure enzyme. It is true that in the twenties J. B. Sumner and J. H. Northrop had obtained crystallized enzymes and stated that the crystals contained protein, but it had been maintained that their products might contain protein merely as an inactive vehicle for the actual enzymes. The slow recognition of their pioneer work is reflected in the fact that they did not receive the Nobel Prize for Chemistry until 1946.

Theorell's classical experiment made it at once obvious that protein is a necessary component of the enzyme. Later, the reversible separation into a prosthetic and a protein part has been performed by Theorell for myoglobin, as well as for peroxidase that decomposes oxygen-rich oxides, and other enzymes have been successfully treated in a similar way by different authors. All enzymes so far isolated have been found to contain protein.

Myoglobin, peroxidase and the cytochromes mentioned above all belong to the haemin proteids, i.e. they contain iron, similarly bound as in haemoglobin. Their mode of action is, however, rather different. The reduced cytochrome *c* in contrast to myoglobin is unable to react with molecular oxygen, and it has the haemin pigment very firmly linked to the protein part. Theorell was able to demonstrate the specific nature of the chemical linkage [via two sulphur bridges from cysteine residues] and showed that the haemin is surrounded by peptide spirals in such a way that the iron is screened off from the contact with oxygen. He has also made numerous other additions to our knowledge of the structure of certain enzymes as well as of the complicated reactions they evoke.

Theorell contributed greatly to our understanding of enzymes and their constitution. His work forms a continuation of that of Warburg, as is also emphasized by the fact that the Caroline Institute awarded THEORELL the *1955* prize 'for his discoveries relating to the nature and mode of action of the oxidative enzymes', a formulation that is very similar to that used in Warburg's case.

An important role in cell oxidation is also played by the fumaric acid itself and by a number of closely related substances, as was shown by the investigations of ALBERT VON SZENT-GYÖRGYI [b. 1893] and his associates. While trying to speed up the dehydrogenation of lactic acid mixed with cleansed muscle by the use of a coenzyme, I. Banga and Szent-Györgyi observed [1933] that this process proceeded much more slowly in oxygen than in the presence of methylene blue. They therefore concluded that in a mixture of lactic acid, muscle and oxygen, something was lacking which could absorb the hydrogen and then convey it to the ferrous enzymes. This was later shown to be the function of fumaric acid, for in 1934 B. Gözsy and Szent-Györgyi discovered that the respiration in minced muscle could be retarded by the addition of malic acid and that it was accelerated by succinic acid as well as by fumaric acid, without these substances being themselves consumed. By a series of subsequent investigations, Szent-Györgyi and associates further established the fact that the substances in question are not to be regarded as products of intermediary metabolism but are themselves carriers of a catalytic action by which a bridge is built between the dehydrogenase system, on the one hand, and the ferrous enzymes on the other. Malic and fumaric acids always appear together in muscle, in the ratio of one to three. In cellular respiration, the malic acid is activated and gives off two hydrogen atoms to the fumaric acid, which is thereby reduced to succinic acid, while the latter, in turn, is oxidized by the ferrous enzymes and then reverts to fumaric acid. Because of its loss of hydrogen, the malic acid simultaneously turns into oxalacetic acid, which, through the influence of the dehydrogenase, then reverts to malic acid. In this way, the original state is restored except that two hydrogen atoms have been forced to become oxidized into water.

Szent-Györgyi has described still another respiratory system, in which the hydrogen is oxidized by degrees, namely, by means of ascorbic acid or vitamin C [cp. p. 230], which in the presence of oxygen, is converted by an enzyme system into dehydroascorbic acid, since the oxygen combines with two unstable hydrogen atoms to form hydrogen peroxide. This, in turn, is broken down by another enzyme, peroxidase, and with the aid of an intermediary substance oxidizes a second molecule of the ascorbic acid. Both molecules of dehydroascorbic acid then take up hydrogen from other substances, possibly with the aid of the sulphuric compounds present in the latter.

SZENT-GYÖRGYI received the *1937* prize 'for his discoveries in connection with the biological combustion processes, with special reference to vitamin C and the catalysis of fumaric acid'.

The vegetable acids referred to above are 'dicarboxylic', which means that each contains two carboxyl groups [cf. p. 200]. Later experiments have shown, however, that these acids must be considered as links in a more complicated system, where tricarboxylic acids play an essential role as the tool, by which certain split products from our food are incorporated and stepwise oxidized. The whole process is centered around the citric acid and is therefore termed the citric acid or tricarboxylic acid cycle. The starting point was the observation that citric acid, discovered in plants in 1784 by C. W. Scheele and found by Thunberg to have a wide distribution also in the animal kingdom, when added to minced mucle tissue, stimulated oxidation to a much greater extent than could be accounted for by its own combustion [an analogy to the effect of fumaric or succinic acids mentioned above]. C. Martius and F. Knoop discovered α-ketoglutaric acid [with two carboxyl groups] as a product of the tissue oxidation of citric acid and suggested that *cis*-aconitate and isocitrate [each of them with three carboxyl groups] were intermediates. These findings were confirmed and extended by HANS ADOLF KREBS [b. 1900] and by W. A. Johnson who also made two further important observations. After the addition of malonate, succinic acid was an essential product of the oxidation of citric acid. But citric acid could not only be rapidly broken down in the tissues; it could also readily be formed there, if oxaloacetic acid was added. They gave the explanation that only part of the oxaloacetic acid [a 4-carbon compound] was oxidized, while another part was condensed with acetate [a 2-carbon compound] or pyruvate [a 3-carbon compound]. The result was the formation of another molecule of citric acid. The cycle thus acts in the following way: citric acid, formed from oxaloacetic acid and acetic [or pyruvic] acid, is disintegrated by passing through the stages of *cis*-aconitic, isocitric, α-ketoglutaric, succinic, fumaric, malic and oxaloacetic acids under the liberation by degrees of water, carbon dioxide and energy. The oxaloacetic acid is then ready to start the cycle anew.

The different intermediates postulated in the cycle have been demonstrated in several ways – partly with the aid of 'labelled' or radioactive carbon – and their stimulating or inhibiting influences according to the concentrations used have been shown. Some additional intermediates have been identified by S. Ochoa and F. Lynen.

Since pyruvate and acetate are products regularly formed in the body when carbohydrates are broken down, there can be no doubt that the citric acid cycle is of fundamental importance for the oxidation of these substances. But there is abundant evidence that it acts in a similar way with fatty acids and many amino aciss. Its seems to be the common pathway for all kinds of foodstuffs and occurs in plants and micro-organisms as well as in mammals. It probably represents the main energy-producing mechanism of living matter. KREBS was awarded one half of the *1953* prize 'for his discovery of the citric acid cycle'.

The numerous steps involved in the tricarboxylic acid cycle require the presence in the cells of a number of specific enzymes, some of which have already been mentioned; others have been found by various authors. It remained, however, to establish the mechanism, by which the acetyl group is incorporated into the cycle. This important problem was solved by FRITZ ALBERT LIPMANN [b. 1899] and his school.

As pointed out in another connection the living organism is deriving the energy form sugar to some extent by splitting it into lactic acid [fermentation] but also–and more economically–through the further oxidation of the split products [respiration]. Lactic acid is then at first transferred into pyruvic or acetic acid. At the pyruvic stage, respiration branches off from fermentation, and Lipmann therefore devoted his interest to the vital oxidation of pyruvic acid. He found it completely dependent on the presence of inorganic phosphate and at first supposed that acetylphosphate is formed as an intermediate. It soon turned out, however, that the situation is more complicated. Studying the well known acetylation [= introduction of an acetyl group] of sulfanilamide, he observed that acetylphosphate did not furnish active acetate, whereas the organic compound adenosinetriphosphate was able to do so–it had already been found by D. Nachmansohn and A. L. Machado to be of importance for the synthesis of the 'neurohormone' acetylcholine [cp. p. 248].

When working with acetylphosphate Lipmann discovered a heat-stable factor which was present in all organs and necessary for biological acetylation. It belonged to the so-called coenzymes [cf. p. 210]; since it enables the transfer of acetyl groups [as well as other acid residues or acyls], it was called coenzyme.

A. Lipmann and his group produced the new coenzyme in pure form. They also settled in the main its chemical structure, though some details have been added by others. It contains adenylic acid [cp. p. 220], pantothenic acid–one of the B-vitamins, the function of which had until then remained obscure–and a derivative of the amino acid cysteine [with a sulphydryl group].

Coenzyme A is able to take up acyls in a labile form. Lynen has shown that this occurs at the sulphydryl groups. With the aid of the easily accessible energy in the acyl-coenzyme A compound, the activated acyls can be transferred to other substances. Special enzymes ['donor-enzymes'] make possible the coupling of acyl-coenzyme A, and others ['acceptor-enzymes'] the transfer of the activated acyl. The activation of acetic acid in this way and its subsequent reaction of the acyl with oxaloacetic acid under the formation of citric acid is only one example of the function of the coenzyme. The recently established fact that plants have no monopoly in taking up carbon dioxide from the air, but that those animal cells which are free from chlorophyll also are able to absorb and fix it [H. G. Wood and C. H. Werkman, 1935], is also explained by the action of coenzyme A. Other examples are the synthesis of acetylcholine and certain steroids [like cholesterol and the hormones of the adrenal cortex], lecithine and haemoglobin, as well as the storing of energy as adenosinetriphosphate. Coenzyme A occupies a key position in many vital processes. LIPMANN was awarded one half of the *1953* prize 'for his discovery of coenzyme A and its importance for intermediary metabolism'.

Great interest has been paid to cholesterol – discovered and isolated in 1815 by M. E. Chevreul. This lipid, with its four ring carbon skeleton, can be found in all cells in the body, and serves as mother substances for bile acids, vitamin D [see p. 231], sex hormones and the hormones of the adrenal cortex [see p. 226], and is also closely related to the glucosides in drugs obtained from Digitalis and used in heart therapy. The distinguished work on the constitution of cholesterol and its structural relation to the bile acids was honoured in 1928, when the 1928 and 1927 prizes in chemistry were given to A. Windaus and H. Wieland, respectively. Through Wieland's analyses and additional work by Rosenheim and King, the question of the total formula of cholesterol was cleared up in 1932. The way in which this vitally important substance is built up from smaller molecules available in the cell remained an open question, a question which, because of the complex tetracyclic molecule with its 27 carbon atoms, presented some exceptionally challenging problems, However, the biosynthesis is now known, and may briefly be described in the following way, starting with acetic acid. First, mevalonic is formed out of acetic acid. Isoprenoid units, derived from the mevalonic acid, combine to form two farnesyl pyrophosphate units, and these condense 'tail to tail' to form squalene, with 30 carbon atoms. Ring closure of this long-chained hydrocarbon results in lanosterol, with the characteristic tetracyclic steroid structure. Lanosterol still contains 30 carbons atoms. In an ensuing series of reactions, however, three methyl groups and the double bonds of lanos-

squalene, with 30 carbon atoms. Ring closure of this long-chained hydrocarbon results in lanosterol, with the characteristic tetracyclic steroid structure. Lanosterol still contains 30 carbons atoms. In an ensuing series of reactions, however, three methyl groups and the double bonds of lanosterol are eliminated, to be replaced by the 5,6 double bond in cholesterol.

The shaping of the tetracyclic ring system, by folding of a long chain precursor, had been tentatively proposed, and R. Robinson [Nobel laureate in chemistry 1947] had suggested that cholesterol may arise by cyclization of squalene. Experimental evidence was lacking, however, until KONRAD BLOCH [b. 1912] at Harvard and FEODOR LYNEN [b. 1911] in Munich began their work on the metabolism of acetic acid, leading to their discoveries concerning the building up of cholesterol and fatty acids. In a series of experiments with radioactive isotopes, Bloch and collaborators [1941–1949] showed that the two carbon atoms, as well as the hydrogen in deuterium-marked acetate, fed to animals, are used for the building up of cholesterol. Lynen, who about the same time was working in Wieland's laboratory on the acetate metabolism in yeast, isolated and showed the nature of the so-called activated acetic acid – a thiolester of co-enzyme A and acetic acid [acetyl co-enzyme A] – achievements of great significance, since the activated acetic acid is the precursor of all lipids in the body and the common denominator of a number of metabolic processes. The intermediate steps from acetate to squalene were elucidated through contributions from several research groups. Thus, K. Folkers and his group at Merck described a growth factor of *Lactobacillus acidophilus* [1956] which was found to be able to subsitute for acetate. It was called mevalonic acid, and was shown to be one of the intermediate substances for which one was searching. A crucial contribution was Lynen's demonstration of how mevalonic acid is formed with the aid of acetyl co-enzyme A. In connection with this work, Lynen also showed the mechanisms behind the action of the vitamin biotin in metabolism. Knowledge about the next step, i.e. from mevalonic acid to squalene, was obtained in the years 1957–61 thanks to work both by Bloch and Lynen and their groups, and by G. Popjak and J. W. Cornforth and their co-workers. Finally, Bloch and his group demonstrated the cyclization of squalene to lanosterol, and also showed how lanosterol is successively transformed into cholesterol. In *1964*, the Nobel Prize was awarded jointly to BLOCH and LYNEN 'for their discoveries concerning the mechanism and regulation of the cholesterol and fatty acid metabolism'.

If the muscle was so fastened that it could not shorten, its entire liberated energy was converted into heat, which could be measured by sensitive thermopiles attached to the muscle. By ARCHIBALD VIVIAN HILL [b. 1886] this method was made extremely accurate and so modified that it faithfully recorded the time-schedule of the heat production. In this way he was able to make the fundamental observation that only some of the heat [the 'initial' heat] is produced during the actual contraction and relaxation of the muscle, while the remainder, which is often more than one-half of the total amount, is evolved during some minutes after the twitches have ceased. This 'delayed' heat production did not appear at all if the muscle was put to work in pure nitrogen, while the 'initial' heat was not affected by this change of atmosphere. The conclusion was that the muscular activity process consists of a working phase which is indifferent to the oxygen supply and covers the entire mechanical action, and of a subsequent recovery phase, which requires oxygen. Hill and his associates then showed that corresponding conditions play an important part during hard muscular work in the human body. In many cases, the need for oxygen during a brief exertion is met almost entirely after the effort is over, which explains the subsequent heavy breathing. The capacity of the organism to carry such an oxygen debt which must be paid for afterwards varies considerably in different people and even in the same person according to his state of health. As long as the work is moderate, a 'steady state' may develop during which the oxygen requirements and the oxygen supply balance each other; the greater the capacity for physical work, the higher the limit for this state of balance usually lies. HILL received one-half of the *1922* prize in 1923 'for his discovery relating to the production of heat in the muscles.'

Hill's demonstration of two separate phases of muscular action gained increased importance from other observations concerning the chemical changes which take place during contraction, some of which had been made earlier and some at the same time. It was known, for instance, that lactic acid is formed in a muscle at work, and the factors which bring this about had been closely studied by W. M. Fletcher and F. G. Hopkins [1907]. They found that, in the absence of oxygen, lactic appears only gradually in a muscle at rest but rapidly in one at work, and in that case accumulates more and more until, reaching a concentration of a few tenths of one per cent, the muscle is no longer able to contract. If oxygen is then supplied, the accumulated lactic acid disappears. The quantitative relations were checked in 1920 by OTTO MEYERHOF [1884-1951], who observed that simultaneously with the accumulation of lactic acid there was a disappearance of a corresponding amount of glycogen, i.e. the compound carbohydrate which in animals plays the same role as starch does in plants. Therefore, it was natural to suppose that the glycogen had disintegrated into lactic acid and that a certain amount of heat had thereby been liberated. If, on the other hand, oxygen was supplied, the glycogen disappeared, too, but there was then no accumulation of lactic acid. Instead, an extra amount of carbon dioxide was given off, and an increased amount of oxygen consumed. It therefore seemed probable that in this case the lactic acid had been oxidized. A quantitative analysis revealed, however, the important fact that the increased oxygen consumption was sufficient to explain the combustion of only a minor part of the accumulated lactic acid. But since the latter had completely vanished, the only explanation left was that the remainder had been converted in some other way, and since at the same time the glycogen content was found to be correspondingly higher than it had been in the tests in an atmosphere of pure nitrogen, Meyerhof concluded that the extra glycogen must have been formed from the lactic acid. Consequently, he assumed [1] that during the contraction period the glycogen is broken down into lactic acid, [2] that the lactic acid is directly involved in the contraction process, and [3] that during the recovery period there is a re-synthesis of glycogen from the major portion of the lactic acid, the source of energy for this conversion being the complete combustion of the remaining, smaller portion of the lactic acid. With this assumption the findings of Hill regarding the generation of heat seemed to fit closely: during the contraction as well as during the realaxation period some heat is produced by the above-mentioned breakdown of glycogen, and the delayed production is explained by the fact that the oxidation of lactic acid does not take place until afterwards. After Meyerhof had made certain corrections, the quantitative figures, too, seemed to fit in with Hill's data. With Hill, MEYERHOF was given a share in the *1922* prize, one-half of which was awarded him 'for his discovery of the fixed relationship between the consumption of oxygen and the metabolism of lactic acid in muscle'.

The chemical action involved in muscular contraction is however, much more complicated. When work is performed there appears in the muscle not only lactic acid but also inorganic phosphoric acid. From juice pressed out of muscle, G. Embden was able to produce a substance, lactacidogen, or hexose-diphosphoric acid, from which both lactic acid and, at the same time phosphoric acid could be liberated through enzymatic action. Meyerhof, therefore, accepted the interpretation that, during its conversion, the glycogen first causes the formation of sugar [hexose] which, in turn, is combined with the phosphoric acid ['phosphorylated'] into hexose-diphosphoric acid. From this substance, lactic acid would then be formed. Embden also noted that a considerable part of the lactic acid formation takes place after the muscular contraction, and since he furthermore felt that he had found support for the assumption that during the actual contraction period the muscular reaction becomes alkaline instead of acid, he could not agree with Meyerhof in attributing to the lactic acid the decisive role in the muscular contraction process itself. Furthermore, other workers discovered a couple of additional organic phosphoric acid compounds in muscle; namely, creatine-phosphoric acid, or phosphagen, and adenosine-triphosphoric acid [ATP]. The first of these is a compound of phosphoric acid and creatine, while the second, as indicated by the name, contains three molecules of phosphoric acid and also adenosine, which, in turn, contains a purine base [cf. p. 200]. If one phosphoric acid group is eliminated from the adenosine-triphosphoric acid, adenosine-diphosphoric acid [ADP] results; if two are removed, adenosine- monophosphoric acid or adenylic acid is produced.

The organic phosphoric-acid compounds attracted particular interest when E. Lundsgaard discovered [1929] that poisoning by mono-iodo-acetic acid, which completely prevents the formation of lactic acid, does not inhibit muscular contraction, though exhaustion then results much more quickly than under normal circumstances. The contraction process is accompanied, however, by a reduction in the phosphagen content. Physiologically phosphagen, identified as N-phosphoryl-creatinine, gives rise to phosphate suitable to be transferred into ADP to form ATP. In the years following upon Lundsgaard's important finding and the debate between the Meyerhof and Embden schools, several of the major questions concerning the mechanisms of muscle contraction were solved. Muscle contains the proteins myosin and actin, joined in a complex called actomyosin. ATP is the immediate source of energy for muscle contraction and enters into specific interaction with the myofibrillar proteins causing actomyosin to contract. The shortening of the contractile elements appears to be brought about by a sliding of the myosin filaments over the actin filaments. Discoveries of importance for the understanding of these different mechanisms were made by several research workers, among whom should be mentioned W. A. Engelhardt and M. N. Ljubimova in U.S.S.R.; A. Szent Gyorgui, F. and G. T. Cori in the United States; A. F. Huxley, J. Hanson and H. E. Huxley in Britain.

It seemed likely that the cyclical processes in muscular activities which had received special attention continued also during periods of rest, so that the contraction of a muscle could be regarded as an intensified form of the conversion of energy that takes place when there is no apparent activity. The specific details of what happens when glycogen is changed into sugar, and vice versa, have been thoroughly studied by CARL F. [b. 1896] and GERTY T. CORI [1896–1957]. They were able to produce from muscle an ester of hexose-phosphoric acid which in some respects differed from the one already known [Embden's ester of hexose-diphosphoric acid, which is really a mixture of the esters of fructose- and glucose-phosphoric acids]. They also succeeded in showing that the new compound differed from the earlier one in that the phosphoric acid was linked to the sugar near carbon atom 1, while in the older compound it came next to carbon atom 6. The new substance, now known as the 'Cori ester,' was found in all the tissues investigated. In the presence of muscle extract it is quickly changed to the 6-ester, but the process requires, partly, the presence of magnesium and, partly, a special enzyme, phosphoglucomutase. After having made clear in great detail the requirements for the different subsidiary reactions, the two Coris were able to reverse the process. After the phosphoglucomutase had been destroyed in the presence of phosphorylase, an enzyme that causes phosphoric acid to be split off, they could build up glycogen from Cori ester with release of phosphoric acid. Small quantities of glycogen had to be present in order to bring about the synthesis. This requirement seems to be explained by the fact that glycogen is made up of short chains with many ramifications, at the end of which additional sugar molecules can be accumulated. The reaction between the Cori ester and the 6-ester could also be made to work in both directions, and when, finally, two of Cori's associates were able to convert glucose into a glucose-6-phosphoric acid ester, the entire glycogen synthesis process became clear. The phosphorylase enzyme which is necessary for the transformation of glycogen into Cori in two different forms. With the aid of one of them, it was possible to synthesize starch, which, unlike glycogen, has long, unramified chains, though in this process the assistance of still another enzyme was required.

C. F. and G. T. Cori were also able to throw light on the effect of the hormone found in the anterior lobe of the pituitary gland, and of insulin on the conversion of sugar. An addition of pituitary gland extract retarded the synthesis of the hexose-6-phosphate ester, while this action was offset or neutralized by insulin. An extract of the adrenal cortex strenghtened the effect of the pituitary gland extract. This gland must, therefore, give off a hormone which, either by itself or in conjunction with the hormone of the adrenal cortex, prevents the phosphorylation of sugar – an action that is blocked by insulin. One-half of the *1947* prize was awarded to C. F. and G. T. CORI jointly 'for their discovery of how glycogen is catalytically converted'.

The metabolism of carbohydrates has been further elucidated by L. F. Leloir and his school, who discovered coenzymes containing glucose, phosphate and uridine [which is one of the purine bases mentioned above combined with ribose]. These 'uridylcoenzymes' are engaged in the biosynthesis of glucose and glycogen, as well as of numerous other carbohydrates, among them the galactose which is one of the two components of the disaccharide lactose or milk sugar [the other half is glucose]. One of the uridylcoenzymes is responsible for the formation of di- and polysaccharides from simpler carbohydrates [monosaccharides] and also for the reversible transformation of galactose into glucose. This was the starting point for another important contribution by H. M. Kalckar and his school, which has shed new light on a rare inborn disease, the galactosemia, in which grave symptoms, such as vomiting, diarrhea, icterus, cataract and psychical debility appear shortly after birth if the child is given milk. If this continues for some time, usually death ensues or grave psychical defects develop. Kalckar et al. found that, in contrast to normal erythrocytes, erythrocytes from patients suffering from the disease accumulated galactose from a medium containing this carbohydrate. This was due to the complete absence of the specific enzyme that causes the transformation of galactose to glucose. In the liver a great reduction of the enzyme also was observed. It is now possible to find out fairly simply whether a child has the disease [e.g. if it runs in the family], and thus to protect it by a diet from which lactose and galactose have been excluded.

HORMONES

During the twentieth century our knowledge of internal secretion both in healthy and in diseased organisms has been greatly increased. For the active substances secreted by the ductless or endocrine glands into the bloodstream or the tissue fluids, W. M. Bayliss and E. H. Starling coined, in 1904, the term hormones. Shortly before that [1902] they had identified one hormone as causing an increased flow of pancreatic juice when the acid contents of the stomach enter the duodenum. Although previously observed, this had been regarded as a reflex reaction, inasmuch as the hydrochloric acid was supposed to stimulate the nerve endings of the intestinal mucous membrane and thus cause increased activity in the pancreas. Byliss and Starling, however, were able to show that from the intestinal mucous membrane the hydrochloric acid releases a specific substance, which they called secretin. When injected into the blood-plasma, it directly stimulates the pancreas. This discovery was found by the Nobel Committee examiner to deserve a prize [1913, 1914], but at that time the First World War intervened and caused a suspension of the prize-awards. When Starling was again nominated in 1926, the discovery was regarded as too old.

The *1909* prize was awarded to THEODOR KOCHER [1841-1917] 'for his work on the physiology, pathology and surgery of the thyroid gland.' A prize-award in this field to a Swiss scientist was connected with the fact that *thyroid* diseases, including enlargement of the gland [goitre or struma], were especially common in Switzerland. Surgeons often had to remove larger or smaller portions of the organ. Kocher perfected the surgical technique employed, so that the operation, previously risky and dreaded, could now be performed with a minimum of immediate danger. In an operation on a girl who had had the entire thyroid gland removed, it was found, however, that certain serious mental symptoms subsequently appeared, similar to those usually found in cretins. This directed Kocher's attention to the problem, especially as J. L. Reverdin informed him that he had observed two patients whose mental powers had decreased after the complete removal of the thyroid gland. A check-up by Kocher showed that all patients in whom only a part of the thyroid had been taken out were well, while of the eighteen who had been deprived of the entire gland, no fewer than sixteen suffered in various degrees from a number of symptoms, such as faintness, anaemia, coarsened skin and loss of hair, accompanied by gradual mental deterioration, sometimes resulting in cretinism. Since these severe after-effects almost always occurred after a complete removal of the thyroid, Kocher concluded that part of it ought to be left in the body. He likewise pointed out that, while cretinism is often caused by the absence of the thyroid, whether congenital or due to an operation, it can also be traced to a goitre which has rendered the gland incapable of functioning. If the disturbances occur in young people, serious inhibition of growth, as well as the mental defects, may ensue while in adults the former effect naturally, does not appear. Kocher's investigations thus proved that the thyroid plays a part in internal secretion. By injecting juice from this gland, and later by simply administering dried thyroid, it became possible to check the symptoms just described. Attempts to produce the hormone in a pure state led, among other things, to the proof that iodine is one of its significant constituents. Not until 1914, however, did E. C. Kendall succeed in isolating the hormone, or rather the constituent of it which brings about the effect – a substance he called thyroxin. Its structure was determined, partly by Kendall himself, and partly by C. R. Harington [1926], whereupon the definitive synthesis was made by Harington and G. Barger [1926].

That the *pancreas*, in addition to its function of supplying the intestine with one of the digestive juices, is also the source of an internal secretion, was shown in 1890 by J. von Mering's and O. Minkowski's classical experiment. They found that a complete removal of the organ causes a serious form of diabetes, while this does not happen if a piece of the gland is implanted under the skin. Proposals for a Nobel Prize were made as early as 1902 and were later repeated, but for some unknown reason were never submitted to a special investigation. The discovery would otherwise seem to have conformed in high degree with Nobel's testamentary stipulations.

The credit for having produced the pancreatic hormone in a practical available form goes to FREDERICK BANTING [1891-1941], C. H. Best and JOHN MACLEOD [1876-1935]. Banting assumed that earlier failures had been due to the fact that trypsin, the protein-splitting pancreatic enzyme, destroys the hormone. In 1901, L. V. Sobolev had shown that a ligature of the pancreatic duct results in destruction of the enzyme-secreting parts, while the other, island-like accumulations of cells, 'islands of Langerhans', which were believed to produce the hormone, remained intact. Hence it should be possible, Banting thought, to extract the hormone in a perfect state after closing the duct of the gland. The experiments were carried out by Banting and Best in Macleod's laboratory, and proved successful; in January, 1922, they could report that, even in human diabetes, injections of insulin, as the new substance was called, reduced the high sugar content of the blood and relieved the general toxic symptoms. Subsequent tests in various places soon demonstrated the great value of insulin in combating the manifestations of diabetes. When the Nobel Prize was awarded in *1923* to BANTING and MACLEOD 'for the discovery of insulin', the stipulation in Nobel's will that prizes should be given for a benefit rendered 'during the preceding year' was, for once, followed to the letter.

The prize-jury has been blamed, rightly enough, for two reasons: it had included Macleod, despite the fact that he had taken no active part in the work, and in fact had been away when the decisive experiment was made; and it had failed to give Best his due share of the honour. Banting expressed his dissatisfaction by sharing his half of the prize with Best, whereupon Macleod gave a corresponding part of his to J. B. Collip, who had collaborated with him in the purification and standardization of insulin.

The laborious nature of the projects had led Banting to seek permission to work in Macleod's laboratory. Owing to the latter's experience in the field, it was well-equipped for the purpose. The work was also facilitated by the previous introduction of convenient methods for determining the sugar content of the blood. Since, furthermore, the first publication on insulin, based on a lecture before the American Physiological Society, bore the names of Banting, Best and Mcleod, there seemed to be good reason for including the last-named in the award. Although it would have been right to include Best among the prize-winners, this was not formally possible, since no one had nominated him – a circumstance which probably gave the Committee a wrong impression of the importance of Best's share in the discovery.

In 1926, J. J. Abel produced insulin in crystalline form. Later advances in this field include the introduction of protamine insulin by H. C. Hagedorn, in 1936. By combining insulin with a basic protein substance, he produced a compound out of which insulin is slowly absorbed by the blood and which consequently, requires less frequent injections than ordinary insulin.

The detailed structure of the insulin molecule was established by F. SANGER, who received the *1958* Chemistry Prize.

The *pituitary gland*, or hypophysis, especially its anterior lobe, has been described as an organ controlling the entire internal secretion, because it produces a large number of hormones, which, by affecting other organs of internal secretion, such as the thyroid, the adrenals, the pancreas and the sex glands, are able to influence their activities to a marked degree. That the pancreas function is influenced by the pituitary gland was indicated by the observation that elimination of sugar from the kidneys usually accompanies the morbid hyperactivity of the pituitary gland which is supposed to be the cause of acromegaly, an ailment resulting in an abnormal enlargement of the face, hands and feet [P. Marie, 1886]. In 1924, BERNARDO HOUSSAY [b. 1887] found that animals whose pituitary glands had been removed became hypersensitive to insulin to such a degree that even small doses considerably reduced the sugar content of the blood. By injecting pituitary extract he was able to offset this extreme reaction to insulin. Houssay then proved that this influence emanates from its anterior lobe. In diabetes, after the pancreas had been removed, the symptoms can be considerably relieved by removing the pituitary as well. Together with A. Biasotti, Houssay also found [1931] that, by injecting sufficient quantities of pituitary extract, it was possible to produce diabetes in test animals. The reason is that the cells in the pancreas which produce insulin are destroyed. These investigations were considered to be of sufficient importance to justify the award, in *1947*, of one-half of the Nobel Prize to HOUSSAY 'for his discovery of the part played by the hormone of the anterior pituitary lobe in the metabolism of sugar'. The other half was given to C. F. and G. T. CORI, whose investigations had revealed the mechanism by which the hormone of the anterior pituitary lobe produces the above effect [see p. 222].

Severe disturbances in the adrenals are the cause of the rare Addison's disease, formerly always lethal. Numerous experiments have shown that it is the *adrenal cortex* which is vital. Attempts to obtain from it substances having a protective effect against Addison's disease, or against the symptoms produced by a surgical removal of the adrenal glands, were at first only partially successful. In 1927, F. A. Hartman was able to extract an active substance from the cortex [cortin], but the method was not dependable. In 1929, W. W. Swingle and J. J. Pfiffner improved the extraction technique, and successful treatments of Addison's patients with cortin were reported in 1931. These investigations can, however, only be regarded as preliminary steps towards the real production in pure form of the hormone, or rather hormones, since a large number of closely related hormones belonging to the sterol group have been found.

Great progress was made through the works of EDWARD KENDALL [b. 1886]. TADEUS REICHSTEIN [b. 1897] and their collaborators. In all, about 30 cortin substances have been isolated, and their chemical structure has been elucidated. The task of distinguishing between these chemically closely related substances has been fraught with immense difficulties, as they are found in the cortex in extremely small quantities and readily form mixed crystals. At least six of the substances have proved to be more or less active on animals whose adrenals had been removed. Half of these were first isolated by Reichstein and a fourth by Kendall. Yet another was first produced by Reichstein, by a semi-synthetic method, from a derivative of bile acid. It is a valuable remedy in Addison's disease and certain other cases of reduced function of the cortex. One more active component – the so-called compound E, or cortisone – was isolated at four different laboratories, among them Kendall's and Reichstein's. Reichstein definitely established the steroid nature of the cortin substances. Thus they are closely related to sex hormones, vitamin D and bile acids, as well as to the active principle in Digitalis leaves or Strophantus seeds. [see p. 216]. The active cortical hormones, which chemically differ from each other very little, are characterized by, among other things, a double bond in the steroid skeleton which is necessary for the biological effects. They are all built up of 21 carbon atoms, but the number of oxygens atoms in the molecule is 3, 4 or 5. The position of the additional oxygen atoms in the molecules was first established by Reichstein and Kendall, thus opening the way for semi-synthetic production.

Largerly owing to the work of Kendall and his school, it has emerged that the comparatively inconsiderable dissimilarities in the cortical hormones structure are accompanied by material differences in their effect.

Great interest was paid to compound E or cortisone. PHILIP HENCH [1896-1965] had observed that the symptoms of chronic rheumatoid arthritis are often alleviated during pregnancy, as well as during jaundice. In both these cases there is an increase in the amount of steroids in the body –namely, female sex hormone and bile acids, respectively. It seemed possible that the adrenal cortex, by one or more of its numerous steroids, might also influence such symptoms, and the production of cortisone in sufficient amounts offered an opportunity to test this hypothesis. Hench, Kendall, C. H. Slocumb and H. F. Polley [1949] showed that, after small doses of cortisone, patients suffering from chronic rheumatoid arthritis were dramatically improved after only a few days. Cortisone was also tried with some success in other diseases which are relieved by jaundice and pregnancy or which involve essentially the same histological types of tissue [muscular, fibrous, collagenous] that are affected in rheumatoid arthritis as well as in certain allergic conditions. Similar results were obtained with ACTH [Adreno-Cortico-Tropic Hormone], a substance produced by the anterior lobe of the pituitary gland and known to stimulate the adrenal cortex. Thanks to the work of H. M. Evans and C. H. Li, it was available in pure form. Unfortunately, the improvement after cortisone or ACTH did not last, and the continuous administration led to certain disagreeable side actions. This greatly reduces the practical value of the new treatment. The discovery of the effect of cortisone on chronic rheumatoid arthritis has, however, led to a better understanding of this illness and is thus an important step forward. The close relationship between the progress made with regard to the purification and nature of the cortin substances and their effects made it natural that the Nobel Prize for *1950* should be awarded jointly to HENCH, KENDALL and REICHSTEIN 'for their discoveries relating to the hormones of the adrenal cortex, their structure and biological effects'.

VITAMINS

The vitamins are closely related to the hormones and, like them, play an important rôle in metabolism, particularly as members of certain enzymatic systems. Although the dividing line between the two categories fluctuates, it is customary to stress as an important difference the fact that, while hormones can be formed inside the body, vitamins must be introduced from without. If they are not supplied in sufficient quantities with the food, certain deficiency symptoms may appear. It was through the study of the latter that the importance of vitamins was clearly demonstrated. While working on beriberi, a serious illness prevalent in certain areas, CHRISTIAAN EIJKMAN [1858–1930] made his famous discovery, in 1897, that corresponding symptoms may be found in fowl which have been fed on polished rice, and also that the effects can be counteracted by adding rice-bran to the feed; that is to say, by restoring the very parts removed by the polishing. Consequently, rice-bran must contain a protective element, and further investigations showed that beriberi in human beings could also be prevented or cured by the same means. At first, Eijkman supposed that the disease was caused by poisoning, and that the poison, which he hunted for in vain, was probably counteracted by a protective element in the bran. In 1901, however, G. Grijns showed that rice-bran contains certain substances necessary for the protection of health – a conclusion endorsed by Eijkman.

Next to Eijkman's investigations, the experiments of FREDERICK GOWLAND HOPKINS [1861–1947] provided the foundations for our knowledge of vitamins. Careful tests with growing rats placed on a diet which, in addition to the necessary salts, consisted of a purified mixture of fat, starch, and protein, revealed [1906, 1909] that after a while the test animals ceased to grow. If a small quantity of milk was added to the feed, the growth was resumed. The milk ration was too insignificant, however, to have any effect as far as an increase in energy was concerned. From his experiments, which were not published in complete detail until 1912, Hopkins concluded that milk contains one or several substances sufficient, even in extremely small quantities, to make growth possible, probably by a catalytic or stimulating action. As a matter of fact, similar observations had been made as early as about 1880, but had then been questioned or remained unnoticed until again brought to light some thirty years later.

When, in 1917, Eijkman's contributions were first submitted to a special investigation, the examiner's attitude was hesitant, partly because of their age. Although it was conceded that Eijkman had opened up a new field of research and that his discoveries had been of great practical value, this attitude was maintained during the next few years. The author of the 1929 report [G. Liljestrand] expressed the opinion that this was a situation covered by the provision in the statutes that older works could also be considered for an award, if their importance had only recently been demonstrated. The value of Eijkman's contribution had been re-emphasized by Hopkin's recent investigations, which had also been proposed for an award that year, as well as by a number of still more recent experiments inspired by these two scientists. Accordingly, the faculty unanimously decided to award one-half of the *1929* prize to EIJKMAN 'for his discovery of the anti-neuritic vitamin' and the other half to HOPKINS 'for his discovery of the growth-stimulating vitamins'.

In fact, as was shown more especially by E. V. McCollum and M. Davis [1913], the growth-promoting effect of milk, demonstrated by Hopkins, depended on two factors, one of which, called *vitamin A*, was soluble in fats, while the other, *vitamin B*, was soluble only in water. In 1918–20, E. Mellanby proved that rickets, or rachitis, is also a deficiency ailment due to the lack of a vitamin soluble in fats. He was able to produce artificial rickets in young dogs by keeping them on a diet containing only a small amount of fats. On the other hand, the symptoms failed to appear if a milk-fat, or better still, cod liver oil, was added. McCollum and his co-workers then found that the antirachitic effect was due to a special, previously unknown substance, vitamin D [see below]. On several occasions the works of both Mellanby and McCollum were declared to merit a prize, but each time other subjects happened to be judged more important than vitamin research.

Vitamin B has been found to consist of a mixture of several different vitamins, as J. Goldberger was the first to prove. Among the different compounds, B_1 or thiamin, which is identical with the substance which gives protection against beriberi, has been shown to be the cornerstone in the coenzyme which participates in building up puruvic acid in the Krebs cycle [see p. 214].

To the group of vitamins soluble in water belongs also the antiscorbutic substance, *vitamin* C, identified in 1907 by A. Holst and T. Frölich, who were able to produce symptoms in guinea-pigs resembling those of scurvy. In 1910, Frölich found that Barlow's disease, which occurs in children, is likewise due to a lack of vitamin C. Holst's and Frölich's experiments, however, were so closely connected with Eijkman's work that, when Frölich was nominated in 1938 [Holst had died in 1931], a special investigation did not seem to be sufficiently motivated. As regards the nature of vitamin C, A. von Szent-Györgyi and J. L. Svirbely have shown [1927] that it is identical with the highly reducing ascorbic acid obtained from the cortex of the suprarenal gland or from certain vegetable substances. This finding was confirmed by a number of other scientists, and the substance's chemical composition has also been clarified. Szent-Györgyi has likewise connected vitamin C with the biological combustion processes, and received the 1937 Nobel Prize in Physiology or Medicine [see p. 213].

The nature of the antirachitic vitamin soluble in fats was elucidated by a number of investigations. In 1919, K. Huldschinsky showed that exposure to ultraviolet rays prevented rickets in children and could bring about cures after the disease had broken out. In 1924, two different groups of scientists, H. Steenbock and his collaborators, on the one hand, and A. F. Hess and his colleagues, on the other, discovered that the antirachitic effect could also be obtained by exposing, not the animals themselves, but merely their food to ultraviolet rays. Since it was known from earlier experiments that vitamin D resists saponification and is therefore found in a fraction of the fats in which cholesterol [see p. 217] is the main ingredient, tests were made to ascertain whether cholesterol, too, could be made antirachitic by irradiation. Both of the two groups of scientists mentioned above and, almost simultaneously, O. Rosenheim and T. A. Webster, found this to be the case. The two last-named then discovered that the substance that became active in this respect was an impurity in the cholesterol. On this subject Rosenheim and Hess then began to work with A. Windaus. With the assistance of J. Phol, Windaus was finally able to show that *vitamin D* is produced by the irradiation of a so-called pro-vitamin, ergosterol, and he was also able to clarify the structure of the vitamin [1927]. The following year, Huldschinsky, Steenbock, Hess and Windaus were proposed for the Nobel Prize. The examiner came to the conclusion that while the discovery of the antirachitic provitamin was the greatest advance in vitamin research since its beginning, the credit was shared by so many scientists that there were insurmountable obstacles to an award. That same year, however, Windaus received the Nobel Prize in Chemistry 'for the services rendered through his research into the constitution of the sterols and their connection with the vitamins'. In this way the culminating discovery in the field of vitamin research was honoured.

The anti-sterility vitamin, or *vitamin E*, is another substance that is soluble in fats. The credit for its discovery belongs essentially to H. M. Evans and his collaborators. While earlier observations [1920] had indicated that rats fed on an apparently adequate diet became sterile, Evans and K. S. Bishop [1922] were the first to be able to remedy this condition by making certain additions to the basic diet. Later on, 1925, Evans and G. O. Burr obtained highly active preparations, whereupon Evans and his associates produced the active element in pure form and also determined its structure.

While experimenting in 1929 with chicks fed on a certain diet, HENRIK DAM [b. 1895] observed that severe haemorrhages occurred under the skin or between the muscles, and that the blood coagulated more slowly than normally. Dam then found that no addition of any known vitamins to the feed had any effect. In 1935, however, he was able to prevent the haemorrhages with the aid of a substance soluble in fats, which he called coagulation vitamin, or *vitamin K*. In the subsequent work of producing the active substance in pure form, a number of scientists in different countries took part, chiefly H. J. Almquist, Dam, EDWARD DOISY [b. 1893], L. F. Fieser and P. Karrer. In 1939, Karrer and his school, in collaboration with

Dam and Doisy with his associates, succeeded in isolating vitamin K and also in determining its structure, whereupon it was synthetized, also simultaneously, in four different laboratories, among them Doisy's. His group also discovered and produced in pure form another vitamin, K_2, which, although it is of a slightly different composition, has the same effect. Dam and his co-workers, above all F. Schönheyder, were also able to explain the mechanism by which vitamin K achieves its results. The coagulation of the blood is due to the transformation of a protein contained in it into a close network of fibrin, in whose meshes the blood corpuscles are caught. This transformation is caused by the action of an enzyme, thrombin, which in turn is derived from a precursor, prothrombin, with the aid of thromboplastin, a substance liberated from the injured cells. The lack of vitamin K was found to cause a drop in the prothrombin content, while a rapid increase occurred after addition of the vitamin. Obviously, vitamin K exerts a direct influence on the formation of the precursor of the enzyme required for the coagulation. Vitamin K soon came to be used extensively as a remedy for conditions caused by reduced prothrombin content in the blood, such as certain infections of the bile ducts, the liver, or the intestines, and characterized by a reduced capacity to absorb fats. It also proved useful in preventing haemorrhages in newborn infants. Such haemorrhages are not seldom due to a distinct lack of prothrombin and are often serious, even fatal. The treatment with vitamin K was, therefore, a great therapeutic advance.

Since the new discoveries had shed additional light on the process of coagulation and had also had important practical results, the Caroline Institute decided in 1944 to award one-half of the *1943* Prize to DAM 'for his discovery of vitamin K' and the other half to DOISY 'for his discovery of the chemical nature of vitamin K'.

To the category of vitamins can be added a substance that is active against pernicious anaemia, a disease which previously had almost invariably been fatal. GEORGE WHIPPLE [b. 1878] and his associates had made a close study of the influence of food on the formation of new blood in dogs. Chronic anaemia was maintained after an initial bleeding by repeated minor blood tappings, so that the percentage of haemoglobin, or red pigment, in the blood was kept at about one-third of the normal figure. From the amount of haemoglobin regularly drawn off, a direct indication was obtained as to the amount of new blood that had been formed. The animals were fed with a bread rich in vitamins, and which also contained proteins, carbohydrates, fats and salts. Among the various additions to the diet, liver, kidneys, meat, and also certain fruits, such as apricots, proved particularly effective. When the dogs were on the standard diet, an acute blood shortage was remedied in from four to seven weeks; but by adding to the diet a liberal amount of boiled liver, the time could be shortened from two to four weeks. When the technique of repeated bleedings was used, even greater differences could be observed. Other viscera than liver and kidney also had a beneficial, albeit a less marked effect.

The results obtained by Whipple and his associates led GEORGE MINOT [1885–1950] and WILLIAM MURPHY [b. 1892] to investigate whether a diet rich in liver would have any effect on pernicious anaemia in man. The results exceeded all expectations. In their very first publication [1926], Minot and Murphy were able to report on forty-five cases of pernicious anaemia favourably affected. Repeated tests proved conclusively that, by administering large quantities of liver, the symptoms of pernicious anaemia can be made to vanish. After only a few days' treatment, the number of immature blood corpuscles goes up, indicating an increased activity in the bone-marrow where the red cells are formed; soon the number of blood corpuscles increases until gradually it may reach the normal amount; while the abnormal types of corpuscles, usually characteristic of the disease begin simultaneously to disappear. If liver is administered in sufficient quantities, there is also often a recession of the nervous symptoms that sometimes accompany the advanced stages of pernicious anaemia. In this way an invariably successful, symptomatic remedy for a disease previously which had defied all other efforts, was found. In view of the close relationship between the experiments on dogs and the treatment of pernicious anaemia in human beings, the Caroline Institute decided to award the *1934* prize jointly to WHIPPLE, MINOT and MURPHY 'for their discoveries concerning liver therapy in cases of anaemia'.

K. A. Folkers and his collaborators have been able to show, simultaneously with an English research team under the leadership of L. Smith, that the anti-pernicious substance consists of vitamin B_{12}, which contains cobalt and is extremely effective. On the basis of X-ray crystalline studies, D. Crowfoot-Hodgkin succeeded in determining the detailed structure of B_{12}, an achievement which mainly falls within the field of chemistry, and in *1964* Dorothy Crowfoot-Hodgkin was awarded the chemistry prize 'for her determinations by X-ray techniques of the structures of important biochemical substances'.

DIGESTION – CIRCULATION OF THE BLOOD–RESPIRATION

Throughout the early 1900's, IVAN PETROVITČ PAVLOV [1849–1936] was repeatedly nominated for the Nobel Prize in Physiology or Medicine. For years his work and his collaborators' work had been adding to our knowledge of the composition and *secretion of the digestive juices*. These scientists had worked out methods by which they were able to extract the digestive fluids from the body without an admixture of food, while at the same time maintaining relatively normal physiological conditions. In this way, for instance, saliva, gastric juice, bile, pancreatic and intestinal fluids could be drawn off through permanently installed fistulas, i.e. artificial passages from the internal organs to the surface of the body, and, by the insertion of a similar tube into the oesophagus, the food itself could be withdrawn after having been swallowed ['fictitious or sham feeding']. In other experiments the natural passage between the oesophagus and the stomach was kept open, while, without interfering either with the innervation or the blood supply, a minor portion of the stomach was closed off, and another fistula was then inserted into it. In this part the gastric juice continued to flow as in the rest of the stomach, thus making possible direct observation of the digestive processes under various conditions.

By such methods Pavlov and his pupils had found that the secretion of gastric juice can be started by the mere sight or smell of food. If the latter is appetizing, 'the mouth waters', and in a few seconds a corresponding 'appetite juice' begins to flow in the stomach. By means of impulses sent along the nerves to the salivary and gastric glands, the cerebral cortex starts the secretion, after receiving news from the sense organs that food is on the way. This action is due to the acquired or developed reflexes commonly called 'conditioned'. The food could also start secretions, it was observed, even after it had entered the mouth or the stomach, but such reactions varied according to the nature of the nourishment. Pavlov assumed that this chemical phase of the gastric secretion was due to a local reflex, because the process went on as before after the vagus nerve, which connects the stomach with the central nervous system, had been severed. More recent research has indicated, however, that the reaction may be caused by one or several hormones. Pavlov also proved that the intestinal juice contains an enzymatic substance which increases the power of the pancreatic juice to digest proteins. Clearly, these discoveries were of fundamental importance, and during the special investigation conducted for the Nobel Committee, it was also brought out that Pavlov had made use of the saliva flow as a clue to mental phenomena.

Although Pavlov's and his associate's observations had been published over a period of several years, they had, in the main, only appeared in Russian; and it was not until 1898 that a comprehensive summary became available in other languages; their importance, therefore, could be said to have been only recently realized. The faculty decided to award the prize for *1904* to PAVLOV 'in recognition of his work on the physiology of gestion, through which knowledge on vital aspects of the subject has been transformed and enlarged'.

Pavlov's concept of conditioned reflexes, mentioned above, has been of basic importance in the study of higher central nervous functions. If the feeding of dogs was accompanied by some form of sensory stimulation which did not elicit salivary secretion, such as flashes of light or certain sounds, and the combination was repeated often enough, the stimulus alone gradually became sufficient to bring about a secretion of saliva. In the central nervous system of the dogs 'new functional paths had been opened' which conveyed the conditioned reflexes thus developed. If salivary secretion ensued, they were described as positive. It was also possible to check the flow of saliva thus developed by the use of suitable new stimuli, which caused an inhibition or negative conditioned reflex. With the aid of conditioned reflexes, excitation and inhibition in the brain were studied, and in this way functional aspects of sleep, alertness, and various kinds of neuroses were obtained. The method has also been used to determine the ability of test animals to differentiate between various kinds of stimuli, such as tones with small intervals, and also to study the localization in the cerebral cortex. On the strength of his works on conditioned reflexes, Pavlov was again nominated for an award [1925 and later], but their significance had long since become obvious, they were not submitted to a special investigation.

Several nominations for prizes in physiology or medicine have referred to investigations of the *circulation of the blood* and the factors connected with it. Our understanding of the heart's mode of action was enormously improved by the introduction of a new and practical method of recording the slight variations in the electrical potentials generated by the heart and transmitted to various parts of the body: the electrocardiogram.

As early as the beginning of the 1880's, a method had been devised to record these potential changes, but, because, of the slow-acting instrument [the capillary electrometer], deformed recordings were obtained. WILLEM EINTHOVEN [1860–1927] felt the need of an instrument capable of recording the actual time relations of the electrocardiogram, and for that purpose he constructed the string galvanometer [1903], which he gradually improved [1906–21]. In the field between two stationary magnets he suspended a slender, silver-coated quartz wire to which the potential changes were transmitted in one of several different ways [from the right to the left hand, lead I; from the right hand to the left foot, lead II; from the left hand to the left foot, lead III]. Because of the magnetic tension between the poles, the quartz wire vibrated in different degrees according to the strength of the electric current passing through it, and these deviations were then enlarged and recorded. The instrument soon became widely used and for a long time was a part of the standard equipment of every sizeable hospital until various technical improvements made it possible to construct a more practical apparatus.

As early as 1906, Einthoven had been able to report that disturbances in the heart activity result in distinct changes in the electrocardiogram. For a detailed analysis it was necessary to have a complete interpretation of a normal electrocardiogram, and here too, Einthoven led the way [1908–13]. He assumed that the systole [contraction process] of the heart and the resulting negativity spread through the cardiac muscle like a wave. The curve in the electrocardiogram is determined partly by the starting-point of the impulse which makes the heart contract and, partly, by the course taken by the wave in passing through the heart. It was known that the impulse originates at the entrance of the superior vena cava into the right auricle, and from there passes through the latter and the left auricle before being conveyed by a special impulse-transmission system on the inside of the two chambers [ventricles] to their respective muscular walls. According to Einthoven, the first negative deflection in the electrocardiogram, the 'p wave', is caused by the excitation passing through the auricles, while the strong subsequent negativity [the 'QRS-complex'] indicates the spread of the excitation wave through the walls of the ventricles. Einthoven called attention to the changes in the entire electrocardiogram when transfers are made from one lead to another, and he showed that variations in the strengths and directions of the resulting potential, the heart's 'electrical axis', can be determined from the synchronous recordings of the three assumed leads.

By means of refined experiments on animals, Einthoven's interpretation was confirmed by T. Lewis [1914–16], and important observations made by him and other scientists threw additional light on the value of electrocardiography in the analysis of pathological heart symptoms.

When Einthoven's work was first submitted to special investigations [1913–17], it was questioned whether the construction of an instrument should be honoured with a prize in physiology or medicine. Such achievements seemed to fall more appropriately under the head of physics. The opinion changed, however, after Einthoven had clarified the main characteristics of the mechanism involved in the electrocardiogram, and after its clinical use had produced valuable practical results. In *1924*, accordingly, EINTHOVEN received the prize 'for his discovery of the mechanism of the electrocardiogram'.

The heart acts like two pumps working synchronously. By one of these 'pumps', the left heart, the blood is driven into the aorta; it is then kept in motion under the influence of a pressure which drives it ahead through the ever smaller arterial blood vessels in all parts of the body; then through the capillaries; and, finally, via the veins back to the right heart [the systemic circulation]. This in turn presses the blood further through the extended network of the lungs to the left heart [the lesser circulation]. The work of the heart is mainly determined by the pressure to be overcome and by the amount of blood to be forwarded. It is of fundamental importance to know each of these two factors. The pressure relations in the auricles and ventricles of the heart were recorded in the horse as early as 1863 by A. Chauveau and E. Marey, after the introduction of narrow tubes into the cavities from the large vessels in the neck. In 1870, A. Fick pointed out that the total blood flow through the lungs could be calculated by dividing the oxygen uptake per minute by the oxygen difference between the arterial and the mixed venous blood entering the right heart ['minute volume of the heart'], and this principle has often been applied in experiments on animals. In man the systemic arterial blood pressure is usually measured without arterial puncture, but after the demonstration [1912] that arteries may be punctured without risking haemorrhage, the direct method can also be applied, and samples of the blood may be taken for analysis. The pulmonary artery, however, is situated deep in the chest and has long been considered quite inaccessible. The same holds true for the right heart, so that the oxygen content of mixed venous blood could only be indirectly determined. In this way the minute volume of the heart has been ascertained.

In 1929, WERNER FORSSMANN [b. 1904], in rather heroic experiments on himself, demonstrated that a fine catheter might be introduced via a vein in the bend of the arm and then pushed forward through the subclavian and upper caval veins, until finally the tip had entered the right heart. This signified that methods analogous to those mentioned above might also be used in man. Obviously important new possibilities presented themselves. The method was used by others, in a few cases to determine the blood flow, but also to obtain X-ray pictures from the lungs after injection of some suitable substance through the catheter – an idea expressed and experimentally supported by Forssmann. On the whole, however, heart catheterization was considered too risky and for most purposes was soon abandoned. Several years later it was again taken up by a group of scientists working on cardiological problems under the leadership of ANDRÉ COURNAND [b. 1895] and DICKINSON RICHARDS JR. [b. 1905]. Some slight improvements of the method were published by Cournand and Ranges [1941], and this time it was not long before it inspired confidence and came into widespread use. It was found that the catheter could also be pushed into the pulmonary artery, in certain pathological cases even into the left heart. Rapid progress was made, to a large extent due to the work of Cournand, Richards and their group, though many other scientists also made important contributions.

Measurements of the pressure in the pulmonary artery revealed that in certain cases the value was raised when the left ventricle was failing. Then blood might be accumulated in the lungs and cause a 'back-pressure'. But Cournand, Richards and their school were able to prove that a rise in the pressure may appear independently of the left heart. This is sometimes the case in chronic lung diseases, e.g. in silicosis and lung emphysema. Closer analysis has revealed that the cause of the increased pressure is to be sought in a number of circumstances, such as reduction of the vascular bed, decreased oxygen saturation of the arterial blood and sometimes a change in the thin membrane itself, through which the oxygen must pass in order to reach the blood. These investigations have meant that diagnosis can now be made earlier and with greater certainty then before, thus increasing the prospects of preventing further deterioration.

In the case of acquired heart disease it has been possible to extend and deepen our knowledge, for example, of the minute volume of the failing heart. Particularly noteworthy, perhaps, are the results obtained in cases of congenital heart diseases. Different kinds of septal defects, abnormal stenoses or dilatations within the heart or the large vessels can now be diagnosed more accurately thanks to the use of blood samples and pressure measurements from different parts of the heart, combined with older methods. It is even possible to calculate separately the blood flow within the lesser and systemic circulations, and thus to find the degree of functional disturbance. These advances have been important to the splendid development of modern heart surgery.

The faculty decided to award the *1956* prize jointly to COURNAND, FORSSMANN and RICHARDS 'for their discoveries concerning heart catheterization and pathological changes in the circulatory system'. It is obvious that though the work of Forssmann was published long ago, this was a typical case where the 'significance has not become apparent until recently'.

A particularly important rôle is played in the blood-circulation system by the capillaries, through whose walls the exchange of substances between the blood and the body tissues takes place. A number of observations have shown that the capillaries can change in size, and these changes play an important rôle in the regulation of the blood-flow in the body tissues. AUGUST KROGH's [1874–1949] demonstration that the gas exchange in the lungs can be fully explained as a physical diffusion process, gave new impetus to the study of a number of classical problems connected with the increased supply of oxygen in the organism when the latter is put under severe strain. Krogh was able to determine the amount of blood the heart pumps around per minute and found that there is a marked increase in the blood-flow when muscular work is performed. Even so, the increased demand for oxygen could not be met entirely by the greater supply of blood, the oxygen of each cubic centimetre of blood being used up faster than when the body was at rest. The most obvious explanation seemed to be that when physical labour is performed, a greater number of capillaries stand open, thus facilitating the diffusion of oxygen. This interpretation was supported by other observations. Thus, for instance, Krogh had measured the speed at which oxygen diffuses through the tissues. From the data thus obtained, and assuming that all the capillaries in the muscles stand open, he concluded that the oxygen pressure in the tissues must be only slightly lower than in the capillary blood. Several direct tests showed, however, that the oxygen pressure in muscles at rest is extremely low. From this lack of agreement between the calculated and the observed figures for the oxygen pressure in resting muscles, Krogh drew the conclusion that not all capillaries are open at the same time. Direct, microscopic examination showed clearly that while the number of open capillaries in resting muscles is extremely small, it goes up quite rapidly after only a few seconds of activity, the increase being proportionate to the work performed per minute, while at the same time the capillaries become enlarged. The ability of the capillaries to contract of their own accord after direct stimulation was also confirmed. These findings were supported by parallel experiments in various places. KROGH received the *1920* prize 'for his discovery of the capillary motor regulating mechanism'.

In recent years, surgery on the heart and blood vessels has undergone a remarkable development. This has been partly due to the use of new anaesthetics, methods for artificial respiration and equipment for extracorporeal circulation, as well as to the introduction of new surgical procedures. Procedures for surgical treatment of pathological changes in blood vessels were much improved by ALEXIS CARREL [1873–1944] in the beginning of this century. When blood vessels are sutured, there is danger of secondary haemorrhages and of blocking the passages, but the risk of a blood clot at the point of incision is still greater. In most cases the latter complication can be prevented by taking care that when the blood passes through the vessel it comes in contact with only its inner side [intima]. Otherwise the development of thrombosis is facilitated. In order to prevent this, E. Payr introduced the use of cannulae made of a swiftly absorbable substance. One of the two vessels that were to be tied together was put through the cannula and then folded over at the end so that its inner side was turned to the outside. The end of the other vessel was then slid over the first, so that the two intimae came in contact only with each other. The procedure was far from reliable, and the need of a better technique was strongly felt. A decidedly superior method was worked out by Carrel. When two bloodvessels are to be joined together, end to end, the Carrel method is to place, at the end of each vessel and at equidistant points in their circumference, three light, supporting threads. The inner surfaces of the bloodvessels near the ends are then cleared of all other tissues, and, by suitable traction on the supporting threads, the cross-sections of the two vessels are formed into triangles of identical size and shape, so that they can be fitted together. The three sides are then sewn together in pairs with extremely fine needles. In this way, only the inner sides of the two vessels come into contact with each other, while at the same time, thanks to the distention that remains after the supporting threads have been pulled out, all danger of constriction is averted.

The effectiveness of the method was convincingly demonstrated by Carrel by means of experiments on animals in which he removed entire organs [e.g. the spleen, a kidney, or even a limb] and then connected them again with the body by sewing together the corresponding blood-vessels, etc. In some cases an organ was sewed back in an entirely different place in the body but was nevertheless able to function fairly satisfactorily. Transfers of organs from one kind of animal to another became technically possible, but the foreign tissues were soon absorbed and gradually disappeared. By such transplantations from one individual to another of the same species, certain permanent results could be obtained, but the most important advantage was that in one and the same animal, a piece of a vein could, for example, be removed and used to replace a defective artery in another part of the body. The new technique introduced contributed greatly to surgery, and the Caroline Institute awarded the prize for *1912* to CARREL 'in recognition of his works on vascular suture and the transplantation of blood-vessels and organs'.

In 1905, Haldane and J. G. Priestley made the important discovery that, in the air of the lung vesicles, carbon dioxide pressure remains practically constant, irrespective of great variations in the composition of the air inhaled, as well as in the general air pressure. As a matter of fact, the carbon dioxide tension is a fundamental factor in the *regulation of breathing*, inasmuch as any increase in it immediately causes an increase in ventilation. This observation led Y. Henderson to use inhalation of carbon dioxide [5 per cent or more] to prevent respiratory standstills in patients during operations or in infants immediately after birth.

In their experiments with the regulation of breathing, Haldane and his collaborators also found, as had already been observed, that a drastic reduction in the oxygen content of inhaled air caused a moderate increase in ventilation. It was then assumed that a shortage of oxygen would result in an accumulation of acid metabolites in the tissues as well as in the blood, and that these, in turn, would stimulate the respiratory centre in the medulla oblongata in the same way as an increase in the carbon dioxide pressure. In 1927, CORNEILLE HEYMANS [1892–1968] was able to demonstrate that the composition of the blood can affect respiration, not only directly, through the respiratory centre, but also by reflex action elicited from the periphery. Lack of oxygen or an accumulation of carbon dioxide was found to stimulate certain chemically sensitive receptors situated at the exit of the aorta from the left ventricle, the impulses thus created being conveyed via the aortic nerves to the respiratory centre. When Heymans studied the pressure sensitive reflexes originating in receptors in the wall of the carotid artery [the carotid sinus] and affecting both blood pressure and heart-rate, he was, in fact, able to confirm previous observations to the effect that respiratory reflexes, too, can originate in that area. Together with several associates [J. P. Bouckaert, L. Dautrebande and U. S. von Euler], he demonstrated that a chemical stimulation of the sinus area induces an increase in respiration. He found that inhalation of air deficient in oxygen accelerated the breathings, but this effect disappeared when the sinus nerves were severed, from which it followed that it was produced wholly through the sinus. In the case of an accumulation of carbon dioxide, on the other hand, it was found that the increased respiration was partly the result of direct stimulation of the respiratory centre, and partly a reflex transmitted from the sinus area. Heymans was able to locate the starting-point of this reflex in a small formation close to the sinus itself, the so-called carotid body. Its function is to respond to changes in the composition of the blood; in fact, it is an internal taste organ with special chemo-receptors, like the aortic body at the base of the aorta. In this way the functions of organs, whose purposes had previously been unknown had been explained. It was also a valuable addition to our knowledge of how respiration is regulated; for a more detailed examination showed that certain drugs, which stimulate respiration, work only through the carotid and aortic bodies; others only through the respiratory centre, and still others through both agencies. In 1939, HEYMANS received the *1938* prize 'for the discovery of the rôle played by the sinus and aortic mechanisms in the regulation of respiration'.

CULMINATION OF CLASSICAL NEUROANATOMY AND NEUROPHYSIOLOGY

Our sense organs are built up of sensory or receptor cells which, depending on their various structural characteristics, react to different types of stimuli. The information from the receptors is transmitted in the sensory or afferent nerve fibres to the central nervous system, represented by the spinal cord and the brain. From the central nervous system run the efferent fibres which, via the motor nerve, innervate the muscles. In man, the central nervous system is built up of some 10 billion nerve cells, which are interposed [intercalated] between the afferent input and efferent ouput. All these neurones, the main part of which constitutes the brain, thus represent a complex system which processes the information received from the sense organs and regulates such patterns of muscular activity as result in posture, walking, hand and face movements, speech and so forth. Part of the information coming from the sense organs is processed in the spinal cord and the lower parts of the brain, and may unconsciously result in reflex movements. The signals are transmitted and integrated in more or less complex so-called reflex arcs, comprising the receptors, the afferent fibres, the interneurones in the central nervous system and the motoneurones innervating the muscles. Part of the information arriving from the sense organs may be transmitted to the highest levels in the brain and induce the special kind of brain activity which results in perceptions and which serves as a basis for alertness, memory, learning and emotions. Analysis of the principles governing the processing of information in the central nervous system has to be based on knowledge of the excitation processes in the receptors, transmission in the nerve fibres, and the functional characteristics of the delicate junctions between the nerve cells, i.e. the synapses. Unless we understand these functions we cannot understand neurological and psychiatric disturbances. Several significant discoveries concerning nervous functions have been rewarded during the past seventy years.

The earliest neuroanatomical and neurophysiological discoveries to be rewarded, and which, in a broader sense than any other, became fundamental to modern neurological research, were those made by the neurohistologist SANTIAGO RAMON Y CAJAL [1852–1934] and the neurophysiologist CHARLES SHERRINGTON [1857–1952]. The classical epoch of neurological research culminated in Cajal's '*Textura del Systema Nervosa del Hombre y de los Vertebrados*' [1897–1899] and Sherrington's '*Integrative Action of the Central Nervous System*' [1906], at a time when modern electronics had yet not been introduced into neurophysiology. To a great extent the research which was to follow, and which, with the aid of refined methods, has brought investigations down to the molecular level, is still guided by Cajal's and Sherrington's ideas. Thus their work also constitutes an introduction to modern neurobiological research.

When Cajal, in the 1880's, began mapping the neurones and their structural interrelations in the retina, brain and spinal cord, he entered a field which was still largely a blank on the scientific map. A prerequisite for his work was, however, the silver-staining technique, developed about ten years earlier by CAMILLO GOLGI [1843–1926].

When under microscopic study, a section of the brain or the spinal cord looks like a jumble of delicate cells and fibres, stained in the traditional way. Golgi's invention of the new staining method amounted to a complete revolution. He observed that after small parts of the central nervous system had, in the usual way, been hardened in a solution of dichromate until hard enough to be sliced thin, and after they had been dipped in a weak solution of silver nitrate, certain nerve elements stood out as dark outlines against a colourless or slightly yellow background. The peculiar value of this method was that individual cells with their processes – dendrites and axones – could now be stained and easily traced to their most delicate ramifications. Thus, it became possible to study, in detail, the structures of the individual cell, as well as the relationship between nerve cells of different types. Because of the way in which it facilitates the visualisation of the three-dimensional arrangements of the cells in the central nervous system, this method, with and without modifications, is still used.

Golgi himself contributed to our knowledge of different types of nerve cells, e.g. in the cerebellum and spinal cord. On the one hand, there are the neurons with short axones and, on the other, those whose extended axones form elongated functional links. One example of the latter type are those which have their cell bodies located in the spinal cord and the axones of which run in the peripheral nerves to the muscles. Later experiments by Sherrington showed that these motoneurones innervate a great many muscle fibres. A mononeuron with connected muscle fibres serves as the unit – the motor unit – in his analysis of the reflex movements.

Golgi's method, however, proved to be rather capricious, and if it was to work, great care had to be taken. In Cajal's hands, modified and applied on young individuals or embryonic material, the method became an extraordinarily effective tool. Cajal made classical studies of the nerve structure in the retina, and later provided detailed descriptions of delicate structures in almost all parts of the central nervous system. He identified several nerve paths in the brain and the spinal cord and described the ramifications of the sensory nerve fibres which enter through the posterior roots of the cord. On a number of points Cajal was able to correct Golgi's findings. Golgi believed that the outermost ramifications of the dendrites are in direct contact with the tissue cells and vessels, and assumed that they convey nourishment plasma to the nerve elements. Cajal proved that the supposed connection does not exist; instead, he took the dendrites to be communication agencies which carry impulses *to*, while the axons convey them *away* from, the nerve cells – an interpretation generally accepted today. W. Waldeyer's theory, according to which the neuron, i.e. the nerve cell together with its various types of processes, constitutes an anatomical and functional unit, was strongly supported by Cajal, while Golgi opposed it – two conflicting interpretations that are well brought out in the Nobel addresses of the two scientists. At the present time, the neuron theory is regarded as one of the fundamentals of the nervous system's anatomy and physiology. In his studies on the spinal cord, Cajal outlined the structural basis of some of the most fundamental reflex arcs, whose functions were analyzed by Sherrington. His description of the neuronal arrangements in the retina, which serves as a basis for our view of the retina as a complex nervous center, guided the electro-physiological research on the eye's manner of processing information, which led to discoveries awarded with the Nobel Prize [see p. 265]. Cajal's descriptions, finally, of the neuronal organization in the cortex of the brain represent the beginning of a new era in the study of the relation between function and structure in this organ, which, in his own words, 'represents the mirror by which nature becomes aware of herself'.

Golgi's work on the fine structures of the nervous system was, nevertheless, obviously of a pioneer nature. His results were published between 1873 and 1890, but did not become generally known until after 1894, when a German edition of his writings appeared. During the first few years of the century, Cajal and Golgi were proposed for a prize, both individually and together, and a corresponding difference of opinion developed within the Committee. This was the first time that a division of the prize in physiology or medicine had been proposed, and views clashed sharply. The Institute decided, however, to award the *1906* prize to GOLGI and CAJAL 'in recognition of their work on the structure of the nervous system'.

As mentioned above, co-operation between different neurons and interpretation of their activity form the basis of the reflex action. Obviously, the reflexes are of fundamental importance, and extensive investigations have been made in order to elucidate their functional organization and their dynamics under various conditions.

To this work SHERRINGTON has contributed more than any other scientist. During an investigation, in 1893, of the familair knee-jerk produced by a sharp tap upon the patellar tendon, which, in turn, causes a reflex twitch of the knee extensor muscle, Sherrington observed that, if the central portion of the nerve leading to the flexor muscle in the back of the thigh was stimulated, no knee-jerk resulted. From this he concluded that the nerve trunk in question contains not only the well-known efferent [motor] fibres, but also afferent [sensory] ones, and that there is a functional correlation between antagonistic muscles. Thus, for example, Sherrington found that from one-third to one-half of all the fibres in the nerves leading to the skeletal muscles are afferent and that they are connected with special sensory organs, viz., the so-called muscle spindles. If these sensory pathways are destroyed, while the efferent paths are kept intact, there ensues a lack of co-ordination of the corresponding muscles, so that the normally precise correlation of their movements disappears. At the same time there is a lowering of the normal muscle tone, which consists of a continuous, though mild, contraction. The tone, therefore, has a reflex background produced by the stimulation of receptors in the muscle itself, in this case initiated by the pull on the muscle spindles [myotatic reflex]. These findings have since been further developed by a number of electrophysiological investigations.

Sherrington and his co-workers – among whom D. Denny-Brown, J. C. Eccles and E. G. T. Liddell may be mentioned – used different types of spinal cord reflexes in their analysis which led to a characterization of synaptic functions. This was done by stimulating various sense organs in the skin, muscles and joints, or by stimulating corresponding sensory nerves electrically and recording the resulting reflex muscle activity. Different co-ordinated reflex patterns were described, and in these experiments, which were mainly performed on cats, the influence from higher levels – brain and cerebellum – on the spinal reflex centers was also investigated.

In careful studies of the strength, duration and distribution of the muscle reflexes in relation to the same parameters of the stimuli, Sherrington and his co-workers obtained functional characteristics of the relay stations in the spinal cord. The information-processing that takes place in these junctions, represented by the synapses, is based on both addition and subtraction, and Sherrington found expressions for the excitatory and inhibitory processes which participate in these processes. He thus showed how, for the resulting reflex activity, the balance between excitation and inhibition are determining factors. The description of synaptic excitation and inhibition, which Sherrington was able to give, influenced subsequent studies of what happens in the membranes of the nerve cells at the synaptic junctions.

Sherrington has contributed more than anyone else to our knowledge about the integrative functions of the nervous system. The exceptional importance of his contribution was early recognized. In many of the nominations, submitted altogether by 134 persons representing thirteen countries, this was stressed with an emphasis unusual even in such cases. It is interesting to note that, in spite of the great esteem which Sherrington enjoyed, he was not awarded the prize until 1932. This was due to several circumstances. In the first investigation, in 1910, the examiner [J. E. Johansson] found that some delay was advisable; while in 1912 and 1915 he came to the conclusion that Sherrington's discovery of the reciprocal innervation of antagonistic muscles deserved a prize. In the Committee it was objected that although it had happened to be forgotten, this discovery, as Sherrington himself had stressed, had already been made in 1826, by the brothers C. and J. Bell. By the time the First World War broke out, several members of the faculty were recommending greater stringency in applying the stipulation in Nobel's will that the prize be given for a definite discovery; whereon the examiner [Johansson] felt he could not, after all, support Sherrington's candidature. After Johansson's retirement, in 1927, there was a certain shift of opinion; but a few more years were to pass before the new attitude could prevail. Sherrington, meanwhile, had continued his researches, and the work of other scientists still further stressed the importance of his discoveries. In *1932* he was awarded the prize, jointly with E. D. ADRIAN [see p. 254].

AUTONOMIC NERVOUS FUNCTIONS – CHEMICAL TRANSMITTORS

Our internal organs, such as blood vessels, heart, lungs and the digestive system, etc., are controlled by a special section of the nervous system not subject to our own will-power and which is therefore said to be autonomic. The autonomic nervous system is thus made up of neurones which innervate the glands, the smooth muscles in the visceral organs and the heart. The efferent fibres originate in the brain or the spinal cord, and the paths from the central nervous system to the effector organs consist of at least two neurones in series. The junctions between these neurones, or synapses, are situated either in the immediate vicinity of, or inside, the different organs, or else are merged into special nerve bundles or ganglia. Afferent nerves also run to the central nervous system. There are two main divisions of the autonomic system; the sympathetic, which is connected with the thoracic and lumbar regions of the spinal cord, and the parasympathetic, which is connected, partly, with the midbrain and the medulla oblongata, and, partly, with the lower or sacral region of the spinal cord. Most organs are innervated both sympathetically and parasympathetically, but the two systems produce opposite effects; if a stimulation of one brings about increased activity in a certain organ, the other, when stimulated, produces the contrary result.

In 1889, J. N. Langley and W. L. Dickinson found that the synapses in the autonomic system could be paralysed by injecting a suitable amount of nicotine into the blood or by a local painting of the ganglia with the same substance. By comparing the effect of an electrical stimulation of the fibres before and after their passage through the ganglion, either with or without the use of nicotine, it was possible to determine whether and where synapses were present. By applying this technique, Langley and his associates mapped out the entire autonomic system. The great significance of these investigations was recognized by the physiologists on the Nobel Committee and they expressed the view that an award would be justified. But opposition was voiced by the member representing neurology.

Nicotine is not the only substance to have a special effect on the autonomic nervous system or portions thereof. HENRY DALE [1875–1968] observed that, like nicotine, large doses of acetylcholine produce, first, a stimulation and then a paralysis, of the synapses throughout the entire autonomic system. Further, adrenaline, which in 1894 had been found in the medulla of the adrenal gland and in 1901 had been the first hormone to be produced in pure form, has striking effects on the glands, smooth muscles and heart. The similarity between the effect of adrenaline and that produced by a stimulation of the sympathetic nerves caused T. R. Elliott [1904] to put forward the theory that the impulses in the sympathetic nerves bring about a liberation of adrenaline in the periphery, and that this can be presumed to be the actual cause of the stimulation effect. Other scientists made similar suggestions. Dale, for instance, hinted that acetylcholine might play a corresponding part in the parasympathetic system. This hypothesis gained in interest, when in 1929, Dale and his associates were able to demonstrate that small amounts of acetylcholine occur normally in various organs of the body.

In 1921, a simple experiment by OTTO LOEWI [1873–1961] cleared up the matter. The heart of a frog, with its nerves attached, was taken out and suspended in a small glass vessel containing saline in such a way that the liquid had free access to the ventricle. When the nerve-trunk was stimulated electrically, the frequency and strength of the heart-beats varied according to circumstances, since the nervestem contains fibres belonging to the sympathetic as well as to the parasympathetic system. When, immediately after such a stimulation, Loewi transferred the liquid which had been pumped back and forth through the heart of the frog to another glass vessel in which a similar heart was suspended, the latter exhibited the same variations in its activity as had just been observed in the first, after the electrical stimulation. The electrical stimulation had therefore released certain substances that cause a typical nervous response. And in fact Loewi was able to prove that different substances are produced by a stimulation of the sympathetic and the parasympathetic fibres. The effects on the parasympathetic nerves, such as the retardation of the heart-beats, brought about the release of a substance which, after laborious experiments, was found to be identical with acetylcholine. As in the case of the latter, its effect was counteracted by atropine, and, like acetylcholine, the unknown substance decomposed quickly in the presence of body tissues. Loewi and E. Navratil, however, succeeded in preventing the breakdown by adding an alkaloid known as physostigmine or eserine, which made it much easier to prove the presence of the substance. Other scientists were able to confirm that, as far as the parasympathetic terminals are concerned, acetylcholine is the normal transmitter substance.

The fact that acetylcholine also stimulates the synapses in the autonomic nervous system made it a matter of urgency to find out whether there, too, the drug has anything to do with the transmission. In co-operation with W. Feldberg and J. H. Gaddum, Dale was able to prove that this is so. Their investigations were also extended to the striated muscles; it was shown that, whenever the latter are stimulated, acetylcholine is also liberated at the terminals of the motor nerves. The discovery of acetylcholine as transmittor substance [cholinergic transmission] in the autonomic nervous system and at the neuromuscular junction was of great importance. The faculty awarded the *1936* prize to DALE and LOEWI, together, 'for their discoveries relating to the chemical transmission of the nerve impulses'.

As to the nature of the substance which the terminals of the sympathetic nerves of the frog's heart give off when stimulated, Loewi assumed that it corresponded closely to adrenaline. W. B. Cannon showed that there is an increase of adrenaline secretion during emotional states, and found also that after removal of the adrenal medulla, emotional stimuli in test animals with denervated hearts can produce accelerated heart-action for a few minutes after the stimulation has ceased. More detailed studies indicated that stimulation of the sympathetic nerves led to the release of a certain substance which entered the blood and in some way affected the heart. Although objections had been raised as early as 1910 by G. Barger and Dale, who proposed that the transmittor might be found among non-methylated catecholamines, adrenaline itself was assumed to serve as transmittor substance at the sympathetic nerve endings [adrenergic transmission]. Cannon's experiment led to the proposal of two adrenergic substances: sympathin E [excitatory] and sympathin I [inhibitory], whereas Z. M. Bacq hinted that noradrenaline might serve as transmittor.

When, therefore, ULF VON EULER [b. 1905] took up this topic in 1945, the situation was somewhat confused. In an introductory paper, 1946, he showed that the effects of spleen and heart extracts on the activity of smooth muscles rather resembled those of noradrenaline than those of adrenaline. The fact that the potency of the spleen extracts, when obtained after transection and degeneration of the nerves, decreased, indicated that the active factor derived from the nerves. Von Euler then prepared extracts from the sympathetic nerves, and with the aid of both biological and chemical tests showed that these extracts contained noradrenaline. Having identified noradrenaline in the sympathetic nerves, he took up the question of its localization in the nerve terminals. Partly in collaboration with N. Å. Hillarp, von Euler demonstrated that noradrenaline is stored in the so-called nerve granules, i.e. small grains in the nerve terminals. Granules, for instance, were isolated from the sympathetic nerves, whereupon chemical tests indicated that these granules contained noradrenaline. In a series of recent studies, von Euler has further investigated the uptake, storage and release of noradrenaline and other related amines. His discovery of the biological significance of noradrenaline as transmittor substance at the sympathetic nerve terminals represents a breakthrough in research on neurotransmittors and has greatly stimulated subsequent scientific work in his field.

Sensitive methods for the study of the building-up, storage and inactivation of noradrenaline have been developed by JULIUS AXELROD [b. 1912]. The mother substance of noradrenaline is the amino acid tyrosin, which is transformed into dihydroxyphenylalanine [DOPA] and, in a following step, to dopamine. In the sympathetic nerves, dopamine is transformed into noradrenaline. There is feed-back, by which the noradrenaline formed influences the transformation of tyrosin to DOPA. This mechanism has been studied by Axelrod. As to the inactivation of the released transmittor, it was known that part of it is decomposed, and this decomposition was assumed to be entirely due to the influence of the enzyme monamine oxidase [MAO] in the nerve terminals. Axelrod, however, found that two other processes are more important for the elimination of the transmittor. He showed that, under the influence of the enzyme catecholamine-O-methyltransferase [COMT], a demethylation occurs and that there is also a significant re-uptake of the transmittor into the nerve. Actually, the re-uptake through the nerve membrane, described by Axelrod, seems to be the dominant factor for the elimination of the transmittor overflow.

Von Euler's and Axelrod's discoveries are of general interest, since noradrenaline has been shown to be one of the brain's important monoamines. Like dopamine, it has been found in neurones which constitute various nuclei and pathways, and the monoamines are therefore assumed to act as transmittors in different central neuronal systems. The actions of several pharmacological substances used in recent years in psychiatry result from interference with the metabolism of the monoamines. Knowledge about the processes described above is therefore of great importance. In this context it should be mentioned that the action of some of these psychopharmacological substances depends on their interfering with re-uptake of the transmittor. Thus, Axelrod's discoveries concerning the formation, inactivation and re-uptake of noradrenaline have been instrumental in the development of research dealing with the phsyiology and pharmacology of neurotransmittors. Von Euler's and Axelrod's discoveries concerning the noradrenergic synaptic transmission, were honoured with the Nobel Prize in *1970*. The prize was shared with B. Katz, whose discoveries concerning the mechanisms by which neurotransmittors are released at the nerve terminals are fundamental to our understanding of synaptic activity in general [see p. 258]. The prize to KATZ, VON EULER and AXELROD was given for their 'discoveries concerning neurotransmittors and the mechanisms for their storage, release and inactivation'.

It has already been mentioned that the autonomic functions are governed by certain areas in the central nervous system, and it has long been known that influences can be exerted on the internal organs from the basal parts of the brain, the midbrain [mesencephalon] and the interbrain [diencephalon]. On this subject the studies by WALTER RUDOLF HESS [b. 1881] with local electrical stimulation through implanted electrodes in alert animals have increased our information.

Electrical stimulation in the study of central nervous functions was used as early as 1870, when G. Fritsch and R. E. Hitzig found that slight electrical stimuli, applied to certain points in the cerebral cortex, caused test animals to make sharply defined movements, which varied according to the location of the points under stimulation. This proved that different parts of the body are represented by specific areas in the cortex. The method of locally stimulating various sections in the central nervous system electrically and observing or recording the resulting activity in glands or muscles or from the nerves innervating them, has routine uses in neurophysiology.

As stimulating electrodes, Hess used metal fibres [0.2 mm in diameter, inserted into the brain of the test animal (cat)]. The metal fibres were insulated except at their very tips, thus making it possible to apply electrical stimuli within limited regions, the localization of which could be ascertained with the aid of a three-demensional map. After the implantation of the electrodes, the animals were in good condition and went about as usual. The stimuli produced more or less typical responses. From certain parts of the interbrain it was possible to influence blood circulation and breathing. Particularly significant was the fact that, from a limited area in the brain-stem, several activities were, as a rule, simultaneously initiated, for example, respiration and blood circulation, salivation and heat regulation, etc. This finding made it seem probable that what is here in question are 'collective centres', through which a co-ordinated action of several different organs can be initiated. It is not only the internal organs, however, that are thus made to act together; the striated muscles can also be brought into simultaneous action, which varies in character according to shifts in the points stimulated. A few other examples may be cited: a stimulation in the posterior or central parts of the midbrain can produce attempts to escape, or agressive reactions similar to those aroused, for instance, when the cat is threatened by a dog. The cat hisses, jumps up on somebody and claws him. If, on the other hand, the electrode is placed a little further forward, it is possible to induce a state of general relaxation in the skeletal muscles, and not far from this point a reaction of the same type as natural sleep was induced. Movements of the face, eyes, head, legs and trunk, sneezing, vomiting, bowel movements, etc., are also initiated from specific points. HESS received one-half of the *1949* Nobel Prize 'for his discovery of the functional organization of the interbrain as a co-ordinator of the activities of the internal organs'.

TRANSMISSION IN NERVE FIBRES AND SYNAPTIC JUNCTIONS

In research into the nature of the message transmitted along the nerve fibres, on the one hand, and the analysis of the synaptic processes, on the other, electrophysiological methods have played an important role. Studies of the electrical characteristics of various tissues can be referred back to Galvani's observations, of 1791, on 'animal electricity'. Most important were the studies, made by Du Bois-Reymond [1843], Von Helmholtz [1852], Bernstein [1871] and Hermann [1879], of the electrical phenomena accompanying nervous and muscular activity. The conclusion was drawn that the nerve is an electrically charged structure, and it was shown that the message is expressed by a negative wave transmitted along it. The galvanometers used at that time to record the electrical activity, however, were incapable of recording fast potential variations. The development of electronic techniques after the First World War opened up new possibilities. Particular reference should here be made to discoveries by P. E. A. von Lenard, concerning cathode rays [prize in physics, 1905], and by G. Marconi and C. F. Braun, concerning the thermionic valve [prize in physics, 1909]. With the aid of the electronic amplifier, the cathode ray tube, small and rapid variations in potential could now be recorded. Discoveries in electronics thus not only played a decisive role in the development of telecommunications. They also opened up new possibilities for the study of signal transmission in our own nervous system.

Pioneer discoveries in this field were made in the 1920's by EDGAR ADRIAN [b. 1889], who realized the great latent possibilities of the thermionic valve amplifier for studying information transmitted in the nerve fibres. With the aid of this device, he and his colleagues demonstrated the characteristics of the impulse code which represents the message in the individual neurons. The complexity of the activity obtained from a whole sensory nerve, in which hundreds of nerve fibres transmit asynchronous impulses from the stimulated sense organ, pointed to the necessity of leading off from single nerve fibres after dissection of fine nerve strands under the microscope. In 1924, Adrian and Y. Zotterman were able to record, from single neurons, the impulse message which occurs in response to natural stimulation of the sense organ in which the nerve fibre under investigation originates. The properties of single sensory receptors could thus be elucidated, and these studies laid the foundations of the unitary analysis of nervous functions. It was found that sensory stimuli of various strengths do not change the amplitude of the nerve impulses, but only their frequency, stimulus strength and impulse frequency being related. Communication in the nerve fibres, that is to say, can be said to function analogously to the principle of frequency modulation in modern telecommunication. In the peripheral sense organ there is a transformation from stimulus strength to impulse frequency, the intensity of the subjective sensation depending upon the impulse frequency in the sensory neurones. During its period of activity, however, the nerve exhibits a lower excitability. The intervals between the separate impulses can, therefore, never be shorter than the so-called absolute refractory period, just as the intervals between bullets fired by a machine-gun depend on the operation cycle of the gun's own mechanism. It was also shown that the sense organs can adjust themselves: a stimulus which, immediately after it has been applied, produces a close succession of impulses, has a weaker effect when sustained. This capacity for adjustment or adaptation to the prevailing stimulus was found to vary considerably as between one sense organ and another.

The fact that the sensory mechanisms could be approached quantitatively with objective methods gave fresh impetus to sensory physiology, which had hitherto been obliged to rely on psycho-technical data. Adrian's fundamental discoveries mark the beginning of a new era in the study of the relationship between the receptor processes, information transmission, and perception. Adrian also studied the characteristics of the messages in the motor nerve fibres which, running from the central nervous system, innervate bundles of contractile fibres in the muscles [the motor unit, see p. 244], and together with D. Bronk had showed how the degree of activity is expressed by impulse frequency. It was because his investigations, which had thrown so much light on the functions of the nerves, the adjustability of the nerve action and the sense organs, also demonstrated anew the value of Sherrington's research, that the Institute decided to award the *1932* prize jointly to ADRIAN and SHERRINGTON 'for their discoveries regarding the functions of the neurones'.

About the time when Adrian had been making his first experiments on single nerve fibres, JOSEPH ERLANGER [1874–1965] and HERBERT GASSER [1888–1963] started to study the nerve action potential led off from the whole nerve in response to electrical stimulation applied at a certain distance from the point of recording. A short time after the application of the electrical shock, a compound action potential is picked up by the recording electrodes and this relatively large negative deflection is built up of the more or less synchronous impulses in the individual nerve fibres. The time interval, or latency, is dependent on the distance between the stimulating and the recording electrodes and the conduction velocity in those nerve fibres which most swiftly transmit the message. Like Adrian, Erlanger and Gasser made use of the modern amplifying technique, and, in order to visualize the action potential, utilized the cathode ray oscillograph, an instrument which proved to be convenient for this type of study. More especially, they concentrated on the transmission and excitability characteristics of various types of nerve fibres, basing their studies on the relation between the latency and shape of the action potential and the nerve fibres' structural characteristics. They found that in the course of transmission a nerve's compound action potential changes appearance: while still close to its starting-point it looks like a triangular wave with a rounded peak; later on the descending wave, it exhibits one or more humps.

The explanation is that the nerve consists of several fibres with different conduction velocities. It could be definitely established that, as the French neurophysiologist L. Lapicque had earlier suggested, the thicker the nerve fibre, the faster it conveys an impulse. Erlanger and Gasser identified three main groups of fibres, the first of which moreover, was, divisible. In mammals the thickest, the A-fibres, have a conduction velocity from 5 to 120 metres a second, the B-fibres 3 to 14, and the slenderest, the C-fibres, 0.3 to 3 metres a second. Within these classifications there are also variations in other properties, such as the threshold of excitation, the refractory period, the magnitude of the impulse, the sensitivity to asphyxia, etc. The individual fibres, which can thus run in the same nerve trunk, serve different purposes. While, for instance, the efferent fibres leading to the muscles have a high conduction velocity, this is much lower in some of the afferent fibres of the sense organs of the skin. They are especially low in the fibres carrying pain impulses.

Gasser and his associates also studied certain details of the action potentials. After the initial compound action potential described above, there may remain a slight deflection which had been called the negative after-potential, and the latter, in turn, may be succeeded by a slight wave in the opposite direction, the positive after-potential. The after-potentials were found to be associated with excitability changes in the neuron. A functional differentiation was made of different nerve fibres on the basis of conduction velocity and differences in threshold, refractory period and in the amplitude and duration of the after-potentials.

The Institue awared the *1944* prize jointly to ERLANGER and GASSER 'for their discoveries relating to the highly differentiated functions of single nerve fibres'.

Much interest has been paid to the mechanism underlying the nerve impulse which, according to classical investigations by Matteucci [1838–1842] and Du Bois Reymond [1848], represents a reduction of the potential difference across the nerve membrane. It had been assumed that the membrane is characterized by a selective permeability, the potassium ions being responsible for the resting potential, and that the reduction of the resting potential during activity depends on a short reversible change in the membrane permeability [Ostwald, 1890; Bernstein, 1912]. According to Overton [1902], sodium ions play a rôle in the impulse formation, a notion which gained support from the experiments of ALAN HODGKIN [b. 1914] and ANDREW HUXLEY [b. 1917] who, with the aid of fine pipettes, introduced into living nerve fibres of the squid, measured the potential difference between the inside and the outside of the membrane while at rest, during activity, and with the nerve fibre surrounded by solutions of varying composition. This intracellular technique was first introduced by R. Gerard and G. Ling, and because of the large diameter [1 mm], the squid giant axon was found to be favourable for this type of study. Hodgkin and Huxley found that during rest – as expected – the interior of the axon is negative in relation to the outside [resting potential 60–70 mV], and that during activity there is not only a drop to zero but even an 'overshoot' by about 40 mV. These studies on the squid axon, which were interrupted by the Second World War, were afterwards resumed, partly in collaboration with B. Katz and R. Keynes. In 1947, Hodgkin and Katz made the supposition that, during activity, there is a momentary influx of sodium ions, followed by an exit of potassium ions. Hodgkin, Huxley and Katz applied the so-called 'voltage clamp' technique, introduced by K. C. Cole, which allowed membrane current measurements while the membrane voltage is electronically controlled. It was found that the membrane current, which ensues when the membrane potential is lowered, is initially due to a temporary sodium influx followed by a delayed potassium outflux. On the basis of the quantitative data obtained on the sodium and potassium currents, Hodgkin and Huxley made a calculation leading to a theoretical description of the nerve impulse and a correspondence was found between the impulse calculated and that obtained by intracellular recording. According to the investigations described, a lowering of the membrane potential to a certain threshold level changes the permeability of the membrane, so that a sodium flux into the axon occurs, followed by a potassium outflow, expressed by the electrical event, the action potential or nerve impulse. The current flow in the nerve fibre engages adjacent segments of the axon, and gives rise to propagation of the activity along the nerve fibre.

While Hodgkin and Huxley were working on the transmission mechanisms of the peripheral part of the neuron – the axon – JOHN ECCLES [b. 1906] took up the functional characteristics of the central part, the cell body, and the transmission mechanisms at the synapses, i.e. at the junctions between the neurons in the central nervous system. Being a pupil of Sherrington, Eccles became interested early in the spinal cord. He had made extensive extracellular electrophysiological studies on spinal reflex transmission when, in 1951, in collaboration with L. G. Brock and J. S. Coombs, he succeeded in penetrating, with fine microelectrodes, the motoneurons in the mammalian spinal cord. This was an admirable technical achievement, which enabled him to measure the membrane potential of the motoneurons and its changes when the motoneurons were activated synaptically through various reflex arcs. Earlier experiments by R. Lorente de Nó, B. Renshaw and D. P. C. Lloyd had yielded knowledge of the time characteristics of the synaptic transmission in the mammalian central nervous system. Lloyd had also presented basic electrophysiological data on the functional organization of excitation and inhibition in certain spinal cord reflexes of various complexity. With his intracellular microelectrodes, Eccles measured the membrane potential of the motoneurons at rest and when synaptically influenced from sensory nerves, whose activity were known to excite or inhibit the motoneurons. As was expected from earlier investigations, stimulation of sensory fibres which excited the motoneurons was followed by a decrease of the motoneuron membrane potential, propagating impulses being fired at a certain level of membrane depolarization. Stimulation of nerves that were known to inhibit the activity was found to increase the membrane potential. An inhibitory inflow from the motoneurons thus tended to drive the membrane potential toward its resting value, which was also measured and found to be much the same as in the peripheral nerve. Eccles interpreted the results on the basis of Hodgkin's and Huzley's ion theory. He and his group also studied the effects of microinjections of various ions into the motoneurons, and this lead him to conclude that the excitatory and inhibitory membrane potential changes are due to changes in membrane permeability. The contributions by HODGKIN, HUXLEY and ECCLES were considered to justify the award of the *1963* Nobel Prize, which was given for 'their discoveries concerning the ionic mechanisms involved in excitation and inhibition in the peripheral and central portions of the nerve cell membrane'.

When, at the end of the last century, Ch. Sherrington introduced the synapse concept for the functional link between nerve cells [see p. 243], he also pointed to the similarity between the interneuronal contacts and the junctions between the nerve terminals and the effector cells, and expressed the view that the processes which serve the synaptic transmission must differ from those which form the basis for the conduction of signals in the nerve fibres. Actually, we are dealing with two quite different mechanisms. Thanks to the electrophysiological investigations mentioned above, we now know a great deal about the nerve impulse. We also know that the impulse cannot jump over the cleft between two nerve cells, although this snyaptic cleft is quite narrow; about 200 Å, according to electronmicroscopic observations. The same is the case at the junction between the nerve fibres and the effector cells, e.g. the muscle fibres.

According to the present view of synaptic transmission in the central nervous system, the activity in the terminals of the presynaptic fibres results in the liberation of a transmitter substance, whose influence on the postsynaptic membrane leads to membrane changes of the type described by Eccles. Our knowledge of these intricate processes in the minute synaptic structure is partly based on discoveries concerning transmission in the autonomic nervous system and at the junction between the motor nerve fibres and the muscle fibres [the neuromuscular junction]. As mentioned earlier, Dale and his co-workers presented evidence that acetylcholine is to be regarded as the transmittor substance at the neuromuscular junction [p. 248]. It remained to show the mechanisms by which the impulses in the nerve terminals release the transmittor and the form in which it is released.

With the aid of intracellular and extracellular microelectrodes, BERNARD KATZ [b. 1911], investigated the electrical activity at the nerve muscle junction. He and his collaborators were able to lead off the activity from single nerve and muscle fibres at rest and in activity, and also in conjunction with local application of various substances through a fine micropipette. When Katz was exploring the nerve muscle junction with his microelectrode, he accidently observed small miniature discharges which occurred spontaneously and which were not to be regarded as impulses.

At rest they had a low frequency – about 1 per sec – and a constant, low amplitude. Katz was able to show that these discharges signal the release from the nerve terminals of small 'packages' of acetylcholine. These packages bombard the specialized muscle fibre membrane at the nerve muscle junction [the muscle endplate], Thus, the transmittor, acetylcholine, is not released in separate molecules, but in packages or 'quanta', which were shown to contain 1,000–10,000 molecules. Katz and his collaborators then demonstrated how, under the influence of the impulse in the nerve terminals, the probability of quantal release increases. Thus, there occurs a summation of bombardments during a short period of time which results in quite a significant depolarization of the muscle membrane at the endplate. As a consequence an impulse arises in the muscle fibre which, transmitted along the fibre, is followed by contraction. Katz shows that the mechanisms responsible for the transmittor release radically differ from those serving impulse transmission in the nerve fibres. As mentioned above, the nerve impulse is dependent on a rapid influx of sodium ions through the nerve membrane, followed by a rapid outflux of potassium ions. By blocking the various links in the transmission process at the nerve muscle junction, Katz found that sodium is not a prerequisite for the coupling between the electrical events in the nerve terminal and the release of the transmittor packages. Instead, calcium must be present if the packages are to empty themselves through the nerve membrane into the synaptic cleft. In electron microscopical studies, small vesicles have been shown to exist in the nerve terminals; these vesicles seem to contain the transmittor substance formed in the nerve. Several investigations indicate that the transmission principle, demonstrated by Katz, equally applies to other synapses, although there exist different transmittors in different neuronal systems [see p. 250]. The discovery of the mechanisms for the release of acetylcholine from the motor nerve terminals in the nerve muscle junction under the influence of nerve impulses forms the basis for the modern concept of synaptic transmission. KATZ was therefore awarded the *1970* prize, which he shared with U. VON EULER and J. AXELROD [see p. 251].

NEUROPHARMACOLOGY

Abnormal variations with regard to the release and breakdown of the transmitter substances in the autonomic system or at the neuromuscular junction, as well as alterations in sensitivity towards them, may cause serious disturbances, e.g. in blood pressure regulation and muscular activity. Consequently it is of practical importance to be able to modify the actions of these substances in one direction or another. Some naturally occurring alkaloids have such effects, but their usefulness is restricted by insufficient specificity and unwelcome side-actions. It is desirable to obtain effective drugs which are free from these drawbacks, and numerous efforts have been made to synthesize such products.

In this field DANIEL BOVET [b. 1907] has made outstanding contributions. Starting with studies on substances acting similarly to adrenaline ['sympathomimetics'] or in the opposite direction ['sympatholytics'], Bovet and E. Fourneau dealt mainly with substances having a certain structural resemblance to the adrenaline group [1933]. G. Ungar, J.-C. Parrot and Bovet succeeded in synthesizing preparations with a pronounced sympathicolytic effect of short duration. In 1937, one of them was also found to counteract histamine, which has powerful effects, mainly by stimulating smooth muscles. Sometimes histamine is released in excess in the body and plays a role in allergic conditions with symptoms analogous to those during anaphylaxis [see p. 176]. This was the first time an antihistamine had been synthesized, and the discovery became the starting-point for comprehensive investigations resulting in efficient antihistaminic drugs. B. Halpern, as well as Bovet and his collaborators, soon obtained preparations that were used in man; their introduction marked a definite improvement of our prospects of successfully treating a number of allergic states, such as urticaria, hay fever, and serum sickness.

Later, Bovet continued his studies on sympathicolytic substances, and he and his group were able to show that the actions on different nervous functions are independent of each other. It was thus possible to produce substances exercising only one of the effects in a fairly pure form. This has given new valuable tools to the scientist and also opened wide perspectives for the future treatment of certain diseases.

A second series of Bovet's contributions concerns substances which paralyze skeletal muscles. The notorious South American arrow poison, curare, has such an action. First the muscles of the head and neck are affected, then those of the legs and arms, and finally the respiratory muscles are paralyzed. When this stage occurs, death follows from suffocation, unless artificial respiration is maintained. The use of curare in order to alleviate certain spastic muscular disorders soon proved too dangerous. The situation improved a little, when the active principle, the alkaloid curarine, became available, thus making possible a more exact dosage. Curarine was tried in surgery to induce complete relaxation without need for deep anaesthesia, which in itself involved certain dangers. Curarine, however, was by no means ideal, the action being long-lasting and the side-effects considerable. The establishment of the structural formula of curarine, by H. King, gave certain leads, which Bovet followed up. He and his collaborators proved that, in spite of great simplifications of the molecule, the paralyzing effect could be maintained. A preparation was obtained which had an excellent paralyzing effect with less side-effects than curarine. This substance, flaxedil, became a valuable aid to surgery. Structurally, it is related to choline, and some choline derivatives were therefore also tested. One of these, succinylcholine, which had already been studied in 1911 by R. Hunt and R. de M. Taveau, displayed remarkable actions, overlooked by earlier investigators. Injected into the bloodstream, within a few seconds it caused blocking of the transmission from nerve to muscle, with resulting paralysis. This occurs in the same order as after curarine, but the risk of respiratory standstill was less, a relatively large dose being required. Furthermore, with the pure preparation, no side-effects occured in man, and the paralysis rapidly disappeared. By continuous infusion it could be maintained at the desired level. Succinylcholine is now used extensively for obtaining muscular relaxation in man and animals.

The faculty decided to award the *1957* prize to BOVET 'for his discoveries relating to synthetic compounds that inhibit the action of certain body substances, and especially their action on the vascular system and the skeletal muscles'.

NEUROSURGERY

One-half of the *1949* Nobel Prize went to EGAS ANTONIO MONIZ [1874–1955] for 'his discovery of the therapeutic value of leucotomy in certain psychoses'. Improved and expanded knowledge of the structure and functions of the nervous system has greatly benefited neurosurgery. In this field. V. Horsley has done pioneer work. He contributed much to the mapping of the motor area of the cerebral cortex and also introduced many important technical improvements. Horsley was the first to operate on tumours in the cerebellum [1886], and in the hypophysis [1906], and he also enjoys priority in having successfully operated on tumours in the spinal cord and cerebrum. The subsequent development of neurosurgery is above all associated with the name of H. W. Cushing. He still further improved the technique, for instance by using electrical coagulations to stop minor haemorrhages, and he made important contributions to the study of brain tumours. Experiments to visualize the blood vessels radiologically started shortly after the discovery of X-rays; at first only in human corpses, but also, from 1923 onward, in living man. In 1927, Moniz made an important contribution by the introduction of cerebral angiography after the injection of a contrast medium into the carotid artery, a significant diagnostic improvement in neurosurgery.

Starting from J. F. Fulton's observation that artificial neuroses cannot be produced in anthropoid apes whose frontal lobes have been removed, while it is possible to produce such neuroses in intact animals, MONIZ made experiments to find out whether a favourable effect could be obtained in mentally disturbed persons by isolating the frontal lobes from the rest of the brain. Observations on human beings had indicated that a mental integration of impressions and experiences takes place in the anterior or prefrontal regions of the brain, in addition to which the areas in question seemed likely to have an important function in reference to emotional states, moral concepts, etc. To some extent the right and left frontal lobes can replace each other; but even if both are destroyed, a considerable part of the higher mental activities can still continue. Several forms of mental disturbances are characterized by a state of tension. Moniz assumed that it ought to be possible to relax the tension in such patients by severing the nerve paths to the prefrontal lobes [leucotomy]. This method was introduced in 1936, and has subsequently been used in thousands of mental cases of various kinds and with a gradually improved technique. More especially, two large categories of patients were treated; namely, those who suffered, respectively, from schizophrenia, the most important and common of all mental disturbances, or from manic-depressive psychoses.

In general, the results of the treatment were found to be favourable, especially in cases with symptoms of extreme anxiety. In many instances it was possible to restore normal mental activities, or what was left of them after prolonged illness. According to the nature of the disease, the operation varied by making the incisions at different distances from the brow. Efforts were made to render the procedure more precise, so as to interfere as little as possible with normal mental activities and also to facilitate healing within the shortest possible time. The method has also proved helpful in a number of chronic cases involving severe pain; the feeling of pain is blunted, and the patient obtains a considerable degree of relief.

As was to be expected, the elimination of the frontal lobes by leucotomy may also involve unfavourable consequences. Emotional reactions may be dulled, lack of tact or even downright rudeness may develop, while in some cases there is impairment of memory and initiative. Nevertheless, prefrontal leucotomy has often enabled a patient to serve a useful purpose in life, while in other cases his care has been greatly facilitated. Since the same goal can now be achieved with the aid of psychopharmaca, the operation is used less today than formerly.

SENSORY PHYSIOLOGY

As already mentioned, the introduction of electronic techniques after the First World War greatly facilitated neurophysiological research. The analysis of the impulse code in single nerve fibres in response to natural sensory stimulation opened up a new avenue in sensory physiology. The discoveries by Adrian and his coworkers on the properties of single sensory receptors, already described, widened our general sensory physiological knowledge [see p. 253]. In analyzing the special mechanisms that underlie energy transmission to, and transformation within, the receptor cells of different sense organs, we are confronted with a variety of special technical problems, inasmuch as the various sense organs, depending on how they are constructed, react to different physical or chemical characteristics in the environment. During the last seventy years, four prizes have been given for contributions in the field of special sensory physiology, viz. concerning vision, hearing and vestibular functions.

Crucial to our understanding of *visual perception* is our knowledge of the way in which the eye forms images. This is done by the dioptric apparatus, by the retinal receptors' photochemical reactions to illumination, resulting in excitation, and by the processing of information from the receptors which takes place in the retina's complex neuronal network before the messages, via the optic nerve fibres, are sent to the brain.

The exactness of the image of the outer world formed on the retina depends on the quality of the lens system: cornea, aqueous humour, crystalline lens and vitreous body. This optical system is highly transparent for light with wavelengths between 300 and 1,200 nm, a range which fully covers the photoreceptors' range of spectral sensitivity [400–700 nm]. Basic data on the eye's optical system were provided about a century ago by the German physicist H. von Helmholtz, who also constructed the opthalmoscope, by means of which the bottom of the human eye can be inspected through the pupil.

An important, albeit not easily appraisable, contribution was made by ALLVAR GULLSTRAND [1826–1930]. It related to optical reproduction in general, and its application to the eye in particular. Previously it had been assumed that every point or straight line in the object-medium is matched by a corresponding point or straight line in the image-medium [so-called co-linear reproduction]. Gullstrand proved, both mathematically and by direct tests, that only in very special circumstances was this theory approximately correct, and that, in general, it fitted actual conditions quite imperfectly and in a throughly misleading manner. As a rule, each point is represented in the reproduction by a diffusion circle, or rather, by two systems of lines. His detailed analysis of the beam of rays under different conditions led to an improved understanding of certain characteristics of the image [the anisotropic coma and the spherical or – better – the monochromatic aberration] which had previously been identified. In order to apply these findings to conditions in the eye, it was necessary to obtain accurate knowledge of its refreactory system; and on this subject Gullstrand made important contributions. Among other things, he improved our knowledge of the shape of the anterior and posterior surfaces of the cornea and the thickness of the latter. The aberration of the light ray in the eye was found to be so marked that, if the diffusion circles were as disturbing to vision as had previously been supposed, it ought to render the clarity of vision which actually obtains impossible. According to Gullstrand's reproduction theory, it is the distribution of light inside a cross-section of the beam of rays, not the size of the cross-section, that is decisive for the accuracy of reproduction. His investigations led to the discovery of intracapsular accomodation, whereby he was able to prove that the gain in the refractive power of the lens, which makes it possible to focus it on the 'near point', depends to only about two-thirds on the increase in its surface curvature, while the remaining one-third is due to a rearrangement of certain elements with varying refractive power. In this way an interpretation of the physiological significance of the heterogeneous structure of the lens was obtained. Gullstrand's careful experiments bore practical fruit in the construction of various instruments useful to ophthalmology, such as the reflex-free ophthalmoscope, the slit lamp and punctual glasses. After a detailed investigation, in which a qualified physicist also took part, the faculty decided to award the *1911* prize to GULLSTRAND 'for his work on the dioptrics of the eye'.

What we call light is the result of the action of a certain portion of the electromagnetic radiation [400–700 nm] on the retinal photoreceptors – the rods and cones. Packets of energy, which combine the properties of waves and particles – the quanta – are caught by the sensory cells, where they initiate a reaction resulting in excitation. The image that falls on the closely packed mosaic of retinal photoreceptors is disintegrated, since different cells respond to various parts and qualities of the image. The primary data are then brought together in the complex nerve net of the retina, in which the messages are translated into a language that can be understood by the brain. Fundamental principles for the structural arrangement of the neurons – in series and in parallel – in the retinal network were presented by Cajal [see p. 245].

Because of their significant contributions to our knowledge of photoreceptor functions and the integration that takes place in the retinal network, RAGNAR GRANIT [b. 1900], KEFFER HARTLINE [b. 1903] and GEORGE WALD [b. 1906] received the *1967* prize, given for 'their discoveries concerning the primary physiological and chemical visual processes in the eye'.

On the basis of earlier knowledge concerning rhodopsin, the photosensitive substance in the rods, Wald and his co-workers – among them R. Hubbard – carried out biochemical investigations which led to the discovery of the primary mechanism by which light triggers off the reaction in the sensory cells. The hundred-year-old history of rhodopsin, its localization in the rods and reaction to light goes back to F. Boll [1867] and W. Kühne [1878]. That the fat soluble vitamin A [see p. 229] is important for the build-up of rhodopsin has been known since the 1920's, e.g. from observations by L. S. Fredericia and E. Holm. In the 1930's, Wald postulated that a chromophore group, consisting of a carotenoid related to vitamin A [retinene], combines with a large protein group [opsin] to form rhodopsin. Later, it was shown by R. A. Morton and T. W. Goodwin that retinene is the aldehyde of vitamin A [retinaldehyde]. Because of several double bonds, vitamin A aldehyde [A_1 in man] may exist in several isomeric forms, the so-called all-trans form being the most stable, and the 11-cis–which is of immediate interest in this context–being unstable. In short, the discoveries of Wald and his group led to the following picture of the molecular primary mechanism leading to excitation. The chromophore group, 11-cis-aldehyde, fits like a hooked puzzle-piece in the profile of the larger protein piece, opsin. When a light quantum is taken up by the visual pigment in the rod, the chromophore changes its form: there is an isomerization from 11-cis to all-trans. The puzzle-piece straightens out and releases itself from its position, so that a successive splitting of the visual pigment follows. This molecular transformation induced by light–the isomerization–triggers the subsequent events in the visual system. All later changes–chemical, physiological and psychological–are, as Wald says, 'dark' consequences of this single light reaction. Wald's conclusion that this reaction applies to the whole animal world also emphasizes the broad significance of his discovery.

Recent absorption measurements on photoreceptors in fish, monkeys and man show the existence of three different types of cones containing different photopigments, whose absorption maxima fall within three ranges of wavelengths, corresponding to blue, green and red. The results of these investigations, performed independently by E. MacNichol and his group, Wald and co-workers and P. A. Liebman in U.S.A., and by W. Rushton in Britain thus support the classical theory of Young and Helmholtz, insofar that, at the receptor level, there is a trichromatic basis for colour discrimination.

The first records of single unit activity in a vertebrate retina in response to monochromatic light of different wavelengths were made on frogs in 1939 by Granit, in collaboration with G. Svaetichin. In these and Granit's following investigations on different mammals, the activity was led off from retinal neurons of higher orders, i.e. those receiving information from several receptor cells. However, Granit and his coworkers were the first to demonstrate retinal units with different spectral sensitivity, and the distribution of the narrow sensitivity curves, obtained by them, pointed to the existence of three types of cones.

In their work on the electrical responses from the whole retina [the electroretinogram], the optic nerve and single retinal units, Granit and his group found several expressions for the important role played by inhibitory processes in retinal integration, a fact which also became very obvious in Hartline's early investigations on single optic nerve fibre activity evoked by point light stimulation in the frog. Thus, the processing in the retinal neurons involves both addition and subtraction, brought about by the excitatory and inhibitory interaction at the synaptic junctions. As a result of such processes, which take place both in the retina and in the visual cortex, there is a re-evaluation of the image projected on the retina. Thus, the external stimulus pattern and the composition of the visual impression do not fully agree. Instead, certain characteristics of the picture are emphasized by heightening contrasts, so that forms stand out more clearly, colours are exaggerated, and movements accentuated.

In experiments on the eye of the horseshoe crab, a creature which offers good possibilities for quantitative studies, Hartline analysed the impulse generation in the light receptors and the impulse response of single light receptors to illumination of different intensity and duration. He then discovered the so-called lateral inhibition, which, because of the relatively simple functional organization of this eye, could be studied quantitatively. This discovery enabled Hartline to demonstrate the fundamental principles according to which the rough data from the sensory cells are re-evaluated in a nerve-net by means of inhibition. In a rather unique manner, his discoveries have contributed to our understanding of fundamental mechanisms whereby heightened contrast sharpens the visual impression of form and movement, and his discoveries also have a wide application in sensory physiology in general.

Our knowledge of the physical problems of *hearing* has been greatly advanced by the Hungarian physicist GEORG VON BÉKÉSY [b. 1899], at present working in U.S.A. In order to study the different steps in the process of hearing, Békésy developed refined methods, including advanced teletechnique and high magnification stroboscopic microscopy. This even enabled him to record membrane movements of the order of thousandths of a millimeter and to follow in detail the important events occurring at various places within the fragile miniature system which makes up the ear. In this transmission system the middle ear represents a link by which energy is transferred from air to the fluid in the inner ear. When energy is transferred from one medium to another, in which the energy propagates at different velocities, part of the energy is reflected at the border between the media, and part is transmitted. Von Békésy's investigations on the dynamics of the delicate mechanical system in the middle ear show how nature solves the problem of decreasing the reflection, thus enabling an optimal energy transfer to the inner ear within a wide frequency range. His main contribution concerns, however, the functioning of the inner ear. He confirmed Helmholtz' view that different wave frequencies engage different parts of the cochlea, high tones stimulating the hair cells at the base of the basilar membrane [which divides the spiral-shaped cavity of the cochlea in its longitudinal direction] and low tones at the top of the cochlea. By direct observations, he has shown that the hair cells are not stimulated by resonance, as postulated by Helmholtz, but that stimulation is caused by the special hydrodynamic conditions prevailing in the cochlea. Via the fluid of the inner ear, the movements of the stirrup's footplate produce movements in the basilar membrane in the form of a travelling wave complex, passing from the stiffer basal part towards the more flexible part in the apex of the cochlea. The highest wave crest first increases, then decreases. The position of maximal deflection was shown to be dependent on the frequency of the stimulating sound, in such a way that at low frequencies, the highest crest of the wave complex is located near the apex, and, at high frequencies, near to the base. Thus, our present knowledge of the way in which the cochlea functions mechanically, and of how it works as a frequency analyzer, is based on von Békésy's discoveries. Von Békésy has also discovered the so-called endocochlear potential at rest and the slow potential shifts taking place upon direct stimulation of the hair cells, processes which are involved in the excitation processes. The faculty decided to award the *1961* prize to VON BÉKÉSY 'for his discoveries of the physical mechanism of stimulation within the cochlea'.

Between 1901 and 1916, the name of G. Retzius was brought up in numerous proposals, particular attention being called to his extensive investigations of the organ of hearing and the nearby *vestibular apparatus*. The latter consists of a pair of small sacs and the semicircular ducts [or canals] which are set in three planes at right angles to each other, the whole system being filled with a fluid. Retzius' most important achievement was his discovery of the actual sense cells [the hair cells] in the above-mentioned sacs and the surrounding nerve endings. Retzius' contributions were deemed by the examiners to deserve a prize; but the Committee found them to be much too old for consideration.

The *1914* prize was awarded to ROBERT BÁRÁNY [1876–1936] 'for his work on the physiology and pathology of the vestibular apparatus'. From investigations made in the 1820's and later, it was known that incisions in the semicircular ducts can cause disturbances in the sense of balance as well as quick rhythmical movements of the eyes [nystagmus], and that infections in the area produce vertigo or giddiness. Gradually, the semicircular canal system came to be considered as a sense organ. Bárány found that when he flushed out an ear with water, some patients complained of dizziness, and he also observed nystagmus effects. Tests showed that these symptoms did not appear when the flushing liquid had the same temperature as the body, while water colder than the body had the same effect as warmer water, though the nystagmus movements then took place in the opposite direction. Bárány saw the explanation of these phenomena to lie in the movements of the fluid in the semicircular ducts, brought about by changes in its specific gravity, according to whether it was warmed or cooled. The effect also proved to be dependent on the spatial position of the semicircular ducts. On the other hand, the effect did not appear if the semicircular ducts had been destroyed by illness. By means of reflexes via the cerebellum, the vestibular apparatus also influences muscle tone. Bárány showed that, when the patient, with his eyes closed, tries to point straight ahead, to flush the left ear with cold water causes an aberration towards the left side, and vice versa. He also found that similar mistakes were made after certain parts of the cerebellum had been detached by local freezing or by pathological changes. On the basis of his findings, Bárány devised methods to investigate the functions both of the semicircular ducts and of the cerebellum. In this way a technique for diagnosing certain ailments, especially various kinds of inflammations in the inner ear, as well as of studying the activities in the cerebellum, became available.

Bárány was also one of the pioneers in the modern surgical treatment of otosclerosis, one of the most important causes of progressive deafness in adult life. The development of osseous changes, with decreased mobility of the stapes, impedes the transmission of sound waves through the oval window to the labyrinthine fluid. To counteract this, attempts have been made to create a new window by establishing a fistula to one of the semicircular canals in the inner ear. The great difficulty, however, has been that the fistula is so easily closed by cicatrization. Various methods have been developed to prevent such cicatrization; until today, in a large number of otosclerosis cases, it is possible to benefit the patients considerably.

IN RETROSPECT

Without exaggeration it may be claimed that a preponderant majority of the really great advances of the past seventy years in physiology or medicine have been mentioned in the proposals on which the Nobel Committee has had to pass judgment. The list includes not only discoveries in the narrow sense of the word, but also many other achievements which, because of their nature, could not possibly be classified as such. Since several of the earliest nominations were based on work performed in the 1880's and 1890's, and many of the contributions made during the past decade have so far been only partially submitted for consideration, the period dealt with is not, strictly speaking, the last seventy years. On the whole, however, it may be said that the work of the prize-jury reflects, in concentrated form, the history of medicine during seventy years of rapid progress.

During the first decades the situation was dominated by the new advances in microbiology and serology, whereby our understanding of the contagious diseases was greatly improved. This important group of ailments was then relegated to the background, only to attract special attention again in connection with the rapid development in chemotherapy. And then during the last twenty years virology and immunology have shown very remarkable progress, reflected in several prizes. Important new areas were also opened by the discoveries of hormones and vitamins, and several prize awards mark the significance attributed to them. Advances in theoretical biology were correspondingly recognized in the rewards for discoveries in genetics. The traditional methods of physiology have continued to bear fruit in discoveries that have been honoured with prizes, while the application to medical research of the new techniques developed in chemistry and physics has also proved most helpful. Medical chemistry, for instance, was able to advance from its exclusive pre-occupation with the composition of the body tissues to a penetrating analysis of the processes connected with the conversion of energy in the organism, and to that progress several prizes bear witness. Similarly, the new techniques of physics, especially those making it possible to measure bio-electrical potential changes, contributed to the rapid growth of our knowledge regarding the functions of the nervous system.

From Fig. 1 [p. 152] it appears that the number of meritorious candidates has invariably been greater than that of the prizes available. In the keen competition that has inevitably resulted, it has quite naturally been insisted upon that the prize awards must not be limited to a few subjects, but must do justice to all branches of medical research in so far as discoveries of fundamental importance are made within them. To appraise achievements in widely differing fields with reference to the somewhat vague expression 'for the benefit of mankind', is naturally extremely difficult. A glance at the list of winners shows, however, that serious efforts have been made to pay due heed to a great variety of claims. The prize has thus been given for discoveries in pure science, as well as for advances in the field of clinical medicine. Not infrequently has a prize been divided between scientists who have worked in the same or related fields, which indicates not only the close relationship between the works that have been honoured, but also the abundance of deserving candidates. On the other hand, a divided prize does not in any way imply a lesser distinction than an undivided one. In view of the high prestige the award has acquired in the public mind, it seems probable that the financial aspect of it is less important than the honour it conveys, and that its real value is therefore the same, whether it is divided or not.

In the decisions the requirement of a fresh discovery has played an important part. Sometimes such a discovery has been made quite independently, but often it has represented the culmination of a long series of investigations. Much consideration has also been given to the desire to reward the opening of new avenues to scientific progress, while mere applications of previous knowledge, no matter how significant, have not been held to be equally valuable. Sometimes difficulties have been caused by the fact that the works proposed for rewards have had several joint authors; as a rule, however, it has been possible to find adequate grounds for limiting the award to the person or persons who have had the decisive share in the discovery. In accordance with the express wishes of the testator, every effort has naturally been made to honour the most recent advances. Often, however, a considerable period of time is required to determine the permanent value of a discovery. This is particularly true of new methods of treatment. There have been risks of awards being made for contributions which in the long run would not prove to be of enduring worth. On a few occasions such awards have actually been made, but it is not humanly possible to avoid such mistakes if the requirement as to recent discovery is to be satisfied. The desire to satisfy this fundamental stipulation has had the result that if for a number of years a candidate has been found to deserve a prize, but has not actually received one, he has gradually been relegated to the group of those whose discoveries must be regarded as too old to receive recognition. In other instances of the same kind, however, new investigations have been ordered, especially if the candidate in question has added to his achievements after the previous examination.

While, as already stressed, awards have been made in many of the different branches of physiology or medicine, the fundamental aim has always been to honour contributions which in one respect or another have been considered to have had, or have seemed likely to have, a decisive effect on future developments in their respective fields. To what extent these efforts have been successful must be left for others to judge.

THE NOBEL MEDICAL INSTITUTE
THE SPECIAL FUND OF THE PRIZE-JURY

The idea of establishing a special Nobel Institute for each of the prize-awarding bodies was broached as early as at the time the will was first made public, and soon after that it was referred to in a written statement which the members of the Special Committee appointed to study the will submitted to the Royal Academy of Sciences and which was later attached to the official minutes regarding the will. As one of the necessary or desirable additions to the will, it was then proposed that under certain circumstances it ought to be possible to devote some of the income from the estate, in other ways than by prize-awards, to the furtherance of the purposes particularly specified in the will, i.e. the promotion of certain sciences and other cultural interests.

'As for as the Academy of Sciences and its share in the income is concerned', ran the Committee's proposal, 'the purpose of such a use of whatever savings may be effected would be, first of all, to establish a well equipped Nobel Institute of Physics and Chemistry, to which foreign scientists would also have access for the purpose of doing their research work.'

Similar views were expressed in a written statement issued shortly afterwards by the teaching staff of the Caroline Institute in which it was declared that it ought to be permissible to employ an unused share in the income 'for the support of physiological and medical research work in general ... In this way it would be possible to establish, in connection with the Caroline Institute in Stockholm, medical research centres which would be available to the scientists of the whole world, who could thus be provided with all the material equipment necessary for the pursuit of their special research work and also, whenever judged appropriate, with the economic support needed to enable them to devote themselves exclusively to such work.'

The proposed use of the funds made available after a prize has been withheld was accepted during the subsequent discussion, though it was stipulated that the money thus retained should be paid into a special capital fund set up for each prize-jury, and that only the interest on this money should be utilized for the purpose indicated. That, in fact, became one of the provisions in the officially approved statutes, according to which the yield of the special funds may be used in other ways than by prize-awards to promote the purposes the testator had ultimately had in mind. Consequently, it is perfectly proper and legal to use it to support the various Nobel Institutes.

In the course of the above discussion regarding the use of prize-money withheld, it was also suggested on a couple of occasions that it might be permissible to use the interest earned by this money for the purpose of organizing a special Nobel Institute to assist in the examination of prize proposals. Otherwise, there has never been any question of using this income except for pure research work, and there has never been any further mention of special assistance in connection with the prize-awards.

At the same time there was also a plan to establish Nobel Institutes of another type. On that point the text of the minutes runs as follows: 'In regard to the method by which works under consideration for prize-awards are to be examined in greater detail, it was proposed... that this critical scrutiny of all or some of the proposals should be performed, as required, by a scientific institution which could properly be called the Nobel Institute. The expenses connected with the various activities of this organization were to be defrayed by a certain percentage of the sums annually set aside for the prizes, and possibly also by the income from the special funds which ... may perhaps be set up'. This plan was further elaborated at a subsequent meeting at which a proposal was made to organize a special institute to serve all the prize-adjudicating bodies, while each of them was to be allowed to decide on the details as to the organization of its own department. The main function of this institute was to make the detailed investigations of such prize proposals as had been received. If required in that connection, thorough studies were to be made 'in order to verify the actual facts on which the claims of a discovery are based as well as the significance of the latter'. It was anticipated that the expenses required for such an institution would be considerable, and it was supposed that the costs of construction and equipment might be defrayed by the income from the main fund before the prize distribution began, while the annual running expenses could be deducted, as a proper part of the cost of making the decisions, from the money set aside each year for the prize-awards. In order to make it possible to affiliate with the proposed institute properly qualified scientists, it was considered necessary to allow them enough time to continue their own research work, 'whereby their power of judgment would be maintained and improved'.

In accordance with the schemes outlined above, the first draft of the proposed statutes included special regulations for the projected Nobel Institute in which its duties were declared to be to assist in the investigation of prize proposals and also to promote work in the cultural fields represented by the awards. The representatives of the Caroline Institute wanted to have a special Nobel Institute for each one of the various groups of subjects and were of the opinion that the expenses of these institutes should be defrayed, first of all, by the funds appropriated to meet the costs of selecting the winners but not wholly expended for that purpose, and that, in addition, it should be permissible to draw on the interest earned by the special funds. Although it was declared in one quarter that the investigation work preliminary to the prize-awards ought to be the primary purpose of the institutes, the statutory regulations regarding future Nobel Institutes were finally formulated in such a way that they placed on the same level 'assistance with the scrutiny necessary for the prize adjudication' and 'the promotion in other ways of the purposes of the Foundation'.

To finance the various Nobel Institutes, there was originally deducted from the main fund for each of the prize-juries the sum of 300,000 Kr. To these appropriations has since been added the money saved from the annual appropriations for the different prize-adjudicating bodies to defray their expenses in connection with the awards [which amount altogether to one-fourth of the total sum set aside each year for the five prizes].

In 1917, the gradual increase in the funds available brought to a head the question of a Nobel Institute for the physiological or medical prize division. In December that year, Professor E. Müller proposed the organization of a special department of physiology at a future, joint Nobel Institute. The subject was taken up by the Nobel Committee, on behalf of which the Rector of the Caroline Institute, Professor F. Lennmalm, drafted a project to set up a Nobel Medical Institute for research work on heredity and race biology. As an argument in favour of such a step the claim was advanced that this line of research was in special need of support and, in view of its importance, also deserved it. During the discussion that followed, it was asserted, however, that an institute for research in race biology and human genetics would serve no purpose in connection with the work of selecting winners of the Nobel Prizes and was rather the concern of the Swedish Government, while a department devoted exclusively to physiology would be valuable also from the point of view of the prize-jury.

At the 1918 session of the Swedish *Riksdag*, a motion was made to appropriate the sum of 50,000 Kr. for each of the four Swedish Nobel Prize juries to help them organize and maintain their projected Nobel Institutes. This proposal, which was based exclusively on the increased need for scientific research work within the country itself, was rejected by the *Riksdag*. In 1919, however, the Swedish prize-juries agreed to petition the Government to submit to the *Riksdag* an official request for the same purpose. In this connection the Caroline Institute decided on its own account that if the requested Government appropriation was granted, a Nobel Medical Institute would be organized by the beginning of 1921, and that at the outset there would be a department of experimental physiology and another of experimental pathology, though a strong minority still preferred the above-mentioned institute for race biology and human genetics. The Government, however, took no action. On the other hand, in the 1920 *Riksdag* a motion was made to address to the Government a request for a study of the proposal to set up a Swedish Institute of Race Biology. In the following year this action resulted in the organization of such an establishment at the University of Uppsala, whereby the previously advanced opinion that this was a direct concern of the Swedish Government was confirmed.

The matter was then left in abeyance until 1935 when a proposal was made to organize a biochemical department of the projected Nobel Medical Institute with Dr. H. Theorell as its head. The time was now ripe for such a step, and in the following year the statutes and by-laws were drawn up and Theorell appointed director of the new biochemical department with the rank of professor, the running expenses being at first wholly defrayed by Nobel money.

Since then another department has been organized for the study of neurophysiology and a third for medical cell research and genetics, with Professors R. Granit and T. Caspersson as their respective heads. In regard to both of these departments the development has differed from that of the biochemical division. For Professor Granit a chair of neurophysiology was set up in 1940 at the Caroline Institute with financial support from the Wallenberg Foundation [in Stockholm] and the Rockefeller Foundation [in New York], and in 1946 its maintenance was taken over by the State. The next year, a state professorship in medical cell research and genetics was provided for Professor Caspersson. The activities of both men have thus been made possible by a combination of liberal private bequests and public funds, while the Caroline Institute has used its Nobel revenue, set aside for the purpose, to construct buildings for the three departments. From July 1, 1956, Theorell's professorship also has been taken over by the State. Thus the Swedish Government and the Nobel Foundation have co-operated in the creation of a Nobel Medical Institute with three departments. Granit and Theorell have now retired and their successors were appointed according to the procedures in use at Swedish medical faculties.

The principal occupation of these departments is their own research work and, at present, the regulations for the activity of these departments are the same as those of other departments at the Institute.

As already stated, the income from the Special Fund may be used not only for the maintenance of the Nobel Institute, but also for the promotion in other ways of the purposes the testator had in mind. For the first time, minor grants in aid of research were paid out from this source in 1918, and on many subsequent occasions such payments have played an important role in promoting scientific investigations. Primarily they have been used to support such work at the Caroline Institute itself, but grants have also been made to workers at other institutions, including some outside Sweden. In 1956 it was decided that the interest from the Special Fund shall be used exclusively for the maintenance of the Nobel Institutes.

CONCLUSION

When the contents of Alfred Nobel's will became known for the first time, they stirred up a lively debate in the Swedish and the foreign press. The views expressed clashed sharply. On the one hand, there were statements which conveyed a sincere and unqualified appreciation of the donor's purposes. In other quarters, however, suspicion and disapproval were voiced. Opinions were even advanced to the effect that the donation would do more harm than good.

As we now look back on the past seventy years, we can conclude that, on the whole, the prize-distributors have performed their duties in a way that has gained general approval. It is evident that many times it has been possible to make a more or less justified criticism of particular awards, as has also been done in regard to certain omissions. But, as is well known, all human efforts are subject to limitations, and the mistakes have probably not been more numerous than could have been expected in view of the difficulties that were bound to be encountered.

It has not been possible to realize Nobel's original plan that the prizes should be large enough to enable the recipients to continue their research work free from financial worries. But in many cases the awards, apart from their monetary value, have indirectly improved the opportunities of the prize-winners to pursue their life-work. By virtue of the prestige the prizes have attained, a recipient is transformed, as C. J. Davisson has expressed it, 'overnight from an exceedingly private citizen to something in the nature of a semi-public institution'. Such a transition has often created more favourable conditions for further work. 'Even the strongest will to research can be crushed by the might of the world about us' F. Bergius once declared. But it is precisely the winner's environment that the prize has most often improved; new laboratories have been built, ample funds have been made available, a greater number of younger scientists have sought his instruction, thanks to which his opportunities to influence future developments in his own field have been greatly enhanced. It is thanks to the impartial, international character of the honour that it has achieved such results and has thereby helped to fulfil the donor's hopes in a different way than he had imagined. On many occasions the winners themselves have called attention to this aspect of the distinction. 'The Nobel awards bring home to the masses of the people of all nations a realization of their common interests. To those who have no direct contact with science they carry a touch of the international spirit, I. Langmuir has maintained. W. Ostwald has pointed out that science has proved itself to be the most important of all human assets, especially as it is completely independent of both race and language, and that, by virtue of its international character, the Nobel Foundation stands out as a rare and brilliant embodiment of this international spirit.

That in many instances the honour has spurred the recipients to new efforts is indubitable. Quite often it has been found that their research work has been carried on after the award with at least as much vigour and success as before. In other instances, the honours have come so late in life that the winner's own activities had already flagged or ceased altogether. But even in such cases, the prize has served an important purpose: it has called attention to various pioneering achievements, and hence has not only helped to create among people in general an increased interest in, and respect for, scientific activities as a whole, but has also attracted the attention of other scientists to fields of endeavour in which important advances might be expected in the near future.

As for the prize-juries, it may be said with justice that the work of carrying out Nobel's wishes has been of great advantage to them. The systematic survey of contemporary research required for the distribution of the prizes has had an inspiring effect on their own scientific activities, and the closer contacts it has established with the scientists of other countries have enabled them to share better in the advances made in various other places. To this the good will gained everywhere by our country through the prize-awards has contributed greatly. The increased responsibility which the work connected with the prize-awards in physiology or medicine has imposed on the Caroline Institute has also brought corresponding advantages. The rapid growth of the Institute during the past seventy years has certainly been greatly facilitated by this aspect of its activities.

The effect of the work done by the Nobel Foundation as a whole is closely connected with the general problem of what modern civilization means to mankind. In spite of our experiences with the frightful dangers which an abuse of the conquests of science may create, it is probably clear to most of us that our entire progress largely depends not only on our increased mastery over the forces of nature, but also on the training in personal responsibility that should accompany it, and, finally, on the success of our efforts to provide a peaceful common existence. Consequently, the following words of P. Curie probably still hold true for all of us: 'I am one of those who, like Nobel, believe that humanity will derive more benefit than harm from new discoveries.' We can therefore agree with H. Schück that 'the Nobel Prizes are an outward expression of our hope that science and literature will some day scatter the shadows of national antagonisms which have descended on the whole world – the hope that at least our descendants will some day see the sun break through the clouds',

THE CHEMISTRY PRIZE

BY ARNE WESTGREN

Alfred Nobel's original intention was that most of his wealth should be used after his death for annual prizes to be awarded by the Swedish Royal Academy of Sciences for the most outstanding discoveries or theories in the wide field of learning and progress as a whole. In his final will, however, he gave up this plan and directed that the prizes were to be awarded in certain specific branches of science and learning only. It was but natural that one of these should have been chemistry.

Nobel's own researches had, after all, been chiefly devoted to problems in chemical technology, so that he had first-hand knowledge of the importance of chemistry in our material progress. At the end of the nineteenth century, this science was making rapid and promising advances. Precision methods were beginning to be applied in the study of chemical phenomena. Scientists trained in the methods of physics had successfully tackled some of the fundamental problems in chemistry, and the no man's land between physics and chemistry was at last being bridged. It had thus been possible to lay a firm foundation for the study of the general laws governing chemical phenomena. The German dye and chemical industry flourished as a result of the work carried out at its own research laboratories and those of the universities. Among chemists there were at that time a number of pioneers whose achievements were obviously of the greatest value to mankind. In his will of 1895, Nobel entrusted the Academy of Sciences with the task of deciding each year which of these scientists had made the most important discovery or improvement during the preceding year and with awarding a prize for this work.

For more than seventy years the Academy has tried to fulfil this task, which is an honourable but by no means easy one.

As has already been mentioned, it was laid down in the will that the prize should be awarded for work during the preceding year. In the statutes of the Nobel Foundation this provision has been interpreted in such a way that the prize shall be awarded for the most recent results in the branches of learning indicated in the will, and for older work provided its significance has only recently been demonstrated. It is further laid down in the statutes that the prize may not be awarded for work which has not proved by experience or expert investigation sufficiently outstanding to fulfil the obvious requirements of the will. Even with these additional explanations of the wording of the will, it is a difficult task to award the Nobel Prize for Chemistry.

In order to assess reasonably accurately the value of a scientific discovery it is necessary to be able to view its effects over a fairly long period. On the other hand, the statutes require that the prize shall be awarded not too long after it has been earned. Those who nominate candidates for the prize must, therefore, be able to some extent to read the future; a gift which human beings possess only rarely and even then with no claim to infallibility. The Academy of Sciences does not, therefore, imagine that its awards of the Nobel Prize will in all cases stand the test of time. Its responsibility is, however, shared to some extent by all the scientists – most of them active research workers in physics or chemistry – who have nominated candidates, since it is only from among these candidates that the Academy may make its choice. In fact, if a scientist is proposed by a large number of sponsors in the preliminary international voting, he is normally selected by the Academy.

In September, 1900, the Academy of Sciences set about its task of awarding the Nobel Prizes for Physics and Chemistry in accordance with special regulations approved by the King in June of the same year. The two Nobel Committees were then appointed, each consisting of five members. Invitations to submit names were sent for the first time to the Swedish and foreign members of the Academy and to the professors of physics and chemistry at Scandinavian universities and colleges and at some ten institutions of higher education outside Scandinavia. About 300 scientists in various parts of the world received a circular letter addressed personally to them, asking them to put forward nominations for the Prize for Chemistry, and an equal number were requested to nominate candidates for the Physics Prize.

Year after year these requests for nominations have been sent out by the Nobel Committees of the Academy. The number of letters has, however, gradually increased. The membership of the Academy has grown, the number of universities and colleges whose professors of physics and chemistry have been approached has increased to about twice the original number, and, finally, an important and valuable group of proposers has gradually been formed, namely the winners of the Nobel Prizes for Physics and Chemistry. During recent years, therefore, about 450 people yearly have had the right to nominate candidates for the Nobel Prize for Chemistry and almost as many for that for Physics. Not quite a third of these

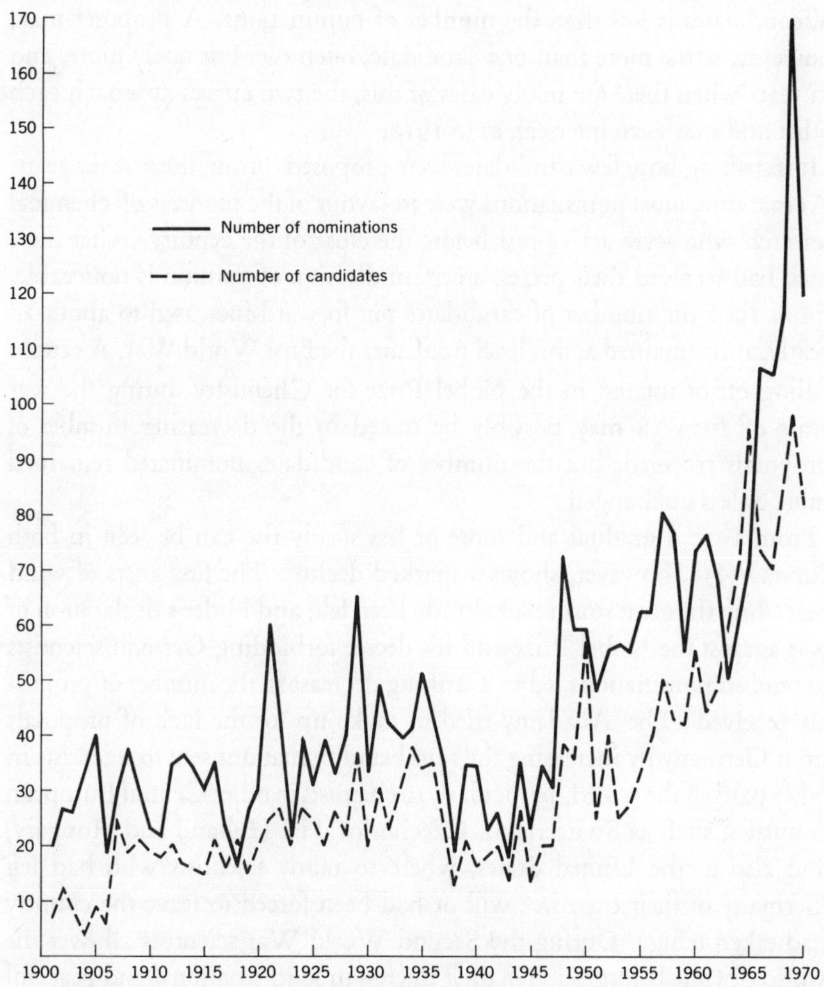

have been Swedes. The foreign universities and colleges have been selected so that the principal language regions in the world are represented each year. They are approached in turn, but in such a way that the more important seats of learning, e.g., the universities of London, Berlin, Paris, Moscow, Chicago, Zürich, Harvard, and the Massachusetts Institute of Technology, recur more often than the smaller universities and colleges.

The diagram above shows how the number of nominations received and the number of candidates proposed have increased during the first sixty years. In many cases the same name was put forward by several proposers so that, with the exception of one single year, 1918, the number of candidates is less than the number of nominations. A proposer may, however, name more than one candidate, often two but rarely more, and in years when there are many cases of this, the two curves approach each other and may even intersect, as in 1918.

It is striking how few candidates were proposed during the first six years. At that time most nominations were in favour of the pioneers of chemical research who were active just before the close of the century. After these men had received their prizes, a certain division of opinion is noticeable. From 1907 the number of candidates put forward increased to about 20 yearly, and remained at this level until after the First World War. A certain falling off of interest in the Nobel Prize for Chemistry during the war years of 1914-18 may possibly be traced in the decreasing number of proposals received, but the number of candidates nominated remained more or less unchanged.

From 1920 a gradual and more or less steady rise can be seen in both curves. 1938, however, shows a marked decline. The first gusts of wind preceding the great storm had already been felt, and Hitler's declaration of war against the Nobel Prize and his decree forbidding German scientists to send in nominations led to a striking decrease in the number of proposals received. The Academy tried to make up for the lack of proposals from Germany by increasing the number of invitations sent to scientists in other parts of the world, particularly to chemists in other Central European countries, such as Switzerland, Czechoslovakia, Holland and Hungary, and also to the United States, where so many scientists who had left Germany of their own free will or had been forced to leave the country had taken refuge. During the Second World War scientists all over the world obviously lost much of their interest in so international and peaceful an activity as the awarding of the Nobel Prize. The circular letters inviting proposals remained unanswered to a greater extent than before. The fact that the prize could not be awarded during the years 1940-43 owing to war conditions naturally also contributed to the slackening of interest.

That Hitler's ban on nominations from Germany was deprecated by at least some of those most concerned is clear from a letter sent by the Nobel Prize winner Max von Laue during a visit to Switzerland in 1939. He urged the Academy of Sciences not to attach any significance to the extraordinary ban imposed by the German authorities. 'They issue so many ill-considered laws', he wrote, 'that they can scarcely keep track of them themselves.'

Many scientists who were invited to submit proposals during the war years regretted that conditions at the time rendered it impossible for them to do so. Many were fully occupied with work of military importance, and access to foreign scientific literature was so limited that they felt unable to form any accurate idea of the progress of research as a whole. Many even questioned the suitability of awarding the Nobel Prize during a period of such violent international discord.

Even during the years immediately following the war the invitations issued by the Academy very often passed unnoticed and the number of candidates nominated was comparatively low. It was not until 1948 that the high level of the years between the wars was again reached. That year the Nobel Committee received 72 letters containing nominations, which later has been only slightly surpassed.

THE CHEMISTRY PRIZES DURING THE FIRST FEW YEARS

Cannizzaro, who lived until 1910, was the last of the great chemists who up to the middle of the nineteenth century were trying to solve the important problem of drawing up a reliable table of atomic weights. In his epoch-making work, *Sunto di un corso di filosofia chimica,* published in 1859, he pointed out that it was easy to settle the current doubt as to whether some atomic weights ought to be halved or not. It was only necessary to determine the vapour density and then apply Avogadro's law that equal volumes of different gases at the same temperature and pressure contain an equal number of molecules, or, if the element could not be studied in this way, to apply Dulong-Petit's law of atomic heats. It was thus possible at last to draw up an accurate table of atomic weights. In the decade that followed, other scientists were able to fit the elements into the comprehensive scheme provided by the periodic system.

Cannizzaro's work was certainly well worth a Nobel Prize, and he was indeed proposed, but strangely enough not until 1907, when he was eighty-one years old. The Nobel Committee agreed unreservedly that his work was of fundamental importance for the atomic and molecular theories and thus for modern chemistry as a whole, but such a long time had elapsed since the publication of his results that the statutes made it impossible to award the prize to him, however much he may have merited it. As already mentioned, the statutes allow older work to be considered only if its significance has not been demonstrated until recently. This, however, was certainly not the case with Cannizzaro, the value of whose work was very quickly recognized – a fact which was even pointed out by the proposers themselves.

The case of another of the pioneers of chemical research in the nineteenth century was quite different. J. Willard Gibbs, professor of mathematical physics at Yale University, was still alive during the first few years of the century. He died in 1903. During the years 1873-78 he published a number of papers in the *Transactions of the Connecticut Academy,* among others a large monograph, *The Equilibrium of Heterogeneous Substances,* which will always remain one of the classical works of chemistry. It contained applications of thermodynamics to such phenomena as thermal dissociation, adsorption, surface tension, and electrochemistry. In this work he formulated the concepts of phase and chemical potential, etc., which are of fundamental importance in modern chemistry, and stated the so-called 'phase rule', which shows how the equilibrium of a chemical system depends on the number of components, the number of phases [i.e. homogeneous parts of a system] and other conditions [temperature and pressure].

Gibbs's work remained practically unnoticed for a long time. It had been published in a little known series, and because of its abstract nature was rather too complicated for his time. At the end of the nineteenth century most chemists were scarcely qualified to follow investigations such as those of Gibbs, which involved the use of mathematical methods. Only certain parts of them attracted attention during the last two decades of the century in connection with the growing interest in the application of thermodynamics to chemistry. Gibbs's phase rule was also applied ast he guiding principle in the studies of the equilibrium of heterogeneous systems carried out at that time by Bakhuis Roozeboom and others. Even by the beginning of the twentieth century, however, the importance of Gibbs's work was not fully appreciated. As late as 1923, when the American chemist G. N. Lewis published his brilliant textbook, *Thermodynamics,* he could write that Gibbs's monograph 'has proved a rich and *still unexhausted* mine of thermodynamic material'.

Gibbs unquestionably deserved to be awarded the Nobel Prize for his work on thermodynamics. The length of time that had elapsed since the work had been carried out would not in his case have precluded an award. But he was never nominated. The time was clearly not yet ripe for a true valuation of his work. This is greatly to be regretted, as the name of J. W. Gibbs as the first or possibly the second on the list of Nobel Prize winners for Chemistry would undeniably have been an honourable addition.

Another two of the prominent figures from the latter part of the nineteenth century were still alive at the beginning of the twentieth century and could, therefore, have been considered for the prize. The most important work of both of them dealt with the heat formed during chemical reactions, and was so comprehensive and of such value that they may together be considered as the founders of thermochemistry. They were the Dane, J. Thomsen, and the Frenchman, M. Berthelot. The former died in 1909 and the latter in 1907. The original aim of their measurements of the heat evolved in the formation of a compound from its components was to find a way of measuring how strongly these components bind one another, or to determine what is known as their affinity. It was thus one of the fundamental problems in chemistry they were trying to solve, a problem that had been studied for a long time.

Later research has shown that the so-called heat of reaction determined by Thomsen and Berthelot is not really a rational measure of affinity, even though it is generally more or less correct if the reaction takes place at normal temperatures. For the lower the temperature at which the reaction takes place, the smaller is the error involved in taking the heat of reaction as a measure of affinity. In actual fact, affinity is not suitably determined by the difference in energy content between the compound and its components, but, as Van 't Hoff suggested on the basis of the second law of thermodynamics, by the maximum quantity of useful work which can be gained when the reaction is carried out in a reversible manner. Serious objections could therefore be raised against the theoretical conclusions drawn by Thomsen and Berthelot from their experimental results. The former soon realized that the criticisms were justified, but the latter sought as long as possible to defend his untenable position. The thermochemical material which they collected by their untiring and very skilful measurements is, however, of great value.

Thomsen was in fact never nominated for the prize, but Berthelot's name was suggested almost every year in the early days. If the thermochemical investigations mentioned above had been honoured with a prize, it ought to have been divided between the two of them. It may be recalled that the Davy Medal was awarded to both of them by the Royal Society in 1883. But since Thomsen's name was never suggested, a division of the prize was not considered, and it is unlikely that this solution would have been preferred by the Academy to the awards that were made at the time to scientists whose work was more recent and of greater merit. In any case, the adjudicators evidently felt that Berthelot should give way to these younger men.

The number of scientists who could be considered as worthy of receiving the Nobel Prize was larger during the first few years than it has ever been since. Is has already been pointed out that chemistry had undergone a period of magnificent development during the last two decades of the nineteenth century. Work of fundamental importance in the sphere of physical chemistry had been carried out by J. H. van 't Hoff, Svante Arrhenius and W. Ostwald. A. von Baeyer, the grand old man of German organic chemistry, had succeeded in synthesizing indigo. He had tackled with striking success the problem of the constitution of tar-dyes. By his studies of the reduction products of benzene and other aromatic substances, he had laid the foundations of the chemistry of the hydroaromatic compounds, thus clearing the way for investigations of the terpenes and camphor, which in fact he carried out himself. E. Fischer had performed a masterly analysis of the structure of the sugars, determined the constitution of the purine derivatives and begun his pioneer work in the field of protein chemistry. Starting from Lord Rayleigh's discovery of the heavy component in the atmosphere, W. Ramsay had isolated this component, thus producing argon for the first time. During subsequent studies of the composition of the atmosphere he discovered helium and the other inert gases. With these discoveries the periodic system was supplemented by a very important group of elements. Other valuable advances in the field of inorganic chemistry were made during the 1880's and 1890's by H. Moissan, who succeeded in isolating the chemically very active gas fluorine and in producing compounds of metals with boron, carbon and silicon in his electric arc furnace, thereby considerably increasing our knowledge of a hitherto little known group of substances.

During the first few years the Academy was chiefly faced with merely deciding the order in which these scientists should be awarded the prize.

They all well deserved to be considered. To compare the value of their contributions to chemistry was not easy, being in such varied fields, but as we have seen, the nominations submitted to the Academy offered good guidance. Of the 20 proposals received in 1901, for example, not less than 11 suggested Van 't Hoff. He was thus clearly indicated by international opinion – in so far as it was expressed by the nominations – as the most deserving candidate for the first Nobel Prize for Chemistry. The Academy in fact followed this clear recommendation. The next year Arrhenius, Berthelot and Fischer received 5 votes each. The Academy then selected Fischer. In 1903, half of the proposals named Arrhenius, who received the prize, and in 1904, not less than 22 of the 32 proposers nominated Ramsay, who was in fact awarded the prize that year. With the next two awards – von Baeyer in 1905 and Moissan in 1906 – the Academy also followed the majority of the proposers.

JACOBUS HENRICUS VAN 'T HOFF [1852-1911] will always be counted as one of the greatest figures in chemical research. As early as 1874, when he was only twenty-two years old, he published an epoch-making work on the asymmetry of the carbon atom. The paper appeared both in French and German and soon made him famous. He had found that the problem of constitution in organic chemistry could only be solved by considering the spatial structure of the molecules. By this discovery he founded a new branch of science, called stereochemistry. Had the Nobel Prize existed at the time, Van 't Hoff would have deserved it. When he was awarded the prize in *1901,* however, it was not for this work – which was of course too old – but for his later fundamental and ingenious work in the field of chemical reactions and for establishing the laws of osmotic pressure. His comprehensive monograph, *Études de dynamique chimique,* published in 1884, is an application of the laws of thermodynamics to chemical reactions and equilibrium with results of great general importance. Svante Arrhenius, reviewing this monograph the following year in *Nordisk Revy,* wrote enthusiastically: 'In the latter part the author exhibits an extraordinary talent for judging a large number of facts in the same light and has also succeeded – with the comparatively insignificant experimental material available – in sketching a magnificent and harmonious plan for the whole field of chemical reactions. Even though the author has already acquired an immense reputation for his genius in robbing nature of her secrets, his previous work is completely overshadowed by what he has achieved here. What a difference there is between him and the present champions of thermochemistry!'

In the autumn of 1885, Van 't Hoff submitted three papers to Professor Otto Pettersson in Stockholm with the request that they should be published in some Swedish journal. Their subject matter was connected with the work of Scandinavian scientists, the pioneer work of the Norwegians Guldberg and Waage on the law of mass action, Thomsen's confirmation of this law, Arrhenius's doctoral thesis, and research data which Pettersson himself had placed at Van 't Hoff's disposal. Van 't Hoff's papers appeared in the Transactions of the Academy under the general title of *Lois de l'équilibre chimique dans l'état dilué, gazeux ou dissous.* The Swedish Academy of Sciences is proud of having received for publication these papers which, together with *Études de dynamique chimique* – 'Révolution chimique' as it has been called – will always be counted among the classical documents of chemistry.

Among the most important results published here was the proof that the osmotic pressure of a solution is equal to the pressure the substance dissolved in the solution would have if it were in gaseous form and had the same volume as the solution, and that the laws of gases, including Avogadro's law, apply to solutions. Hence it was only necessary to consider osmotic pressure instead of gas pressure. By measuring osmotic pressure one could also obtain a measure of the molecular weight. Unfortunately it is not easy to measure osmotic pressure direct with any accuracy, but Van 't Hoff proved thermodynamically that the lowering of the freezing point caused by the dissolved substance is proportional to the osmotic pressure. As this change in temperature can be measured easily with great precision, it is thus possible – as Raoult had, moreover, found out empirically shortly before – to determine the molecular weight of a dissolved substance simply and accurately.

Van 't Hoff found that the results of experiments on solutions of organic substances in water fitted in well with his theory, but in the case of solutions of inorganic salts, acids, and bases the freezing point was lowered more than the calculated amount. He described this anomaly in detail in a paper published in 1887 in the first volume of Ostwald's *Zeitschrift für physikalische Chemie.* An explanation of the deviations was given in the same volume in a memoir by Arrhenius, which was practically identical with two papers published by him in the same year in the Transactions of the Swedish Academy of Sciences.

In these papers Arrhenius pointed out that the solutions which caused

Van 't Hoff's difficulties were electrolytes. They contained ions and if these could be considered as osmotically equivalent to molecules, as seemed reasonable, the solutions in question must have a higher osmotic pressure and consequently produce a greater lowering of the freezing point than solutions containing only undissociated molecules. Arrhenius had studied how the electrical conductivity of a solution of a salt changes with the concentration, and since the electric current is carried by the free ions, he was able to measure the dissociation. He then used his experimental results to calculate how great the fall in the freezing point ought to be for the electrolytes studied by Van 't Hoff, taking into consideration the degree of dissociation into ions. The values he obtained agreed trhoughout with the experimental results. His theory of electrolytic dissociation was thus definitely confirmed, and the general validity of Van 't Hoff's law of osmotic pressure in solutions was proved.

When the Academy of Sciences was considering the award of the Nobel Prize for 1901, Arrhenius made a statement in which he said, among other things: 'Several circumstances led to the relatively early recognition of Van 't Hoff's discovery. At an early age [1874] he published a work on stereochemistry which brought down on his head the ridicule of conservative chemists, the ridicule which usually follows immediately after a great discovery. Since then his stereochemical work has received the recognition it so highly deserved. In 1876 appeared his brilliant book, *Ansichten über organische Chemie,* which although it was loftily ignored by most chemists, considerably increased his reputation with the rest. Finally, his splendid work, *Études de dynamique chimique* [1884], made him at once the most prominent man in physical chemistry. This treatise should be regarded as leading directly up to the great work for which it is proposed to offer him the prize. Quite apart from the fact that Van 't Hoff had thus already made a name for himself, which naturally made it easier for him to win recognition for his new work, the theory of electrolytic dissociation published simultaneously protected him from really violent attacks. Although the main controversy between the old and the new ideas during the past fifteen years has concerned the problem of electrolytic dissociation, there have nevertheless been isolated and virulent attacks – for example that by Lothar Meyer – against Van 't Hoff's law. These attacks have been convincingly answered by Van 't Hoff himself.'

As early as in his doctoral thesis in 1884, SVANTE ARRHENIUS [1859–1927] published the results of his studies of the electrical conductivity of solutions, so that his thesis can be said to contain the first draft of the theory of dissociation, even if it was still rather vague. It is not surprising that the ideas expressed there were not immediately appreciated. Unusual acumen and a lively intellect were necessary to understand the significance of Arrhenius's ideas at this early stage. Two scientists proved, however, to possess these powers. They were Otto Pettersson in Stockholm and Wilhelm Ostwald in Riga.

Pettersson reviewed the thesis in *Nordisk Revy* and praised it very highly. He ended his article with the following words: 'The faculty have awarded the mark *Non sine laude* to this thesis. This is a very cautious but very unfortunate choice. It is possible to make serious mistakes from pure cautiousness. There are chapters in Arrhenius's thesis [e.g., the discovery of the connection between conductivity and speed of reaction] which alone are worth more or less all the faculty can offer in the way of marks.'

Ostwald has related that he found the ideas propounded in Arrhenius's thesis so strange at first that he was inclined to consider the whole thing as rubbish. But then he discovered some calculations of this 'obviously very young' writer which made him see his own results in an entirely new and clearer light. From that moment he was a keen supporter of the new ideas.

Professor P. T. Cleve, in his speech in honour of Arrhenius at the Nobel banquet in 1903, confessed how little he had realized at first the value of this new theory of the connection between chemical affinity and electrical conductivity. 'These new theories also suffered from the misfortune that nobody really knew where to place them', he said. 'Chemists would not recognize them as chemistry, nor physicists as physics. They have in fact built a bridge between the two.'

When Cleve said this he must certainly have had in mind certain differences of opinion which had arisen when the question of awarding Arrhenius the prize was discussed in the Academy. Should he receive the Prize for Physics or for Chemistry? He had been nominated for both. A large majority of the proposers for each of the prizes had suggested his name. His work was of great importance in chemistry but had resulted from studies of a problem in physics and therefore belonged to the field of physics. Arrhenius's methods were those of a physicist, and presumably the fact that he was by profession a physicist could not be overlooked.

When considering the question, the Nobel Committee for Chemistry hit upon the peculiar idea of suggesting that he should be awarded half the Prize for Chemistry and half that for Physics. This ingenious solution did not please the physicists, who turned down the suggestion pointing out that it would be difficult to award the other half of the Prize for Physics. In its report for *1903* the Nobel Committee for Chemistry wrote: 'Since it is a question of awarding the prize for the theory of electrolytic dissociation, the origin and scope of which go far beyond the boundaries of chemistry, the theory should be judged as a whole and in its context. To single out certain parts of it which are particularly important in chemistry and to award them the Prize for Chemistry would give the scientific world the idea that neither the significance of Arrhenius's discoveries nor his scientific standing were fully appreciated in his mother country.' When the physicists would not agree to the proposal made by the Committee for Chemistry, a majority of three members of the latter committee voted for postponing the decision on Arrhenius until the following year. At a later meeting is was pointed out, however – and by a chemist – that such a postponement would more than anything else give scientists as a whole the impression that Arrhenius's merits were not fully appreciated in his own country. Fortunately the Academy followed the minority of the Committee, including P. T. Cleve, which wanted to award the entire 1903 Prize for Chemistry to Arrhenius.

Had the Chemistry Committee had its way and half of each prize been awarded to one scientist, a precedent would have been created which would have rendered the treatment of similar questions later on unnecessarily complicated. Chemistry also overlaps medicine. The logical consequence of such a decision would have been that a similar procedure would have to be applied to other borderline cases, and in such cases prizes for chemistry and medicine could scarcely be awarded without joint discussions between the Academy of Sciences and the Caroline Institute.

The Academy has often been faced with having to decide which prize should be awarded for some special piece of research. It is now generally recognized that the important thing is to decide whether work which can with equal justice be reckoned as chemistry and physics or chemistry and medicine, is in fact worthy of a Nobel Prize. If it is, then a prize should be awarded, which prize is of secondary importance. In order to insure that no worthy candidate falls between two stools because he happens to be a borderline case, close co-operation is necessary between the Nobel Committees, and the committees have in fact always tried to collaborate.

Just as Van 't Hoff's and Arrhenius' pioneering discoveries bore a certain relationship to each other, there is, as we have already seen, a connection between the work of Arrhenius and that of WILHELM OSTWALD [1853-1932]. At the beginning of the 1880's Ostwald carried out in his laboratory in Riga a series of experiments on chemical dynamics. He studied, for example, the influence of acids on decomposition processes such as the saponification [splitting up into acid and base] of the esters and the inversion of cane sugar [splitting up into fructose and glucose]. He found that the rate of these reactions was directly related to the strength of the acid, which he was able to determine in different ways. The rate of decomposition was found in further investigations to be proportional to the conductivity of the acids. At this time Arrhenius's thesis appeared. After studying it more closely, Ostwald recognized that the acid molecules, which Arrhenius described as 'active' in the conduction of the electric current, must be the ones which influence the process of decomposition. He completed his investigations in order to test this idea, and when Arrhenius published his theory of dissociation some years later in its final form, Ostwald had collected experimental material which provided excellent support for the theory. He was able to summarize his results as follows: the rate of saponification of esters or the inversion of cane sugar is approximately proportional to their content of hydrogen and hydroxyl ions, respectively.

The influence of ions in speeding up reactions belongs to the group of phenomena which Berzelius called catalytic. Up to the time when Ostwald published his results, the concept of catalysis was mainly used for purposes of classification and, like Berzelius's electrochemical theory, had been largely discredited. It was now shown to represent an objective reality. In the processes investigated by Ostwald, hydrogen and hydroxyl ions act as catalysts, i.e., they speed up the reaction without being used up themselves. This acid and base catalysis has since proved to be more complicated than it appeared at first. It is, for example, also influenced by the presence of neutral salts, a phenomenon which was discovered by Ostwald and has since been the subject of much research up to the present day. In *1909*, OSTWALD was awarded the Nobel Prize for his pioneer work in this field.

Thus, the third of the triumvirate of brilliant scientists – Van 't Hoff, Arrhenius and Ostwald – who had contributed more than any others to the tremendous advance of physical chemistry at the end of the nineteenth century, was also awarded the Nobel Prize. By the number and excellent style of his writings, by his success as a teacher in both Riga and Leipzig and by founding the *Zeitschrift für physikalische Chemie*, in which the champions of the new theories could publish their results, Ostwald contributed perhaps more than Van 't Hoff and Arrhenius to the universal acceptance of these theories. The reason why he received his prize later than Arrhenius was that the statutes do not allow the prize to be awarded for a life's work but for 'a discovery or improvement', i.e., a definite piece of work or series of related researches. The importance of his contribution can scarcely compare with the revolutionary and far-reaching significance of Arrhenius's theory of dissociation, and his discoveries were evidently not considered to be of such value as those of other scientists rewarded during the intervening years.

When awarding the prize for the first few years, the Academy could, moreover, hardly favour exclusively the founders of this newly discovered branch of chemistry – bordering on physics – even if the most sensational advances in the immediate past had been made in this particular field. Great progress had also been made in other fields, and these discoveries had to receive their just reward.

During the nineteenth century synthetic organic chemistry had developed into a science of imposing dimensions and well-established methods. Many of the century's most distinguished scientists had helped to build it up, especially in Germany. The investigation of the frequently very complicated molecular structure of organic substances requires a perfect command of established analytical methods and the ability to invent new ones where necessary, systematic work, accuracy and perseverance; all qualities considered to be typically German. It is thus probably no accident that organic chemistry flourished in Germany.

When the Academy started to award the prizes, two of these German scientists, ADOLPH VON BAEYER [1835-1917] and EMIL FISCHER [1852-1919], were in the front rank of prospective candidates. Fischer was the younger of the two – he had in fact studied under von Baeyer – so that one might have thought that the latter should have received the prize first. The opposite occurred; FISCHER was awarded the prize in *1902* and VON BAEYER in *1905*. The reason was that Fischer had done his most important work during the period immediately preceding the award. Von Baeyer's principal contributions had been made much earlier and their industrial importance was not realized until rather late. His candidature was in fact based partly on work done comparatively late in life.

Fischer had tackled with great success a problem that had long been regarded as one of the most difficult in organic chemistry, the structure of the sugars. He found in phenylhydrazine – which he had prepared himself – a reagent for transforming these substances into well crystallized compounds which were only slightly soluble, the so-called hydrazones and osazones. He also developed a method for recovering the pure sugars from the osazones, which could be comparatively easily identified and separated from one another. In this way he was able to investigate successfully a field which had previously been particularly inaccessible. The different sugars could now be isolated. Their properties could be determined systematically and their mutual relationships unravelled. Fischer soon succeeded in producing carbohydrates of various kinds from synthetic substances, not only the natural ones but a large number of others with shorter and longer carbon chains. The elucidation of the molecular structure of these substances made rapid progress as a result of his work. Finally, his research threw fresh light on the formation of carbohydrates in nature and furnished important data on the connection between the fermentability of these substances and their molecular structure.

In its report in 1902 the Nobel Committee wrote: 'The particular type of research characteristic of organic chemistry during the last few decades of the century that has just ended, reached its culmination and most elegant form in Fischer's investigations of the sugars. From the point of view of experimental technique his work can be considered unsurpassed.' Of his determinations of the molecular structure of the carbohydrates the Committee said: 'Since the complications are considerable here and the theory can be proved down to the smallest detail, our conception of the grouping of the atoms has been so firmly established by these investigations that one may be justified in concluding that it will never be seriously upset, even if our ideas on the nature of atoms and particularly of valencies undergo a complete transformation in the future.' This was a little rash. Thirty-five years later the Nobel Prize was awarded again for studies on the structure of the carbohydrates. The subject was not exhausted by Fischer's work, even if he brought the problem nearer to its final solution and therefore unquestionably deserved the prize.

Alongside his studies of the carbohydrates, and particularly after he had achieved his most important results in that field, Fischer had taken up another problem, the study of which also led to a great number of important results. He attacked the problem of the constitution of the uric acid group. In addition to uric acid – discovered by Scheele in stones in the bladder – this group contains a large number of physiologically important substances, including theobromine, theophylline and caffeine, which are found in the vegetable world and are the stimulating constituents in cocoa, tea and coffee. He established the constitution of these substances, synthesized the parent substance, purine, from which they were derived, and in addition to the natural derivatives prepared a large number of hitherto unknown ones. By the time he received the prize he had studied no less than 150 substances belonging to the purine group.

In 1899 Fischer attacked an even harder task, the problem of the structure of the proteins. In this field, too, he made brilliant progress, but by 1902, when he received the prize, his work had not advanced sufficiently far for it to be cited as a ground for the Academy's decision.

No real conception of the chemical nature of indigo dye had as yet been arrived at – on the contrary, it had been realized what great difficulties a full investigation would involve – when von Baeyer tackled the problem in 1865. After five years he succeeded, in collaboration with Emmerling, in carrying out the first synthesis of indigo, an achievement which created a sensation among chemists at the time. In 1880 he discovered a new method for producing the dye, which appeared to open up the way for commercial production – something which had long been one of the wildest dreams of the chemist. He tried to realize this in collaboration with two of Germany's largest chemical concerns, and manufacture of the substance was started, based partly on his 1880 method and partly on a new one which he worked out two years later. The synthetic product could not, however, compete financially with natural indigo – which was not surprising as neither of the two methods had originally been worked out with a practical end in view. In 1890, however, Heumann succeeded with the aid of Baeyer's results in producing the most important basic material, indoxyl, more cheaply, and it was now possible to introduce a method of production which satisfied industrial requirements. By 1897 everything was ready for the synthetic product to start competing with the natural one.

The natural product was obtained from a glucoside, a compound of sugar and indoxyl, found in the leaves of certain plants, especially those belonging to the *Indigofera* and *Isatis* genera. In India, particularly, the growing of *Indigofera* for the production of indigo played an important economic role at the end of the nineteenth century. Manufacture of the dye, however, made it so cheap – the price fell in a few years to about a third of the old one – that the cultivation of *Indigofera* no longer paid.

Side by side with his researches on indigo, which stimulated the development of organic chemistry by introducing new methods and opening up new fields of research, von Baeyer worked on other problems in the chemistry of dyes. He discovered a group of dyes, the so-called phthaleins, which also became of great industrial importance. The lovely red eosin belongs to this group. During the first few years of the twentieth century he devoted himself to the important question of the connection between the optical properties of chemical compounds and their molecular structure. His main purpose was to solve the central problem of how colour is determined by constitution.

By his work in the 1890's on the reduction products of benzene and its derivatives, von Baeyer linked up the two main fields of organic chemistry, viz. the aromatic compounds and the aliphatic ones. The reduction products proved to have the ring structure of the original aromatic substance but the properties of the aliphatic series. This discovery opened up a large new field of organic chemistry, that of the hydroaromatic or alicyclic compounds. To this group belong the industrially and medically important terpenes and camphors, studies of which were successfully begun by von Baeyer and later continued by his pupils.

When von Baeyer was awarded the Nobel Prize, his work was described by O. Widman, a member of the Nobel Committee for Chemistry at the time who had once studied under von Baeyer and remained a devoted admirer of his ever since. He wrote: 'Baeyer has worked in all possible fields of organic chemistry. Everywhere his work has broken new ground. There is scarcely one of his innumerable papers which does not contain some original idea or some new method. To admirable discernment and a phenomenal experimental skill he adds great perseverance in the accomplishment of his aims and, even after reaching the age of seventy, an unbelievable thirst for work. He has shown comparatively little interest in theories, even though we owe to him several brilliant ones. In this respect he has been, as he himself said recently, the direct opposite of his teacher Kekulé. Kekulé was the born general who wanted to command nature. Baeyer's guiding principle has been that a natural scientist should not *rule* but *listen* to what nature herself has to say. For this reason he has never stuck obstinately to his own opinions but readily accepted other people's views when he considered them well founded. A striking example of this is seen in his work on the base-forming properties of oxygen, in which, although over sixty-five years old, he adopted with youthful eagerness the theory of the quadrivalency of oxygen, while most older chemists just shrugged their shoulders at it.'

Like the other physical and organic chemists who were awarded the Nobel Prize during the first few years, Sir WILLIAM RAMSAY [1852-1916] had carried out, as early as the 1880's, investigations which attracted considerable attention. The discovery which won him the *1904* Nobel Prize was not, however, made until the next decade and led to work which was not fully completed at the time of the award.

In his Nobel Lecture Ramsay said that, a long time before, he had read with great interest Cavendish's account, published in 1785, of the combustion of atmospheric nitrogen in an excess of oxygen by passing electric sparks through it. In this experiment the nitrogen oxides formed were absorbed by potash lye with formation of saltpetre and the unused oxygen removed with a solution of liver of sulphur. A small quantity of gas remained, which according to Cavendish certainly did not exceed 1/120 of the original volume of nitrogen. At this point in the description Ramsay had noted in the margin: 'Look into this.'

He was reminded of this when, at the beginning of the 1890's, he was speculating on certain obscure discrepancies which Lord Rayleigh came up against when making precision measurements of the density of nitrogen. If the gas was extracted from the air by removing the oxygen, moisture and carbon dioxide, it was found to have a slightly greater density than when produced chemically, from ammonia for example. Lord Rayleigh wondered whether the gas obtained from compounds of nitrogen could possibly be partly dissociated. He clearly did not really believe this, however, as in September 1892 he wrote in an open letter to *Nature:* 'I am much puzzled by some results as to the density of nitrogen and shall be obliged if any of your chemical readers can offer suggestions as to the cause. According to two methods of preparation I obtain quite distinct values. The relative difference, amounting to about 1/1000 part, is small in itself; but it lies entirely outside the errors of experiment.'

Rayleigh and Ramsay took up the problem together and in 1894 were able to report that they had found a new gaseous element, amounting to about one per cent of atmospheric air. It was clearly a bubble of this gas that Cavendish had isolated in his experiment a hundred years before. He was thus on the verge of the great discovery that Rayleigh and Ramsay were to make a century later.

The new gas was found to be chemically inactive and was given the name argon [from Greek *argon,* inert]. It proved to have a density about 40 per cent greater than that of nitrogen, which explains the high value of the specific weight which Rayleigh obtained for the specimens of the gas isolated from air. He had, of course, actually examined nitrogen mixed with argon.

In his search for possible compounds of argon, Ramsay studied, among other substances, minerals containing uranium, which, when dissolved in acid, were known to give off a gas presumed to be nitrogen. As he suspected, he found that this was a mistake. The gas was not nitrogen. It certainly contained argon, but consisted mostly of another new element. Its spectrum showed a clear, brilliant yellow line indicating it to be helium. This element had never before been found on earth. The French astronomer, Janssen, had found the line in a spectrum of the atmosphere of the sun, and Frankland and Lockyer assumed it to be due to an unknown element present in the sun for which they suggested the name of helium. In a letter to his wife on March 24, 1895, Ramsay described his discovery as follows:

'Let's take the biggest piece of news first. I bottled the new gas in a vacuum tube, and arranged so that I could see its spectrum and that of argon in the same spectroscope at the same time. There is argon in the gas; but there was a magnificent yellow line, brilliantly bright, not coincident with but very close to the sodium line. I was puzzled but began to smell a rat. I told Crookes, and on Saturday morning when Harley, Shields, and I were looking at the spectrum in the darkroom a telegram came from Crookes. He had sent a copy here and I enclose that copy. You may wonder what it means. Helium is the name given to a line in the solar spectrum, known to belong to an element, but that element has hitherto been unknown on earth... It is quite overwhelming and beats argon.'

Helium proved to be a light gas, only twice as heavy as hydrogen. Chemically it was found to be of the same nature as argon and like argon did not form any compounds.

The fitting in of these two new elements into the periodic system led Ramsay to search for more gases of this kind. In 1898 he was able to report that, in addition to helium and argon, the air contains extremely small quantities of three other elements of the same type. He called them neon, krypton and xenon. The first of these has a density between those of helium and argon, while the other two are heavier than argon. Later, radium emanation, radon, which is the heaviest of them all, was added to this group of so-called inert gases.

Ramsay's achievement is unique in the history of the discovery of the chemical elements. Never before had a single scientist found a whole group of new elements. Moreover, they were chemically inert, and thus of a hitherto unknown type of great theoretical interest. By carefully determining the constants of the inert gases, Ramsay was able to fit them into their places in the periodic system, which was thus enriched by a whole new column. The abrupt change in the system from the halogens to the alkali metals, which are completely different in electropolarity, had always been striking and appeared to conflict with the long confirmed law that nature does not make any jumps. Thanks to Ramsay's discovery this gap had been filled. In the inert gases, which lacked valency and electric polarity, one could *a priori* envisage a natural transition between the different periods of the system. On the basis of their atomic weights they do in fact fit in as a connecting link between the most negative of all elements, the halogens, and the most positive, the alkali metals.

It was Lord Rayleigh's researches that prompted the work which led to these brilliant results. The same year that Ramsay received the Prize for Chemistry for his discovery of the inert gaseous elements in air and his determinations of their place in the periodic system, Lord Rayleigh was awarded the Prize for Physics for his researches on the density of the most important gases and his discovery of argon in connection with these investigations.

The completion of the periodic system by the inclusion of the inert gases focused the attention of chemists on this survey of the elements showing their mutual relationships. As has already been pointed out, the periodic table could not be drawn up until Cannizzaro had definitely established certain atomic weights which had previously been doubtful. In 1869 Dmitri Mendeleev, a Russian, and Lothar Meyer, a German, discovered independently of each other that, if the elements are arranged in the order of their atomic weights, an obvious periodic recurrence appears in their chemical properties. From this regularity Mendeleev concluded that there were certain gaps still to be filled, and he could even foretell the most important properties of the elements not yet discovered and their compounds. In the 1870's and 1880's gallium, scandium and germanium were discovered, and their atomic weights and properties agreed exactly with Mendeleev's predictions. As a result of this, his system quickly won general acceptance.

The validity of the periodic system was tested even more thoroughly when it came to fitting in the inert gases. After various possibilities had been considered, they were finally included as a special column of zero-valent elements. That this was possible showed that the system was capable of unexpected development. The value of Mendeleev's system, which had previously been confirmed by the discovery of the three elements mentioned above, was thus shown in a new and clearer light.

Although considerable time had elapsed since the discovery of the periodic system, several scientists who sent in nominations for the prize considered that its significance had only just been fully recognized. They pointed out that work on the system was still going on, that it still offered promising fields for research and was a valuable guide in chemical investigations. Meyer had died in 1895, but Mendeleev was nominated by various proposers in 1905 and 1906.

In the latter year the Nobel Committee took up the suggestion as its own. One of the five members, who represented chemical technology on the Committee and had at its request investigated the work of the French chemist, HENRI MOISSAN [1852-1907], had, however, been so impressed by this that he dissented from the opinion of the majority, proposing Moissan instead. He opposed the view that the significance of the periodic system had only recently been fully recognized and wrote: 'The system has in fact been lectured on from all the chairs of chemistry in the world and treated in all textbooks as something which, in spite of its imperfections, has its firm foundations in nature herself.' He also pointed out that it was Cannizzaro's work that had rendered Mendeleev's system possible and that it would not be just 'to award the Nobel Prize to the inventor of the periodic system when the man who had laid the solid foundation of the determinations of the atomic weights on which the periodic system rests, is still unrewarded'.

When the question was considered by the next body, the chemistry section of the Academy, the dissentient won support for his view. Four of the ten members of the section agreed with him, and one declared himself unable to judge. Five votes were therefore cast for Moissan and four for

Mendeleev. The Academy accordingly decided to award the *1906* Nobel Prize for Chemistry to MOISSAN. This proved to be the last opportunity of rewarding Mendeleev for drawing up the periodic system, which has had such a revolutionary and stimulating effect on the development of chemical research. He died at the beginning of 1907. It is to be regretted that the Academy felt unable on formal grounds to offer its prize to the author of one of the most important advances in chemical theory during the latter part of the nineteenth century. Had the Nobel Prize existed in the 1870's and 1880's, he would certainly have received it.

The achievements for which Moissan was honoured – the isolation of fluorine and the introduction of the electric furnace into the service of science – may appear to have little in common. In actual fact these processes were used for the same purpose, to find a method for producing artificial diamonds. Moissan at first tried to achieve this by making compounds of carbon and fluorine, which were decomposed in different ways. He hoped that the carbon would then crystallize in its most noble form, as diamonds. This did not happen, however; instead he always obtained a residue of graphite. Later on he used his electric furnace to alloy carbon with iron or silver at high temperatures, after which he cooled the melt quickly by plunging it into water. After dissolving the metals in acid a silt remained, which on examination under the microscope was found to contain small, hard, glittering, octahedral crystals. Moissan thought these were diamonds. Later research has, however, shown that they were in all probability spinels, which are sometimes found in the silt in melts of this kind. In any case Moissan did not succeed in finding any practical solution to the problem of producing diamonds.

The news that he had produced artificial diamonds caused a great sensation at the time and was, moreover, stressed in the speech in his honour when the prize was awarded in 1906. The Academy's official statement did not, however, make any mention of it. It cited other contributions to inorganic chemistry of such importance that they can almost be said to have caused a renaissance in this branch of science which had been somewhat overshadowed during the latter part of the nineteenth century by research in organic chemistry.

Ever since Scheele's discovery in 1771 of hydrofluoric acid, many attempts had been made to isolate fluorine from it or its salts, but all had failed owing to the great reactivity of the element. On electrolysis of fluorides dissolved in water the liberated fluorine combines instantaneously with the hydrogen in the water or with other substances present. Dry hydrofluoric acid is not, on the other hand, an electric conductor. Moissan found, however, that a solution of potassium hydrogen fluoride in dry hydrofluoric acid was a suitable substance for electric decomposition. By carrying out the electrolysis at a low temperature in a platinum vessel and by using platinum–iridium electrodes, he was able to prevent any great losses of fluorine and the problem was solved. This was in 1886. Later it was found that the expensive platinum could be replaced by copper, which, it is true, is attacked to some extent by the fluorine but at the same time becomes coated with a protective film of copper fluoride. In this way Moissan prepared large quantities of the element that had so long been searched for in vain, and it was now possible to study its properties. A great many new fluorine compounds could also be prepared, by means of which our knowledge of the chemical nature of the element was greatly increased.

Moissan's electric furnace was not built for technical but for purely scientific purposes and was very simple. It was made of two suitably shaped blocks of limestone, surrounding a cavity in which the crucible containing the substance to be heated was placed. Graphite electrodes were introduced into the furnace through channels hollowed out in the blocks, and the electric arc between them produced temperatures up to about 3,500° C. Copper, silver, platinum, iron, and many other metals could not only be melted but even vapourized in this heat. Moissan carried out comprehensive investigations of the compounds of various elements with carbon, boron and silicon. From calcium and carbon he produced calcium carbide, which has proved to be of great technical value. From silicon and carbon he obtained silicon carbide – carborundum – which, on account of its hardness, is excellent for grinding and has therefore played a considerable role in modern industry. Moissan's method for producing it, was, however, scarcely an economic one. He first noticed crystals of silicon carbide in his melts in 1891, but did not immediately publish his observation. Some months later E. G. Acheson patented in the United States a method for producing silicon carbide by heating sand and coke in an electric furnace. Acheson, who had been working independently of Moissan, must therefore be considered as the actual discoverer of carborundum.

Moissan's work was not prompted by a desire to achieve results which would be chiefly of practical use. He took out no patents. The satisfaction of breaking new ground in his own field of science was sufficient for him. In the introduction to *Le four électrique,* in which he collected the results of his work on high-temperature chemistry, he wrote: 'But what I cannot convey in the following pages is the keen pleasure which I have experienced in the pursuit of these discoveries. To plough a new furrow; to have full scope to follow my own inclination; to see on all sides new subjects of study bursting upon me; that awakens a true joy which only those can experience who have themselves tasted the delights of research.'

After the scientists whose work has been outlined above had been rewarded, the Nobel Prize for Chemistry was given for work entirely or almost entirely carried out during the present century. The history of the prize is, therefore, largely the history of the advance of chemistry during the last seventy years. In order to make the survey more readable, the various fields of chemistry will now be dealt with separately.

RADIOACTIVITY AND ATOMIC CHEMISTRY

In 1896 a discovery was made in France of overwhelming importance in the study of matter. H. Becquerel found that substances containing uranium emit spontaneous radiation of a complex nature. Some time later MARIE CURIE [1867-1934] reported that thorium also possessed this property and that the mineral pitchblende gave off much stronger radiation than could be accounted for by its uranium content. Together with her husband, Pierre Curie, she analysed the mineral and by treating large quantities of it they were able to show that it contained two new radioactive elements, polonium and radium. This work, which gave rise to the nuclear physics and chemistry of our day, was rewarded with the Nobel Prize for Physics in 1903, half being given to Becquerel and the other half to the Curies. It was awarded 'in recognition of the excellent service rendered to mankind by the three scientists in their joint work on the phenomena of radiation discovered by Becquerel'. It was thus the discovery of radioactivity for which the prize was given; no mention was made of the new elements discovered in pitchblende.

When Mme Curie, who continued her chemical studies of radioactive substances, was again nominated for a prize – this time the Prize for Chemistry – the Nobel Committee was thus able to point out that the discovery of radium, which one of her nominators [Arrhenius] described as the 'most important during the last century of chemical research', had not yet been made the subject of an award. In *1911,* when the nomination was submitted, the Committee did not hesitate, therefore, to recommend it to the Academy, and the prize was awarded to Mme CURIE 'for her services to the advancement of chemistry by the discovery of the elements radium and polonium, by the isolation of radium and the study of the nature and compounds of this remarkable element'. Her husband had died in 1906, otherwise they would naturally have shared the award. This is the only occasion on which a Nobel Prize has been conferred twice on the same recipient.

In this unique case the award was, however, made for work carried out with unusual determination and skill under difficult conditions and which had opened up a field where further research could be expected to yield valuable results. That it was no easy task to isolate radium from pitchblende can be seen from the fact that the uranium contains only 3.4 parts of the element in 10,000,000. In one ton of the mineral, which contains 60 per cent of uranium, there is only 0.2 g of radium. The polonium content is even smaller. That it was at all possible to concentrate measurable quantities of these two rare elements was due to their radioactivity. Their radiation ionizes the air in their immediate neighbourhood, making it a conductor. By systematically measuring this effect for the various residues and crystal fractions as the work proceeded, Mme Curie was able to raise the concentration of the radioactive elements. Polonium was precipitated along with bismuth, radium followed barium. By fractional crystallization of the chlorides of the two latter elements, it was possible to separate them, and Mme Curie finally obtained 100 mg of pure radium chloride from 1 ton of pitchblende. It was now possible to determine the atomic weight and chemical properties of radium and, finally, to isolate the element itself by electrolysis. It belongs to the group of alkaline earth metals, thus joining the series calcium, strontium and barium. Its properties are most similar to those of barium.

As pitchblende contains only 1/5,000 as much polonium as radium, it was impossible to isolate the former in its pure form. Together with A. Debierne, Mme Curie succeeded, however, in obtaining from several tons of pitchblende a few mg of a substance containing sufficient polonium to be about 50 times more active than an equal amount of radium.

The spectrum of this substance included lines which could be attributed to polonium.

Mme Curie was able by her work to confirm a theory she had put forward previously that radioactivity is a property of the atom. Her own researches and those of other workers soon furnished the proof that the radiation emitted by radioactive elements is due to the successive disintegration of their atoms. The rate of transformation differs from element to element. Polonium is half transformed in 140 days, while the corresponding time for radium is 1,580 years.

New active elements were discovered in rapid succession. When working on residues of uranium for the Curies, Debierne found them to contain a substance with strong radiation which was precipitated together with iron. It was given the name actinium. Substances containing radium, thorium and actinium were found to emit active gases, so-called emanations, which left an active coating on the surfaces of solid objects with which they came into contact. These emanations were not identical, as they differed in the rate of decay. The half-life period for radium emanation was found to be a few days, that of thorium emanation a few minutes and of actinium emanation a few seconds. Pitchblende was also found to contain radioactive lead, which could not be differentiated chemically from ordinary lead, and an active thorium, ionium, which differed from ordinary thorium in its radioactive properties.

Order was brought into this chaos of newly discovered elements by a theory of radioactivity put forward in 1903 by ERNEST RUTHERFORD [1871-1937] and F. Soddy. According to this theory, radioactive elements undergo a series of successive changes in which new elements are continuously formed, each of which differs chemically from that from which it is derived. The intermediate products are characterized mainly by the decrease in their radioactivity, which takes place quite independently of temperature. The half-life period already mentioned is a constant, depending on the proportion of the atoms in a radioactive element that disintegrate in unit time. The active elements differ considerably in this respect, their half-life periods varying from a fraction of a second to ten thousand million years.

Rutherford and his associates – at McGill University in Montreal from 1898 to 1907 and then at Manchester – took the lead in further research on radioactive elements. In the light of his disintegration theory it soon became clear that they could be arranged in three main groups, one containing radium and the elements derived from it, the parent element being probably uranium, one with thorium as the parent element, and the third comprising actinium and its disintegration products.

The disintegration of radioactive elements is accompanied by emission of radiation. Rutherford also studied this aspect of the phenomenon. He tested the ability of radiation to pass through a thin sheet of aluminium, and found that some of it was slightly slowed down by the sheet whereas some was more penetrating. The former he called α-radiation and the latter β-radiation. Both are accompanied by so-called γ-radiation, which passes through solid matter even more easily than β-radiation. The γ-rays, the 'hardest' type of radioactive radiation, have since proved to consist of electromagnetic waves of the same type as light and X-rays but with a shorter wave-length than the latter. As early as 1899 Giesel demonstrated that β-radiation is deflected in a magnetic field in the same way as cathode rays. It must, therefore, consist of a stream of negatively charged elementary particles or electrons.

Rutherford solved the problem of the nature of α-radiation, a problem which was of the greatest importance in the study of radioactive processes. By studying their deflection in magnetic and electric fields he was able to show that they consist of relatively heavy, positively charged particles, and to determine the relationship between their mass and their charge. From this he could conclude that they were either hydrogen molecules with the same charge as a univalent positive ion or helium atoms with double this charge. The latter seemed more likely as radioactive substances had been shown to contain helium. Finally, Rutherford devised a method for counting the number of α-particles emitted by a radioactive substance in a given time and then measured the total amount of electricity they carried. These measurements indicated that an α-particle is charged with two positive units, and hence has the same weight as a helium atom. Rutherford and Royds eventually succeeded in proving that α-particles are helium atoms. They sealed a fairly large quantity of radium emanation in a glass tube with sufficiently thin walls for the α-particles emitted by the active gas to be able to penetrate them. The particles were then caught up in a closed outer vessel. After a time this vessel was found to contain a gas showing a clear helium spectrum.

In 1908, the Nobel Committee reported as follows on Rutherford's pioneer studies on the transformations of radioactive substances: 'The disintegration theory and the experimental results on which it is based have led to a new and considerably wider interpretation of nothing less than the fundamental concepts of chemistry. In the nineteenth century the atom and the element represented the final units in the process of chemical decomposition and as such the limit of experimental research. Questions as to what existed beyond that limit were a matter of more or less vague and fruitless speculation. This long insuperable boundary has now been removed, at least in theory. The law of the immutability of the elements can no longer be upheld, and like that of molecules before them, the structure of atoms and the laws governing it can now be studied by scientific methods based on exact measurements. The results which have so far been achieved are not only of great importance themselves but perhaps even more important for the rich possibilities they open up for future research.' Later developments have proved how well founded the Committee's hopes were.

Rutherford had also been suggested by several nominators for the Physics Prize, but at a joint meeting the two Nobel Committees decided that it would be most suitable, considering the fundamental importance of his work for chemical research, to award him the Prize for Chemistry. On the unanimous recommendation of the Committee for Chemistry, RUTHERFORD was consequently awarded the *1908* Nobel Prize 'for his investigations into the disintegration of the elements, and the chemistry of radioactive substances'.

Rutherford not only laid the foundations of the theory of radioactivity, but has also the principal credit for the subsequent rapid progress in this field, which has revolutionized both physics and chemistry. He was one of the greatest scientists of all time.

Rutherford recognized that, on account of the extremely concentrated form of energy it represented, α-radiation must be a valuable tool in studying the structure of the atom. By investigating the scattering of α-radiation on passing through a thin metal foil he made his most important discovery. The number of strongly deflected particles was so great that their deviation from the angle of incidence could not be the result of a number of collisions with atoms in the metal foil but must be due to isolated collisions with minute, positively charged particles. This observation led him to construct his well-known atom model on which all later developments in atomic physics are based. From his experiments he concluded that the mass of an atom is concentrated in a positive central body, the nucleus, whose linear dimensions are about 1/10,000 those of the atom. Round the nucleus is a system of negative elementary particles, electrons, sufficient in number to render the atom as a whole neutral.

Rutherford formulated his theory of the structure of the atom in 1911, and it soon proved a valuable aid in the interpretation of certain obscure phenomena in the chemistry of radioactive elements. Some of these elements were strikingly similar chemically, so similar even that they could not be separated by any chemical operation. This was the case with ionium and thorium. The primary distintegration product of thorium, mesothorium-I, discovered in 1907 by Otto Hahn, could not be separated from radium, and some of the active elements of the uranium series had exactly the same chemical properties as common lead.

A first attempt to explain these anomalies was made in 1909 by D. Strömholm and The Svedberg at Uppsala, who studied the isomorphy of radioactive elements in order to determine their chemical nature. They described their observations in two papers in Swedish, published in the *Arkiv för kemi.* The latter of the two papers concluded with the following statement: 'One might suppose that the genetic series continue right down through the periodic system, but that the three elements of the various genetic systems which occupy the same place in the periodic system are always so alike in their chemical properties that they constantly occur together in nature, and cannot be separated in the laboratory. Perhaps there is a hint of this in the fact that Mendeleev's table only gives an approximate rule for atomic weights but lacks the exactitude of a law of nature; this would not be surprising if the elements in the table were a mixture of several similar elements with almost, but not quite, identical atomic weights. In actual fact, however, we have not been able to establish any chemical differences, not even purely quantitative ones, between the three related elements radium, actinium-X and thorium-X.' Strömholm and Svedberg pointed out, however, that they lacked sufficient material to pass any judgment on this hypothesis.

It remained, therefore, for Rutherford's collaborator from his Montreal days, FREDERICK SODDY [1877-1956], to clarify fully the question of this extraordinary similarity between certain radioactive elements. A survey which he wrote in 1910 contains the first hints of the correct solution; it took firmer shape in a communication the following year and developed, finally, in 1913 into the theory of the isotopic radioactive elements.

An α-transformation, in which a particle with two positive unit charges and a mass of four units of atomic weight is expelled from the nucleus of the active element, gives rise to an element two columns to the left of the parent element in the periodic system and with an atomic weight four units less that of the parent. In a β-transformation, when a practically weightless negative elementary particle, an electron, is expelled, an element is formed one column to the right of the parent element and with very nearly the same atomic weight. This so-called *displacement law* was formulated by Soddy, Fajans, and Russell more or less independently of one another in 1913.

To eight α-transformations in the uranium–radium family there are six β-transformations, and the proportions are roughly the same in the thorium and actinium series. The three distintegration series are also in general very similar to each other chemically. It follows from this that many radioactive elements must have similar chemical properties but different atomic weights. In the case of such similarity as, for example, between thorium and ionium, between radium and mesothorium-I, between the three inert gaseous emanations radon, thoron and actinon, etc., the charges on the atomic nuclei are the same in each group, but the atomic weights differ. The decisive factor for the chemical properties of an element is the charge on the nucleus, because this determines the number of electrons in the atom and the chemical properties reside in the electron shell. The various elements in one group are *isotopes.* Their atoms are, as Soddy briefly expressed it, alike on the surface but unlike inside.

The displacement law and the theory of isotopes were certainly the results of the work of many different scientists, but the main credit for having furnished the experimental proof belongs to SODDY. In 1922 he was awarded the *1921* Nobel Prize 'for his contributions to the chemistry of radioactive substances, and his investigations into the origin and nature of isotopes'.

At the same time as Soddy, FRANCIS WILLIAM ASTON [1877-1945] received the *1922* prize 'for his discovery, by means of his mass spectrograph, of the isotopes of a large number of non-radioactive elements, as well as for his discovery of the whole-number rule.' He had succeeded in determining accurately the mass of the positively charged atoms in positive radiation and discovered that most of the elements investigated were not simple but made up of two or more types of atoms with different weights.

In an electric discharge tube a stream of positively charged gas ions moves towards the cathode. If the cathode is perforated, these particles pass out through it with the speed they have acquired in the electric field. As they can get their charge in different parts of the field and as their charge can vary during their passage through the field, they do not pass out through the cathode with the same speed even if their masses are the same. Aston perfected a spectrograph in which it was possible to split up a narrow pencil of positive radiation into subsidiary pencils each of which contained particles with the same *e/m,* i.e. relation between charge and mass. To this end the original pencil of rays was deflected first by an electric field between two condenser plates and then by a magnetic field at right angles to the electric one formed by a powerful electromagnet. If a photographic plate is adjusted so that its plane cuts the original direction of the radiation at the same angle as most of the electrically deflected rays, then from simple geometrical considerations rays with the same *e/m* must strike the plate at the same point regardless of the speed of the particles. In this way a so-called mass spectrum is registered. Aston was able to determine the *e/m* values to which the various lines in such a spectrum correspond by calibrating his mass spectrograph. This was done by analysing positive radiation with a few easily identified *e/m* values. Since *e* consists of one or two and only exceptionally of more unit charges, it is easy to determine the various values of *m,* i.e. the atomic or molecular weights of the gas ions.

At the time of his award Aston had perfected his method until he considered that he could determine atomic weights with an accuracy of 1 pro mille. Since then both he and others have improved it even further.

By 1922 Aston had investigated over 30 elements and shown that the majority of them were mixtures. This was in itself a striking result, but even more remarkable was the fact that all the atoms he studied proved to have isotopic weights which were very nearly, but not quite, whole numbers on the oxygen [= 16] scale. This so-called whole-number rule was thought by the English physician William Prout to hold for all atomic weights determined by the usual chemical methods, and in 1815 he had formulated on the basis of this the daring hypothesis that all elements are ultimately made up of hydrogen. His idea had been tested and rejected by such masters of atomic weight determination as Berzelius and Stas as they could not verify his basic assumptions. The atomic weight of chlorine, for example, was found to be 35.5, and thus as different as is possible from a whole number. But Aston showed with his mass spectrograph that chlorine is a mixture of two main isotopes, one with atomic weight

35 and the other with atomic weight 37, and that these two isotopes occur in such proportions that the average atomic weight of the mixture is 35.5. Thus Prout's hypothesis came into its own again although in a slightly modified form in so far as it was now assumed that the atoms of all the elements were made up of hydrogen nuclei, or *protons,* and *electrons.* This theory of the structure of the atomic nucleus was again modified ten years later when Chadwick discovered the neutron – an uncharged particle with the same weight as a proton – and showed that the atomic nucleus is composed of *protons* and *neutrons.*

Hydrogen, whose atomic nucleus consists of only one elementary particle, a proton, occupies a special position among the elements in that its atomic weight differs rather considerably from a whole number. With his later, much improved mass spectrograph Aston arrived at the value 1.00778. The most accurate determination of the atomic weight of hydrogen by chemical methods gave the value 1.00777. The agreement was of course excellent.

In 1929, however, an important discovery was made which at once altered the situation. The Americans Giauque and Johnston found on studying very carefully the band spectrum of oxygen that the gas consists not only of atoms with atomic weight 16 but also of atoms with weights 17 and 18, the latter being as frequent as 1 in 630. This means that the scale of chemical atomic weights, in which the weight of the mixed element oxygen is equated to 16, is not the same as Aston's mass-spectrographic scale in which the atomic weight of the lightest of the isotopes of oxygen forms the base 16. Aston's value for the atomic weight of hydrogen, 1.00778, must, therefore, be reduced to 1.00756, if we are to compare it with the 'chemical' atomic weight of hydrogen, 1.00777. The difference seemed too great to be explained away as due to experimental errors. In 1931 Birge and Menzel, therefore, put forward the hypothesis that hydrogen contains atoms of weight approximately 2 in addition to those of weight approximately 1, and that the concentration of the former is about 1 in 4,500.

This hypothesis led the American chemist, HAROLD C. UREY [b. 1893], to look for a heavy isotope of hydrogen. That he finally succeeded in proving the existence of heavy hydrogen was chiefly due to his excellent mathematical and physical training which enabled him to calculate in what way the heavy atoms could be concentrated. He predicted that the vapourization of liquid hydrogen at a very low temperature would result in a concentration of the heavy hydrogen atoms in the unvapourized part of the liquid. His discovery was thus the result of methodical research, not of a lucky chance.

By vapourizing 4 litres of liquid hydrogen to within a few cubic centimetres at a temperature just above its melting point, Urey produced samples in which, according to his calculations, the heavy hydrogen should have been considerably concentrated. Spectroscopic investigation proved him to be quite correct, the samples giving rise to lines corresponding to a spectrum of hydrogen with atomic weight 2. The existence of heavy hydrogen was thus definitely established.

Urey tried to work out theoretically the possibilities of separating the two isotopes by electrolysis of water and to this end he calculated their electrode potentials. The difference between them was not large and the chances of succeeding by this method did not appear to be great. Fortunately, as Urey himself said, E. W. Washburn of the Bureau of Standards in Washington did not trouble to make such calculations but went straight ahead with experiments, helped by Urey who analysed his samples spectroscopically. It appeared that the concentration of heavy hydrogen increased very much in a solution electrolysed under suitable conditions. Washburn, who died in 1934, was thus the first to indicate an effective method for producing high concentrations of heavy hydrogen.

Washburn's suggestion was followed up not only by himself but by other scientists. The American chemist G. N. Lewis, who had already worked on the separation of isotopes, was the first to succeed in preparing practically pure heavy water. Communications followed in quick succession from his institute, describing the remarkable properties of the new gas and the heavy water. Urey, too, continued his investigations of heavy hydrogen and its compounds. When he found, like other scientists, that its properties differed appreciably from those of ordinary hydrogen, he decided that it was best to give the two kinds of hydrogen different names. At his suggestion the heavy isotope was called deuterium and the light one protium. Since then a third isotope of hydrogen with atomic weight 3 has been discovered and given the name of tritium.

UREY has the credit 'for the discovery of heavy hydrogen' and he was awarded the Nobel Prize for it in *1934*. When his Nobel Lecture was about to be printed the following year in *Les Prix Nobel*, he added this note to the proofs: 'Since this was written, Aston has revised his mass-spectrographic atomic weight of hydrogen [H] to 1.0081 instead of 1.0078

[Aston, F. W., *Nature* 135, 541, 1935]. With this mass for hydrogen, the argument by Birge and Menzel is invalid. However, I prefer to allow the argument of this paragraph to stand, even though it now appears incorrect, because this prediction was of importance in the discovery of deuterium. Without it, it is probable that we would not have made a search for it and the discovery of deuterium might have been delayed for some time.'

The Hungarian, GEORGE DE HEVESY [1885-1966], used the chemical agreement between isotopes of the same element to work out an ingenious method for studying chemical processes by means of so-called tracer elements.

When working at Rutherford's institute at Manchester he had not succeeded in the task he had been set of separating radioactive radium D from the final disintegration product in the radium series, inactive radium G. The discovery of isotopes explained why he had failed. Radium D and radium G are different kinds of lead. Their atoms have the same nuclear charge and hence the same number of electrons in their outermost shells, but radium D has a heavier atomic nucleus than radium G. The former disintegrates with emission of β-radiation, whilst the latter is stable.

If ordinary lead is added to radium D, we obtain a metal whose atoms behave in exactly the same way chemically though some of them are earmarked. They are shown to be present by their radiation and, since they always accompany the inactive atoms, they act as a tracer for these. Very small quantities of such tracers are needed, as the intensities of radiation can be measured with such precision that unweighable quantities are susceptible to measurement.

Hevesy used his method to investigate the solubility and reactions of lead salts. He studied how lead was taken up by plants and how it was reabsorbed and secreted by animal organisms. The displacement of the atoms in solid lead, i.e. the self-diffusion in the metal, could now be determined, a process which it had previously been impossible to measure.

As long as only natural radioactive elements could be used as tracers, the usefulness of the method was very limited. In fact, only the heavy metals lead, thorium, bismuth and thallium and their compounds could be studied by it. The position was altered, however, at the beginning of the 1930's when radioactive isotopes were produced of a whole series of elements. Studies of chemical processes by means of radioactive tracers were begun in laboratories all over the world. Hevesy was the leader in this field of research, and a large number of important investigations were carried out by him and his co-workers.

Particularly valuable results were achieved in the field of biology. Using radio-phosphorus, injected in the form of physiological sodium phosphate into animals and human beings, it was possible to study where and how quickly the various organic compounds of phosphorus are formed and to follow their passage through the living organism. Similar studies were carried out with radioactive sodium and potassium. Other active isotopes, such as those of carbon, magnesium, sulphur, calcium, chlorine, manganese, iron, and zinc, were also used.

For the lighter elements inactive isotopes have been used, for example, heavy hydrogen with atomic weight 2, carbon with atomic weight 13, nitrogen with atomic weight 15, and oxygen with atomic weight 18. It is naturally not so easy to determine the proportion of an inactive tracer as it is to determine that of an active one, but it can be done by means of density measurements or with a mass spectrograph. To find the concentration of deuterium is comparatively easy as it is twice as heavy as ordinary hydrogen.

In 1944 HEVESY was awarded the prize for *1943* 'for his work on the use of isotopes as tracer elements in researches on chemical processes'. His method for studying the mechanism of biological processes has revolutionized research in physiological chemistry. In organic chemistry, too, the importance of his method in elucidating the course of a reaction can scarcely be overestimated.

As has already been mentioned, Hevesy got the first idea of the work for which he received the Nobel Prize while he was visiting Rutherford at Manchester, and it was also at the institute of this English physicist – from 1919 the Cavendish Laboratory at Cambridge – that the possibility of transforming atomic nuclei was discovered. When studying collisions between α-particles and nitrogen nuclei, Rutherford found that the latter ejected fragments which could be identified as hydrogen nuclei. This was the first successful experiment with nuclear fission. Other light elements also reacted in the same way to the swift α-particles. The phenomenon was regarded as being mainly a fission reaction. What happened to the bombarded atomic nucleus attracted at first relatively little attention. Using the Wilson cloud chamber, which shortly afterwards won its inventor the Nobel Prize for Physics, Blackett was able in 1925 to show that the reaction between the α-particle and the bombarded atomic nucleus had chiefly the nature of a synthesis. The two bodies unite on collision and, after a proton has been ejected, the result of the whole process is an atomic nucleus with a one unit greater charge and a three units greater atomic weight than the original nucleus. An isotope of oxygen with atomic weight 17 is produced from nitrogen, and from aluminium a silicon isotope with atomic weight 30.

In these first attempts to transform atoms by means of α-particles, stable nuclei were always formed after the emission of the proton. In 1934 IRÈNE JOLIOT-CURIE [1897-1956] and her husband FRÉDÉRIC JOLIOT [1900-1958] discovered that meta-stable isotopes of light elements can in certain cases be produced by bombardment with α-particles and that these meta-stable types of atoms disintegrate in the same way as the natural, heavy radioactive elements. The year before, they had found that the reaction of α-particles with aluminium not only involved the emission of protons but that simultaneously there occurred, on a relatively insignificant scale, another process involving the emission of neutrons. On investigating the problem further they found that α-particles react with the nuclei of aluminium atoms in yet a third way, during which process bodies with unit positive electric charges are emitted, positrons – the type of particles for whose discovery in the autumn of 1933 C. D. Anderson was awarded the Nobel Prize for Physics in 1936. When trying to establish the connection between the energy of the bombarding α-particles and the intensity of the positron radiation, they made the surprising observation that positrons are emitted in greater numbers after the bombardment has been in progress for some time and that their emission does not cease immediately the bombardment with α-particles is cut off but continues for some minutes. It was obvious that a radioactive element had been formed which, like natural radioactive elements, distintegrated with a speed characteristic of the element, and that this activity decreased according to the same laws as those governing the natural active elements.

Other light elements were bombarded with α-particles and studied in the same way as aluminium. Boron and magnesium could also be transformed into radioactive elements in this way. These results were published in January 1934. Some weeks later the two scientists presented further evidence of the genesis of new active elements. They had isolated the substance formed by α-bombardment of boron and shown that it had the chemical properties of nitrogen. Radioactive nitrogen had thus been produced from boron. In the same way aluminium was transformed by α-particles into radio-phosphorus.

During the years that followed the Joliot-Curies and others produced a large number of radioactive isotopes. Thus the transmutation of the elements that the alchemists had dreamed of was at last realized. The atoms first formed in these nuclear reactions are, it is true, unstable, but in their transformation they give rise to types of atoms which are not identical with the original ones. The lifetime of the intermediary products varies considerably. Some are half-changed in a fraction of a second. Others are more long-lived and have a half-life period of hours, days, weeks or more.

As has already been mentioned, these artificial radioactive isotopes have become very important as tracers in investigations by Hevesy's method. They have also been widely used in radiotherapy, where they are better for certain purposes than the expensive natural radium preparations. They have proved an exceedingly valuable asset in this branch of medicine and their use should open up possibilities for further advances. IRÈNE JOLIOT-CURIE and FRÉDÉRIC JOLIOT were awarded jointly the *1935* prize 'for their synthesis of new radioactive elements'.

The prize-winners themselves realized that projectiles other than α-particles could be used for the transmutation of elements. Nor was it very long before methods had been worked out both in England and America for accelerating charged particles of different kinds, and new radioactive elements were synthesized by adding ordinary and heavy hydrogen nuclei, protons and deuterons, to atomic nuclei. The two French scientists had pointed out at an early stage that neutron bombardment ought also to cause these nuclear reactions, but before they had time to prove this, E. Fermi in Rome [Nobel Prize winner for Physics in 1938] had shown their assumption to be correct. Since neutrons are electrically neutral they are able on collision to come into closer contact with the atomic nuclei than are α-particles, protons and deuterons, which owing to their charges have to force their way through the repelling electric fields around the nuclei they hit. With Fermi's method it was, therefore, possible to transform even heavy atomic nuclei.

In 1939 it was discovered that cosmic radiation coming from outer space produces neutrons at about 30,000 feet and higher in the atmosphere, which there combine with nitrogen nuclei forming carbon with an atomic weight of 14. These carbon atoms have a high energy at the moment of their formation and are rapidly oxidized to carbon dioxide, which spreads out and distributes itself evenly in the atmosphere.

The ratio of carbon-14 in the carbon dioxide of the atmosphere is very low. In about 10^{12} of its carbon atoms, there is only *one* which has an atomic weight of 14. But nevertheless, this ratio can be determined, for carbon-14 is a radioactive isotope and manifests itself by its radiation. It is converted into nitrogen by the emission of an electron, which can be detected by a sensitive apparatus. The disintegration is, however, a slow procedure. The half-life period is 5,600 years.

If it is assumed that the intensity of cosmic radiation has been constant during the last few tens of thousands of years, then the average lifetime of carbon-14 – which is approximately 8,000 years – should be sufficiently long to allow for the formation of a stationary state in the concentration of this isotope, not only with reference to the atmosphere, but also to the hydrosphere and biosphere as well. Active and non-active carbon dioxide are dissolved in water of the seas and lakes, they are assimilated by trees and plants, and finally also by the animals, which ultimately live on plants. The ratio between active and non-active carbon in all living organisms is the same as that in the air.

When an organism dies, the exchange of carbon with its surroundings ceases and the carbon atoms are inexchangeably held fast in the big molecules of the biological substances. Because the activity of the carbon atoms decreases at a known rate, it should be possible, by measuring the remaining activity, to determine the time elapsed since death, if this occurred during the period between approximately 500 and 30,000 years ago.

This hypothesis was published by the American WILLARD F. LIBBY [b.1908] in 1947, and with his great experimental skill it did not take him long to prove the validity of the theory. Recently-dead biological substances, such as wood and plant materials, seal oil and others, showed an activity which could be calculated from the knowledge of the production of carbon-14 in the atmosphere, and its rate of decomposition. Fossil material, such as petroleum, was completely inactive; it comes from organisms which lived millions of years ago.

These first control experiments were preceded by a complicated enrichment procedure, but thanks to Libby's experience in working with substances of low activity, he succeeded in refining the activity measurements so that the preliminary concentration procedures became unnecessary. If this had not been possible, his method of age-determination would not have turned out to be the important tool for the advancement of science it has now become.

This refined method was then tested by Libby and coworkers on, among other things, charcoal and wood found in Egyptian graves, for all of which Egyptologists had been able to determine the time when they were built. It was also checked by determining the age of heartwood from the trunks of redwood trees [*Sequoia sempervirens*], and of Douglas firs [*Tsuga Douglasii*], which were several thousand years old and whose exact age could be determined by counting the annual rings. The results Libby thus obtained from these control experiments left no doubts about the reliability of the method.

It was then used to solve problems met with by archaeologists and geologists. Important results were obtained in rapid succession. Egyptologists received important support in their efforts to create a chronology dating back to about two thousand years earlier than the first royal dynasty. It was proved that the last great glacial period in the northern parts of Europe and North America was simultaneous, and took place about 11,000 years ago. Traces of the first human habitations in these regions were dated to about 10,000 years ago.

It is true that archaeologists and geologists have had methods at their disposal by which they could date their materials within the periods mentioned here. Especially pollen analysis has been a very efficient tool for this purpose. The carbon-14 method is a complement to these older means of investigation and enables more accurate measurements to be made.

The carbon-14 method has also been applied in oceanography, for example, for the dating of relatively recent sea sediments. It has made possible more and more accurate determinations of the turnover of the oceanic deep water, and therefore plays an important role nowadays in connection with one of the central problems of physical oceanography, i.e. water circulation in the sea.

One of the scientists who suggested Libby as a candidate for the Nobel Prize has characterized his work in the following way: 'Seldom has a single discovery in chemistry had such an impact on the thinking in so many fields of human endeavour. Seldom has a single discovery generated such wide public interest'.

Libby was awarded the *1960* prize 'for his method of using carbon-14 as a measurer of time in archaeology, geology, geophysics, and other sciences'.

By bombarding uranium, the heaviest natural element, with neutrons,

Fermi thought he could produce so-called transuranium elements, which would continue the periodic table. Many scientists questioned this, but OTTO HAHN [1879-1968] and Lise Meitner considered they could confirm his conclusion. During the years 1936-38 they studied together products formed by neutron bombardment of the heaviest elements, thorium and uranium. At the end of 1938, however, Hahn and his young collaborator, F. Strassmann, on investigating one of the products formed by the reaction between neutrons and uranium, found that, instead of being an isotope of radium as had been supposed, it behaved chemically like barium. In January 1939 they reported this finding, and Hahn tentatively put forward the daring hypothesis that the heaviest elements, after absorbing neutrons, are simply split into two more or less equal parts, thus giving rise to elements somewhere in the middle of the periodic table. Only a month later he was able to produce experimental proof of his hypothesis, and further confirmation came almost simultaneously from scientists in various parts of the world.

Hahn's discovery came as a complete surprise and aroused the greatest sensation among nuclear chemists and physicists everywhere. It became the immediate subject of important theoretical studies by Lise Meitner and Frisch based on Bohr's view of the structure of atomic nuclei. These scientists pointed out that the splitting of the nucleus must give rise to an enormous increase in energy due to the transformation of matter into energy, and calculated that the two parts formed would fly apart with tremendous force. This was proved experimentally by Frisch. His findings and Joliot's observation that certain products of the fission process disintegrate with emission of neutrons, suggested the possibility of initiating by the disintegration of uranium a so-called chain reaction which would produce large amounts of energy. Magnificent perspectives were thus opening up for future research.

As the acknowledged master of the art of identifying traces of radioactive elements chemically, Hahn together with his young collaborators took the lead in the study of the numerous products formed by the nuclear fission of heavy atoms. Not only can the fission take place in many ways depending on the nature of the reacting nuclei and the energy of the bombarding neutrons, but its primary products are unstable and disintegrate successively with emission of elementary particles, so that each of them forms the starting-point of a long or short series of different types of atoms. Within a few years a hundred direct and indirect fission products were obtained, belonging to twenty-five different elements occupying positions in the periodic table between selenium and praseodymium. In 1945 HAHN was awarded the *1944* prize 'for his discovery of the fission of heavy nuclei', but owing to post-war conditions in Germany he was unable to receive his prize until 1946.

It is deeply to be regretted that Hahn's discovery was first used technically for making the atom bomb. The war compelled this development. It was unfortunately easier to use atomic energy for destructive purposes than for peaceful ones. Great efforts are, however, now being made to utilize atomic energy for the benefit of mankind. There is every reason to believe that this problem can be solved, so that we may hope that Hahn's gift to humanity will prove a blessing in the end.

Much of the research necessary for the construction of the atom bomb had naturally to be kept secret during the war. In so far as the curtain has now been raised, important scientific discoveries made in this connection have been revealed. The existence of the transuranium elements has been confirmed. Not less than eleven such elements have so far been discovered and their chemical properties so completely determined that the periodic table has been significantly rounded off. We stand to-day only on the threshold of the atomic age and the future will certainly bring rich harvests in this field of science.

The first transuranium element of which there was definite proof was produced by EDWIN MATTISON MC MILLAN [b.1907] and P. H. Abelson in May 1940 at the university of California, by irradiating uranium with neutrons with the aid of the cyclotron built by E. O. Lawrence. It was obtained as a disintegration product of a β-radiating uranium isotope, which has a half-life of 23 minutes. Hahn and Meitner had also discovered this species, but their preparation was too weak for its daughter-product to be demonstrated. The Americans were able to investigate this thoroughly, and showed that it forms an isotope of element 93, that is to say, a transuranium element. They called it *neptunium* after the planet Neptune, whose orbit lies next outwards after Uranus in the solar system. By irradiating uranium with rapid neutrons or with heavy-hydrogen nuclei [deuterons], other neptunium isotopes were soon produced in Berkeley.

In 1940 McMillan and GLENN THEODORE SEABORG [b. 1912] and their fellow-workers had already reported that when neptunium disintegrates it gives rise to an element 94. By analogy with the way in which names had been found for uranium and neptunium, this second trans-uranium element was called *plutonium,* after the planet Pluto, which has its orbit next outside that of Neptune. The first isotope of this element, which has a half-period of 24,000 years and thus is relatively stable, is what is called an atomic fuel. This plutonium isotope reacts with slow neutrons in the same way as the uranium isotope ^{235}U, that is to say – when it is split it develops great energy and gives off neutrons. In this way it came to play an important part in the atomic-bomb project during the war, and methods were developed for its production on a large scale.

After these problems, conditioned by the war, had been solved, Seaborg, as leader of a comprehensive group of able colleagues, completed the studies of the transuranium elements. In doing this, he has written one of the most brilliant pages in the history of the discovery of chemical elements.

Several more transuranium elements have later been produced. The chemical characteristics of all these new elements have been established by developing a refined ultra-microchemical technique. A prophesy of Bohr that in the transuranium elements we are dealing with a group of substances of the same sort as the rare earth metals has been confirmed. This series of closely associated elements begins with 89 actinium. Thus, corresponding to the rare earth elements, the lanthanides, there are the actinides, and a certain agreement can be found between corresponding members of these two series. Seaborg therefore proposed for the transuranium elements 95 and 96 the names *americium* and *curium,* in analogy with their corresponding rare earths europium and gadolinium [after Europe and the Finnish chemist Gadolin respectively]. The seven transuranium elements more recently produced are 97 *berkelium,* 98 *californium,* 99 *einsteinium,* 100 *fermium,* 101 *mendelevium,* 102 *nobelium* [named after Alfred Nobel], and 103 *lawrencium.*

By irradiating different sorts of heavy atoms with neutrons, protons, deuterons, helium nuclei, or, more recently, carbon, nitrogen, oxygen, and neon nuclei, a great number of isotopes have been produced from the transuranium elements. The study of the formation and properties of these isotopes has yielded a wealth of scientific material.

The two pioneers and leaders in this field of research, MC MILLAN and SEABORG shared the *1951* prize 'for their discoveries in the chemistry of the transuranium elements'.

CHEMICAL THERMODYNAMICS AND ITS TECHNICAL APPLICATIONS

Chemical thermodynamics, which was built up during the latter part of the nineteenth century, mainly by Gibbs and van 't Hoff, was extended in 1906 by the German chemist, WALTHER NERNST [1864-1941], by what he himself called its third [and last] law. Its formulation was the result of attempts to find a general method for calculating chemical equilibrium from thermal data. The driving force in a chemical reaction, the affinity of the reacting substances, regulates the equilibrium between the initial and the final products. As has already been mentioned, the affinity is not equal to the heat of reaction but to the maximum useful work which can be gained when the reaction is carried out in a reversible manner. How this quantity, which is also called the thermodynamic potential and denoted by Gibbs by $\triangle G$, varies with temperature can be calculated if we know the change in the heat content $\triangle H$ of the reacting system. This connection is apparent from the first two laws of thermodynamics. The first of these is the well-known law of conservation of energy, which has defeated all attempts to construct a perpetuum mobile. The other indicates in which direction the conversion of energy will take place in a closed system and gives the limiting value for the effectivity of a heat engine. The two are not, however, sufficient to calculate the absolute value of the thermodynamic potential. To do this we must know the relation between $\triangle G$ and $\triangle H$ at any given temperature. Nernst's principle gives this relation for temperatures just above absolute zero.

On the basis of a few experimental data, 'wie von einem glücklichen Zufall geleitet', as he said, Nernst formulated the bold theory that the limiting value of $[\triangle H - \triangle G]/T$ is 0 for $T = 0$, where T is the absolute temperature. The fraction represents the change in the so-called entropy, a property of a chemical system which is used with advantage in this connection. Nernsts' principle also implies that all processes take place without change in entropy at absolute zero. This does not rule out the possibility that the entropy itself may be minus infinity at $T = 0$, if it is given a limited value at a slightly higher temperature. In 1911 Planck supplemented the law by the assumption that this is not the case and stated it as follows: at absolute zero the entropy is equal to zero for every chemically homogeneous solid or liquid body.

To test the validity of this law was not easy. Nernst was forced to collect most of the necessary experimental data himself, and his heat law thus led to comprehensive determinations of specific heats, transition points and equilibria. Unfortunately for rather a long time he applied a somewhat irrational method, so that, in spite of the fact that data were gradually accumulated which supported his theory, it took a long time before it could be considered proved. The application of the quantum theory played a decisive role in the final proof.

It finally became clear that by formulating his principle and by his comprehensive determinations of specific heats at low temperatures, NERNST had made a contribution of fundamental importance to the development of chemistry. The *1920* prize was, therefore, awarded to him in 1921 'in recognition of his work in thermochemistry'.

Planck had already stated that a solution cannot have zero entropy at absolute zero, but G. N. Lewis pointed out in 1927 that Planck's modification of Nernst's law is not enough. Only a pure, perfect crystal has zero entropy at absolute zero, whereas this is not true of liquids or amorphous bodies. This was proved experimentally at Lewis's institute in Berkeley, California, by Gibson and Giauque who found that amorphous glycerol possesses a definite zero-point energy, but that crystalline glycerol does not.

During several years round about 1920 Lewis and his associates carried out a series of very elegant investigations to test the validity of the third law. This work has since been continued and brought to a high degree of precision by his pupil, WILLIAM FRANCIS GIAUQUE [b.1895].

In order to reach very low temperatures he introduced the adiabatic demagnetizing method. By quick evaporation of liquid helium it is possible to reach a temperature of a little less than one degree above absolute zero, but by Giauque's method temperatures of only a few thousandths of a degree above it can be achieved. Entropy is a measure of the lack of order in the molecules or atoms in a substance. If a paramagnetic salt, e.g. gadolinium sulphate or potassium chromium sulphate, which has been cooled as far as possible with liquid helium, is acted upon by a strong magnetic field, the metal atoms of the salt tend to arrange themselves in a certain way which involves a lowering of entropy. Heat is given off to the surroundings. If the salt is then demagnetized adiabatically, i.e. when isolated from the surroundings, by uncoupling the current to the electromagnet, the arrangement of the atoms caused by the magnetization disappears, causing the temperature to fall.

With his cooling method Giauque has been able to carry out experiments within a temperature region where the thermal motion of the atoms practically ceases, and to measure energy changes connected with transitions in the state of the atoms themselves. Besides his thermodynamic determinations he also studied molecular spectra and calculated values for the entropy from these. His measuring technique is sufficiently accurate for him to have reduced the study of the difference between calorimetric and spectroscopic entropy to an exact science, and he has applied and worked out methods used in statistical thermodynamics and quantum mechanics for the theoretical analysis of his experimental results. His work has considerably widened our knowledge of the structure of matter, and GIAUQUE was awarded the *1949* prize 'for his contributions in the field of chemical thermodynamics, particularly concerning the behaviour of substances at extremely low temperatures'.

At the beginning of this chapter [p. 286] mention was made of the many years that had to elapse before chemists realized the value of Gibbs' pioneer work in thermodynamics. The same delay occurred in exploiting another theoretical thermodynamic study of great importance made by the Norwegian-American LARS ONSAGER [b. 1903] one-half century later. First published in 1929 at a scientific congress in Copenhagen, it was presented in its complete form in *The Physical Review* in 1931. That year, the journal printed two articles by Onsager, entitled 'Reciprocal Relations in Irreversible Processes.' They were so concisely written that one article comprised only 22 printed pages and the other only 15 printed pages. In point of size, it has been said, these writings must be the slenderest works ever to be rewarded with a Nobel Prize. The brevity of the articles has been more than offset by their far-reaching influence on the development of chemistry. However, twenty years were to pass before this was generally realized. Like Gibbs, Onsager was before his time.

The three laws of thermodynamics, referred to above, are among the cornerstones on which the entire edifices of modern physics and chemistry rest. But they can only be used to describe static states, and in chemistry are only applicable to systems in a state of reversible equilibrium. Most processes occurring in nature, however, are irreversible; they cannot, of their own accord, go backwards.

In irreversible thermodynamics it is now commonplace to speak of forces [generalized], and the sign X is used for quantities, such as gradients of temperature, concentration, potential or chemical affinity, which can give rise to irreversible phenomena. Corresponding to these are fluxes of heat, diffusion, electric current and chemical reaction velocity. They are generally referred to as fluxes, and denoted by J.

It is natural to assume that – at least in the proximity of equilibrium – there exists a linear relationship between force and flux, i.e. $J = L \times X$. A relationship of this sort is called a [linear] relationship of phenomena, since it represents experimentally verified laws and is not based on a general theory of irreversible processes. The proportionality coefficients L are called phenomenological or transport coefficients.

In many cases of current scientific interest, however, several irreversible processes can occur simultaneously; they can also mutually influence one another. For two processes, therefore, we can write

$$J_1 = L_{11}X_1 + L_{12}X_2$$

and

$$J_2 = L_{21}X_1 + L_{22}X_2.$$

According to Onsager, it is now generally valid that

$$L_{ik} = L_{ki} \qquad (i,k = 1,2,3,\ldots,n),$$

where forces and fluxes are adequately defined. This relationship has been termed 'Onsager's reciprocal relations' and is the core of his epoch-making extension of thermodynamics. By a brilliant and mathematically impressive use of statistical mechanics, Onsager has presented very strong arguments for the validity of his ideas; and the results of calculations based on them have also been shown to agree with experimental data.

In physics Onsager's laws have made possible a description of thermodynamic phenomena and of the Peltier effect. They have been successfully applied to explorations of the function of membranes, and thus have been of great importance to biochemistry and biology. At present, Onsager's irreversible thermodynamics have proved to be immensely useful in investigating the velocity of very fast reactions [cf. p. 343].

ONSAGER was awarded the *1968* Chemistry Prize 'for his discovery of the reciprocal relations which bear his name, and which are the basis of irreversible thermodynamics'.

During his first attempts to verify his theorem Nernst worked out an approximate formula for the equilibrium between ammonia and its components, hydrogen and nitrogen. His theoretical considerations were, however, so over-simplified and his basic thermodynamic data still so uncertain that his formula could not be used without considerable modification of one of the constants involved. Experimental determinations of equilibrium in question had been made by the pioneer of direct synthesis of ammonia, FRITZ HABER [1868-1934], who began his work in this field in 1904. Four years later he submitted an account of his results to the Badische Anilin- und Soda Fabrik at Ludwigshafen, Germany, which based its manufacture of ammonia on them.

Haber's report indicated that the formation of ammonia takes place immeasurably slowly at ordinary temperatures, but that the speed of reaction increases if the mixture of gases is heated. Unfortunately this shifts the equilibrium in an unfavourable direction, so that the relative amount of ammonia formed decreases. The important thing is thus to select the most suitable temperature for the reaction. Haber found heating to about 500° the most suitable, but the reaction must then be speeded up by an efficient catalyst. Since the synthesis of hydrogen and nitrogen into ammonia involves a reduction in the number of molecules in the reacting mixture of gases, it should be possible to increase the yield by increasing the pressure. Haber's report concluded with the statement that a direct synthesis of ammonia should be economically possible at the temperature indicated and at a pressure of 200 atmospheres with powdered osmium or uranium as the catalyst.

A great deal of work proved to be necessary before the method could be applied with advantage to mass production. Two difficulties had to be overcome. The reaction chamber did not stand the strain and the catalysts were too expensive and too sensitive to the action of impurities in the gases. In Haber's experiments the reaction mixture was enclosed in a tube of ordinary carbon steel which must, therefore, withstand a pressure of 200 atmospheres at a temperature of about 500°. Hydrogen, however, tends to decarburize and penetrate red-hot iron, making it brittle and full of cracks. The large number of explosions indicated that an improved reaction chamber was an urgent necessity.

At this point CARL BOSCH [1874-1940] made an important contribution. He replaced Haber's single-walled vessel by two tubes, one inside the other. He constructed the outer of these, which was kept at a relatively low temperature and only had to stand the high pressure, of ordinary steel. The inner tube, which is not exposed to any pressure but must be able to withstand the chemical action of the hot gases on its inner wall, was made of alloy steel. His double-walled chamber also made it possible to apply the so-called counter-current principle which Haber had already used. The mixture of gases was passed through the space between the tubes before it was allowed to enter the inner tube where the reaction took place. As heat is formed during the process, the cost of producing the ammonia is thus reduced. Bosch and his collaborators also carried out a great many experiments to discover suitable catalysts and found iron oxide mixed with a little aluminium oxide to be an excellent contact substance.

The Haber-Bosch synthesis of ammonia is now used in almost every country in the world for producing nitrogen fertilizers. The total annual production of nitrogen fixed in this way is measured in millions of tons and its value in millions of pounds. Most credit for this epoch-making method of providing nitrogen for agricultural purposes must be given to HABER, whose idea it was to synthesize ammonia directly and who succeeded in developing the method that rendered industrial production possible. He was awarded the *1918* prize in 1919 'for his synthetic production of ammonia from its elements'.

During the next ten years it became increasingly evident that Bosch's contribution to the practical realization of Haber's idea represented a great advance in the field of chemical technology. High-pressure methods proved useful for many purposes.

FRIEDRICH BERGIUS [1884-1949] applied them with great success for the hydrogenation of coal by means of which process it could be transformed into liquid oils. The idea of making oil from coal came to him while he was investigating the formation of fossil coal. He tried in his laboratory to do in a short space of time what it had taken Nature millions of years to achieve, namely, the transformation of vegetable matter into substances of the nature of mineral coal. He was able to elucidate the structure of fossil coal and was led to the assumption that these complicated organic substances could be broken down by hydrogenation under pressure in a less violent way than by dry distillation. His assumption was confirmed by experimental investigations.

These experiments indicated that the transformation into oil takes place with considerable production of heat. In order for it to be carried out successfully it must, therefore, be done within a rather limited range of temperature, varying for the different types of coal. For the temperature to be regulated accurately it is necessary for the coal to be suspended in a substance which does not take part in the reaction. The final product, the so-called Bergin oil, could be used for this purpose. When carrying out his first experiments Bergius did not believe that the process could be facilitated by catalysts as he considered that they would be immediately destroyed ['poisoned'] by the reaction products. However, Bosch, who also applied to this field his extensive experience in high-pressure technique, succeeded, at the laboratory of the large concern I. G. Farben in Ludwigshafen, in finding suitable catalysts for the Bergin process too. There he perfected and modified the method for obtaining oil from coal. In its new form it was called the I. G. process, though it was naturally based on Bergius's original idea.

Side by side with the production of liquid fuel and lubricating oils from naphtha and crude mineral oils the manufacture of similar products from coal by treating it with hydrogen under pressure plays a very important role. It is generally known what this method of producing petrol meant to Germany during the last war. By their work BOSCH and BERGIUS created the technical basis for industries which are now an essential part of world economy. They shared the *1931* prize 'in recognition of their contributions to the invention and development of chemical high pressure methods'.

COLLOIDS, CHROMATOGRAPHY, AND SURFACE CHEMISTRY

In 1926 three prizes were awarded for work on colloids. RICHARD ZSIGMONDY [1865-1929] received the *1925* Prize for Chemistry 'for his elucidation of the heterogeneous nature of colloid solutions and for the methods he has devised in this connection, which have since become of fundamental importance in modern colloid chemistry', THE SVEDBERG [1884-1971] was awarded the *1926* Chemistry Prize 'for his work on disperse systems', and J. Perrin received the Physics Prize for the same year for similar work but with special reference to his discovery of the so-called sedimentation equilibrium.

Together with the famous optician H. Siedentopf at the Zeiss factory at Jena, Zsigmondy constructed the ultramicroscope, which became of such importance for the progress of colloid research. In this instrument, which was Zsigmondy's idea, the solution to be examined is illuminated by a powerful beam of light and observed through a microscope from the side, i.e. at right angles to the axis of the rays. If the solution contains particles, these are made visible by the light they scatter and are shown as small bright specks against a dark background. In this way it is possible to observe particles too small to be seen in an ordinary microscope. Zsigmondy was able with his ultramicroscope to prove definitely that colloids are not, as had sometimes been assumed, molecular solutions of certain allotropic modifications of the substances they contain but simply fine-grained suspensions of these substances.

His principal researches dealt with colloidal gold. He solved the problem of the formation and structure of gold ruby-glass and elucidated the nature of gold in water solution, the *aurum potabile* which had puzzled chemists since the time of Paracelsus and was studied both by Berzelius and Faraday. The ultramicroscope made it possible to determine the size of colloidal particles so that the important problem of how the properties of colloids alter with the degree of fineness or dispersion could be successfully tackled. Together with the Polish physicist, Smoluchowski, Zsigmondy elucidated the mechanism of coagulation, i.e. what happens when particles in unstable colloids combine into larger aggregates, and extended our knowledge of the structure of coagulates or gels.

In his doctoral thesis, *Studien zur Lehre von den kolloiden Lösungen,* published in 1907, Svedberg communicated his first results in the field of colloid research. He described a method he had worked out for the production of metal colloids in various media by electric pulverization, with which he had succeeded in producing an entire series of new systems of great interest. His thesis also included investigations of the peculiar movement of colloidal particles called the Brownian movement after its discoverer, the English botanist, Robert Brown. It seemed likely that it is caused by the collisions between the molecules in the liquid and the particles. On this assumption Einstein and Smoluchowski had worked out a theory for the phenomenon, which was tested by Svedberg by studying the movement of the particles in Zsigmondy's ultramicroscope. The results of his measurements confirmed the theory, thus proving the existence of molecules.

Ostwald, who had maintained that the atomic theory ought to be abandoned, since, in his opinion, it could not be proved and had a retarding effect on research, and who had consistently discarded the concepts of atoms and molecules from his textbooks, confessed in a review of Svedberg's thesis that he had been converted. He wrote: 'The reviewer has already on a previous occasion expressed the opinion that we have here in fact obtained the long-sought-for proof of the kinetic theory. He does not hesitate to admit that since satisfactory proof has now been furnished, he is no longer justified in rejecting the theory, his reason for doing so being precisely the previous absence of such proof.' He ended his review with the surmise that important results could also be expected in the future from the 'young, talented and energetic' author of this thesis, and in that he was certainly correct. During the years that followed Svedberg intensified his studies of colloids and allied phenomena, particularly the Brownian movement. Together with Zsigmondy he became the leader of further advance in this field.

Some years before he was awarded the Nobel Prize, Svedberg had made what was perhaps his most important contribution, the invention of the ultracentrifuge. Overcoming great experimental difficulties he succeeded in constructing an apparatus in which samples of colloids or high molecular solutions could be subjected to the effects of a very strong centrifugal field. By photographic registration of the displacement of the particles and of their distribution when the so-called sedimentation equilibrium was reached, it was possible to determine their masses or molecular weights. Data could also be collected on the shape of the particles or molecules. This apparatus has since been perfected by its inventor, and the ultracentrifuge is now an indispensable aid in studying high molecular substances. Svedberg has succeeded in determining the molecular weights of a large number of these and, particularly in the case of the proteins, found that they follow laws of great importance for a more detailed characterization of these biologically important substances.

In addition to ultracentrifugation two other valuable methods for investigating colloids and high molecular substances have been worked out at Svedberg's institute at Uppsala. His pupil ARNE TISELIUS [1902-1971] developed a method for isolating and purifying such substances based on two phenomena, electrophoresis and adsorption.

When a colloid or a solution of a high-molecular substance is exposed to the effect of an electric field, i.e. when an electric current is passed through it, the particles or molecules dispersed in the liquid are displaced towards one or other of the electrodes according to their charges, which in their turn depend on the constitution of the surrounding medium. The phenomenon has been called electrophoresis. The speed of the particles depends on their charge, size and shape in addition to the potential gradient in the solution. It is thus possible to separate the different particles or types of molecules from one another and to purify them.

Tiselius started by making a detailed study of electrophoresis with its many interfering subsidiary phenomena and worked out a rational method on the basis of his observations. He gradually improved it over a period of years and finally achieved a high degree of perfection. In applying it he has made a number of important discoveries, particularly on proteins. It is true that it had previously been assumed that the globulin found in blood serum is not a uniform substance, but Tiselius divided it into three distinct fractions and observed that at least two of these included groups of slightly different types of molecules. Their further division has since been continued. The results of electrophoretic studies by Tiselius and his collaborators on the antibodies and protective substances formed in the blood after immunization are also of great value medically.

Adsorption analysis was used more than fifty years ago by the Russian botanist Tswett for separating vegetable dyes. The method is based on a phenomenon which has since been utilized in the construction of the modern gas-mask. This is provided with a charcoal filter, which frees the inhaled air from harmful substances. In the same way a liquid passing through a closely-packed, finely pulverized substance or other porous body loses some of the substance dissolved in it. Varying quantities of the substance adhere to the surface of the solid medium, a phenomenon which is called adsorption. If several substances are present in the solution, they are usually adsorbed to different degrees, so that this property can be utilized in order to separate them. After a systematic study of the conditions for adsorption analysis, Tiselius worked out various methods for performing it. In all of them the methods of observation are such that it is irrelevant whether the substances to be analysed are coloured or not. Another decisive step forward was that Tiselius found a means of carrying out adsorption analyses not only qualitatively but also quantitatively. His work in this field has been full of new ideas which he has carried out with great constructive ingenuity. He has achieved fine results with analyses of mixtures containing aminoacids, peptides or carbohydrates.

In *1948* the Chemistry Prize was awarded to TISELIUS 'for his researches on electrophoresis and adsorption analysis, especially for his discoveries concerning the complex nature of the serum proteins'.

In the 1940's two British scientists ARCHER JOHN PORTER MARTIN [b.1910] and RICHARD LAURENCE MILLINGTON SYNGE [b. 1914] developed another extremely valuable method to separate substances, especially those built up of big molecules, and thus to purify them. In *1952* they received the prize jointly 'for their invention of partition chromatography'.

This procedure has proved to be greatly effective in the cases when substances are to be isolated from mixtures of similar components in which they are present only in relatively small quantities. It is here that Martin and Synge's method has enjoyed great success, especially in what is perhaps its most important form called filter paper chromatography. A drop of a liquid containing the mixture to be investigated is allowed to fall onto a strip of filter paper, to form a little spot. This paper is then caused to draw up some suitable mixture of liquids, for example butyl alcohol and water, by capillary action. The spot begins to move, and one can see how it then gradually segregates into several spots, some of which rapidly follow the liquid which has been drawn up, while others lag behind. Thus a resolution of the mixture into its component parts results, a resolution which in this example would depend on the different *partition* of the substances between the water held by the filter paper and the freely moving butyl alcohol. Hence the name partition chromatography. Instead of resorting to a series of intricate chemical operations, one can in this simple way make a complete analysis of even the most complicated mixtures; and a single drop of the starting material is fully sufficient for the purpose.

The method of Martin and Synge, in different forms, has found extensive application in all branches of chemistry and important discoveries have been made with it. New and interesting substances have been traced and isolated with its help. Metabolic pathways in the organism can be studied, and formerly unknown intermediary products identified. This has been done, for example, with studies of the way in which the green leaves of plants build up starch out of the carbon dioxide of the air.

Partition chromatography has had other extremely important applications when it has been used as a means of studying the structure of giant molecules. It has been possible in this manner to attack problems of the structures of proteins and carbohydrates with considerably greater prospects of success. Synge has shown this in some very beautiful investigations on the structure of gramicidin, an antibiotic active against certain bacteria. In such work as this, it is of special importance that the method is suitable for the isolation, not only of the smallest building blocks [the amino acids], but also of larger fragments [peptides]. It is as if one had a puzzle to put together: if by chance several pieces happen to hang together, the problem immediately becomes much more simple. The young English chemist F. Sanger has succeeded in putting together an unusually difficult puzzle of this sort; from the mixtures which were separated with Martin and Synge's method, among others, he has been able to get an almost complete picture of the structure of the *insulin* molecule – a result which perhaps more than any other, shows the method's great scope and principal significance [cf. p. 379].

It has already been pointed out in this survey that in his fundamental thermodynamic studies of chemical problems Gibbs also carried out detailed investigations of surface tension and adsorption. Since his day the scientist who has most successfully treated these phenomena is the American, IRVING LANGMUIR [1881-1957], who was awarded the *1932* prize 'for his discoveries and investigations in surface chemistry'.

While working on improving the electric incandescent bulb at the General Electric Company at Schenectady – work which resulted in the revolutionizing invention of the gas-filled bulb – Langmuir found that the residue of gas remaining in the so-called vacuum bulb adhered tightly to the walls in quantities corresponding to a single layer of atoms arranged side by side. They form a monatomic layer. He thus arrived at an entirely new theory of the mechanism of adsorption, i.e. the adhesion of a gas, liquid, or dissolved solid to an adjacent surface of a solid or liquid substance. According to Gibbs this adhesion is chiefly regulated by surface tension. Langmuir pointed out that one must also take into consideration the existence of unsaturated valency forces in the surface of a solid or liquid body which, under certain circumstances, could come into operation and bind a film of foreign atoms or molecules. The surface of a crystal ought, therefore, to resemble a chessboard where there is room in each square for one foreign particle bound by the valencies operating there. This theory has been confirmed experimentally in a large number of cases. Investigations of surface layers with electron diffraction diagrams have shown that Langmuir drew a correct picture of adsorption on the surfaces of metals and other crystals.

His work in this field has proved of great importance, since it has provided a means for further research on the so-called heterogeneous catalysis, i.e. the accelerating effect of certain solid substances on chemical reactions in gaseous and liquid systems.

Langmuir also carried out important investigations on the conditions existing in the dividing layer between liquids and gases. Particularly far-reaching results were arrived at in his studies of the spreading of oils and fats on water. He measured the resistance against reducing the surface area of the films thus formed and found that it was very small as long as the film extends over a considerable area. After a certain reduction in the film the resistance to further reduction increases suddenly. According to Langmuir this point corresponds to the formation of a continuous unimolecular layer. The molecules in the layer are elongated and stand with one end dipped into the water while the rest of the molecule stands up rather like a stalk in a cornfield. At the moment when the lateral pressure has reached its critical value, i.e. when, according to Langmuir, the molecules are in contact with one another throughout, it is possible to calculate their dimensions from the extension of the film. Langmuir found, for example, that the molecules in certain fatty acids have a cross-section of 4 to 5 hundred millionths of a centimetre. This and other similar results have since been confirmed by X-ray analysis of fatty acid crystals. Langmuir's work in this field has facilitated an understanding of the properties of lubricating oils and of the mechanism of ore flotation.

X-RAY AND ELECTRON INTERFERENCE BY GASES AND VAPOURS – DIPOLE MOMENTS – VALENCE FORCES

The Dutch physicist, PETER JOSEPHUS WILHELMUS DEBYE [1884-1966], has made important contributions to various fields of physical chemistry. He found a simple law for the relation between atomic heat and temperature, a law which played an important role in discussions on the third law of thermodynamics. With his assistant, E. Hückel, he calculated the effect of the so-called interionic forces on the motion of ions, thus carrying the theory of electrolytic dissociation a considerable step forward. Independently of Giauque, he has also stated the principles of the method for reaching low temperatures by adiabatic demagnetization. When he received the Nobel Prize for Chemistry in *1936,* it was, however, 'for his contributions to the study of molecular structure through his investigations on dipole moments and on the diffraction of X-rays and electrons in gases'.

When atoms unite to form molecules it may happen that their charges are partly transferred from one to another so that they build up an aggregate of particles consisting of combined ions. If the molecules are subjected to the effect of an electric field, the nucleus of each atom is displaced a little in relation to the surrounding system of electrons, which is deformed to a certain extent; the configuration of the ions is slightly changed, and, finally, if the distribution of the charge on the molecule as a whole is asymmetric – if it has what is called a dipole moment – the field tries to arrange the molecules in a given way. Debye worked out a theory for the total polarization and indicated methods for determining the dipole moment of molecules. This could be determined either by measuring the changes in the dielectric constants and the density resulting from changes in temperature, or by investigating molecular refraction extrapolated to radiation of infinite wave-lengths. Strictly speaking, Debye's theory holds only for rarefied gases in which it is not necessary to take into consideration the interaction between the molecules. As it is difficult to obtain the necessary experimental data for calculating the dipole moment of gases, it is fortunate that the theory has proved to hold without appreciable errors for dilute solutions of substances in non-polar solvents. Much insight has been gained into the structure of both inorganic and organic molecules from measuring their dipole moments. In organic chemistry particularly, investigations on the symmetry of the charges on molecules have proved of very great value.

When treating theoretically the interaction between X-rays and atoms, Debye found that even the arrangement of atoms in the molecules of a gas – which is conditioned by the fact that they all have the same structure – can be sufficient to give rise to an appreciable interference effect. The scattering intensity must here, as in the interaction between X-rays and crystals, pass through a series of maxima and minima as the scattering angle increases. Debye formulated a complete theory for this phenomenon and was thus able to devise a valuable method for determining molecular structure. A narrow beam of X-rays of known wave-length strikes a gas, and the scattered radiation is registered photographically. Debye's theory is then used to test whether any conceivable molecular model fits in with the intensity distribution of the scattered radiation, and if any such arrangement of the atoms is confirmed, its dimensions can be determined and important data thus obtained on the molecular configuration. Cathode rays, which consist of fast-moving electrons and are therefore also called electron radiation, were found by De Broglie to be of wave type and can therefore also be used for studying the structure of molecules. A large number of substances have now been investigated in this way and their structure determined.

Very comprehensive and profound research on the structures of crystals and molecules have been performed by LINUS PAULING [b.1901] and his collaborators at the California Institute of Technology, Pasadena, Cal. For this purpose they used X-ray crystallographic as well as electron diffraction methods. Their work has not, however, aimed only at unraveling structures, but was performed mainly in order to form an experimental base for studies on the connection between the nature of valence forces and the building of chemical substances.

According to Pauling, the chemical bond is essentially of three main types: the *ionic* bond, which, at least partly, is characterized by electrostatic forces, the *covalent* bond, which implies two electrons and two electronic orbits, one for each of the atoms bound together, and the *metallic* bond, which is explained as some kind of resonance of a covalent bond between all possible positions in the atomic lattice. Using 'elementary' quantum mechanics* in a very clever way Pauling has endeavoured to elucidate, as exactly as possible, the connection between valence forces and structure. Already in the 1920's he performed a series of investigations of the covalent bond, the structure of simply built molecules, such as H_2, the distances between the centres of adjacent atoms and ions in crystals and molecules, etc. During the 1930's this research was followed by a series of very important quantum mechanical investigations in which a more quantitative and uniform view of the chemical bond was applied and the concept of resonance played a more prominent part. Resonance implies that the state of a molecule does not necessarily have to be represented by only one classical valence pattern, but corresponds to an intermediate of several such patterns which makes it more stable.

A comprehensive survey of his main results in this domain has been given by Pauling, 1939, in his book *The Nature of the Chemical Bond* which to many chemists of our day has become one of the main sources of information on the chemical valence forces.

* Cf. p. 444 ff.

Pauling has used his wide and profound knowledge of bond types, atomic distances and bond directions in investigations of the structure of complicated compounds. He has, for example, performed brilliant studies on the structure of proteins. Already at the end of the 1930's he and his collaborators determined the structures of several amino acids and dipeptides which, as relatively simply built links, form part of proteins. Starting from these results, some conceivable structures for the building elements of proteins were worked out and the patterns thus arrived at have been controlled by means of X-ray data. There is strong evidence that the structures discovered are present in synthetic polypeptides, fibrous proteins, including hair, finger-nail, and other α-keratin proteins, silk and the β-keratin proteins, and haemoglobin and many other globular proteins.

PAULING received the *1954* prize 'for his research into the nature of the chemical bond and its application to the elucidation of the structure of complex substances'.

In 1916, G. N. Lewis, by a stroke of genius, established the hypothesis that covalent bonding is caused by two electrons in one way or another belonging together – an electron pair. These are found in the space between the atoms which they bond together, and can be regarded as belonging to both of them. His idea was subjected to quantum mechanical treatment, first by Heitler and London in Germany, and afterwards by Slater and Pauling in the United States. Their work resulted in the so-called valence-bond, or VB, method, which can be used to study the electronic structure of molecules and their ways of reacting. It was by using this method that Pauling came to have his brilliant insights into valency.

Parallel with this approach, another more profound and comprehensive method of studying molecular binding forces was developed. The idea came from the American ROBERT SANDERSON MULLIKEN [b. 1896], who had long devoted himself to the study of molecular spectra. In order to interpret these, he had to create a rational molecular model. In doing so, he applied an approach to the subject analogous to that which, some ten years earlier, had led to the establishment of Bohr's atomic model. It is true that in a molecule not merely a single positive nucleus with its surrounding electrons is in question; a molecule has several positive nuclei, surrounded by a cloud of electrons characteristic of the molecule as a whole.

From 1925 onward, Mulliken applied a quantum-mechanical approach to these ideas, and calculated the paths of electrons in the field of force formed by the molecule's positive and negative particles. These were difficult and time-consuming calculations, and could only be carried out for simple cases. But the results were promising, and the work continued. The theory was developed in depth by a number of scientists, chief among them F. Hund and R. Mulliken. In the course of these investigations, the latter introduced the concept 'molecular orbital' in order to describe the movement of an electron extending over the entire molecule – an approach which has come to be known as the molecular-orbital, or, more succinctly, the MO method.

The possibilities for exploiting this new method for molecular studies were greatly extended in the mid-1950's when computers could be employed for the calculation work. Mulliken took the lead in developing his method in such a way that it became amenable to computerization. By now the electronic structure of small molecules had been established with such a degree of accuracy that certain of their characteristic quantities, such as interatomic distance, dipole moment and many others, could be calculated with such accuracy that they differ from experimentally determined values by only a few per cent. In many cases, too, these calculations have yielded valuable complementary information concerning the bonding forces in the molecules investigated.

In organic chemistry, too, important results have also been achieved by the MO method. The first and only fully adequate description of the electronic structure of the benzene molecule and an explanation found for the special stability of a cyclic system with six electrons [the electron sextet] has been obtained. Purely quantitive calculations, it is true, have so far proved impossible for large molecules, but Mulliken has established the principles of a valuable method for combining theoretical research with information about the structure of molecules in the MO method. Mulliken's method has also been used for structurally complicated biochemical substances. In most chemical fields it has furthered developments.

'For his pioneer work on chemical bonding and the electron structure of molecules by the molecular-orbital method' MULLIKEN was awarded the *1966* Nobel Prize in Chemistry.

CHEMICAL CHANGE

Reaction kinetics is a branch of chemistry which has as one of its main objects the investigation of the course of chemical processes. Nobel Prizes had, until 1956, only twice been awarded in this important field. In *1901* VAN 'T HOFF received a prize for his discoveries of the laws of chemical dynamics, i.e. the laws of the rate of chemical reactions, and in *1909* OSTWALD was rewarded for his work on catalysis and for his investigations into the fundamental principles governing chemical equilibria and rates of reaction. During later years, great progress has been made in reaction kinetics, and this subject now plays a role that can hardly be overestimated. Its results are of fundamental importance to pure chemistry and are also of very great value to the technical applications of this science. Of the scientists working in this domain, Sir CYRIL HINSHELWOOD [1897-1967] and NIKOLAI NIKOLOJEVIČ SEMENOV [b. 1896] are those who have most contributed to this progress during recent years and the *1956* prize was divided between them 'for their researches into the mechanism of chemical reactions'.

Already in the 1880's van 't Hoff and Arrhenius stated that it is not enough for molecules to collide in order to react. The collision must be sufficiently vehement to loosen the coherence of the molecules so that their atoms may rearrange themselves into new combinations. Hinshelwood has, in many respects, developed this collision theory and by his investigations he has thrown much light upon what happens when molecules take part in chemical transformations.

Van 't Hoff was, however, aware that there are many reactions which do not seem to follow his laws. The explanation of this fact is based upon the idea of so-called chain reactions. It was originally propounded by the German Max Bodenstein who already in 1913 resorted to this idea in order to explain the mechanism of chemical reactions which are strongly influenced by light. A chain process implies that, besides the final products, there are intermediary unstable products formed during the reaction which may react with the original substances without especially forceful collisions. Therefore, if a pair of molecules react somewhere in the gas mixture, they start a series of reactions in a great number of molecules, and thus form the starting point of a chain process.

In 1923 the Dane J. A. Christiansen and the Dutchman H. A. Kramers suggested that it might be possible, by means of the idea of chain reactions, to explain the mechanism of explosions which are very rapid and vehement chemical reactions. They supposed that reaction chains in some cases may branch so that a transformation of a pair of molecules is succeeded not by only one but by several reactions. They did not develop their idea further, but this was done during the following years by SEMENOV and HINSHELWOOD. These latter found, independently of each other, one in Leningrad, the other in Oxford, that a great number of chemical processes, not only explosions, are chain reactions.

The investigations of the two scientists supplement each other. Of great value is the fact that in their work, theory and experiment have generally supported each other. The contributions of the two scientists in this progress seem to be fairly alike. Semenov started a little earlier with investigations on explosions, but Hinshelwood's work has been of a somewhat wider scope. He has dealt with many different problems of reaction kinetics.

The insight into the course of reactions is fundamental to all branches of the chemical industry where it is essential to find the conditions for the best way to produce a material. Substances may react with each other in different ways. By means of investigating reaction rates it is possible to find out which precepts should be followed in order that a reaction comes to pass in the right direction so that the process leads to the product wanted.

Nowadays, the main part of our energy supply is founded upon the use of combustion motors, and the present very effective work on their improvement has its chemical basis in the work done by Hinshelwood and Semenov. The technicians in the field of explosives have also great use for this work in their efforts to gain an insight into the mechanism of explosion reactions.

As late as a few decades ago, it was supposed that many chemical reactions occur instantaneously. The neutralization of acid by alkali, it was thought, was one such process. Long ago, Bodenstein, among others, had demonstrated that many chemical transformations occur by stages, and thus consist of part reactions, some of which were said to be immeasurably fast. In point of fact, up to the time in question, it had only in certain cases been possible to measure the speed of reactions occurring in less than one thousandth per second or so. But in view of the fact that the cycles of the atoms in a molecule occur at a frequency of about one billion per second, the possibility of reaction times down to a microsecond, even a nanosecond (10^{-9} sec), could not be excluded.

Around the year 1950 a thorough revolution occurred in this field. At that time generally valid methods for determining the speed of very fast reactions were worked out. Chemical processes, regarded until then as 'instantaneous', or 'immeasurably fast', could now be studied. The men behind this fundamental progress in reaction kinetics were MANFRED EIGEN of Göttingen [b. 1927], RONALD GEORGE WREYFORD NORRISH [b. 1897] and GEORGE PORTER [b. 1920] in Britain.

These new methods are based on the effect of pulses of energy on systems in a state of equilibirum. This leads to the formation of molecules or molecular fragments [e.g. dissociation products] in such high concentration that their transformation as the system returns to a state of equilibrium can be measured by fast physical methods, based on photoelectric, conductometric or refractometric observations.

The first electrolyte solutions studied by Eigen were subjected by him to rapid increases in pressure by means of a membrane arrangement that was suddenly forced to burst; or else he caused sound or supersonic waves to pass through the solution where they were absorbed when transferring energy to the dissolved molecules. He also made great use of electrical shocks, i.e. for short periods – one microsecond or so – strong electric fields were allowed to influence the system under examination, in many cases in the form of waves of alternating current. This leads to a rise in temperature of 5–10°C, which can have a certain effect on the system's state of equilibrium. Eigen has cleverly used this temperature-rise effect to achieve velocity constants for extremely fast reactions.

In the objects studied by them, Norrish and Porter disturbed the equilibrium by violent ray pulses in the visual or ultraviolet regions – quantities of energy of thousands, even hundreds of thousands of joules from flash-bulbs being released for about one microsecond. This method has been called flash photolysis. The effect of such an intense radiation on a system in equilibrium is such that virtually all its molecules are transformed into activated particles. The subsequent swift return to equilibrium could be registered in the manner described above, most often spectrophotometrically.

These methods, developed by Norrish and Porter and Eigen, opened up an entirely new field of research. Rich harvests have since been reaped in it both by the pioneers in the field and by many other scientists all over the world who have followed in their footsteps. A large number of electrolyte dissociations and many other fast processes have now been studied, and recently information has been obtained on the reactions of complex substances. Furthermore, owing to these new methods, greater insight has been gained into the properties of molecules and radicals.

EIGEN was awarded one-half of the *1967* Chemistry Prize, and NORRISH and PORTER, received jointly the other half, all for 'their work on very fast reactions'.

INORGANIC CHEMISTRY

In *1913* the Swiss ALFRED WERNER [1866-1919] was given the prize 'in recognition of his work on the linkage of atoms in molecules by which he has thrown fresh light on old problems and opened up new fields of research, especially in inorganic chemistry', and in 1915 the American THEODORE WILLIAM RICHARDS [1868-1928] received the *1914* prize 'for his accurate determination of the atomic weight of a large number of chemical elements'.

WERNER was a brilliant systematist who succeeded with admirable ingenuity in determining certain fundamental characteristics in the linkage of so-called complex compounds by studying comprehensive experimental data collected by himself and his many collaborators. These complex compounds are built up by the uniting of two or more simple compounds and are characterized by the fact that when dissolved in water they do not dissociate into their original components. Most of the heavy metals are able to form such complex compounds. Werner studied those of cobalt and chromium in particular detail. He assumed that the metal atoms attach to themselves molecules or atoms whose number is determined by the so-called co-ordination number of the central atom. To begin with he considered this number to be 4 or 6. These atoms or groups of atoms which are bound in the so-called inner sphere do not detach themselves when the compound is dissolved in water. Moreover, they are grouped regularly round the central atom. If the co-ordination number is 4, they assume a tetrahedral or quadratic formation, and if the co-ordination number is 6, they lie at the corners of an octrahedron whose centre lies in the central atom. If the atoms and molecules in the inner sphere are not all of the same kind, different compounds – a number of isomers – are formed according to the relative position of the different atoms or molecules. Under given conditions it is easy to determine the isomeric possibilities.

Werner was able to prove the validity of his assumptions partly by measuring the electric conductivity of water solutions of the complex compounds and partly by studying their isomerism. He was able to determine from the conductivity which parts of the dissolved compound split off in the form of ions and could therefore not be co-ordinated with the central atom. The number of isomers indicated the arrangement of the particles directly attached to the central atom.

Werner also tried to extend the theory of chemical valency by differentiating between principal and subsidiary valencies, the latter coming into force after the former are saturated. He was unable, however, to build up a completely coherent and convincing theory. Time was not yet ripe for a solution of the problem of the chemical bond. Arrhenius, who supported him for the prize, wrote when nominating him: 'It has been said of Werner's epoch-making work that it is partly incomplete. That this is correct, I am only too willing to admit, particularly as I have already said so in my book, *Theorien der Chemie*. If, however, we are to demand perfection in all details of work proposed for the prize, we should in all probability be forced to turn down everything.'

Werner's theory brought order into the chaos then existing in the chemistry of inorganic complexes. He laid the foundations of, and to a great extent built up, the stereochemistry of inorganic compounds. The structural formulae he proposed, which it has since been possible to test by determining the positions of the atoms by X-ray crystallographic analysis of the complex compounds, have almost without exception proved to be correct.

G. N. Lewis, in his pioneer work on chemical valency published in 1923, speaks of Werner as follows: 'His *Neuere Anschauungen auf dem Gebiete der unorganischen Chemie* [1905] marked a new epoch in chemistry; and in attempting to clarify the fundamental ideas of valency, there is no work to which I feel so much personal indebtedness as to this of Werner's. While some of his theoretical conclusions have not proved convincing, he marshalled in a masterly manner a great array of facts which showed the incongruities into which chemists had been led by the existing structural formulae of inorganic chemistry.'

RICHARDS made sensational contributions in the field of atomic weight determinations, where after Stas' accurate analyses in the 1860's most chemists thought that there hardly remained anything of importance to be done. By intensive, systematic and careful work, which took him more than a quarter of a century, Richards showed that many of Stas' values were not acceptable. Moreover, among the elements whose atomic weights had to be revised were oxygen, silver, chlorine, bromine, iodine, potassium, sodium, nitrogen, and sulphur upon which the atomic weight determinations of the other elements are based.

When Richards arrived at results different from those of his predecessors, he was usually able to point out the sources of error which had complicated earlier determinations. Stas had worked throughout with large quantities of the substances in order to eliminate errors in weighing. In his precipitation reactions, which were therefore carried out with far too concentrated solutions, were included foreign substances – by adsorption or otherwise – which could not be eliminated by washing. Richards avoided these errors by working with small quantities and dilute solutions. He also introduced a large number of other improvements in existing methods of measuring atomic weights and worked out a great many new ones, which were not only useful for the purpose for which they were intended but for the preparation of chemically pure substances in general.

In the spring of the same year in which he received the Nobel Prize he applied his skill as an atomic-weight expert to an investigation of the isotopes of lead. In so doing he confirmed the results of the disintegration theory as far as lead is concerned.

MICROCHEMISTRY

When in *1923* the prize was awarded to the Austrian FRITZ PREGL [1869-1930], the winner was, like Richards, an analytical chemist but one whose studies were chiefly devoted to organic substances. He received the prize 'for his invention of the method of micro-analysis of organic substances'. In his speech at the presentation ceremony, O. Hammarsten, the Chairman of the Nobel Committee at the time, pointed out that it was not for a discovery but for modifying and improving existing methods that Pregl was being awarded the prize.

The contents of carbon and hydrogen can, it is true, be determined in the same sample, but nitrogen, sulphur, chlorine and many other elements each need a special analysis. When one considers that every such analysis carried out by the older methods requires 0.17-0.20 g of the substance whereas Pregl's micro-analysis can be carried out with as little as 0.003-0.005 g, one realizes what an important advance this new method was in organic chemistry. The amount of substance which had previously been necessary for one analysis was now sufficient for about fifty. Working with very small quantities naturally requires a certain amount of manual skill, but this can be acquired with a little practice. There is nothing particularly difficult in the technique, and micro-analyses which are carefully performed give just as accurate results as macro-analyses.

Pregl's method is based almost entirely on the same principles as the methods already in use, but nevertheless required the working out of entirely new devices. Pregl constructed apparatus not only for determining the elementary constitution of a compound but also for finding out its molecular weight and fixing the amounts of the most important groups of atoms included in it.

Micro-analysis is an invaluable aid to scientists working on substances which are rare or otherwise difficult to obtain, such as enzymes, hormones, toxins, etc. The method was, it is true, first developed for the study of organic substances, but has since become widely used in inorganic chemistry as well. Microchemistry has grown into an important science with periodicals and a comprehensive literature of its own.

Polarography, invented by JAROSLAV HEYROVSKÝ [b.1890], working in Prague, is another analytical procedure which may be performed on small amounts of substances and which thus also may be termed a micro-method. It is based on the use of a dropping mercury electrode as an indicator in the determination of current–voltage curves in voltametric investigations of electrolytic solutions.

Mercury from a reservoir flows through a thick-walled capillary glass tube at a rate of 20 to 40 drops per minute into the solution which is to be analysed. The solution is contained in a glass bulb, the bottom of which is covered by a layer of mercury. By means of a platinum wire sealed into the glass vessel this mercury may be connected with the one pole of a battery. The other pole is connected with the mercury of the dropping electrode. The latter is the cathode. A branching device makes it possible to vary the applied voltage continuously. The current passing through the solution is registered on a galvanometer.

By means of two side tubes in the vessel the solution is saturated before analysis with hydrogen or nitrogen, as the presence of oxygen may have a disturbing influence on the measurement. As a rule, an electrolyte with a high decomposition potential, usually potassium chloride, is present at a fairly high concentration in the solution to take care of the electricity transport. In this way the substances whose reactions at the indicator electrode are to be studied do not take part in the conduction, but arrive at the surface of the mercury drops only by diffusion.

At low voltages there is only a weak current, the so-called residual current, passing through the solution. When the voltage is raised to the vicinity of the decomposition potential of an ion species the current increases more and more and grows proportionally to the voltage increase when the ions are discharged on the mercury drops. Within this interval the current-voltage curve has thus a rectilinear portion. When the mercury drops are saturated with discharged ions, the curve deviates and finally becomes again practically parallel to the voltage axis. Each kind of ions thus produces a 'wave' on the curve. The central point of the rectilinear part in the diagram is termed by Heyrovský a 'half-wave potential'. It is characteristic of the ion in question which thus may be identified in this very simple way. Moreover, the height of the wave gives a measure of the concentration of the ion in the solution. The analysis is thus both qualitative and quantitative.

The dropping mercury electrode has a great advantage in the incessant renewal of the cathode surface. Concentration polarization is thus avoided. If the solution contains depolarizing anions, the mercury layer on the bottom of the cell maintains a well-defined potential and may thus be used as a reference electrode.

Heyrovský performed his first work in this domain already in the 1920's. After a few years he succeeded in making the registration of the current–voltage curves an automatic procedure. With an apparatus of this kind, a so-called polarograph, an analysis may be performed within a few minutes. Strangely enough, however, his first achievements attracted relatively little attention and it took, in fact, a considerable time before chemists became aware of the valuable tool Heyrovský had developed for routine and research analyses.

Polarography is a quick method and is thus of great use in the industry where it is often important to make rapid analyses, e.g. in controlling chemical processes. Nowadays it has acquired general application in factory laboratories. In many cases several components may be determined in a single polarogram. It may be mentioned as an example that in a mixture of thallium, cadmium, zinc, cobalt, and manganese salts the concentration of all these five metals may be established in one and the same analysis.

The method has also been developed so that it may be applied to organic substances. The reduction of such compounds produces bends or waves on the current-voltage curve which are somewhat different from those due to the discharge of inorganic ions but, by means of calibration procedures, they have, with great success, been used for analytical purposes. The method may also be employed for gas analyses. In recent years polarography has gained an extra-ordinarily wide application and has turned out to be an indispensible tool in chemistry. Its originator was therefore awarded the *1959* prize 'for his discovery and his development of polarography'.

PREPARATIVE ORGANIC CHEMISTRY

The development of synthetic organic chemistry in the nineteenth century was facilitated by frequent discoveries of certain reagents and types of reactions which could be widely used. For example, it was found that the organic compounds of zinc, the so-called zinc alkyls, discovered in the middle of the century, could be used for various kinds of syntheses on account of their marked reactivity. The corresponding compounds of magnesium have, however, proved of much wider and more varied use.

During the years 1900 and 1901 the French scientist VICTOR GRIGNARD [1871-1935] showed in a series of fine experiments that metallic magnesium reacts with organic halogen derivatives in ether solutions, forming the corresponding organic halogen compounds of magnesium to which one or two molecules of ether are bound chemically. These magnesium alkyl halides have the advantage over the corresponding zinc compounds that they do not ignite spontaneously at ordinary temperatures. They are normally soluble in ether, and even in such solutions, the so-called Grignard reagents, they react extremely easily with a large number of different types of organic compounds, during which reactions carbon is bound to carbon so that a real organic synthesis takes place.

Grignard summarized his results in his doctor's thesis published in 1901. His method was by then worked out except for small details, and its usefulness demonstrated in a number of widely different cases. It allows of unlimited combinations; it may well be said that no branch of organic chemistry is beyond its reach. In this respect his method was unsurpassed by any other. It has also been widely used not only in preparations but also for solving purely theoretical problems which could previously not be treated at all or only with difficulty. The organic compounds of magnesium have often been used in determinations of chemical constitution.

Another method used in organic chemistry which attracted attention at the turn of the century because of its scientific and technical importance was the Frenchman PAUL SABATIER's [1854-1941] hydrogenation of organic compounds using finely powdered metals as catalysts.

Since the beginning of the nineteenth century it had been known that platinum sponge accelerates the process of oxidation, but it had only exceptionally been used to carry out hydrogenation. Oxides of nitrogen had been reduced to ammonia, and it was known that, in the presence of finely powdered platinum, iodine and hydrogen quickly combine to form hydrogen iodide at low temperatures.

At the end of the 1890's, Sabatier, together with his pupil J. B. Senderens, noticed that a similar catalytic effect could be achieved by finely powdered nickel, cobalt, copper, and iron. This observation led to a series of attempts to hydrogenate unsaturated compounds in general, not only those containing double bonds between carbon atoms but also between carbon and other elements. The experiments were highly successful, and an extremely fruitful method in organic chemistry was thus been developed. The method is very simple to use. A suitable amount of the pure oxide of one of the metals is introduced into a glass tube and reduced with hydrogen gas at about 300°. After the reaction is finished, the temperature is suitably lowered – sometimes completely cooled down, but most often to about 180° – after which the current of hydrogen gas is mixed with the vapours of the organic substance to be hydrogenated. The reaction runs easily and when properly carried out usually gives a good yield, in so far as only limited amounts of by-products are formed and molecular rearrangements seldom occur.

The method has found important applications. In its original form it could only be used for compounds which can be vapourized without decomposing, but it has since also been applied indirectly to substances which cannot be distilled but which are soluble in water or in some organic solvent.

Sabatier's hydrogenation method is now used on a large scale for in-dustrial purposes. With nickel as the catalyst, hydrogen is introduced into unsaturated oils – both vegetable oils, such as olive oil, linseed oil and cotton-seed oil, and animal oils, such as fish liver oil and whale oil. The raw materials thus treated become more solid, so that the process is called *fat hardening*. Hydrogenation also has the advantage that the unpleasant taste and smell of raw materials such as fish oils and whale oil almost entirely disappear. Such products can therefore be used for manufacturing stearin and soap and even fatty foodstuffs. The use of whale fat in the margarine industry, made possible by Sabatier's fat-hardening process, has revolutionized the economic development of whaling.

The *1912* prize was divided between GRIGNARD and SABATIER for their methods of synthesis 'whereby the progress of organic chemistry has been greatly advanced'.

In the 1920's and 1930's OTTO DIELS [1876-1954] and KURT ALDER [1902-1958] worked out a procedure of organic syntheses which in its wide applicability ranks with the Grignard method. It is based on the fact that two molecules, one with two conjugated double bonds [the diene] and one with a single double bond [the dienophile], easily close together to form a 6-membered ring, if certain structural conditions are fulfilled. It is true that certain instances of such reactions had been observ-ed earlier, but they had hardly been correctly interpreted or met with the attention they merited. The German chemists were the first [1928] to explain definitely the course of the reaction and to emphasize that in this case they had to do with a discovery of great general usefulness.

The so-called diene-synthesis of Diels and Alder was rapidly developed into one of the most important expedients of modern organic chemistry and is now treated at great length in handbooks on its methods. It has also proved very valuable for analytical purposes. Maleic anhydride is readily disposed to take part in a synthesis of this kind and is now com-monly used as a sensitive reagent on conjugated double bonds. This sub-stance has become of great importance for elucidating structures of com-plicated products occurring in Nature, such as, for example, steroids and terpenoids. In the rather frequently occurring cases, where natural prod-ucts are easily isomerised by displacement of double bonds, their reaction with maleic anhydride may render valuable information on the course of the isomerisation process. The diene synthesis has also proved to be of technical value in the industry of plastics and for the working up of cracking products. In the formation of more intricately built systems, stereochemical problems may arise which have great theoretical interest. They have been successfully treated by Alder.

The *1950* prize was divided equally between DIELS and ALDER 'for their discovery and development of the diene synthesis'.

During the last few decades, studies of the structure of complicated natural products have been of great interest to chemists. Today, owing to the introduction of new physical and physico-chemical methods, the possibilities of successfully comprehending such structures have increased. An unchallenged master in this field of research is the American ROBERT BURNS WOODWARD [b. 1917], who succeeded in synthesizing a large number of complex structured substances that had until then defied all attempts at synthesis. Proposals received in the early 1960's by the chemical Nobel committee, nominating him as a candidate for the prize, contain such phrases as these: 'He has shown that almost no synthesis is impossible'. And: 'Now there is no limit for organic synthesis'.

Woodward not only possesses a broad knowledge of classical organic procedures, he has also successfully exploited contemporary experimental methods [among them infrared spectral measurements] in studying the substances involved in his chain of syntheses. During the Second World War, Woodward succeeded in synthesizing quinine, the well-known antidote to malaria; and, in the years immediately following the war, he also synthesized the steroids, cholesterol and cortisone. His synthesis of strychnine, the poison found in St. Ignatius' beans, achieved in 1955, and soon afterwards, his synthesis of the medically important alkaloid reserpine attracted wide attention. He has also chemically synthesized a whole series of other important substances in the alkaloid field. He has contributed much to our knowledge of antibiotics, and among other things he has investigated the problems surrounding the structure of Aureomycin and Terramycin. If this work on numerous medically effective substances has been so valuable, it is because it has offered methods for varying their composition. In certain cases, by producing synthetic substitutes, which in some respect have been modified as compared with the natural substance, it is possible to obtain products still more therapeutically efficient, or medical preparations whose contraindications are somewhat less dangerous, than those of the natural product.

Finally, Woodward has succeeded in carrying out the very difficult synthesis of chlorophyll, and thereby in certain respects has complemented our knowledge of its molecular structure.

A characteristic dominant in all of Woodward's research has been his predilection for tackling seemingly insuperable problems. 'For his meritorious work in the development of organic synthesis' he was awarded the *1965* Chemistry Prize.

THE CONSTITUTION OF ORGANIC COMPOUNDS AND BIOCHEMISTRY

The properties of organic compounds depend not only on their composition but also on their structure, i.e. the arrangement of the atoms in the molecule. For a successful synthesis of substances with complicated structures, such as dyes, medicines and other technical preparations from simpler molecules, it is necessary to ascertain the molecular constitution not only of the original substances but also of the final products of the synthesis. Determining the constitution, at least of complex compounds, makes great demands on the skill and ingenuity of the scientist.

The work of countless organic chemists has, however, led gradually to the elucidation of the structure of a great number of compounds and of the connection between their constitution and their physical and chemical properties. In order to determine the structure of an organic compound one normally acts upon it with various, not too strongly reactive chemical agents so that it is broken down into a number of simpler constituents which can be identified. In the light of the data thus obtained an attempt is then made to build up the original substance from the recognizable parts. The constitution cannot generally be considered definitely established until such a resynthesis has been carried out.

When a chemist wants to form a three-dimensional picture of a molecule that can be composed in the above manner, he must observe the rules for the stereochemistry of the carbon atom, established nearly one-century ago by Van 't Hoff and Le Bel [cf. p. 289]. Even by allowing for this limitation, it can happen that he will arrive at more than one possible model molecule. He can find himself faced with a choice of several conformations. Which of these is the most stable and probable can be elucidated by so-called conformational analysis, a procedure developed by the Englishman

DEREK HAROLD RICHARD BARTON [b. 1918] on the basis of diffraction determinations of structure, carried out by the Norwegian ODD HASSEL [b. 1897].

By applying various physical methods, but above all by X-ray and electron diffraction analysis, Hassel, who had early made a name for himself as a brilliant X-ray crystallographer, studied the molecular structure of cyclohexane, decalin [fully hydrogenated naphthalene] and a large number of derivatives of these hydrocarbons. Cyclohexane can appear in two conformations; its molecule can have either the chair or the boat form. Hassel found the former to be incomparably more stable than the latter. He has disproved long-standing notions of the molecular structure of *cis*-decalin, and instead has put forward an energetically favoured molecular model for this substance.

Hassel has drawn attention to the fundamental differences existing between the carbon atoms' *a*- and *e*-positions in a cyclohexane. The former are closely parallel to the trigonal axis of the molecule: three are oriented in one direction, three in the opposite direction, with the latter six *e*-valences virtually at right angles to them. It was found that the *a*-position is more sterically hindered and that heavier or more bulky substitutes prefer the *e*-position. Hassel has applied these ideas to a great number of derivatives of cyclohexane and decalin, and has also drawn their consequences for the carbohydrates.

The six-membered carbon ring is a common structural element in many natural products, and the knowledge gained of its properties, owing to Hassel's work, has proved applicable to research into these substances' structure. In this way Barton, who had long been interested in the structure of steroids, was able to give a natural and simple explanation of a whole series of empirical results in the stereochemistry of these substances, which until then had been hard to interpret. He carried out similar research into alkaloids, terpenes and polyterpenes, and was able to establish general rules as to how to apply conformational analysis. He has made conformational analysis, which today sets its stamp on virtually every branch of chemistry, into a powerful tool in the hands of chemical research. For the knowledge it yields of the reactive paths of molecules, conformational analysis has been of particular importance in preparative chemistry. By showing which part of a molecule can most easily combine with some other substance, it is also in constant use in medical research.

When proposing Barton's and Hassel's candidature for a Nobel Prize in Chemistry, one eminent authority wrote: 'Conformational analysis is the first real advance in stereochemistry since the theory of Van't Hoff-Le Bel, i.e. since 1874'.

BARTON and HASSEL shared the *1969* prize for 'their contributions to the development of the concept of conformation and its application in chemistry'.

For many reasons the compounds occurring in Nature, in plants or animals, are particularly interesting, and many such substances were described in the early period of organic chemistry. Pioneer work in this field was done, for example, by Scheele and Berzelius. During the first half of the nineteenth century it was normally only possible to determine the structure of the simplest of the naturally occurring substances; scientists were not equipped to tackle successfully more difficult constitutions until towards the end of the century. Reference has already been made to the important investigations carried out by Emil Fischer and A. von Baeyer.

The latter, it will be remembered, opened up an entirely new field of organic chemistry by his discovery of the alicyclic compounds. These compounds occur, for example, in a large group of vegetable products characterized by a more or less strong smell and play an important role in the biological functions of plants. Because of their volatility they have been termed ethereal oils. They contain hydrocarbons of a special kind, which since they occur in ordinary turpentine have been called terpenes. Closely related to these liquid terpenes are the solid substances obtained from the ethereal oils, the camphors.

Many attempts had been made to elucidate the constitution of these substances, but the German scientist OTTO WALLACH [1847-1931] was the first to introduce any order into the chaos of puzzling phenomena in this field. He began his studies of the terpenes and the camphors in 1884 and for six years collected a comprehensive and valuable experimental material. He succeeded in isolating and identifying about ten terpenes, found that they are liable to undergo changes under the influence of chemical reagents, that their molecules have a tendency to rearrangement and that they tend to form addition compounds both with themselves and with other substances. Wallach managed, however, to overcome the difficulties caused by these properties and was thus the first to gain any real insight into the chemical nature of the terpenes. The genetic relationship between a large number of these compounds could now be elucidated, and after von Baeyer had shown the connection between aromatic and alicyclic substances, Wallach was able to solve a number of structural problems of fundamental importance. Great advances were thus made in the study of this new series of substances, which von Baeyer's work had opened up for research. The results achieved were not only of scientific importance but had a far-reaching influence on the chemical industries concerned with the production of ethereal oils and artificial perfumes. WALLACH was awarded the *1910* Nobel Prize for his work in the field of alicyclic compounds.

This field of study was far too wide for Wallach alone to be able to exhaust it. Many chemists, both his contemporaries and later workers, have contributed to our knowledge of the alicyclic compounds of the ethereal oils. Among them the French scientist, A. Haller, and the two Finns, O. Aschan and G. Komppa, deserve special mention.

Very important advances in the field of the terpenes were made about 1930 by LEOPOLD RUZICKA [b.1887], who was Croatian by birth but had been a Swiss citizen for thirty years. He solved the problem of the structures of the so-called sesqui-, di- and triterpenes which have $1\frac{1}{2}$, 2 and 3 times as many carbon atoms in their molecules as the monoterpenes studied by Wallach. Ruzicka tackled the problem by careful dehydrogenation, i.e. eliminating some hydrogen which is the most easily removed constituent of these complex hydroaromatic compounds, and thus converting them into the corresponding aromatic compounds which could be identified. As a working hypothesis he formulated the so-called isoprene rule, according to which the carbon framework of the molecules of the higher terpenes is composed of a number of remnants of isoprene, each comprising five carbon atoms arranged in the way characteristic of this hydrocarbon. This rule proved to be a good working guide and has thrown much light on the chemistry of the terpenes and the compounds related to them.

During his successful studies of the terpenes, Ruzicka, like Wallach, was led to investigate the structure of certain odoriferous substances and made many remarkable discoveries. He showed that the molecules of the ketones, muskone and civetone, present in the secretions of the musk-deer and the civet, contain closed rings of no less than 15 and 17 carbon atoms, respectively. It had not previously been thought possible that there could exist molecules with so many atoms linked together in a ring, so that Ruzicka's discovery attracted considerable attention. Up to that time chemists had not been able to synthesize compounds with more than at most 8 atoms in each ring. Ruzicka and his co-workers succeeded, however, in preparing cyclic ketones containing from 9 up to over 30 atom rings in their molecules, and thus introduced a very remarkable group of substances into organic chemistry.

The series of ring ketones illustrates very clearly how physiological properties change with the molecular structure. The ketones with 5 to 8 atoms per ring smell of bitter almonds, caraway seeds and peppermint all at the same time, those with 10 to 12 atom rings smell of camphor, and those with 14 to 18 of musk, which is strongest in those with 15 carbon atoms in each ring.

Ruzicka found that the polyterpenes he examined bear a certain relation to a group of substances of great physiological and medical importance, namely, the bile acids, the sterols and the sex hormones. He was the first to prepare a sex hormone from a sterol, and to elucidate its constitution in detail, and he also worked out methods for producing male sex hormones. As his work in this field was closely connected with the pioneer work on sex hormones by the German scientist, ADOLF BUTENANDT, they were awarded jointly the *1939* Prize for Chemistry, half of it being given to RUZICKA 'for his work on polymethylenes and higher terpenes'. We shall return to Butenandt's work later on in this survey.

In the 1920's HERMANN STAUDINGER [1881-1965] suggested that, in many cases instead of the cyclic compounds expected, e.g. such as studied by Ruzicka, highly polymeric products were formed. This may happen when steric conditions put obstacles in the way of ring-formation, i.e. in such cases when, because of certain features of the molecular structure, the two ends of the atomic chains have difficulty in finding each other. In such cases the atomic chains may attach themselves one to another, and this process may go on until very long and eventually also highly ramified macromolecules are formed.

In the beginning this view had many adversaries – the time was not ripe for its acceptance. The objection was made that the ordinary chemical valence forces were insufficient to keep together the big molecules assumed to be formed. Many old-fashioned chemists found it also hard to believe that the polymerized products could consist of molecules of different size. If Staudinger's view on the formation of the polymers was true, the length of the molecular chains must to a certain degree depend on chance, even if they were built according to one and the same plan and were of an average size.

During the following decade, however, the ideas of Staudinger began to gain ground. X-ray crystallographic investigations which indicated the correctness of his concept contributed to this to a great extent. At this time polymerized products were also used to an ever increasing extent for technical purposes. The industry of plastics began to flourish. Staudinger's ideas on the molecular structure of its products were found to be of fundamental importance to its development. His work formed a solid theoretical base for the attempts to find new plastic materials and to vary their qualities. Thanks to his achievements, rapid progress was made possible. His work had also a remarkable influence upon the advance of pure science. At last it was clear that STAUDINGER's work was to count among the great conquests in chemistry and he received the *1953* prize 'for his discoveries in the field of macromolecular chemistry'.

In the 1950's, significant progress was made in the high polymer field owing to contributions by the German KARL ZIEGLER [b. 1898] and the Italian GIULIO NATTA [b. 1903]. They were awarded the *1963* prize 'for their discoveries in the chemistry and technology of the high polymers'.

As a specialist in organometallic substances, Ziegler had, among other things, produced lithium compounds. As chemical reagents these were in certain respects an improvement on Grignard's magnesium compounds [cf. p. 350]. Far more important, however, were his synthesis of organo-aluminium compounds, and his discovery, made in 1953, that the latter, together with compounds of certain heavy metals such as titanium, zirconium, molybdenum, cobalt, etc., could be used as catalysts to produce high polymers. Owing to this discovery, it became possible to control and direct processes of this sort with greater efficiency than had been the case by the previously utilized condensation methods. By Ziegler's addition method, for instance, it is possible under normal pressure and with only a slight rise in temperature to produce polyethene from ethene. In some respects the product thus obtained is also superior to that produced by high pressure condensation.

By using empirical practical methods Ziegler perfected his methodology, and finally got so far as to gain a high degree of control over the polymerization process. Using various catalyst mixtures and suitable experimental conditions, he was able to produce dimers, i.e. to join molecules together in pairs, produce polymers of any desired medium chain length, and also produce extremely long molecular chains, having up to hundreds of thousands, even millions of bonds. He was also successful in bringing about extremely interesting ring closures of a rather unusual type. By a happy chance he found that finely divided nickel pulls off the catalyst group from the carbon chain. This gave him a means of interrupting the polymerization process at a convenient stage.

This pioneer research has been further developed and, in certain crucial aspects, more deeply investigated by Natta. Natta is primarily a physical chemist, who began his career as an X-ray crystallographer. His most important results have been achieved in determining structure by X-ray diffraction. An instance of his research is his studies of addition polymers of propene – hydrocarbons which are the next highest homologues to ethene and which can be obtained from ethylene by replacing one of its hydrogen atoms by a methyl group. When polymerizing propene, three structurally different products can be obtained. The methyl groups, which form what are called side chains, can, first, be arbitrarily distributed on either side of the carbon chain; second, all be found on one side of it; and, third, alternate regularly from one side to the other. Lastly, one further form of addition polymer can be formed, namely those polymers that Natta has called stereoblocks – molecules whose radical side chains point, over certain of their longer sections, in one direction, and over other long sections in the opposite direction. By experiment, Natta has also found other catalyst complexes for achieving stereospecific polymerization than those used by Ziegler. He has also done much valuable work in exploring the central problem of the mechanism of catalysis.

Owing to Natta's research, valuable insight has been gained into the relationship between the structure of high polymers and their technical properties. Previously, it had been possible to obtain products which are very similar to the two substances obtained from the sap of the rubber-tree – rubber and gutta percha. But not until Ziegler and Natta had done their work was it possible to synthesize highly polymeric substances that are completely identical with these natural products. Nature's monopoly in this field had seemed hard to break; but at last it was broken.

It is a well-known fact that the chlorophyll present in the leaves of plants plays an important role in their assimilation of carbon dioxide. Research on the structure of this substance was begun by Berzelius, but the problem could not be solved with the limited resources then available. Certain of his results have, however, proved valuable to later workers. Interest in the chemical nature of chlorophyll increased when it was shown that it was not homogeneous as had previously been assumed but probably made up of at least two components and chemically related to haemoglobin. The researches of the German chemist, RICHARD WILLSTÄTTER [1872-1942], and his associates threw much light on the chemistry of chlorophyll.

He found that its magnesium content is not an impurity but that the metal is an integral part of the molecule, in which it is bound to the nitrogen atoms in the same complex way as is iron in haemoglobin. He confirmed that the green pigment in plants is made up of two components, one blue-green, chlorophyll *a*, and the other yellow-green, chlorophyll *b*, normally occurring in plants in the ratio 3:1. He also worked out methods for preparing both substances in a pure state and went a long way towards finding out their chemical constitution. They are diesters, which on saponification split up into two alcohols, methyl alcohol and phytol, and the colour components chlorophyll *a* and *b*, which contain magnesium. This splitting up can also be brought about by the action of an enzyme, chlorophyllase, present in leaves. Willstätter's studies of the chlorophylls and chlorophyllides and their derivatives are specially interesting because of the relationship between haemoglobin and chlorophyll. He was able to produce the same parent porphyrin from both these pigments.

Willstätter also carried out pioneer investigations on other plant pigments, such as the carotenoids, which are found in leaves together with chlorophyll, and the different coloured anthocyanins in flowers and fruits. The latter are glucosides, i.e. made up of a sugar, usually grape sugar, and a colouring matter, a cyanine. He studied the constitution and mutual relationships of the latter group of substances and made clear their connection with the natural yellow pigments occurring in the flavin or flavonol groups.

WILLSTÄTTER was awarded the *1915* Nobel Prize 'for his pioneer researches on plant pigments, especially chlorophyll'.

In *1930,* investigations on chlorophyll were again rewarded when HANS FISCHER [1881-1945] of Munich received the prize 'for his researches into the constitution of haemin and chlorophyll and especially for his synthesis of haemin'. In this case the Academy was pleased to be able to make an award which fulfilled literally the condition laid down in Nobel's will that the prizes should be awarded for work done 'during the preceding year', because Fischer's greatest piece of research, his synthesis of haemin, had been carried out in 1929.

This work formed the last link in a chain of investigations extending over a period of twenty years or so, the chief aim of which was to solve the problem of the constitution of a group of substances with complicated structures, the so-called porphyrins, to which belong the basic substances of the pigment in blood and leaves. The porphyrins occur in human urine, normally, it is true, in minute quantities but in larger amounts during a certain illness, the so-called porphyrinuria. Fischer was able to determine the structure of these substances in detail and succeeded in synthesizing a number of them. By introducing iron into the molecules of one of them, protoporphyrin, he produced artificial haemin, which proved to be identical with that obtained by splitting up haemoglobin.

Fischer confirmed that the colouring matter in blood is closely related to that occurring in leaves and that they can both be derived from the same porphyrin. The chemical structure of this substance had not, however, been fully elucidated by Willstätter. Fischer therefore examined the breakdown products of chlorophyll, ascertained their constitution by syntheses and in other ways, and by 1930 he had partly succeeded in determining the structure of the chlorophyll molecules.

The yellow pigments were also studied in detail by Fischer. He elucidated the constitution of bilirubin, the most characteristic of these substances, and determined its relationship to haemoglobin.

Sir ROBERT ROBINSON [b.1886], of Oxford, who was awarded the prize in *1947* 'for his investigations on vegetable products of biological importance, especially the alkaloids', may also to a certain extent be looked upon as a successor to Willstätter. He has carried out, for example, fine work on the usually beautifully coloured anthocyanins which are common in the plant world. His extensive researches, however, cover a much wider field. He has made valuable contributions to our knowledge of the sex hormones and has synthesized substances with similar properties. In the sphere of medicine he has achieved important results by his studies of synthetic remedies for malaria and by his participation in the research on penicillin. He is also one of the group of English scientists who have recently thrown fresh light on the mechanism of organic reactions.

In giving their reasons for Robinson's award the Academy mentioned especially his studies on alkaloids. These heterocyclic nitrogen compounds of basic character, which occur in plants in the form of salts, are used, most often in extremely small doses, for medical purposes because of their marked physiological effects. Their chemical structure, which is extremely complicated, has been the subject of investigation by many prominent scientists. Robinson, who is at present the unsurpassed master in this field, has succeeded in solving completely the difficult problem of the arrangement of the atoms in the molecules of morphine and strychnine and thrown much light on the structure of many other alkaloids. He has also put forward a theory for the genesis of the alkaloids in plants, which is confirmed, for example, by his synthesis of tropine, a substance closely related to cocaine. This theory has made it possible to co-ordinate the comprehensive and apparently heterogeneous data in this difficult field resulting from the work of many scientists over a long period of years. It has also proved useful in determining molecular structures.

As mentioned above, the pigments in the leaves of plants, especially the chlorophyll, play an important role in their assimilation of carbon dioxide. Willstätter was interested in this process, too, and dedicated much work to its elucidation. It is of fundamental importance to all life on earth because by means of their utilization of the carbon dioxide of the atmosphere the green plants are able to produce sugars, cellulose, starch, fats and other substances which they need for their vital activity and which again become the food and the source of energy in animals. This assimilation process is a photosynthesis by means of which the energy of radiation of sunlight is transformed into chemical energy which is thus stored up and may be used for industrial purposes.

It stands to reason that, for a very long time, chemists have speculated on the question of which reactions occur in this basic process. Among those who have attacked this problem may be mentioned the great German chemist Liebig, the founder of agricultural chemistry, the Nobel Prize winner von Baeyer, mentioned above, and as just pointed out Willstätter. None of them was, however, able to overcome the difficulties of the problem. The methods available for their research were all too crude to enable them to succeed. Two ways of investigation had first to be developed before the riddle of these intricate reactions could be solved. One was Hevesy's method of using isotopes as indicators for the study of chemical processes, the other was partition chromatography, developed by Martin and Synge [see pp. 334 and 335].

With great skill MELVIN CALVIN [b.1911] at the University of California employed these modern research methods on the carbon dioxide assimilation. In these investigations he used as radio-indicator carbon-14, the same isotope that Libby made use of for his famous dating method. It had been produced in Berkeley, California by radiation of nitrogen-containing substances with neutrons in the cyclotrone of Lawrence.

Calvin arranged that carbon dioxide containing carbon-14 atoms was assimilated by suspensions of green algae. After certain definite time intervals he took out small samples from the reacting system and mixed them with boiling 80 per cent ethyl alcohol to stop the enzymatic processes. The substances present in the samples were extracted and the solutions thus obtained analysed by means of paper chromatography. After long and persevering work Calvin had identified most of the components present in the samples. He found some twenty different substances forming links in the reactions which constitute the assimilation process. He was also able to draw up reaction sequences according to which the different carbohydrates are produced from the primary products.

The shorter time the suspension had been illuminated the more predominant in the samples was a substance with three carbon atoms in its molecule, which was identified as 3-phosphoglyceric acid [PGA]. Even if this is the first detectable compound to be labelled it is not this substance which incorporates the carbon dioxide or forms what is called the acceptor. Surprisingly enough, Calvin found that the acceptor was a compound with five carbon atoms in its molecule, a derivative of a ketopentose, ribulose-1,5-diphosphate. At the fixation of carbon dioxide this substance is transformed into a compound with six carbon atoms in its molecule which is not stable but spontaneously splits up into two molecules of PGA.

The ribulose-diphosphate plays an important role in the reactions converting one carbohydrate into another. By studying such transformations Calvin found many different ways for the regeneration of this compound which has a central function in the photosynthesis and must be regenerated in order that the assimilation process may proceed.

Reduced diphosphopyridine-nucleotide [DPNH] plays an essential role and adenosine-triphosphate [ATP] must be present when the ribulose-diphosphate is regenerated. These substances are old acquaintances from investigations of the breaking down of carbohydrates in animal cells. For their regeneration they need an addition of energy and it is evidently in this part of the reaction system that the light absorption of the pigments influences the carbon dioxide assimilation.

This concerns the so-called energetic side of the process. Calvin has rendered valuable contributions to its elucidation and many other scientists have treated this part of the complex problem. The outcome of their work is, however, still somewhat doubtful. It is based on too many speculations. It is quite another thing with the material side of the process or 'the path of carbon in photosynthesis' as Calvin calls it. Its problems are solved by him. With great dexterity he has established the experimental data necessary for this task and by ingenious study of them he has succeeded in disentangling the apparent confusion met with. CALVIN was rewarded with the *1961* prize 'for his investigations on the carbon dioxide assimilation of plants'.

In 1928 two German scientists were awarded prizes for closely connected researches. HEINRICH WIELAND [1877-1957] received the *1927* prize for 'his researches into the constitution of the bile acids and related substances', while ADOLF WINDAUS [1876-1959] was given the *1928* prize for 'his researches into the constitution of the sterols and their connection with the vitamins'.

The bile acids occurring in the gall-bladders of animals are of great importance in metabolism. When WIELAND began to study them in 1916 it was thought that there were three of them, but he soon found that one was in reality only an addition product of one of the others and a fatty acid. This and other similar addition products proved to be soluble in water, and Wieland could thus explain how the gall-bladder can make some substances which are in themselves insoluble in water susceptible to absorption.

Shortly after, Hans Fischer succeeded in isolating another bile acid from gall-stones in cattle, and Wieland then proceeded to investigate the constitution of this acid, too. From 100 kg of gall-bladder contents of oxen he could only produce 1 g of it. In spite of the fact that he had in all only 3 g of the substance, he was able to find out its relationship to the bile acids already known. Finally, Wieland succeeded in producing the parent substance, from which all three acids were derived, and was thus able to determine their complicated structure almost completely. The parent substance proved to be closely allied to cholesterol, a compound which also occurs in gall-stones and has been closely studied by Windaus.

Wieland then turned his attention to a substance which may be thought to have rather a curious origin but is of interest, since it belongs to a group which plays an important role in medicine as heart stimulants, namely toad venom. One of the constituents in the skin of toads, bufotalin, had, it is true, already been isolated, but its constitution was unknown. Wieland found it to be closely related to the bile acids. He then investigated the real toad venom, bufotoxin, which he succeeded in isolating from certain secretions of toads. It turned out to be a compound of bufotalin with an amino-acid, arginine, and suberic acid. This acid had hitherto only been found in plants. The toxic properties of bufotoxin could now be explained, and it was obvious that it must influence the heart as its physiological effects were comparable to those of digitalis, the drug normally used as a heart stimulant.

Wieland also put forward a theory to explain the chemical reactions involved in the process of respiration, a theory which had a highly stimulating influence on physiological research.

The sterols studied by Windaus occur in both plants and animals. One of the most important of them is cholesterol, which has already been mentioned above. Although it is most easily prepared from gall-stones, it is nevertheless found in many different places in the animal organism, and evidently plays an important role in the vital processes of living beings. Windaus's decisive contribution to this field was his discovery that the sterols are derived from the same parent substance as the bile acids studied by Wieland. He was able by a very simple chemical reaction to convert the sterol present in the human intestine, the so-called coprosterol, into a substance identical with the parent substance of the bile acids found by Wieland. By the time he received the prize Windaus had progressed very far in his detailed studies of the structures of the various sterols.

In addition, Windaus investigated with great success the glucosides occurring in the *Strophanthus* and *Digitalis* genera. These act as heart stimulants and are, therefore, of great medical interest. He succeeded in producing many of them in a pure state, and found that they, too, were closely related in structure to the bile acids and thus to the bufotoxin studied by Wieland.

His studies of the sterols led Windaus into the field of vitamin research, and he made an important discovery concerning one of these substances, which are essential components in the foodstuffs of the higher animals. English and American scientists had reported that if certain foodstuffs, milk for example, are subjected to ultraviolet radiation they became actively antirachitic. Vitamin D must, therefore, be formed in this process as it is the antirachitic factor. Windaus tried to ascertain whether it could possibly be the cholesterol present in the foodstuffs that is converted into vitamin D by irradiation. However, in spite of extensive experiments he failed to obtain any product from it which could be activated. Finally, he found that it was another sterol, ergosterol, the chemically most unsaturated of those he had isolated and, therefore, that with the highest reactivity, which in this case played the role of a so-called provitamin. Ergosterol, which can be produced from ergot or yeast, is changed into vitamin D by irradiation and has a very strong antirachitic effect in this form. If rats suffering from rickets are fed with 0.0001 mg of irradiated ergosterol daily, all symptoms of the disease disappear.

Windaus has since led further research on the vitamin D group of substances.

Vitamins attracted ever increasing interest during the 1930's, and it was not long before another prize for chemistry was awarded for work in this field. In *1937* the Englishman WALTER NORMAN HAWORTH [1883-1950], and the Swiss PAUL KARRER [1889-1971] shared the prize, the former 'for his researches into the constitution of carbohydrates and vitamin C' and the latter 'for his researches into the constitution of carotenoids, flavins and vitamins A and B_2'.

The carbohydrates, to which group belong the sugars, starches, dextrin, and cellulose, are extremely important in physiology, particularly nutritional physiology, and technically. No organic substance occurs so abundantly in Nature as cellulose. The carbohydrates are also important constituents of a large number of natural products, in which they combine with alcohols and phenols or with acids of various kinds to form the so-called glucosides and tannins. It is therefore only natural that chemists should have worked assiduously to elucidate the structure of these substances.

Emil Fischer's pioneer work in this field has already been mentioned. Even though his structural formulae rendered possible a general survey of the chemical nature of the sugars, they could not explain phenomena which hinted at molecular rearrangements in these substances on being dissolved. It was obvious that they could take on many more forms than those indicated by Fischer's formulae. Gradually scientists became more and more convinced that the framework in sugar molecules consists not of an open carbon chain, as Fischer envisaged it, but of rings.

Our present detailed knowledge of the structure of these cyclic carbohydrate molecules is based on Sir Norman Haworth's researches. The work which led to this magnificent result was started at the University of St. Andrews in Scotland. The professors of chemistry there, Thomas

Purdie and his successor, Sir James Irvine, of which the former had been Haworth's teacher, had worked out an excellent method for investigating carbohydrates and made valuable contributions to the chemistry of these substances. Irvine, especially, made important discoveries in this field. Haworth improved their method very considerably, and introduced what has been described as a renaissance and a second classical period in the chemistry of the carbohydrates. After the structure of the simpler sugars had been unraveled, he was able to determine the constitution of the more complex carbohydrates, such as the disaccharides, various types of starches and, finally, the most difficult of all, cellulose.

In 1925 Haworth was appointed professor at Birmingham. There, together with E. L. Hirst, he turned his attention to the problem of the molecular structure of ascorbic acid. This substance is the vitamin C which counteracts scurvy. Szent-Györgyi, who had prepared it from paprika, considered that chemists accustomed to working on carbohydrates were particularly fitted to tackle the structure of ascorbic acid and, therefore, asked Haworth to study it. It was not long before Hirst was able to suggest a formula for ascorbic acid, and this was subsequently confirmed by Haworth and Hirst. Important contributions to the study of the structure of ascorbic acid and related substances were also made by Karrer and H. von Euler. During 1933, T. Reichstein in Switzerland and Haworth and his associates in Birmingham succeeded in preparing synthetic ascorbic acid.

The biological effects of vitamin A and its presence in fish-liver oils have been known since 1906. A deficiency of this vitamin inhibits growth, reduces resistance to infections and can lead to a disease of the eye, xerophthalmia. Many attempts had been made to isolate the vitamin and determine its constitution, but they were not successful until 1931. Karrer was responsible for this achievement, and was thus the first to elucidate the chemical structure of a vitamin.

His discovery resulted from studies of the constitution of the carotenoids which he had been working on since 1927. These substances are the fat-soluble, yellow colouring matters which, as has already been mentioned, are very widespread in Nature and occur, for example, in the leaves of plants. They are named after carotene, the yellow pigment in carrots [*Daucus carota*]. Isolated carotenoids had been prepared in a pure state by Willstätter, but Karrer was the first to clarify their structure, and by his skilful investigations in this field he added a new and important chapter to the history of organic chemistry.

During the 1930's Karrer also studied the structure of the flavins. The most important of these is riboflavin, which was shown by Szent-Györgyi [Nobel Prize winner for Medicine in 1937] and R. Kuhn to belong to the growth-promoting vitamin B_2 complex. Otto Warburg [Nobel Prize winner for Medicine in 1931] found, together with Christian, that it is a component of the so-called yellow enzyme which plays such an important role in the combustion and fermentation reactions in living tissue. Karrer succeeded in determining the constitution of this vitamin, too, and could confirm his result by a synthesis of the substance.

As a result of this work it became possible to prepare artificial ascorbic acid and riboflavin more cheaply than by isolating them from the natural substances in which they occur. Vitamin A could not, it is true, be produced with certainty at the time of Karrer's award without the assistance of living processes, but his investigations showed that it was built up by the living organism from a variety of carotene which could thus act as a provitamin. This latter substance could be prepared in various ways relatively cheaply. The successful synthesis of several vitamins has rendered possible the production of concentrated and comparatively inexpensive artificial preparations which can be used to cure avitaminosis in patients suffering from a deficiency of these substances.

Willstätter's pupil, RICHARD KUHN [1900-1967], has greatly increased our knowledge of the carotenoids and the vitamin B group. His investigations were based on studies over a period of nearly twenty years of compounds containing so-called conjugate double bonds. These polyenes and diphenylpolyenes, as they are called, proved to be of great interest in connection with the study of the chemical nature of the carotenoids, since the molecules of one of the latter, crocetin, had been found to contain polyene chains. Kuhn discovered no less than eight new carotenoids, which he prepared in a pure state and whose constitution he was able to analyse. The carotenoid derivative crocetin studied by Karrer, which is a constituent of the glucoside crocein, was found by Kuhn to be of great biological interest, since it is necessary for the fertilization process of certain algae. Together with his co-workers he therefore isolated and investigated several crocetin compounds.

As has already been mentioned, Kuhn also carried out work of fundamental importance on vitamin B_2. He was the first to isolate the substance. From 53,000 litres of skimmed milk he prepared 1 g of riboflavin. A breakdown product of riboflavin, lumiflavin, proved to be identical with the yellow enzyme obtained by Warburg and Christian from yeast, and by determining the structure of the enzyme, Kuhn was able to unravel the constitution of riboflavin.

In the spring of the same year that Kuhn was awarded the Nobel Prize he succeeded, together with Wendt, Andersag and Westphal, in isolating an extremely important member of the vitamin B group, the antidermatitic B_6, which he called adermin. The constitution of this substance was also determined.

In 1939, KUHN was awarded the *1938* Prize for Chemistry 'for his work on carotenoids and vitamins'.

It has already been mentioned that the Academy decided in the same year to divide the *1939* prize equally between LEOPOLD RUZICKA and the German ADOLF BUTENANDT [b.1903], whose work bore a certain relation to each other. The latter was awarded the prize 'for his work on sex hormones'.*

These substances, which are secreted by the sex glands in man and animals, have a controlling influence on the sexual functions. Research into their chemical nature took a decisive step forward in 1929 when Butenandt and Doisy [Nobel Prize winner for Medicine in 1943] succeeded independently of each other in isolating and preparing in a pure state the female hormone oestrone from the urine of pregnant women. Butenandt determined its constitution and certain characteristics of its chemical nature. When, shortly after, an even more active female hormone, oestriol, was isolated from the urine of pregnant women, Butenandt studied this, too, and proved its relationship to oestrone. In a few more years he succeeded in unravelling the chemical structure of both these substances and in showing their connection with the bile acids and the sterols.

* After Kuhn and Butenandt had been informed of the Academy's decision to award them the Nobel Prize, they replied that Germans had been forbidden to accept the Nobel Prize from then onwards by their government and that they, therefore, declined the prizes offered to them. As they had not drawn their prize money by the 1st October, 1940, it reverted to the funds in accordance with the statutes of the Nobel Foundation. It was rumoured that the prize-winners had been forced to take this step by the Nazi government. This rumour was confirmed when Kuhn and Butenandt wrote to the Academy in 1948 expressing their gratitude for the honour that had been accorded them and their regret that they had been forced under threat of violence to refuse the prizes in 1939. By this time the prize money was no longer available, but the Academy decided to award Kuhn and Butenandt the gold medals and diplomas due to them, the awards being made in July, 1949.

The corpus-luteum hormone, progesterone, which plays an active part in pregnancy, was also prepared in a pure state by Butenandt, and synthesized from cholesterol in 1939.

As early as 1934, Butenandt had succeeded in isolating the male hormone, androsterone, from an extract of male urine in chloroform. It proved to be closely related chemically to oestrone. When, in the following year, Laqueur obtained the still more active testosterone from an extract of the testicles, it was easy to determine its structure because of its close relationship to androsterone. Ruzicka and Butenandt succeeded independently of each other in converting androsterone derivatives into testosterone.

During the last decades brilliant research on vitamins and hormones have been performed also by VINCENT DU VIGNEAUD [b.1901] at Cornell University Medical College in New York. This chemist is a specialist on sulphur-containing organic compounds and it is certainly due to a great extent to his profound knowledge of this part of organic chemistry that he has his safe grasp on the problems and has been extremely successful in his work.

Already in the 1920's du Vigneaud investigated the function of sulphur in insulin, which at that time was recently discovered. This entailed very important work on sulphur-containing amino acids, first on cystin, homocystin, and methionin. Studying the importance of these amino acids in the metabolism of rats used for experiments, du Vigneaud found that methionin plays a very prominent part in the transmission of the methyl group to life-sustaining substances containing this group. Using Hevesy's isotope technique for marking the methyl group, he could follow its course during metabolism and discovered that a methyl group in a certain chemical combination is fundamental for life and may be considered to act as a vitamin.

In 1923 du Vigneaud started investigations of the hormones of the posterior lobe of the pituitary gland. One of them, oxytocin, governs the contraction of the uterus; another, vasopressin, raises the blood pressure. Both are polypeptides, i.e. composed of amino acids in the same way as proteins, although their molecular weight is lower. Du Vigneaud has succeeded in unraveling the constitution of both of these substances. Each of them contains eight amino acids forming a chain which at one point is closed to a ring by sulphur atoms [a sulphur bridge]. Finally, du Vigneaud has succeeded in the difficult task of synthesizing oxytocin by building up the molecular chain step by step and then making it close into a ring. By this achievement, the first structural determination and the first synthesis of a polypeptide hormone have been performed. As this class of substances has an important function in controlling life processes, this accomplishment was a most remarkable advance in chemistry and medicine. It constitutes a brilliant attainment in organic chemistry.

Recently du Vigneaud played an outstanding part in the research on penicillin and he succeeded even in the synthesis of this complicated substance, although only in a very small quantity. Also of great importance is his work in the structural determination and the synthesis of biotin, a sulphur-containing substance which first attracted attention as a necessary factor for yeast growth. Later on, biotin has been found to be of great importance to many higher and lower organisms, although present in very small quantities.

DU VIGNEAUD was awarded the *1955* Nobel Prize 'for his work on biochemically important sulphur compounds, especially for the first synthesis of a polypeptide hormone'.

Sir ALEXANDER R. TODD [b.1907] was awarded the *1957* prize 'for his work on nucleotides and nucleotide co-enzymes'. His research in this field had then been in progress for nearly 15 years.

The name nucleotide refers to the fact that the compounds in question are present in cell nuclei, where they form a regular constituent of chromosomes. They occur also in other biological systems; for example, together with proteins they form part of virus molecules, and further, various co-enzymes are nucleotides of special structure. They are thus substances of fundamental biological significance.

A simple nucleotide is built up of a molecule of phosphoric acid, a molecule of a certain type of sugar [ribose or deoxy-ribose] and a molecule of a nitrogen-containing base. A large number of these simple nucleotides are then bound together to form macro-molecules which are usually called nucleic acids or polynucleotides. These facts were established relatively early by breaking down the macro-molecules [p. 200]. However, by this method one could not arrive at any precise knowledge of how the various structural elements are combined. It is, of course, clear that the structure of the molecules must be of fundamental importance in determining their mode of chemical reaction and thus their biological function.

Todd and his co-workers had attacked these problems systematically and their work had finally advanced far enough to give a clear understanding of the principles governing the building-up of polynucleotides.

These are now nearly as well understood as in the case of proteins and carbohydrates. The work had to a large extent been planned using synthetic methods. Thus, various substances of known structure were synthesized and then compared to the break down products of nucleic acids. Many possible alternatives had to be rejected. The work was rendered difficult by the peculiar characteristics of the nucleic acids due to the fact that they contain many acidic and basic groups in equal number and that hardly any ordinary chemical methods were directly applicable. Many special procedures had to be worked out and it was often necessary to work under very delicate conditions.

The nucleic acid molecule appears to consist of a main chain of alternating sugar and phosphoric acid molecules, each sugar molecule having a nitrogen-containing group attached to it as a small appendage. The number of different nitrogen-bases occurring in a certain nucleic acid is limited, usually only four types being present. In other respects the structural plan is uniform. For instance, it is always one certain atom of the nitrogen-base which acts as the connecting link to the sugar molecule. The difference between various nucleic acids seems to depend on the order in which the nitrogen-bases occur. Obviously, in a giant molecule the number of possible combinations is very large.

Todd's results have been used by other scientists as the foundation for highly interesting theories postulating spiral formation of the chains. It is possible that one can thus find an explanation of how a nucleic acid can act intermediary in the formation of another nucleic acid molecule or even a protein.

Todd's methods have also been found extremely fruitful in the study of coenzymes of the nucleic acid type, and it has been possible to synthesize several of these, for example, the alcohol-fermenting co-zymase. Now that the structure of co-enzymes can be elucidated by means of syntheses, interesting perspectives in biochemical research have been opened.

Finally it may be mentioned that Todd has also made particularly important contributions in the investigations of vitamin B_{12}, the substance present in liver which is active against pernicious anaemia. According to the structural formula suggested by Todd and Dorothy Hodgkin, this substance may be regarded as a nucleotide of very peculiar structure.

The enzymes, like the vitamins and hormones, play an extremely important role in the vital functions of living organisms, so that their chemical nature and behaviour have been the subject of much research during the last sixty years. Great advances have been made in this field, and particularly valuable data were obtained at an early stage on the group of oxidation-reduction enzymes which activate the process of alcoholic fermentation.

Berzelius had assumed that the fermentation of sugar to alcohol and carbon dioxide was catalyzed by certain substances in the same way as hydrogen peroxide is made to decompose by the action of finely powdered platinum. In the middle of the nineteenth century, however, Pasteur showed that all fermentation reactions are caused by micro-organisms and his vitalistic explanation was summed up in the law: 'No fermentation without life.' Liebig gave a third explanation. He attributed the decomposition of sugar to the influence of specific fermentation substances, so-called ferments, whose particles he assumed to be in violent motion which they transmit to the sugar molecules. Shortly before the turn of the century, the German chemist, EDUARD BUCHNER [1860-1917], proved that, as Berzelius had assumed, fermentation is due to the catalytic action of enzymes. These are produced by living organisms, but the presence of the latter is not necessary for fermentation to take place.

Buchner mixed fresh yeast with fine sand and kieselguhr, and ground the mixture together until the membranes of the cells were broken and the content of the cells freed. The plastic mass was then subjected to considerable pressure in a hydraulic press, whereby an almost clear, yellow or brownish-yellow liquid rich in proteins was obtained. When this juice was mixed with a solution of sugar, powerful and violent fermentation occurred, whether with cane, grape, fruit or malt sugar. Both carbon dioxide and alcohol were formed and, as closer investigations proved, in the same proportions as in fermentation of sugar with yeast-fungi. Buchner's investigations thus showed that alcoholic fermentation is an enzymatic process which can take place independently of the cells.

In order to meet the objection that the pressed juice might still contain living remnants or parts of yeast cells, Buchner and his collaborators carried out a series of investigations which proved conclusively that fermentation takes place independently of living organisms. Toxins which are known beyond any doubt to kill the activity of the cells scarcely reduced the action of the pressed juice. The fermentation enzyme, which Buchner called *zymase*, was precipitated out of the pressed juice with ethyl alcohol. Such precipitation could be carried out at least twice without the zymase losing its activity, but yeast cells are killed by such treatment. Buchner also showed in other ways that alcoholic fermentation is an enzymatic process which can continue after the cells are dead.

The significance of Buchner's discovery lies in the fact that he recognized that yeast fermentation, the very prototype of the fermentation processes, belongs to the category of enzyme reactions which are of such importance in animal and plant life. He thus opened the way for exact chemical investigations in this field. In *1907* BUCHNER was awarded the Nobel Prize 'for his biochemical researches and his discovery of cell-free fermentation'.

Buchner considered it possible that zymase was not homogeneous but composed of at least two components, but he was unable to put forward any convincing proof of this. It remained for the Englishman, ARTHUR HARDEN [1865-1940], to throw light on this problem.

Harden investigated the possibility of preventing the so-called autolysis – self-destruction or decay – of Buchner's pressed-yeast juice, and discovered that the addition of filtered, boiled-yeast juice to a sugar solution has a marked accelerating effect on fermentation. Closer investigation showed that this increased fermentation was due to two important ingredients in the boiled juice, namely a phosphate and an enzyme component, the so-called co-zymase, both of which must be present for fermentation to take place.

Harden studied the function of the phosphoric acid more closely in a series of experiments carried out together with Young. They succeeded in isolating certain compounds of sugar and phosphoric acid, among them a hexose diphosphoric acid ester, the so-called zymophosphate. The fermentation yield proved to have a definite relation to the amount of phosphate added. The fundamental importance of phosphoric acid in the process of fermentation was thus clearly established.

In order to study more closely the role played by co-zymase in fermentation, Harden and Young carried out the following important experiment. Pressed-yeast juice was forced under great pressure through porous porcelain, impregnated with gelatine. By means of this ultra-filtration the juice was split up into two components, neither of which had any fermenting effect alone but had the original property of the yeast juice when mixed together again. Addition of phosphate did not increase the fermentation effect of either of them. From this Harden concluded that fermentation is caused by the simultaneous presence of an enzyme, consisting of the larger of the molecules separated by the ultra-filter – this was thought to be the actual zymase – and of a complementary substance with relatively small molecules, the so-called co-enzyme.

Harden and Young tried to concentrate the co-enzyme so as to be able to determine its chemical nature, but their attempts met with little success. It remained for HANS VON EULER-CHELPIN [1873-1964] and his collaborators in Stockholm to overcome the difficulties in the way of solving this problem.

Euler continued Harden's investigations of the function of phosphoric acid and the co-enzyme in the process of fermentation and made a detailed study of the reactions connected with this process. He proved that the co-enzyme plays an important role in the formation of Harden's hexose diphosphoric acid ester, either directly or – as Euler's collaborator Ragnar Nilsson thought – indirectly by the transformation of the monophosphoric acid ester discovered by Harden and Robison in 1914. The experiments showed, moreover, that co-zymase also effects the transformation of aldehydes into alcohol and acid. As its effect on carbohydrate and aldehyde reactions must be the same in fermentation and in living processes, one can easily understand the far-reaching importance of these detailed studies of the reactive properties of co-zymase.

By a series of purifying operations Euler and Karl Myrbäck succeeded in preparing a solution of the co-zymase with an activity of five to eight hundred times that of the original yeast juice. As a result of this considerable concentration it was possible to study its chemical nature successfully. Its molecular weight was fixed at about 490. It appeared likely that it was some kind of nucleotide, since it lost its activity under the influence of an enzyme, the so-called nucleosidase, which splits up such substances. Its base was assumed to be adenine and its carbohydrate, at least most of it, a pentose, since co-zymase gave a pentose reaction when distilled with acid.

In connection with his investigations of fermentation processes Euler also studied the oxidation-reduction enzymes which occur in living cells and influence the biological respiration processes. He found that these enzymes required the presence of a co-enzyme to become active. This is an extremely important result, since it explains why co-zymase occurs so frequently in vegetable and animal tissues. It is a substance of basic importance in all living processes.

EULER's investigations showed clearly the value of HARDEN's pioneer work on fermentation processes, and the *1929* prize was divided equally between them 'for their investigations on the fermentation of sugar and of fermentative enzymes'.

A peculiarity of enzymes is that they can transform millions of times their own weight of the substances they act on. In living organisms they are active in extremely small quantities. Since they occur so sparingly and are sensitive and easily transformed or destroyed, it has proved very difficult to prepare them in a pure form.

It therefore caused a great sensation when, in 1926, the American JAMES B. SUMNER [1887-1955] reported that he had devised a surprisingly simple method for preparing crystals of the enzyme urease which splits up urea. He had started out with a substance whose enzymatic activity surpassed all previous sources of urease, namely, a meal made of beans from a plant unusually rich in this enzyme, *Canavalia ensiformis,* which the Americans call 'jack bean'. The meal was ground with dilute acetone and the suspension filtered and chilled. If the filtrate was kept in a refrigerator for 24 hours, crystals appeared which were separated from the solution by centrifuging. The substance thus isolated had about 700 times the activity of *Canavalia* meal. It could be recrystallized without losing any of its activity. It was found to be a protein, which on examination in Svedberg's ultracentrifuge proved to be homogeneous and to have a molecular weight of not less than 483,000.

Sumner's report that he had succeeded with his simple method in isolating an enzyme at first met with a certain amount of scepticism. Such a prominent scientist as Willstätter had devoted a great deal of work to the purification of invertase, which splits up cane sugar, but could not obtain it even in a highly concentrated form. He doubted whether enzymes were proteins.

Sumner's fellow-countryman JOHN HOWARD NORTHROP [b.1891] however, started similar purifications of enzymes on a large scale, concentrating on those which, like urease, were characterized by their relatively high stability. By 1930 he was able to report that he had prepared crystals of the enzyme pepsin, which is present in the gastric juice and splits up proteins. Shortly after he succeeded in isolating two proteinases occurring in the pancreas, which he called trypsin and chymotrypsin. He also prepared pepsinogen, the inactive pro-enzyme of pepsin, in crystalline form. During the following years Northrop and his associates could record similar successes with several other enzymes. They also studied in detail the homogeneity and purity of the substances isolated and established conclusively the protein nature of enzymes. The methods devised by Northrop and his co-workers for preparing pure enzymes have been of great value for subsequent research.

Sumner's and Northrop's pioneer work made possible detailed studies of the chemical nature of enzymes, and as chemists could now use well-defined enzyme preparations they were able to investigate the changes brought about by these substances in a far more systematic way than before and with far greater chances of success.

The successful purification of enzymes had a stimulating effect in other fields of research. The American WENDELL M. STANLEY [1904-1971], had tried to show that the virus contagions are proteins by subjecting them to the action of the protein-splitting enzymes, the proteinases, but in 1934 he modified his investigation method in accordance with that used so successfully by Sumner and Northrop. In the following year he was able to isolate from a large number of tobacco leaves, attacked by the so-called mosaic disease, a crystalline substance which proved to have all the properties of a protein, being at the same time highly infectious. This was clearly the contagious agent. It has since proved to contain nucleic acid as an important ingredient.

The virus particles are too small to be observed in an ordinary microscope, but they can be made visible in an electron microscope and are sufficiently large not to pass through an ultra-filter. Viruses, like bacteria and other living organisms, are able to multiply but probably only in contact with living cells. Research on this subject deals with the borderland between living and dead matter. The progress made in this field, particularly owing to Stanley's work, is most impressive and has attracted much interest among scientists.

Owing to the close connection between the researches described above, the three Americans were awarded a prize jointly. One half of the *1946* prize was given to SUMNER 'for his discovery that enzymes can be crystallized' and the other half divided equally between NORTHROP and STANLEY 'for their preparations of enzymes and virus proteins in a pure form'.

Ever since the late 1940's and up to our own time the Argentine scientist LUIS FEDERICO LELOIR [b. in France in 1906] has been carrying out a series of works of epoch-making importance to our knowledge of the metabolism of the carbohydrates in living organisms. He was awarded the *1970* Prize 'for his discovery of sugar nucleotides and their function in biosyntheses of carbohydrates'.

About 1943, turbulent political conditions in Argentina obliged Leloir in that year to leave the country. He was able to carry on his work in St. Louis, Missouri, with the Coris, who themselves had been given the Nobel Prize for Medicine for their research into the processes involved in the catalytic transformation of glycogen [cf. p. 221]. Here Leloir attacked the problem of the opposite reaction, the building up of high-molecular carbohydrates from simpler ones, including the question of the biosynthesis of glycogen. In itself the idea suggested that the same enzyme might be active in both processes. But Leloir soon discovered that this was not so.

After a few years he returned to Buenos Aires, where a modern research institute had been placed at his disposition, and there went on with the work he had begun at St. Louis. In 1949, he was able to announce that a sugar nucleotide, uridine diphosphate glucose, [UDPG] influences the formation of glycogen from glucose. Later, he discovered a great number of analogous sugar nucleotides, which are of fundamental importance in the conversion of carbohydrates and their derivatives, as also for the syntheses of compound sugar species and of other simple glycosides, oligo- and polysaccharides.

In the nominations recommending Leloir for a Nobel Prize, it was stressed that the real evidence of the importance of a discovery lies in the extent of the new research which it has precipitated, the hitherto unknown paths it has opened up and the secondary discoveries it has made possible. Leloir's achievements are certainly exemplary of this. Few discoveries in biology and chemistry have had such extensive consequences; and in the work being done in those fields of research in which he has delved, it has always been Leloir who has been the leading figure. It is he who has made all the most significant discoveries of new principles concerning the sugar nucleotides and their function.

In point of fact, Leloir's discoveries could just as well have been rewarded with a Nobel Prize in Medicine or Physiology. If properly exploited, they are regarded as opening up possibilities of a more effective cure for diabetes than has hitherto been available.

At the beginning of this century Emil Fischer took the first step in elucidating the structure of proteins [cf. p. 297]. He found that their molecules consist of chains built up of amino acid residues and succeeded in linking together series of such radicals into substances, so-called polypeptides, which have properties very similar to those of the proteins. Ever since that time chemists have toiled with the task to find out the sequence of the amino acids in a protein molecule in order to determine its structure more completely. This difficult problem was solved in the 1950's by FREDERICK SANGER [b.1918], of Cambridge, who received the *1958* prize 'for his work on the structure of proteins, especially that of insulin'.

About 25 different kinds of amino acids have been met with in Nature. A protein may have 20 to 100 links of them in its molecular chains, ordered in a definite sequence, chemically and biologically characterizing it. In order to determine this sequence a molecule has to be broken down into smaller parts, which consist of only a few links and are simple enough to be identified. Such fragments, so-called peptides, are obtained if proteins are treated with acids or with certain enzymes.

A very great number of peptides are formed during such a procedure, and it is a hard task to separate and identify them individually. Sanger treated proteins or their fragments with dinitrofluorobenzene which forms coloured and stable so-called DNP-compounds with the chain-ending amino acids. Peptides from the end of a protein molecule are thus marked in this way. The method was applied also to the broken-down protein in order to facilitate the identification of its peptides.

With great skill and perseverance Sanger also used electrophoretic [cf. p. 332] and chromatographic [cf. p. 334] methods for the separation and identification of the products obtained by breaking down proteins with acids or enzymes. He managed in this way to determine the amino acid sequence of the insulin molecule. He had found that this molecule is formed of two chains [A and B] which have different end-groups and are held together with bridges of sulphur atoms. Each chain was studied separately.

In order to find out how the peptides of a protein are arranged in their molecule chains a method was used that reminds one of putting together the pieces of a puzzle. If the different amino acids are denoted with *a, b, c, d,* etc. and Sanger found for example in the fragment mixture of insulin a peptide with the composition *abcdef* and another with the composition *defgh,* he could conclude that a domain of the insulin molecule must have the sequence *abcdefgh.* In this way it was possible to reconstruct complete series of the two chains of the insulin molecule. The A-chain was found to consist of 21 amino acids and the B-chain had 30 links of that kind. Sanger could also establish the position of the sulphur bridges. They connect amino acids number 7 and 20 in the A-chain with number 7 and 19 respectively in the B-chain.

By this pioneer work on the structure of insulin Sanger has opened an extremely important and vast field of research. His methods are now applied by himself and many other scientists to the task of determining the structure of other proteins. These complicated substances play a dominant role in biological phenomena. Many hormones, all enzymes so far known, toxins, and antibodies are proteins. Proteins are also essential functional constituents of human and animal bodies. Important advances have been made in the study of these substances by means of Sanger's ingenious methods.

In the early summer of *1962* the medical and chemical Nobel committees held a joint meeting to discuss eventual awards to common prize candidates. The result was that, at the end of that year, five scientists, who had applied X-ray diffraction methods to the study of vital substances of exceedingly complicated structure, were rewarded. Crick, Watson and Wilkins together received the Physiology and Medicine Prize for their research into nucleic acids [cf. p. 202], while the Chemistry Prize was divided equally between the Englishman JOHN COWDERY KENDREW [b. 1917] and the Austrian MAX FERDINAND PERUTZ [b. 1914] 'for their research into the structure of globular proteins'.

This research had extended over many years, beginning in the mid-1930's when Perutz had moved from Vienna to Cambridge, where he came to work at the Cavendish Laboratory. In his native country he had been occupied in X-ray crystallography, and in Britain he continued in the same field. After a short time in association with the eminent X-ray cystallographer J. D. Bernal, he succeeded in producing X-ray patterns from horse haemoglobin crystals which, by reason of their sharpness and wealth of detail, attracted wide attention. During the same period, Sir Lawrence Bragg, one of the pioneers in the field of X-ray crystallography [cf. p. 434] succeeded Rutherford as director of the Cavendish Laboratory. Even at that date he took a great interest in the Institute's protein research and supported it in every way.

Some ten years later Kendrew joined Perutz' research group. It became his task to try to determine the structure of myoglobin. Like haemoglobin, myoglobin is a substance responsible for the red colour in blood and shares the same function in helping to carry oxygen from the lungs to the tissues; but it also serves as an oxygen resevoir and is, therefore, especially plentiful in deep-sea creatures, such as whales, seals and penguins.

A haemoglobin molecule has four so-called haem-groups [iron-porphyrin complexes], each with one iron atom. In the myoglobin molecule, however, there is only one such group, and therefore only a single iron atom. Additionally, myoglobin contains 153 amino-acid residues and is built up from about 2,600 atoms. Its molecular weight is about 17,000. The molecular weight of haemoglobin is four times as great.

To interpret the X-ray patterns of these crystals' exceedingly complicated structure was a most difficult task. But in 1955 the experimenters made some progress, when it was proved possible to introduce five or six atoms of such heavy metals as mercury and gold at decisive sites in the crystal lattice of the proteins. This led to no significant change in the lattice structure as a whole. But it does have an effect on the beams of X-rays deflected in the crystal: the intensity of the spots in the X-ray pictures are somewhat modified, and this can be exploited for their interpretation. After quite a short time the method proved viable, and finally, after much pains and trouble, the goal was reached, the work having occupied a large staff of workers over a number of years. The first clarification of the crystal structure of myoglobin was based on an examination of 110 crystals, and the intensity was determined for about 250,000 spots in their X-ray pictures. To treat this gigantic amount of data an electronic computer of great capacity was required.

In all essentials the structure of myoglobin had been elucidated by 1962, but haemoglobin's more complicated structure was not so thoroughly understood. Kendrew and Perutz, however, have continued their work and in greater detail determined the atomic arrangement of these substances. The results of Pauling's protein studies [cf. p. 339] have been confirmed. Sanger's studies of the amino-acid sequence in polypeptide chains, described above, have in certain respects been complemented. By their successful X-ray analyses Kendrew and Perutz have shown the way of other scientists in this field, and X-ray diffraction studies of various types of proteins, e.g. enzymes, have now been taken up and brought to a successful conclusion, not only at Cambridge but also in many other places.

Penicillin was discovered shortly after the outbreak of the Second World War. It was quickly recognized as an exceedingly effective antidote against infections. Soon, output could not keep pace with demand, and science was faced with the task of producing this vital medicine by chemical synthesis. Thus, it was important to understand its nature. Both in Britain and the United States research was devoted to this end.

An Oxford research team, led by DOROTHY CROWFOOT-HODGKIN

[b. 1910], attempted to determine the crystal structure of penicillin and some of its compounds, and thus decide which of the many hypothetical structures for penicillin proposed by chemists was the right one. The penicillin molecule contains one atom of sulphur; and after a number of tentative and unsuccessful experiments it become possible to determine the orientation of the sulphur atoms in the crystal lattice. This, in turn, made it possible step by step to elucidate the structure of the lattice as a whole.

Although the chemical constitution of penicillin had been fully established, its large-scale production by chemical synthesis continued to present insuperable difficulties. The substance was too sensitive to acid solutions. A firm foundation had been laid, however, for the future development of the chemistry of penicillin and, subsequently, derivatives of penicillin and allied compounds possessing greater stability in acids than the original type, obtained from mould [penicillin G] have been synthesized. Some of these have proved possible to produce chemically on an industrial scale. They have the advantage of tolerating the digestive juices, and can therefore be taken orally.

In 1948, medical laboratories in Britain and the United States succeeded simultaneously in growing crystals from the factor in the liver material that protects the organism against the dangerous illness, pernicious anaemia [cf. Liljestrand, p. 233]. In the United States this has been named vitamin B_{12}. This substance is produced by certain microorganisms and moulds in the alimentary canal of certain higher animals, particularly the ruminants, who seem to stand in special need of it. In some other higher animals, such as the human being, it is only produced in insignificant quantities, and therefore must be supplied in the form of food.

The B_{12} molecule comprises 181 atoms. Of these, one consists of cobalt, a relatively heavy particle; but to this cobalt atom a cyano group is attached. This can be replaced by thiocyanogen, and in the thiocyanogen radical the sulphur can be exchanged for selenium. Thus it is possible to introduce various heavy atoms into the crystal lattice. By this means, and by using a suitable experimental method then newly developed by the Dutchman, J. M. Bijvoet, Mrs. Hodgkin finally succeeded in thoroughly elucidating the molecular structure of vitamin B_{12}.

In doing so, she had solved a far more difficult problem than any she had so far tackled. She had become a complete virtuoso in X-ray crystallography, and had shown that she possessed all the qualities necessary to assure the success of the difficult enterprise she had undertaken. She had given proof of unbending perseverance, an extraordinary imagination and brilliant intuition. In an article written on the occasion of the fiftieth anniversary of X-ray diffraction methods, one of the most eminent X-ray crystallographers of our time wrote, concerning her analysis of vitamin B_{12}, as follows: 'As a complete structure determination it can be considered the crowning triumph of X-ray crystallographic analysis, both in respect to the chemical and biological importance of the results and the vast complexity of structure'.

She was awarded the *1964* prize for 'her determinations of the structure of biochemically important substances by X-ray methods'.

AGRICULTURAL CHEMISTRY

The work of the Finn ARTTURI ILMARI VIRTANEN [b.1895], like the researches just described, belongs to biochemistry. It has, however, proved to be most important in the field of agriculture. Virtanen has stated the aim of his experiments as follows: 'The fertility of the soil in Scandinavia is limited by the deficiency of nitrogenous substances, and the proper feeding of cattle is also hampered by the lack of such substances, i.e. proteins... A successful solution of the nitrogen problem should thus also contribute towards a satisfactory solution of the economic problems of farming'. To achieve this end Virtanen worked along two main lines. First he tried to find out how green fodder, rich in proteins, could be produced economically and for this purpose studied the assimilation of nitrogen by plants and its conversion by them into proteins. Secondly he worked out a method, based on purely theoretical considerations, for the storage of fodder so as to reduce the losses of proteins and vitamins to a minimum.

It has been known for a long time that the addition of organic or mineral acids to fodder ensilage inhibits the respiration of the plant cells and all fermentation processes, and many attempts have been made to make use of this observation in practice. They were, however, rather unsystematic and did not include any detailed studies of the conditions necessary for preserving the nutritive value of the fodder or of the suitability of ensilage as cattle food. Virtanen was the first to solve this problem and his success was due to his detailed and rational methods of research.

By the so-called AIV-method – named after his initials – the fodder is acidified with hydrochloric acid to which some sulphuric acid has been added. By arduous and comprehensive investigations Virtanen determined the limits within which the acidity of the fodder ensilage should be kept.

There are many advantages in storing fodder by the AIV-method. The farmer is more independent of the weather and can avail himself of regrowths in the form of late harvests which could not be preserved by the normal method of drying in the open. AIV fodder, particularly if rich in leguminous plants, forms an excellent substitute for concentrated foodstuffs, such as oil-cakes, etc. The method thus considerably increases the possibility for many countries to become self-supporting in cattle fodder. In recent years it has become very widely used. VIRTANEN was awarded the *1945* Nobel Prize 'for his researches and inventions in agricultural and nutritive chemistry, especially for his fodder preservation method'.

This brings us to the end of our survey of the Nobel Prize for Chemistry from 1901 to 1970. In all, 79 scientists have received the award. They have been divided between the various branches of chemistry as follows: 38 physico-chemists, 5 inorganic chemists, 34 organic chemists and biochemists, and 2 technologists; 22 of the prizes have gone to Germany, 18 to Great Britain, 16 to the United States, 6 to France, 4 to Sweden, 3 to Switzerland, 2 to The Netherlands and one each to Argentina, Austria, Czechoslovakia, Finland, Hungary, Italy, Norway and the Soviet Union.

It is for others to judge whether the Academy's awards have justified the trust Alfred Nobel placed in its hands. It cannot, however, be denied that it has honestly tried to do its best. The awarding of the Nobel Prizes has been a great responsibility and has involved much work, but it has also been a great advantage to the Academy. The annual letters from abroad containing nominations have kept its physicists and chemists in constant touch with the latest advances in their sciences, and the studies necessary to judge these nominations have caused them to follow in detail the progress in their own particular branches of science. In this age of specialization it is highly useful to be forced yearly to survey and compare research as a whole. The meetings and discussions with the great men of science who have come to Stockholm to receive their prizes have also had a stimulating effect on Swedish scientific life.

The Nobel Prizes have led to close and valuable contacts with research abroad. For a country lying on the edge of the world as ours does, this is of the utmost importance. Thus, not only the prize-winners themselves but also those within the Swedish Academy of Sciences who have taken part in awarding the prizes have every reason to thank the great benefactor Alfred Nobel.

THE PHYSICS PRIZE

BY MANNE SIEGBAHN AND KAI SIEGBAHN

According to the present statutes of the Nobel Foundation, the Swedish Academy of Sciences has to award two of the five annual Nobel Prizes. One of these is to be given to 'the person who has made the most important discovery or invention within the field of physics'. According to Nobel's will these awards should be made for investigations presented during the preceding year – a provision clarified in the statutes by the statement 'that the awards shall be made for the most recent achievements in the fields of culture referred to in the will and for older works only if their significance has not become apparent until recently'.

In view of these provisions, it is clear that a survey of the prizes distributed during the past seventy-years will be essentially a summary of the development of physical science during that period. But the second quotation from the statutes, authorizing awards even for earlier research, implies that the activities rewarded actually cover a period extending considerably before 1901, the year when the first prize was awarded. Indeed, a scrutiny of the list of names proposed for the first award reveals that of the eleven candidates nominated no less than eight received Nobel Prizes during the next ten years, thus essentially for work done before the establishment of the prizes. Only after the first decade of the activities of the Foundation is it possible to consider that the distribution of prizes, at any rate in physics, has taken a more normal course. In awarding the earlier prizes one could, of course, hardly disregard those fairly recent discoveries which at that time formed the basis of current research, and this point of view was stressed in the prize-adjudicating body during the early years.

When the statutes of the Nobel Foundation were issued in 1900, physical science was on the verge of an entirely new phase of development. Towards the end of the nineteenth century classical physics had reached a certain measure of completion, and some people were inclined to maintain that on the whole nothing remained for future generations of investigators but to fill in a few details here and there.

In dynamics, i.e. the theory of the motion of rigid bodies, the elegant mathematical formulation of the equations of motion, derived from Lagrange's formulae by Hamilton in the 1830's, seemed to represent the final form of the laws which served as the most important foundation of physics. In the simplest case Hamilton's equations are equivalent to the laws of

Newton, according to which the motions of the celestial bodies may be explained by the theory of gravitation.

The elastic properties of solids, which are of fundamental technical and practical importance, had been elucidated by elaborate theories of elasticity on the basis of which, knowing certain characteristic constants of the material in question, one could calculate in advance the changes in an elastic body under given stresses.

In hydrodynamics, dealing with the laws of motion of liquids, a system of equations had been obtained, permitting of a satisfactory and quantitatively correct description of the phenomena. The same was true in aerodynamics, though in both cases the calculations were hampered by mathematical difficulties even under idealizing assumptions.

Finally, in the kinetic theory of gases one had succeeded in finding a statistical-mechanical interpretation and method of calculation, allowing a detailed computation of many characteristic properties of gases.

The principal foundations of the natural sciences were the law of the conservation of mass and the corresponding law for the total energy. It is true that, after the Frenchman Carnot had laid the first foundations of thermodynamics through his famous treatise, *Réflexions sur la puissance motrice du feu et les machines propres à développer cette puissance* in 1824, considerable time elapsed before the connections between heat, work, electric energy, radiant energy, and other forms of energy were fully understood. The proof of the fixed ratio between heat energy and mechanical energy – the mechanical equivalent of heat – by Robert Mayer in Germany, by Joule in England, and by Colding in Denmark, independently of each other at the beginning of the 1840's, together with the fundamental theoretical investigations of Helmholtz in his classical memoir, *Erhaltung der Kraft* [1847], were the achievements that primarily created the firm foundations of the modern concept of energy. The final form of thermodynamics was due mainly to William Thomson [subsequently Lord Kelvin], who published his famous treatise on the theory of heat in 1851.

An important contribution to the question of the conservation of energy had been made by the Dane, Julius Thomsen, who showed in 1853 that this law is valid also for chemical reactions. The ingenious development of the thermodynamics of chemical equilibrium by the American scientist J. Willard Gibbs [1877] stands out as the final monument to this phase of development of one of the most important foundations of all scientific research.

During the last century research in optics had apparently led to a complete elucidation of the phenomena connected with the propagation of light, its polarization, refraction, interference, double refraction in crystals, etc. The old controversy between the corpuscular and the wave theories for the nature of light had been finally settled, chiefly through Fresnel's classical treatise, *Mémoire sur la diffraction* [1818]. On this basis, a large number of optical phenomena had been studied in detail, and the results all confirmed the correctness of the wave theory in a brilliant manner. Fresnel had also [1821] been able to indicate values for the wave-lengths to be expected for light: for red light about 16,000 wave-lengths per cm and for violet about 32,000 per cm.

Newton had already made use of a glass prism for the separation of light into its component colours. Another method of attaining the same result had been introduced in 1823 by Fraunhofer of Munich, who passed the light through a 'grating' made by ruling many parallel equidistant lines on a glass plate with a diamond point. In passing through the grating the light is 'diffracted' into rays in different directions, each direction giving a definite colour component of the light. This method of analysing the different colours of light had the advantage that, given the distance between the lines on the grating, the wave-lengths of the different components could be determined directly by measuring the angle of deflection. A further study showed that, outside the long-wave limit of the visible light spectrum, there is a radiation, not perceived by the eye but detectible and measurable by instruments sensitive to heat, constituting the infra-red spectral region. After the photographic method, discovered by Daguerre about 1840, had been employed for registering spectra, it could be shown directly on the photographic plate that beyond the short-wave limit of the visible spectrum there is an ultra-violet spectral region. Spectral analysis became of epoch-making importance, not merely for physics but also for most of the other natural sciences. Bunsen and Kirchhoff, to whom the credit of having constructed spectral instruments and of having introduced the method into the laboratory is chiefly due, discovered with its aid two new chemical elements, viz. rubidium and caesium. The same method led to the discovery of the elements thallium, indium, gallium, etc., by other scientists. By way of spectral analysis known elements could be identified in the celestial bodies. This device proved capable of being developed into an extremely accurate and sensitive method of chemical analysis.

An extreme refinement of the spectroscopical methods of measurement was introduced by H. A. Rowland [1882], who produced gratings on concave mirrors and succeeded in raising the precision of the gratings considerably. With these new aids for measuring spectra, Rowland and a number of other scientists, in the first place A. J. Ångström, H. Kayser and C. Runge, effected a very complete determination of the wave-lengths of the known elements. In the resulting immense mass of figures certain regularities were found. Thus Balmer of Basle [1882] found that the wave-lengths of the spectral lines of hydrogen could be represented by a simple formula. Kayser and Runge showed, in the case of some elements, that certain spectral lines could be grouped into a series. The most important contribution to the utilization of the extensive spectral measurements was made, however, by J. R. Rydberg of Sweden, who found that by employing the wave-number, i.e. the number of wave-lengths per unit of length, instead of the wave-length itself, groups of analogous spectral series of a number of elements could be represented by a simple difference formula. A constant, characteristic of the series, was found and later called 'Rydberg's constant'. Though these investigations had revealed certain important regularities in the composition of the light emitted by the different elements, yet a deeper insight into the process of radiation was still lacking, in spite of the comprehensive and exact observations available.

For electric phenomena Maxwell's equations had finally [1856] provided a universal basis in terms of which all electromagnetic phenomena could be expressed and calculated. The discovery of the effects of an electric current on the magnetic needle was made by Örsted of Denmark in 1820 and furnished a point of departure for the later development. It gave rise to intensive research concerning the connection between the electric phenomena. Biot and Savart supplemented Örsted's discovery by accurate quantitative measurements, and in his famous treatise, *Mémoire sur la théorie mathématique des phénomènes électrodynamiques, uniquement déduite de l'expérience* [1827], Ampère furnished a comprehensive mathematical treatment of the observations. Faraday's remarkable discovery of induced electric currents, the foundation of modern electric industry, followed shortly afterwards in 1831.

Faraday, whose brilliant experiments enriched physical science with so many discoveries, also gave theoretical research a new trend by replacing the concept of action at a distance by the theory of electric and magnetic fields as carriers of the effects. These ideas were formulated mathematically by his fellow-countryman Clerk Maxwell in the previously mentioned electromagnetic theory. Apart from the predominant importance of Maxwell's theory for the calculation of all kinds of electromagnetic phenomena, it also furnished an interpretation of light in terms of electromagnetic waves. A complete description of the propagation of light, its refraction, interference, etc. had previously been given on the assumption that light is a wave motion. Maxwell proved in 1864 that light waves could be interpreted as an interplay of electric and magnetic forces in accordance with his general electromagnetic equations. A couple of decades passed before this interpretation was generally accepted, and when it was, this was due to some extremely interesting experiments by the German scientist, Heinrich Hertz [1887], who opened up one of the most important fields of modern physical research, namely that of electromagnetic waves. In its simplest form, Hertz's experiment consisted in charging two metal balls, separated by a small air space only, until a spark passed from one to the other. When this happens, the electric charge oscillates between the two spheres, thus giving rise to an oscillatory change of the electric and the magnetic forces in the neighbourhood. This change proceeds successively outwards from the spheres, in other words, they emit electromagnetic waves. By placing a 'receiver' at some distance from the spheres, Hertz was able to intercept these waves and force them to produce an effect there, e.g. a spark between two wires. Even though in this case the wave-lengths were of quite a different order of magnitude from those of light waves, no one doubted any longer but that the same kind of phenomenon occurred in both cases. From the point of view of general principles, the most important result obtained in this manner was that optics could be integrated with electricity into a unit. The efforts to assemble different phenomena into a single concept had thus been considerably advanced. In technology these discoveries led within a few decades to a fantastic development which has greatly transformed the way of life.

THE FIRST AWARD

The above brief survey will have shown that towards the end of the last century physical science had arrived at a picture of the natural phenomena and their interplay which was apparently very satisfactory and to a certain extent complete. Everything seemed to fit well into a mechanical conception of the universe, including electric, magnetic and optical phenomena.

It was hardly expected that there would be any revolutionary innovations, when quite unexpectedly in the middle of the 1890's some laboratory experiments suddenly gave research an impulse the effects of which were extremely far-reaching.

Scrutinizing the historical course of the majority of great discoveries, one finds that they are seldom so spontaneous as they appear to be on the surface. In reality they are the results of systematic research, often protracted and time-consuming, which at a certain moment has been carried to a stage where the discovery comes more or less by itself to a scientist with an open mind. This does not detract from the value of the contribution of the scientist. Only he who has the god-begotten gift intuitively to separate from the trivial observations just the little something which on closer analysis leads to the discovery – only he finds what has escaped many who, in their hands and before their eyes, had the same possibilities of making the discovery.

In 1895 when WILHELM CONRAD RÖNTGEN [1845-1923] discovered the new kind of rays, called X-rays by him, he was engaged in experiments of a type common at that time and during preceding years in physics laboratories all over the world. The very first lines of his famous paper *Über eine neue Art von Strahlen* sufficed to make his experimental arrangements clear to every scientist, for they run: 'If the discharge of a rather large Ruhmkorff induction coil is allowed to pass through a Hittorf vacuum tube, or a sufficiently evacuated Lenard tube, Crookes tube, or similar apparatus, and the tube is covered with a fairly closely fitting mantle of thin black cardboard, it is seen...' Investigations into electric discharges through rarefied gases in tubes had been made earlier by a number of scientists, not merely by Hittorf, Lenard and Crookes, whom Röntgen mentions explicitly. The great Faraday had already been engaged in such experiments. In 1869 Hittorf published his investigations, which attracted much attention. Crookes' work of 1879 had aroused a great sensation, perhaps not least owing to the pregnant formulation concluding his lecture before the Royal Society in December 1878: 'The phenomena in these exhausted tubes reveal to physical science a new world – a world where matter may exist in a fourth state, where the corpuscular theory of light may be true, and where light does not always move in straight lines, but where we can never enter, and with which we must be content to observe and experiment from the outside.' A German translation of this lecture was also published. Lenard, who, according to his own statement, was stimulated into making his investigations by Crookes' paper, published in 1893 his first results on cathode rays, i.e., what Crookes called 'radiant matter'. Many of the very prominent scientists who had worked on these problems had certainly also used fluorescent screens in their experiments and thus had had all the prerequisites enabling Röntgen to discover the new radiation. It may have been due to chance that Röntgen observed this peculiar radiation, but his communication about the discovery does not merely mention the unexpected light effect on the fluorescent screen, it also gives an analysis of the most important properties of the rays. Thus he demonstrated their power of penetrating matter which is impervious to ordinary light, and their power of giving rise to fluorescence in substances which are usually called phosphors, such as uranium glass, ordinary glass, calcite, rock salt, etc. He also observed that a photographic plate was blackened by the radiation. Further, he found by experiment that the rays were not, like the cathode rays, deflected by a magnet, and that primarily they appeared to proceed from the place in the vacuum tube struck by the cathode rays. On deflecting the latter by a magnet, he found that the place of emission of the new rays moved accordingly. In this connection Röntgen established something important for the further development, namely, that if the cathode rays were allowed to strike platinum, a far stronger X-radiation resulted than from aluminium, glass or other light substances. On the other hand, in spite of eager attempts made with a number of different substances, Röntgen could not observe any refraction of the rays by a prism or reflection or concentration by a lens in distinction from the behaviour of ordinary light.

These brief indications of the contents of Röntgen's first communication may suffice to show how supremely and rapidly he created order in a sphere which was entirely outside all previous human experience. It need only be added that nearly twenty years were to elapse before any palpable advance could be noted in our knowledge of the properties of X-radiation, over and above what Röntgen himself had obtained.

The very important medical uses – the first photographs of skeletons were taken by Röntgen himself – were of course obvious and contributed more than anything else to spreading a general knowledge of this new remarkable radiation.

In *1901*, when the Swedish Academy of Sciences had to distribute the Nobel Prizes for the first time, it was natural that the choice for the Prize in Physics should fall on Röntgen. It may be said without exaggeration that a more worthy scientific achievement and one more in the spirit of the Nobel Prizes than Röntgen's cannot be imagined. It was certainly a great satisfaction to the Swedish Academy of Sciences, which had undertaken this difficult and responsible task with much hesitation, that such an eminent achievement could be rewarded at the first distribution. It had certainly not been made 'during the preceding year', as laid down in Nobel's will, but it was so new that it had hardly had time to be more than tested and fully accepted by international professional criticism, and it could be said with assurance that it implied an immense contribution of lasting value to research.

RÖNTGEN was awarded the prize 'in recognition of the extraordinary services he has rendered by the discovery of the remarkable rays which have subsequently been called after him'.

When development in this field took the next important step forward in 1912, the situation had materially changed, owing to a series of advances within other branches of physical science whereby new points of view had become available also for a further elucidation of the phenomena connected with Röntgen radiation.

At this juncture it may be of some interest to indicate the situation within the Academy of Sciences at the time of the first distribution of the Nobel Prizes. According to the statutes, no minutes may be kept of the meetings of the Academy for the awarding of the prizes. On the other hand, the nominations received in 1901 by the Nobel Committees from a large number of prominent scientists all over the world are still extant and may be considered as forming a kind of ballot among international experts for the guidance of the Academy in their choice. The following persons had been proposed for the 1901 Nobel Prize for Physics:

Professor S. Arrhenius, Stockholm
Professor Henri Becquerel, Paris
Professor W. W. Campbell, Lick Observatory, Cal., U.S.A.
Lord Kelvin, Edinburgh
Professor G. Lippmann, Paris
Mr. G. Marconi, London
Professor A. E. Nordenskiöld, Stockholm
Professor W. C. Röntgen, Munich
Professor J. J. Thomson, Cambridge
Professor J. D. van der Waals, Amsterdam

Dr. P. Zeeman, Amsterdam
Division of the prize between W. C. Röntgen, and Ph. Lenard of Kiel.

However, the great majority of the proposers, i.e. seventeen out of twenty-nine, had joined in proposing Röntgen, while the other candidates received only a stray vote or two. Of those proposed, Arrhenius, who incidentally was a member of the Nobel Committee for Physics, was granted the 1903 Prize for Chemistry. Becquerel shared the Physics Prize in 1903 with Pierre and Marie Curie. Lord Kelvin, who was looked upon by many as the foremost physicist then living, was proposed by Röntgen, formally on the basis of a couple of papers published in 1900, but reference was also made to his outstanding life-work within physical science. However, the Committee pointed out that Lord Kelvin's work had been done at too early a period for it to be rewarded under the terms of the statutes. In 1908 Lippmann was awarded the Physics Prize, and in 1909 Marconi shared it with F. Braun of Strasbourg. Van der Waals received the Physics Prize in 1910. In 1902 Zeeman shared the prize with his fellow-countryman, H. A. Lorentz of Leyden. Campbell, one of the foremost astronomers of the time, could not be considered since his work lay outside the fields of research for which the Nobel Prizes are intended. The prominent Swedish explorer, A. E. Nordenskiöld, had been proposed for a prize by a Swedish member of the Academy of Sciences for 'his invention for obtaining drinking-water from crystalline rocks' [well-boring in primeval formations]. This candidature, however, never materialized, as Nordenskiöld died on August 12, 1901, before the Academy had dealt with the question of prizes.

The discovery which received the first award was of such a nature as to arouse enormous interest far outside professional circles, and its importance – after it had been confirmed in many different quarters – was manifest to people at large, and this is not always the case where scientific discoveries are concerned. But the work of Röntgen also led indirectly to a discovery which opened up one of the most fascinating fields of research so far cultivated by natural science. Its consequences have culminated during the last decades in releasing natural forces vastly surpassing those of our earlier experience.

RADIOACTIVITY

Shortly after Röntgen's discovery some photographs taken with the new radiation were shown at a meeting of the French Academy of Sciences, and there gave rise to a discussion concerning the nature of the radiation. The great mathematician Henri Poincaré, one of the most prolific scientists of all times, put forward the idea that X-radiation might be directly connected with the fluorescence exhibited by the glass of the evacuated tube at the spots from which the X-rays seemed to depart. Although this idea could not be quite correct, since Röntgen had found that the non-fluorescent platinum radiated much more intensely than the glass wall, the idea was taken up by another French physicist, HENRI BECQUEREL [1852-1908], an international authority in his field. At the 'Musée d'Histoire Naturelle' in Paris the chair in physics had passed from father to son in the Becquerel family through three generations, Henri Becquerel being the incumbent at this time. His father, Edmond Becquerel, had carried out investigations, which had attracted much attention, into the phenomena of phosphorescence and fluorescence, and consequently the museum had a large collection of substances exhibiting these properties. From these Henri Becquerel selected a uranium salt which was first exposed to sunlight until it showed strong fluorescence and then placed against a photographic plate wrapped in black paper. Upon developing the plate, he found that it had been blackened though it had not been exposed to ordinary light. This would seem to confirm the hypothesis of the connection between fluorescent light and X-radiation. But when Becquerel decided to investigate how long the effect of the fluorescent light lasted, he found to his surprise that the photographic plates were blackened long after the fluorescence had ceased. Further, in continued experiments he found that it was just the uranium salts which exhibited the new effect, but that the latter was independent of what particular uranium compound was used. This was evidently a new type of radiation from the uranium atom, entirely unaffected by external conditions, and it seemed to persist with undiminished strength indefinitely. Becquerel had discovered *radioactivity* [1896].

To develop X-radiation an evacuated tube and high electric tension were required, but the new radioactive radiation was emitted permanently by the uranium without any external influence.

Of special importance for further research was Becquerel's observation that this radiation – like the X-rays – could discharge an electroscope. Thus a method was obtained, not only for detecting radiation, but also for measuring radioactivity, as the rate of discharge of the electroscope gives a measure of the strength of the radiation. By this method Becquerel could prove quantitatively that the radiation was constant and did not diminish with time.

As mentioned above, Becquerel had found that this radiation, during the immediately following years called 'Becquerel radiation', was emitted by uranium. Using this new method of electric measurements, Mme MARIE SKLODOWSKA CURIE [1867-1934] began a systematic investigation with a view to ascertaining if other substances than uranium exhibited similar properties of radiation. In 1898 Mme Curie – simultaneously with Schmidt in Germany – found that thorium, next to uranium the heaviest of the known elements, was 'radioactive'. But apart from uranium and thorium, Mme Curie could not find among such chemical elements as were produced or were in use in the laboratories any other emitting Becquerel rays. However, in the course of her investigation of uranium and thorium compounds, she observed that some of them emitted a stronger radiation than corresponded to the content of uranium or thorium. From this she concluded that these substances also contained unknown radioactive elements.

Together with her husband PIERRE CURIE [1859-1906], then Professor of Physics at 'l'École de Physique et de Chimie industrielles' in Paris, she made a chemical analysis of the uranium mineral pitchblende, every separation product being tested for its strength of radiation. The first product found in this manner, exhibiting considerably stronger radiation than uranium, had chemical properties resembling those of bismuth. In honour of Mme. Curie's native country, this element was called *polonium*. In the continued work of separation, in which Bémont now also took part, a substance was then found which emitted extremely strong Becquerel radiation. The corresponding element, which later turned out to be the most specific in the group of radioactive elements, was given the name of *radium*. In its chemical properties it resembled barium, but it could be separated from the latter by fractional crystallization.

Side by side with this work Becquerel studied the properties of the new radiation, and for these experiments the more strongly radiating preparations produced by the Curies were successively placed at his disposal.

Even though the radiation, as already mentioned, exhibited certain properties characteristic of X-radiation, especially great penetrating power, it was manifest that it could not be identical with the latter. Becquerel pointed out that the new radiation also had some properties resembling those of the cathode rays, i.e. the rays emitted from the negative electrode [the cathode] in an evacuated tube, whose chief characteristic is the fluorescence they give rise to on the glass walls of the tube. These rays, about the nature of which different opinions were held at that time, appeared to proceed in rectilinear paths from the cathode, but they could easily be deflected by a magnet placed close to the vacuum tube.

Employing a preparation of radium produced by the Curies, Becquerel proved in 1899 that the radiation from this element could be deflected by a powerful magnet. Similar experiments giving the same results had been carried out at the same time by F. Giesel in Germany and by St. Meyer and E. v. Schweidler in Austria. On the other hand, the radiation from polonium did not appear to be affected by the magnet. Further experiments concerning the penetrating power of radium and polonium radiation, respectively, had shown that the latter was very much less penetrating than the former. Thus Becquerel considered that he had established the existence of two kinds of rays. After a closer study of the radiation from radium, the Curies found that it emitted both kinds of rays simultaneously.

At this stage of development in radioactivity a young physicist, Ernest Rutherford from New Zealand, began to take a very active part in the researches within this field. During the years 1895-98 he worked as a research student at the Cavendish Laboratory in Cambridge under J. J. Thomson. Showing exceptional energy and an extraordinary capacity for finding the right ways and means intuitively, Rutherford tackled the problem of radioactivity, and soon became the leading figure in the development of this branch of physics. In a paper published in January 1899, in which he reported an exhaustive study of the radiation from uranium with respect to its power of penetrating thin aluminium foil, he writes: 'These experiments show that the uranium radiation is complex, and that there are present at least two distinct types of radiation – one that is very readily absorbed, which will be termed for convenience the α-radiation, and the other of a more penetrative character, which will be termed the β-radiation.' Thus the two types of radiation had been given the designations subsequently generally accepted.

Finally, the Frenchman Villard called attention to the fact that, apart from these two kinds of rays, a third type was also emitted, which was not affected by magnetic fields and showed great resemblance to X-radiation. This type was given the name of γ-rays.

With the work of these scientists the first chapter in the history of radioactivity had been written, and a new field of research opened up, which, more than any other, was to dominate physical research during the following half-century.

For these important contributions the *1903* prize was awarded to BECQUEREL 'in recognition of the extraordinary services he has rendered by the discovery of spontaneous radioactivity', and to PIERRE and MARIE CURIE 'in recognition of the extraordinary services they have rendered by their joint work concerning the radiation phenomena discovered by Professor Henri Becquerel'.

Mme CURIE later [*1911*] received the Prize for Chemistry for her work on the chemistry of radioactive elements. RUTHERFORD, too, was awarded the Nobel Prize for Chemistry [*1908*] for his extremely important investigations into radioactivity [see p.373].

These remarkable discoveries led to a profound change in the earlier concept that a uniform mechanical interpretation could account for all natural forces and natural processes, including electromagnetic and optical phenomena. In reality the phenomena discovered by Röntgen, Becquerel and the Curies represented something lying quite outside the experiences previously studied. In fact, each of these discoveries applied to a specific sphere of its own in the hitherto unknown world of matter.

As shown by subsequent research, chiefly thanks to the work of Rutherford, the radioactive phenomena have their origin in what is nowadays called the nucleus of the atom, a positively charged central body within the atom. Although the diameter of the nucleus amounts to only about one hundred-thousandth part of that of the atom, yet the nucleus accounts for practically the whole mass of the latter. The radioactive radiation is the means of communication through which we get an idea of what goes on in this world concealed until then. The three kinds of rays which could be distinguished during the first phase of development, namely the α-, β-, and γ-radiations, may be briefly characterized thus: α- and β-radiations are rays of particles, while γ-radiation has a wave nature and is of the same character as light though with a very much shorter wave-length.

More detailed insight into the properties of particle radiations was obtained, firstly, by determinations of their penetrating power in different substances, and, secondly and chiefly, by studying their deflection in electric and magnetic fields. Observations on the latter phenomenon showed, as a first result, that the α-particles were positively charged and the β-particles negatively charged.

What above all made the radioactive radiation seem to be so inexplicable was perhaps the circumstance that it appeared to continue with undiminished strength indefinitely. According to the measurements of the Curies, 1 g of radium emits a heat effect of about 100 calories per hour. The law of the conservation of energy, one of the most important principles of physics, appeared to be in danger. As we now know, however, the explanation is found, firstly, in the great supply of energy in the nucleus of the atom, and, secondly, in the fact that the nuclei of the radioactive elements disintegrate more or less rapidly, giving rise to nuclei with less energy. In the case of radium this process is fairly slow – it takes about 1600 years before one half has been so transformed. These facts were elucidated by the transformation theory of Rutherford and Soddy in 1903. Since these questions were considered to lie within the domain of chemistry rather than that of physics, these two scientists were awarded prizes for chemistry [RUTHERFORD in *1908* and SODDY in *1921*]. A more detailed discussion of related matters is consequently to be found elsewhere in this publication [see pp. 319 ff.].

Even though the other type of newly discovered radiation, the X-rays, showed a certain resemblance to that just described as emanating from the nucleus of the atom, it had quite a different origin. However, it may be mentioned in passing that in radioactive radiation there may also occur a secondary X-radiation in addition to the normal α-, β-, and γ-radiations.

To throw light on these questions, however, an account of the investigations into cathode rays and related phenomena is necessary.

THE ELECTRON, ITS CHARGE AND MASS

As mentioned above, during the later decades of the nineteenth century many laboratories directed their attention to the passage of electricity through gases. The conduction of electricity through *solids,* primarily metals, had of course been well known and was summed up by Ohm's law of 1825. The passage of electricity through *liquids* had been explained in some essential features by Faraday in 1834, and the subsequent development finally led to the theory of electrolytic dissociation of Arrhenius [1887] with its far-reaching significance for chemistry. In the case of the passage of electricity through *gases,* the conditions were obviously very complicated and, therefore, difficult to elucidate. When this task was finally accomplished, the results were of so much greater importance, because they led to a better understanding of the nature of electricity and to the discovery of the electrical counterpart of the atom of matter, namely the electron.

The main features of this development were as follows. When electricity passes through a more or less evacuated glass tube, a great variety of very bright colour effects appear. If the air is considerably rarefied, it is found that the glass tube begins to exhibit a strong fluorescence which is obviously developed by rays proceeding from the cathode. The discovery of these 'cathode rays' is ascribed to Plücker [1859]. Their importance for the discovery of the X-rays has already been indicated above. In 1871 Varley put forward the suggestion that the cathode rays consist of small electrically charged particles thrown off from the cathode and hence negatively charged. By means of an experiment, as elegant as it was simple, William Crookes in 1879 was able to give very tangible support to such a concept of the cathode rays. The arrangements in this test, which subsequently became an ordinary demonstration experiment, were as follows. Between the cathode and the opposite glass wall in the vacuum tube was placed a Maltese cross of mica which could be made to fall down by inclining the tube. When the cross was upright, its shadow fell on the glass wall, thus proving that the cathode rays followed rectilinear paths from the cathode, but were checked by the mica cross. If a magnet was applied near the tube, the shadow moved, owing to the deflection of the rays, and in such a manner as would be expected if the cathode radiation was a flow of negative particles. Crookes, and with him the British scientists, therefore conceived of the cathode rays as a particle radiation. Remarkably enough this theory was not accepted by the German physicists, who instead adopted an interpretation of the cathode rays put forward by Goldstein in 1876, according to which these rays had the character of waves. One of the strongest arguments in favour of this interpretation was advanced by Heinrich Hertz, at that time the foremost experimental physicist in Germany, who proved that cathode rays could pass through thin foils of gold, silver and aluminium. No particles of matter of a kind then known could very well penetrate such foils.

In connection with his experiments on the transmission of cathode rays through metal foils, Hertz initiated experiments which attracted great interest. As he related later in his Nobel lecture, PHILIPP LENARD [1862-1947], who at that time [1892] was an assistant at Hertz's institute, was one day summoned to his great master – something which to Lenard's regret very seldom happened – and Hertz said to him: 'One ought to separate two spaces by means of an aluminium foil; in one space the rays could be produced as usual, on the other they could then be observed more clearly than before, and even if, owing to the delicacy of the foils, there would be only a very slight difference in air pressure between the two spaces, one could perhaps completely empty the space under observation and see whether this was an obstacle to the spreading of the cathode rays or not, that is, whether they are phenomena in matter or in the ether.' Lenard had previously made vain attempts to cause the cathode rays to pass out of the evacuated tube with a view to being able to study their properties more easily outside. As an exit window he had used a quartz plate which was known to be transparent to ultraviolet light. Since Lenard shared the notion then current among German physicists that cathode rays are a kind of ultraviolet radiation, he thought that a quartz plate would also let this type of radiation through. The attempts had been unsuccessful, but when Lenard followed Hertz's advice and replaced the quartz plate by thin metal foils mounted on a metal plate with a number of fine holes, he found at once that the cathode rays passed out into space immediately in front of the plate. For instance, they could produce light effects on a fluorescent screen placed there.

During the next few years cathode ray tubes with 'Lenard windows' were much appreciated in demonstration experiments. The elucidation of the nature of the cathode rays, however, was obtained in other ways. In *1905* LENARD was awarded the Nobel Prize for his 'work on cathode rays'.

It was above all thanks to JOSEPH JOHN THOMSON [1856-1940] in Cambridge and his progressive school of young physicists that the enigma of the cathode rays was definitely solved, and the corpuscular theory triumphed over the wave theory. The cathode radiation was shown to consist of negatively charged particles, small in comparison with the atom, to which the name of electrons was given. Nevertheless, thirty years later a Nobel Prize in Physics was awarded 'for the discovery of the wave nature of the electrons'! As has already been indicated, what was gained at about the turn of the century from the study of the cathode rays was of far-reaching importance for an understanding of the nature of electricity. The decisive experiments were briefly as follows: by exposing the beam of cathode rays to the influence not only of a magnetic field but at the same time also of an electric field – by causing the beam to pass between two electrically charged metal plates – a combined effect was obtained allowing a calculation of the velocity of the particles. In this way Thomson found that, at very low pressures of the gas in the tube, the velocity of the cathode particles amounted to about one-third of the velocity of light, or about 100,000 km per second; at higher pressures, velocities below 10,000 km per second could be observed. After the velocities of the particles had thus been determined, it was possible, by exposing the beam of cathode rays to the electric cross field only, to measure the ratio between the mass and the charge of the particles. It was found that this ratio was independent not only of the velocity of the particles but also of the material used for the cathode and of the gas present in the tube. The latter observation at first appeared extremely remarkable as of course it was to be expected that the particles originated either from the electrode or from the gas. The value obtained by Thomson in these first measurements for the ratio between mass and charge proved to be only 1/1700 part [the most recent measurements give the value 1/1840] of the corresponding ratio for the electrically charged hydrogen atom.

As Thomson was able to prove convincingly by experiments based on a discovery by C. T. R. Wilson [to be described more fully later] that the electric charge was the same in both cases, the conclusion was inevitable – the mass of the cathode particles is only about 1/1700 part of that of the hydrogen atom, i.e. the lightest known atom. Thomson was now able to show that the same electric particles were also met with in connection with many other phenomena besides the cathode rays. They are emitted, e.g., by metals heated to a sufficiently high temperature and also by metals and other bodies when exposed to light, especially ultraviolet light. The β-rays emitted in the case of radioactive radiation consist of the same kind of particles, although here the initial velocity is considerably higher than in the case of cathode rays. This particle, to which Thomson gave the name of 'corpuscle', and which has later been called electron, was thus found to be present everywhere in matter. The carrier of the negative electricity had been finally found, and accurate data for its most important properties, its *mass* and its *charge,* had been obtained. On the other hand, no particle of correspondingly small mass carrying a positive charge had been observed. An old subject of controversy, where different hypotheses had succeeded each other, was now settled. THOMSON was awarded the *1906* Prize for Physics 'in recognition of the great merits of his theoretical and experimental investigations into the transmission of electricity through gases'.

A new, extremely exact measurement of the elementary charge of electricity – one of the most important of the natural constants – was made in 1912 by Robert A. Millikan. He employed a method which was very simple in principle. An extremely small drop of oil, falling between two horizontal metal plates, one charged positively and the other negatively, is observed through a microscope. If the droplet is not charged, it falls at a rate determined by gravity and air friction. On the other hand, if the drop carries an electric charge, the velocity of its fall will increase or decrease according as the electric force from the plates acts in the same direction as gravity or in the opposite direction. Millikan found that the velocity of the drop changed by steps, obviously owing to one or more unit charges having joined the drop. From these measurements he was able to calculate with great accuracy the size of the elementary unit of electric charge. We shall return later to another of Millikan's important contributions to our knowledge of the foundations of physical science [p.429].

EFFECTS OF ELECTRIC AND MAGNETIC FIELDS ON OPTICAL SPECTRA—RELATIVITY

As previously mentioned, the Faraday-Maxwell theory, without resorting to atomistic concepts, had succeeded in giving a good mathematical description of electromagnetic phenomena. After the famous experiments of Hertz, this theory had been generally accepted as an explanation of the propagation of light. For several reasons it had become obvious, however, that the electromagnetic theory of light called for amplification. The theory had to take account of the three parts constituting the material world: ordinary matter, electrons, and the medium carrying the electromagnetic forces and waves. This medium had been called the 'ether', but only the vaguest notions could be formed about it. The credit for having extended

Maxwell's theory to comprise also the phenomena occurring in matter through the agency of the electrons, goes in the first place to the Dutchman, HENDRIK ANTOON LORENTZ [1853-1928], even though many other scientists, such as H. Poincaré in Paris, Wiechert in Göttingen, and Larmor in Cambridge, contributed to the formulation of the theory in this field.

When Lorentz had completed the main features of this 'electron theory', his young fellow-countryman PIETER ZEEMAN [1865-1943] made an experimental discovery which, apart from its great general significance, became a touchstone for the new theory. If, as had been imagined, light was really of an electromagnetic nature, then it should be expected that it could be affected by magnetic and electric forces. Faraday had already shown that magnetic forces had some influence on the propagation of light in that its polarization was affected, and several years later Kerr had found similar effects when light was reflected by the pole plates of a magnet.

However, Zeeman's discovery concerned a question of far greater scope, namely, whether or not the emission of light could be influenced by magnetic forces. In order to test for such an effect, Zeeman in August 1896 placed a gas burner between the poles of a strong electromagnet and introduced common salt into the flame, producing a sodium spectrum. If this light is examined with a Rowland grating, two very strong yellow lines are found whose wave-lengths differ only by about 0.1 per cent. As soon as the electric current was connected with the magnet, both these lines, which had previously been very narrow, showed a substantial increase in width. This could be interpreted only in the sense that, owing to the effect of the magnetic field, the frequency of vibration in the light-emitting atom had been changed. Experiment and theory now advanced hand in hand. According to the electron theory of Lorentz, a splitting of the frequency of the original line into two components was to be expected when the flame is viewed in the direction of the magnetic field, but into three components when the flame is viewed perpendicularly. With a sufficiently powerful magnet and a strongly diffracting grating, Zeeman was able to verify these theoretical conclusions. In addition, the theory afforded detailed information as to the orientation of the vibration [the 'polarization'] of the different components; these predictions were tested experimentally and confirmed by Zeeman. Finally, empirical justification had been obtained for calculating from the theory the data for the particle whose oscillations in the atom were presumed to generate the light. The theory gave a value for the ratio of the charge to the mass of the particle, agreeing, within the limits of accuracy, with the value found by Thomson for the electron at this time. In this manner Zeeman's discovery had given the electron theory a wider and more secure basis, influencing our entire concept of the nature of electricity and matter. It should be added that, in the form it then had, the electron theory well interpreted the typical simple splitting of spectral lines, but that in several cases Zeeman found far more complicated effects when the lines were split into more components.

LORENTZ and ZEEMAN were awarded the *1902* Nobel Prize 'in recognition of the extraordinary service they had rendered by their investigations of the influence of magnetism upon the phenomena of radiation'.

After Zeeman's discovery of the effect of the magnetic field on the emission of light, the question presented itself whether or not it would be possible to find a similar effect in the case of electric fields. A good many years passed, however, before anyone succeeded in finding the right experimental conditions. The difficulty was that a flame conducts electricity and, when placed between two electrodes, it discharges them as soon as one tries to establish an electric field between them.

It was not until 1913 that the electric effect on the emission of light was successfully demonstrated with the aid of the so-called canal rays. These rays had long been known as a positive counterpart to the negative cathode rays. They appear if a hole is bored in the cathode of the discharge tube, whereupon rays passing through this 'canal' in opposite direction to the cathode rays are observed. They consist of atoms or atom complexes, in general carrying a positive electric charge. From this canal radiation, light is emitted by the substances making up the rays. By arranging a strong electric field around the canal rays, the German physicist JOHANNES STARK [1874-1957] in 1913 found the long-sought-for effect which proved to be very complicated. Thus the red line of hydrogen was split up into no less than nine components. Remarkably enough, at the same time and independently of Stark, the Italian physicist La Surdo, experimenting with canal rays, had found the effect but without realizing how it should be interpreted.

STARK was awarded the *1919* prize 'for his discovery of the Doppler effect in canal rays and the splitting of spectral lines in electrical fields'. The theoretical interpretation of this complicated phenomenon could be obtained from Planck's quantum theory for radiation phenomena.

As mentioned above, the existence of a special medium, the ether, conceived of as filling the space not occupied by ordinary matter, had been postulated for the propagation of light. Conceptions as to the character of this hypothetical medium were very obscure, however. Hardly anything more could be said about it than that the electromagnetic equations were valid in this medium. Every attempt at obtaining empirically tangible concepts had failed to attain results. One of the most significant experiments in this connection was made by ALBERT ABRAHAM MICHELSON [1852-1941] in 1880 and continued by him during the following years, partly in collaboration with Morley, with constant improvements in the apparatus. His object was to establish the motion of the earth relative to the ether, and even though the result of his experiment was negative, it became of extraordinary significance in two respects. The brilliant method evolved by Michelson subsequently became one of the most effective tools of optics, and his experiments furthermore served as an incitement for the considerations which ultimately led to Einstein's theory of relativity.

The experiment performed by Michelson was based on known optical phenomena, namely the interference of light. He found a way of utilizing such observations for analysis and precision measurements in other fields, resulting in an enormous progress over earlier methods. The principle of Michelson's interferometer was briefly that he allowed a ray of light, after separation and reflection in two mirrors at varying distances, to reunite. If the wave crests of the two rays happen to coincide after the reflection, the rays reinforce each other, otherwise a reduction in the strength of the light takes place. By slowly displacing one mirror with respect to the other, and observing the successive changes in the intensity of the light, one can find how many wave-lengths of light the mirror has been moved. As the wave-length of light is only some ten-thousandths of a millimetre and it is possible to detect a change of less than one-tenth of this, we have at our disposal a method for measuring lengths with an accuracy of a few hundredthousandths of a millimetre. To obtain a correct millimetre scale, i.e. one in accordance with the metre agreed upon at the international metre convention in Paris in 1918, it was necessary to measure the prototype metre with the interferometer and to express it in terms of light wave-lengths. Partly because the exactitude of this method of measuring is far greater than that obtainable by directly observing the graduation lines on the prototype metre, and partly because the wave-length of a definite spectral line is a length provided by nature and constant for all time, the latter is nowadays taken as the basic length.

The interferometer has opened up unthought-of possibilities for the analysis of the finer details in spectral lines, such as for example are important for the study of the Zeeman and the Stark effects, and for the conclusions to be drawn from them for the theories of the emission of light, the structure of the atoms, etc.

MICHELSON was awarded the *1907* prize 'for his optical precision instrument and the spectroscopic and metrological investigations he has carried out with it'.

Though a discussion of the theory of relativity lies outside the scope of the present survey, it should be mentioned, however, that when Einstein in 1905 presented the theory in its earlier form, the 'special' theory of relativity, he took two postulates as his point of departure. The first of these, according to which the velocity of light is independent of the motion of the light source, was based on the empirical result of Michelson showing that no motion of the earth relative to the ether could be detected. The second postulate is of a very general nature; it implies that the mathematical formulation of the laws of nature is the same for all systems moving with uniform velocity relative to each other. For instance, if one measures the force of gravity in a railway train, moving at a uniform rate, the same result is obtained as when the measurements are made in a room at rest. In one sweep the special theory of relativity removed a number of difficulties in the electrodynamical theories of moving bodies. The most remarkable consequence of the theory was perhaps Einstein's mass-energy equation, stating that mass when transformed into energy will produce an amount of energy equal to the mass multiplied by the square of the velocity of light. This law has been verified experimentally for several different phenomena and, as is well known, it is basic for problems relating to atomic energy.

For the broader basis on which Einstein built his 'general' theory of relativity in 1916, one starts from the conditions holding when – to continue the example used above – the observations are carried out in a train, *not* moving at uniform velocity, and the speed is raised or lowered. In this case the force of gravity does not appear to be directed vertically downwards but forming an angle with the vertical. The same effect is attained if the measurements are made in a room at rest where an attracting mass is placed in front of or behind the recording instruments. This equivalence of a 'field of attraction' with a 'field of gravitation' serves as the basis of the general theory of relativity and led Einstein to a law of gravitation, more general than that of Newton but containing the latter as a special case.

ELECTRONS FROM METALS

As previously mentioned, J. J. Thomson, in his investigations into the properties and occurrence of electrons, established that these particles are also emitted by metals at high temperatures. It had long been known that the air in the neighbourhood of incandescent bodies conducted electricity, although the nature of the phenomenon was not clearly understood. At the turn of the century it was still an open question whether the electrons were released from the metal by a purely thermal effect or by chemical action due to the surrounding gas, or, possibly, by the effect of light radiation. After overcoming great experimental difficulties, OWEN RICHARDSON [1879-1959] at the Cavendish Laboratory in Cambridge succeeded in showing that the phenomenon was purely thermal. To prove this, it was necessary to carry out the experiment in such a high vacuum that the remaining gas could not possibly have any influence. With the methods of evacuation available at that time this involved immense difficulties. After weeks of pumping, however, Richardson succeeded in getting the experimental apparatus so free of gas that the experiments gave unquestionable results. The electrons were emitted by the metal without the co-operation of the gas, and it could be proved that the phenomenon was due only to the temperature of the incandescent wire.

According to the current theory of the conduction of electricity in metals, developed chiefly by J. J. Thomson, H. A. Lorentz, E. Riecke and P. Drude, the transportation of electricity in a metal was effected by electrons moving freely within the metal approximately like a gas. The electrons were assumed to have all possible velocities and directions and the same average energy as the kinetic theory of gases assigns to a monatomic gas on the basis of Maxwell's statistical law of distribution.

Richardson was now able to develop a simple mathematical formula for the number of electrons emitted by the incandescent body at different temperatures, based on the assumption that all electrons striking the surface of the metal from the inside with a certain minimal velocity were emitted.

This minimum value of the velocity component at right angles to the surface was necessary to overcome a certain exit resistance in the surface layer. By means of *Richardson's law* and the experiments he carried out to verify it, valuable direct confirmation was gained of the ideas concerning the electric properties of metals which had been arrived at in other ways. After a renewed thermodynamical treatment, Richardson in 1911 modified the formula he had given for the connection between temperature and electron emission. The difference between the two formulae was slight, however, and both agreed numerically with the observations within the experimental limits of error. At the time Richardson's findings were of purely theoretical interest, but the data obtained were later supplemented by observations on other similar phenomena and became of fundamental importance as an aid to research and for technical purposes. It is enough to recall that modern radio technique is largely based on the thermionic emission of electrons.

RICHARDSON was awarded the *1928* prize 'for his work on the thermionic phenomenon and especially for the discovery of the law named after him'.

RADIO WAVES, SOLIDSTATE ELECTRONICS AND QUANTUM ELECTRONICS

Mention has been made above of the great importance of the experiments of H. Hertz with electric waves in 1887 for the general acceptance of the electromagnetic theory of light. At the same time, however, these brilliant experiments opened up an entirely new field for research and technology, that of the electromagnetic waves. Hertz' investigations of the generation and propagation of electric waves clarified all essential facts about them. Experiments to demonstrate the 'Hertzian waves' and their properties were soon introduced into physical laboratories all over the world, and research in this field was begun in many quarters.

The interest of the general public was naturally enough particularly attracted to the experiments with Hertzian waves for 'wireless telegraphy'. Hertz had shown that waves emanated from his oscillator and could be caught up by a receiver without there being any direct connection between them. Thus he had realized the wireless transmission of signals, although merely over a very short distance in the laboratory. Hertz' interests were centred on other things than trying to exploit his discovery for such purposes.

Everyone knows that the name of GUGLIELMO MARCONI [1874-1937] is closely associated with the technical development of the new method of communication. In his Nobel lecture Marconi pointed out that he had never pursued regular studies, either in physics or in electrical engineering, although as a boy he had been keenly interested in these subjects. On one occasion, however, he attended a course of lectures in physics given by Professor Rosa at Leghorn, and, according to his own statement, he was quite familiar with the publications of Hertz, Branly and Righi. He began his experiments with wireless telegraphy in 1895.

Among the many who were working with the Hertzian waves at this time, with the idea of using them for communication purposes, mention should be made of the Russian scientist Popov, who gave an account of his experiments as early as the beginning of April, 1895. Like many others at that time, he used a Branly coherer as the receiver. The coherer, incidentally, had been used by many scientists before Branly but had fallen into oblivion. It consists of a glass tube in which metal filings have been placed between two metal cylinders. Normally the coherer has a high electric resistance, but when struck by electric waves it becomes a conductor and will transmit a current from a battery. If a galvanometer or other sensitive current-measuring instrument is placed in the coherer circuit, a current is registered which ceases, however, when the coherer is shaken. Popov placed an electric bell in the circuit; as soon as a signal was registered, the bell would automatically shake the coherer, thereby restoring it to its normal state. In these experiments with Hertzian waves, Popov succeeded in transmitting signals over distances up to 5 kilometres.

Marconi's first important invention for sending signals over great distances with the Hertzian waves consisted in connecting one of the spheres of the oscillator with the earth while the other was connected to a vertical conductor, the 'antenna'. The latter was also provided at the top with a large metal body, a 'capacity'. There was a similar arrangement at the receiving side, where the coherer was both grounded and connected to an antenna. In the first experiments carried out by Marconi at his home in Bologna, he was able to transmit signals over 2,400 metres. In September 1896 Marconi continued these experiments in England for the British Government and then attained distances of 2.8 km. In March 1897 he had increased the distance to 6.4 km. and in May of the same year to 14.5

km. In July of that year the Italian War Ministry, under the direction of Marconi, carried out experiments with antennas 28 metres high and were then able to attain a distance of 18 km.

From these experiments Marconi found that the range of the signals could be increased by using higher antennas; the range varies as the square of the height of the antenna. Here practical reasons set a somewhat narrow limit for the increase of the range in this way. Another method was of course to increase the electric energy fed into the oscillator or to increase the sensitivity of the receiver, but, with the transmitting and receiving arrangements employed, the possibilities of materially increasing the range were fairly limited.

Marconi's experiments were guided entirely by the inventor's intuition, but parallel to them FERDINAND BRAUN [1850-1918], then professor of physics at the University of Strasbourg, was attempting to work out methods of wireless telegraphy on the basis of exhaustive research. In the cathode-ray oscillograph, constructed by him in 1897, he had an extremely effective device for studying the rapid electric phenomena in transmitter and receiver. 'Braun's tube', in its modern construction, is now an indispensable tool in every laboratory and its technical use was later extended to radar and television, etc. It is simply a cathode-ray tube of the type mentioned above, where, however, the beam of rays has been limited to a thread-like ray which may be affected by external electric currents in coils outside the tube or voltages on electrode plates fused into the tube.

In Marconi's transmitting arrangement the antenna was directly connected to the two spheres and thus formed with them a single oscillating circuit emitting Hertzian waves. Braun introduced a new principle by dividing both the transmitter and the receiver into two oscillating circuits. The main oscillator was a closed circuit containing the spherical spark-gap, a condenser and an adjustable wire coil ['self-induction']. In this circuit the electric oscillations were generated by the spark-gap which as usual was connected with a high tension generator [an induction coil]. The electric oscillations in this closed circuit were then transmitted to the antenna circuit either by direct connection between the circuits or by 'inductive' coupling.

The essential advance implied by the two 'coupled' circuits was that, by tuning them, relatively undamped outgoing oscillations were obtainable, instead of the short-lived current pulses produced by the single circuit. By utilizing the additional possibilities of regulation and the ability of the condenser of storing electric energy, the output of the antenna could be considerably increased. Thus prerequisites had been created for increasing the transmission range.

With regard to the receiver arrangements, a contribution by Braun should be mentioned, as it subsequently came to play a great role when radio became the property of the general public. In his youth [1874] Braun had studied the electric properties of certain crystals, among others, galena and pyrite, and had found that they transmitted an electric current more readily in *one* direction than in the opposite one. In 1898 he made an attempt to use these crystals as receivers instead of the coherer and found that they could certainly replace the latter but not to any advantage. When later the telephone receiver was introduced in 1901, Braun again took up his experiments with crystal detectors. Some years later, at Braun's suggestion, a large German radio firm started manufacturing earphones with these crystal detectors, which were subsequently very widely used.

Continuing his efforts to increase the range of radio transmission, Marconi made use of circuits built on the resonance principle, and in 1901 he succeeded for the first time in establishing wireless connection across the Atlantic between Poldhu in Cornwall and St. John's in Newfoundland, a distance of about 3,400 km.

MARCONI and BRAUN were jointly awarded the *1909* prize 'in recognition of their services in the development of wireless telegraphy'.

Even after Marconi had succeeded in establishing radio communication across the English Channel, doubts were expressed as to whether it would be possible to reach appreciably greater distances on account of the curvature of the earth. Reference was made to the analogy with light waves. There was a difference, however. In radio transmission 'free' waves were not used as in Hertz's experiment; as mentioned above, one part of the oscillator was grounded and this might be anticipated to affect the prospects favourably. But even this explanation appeared insufficient after Marconi had succeeded in sending signals such great distances as across the Atlantic Ocean.

Independently of each other, Heaviside in England and Kennelly in America pointed out that if the existence of an electrically conducting layer in the upper atmosphere was assumed, the radio waves would be guided between the earth and this layer, and thus the energy would not be dissipated into space. As there was no direct proof of the existence of such an ionized layer in the atmosphere, other explanations were also sought for, but the theory advanced by Heaviside and Kennelly remained in the foreground. It was not until 1924 that the existence of the conducting layer in the atmosphere, postulated by this theory, was proved experimentally and its distance above the surface of the earth was measured and found to be about 90 km. The first measurements were made by the English physicist EDWARD VICTOR APPLETON [b.1892], using a method developed by him which permitted a detailed study of the propagation of electromagnetic waves in the atmosphere. Appleton argued as follows: if the strength of the signals received at an appropriate distance from a transmitter is measured, it is to be expected that the direct wave and the wave which is turned back by the reflecting layer in the atmosphere, and which strikes the receiver somewhat later than the direct wave, should either reinforce or impair each other. The strength of the signals should then also change with the wave-length or frequency of the emitted signals. By varying the frequency one can obtain the height of the reflecting layer from these measurements by a simple calculation. In addition to the so-called Heaviside-Kennelly layer, Appleton a couple of years later found by his method another conducting layer in the atmosphere at a considerably greater height, namely at about 230 km. It would take us too far here to describe the many results which have been reached in this field by Appleton and his collaborators as well as a number of other workers; the importance of their researches extends far beyond the applications to radio telegraphy and other practical uses of radio waves. It may suffice to point to the direct connection between these phenomena and others, such as the variations in the magnetic field of the earth and the occurrence of sun spots. It should also be mentioned that a new method of measurement, having advantages for certain investigations over that used by Appleton for his fundamental discoveries, was indicated by Breit and Tuve in 1925.

APPLETON was awarded the *1947* prize 'for his investigations into the physical properties of the higher layers of the atmosphere and especially for the discovery of the so-called Appleton layer'.

The industrial development of different kinds of electron tubes like diodes, triodes, tetrodes and pentodes has created a new field in physics, called electronics. By means of such tubes and the appropriate circuitry, it became an easy matter to rectify or amplify any small input signal, e.g.

radiowaves, or to create undamped electrical oscillations of various frequences. In these tubes the electricity is carried between the different electrodes by means of free electrons in vacuum. The transportation of electric charges through solid material is a much more complicated problem. For pure metals, which always have good conductivities, the transportation is performed by the free conduction electrons in the metal. In semiconductors like germanium and silicone with minute amounts of impurities [e.g. arsenic or indium], the current can be transported by electrons or by 'holes'. It turns out that such semiconducting crystals under certain circumstances can act as very efficient rectifiers and a closer study of these phenomena finally created another important field in physics, namely, the 'solid state electronics'. Because of its obvious practical applications, this field was intensively explored in many industrial research laboratories during the forties and later. A most spectacular discovery was made in the Bell Telephone Research Laboratory in 1948 when a research team consisting of WILLIAM SHOCKLEY [b.1910], JOHN BARDEEN [b.1908] and WALTER H. BRATTAIN [b.1902] was able to show that a particular arrangement of semiconducting layers in contact with electrodes could not only rectify but also amplify currents and voltages. They called their invention a 'transistor'. It has several distinct advantages above the ordinary electron tubes, e.g. extremely low power consumption, small dimensions, longer lifetime, etc. Already, it is possible days replace the ordinary vacuum tubes in most cases.

SHOCKLEY, BARDEEN and BRATTAIN were awarded the *1956* prize 'for their investigations on semiconductors and the discovery of the transistor effect'.

Recent years have seen rapid developments in electronics. Owing to a number of scientists' penetrating analysis of the atomic processes that take place in gases and crystals when these are 'excited' in various ways, there have been new and spectacular achievements. The connexion between this new sort of electronics and modern atomic quantum theory finds expression in the name 'quantum electronics'. For all these new developments the foundations were laid by Einstein as early as 1917 in a paper in which he established an equation the manner in which light is absorbed by and emitted from a gas. Not until some thirty-five or forty years later, however, did it become clear that, under special conditions, a term so small as to be apparently negligible, which Einstein had appended to his equation, could have a dominating influence. In the early 1950's CHAR-

LES H. TOWNES [b. 1915], from the United States, and the Russian scientists Alexander Mikhailovich Prochorov [b. 1916] and Nikolai Gennadievich Basov [b. 1922] began speculating on these questions. Independently they discovered that, if energy is applied to a gas in sufficient quantity and under suitably selected external conditions, it is possible to 'stimulate' the gas into a state which is to some extent reminiscent of an atomic reactor; the difference being that the radiation generated in enormous quantities in the gas is short-wave [microwave] or indeed ordinary visible light. Townes called the first apparatus of this sort a 'maser', an abbreviation of 'microwave amplification by stimulated emission of radiation'. The wavelength of the radiation emitted is determined by the 'inner' frequency changes of the atoms and molecules. These do not vary, and are exceedingly sharply defined. The new 'atomic clocks', so-called, are based on these scientists' discoveries. Characteristic of these new instruments is their extremely high frequency stability. Ammonia, caesium and hydrogen masers, in rising order of accuracy, have been put to a wide range of uses, and today, following an international decision of the 'Conférence Général des Poids et Mesures', are utilized as standard measures of time. The maser has one further enormously important characteristic: it generates virtually no inherent radio interference, as other amplifiers do. This has made it possible to register and amplify, for example, the radio waves emitted by remote celestial bodies and galaxies, thus opening up new perspectives for astronomy.

Science has also succeeded in obtaining corresponding stimulated emissions from ordinary optical light from gases and certain types of crystals. Such instruments are called 'lasers': [l = light]. A great range of technical and scientific applications have followed from the development of these lasers, and many future applications, for instance within telecommunications, now lie within reach.

Closely allied to the above-mentioned progress in quantum electronics is the elegant research carried out during more or less the same period by ALFRED KASTLER [b. 1902] and his colleagues, notably Jean Brossel, in Paris, into the Hertzian resonances of atoms and so-called 'optical pumping'. By exposing gases to radiation by light and microwaves, often in combination with applied magnetic fields, Kastler has succeeded in bringing atoms into a state of excitation lasting long enough for detailed studies to become possible. Among other things, the above-mentioned Zeeman effect has become accessible and with considerably increased sharpness, a development in which the polarization of light has played a crucial rôle. Kastler's technique is a striking example of how a refined combination of experimental parameters can be exploited to find out to what extent quantum mechanics applies at these extreme limits.

The prize for *1964* was awarded, one-half to TOWNES, and the other half jointly to BASOV and PROCHOROV, for their fundamental work in the field of quantum electrodynamics, with deep-ploughing consequences for the physics of elementary particles'.

KASTLER received the *1966* prize for 'the discovery and development of optical methods for studying Hertzian resonances in atoms'.

MAGNETO-HYDRODYNAMICS

An ionized gas is also commonly known as a 'plasma'. In this plasma are positive ions, electrons and, depending on the degree of ionization, a certain number of remaining neutral molecules. The plasma's characteristics have long been a subject of research, particularly in connection with gas discharges and conditions at electrodes in various sorts of electron tubes. Here I. LANGMUIR [1881-1957] made some important contributions, and among other things was successful in showing how oscillations could arise in the plasma as a result of electric influence from the ions. In *1931*, Langmuir was awarded the Nobel Prize for Chemistry for his research in another area, namely surface chemical phenomena. In 1942, the Swedish scientist HANNES GÖSTA ALFVÉN [b. 1908] demonstrated that a new type of wave movement can arise in a plasma as a result of coupling between the movements of the particles and the magnetic fields which accompany the movements of the charged particles. Alfvén was also able to find an expression for the speed with which the 'magneto-hydrodynamic' waves reproduce themselves in a plasma. Such 'Alfvén waves' have afterwards been experimentally verified in his own laboratory and play a crucial role in explaining the conditions that prevail in ionized matter. Cosmically speaking, this is an ordinary state of aggregation, e.g. in the stars. Thus the plasma constitutes a fourth state of matter, over and above gases, liquids and solids. Alfvén has laid the foundation for and developed so-called magneto-hydrodynamics, which is essential to our understanding of a number of phenomena in plasma physics and cosmology. He has also shown that physical occurrences in which the magneto-hydrodynamic aspects are decisive are involved in such phenomena as the Northern Lights, sun-spots and the origin of the solar system. Magneto-hydrodynamics is also of crucial importance in current research into fusion, i.e. attempts to release nuclear energy from a hydrogen plasma shut up in a 'magnetic bottle'.

Alfvén was awarded one-half the *1970* prize for 'his fundamental contributions and discoveries in magneto-hydrodynamics with fruitful applications within various fields of plasmaphysics'.

ATOMIC THEORY APPLIED TO GASES AND LIQUIDS – LOW TEMPERATURES AND HIGH PRESSURES

Around the turn of the century opinions were divided about one of the most important concepts of natural science: the *atom.* Many scientists believed that the atom should be looked upon only as an auxiliary hypothesis without any real or material foundation. The term 'atom' itself had of course been taken over from older, purely philosophical arguments, where in certain cases the significance of empirical experience was utterly rejected. On the other hand, all modern scientific research is based on a thorough experimental study of the phenomena of Nature, and these observations are regarded as the foundation and guiding principle in the formation of our theories. The atomistic concept of present-day science has nothing but the name in common with that of the ancient philosophers; the latter might almost be characterized as the limit of the power of abstraction of the human brain when attempting to analyze the concept of matter. The concepts of atom and of molecule at which chemists and physicists have arrived through their observations are notions with a concrete meaning expressible in terms of exactly defined data. This applies for instance to the information obtained by physicists from a study of gases. In the kinetic theory of gases, mentioned in the introduction, one starts from the assumption that in a gas the atoms [in the case of monatomic gases] or molecules move in rectilinear paths until they collide with one another or are reflected by the walls of the vessel. With this point of departure, the observations gave the result that, e.g. in the case of hydrogen, whose atoms are the lightest of all, the molecules at room temperature move at an average velocity of about 1 km/sec. The dimensions of the particles could be estimated to be of the order of magnitude of ten-millionths of 1 mm, and the total number of atoms in a given amount of gas could also be found. In spite of these and a number of other concrete data about the atom, great scepticism prevailed concerning its actual existence, even among natural scientists, and the more extreme doubters spoke of a 'chimera'. It was not until the beginning of the twentieth century that experiments finally carried the concept of the atomic structure of matter to victory. And not only that, but, as mentioned above, the atomic concept was also applied to the structure of electricity. Subsequently it was extended in a modified form to embrace the phenomena of radiation and conversion of energy through the quantum theory, which has revolutionized physics during the last 60 years.

Before we pass on to the theoretical and experimental phases of this development, we shall give a brief account of some advances in our knowledge of the structure and properties of matter. Concerning the gases we may start by mentioning a discovery which supplemented our knowledge in one very essential respect, namely with regard to what chemical elements exist. It had long been known that atmospheric air contains nitrogen and oxygen in the ratio of 79 to 21. In experiments with the object of testing Prout's hypothesis that all elements are built up of hydrogen atoms, JOHN WILLIAM STRUTT, Lord RAYLEIGH [1842-1919], discovered a previously unknown constituent of the atmosphere, namely argon. Though there is about one per cent of this gas in the atmosphere, it had so far escaped attention, chiefly owing to its chemically inert character. This discovery was an achievement which rightly aroused admiration. According to Prout's hypothesis, it was to be expected that the density of oxygen would be exactly 16, if that of hydrogen is taken to be 1, while the best existing determination due to Regnault had given the value 15.96. The deviation from the value 16 was within the limits of experimental error. When, however, Rayleigh made a new determination by a considerably improved method, the value obtained, 15.88, differed still more from the desired integral value 16. When he subsequently continued his measurements for nitrogen, it proved to his great surprise – after he had carried out a whole series of control experiments of various kinds – that nitrogen taken from the atmosphere was slightly heavier than nitrogen produced chemically from nitrogen compounds. In the former case the weight of the nitrogen in the container weighed by Rayleigh was 2.3102 grams, in the latter 2.2991 grams, a slight difference of 11 milligrams, which, however, far exceeded the limits of error for his very exact measurements. By continued analysis of his results, in the later stage of which the chemist William Ramsay took part, Rayleigh was able to explain the higher weight of nitrogen from the air by the fact that the latter was mixed with a hitherto unknown gas, the density of which he determined as 19.94.

In *1904* RAYLEIGH was awarded the Nobel Prize 'for his investigations concerning the density of the most important gases and his discovery of argon, made in connection with these investigations'.

This discovery led to the finding of a whole series of similar, chemically inert gases, namely helium, neon, krypton and xenon. All these occur in the atmosphere, although in minute amounts. William Ramsay, who discovered all these elements, isolated the most important of them – helium – from the mineral cleveite. This element, which was known from its spectrum to exist in the sun [whence the name], became immensely important for reaching extremely low temperatures – as we shall soon show. RAMSAY's discoveries were rewarded with the Nobel Prize for Chemistry for *1904* [see p. 300].

From the kinetic theory of gases a formula could be deduced giving the relation between the pressure, volume and temperature of a mass of gas. Even though this simple formula agreed on the whole with the observations already made, there were small but palpable deviations and these became more striking the more the gas was compressed. The Dutch scientist, JOHANNES DIDERIK VAN DER WAALS [1837-1923], tried to modify the formula so as to make it valid both for the gaseous and the liquid states. As a matter of fact, by changing the temperature continuously one can, under certain circumstances, transform a gas into a liquid. In order to be able to use the kinetic formula also at higher pressures, when the distance between the molecules becomes less and less, it ought to be observed, according to Van der Waals, that the molecules themselves occupy an appreciable part of the volume. In the formulae the volume ought therefore to be decreased by the total volume of the molecules, since only the remaining space is available for the motion of the molecules. Furthermore, the attraction exerted by the molecules on one another had not previously been taken into account. With a great increase in the external pressure which brings the molecules very close to one another, this attraction must be appreciable and must have the same effect as an increase in the external pressure. From this approach Van der Waals set up a 'law of corresponding states', and this tallied in its main features with the observations on the gaseous and liquid phases of a homogeneous substance. The deviations were partly due to the unavoidable simplifying assumptions. Van der Waals pointed out especially that the volume occupied by the molecules themselves is not quite independent of the pressure. In many cases deviations were also caused by the presence of more than one type of molecule. In connection with these investigations Van der Waals set forth certain general theorems for the relation between a gas and a liquid applicable to different substances, which became of great value for further research.

VAN DER WAALS was awarded the *1910* prize 'for his work concerning the equation of state of gases and liquids'.

Investigations made at very low temperatures proved to be the line of research which led to the most fruitful results in this field. The problem of producing low temperatures is intimately connected with the question of condensing gases into liquids. In this sphere, too, Faraday had carried out important pioneer work [1823, 1845]. By 1877, thanks to his work and that of others, all the known gases had been liquefied, with the exception of six [among them oxygen, hydrogen and nitrogen] which were therefore characterized as 'permanent' gases. However, after Wroblewski and Olszewski of Cracow had found a device in 1883 for producing liquid oxygen in large quantities, and Linde of Germany and Hampson of England had introduced a new method in 1895, based on the so-called Joule-Kelvin effect, of producing liquid air on an industrial scale, Dewar finally succeeded in condensing hydrogen in 1898. Thus, in successive stages, temperatures down to —259° had been reached. Liquid hydrogen boils at —253°, and at a pressure of 55 mm of mercury it freezes to a solid with melting point —259°. The leading role in this field was now taken over by the Dutch physicist HEIKE KAMERLINGH ONNES [1853-1926]. He had already started experimental work on the state of matter at low temperatures in the 1880's, largely guided by the theories of Van der Waals. Gradually he built up a low-temperature research laboratory in Leyden, where equipment was available for experimental work at a series of low temperatures; with methyl chloride —90°, with ethylene —145°, with oxygen —183°, and finally with hydrogen down to —253°.

In order to get nearer to the absolute zero point, —273°, Kamerlingh Onnes started a thorough study of the newly discovered inert gas, helium, and finally succeeded in condensing it into liquid form in 1908. In this way it was possible to reach *absolute temperatures* between 4.3° and 1.15°. For our knowledge of matter this turned out to be a most important result. Comprehensive investigations into different phenomena at these extremely low temperatures were carried out in Kamerlingh Onnes's cryogenic laboratory during the immediately following years, partly by himself and his co-workers, partly by a large number of specialists in different fields who visited his institute to study various physical and technical problems at such temperatures. A number of sensational and important results were obtained. One of the most remarkable was the discovery that the electric properties of certain metals, among them mercury, are changed completely and in a discontinuous manner. At such low temperatures the electric resistance suddenly drops to less than a thousand-millionth of its ordinary value. The metal becomes what is called 'super-conductive'. This implies, e.g., that an electric current generated in a loop of the cooled metal continues to flow in the conductor for hours without losing its strength appreciably.

KAMERLINGH ONNES was awarded the *1913* Nobel Prize 'for his investigations into the properties of matter at low temperatures which led, amongst other things, to the production of liquid helium.'

Ever since Kamerlingh Onnes succeeded in condensing helium, the interesting phenomena which arise at extremely low temperatures have been the main theme of research at several of the world's most famous laboratories. One of the scientists who made eminent contributions was the Russian, Peter Kapitza. Among other things, he studied the remarkable change which occurs in condensed liquid helium when it is still further cooled from 4 °C to about 2 °C. At this temperature the liquid helium suddenly becomes unlike anything so far discovered; its mobility becomes wholly abnormal. The liquid moves with ease through tubes and capillaries, precisely as if there were no obstacle at all. Strange fountain effects of a seemingly paradoxical nature can also be observed. LEO DAVIDOVIC LANDAU [1908-1968], who had been working with Kapitza since 1937, succeeded in getting a new and original grasp on these phenomena when he applied the modern quantum theory to the entire movement of the liquid, and not merely to the movement of the atoms, as other scientists had done. Landau took as his starting point the state of the liquid at absolute zero, and the movement found certain fictive particles, so-called quasi-particles, characteristic of its excited, viz. higher state. In this way Landau was able to achieve agreement with experimental results. In this connexion he also succeeded in discovering that, in liquid helium, besides ordinary sound-waves, a so-called second sound can occur. Helium consists of two different isotopes, one, by far the most common, with a mass of 4, and one with a mass of 3. The latter variant, helium 3, can also be condensed, and turns out to have quite different qualities from helium 4. Landau's theory was successful in explaining the characteristics of this liquid, too, and furthermore predicted a new type of wave-movement, which he called zero sound.

LANDAU was awarded the *1962* Nobel Prize 'for his pioneering theories for condensed matter, especially liquid helium'.

The actual existence of atoms and molecules, though it had already received strong support through the above-mentioned investigations into the gaseous state and through the successful applications of the kinetic theory of gases, was still looked upon with scepticism in some quarters. A series of investigations concerning a phenomenon generally called the 'Brownian movement' led, however, to a change in attitude among these doubters. The British botanist, Robert Brown [1827], had observed in the microscope that small grains of pollen, suspended in a liquid, are always in a state of slow, irregular motion. The phenomenon is very often encountered in Nature; wherever there are particles of sufficiently small dimensions, microscopical or 'ultra-microscopical', they will exhibit Brownian movements. The explanation is simple on the basis of the kinetic theory of gases. When the molecules of the liquid or gas surrounding the particle knock against it, the collisions combine to set the minute particle in motion. Owing to the chance distribution and force of the blows received by the particle, the motion is very irregular. Since the number of collisions is very large, however, one can treat the problem statistically, and a mathematical theory for the Brownian movement was advanced by Einstein in 1905. His theory was investigated experimentally and fully confirmed by observation. Of special importance was the fact that with the aid of Einstein's theory a value for the number of molecules in a given mass of liquid could be computed from certain measurements. For these determinations the French physicist, JEAN PERRIN [1870-1942], used microscopic particles of gamboge suspended in water and prepared in such a manner that they were of known uniform size. The value obtained for the number of molecules agreed, as expected, with values obtained by entirely different methods in connection with other phenomena. Perrin was also able to obtain a value of the same quantity studying the distribution of the gamboge particles in the vertical direction in the water container. In spite of the effect of gravity on the particles, they do not fall down to the bottom of the vessel when they are of microscopic dimensions, but remain suspended with concentration decreasing upwards. The number of molecules determined on the basis of this sedimentation equilibrium was in agreement with that obtained in other ways.

PERRIN received the *1926* prize 'for his work concerning the discontinuous structure of matter, and especially for his discovery of the equilibrium of sedimentation'.

Attention has been drawn to the results gained from the study of the state of matter at extremely low temperatures and to the new phenomena revealed by such investigations. This work also led to research on the behaviour of gases under *high pressure,* but such investigations presented considerable technical difficulties. The highest constant pressure attained at the turn of the century was 3,000 kg per square centimetre. In this field PERCY WILLIAMS BRIDGMAN [1882-1961], of Harvard, introduced new methods with the aid of which he carried out work of an epoch-making nature. In successive steps Bridgman raised the pressure limit first to 100,000 kg per cm^2 and subsequently up to 500,000 kg per cm^2 by using double high-pressure vessels made from special alloys. Among the numerous sensational results of Bridgman's researches concerning the behaviour of matter under very high pressures may be mentioned his discoveries of new modifications of various substances. Thus, for example, he found that phosphorus can exist in a form previously unknown, the so-called black phosphorus. Water in solid form proved to be a far from simple substance – no less than six different modifications of ice were detected. Bridgman also studied the effect of high pressures on the electric properties of metals, on the viscosity of liquids, and on the heat conduction of gases, all problems of the very greatest technical importance.

In *1946* BRIDGMAN was awarded the prize 'for the invention of apparatus for achieving extremely high pressures, and for the discoveries he made therewith in the domain of the physics of high pressures'.

THE QUANTUM NATURE OF ENERGY

The epoch-making experimental discoveries which set their stamp on physical research at the turn of the century and opened up entirely new fields were followed after the first decade by an extremely remarkable phase of development in our understanding of the processes of Nature. An atomic structure had been found both for matter and for electricity. But for energy, another of the primary constituents of physical reality, the fundamental laws of thermodynamics appeared to give all that was desired. Their validity and general applicability had been tested on a multitude of different problems, physical, chemical and technical. Nevertheless, investigations of one of the basic problems in the conversion of energy, viz. radiation of heat, led to results that could not be deduced from these laws.

Heat radiation is one of our most common place experiences and naturally it had long engaged the attention of physicists. Stefan in 1879 had found experimentally a simple relation between the amount of heat radiating from a body and the temperature of the latter; according to this law, the amount of energy radiated per unit of time is proportional to the fourth power of the absolute temperature, and this result was derived theoretically by Boltzmann in 1884. It had also become clear that heat rays are of the same nature as light rays, although as a rule they have considerably greater wave-lengths than the latter.

Using the laws of thermodynamics, the German scientist, WILHELM WIEN [1864-1928], in 1893 deduced a further important law for heat radiation. It is well known that with rising temperature an iron rod, for instance, passes from a red glow to a white glow. The heat radiation emitted by a hot body is composed of rays covering a long range of wave-lengths; it has what is called a 'spectral distribution' with a maximum intensity at a certain wave-length. From the simple observation just mentioned, it is obvious that with rising temperature the portion of the spectrum having this maximum intensity is displaced towards shorter wave-lengths in the spectrum. The quantitative expression for the displacement is known as 'Wien's displacement law'. Since the position of the maximum is easily determined experimentally, the law affords a possibility of calculating the temperature of a radiating body from such a determination.

As stated above, Wien deduced his law from thermodynamical considerations. He verified it by measurements in the laboratory, and could then use it for calculating, for instance, the temperature of the sun from observations of the spectral composition of its radiation. Together with Stefan's law, Wien's displacement law forms the foundation of our knowledge of heat radiation. It should be pointed out, however, that, strictly speaking, these laws hold only under ideal conditions, viz., when the body neither reflects nor transmits incoming radiation. Not even a sooted surface entirely satisfies the first of these conditions. The experimental procedure is, therefore, to observe the radiation emitted from a small opening in a furnace the temperature of which can be regulated and measured.

The two laws thus found afforded no information, however, as to how the energy in the radiation is distributed over the different wave-lengths comprised in the radiation. The problem of finding this distribution now called for a solution. In 1894 Wien and Lord Rayleigh, using different modes of approach, each deduced a formula closely agreeing with the observations. Wien's formula indicated correctly the distribution for the short wave-lengths, while Lord Rayleigh's gave good agreement in the long-wave range.

It was in attempting to find the correct formula for the energy distribution over the whole range of wave-lengths that MAX PLANCK [1858-1947] put forward his revolutionizing hypothesis of *radiation quanta.* According to this theory, the radiation is emitted or absorbed in definite quanta, the energy of which has a different magnitude for different wave-lengths. If the amount of energy is assumed to be proportional to the frequency of the light ray in question, the statistical calculation leads to a formula which agrees completely with the observations. The numerical factor defined as the ratio between the energy and the frequency of a radiation quantum, which Planck introduced in his hypothesis, is usually referred to as Planck's constant and is denoted by the letter h.

Planck's theory thus gave the correct law for heat radiation, embodying both Stefan's law and Wien's displacement law. Not only had this long-sought goal been reached, but the importance of Planck's hypothesis extended far beyond this special problem. Is transformed our whole concept of energy.

In addition to the derivation of the law of radiation, Planck's hypothesis, extended in some respects by ALBERT EINSTEIN [1879-1955], was shown by the latter to give a quantitatively correct interpretation of several physical phenomena, among them the so-called photoelectric effect. This phenomenon is observed when a ray of light strikes, for example, a metal surface. If the frequency of the light exceeds a certain minimum, electrons are released from the surface, and above the latter frequency the *velocity* with which the released electrons leave the surface increases as the frequency increases. The law which Einstein deduced for this effect gave the relation between these various magnitudes with Planck's constant entering as the basic factor. ROBERT ANDREWS MILLIKAN [1868-1953] in 1914 carried out a very exhaustive experimental test of the law with a view to arriving at an exact value for Planck's constant. The value obtained agreed exactly with that computed by Planck from heat radiation. Einstein proved further that Planck's hypothesis could be used for interpreting a number of other phenomena in different fields of physics and chemistry. Among other things it enabled him to deduce a formula for the specific heat of solids, on the whole in good agreement with the measurements. The characteristic feature of all these phenomena was the fact that Planck's constant recurred in all of them with the same value. This constituted the most convincing proof that with his hypothesis Planck had found a basic and universal property of energy.

WIEN received the *1911* prize 'for his discoveries regarding the laws governing the radiation of heat', and PLANCK that for *1918* 'in recognition of the services rendered by him to the development of physics by his discovery of the elementary quanta'.

In 1922 EINSTEIN was awarded the *1921* prize 'for his services to theoretical physics, and especially for his discovery of the law of the photoelectric effect', and finally MILLIKAN received the *1923* prize 'for his work on the elementary charge of electricity and on the photoelectric effect'.

The German physicists JAMES FRANCK [b. 1882] and GUSTAV HERTZ [b. 1887, a nephew of the previously mentioned H. Hertz] carried out an investigation of great importance for the experimental verification of Planck's quantum theory. These two scientists found that an electron of known velocity, when shot at an atom of a gas, does not cause it to emit light until the velocity of the electron has reached a certain minimum value. Thus a very elementary process is involved here. An electron with a certain critical velocity or energy releases a light wave whose frequency can be accurately measured. The result of the measurements showed that the minimum energy of the electron equals the product of Planck's constant and the frequency of the light ray. Or, formulated in another way: from the two quantities directly observed, viz. the energy of the electron and the frequency of the light, one finds, upon dividing the former by the latter, a numerical constant having exactly the same value as the constant postulated by Planck in his theory of heat radiation.

FRANCK and HERTZ shared the *1925* prize 'for their discovery of the laws governing the impact of an electron upon an atom'.

THE QUANTIZED ATOMIC MODEL

Thus from different fields of physics an overwhelming body of evidence in support of Planck's quantum theory had been assembled. The most brilliant application and at the same time the strongest confirmation of the new idea was furnished, however, by the atomic theory propounded by the Danish physicist NIELS BOHR [b.1885]. This theory laid an entirely new foundation for our understanding of the processes within the world of matter. Apart from the quantum theory, the atom model proposed by Ernest Rutherford served as the point of departure for Bohr's theory of the atom. From his experiments on the scattering of alpha particles when passing through very thin foils, Rutherford concluded that the atom contains an inner positively charged nucleus of very small dimensions compared with the whole volume of the atom. He estimated the diameter of the nucleus at a hundred-thousandth part of that of the atom. In spite of this it must be presumed that the greater part of the mass of the atom is concentrated in the nucleus. In the residual space of the atom outside the nucleus, electrons are to be found whose total negative charge equals the positive charge of the nucleus so that the atom as a whole is electrically neutral. The simplest of all atoms, that of hydrogen, contains only one electron circling around the minute nucleus, the *proton,* which has a single positive charge and a mass which is about 1840 times that of the electron.

As mentioned in the introduction, very comprehensive and exact measurements of the spectra of the various elements were available. Rydberg had shown that in the spectra of the different elements there occur analogous series of spectral lines and that these could be expressed by a simple formula containing a constant, the same for all series, known as *Rydberg's constant.*

These facts form the background to Bohr's extraordinary contribution in this field. The classical theories had been unable to give any interpretation of the large amount of empirical data concerning the radiation of light from the atom which had been collected. Bohr based his theory on two postulates, both of which were in sharp conflict with the prevailing ideas on electromagnetic phenomena. The first of these asserts that among the orbits of the electrons in an atomic system which are possible on the basis of the classical laws of mechanics there are a number of *stationary states.* Every lasting change in the motion of the atomic system involves a transition from one of these stationary states to another. According to the second postulate, when such a transition takes place, an electromagnetic radiation is emitted with a frequency completely determined by the difference in energy between the two states, the ratio between the energy difference and the frequency being equal to Planck's constant.

How violently these postulates conflicted with the then current concepts can be made clear on two points. According to Maxwell's electromagnetic theory, the motion of the electron along a circle in the simplest stationary case should lead to a steady radiation with a continuous loss of energy and, furthermore, the electromagnetic waves should be emitted with a frequency agreeing with that of the oscillator. But in Bohr's second postulate there is no direct connection between the rotation frequency of the electron and the frequency of the emitted radiation, since the latter is determined solely by the energy difference between the two states of motion.

Thus Bohr's theory implies that the conditions in the atom require essential departures from the laws governing ordinary phenomena.

Already in his first communication of 1913, Bohr showed that, with his assumptions, the theory covered the experimental facts concerning the light emission of atoms to a great extent. Among other things – and this was a very strong support for the theory – Bohr could deduce Rydberg's constant from known elementary natural constants, namely the charge and the mass of the electron and Planck's constant. Still more convincing evidence for the correctness of Bohr's theory was afforded when in 1915 Sommerfeld extended the discussion to more complicated systems. Using the relation between mass and velocity indicated by Einstein's theory of relativity, he was able to explain the fine structure of certain spectral lines which are observable only with spectroscopic instruments of the highest resolving power.

In the further development of his theory, Bohr found a very fruitful method – 'the correspondence principle' – for utilizing to some extent the concepts of the classical doctrine in order to deduce and interpret results according to the new theory. Thus a quantum-theoretical interpretation could be given of the Zeeman effect, and this agreed with the previously mentioned explanation of the phenomenon which had been suggested by Lorentz on the basis of the classical theory. Even the Stark effect, which could not be fitted into the earlier theories, now received a satisfactory interpretation. After Bohr's theory of the atom had shown its usefulness, it became for a time the lodestar of atomic research and was an essential prerequisite for the magnificent advance in this field of physics.

BOHR was awarded the *1922* prize 'for his services in the investigation of the structure of atoms, and of the radiation emanating from them.'

X-RAYS IN ATOMIC RESEARCH

Shortly after the advent of the quantum theory, while its applicability to different problems of physics and chemistry was being tested in many quarters, an experimental discovery of far-reaching importance was made, which was to form the starting-point for subsequent attempts to elucidate the structure of the atoms with the aid of the quantum theory. Since Röntgen's discovery no noteworthy advance had been made in our knowledge of the nature and origin of X-radiation. Medical requirements had, it is true, led to the construction of more effective X-ray tubes which proved helpful also for research purposes. But all the experiments carried out with the object of settling the old dispute as to whether X-rays were particle radiations or whether they consisted of electromagnetic waves, had not yielded any definite results. As the rays are emitted from the place in the vacuum tube where the cathode rays are stopped, and as J. J. Thomson had shown that the latter consist of electrons, it was possible, in accordance with Maxwell's theory, to explain the X-rays as an electric impulse caused by the sudden checking of the electrons. In this way it was also possible to estimate the length of the impulse wave, and a value of about one-tenth of the diameter of the atom was obtained.

Direct attempts to discover interference phenomena of the type that had long been studied in light waves, and which even Röntgen had tried in vain to find, had led only to very uncertain results. It was then understandable that, as late as 1912, prominent physicists still maintained that the X-rays were of a corpuscular nature.

The whole question was suddenly decided by a brilliant experiment suggested by MAX VON LAUE [1879-1960], then working at the University of Munich where Röntgen was director of the physical laboratory. At the request of Röntgen's colleague in theoretical physics, A. Sommerfeld, a versatile and exceptionally productive scientist, Laue had written the article 'Wellenoptik' for the *Enzyklopädie der mathematischen Wissenschaften* and had thus been led to study the theory of the diffraction of light waves in ordinary gratings and in crossed gratings. One of Sommerfeld's pupils, P. P. Ewald, later one of the most famous workers in this field, had been assigned the task of giving a mathematical treatment of the behaviour of Hertzian waves when passing through a space-lattice. This led von Laue to pose the question whether X-rays – assuming that they were electric waves of the expected wave-length – might give rise to interference phenomena in the space-lattices found in Nature, namely in crystals. According to the traditional view, the atoms in crystals lie regularly arranged in layers, and the distance between adjacent atoms was estimated on good grounds to be of the order of magnitude of some ten-millionths of one mm. Such a distance would have the right relation to the supposed wave-length of the X-rays for the production of interference phenomena.

W. Friedrich in Röntgen's laboratory, who had done work with X-rays, offered to test von Laue's idea experimentally. Remarkably enough, Röntgen himself was very sceptical about and uninterested in the planned experiments, clearly on account of the many vain attempts which had already been made to prove interference in the case of X-rays.

The experiments which Friedrich carried out together with Knipping gave indications of a positive effect. In this case a copper sulphate crystal had been placed in a narrow beam of X-rays without being oriented with respect to the direction of the ray. On a photographic plate, placed behind the crystal and at a distance from it, there appeared after development, apart from a blackened dot where the direct ray had struck the plate, also a number of irregularly distributed spots. The latter were manifestly due to the ray having been split up into several beams as a result of interference in the crystal. In further similar exposures, but with the axes of the crystal oriented in the direction of the rays, regularly arranged spots appeared. Their position could be related to the geometrical properties of the crystal grating.

This discovery proved both that the X-rays are of the same nature as light, i.e. of a wave nature, and that their wave-length, at any rate under the experimental conditions used, is only about one ten-thousandth part of that of visible light. At the same time, support was obtained for the correctness of the view of crystal structure as a space-lattice, a theory which had already been put forward, but rather as an idealized picture than as a concrete reality.

VON LAUE was awarded the *1914* prize 'for his discovery of the diffraction of Röntgen rays by crystals'.

Thanks to von Laue's discovery, the wave nature of X-rays and the order of magnitude of their wave-length had thus been established. The photographic interference pictures taken by Friedrich and Knipping with crystals were difficult to interpret in detail. The problem was taken up in several quarters, but it was mainly through the work of WILLIAM HENRY BRAGG [1862-1942] and WILLIAM LAWRENCE BRAGG [1890-1971] that the phenomenon was quantitatively elucidated and turned to account. They found a simplified interpretation of the interference pictures which, although it agreed with von Laue's space-lattice theory, presented advantages greatly contributing to the rapid development in this field. According to W. L. Bragg, the X-rays are reflected from certain definite planes in the crystal, in accordance with the normal law of reflection, with equal angles of incidence and of reflection. Such planes are, for instance, the naturally formed surfaces in crystals, but also any plane laid through the regularly arranged atoms in the space-lattice. However, for reflection to take place, co-operation is required among a number of such 'atom planes' parallel to one another. The distance between these planes determines the angle at which reflection can take place for a definite wave-length of the X-rays. This simple relation, usually known as *Bragg's law,* rendered possible a direct measurement of the wave-lengths of the X-rays by determining the angles, on the assumption that the distances between the atoms had been computed in another way. For crystals of simple structure, such as common salt, these distances could be calculated from previously known data.

Two ways were now open for further research. On the one hand, the X-rays could be used as an aid in the study of the structure of solids and, especially, crystals, i.e., of how the different kinds of atoms are placed in the regular patterns forming the crystal lattices. On the other hand, by using some suitable crystal, the X-rays, their wave-lengths and composition under different conditions of emission could be investigated, and thus attempts be made to find out how they are generated.

The first of these tasks was tackled primarily by the two Braggs, father and son. Instead of the photographic methods employed by Friedrich and Knipping, the Braggs used a method of electric registration, based upon the property of X-rays to make the air conducting. With such an arrangement, a so-called 'ionization chamber', data could also be obtained of the relative strength of the reflected rays, a factor of decisive importance for gaining information from the measurements as to the structure of the crystals. Thanks to the pioneer work of the Braggs, the structure of a large number of simple substances was elucidated, and a firm foundation was laid for further research in this field, which soon resulted in a detailed knowledge of the structure of solids.

W. H. BRAGG and W. L. BRAGG received the *1915* prize 'for their services in the analysis of crystal structure by means of X-rays'.

The other field of investigation opened by von Laue's fundamental discovery was, as already mentioned, the study of the X-rays themselves, their conditions of emission and the connection of the latter with other phenomena of radiation. With the methods available for the study of X-rays before von Laue's discovery, CHARLES GLOVER BARKLA [1877-1944] had found a number of characteristic properties of the radiation emitted by a substance when it is irradiated with X-rays. He had observed that, in its turn, the irradiated substance emits 'secondary X-rays', of which there are two kinds. One of them completely conforms in character, i.e. absorption qualities, with the incoming 'primary' radiation. On the other hand, the second kind proved always to be of the same character for a given element, irrespective of the penetrating power of the primary radiation and of the form or the chemical state of the element. Thus every element emitted its own well-defined X-radiation, and Barkla therefore called it the *characteristic radiation* of the element in question. Further, by determining the degree of absorption of these rays, for instance, in aluminium, he found that the absorption of the characteristic radiation decreases step by step with rising atomic weight without showing the well-known periodicity governing the chemical properties of the elements. Barkla also discovered that the elements exhibited two characteristic rays with a fairly great difference in penetrating power.

As had already been mentioned, these results of Barkla's had been obtained some years before von Laue's discovery, thus before the nature of X-rays was clear. In some respects Barkla's observations argued in favour of the wave concept. At that time no explanation could be given of the origin of the characteristic radiation or of its connection with other atomic properties. The value of Barkla's pioneer work had already shown itself in the investigations of the Braggs which called for strong rays of a wave-length giving appropriate penetrating power. Barkla's measurements suggested that an element of atomic weight about 100, i.e. palladium or rhodium, ought to have a characteristic radiation with the desired properties, and this proved to be the case. As a result of systematic research, it was found that these characteristic rays had well-defined wave-lengths, of the same character as the monochromatic rays of ordinary light, the spectral lines. Hence these X-rays were used in the investigations of the structure of solids or crystals mentioned above, the elements in question, rhodium, palladium, copper, etc., being placed in the X-ray tube so that they were directly hit by the cathode rays, causing the characteristic radiation to be emitted. The great importance of Barkla's result concerning the characteristic X-radiation of the elements showed itself, however, chiefly in further researches with the new and exact methods of studying X-rays evolved on the basis of von Laue's discovery.

In 1918 BARKLA was awarded the *1917* prize 'for his discovery of the characteristic Röntgen radiation of the elements'.

It has already been mentioned that, using the law indicated by them the Braggs determined the wave-lengths of some of the characteristic rays found by Barkla. In many quarters the study of these 'X-ray spectra' of the elements was now taken up, and the photographic method of registration proved to be more suitable than the rather time-consuming electric measurements. The investigations carried out by Maurice de Broglie at Paris and H. G. J. Moseley at Cambridge were of special importance for the advance in this field. The former introduced an elegant method in which, by turning the reflecting crystal, a very large range of wave-lengths could be registered on the same photographic plate. In this connection he also found, apart from the complicated structure of some of Barkla's characteristic radiation, a sharply marked absorption for certain definite wave-lengths which was ascribed to the elements found in the photographic emulsion layer. These 'absorption spectra' actually correspond to certain observations made by Barkla concerning the absorption conditions of X-rays in various substances and afford direct information as to the atomic structure of the elements involved, as was shown by the interpretation given later.

The investigations which the young scientist, Moseley, published in 1913-14 attracted the greatest interest. One of the most brilliant careers in physical research was prematurely brought to an end when he fell in the Gallipoli campaign of 1915 during the First World War.

Moseley was the first to use the new methods for a systematic study of the characteristic radiation of the various elements. Following this radiation from one element to the other in the periodic table, i.e., essentially in the order indicated by their atomic weights, he found for several groups of elements that it obeys an extremely simple law. On the basis of the Rutherford–Bohr theory of the atom it now became possible to localize the source of the X-radiations emitted by the elements. While the ordinary spectra of the elements are emitted by electrons moving in the outer electron shell of the atom, the X-rays on the other hand originate from rearrangements of electrons in the inner shells. This interpretation immediately makes it clear why the ordinary spectra show an intimate connection with the chemical properties of the elements, which are also determined by the more or less free electrons in the outer shell of the atom, while the X-ray spectra show no trace of the periodic changes appearing in the chemical properties of the elements.

After it had thus become clear, thanks to Moseley's prematurely interrupted work, that a study of X-ray spectra might throw light on the energy conditions of the atoms as far as the electron shells are concerned, it became an urgent matter to develop further the methods of investigating the X-radiation of the elements. Here the aim was partly to achieve such accuracy in the measurements that a reliable quantitative analysis could be made, and partly to attain a complete registration of all components of the radiation. For the latter purpose one needed measuring and registering instruments capable of recording both the more penetrating radiation and the part which is readily absorbed by ordinary air.

With the aid of the new methods developed by the Swedish physicist MANNE SIEGBAHN [b.1886], and the instruments designed for this purpose, a large number of new series within the characteristic X-radiations of the elements were discovered. At the same time the absorption of the X-radiation of the various elements was determined. The 'X-ray absorption spectra' thus obtained exhibited a relatively simple structure: for the lowest energy level *one* characteristic energy value, for the next *three,* for the following one *five,* etc. Combining the exact values of the measurements for emission and absorption spectra of the elements, detailed quantitative information was obtained, firstly of the structure of the electron shell of the atom, and secondly concerning the laws governing the changes of energy in the latter which cause the emission of the radiation. The investigations showed how successive electron shells are added in passing from the lighter elements to the heavier ones, and the measurements gave exact energy levels for the different shells. From the empirical data it was possible to establish with great accuracy how many electrons enter into the different shells of the various elements. By employing quantum-theoretical considerations, some simple laws were found, which proved to be generally valid. These laws concerned, firstly, the rules governing the transition of electrons from one configuration to another, and, secondly, the number of electrons which could be accommodated in each shell for a given configuration.

With the accuracy required and attained for these measurements by the new methods, it was found that the above-mentioned reflection law of the Braggs called for a refinement in view of the previously unobserved diffraction of X-rays when passing through the surface of the crystal.

By way of summary it may be said that the new precision technique for the study of X-ray spectra led to a practically complete knowledge of the energy and radiation conditions in the electron shells of the atoms. At the same time a solid empirical foundation had been created for the quantum-theoretical interpretation of attendant phenomena.

In *1924* the prize was awarded to SIEGBAHN 'for his discoveries and investigations in X-ray spectroscopy'.

The study of X-rays, which in so many respects widened our knowledge of the structure and properties of matter, also contributed towards the understanding of radiation. Planck's hypothesis, mentioned above, concerning the existence of radiation quanta of fixed magnitude for a given wave-length, received elegant and very clear confirmation through experiments carried out in 1923 by the American ARTHUR HOLLY COMPTON [1892-1954]. While in the case of earlier studies of the validity of this hypothesis, the experiments had dealt with ordinary light, experiments with X-rays involved a testing of the hypothesis within an entirely new energy range, where the magnitudes of the radiation quanta are 10,000 to 100,000 times as large as those in the range of ordinary light.

The immediate purpose of Compton's investigations was to clear up the scattering of X-rays in matter. He then made the remarkable discovery that an incident 'monochromatic' X-ray gives rise to a secondary ray with a somewhat greater wave-length, and that the change in wave-length is greater the more the direction of the outgoing ray deviates from that of the incident ray. According to Planck's quantum hypothesis, this of course implies that the energy of the outgoing ray is less than that of the incident ray. According to the law of conservation of energy, it must be expected that the surplus energy is to be found elsewhere. Actually this energy is absorbed by an electron emitted during the same process. This could be proved by the English physicist CHARLES THOMSON REES WILSON [1869-1959] by a method which he had indicated a long time previously for making visible tracks of the trajectories of electrically charged particles. The method, which has been of immense importance for research, is based on a very simple principle. Along its path in a gas an electrically charged particle, on colliding with the gas molecules, causes the latter to split up into negatively and positively charged ions. If the gas is enclosed in a vessel [the 'Wilson cloud chamber'] saturated with water vapour, and suddenly expanded, the fall in the temperature results in a condensation of water vapour on the ions which act as nuclei for the formation of small drops. Strong illumination reveals the drop formations along the track of the particle.

Exhaustive investigations by this method enabled Compton to show that the phenomenon he observed can be quantitatively explained on the assumption that an incident radiation quantum, a 'photon', is transformed into a new photon with less energy and a different direction, and that at the same time an electron receives the surplus energy in the form of a velocity component in a direction determined by the law of conservation of momentum. This simple mechanical explanation proved to agree with the formulae derived from the later developed wave mechanics.

COMPTON received one-half of the *1927* prize 'for his discovery of the effect named after him', the other half being awarded to WILSON 'for his discovery of the method of making the paths of electrically charged particles visible by condensation of vapour'.

Compton's discovery of the change in wave-length when X-rays are scattered in matter gave rise to an extremely important observation relating to the scattering of ordinary light. One effect of this phenomenon belongs to our everyday experiences. The blue colour of the sky is a result of the scattering of sunlight and is due to the fact that in the atmosphere the shorter wave-lengths, the blue light, are more strongly scattered towards the sides than the long-wave red rays. The red colouring of the sunset is the complementary phenomenon, due to the blue rays being deflected in the intervening layers of the atmosphere, so that the remaining light becomes relatively more abundant in red rays.

In experiments on the phenomena connected with the scattering of light in different substances, the Indian physicist, Sir CHANDRASEKHARA VENKATA RAMAN [b.1888], found that the relevant theory put forward by Lord Rayleigh and other workers did not seem fully to agree with actual observations.

In Raman's investigations on the scattering in both solid, liquid and gaseous substances, phenomena appeared which could not be interpreted by the existing theories based on classical physics. According to these theories, it was to be expected that the scattered light should have the same colour or, more precisely, the same wave-length as the incident light. This seemed not to be the case however, as was shown by experiments with colour filters, even though the observations were somewhat uncertain owing to the extreme faintness of the scattered light.

With improved instrumental aids which rendered possible a considerable increase in the brightness so that direct photographs of the colour composition of the scattered light could be made, Raman and Krishnan found that, when scattered, a monochromatic ray in the incident light is split up into a number of components with wave-lengths greater or smaller than that of the original light. The interpretation of this phenomenon, which is called the Raman effect after its discoverer, could be given – at any rate as far as the essential features were concerned – by the then accepted form of the quantum theory. An incident light quantum, upon meeting a molecule, may either absorb the same energy quantum as that emitted by the molecule itself when passing from one possible energy state to another, or it may yield up part of its energy to the molecule, in which case the latter can only absorb energy quanta of a magnitude determined by the fixed proper energy states of the molecule. Hence a study of the components in the Raman effect affords direct information on the different energy states of the scattering molecule, and in many cases this is the simplest method of determining the energy levels of molecules.

RAMAN was awarded the *1930* prize 'for his work on the scattering of light and for the discovery of the effect named after him'.

PHYSICS AND TECHNOLOGY

In *1912* the Academy of Sciences awarded the Nobel Prize for Physics for a brilliant Swedish invention based on the difference in the heat radiation from a reflecting body and that from a blackened one. GUSTAF DALÉN [1869-1937] took advantage of this phenomenon for the construction of an automatic 'sun valve' which could be used, for example, for beacons, to turn off or to open the supply of gas to the light source in daylight or darkness respectively. The regulating device consisted of one blackened and three polished parallel bars which, owing to their different heat radiation properties, undergo varying changes in length due to the irradiation. The valve is then affected in the desired manner by means of a lever. By combining these valves with improved gas accumulators, Dalén constructed new types of beacons and buoys which functioned automatically and needed only occasional supervision. They were rapidly introduced all over the world and became of immense importance to navigation.

DALÉN received the *1912* prize 'for his invention of automatic regulators to be used in conjunction with gas accumulators for lighting beacons and light buoys'.

Physical measurements are very often based upon exact determinations of lengths or of angles, and in the former case it is usually necessary to refer the measurement to the international unit of length, the standard metre kept in the Pavillon de Breteuil in Paris. For measurements calling for the highest precision, the change with temperature of the metre scale employed must be taken into account, and this often involves an element of uncertainty. An immense advance for precision physics was therefore attained when, after many years of research entailing the systematic production of a large number of metal alloys, in particular nickel steels, the Swiss-French physicist, CHARLES ÉDOUARD GUILLAUME [1861-1938], succeeded in finding a material which, practically speaking, did not change its length within reasonable temperature limits. This nickel steel alloy, which contains 35.6 per cent of nickel, Guillaume called *invar.* Apart from its great value for measurement technique, especially in physics and geodesy, where it was of revolutionary importance, this alloy has also been widely used in precision instruments where independence of temperature is an essential factor. Guillaume later produced another alloy, called *elinvar,* with the important property of not changing its elasticity within a wide temperature range. By systematic investigations, he was also able to indicate suitable alloys for a number of different purposes. The practical importance of these is very far-reaching. As an example it may be mentioned that several millions of watches of a precision type are manufactured annually with parts made of these steel alloys. In the incandescent light bulb industry they replaced the expensive platinum for lead-in wires, a saving calculated at that time to amount to twenty million francs annually.

GUILLAUME was awarded the *1920* prize 'in recognition of the service he has rendered to precision physics by his discovery of anomalies in nickel steel alloys'.

The prominent French physicist GABRIEL LIPPMANN [1845-1921] attempted to utilize the interference of light for producing photographs in natural colours. Suppose that a mirror is placed in contact with the light-sensitive emulsion of a photographic plate. If light strikes the plate on the glass side, reflection in the mirror gives rise to standing waves in the emulsion. When the plate is developed, the precipitation of the grains of silver will show a stratification corresponding to the different wavelengths of the light. When the plate is looked at in a mirror, the picture will consequently be reproduced in its right colours. This idea, incidentally, had been tried earlier by Wiener [1890] in an attempt to find in it a confirmation of the wave theory of light. After many years of experimenting Lippmann succeeded in producing extremely beautiful colour photographs by this method. As is well known, the technique of colour photography has, however, progressed along other lines, chiefly because Lippmann's method required too long an exposure to be used in practice.

LIPPMANN was awarded the prize in *1908* 'for his method, based on the interference phenomenon, for reproducing colours photographically'. He concluded his Nobel lecture with the significant sentences: 'Perhaps progress will continue. Life is short and progress is slow.'

The microscope is one of the most important optical instruments with a very wide application in many branches of the natural, biological and medical sciences. The classical theory of the microscope, given by Ernst Abbe at the end of the last century, was for a long time considered as the final solution of the problems connected with the formation of the image and the limits of the power of resolution of the microscope. It was therefore a surprising event when professor FREDERIK ZERNIKE in Groningen was able to show that this theory needed a complement, which also had an important bearing on the practical use of the microscope. Abbe had, in his study of the formation of an image, considered an object consisting of fine transparent lines separated by dark lines. Zernike pointed out that an object where the alternating lines were *equally transparent* but did show a difference in refractive index, could under suitable conditions, be made visible under a microscope. The method to obtain images of such objects is called the 'phase-contrast method'. The technical method to do this depends on the difference in phases between the light waves which have passed through different parts of the object. In this *phase-contrast method* a specially formed 'phase-plate' is introduced into the microscope.

The phase-microscope has an extensive application especially for biological purposes. However, the phase-contrast method has also been used in other connections – e.g. for correcting errors in lenses or mirrors where highest accuracy is needed.

ZERNIKE was awarded the *1953* prize 'for his demonstration of the phase-contrast method, especially for his invention of the phase-contrast microscope'.

WAVES AS QUANTA – PARTICLES AS WAVES

The discoveries which above all set their imprint on the development of physics during the first quarter of this century were those relating to the atomic or quantum nature of light radiation and the similarly quantized structure of the particles of matter, the atoms and the molecules. A relatively very simple and in most respects satisfactory interpretation of the interplay of matter and radiation could be given in the light of these findings. They also led to a number of new empirical discoveries, and in this way a considerable amount of data could be co-ordinated on the basis of a few fundamental postulates. Furthermore, quantitative tests could be carried out with extreme numerical precision, and even fine details in the results of the observations could be explained. Nevertheless it gradually became manifest that the current formulation of the quantum theory was not entirely satisfactory. One simple fact, however, could not be upset: in the case of radiation and atomic phenomena one fundamental quantity, Planck's constant h, steadily recurred, and its numerical value could be established with considerable accuracy in many different ways and for many different phenomena. This basic element of the theory consequently remained beyond doubt. A more satisfactory quantum theory had to be built on it, capable of explaining the empirical data with at least the same accuracy as the existing one. Furthermore, it was demanded of any new theory that it should cover a large number of more complicated phenomena for which the current quantum theory seemed unable to furnish an adequate explanation. This was true, for example, of the optical phenomena described above where the theory gave expression to the simple ideal cases, but did not seem to be applicable to more complicated structures. Also in the case of atomic structure, the scope of the theory seemed to be limited to the simplest cases only.

The logical defect of the existing quantum theory was that whilst it was based on the application of classical mechanics to atomic phenomena, concepts had also been introduced into it which were in obvious conflict with classical mechanics. For these reasons it was clear that any new theory would have to involve a radical change even in the fundamental assumptions. The years 1924-26 saw the beginning of a new epoch in theoretical physics, that of *wave mechanics* or *quantum mechanics.* This revolutionizing theory was to become the dominant factor in physical thinking, and still serves as the firm foundation of our concepts of Nature.

In 1924 the thirty-two-year-old scientist Prince LOUIS VICTOR DE BROGLIE [b.1892] presented his remarkable dissertation, *Recherches sur la théorie des quanta,* to the Faculté des Sciences in Paris. The basic idea of this memoir is briefly as follows. Natural phenomena appear to consist of two different worlds, matter and radiation. One of them is built up of small particles, atoms and electrons, the motions of which are governed by Newtonian mechanics or, in the case of the highest velocities, by the principles of the theory of relativity. Radiation, on the other hand, is a wave motion in the hypothetical ether determined by the electromagnetic equations. Through Planck's theory, however, a certain synthesis had been attained in the case of radiation between the two earlier competing theories of light as consisting either of waves or of light corpuscles. In the theory of radiation quanta it was assumed that they had definite fixed energies determined by the frequency or wave-length of the radiation. This dualistic concept of radiation had proved very fruitful in interpreting both the older and the newly discovered radiation phenomena. Ought it not to be possible to apply a similar dualism to the particles of matter also? There were, however, no phenomena indicating directly that atoms and electrons were of a wave nature. However, proceeding from certain analogies in the mathematical treatment of some mechanical and optical phenomena – the principles of de Maupertuis and of Fermat respectively – de Broglie developed a theory according to which every particle is associated with a wave motion. The wave-length of the latter is determined by the momentum of the particle and by Planck's constant in a manner fully analogous to that holding for radiation quanta. On these fundamental assumptions, de Broglie tried to formulate a new quantum theory free from the defects inherent in the earlier one.

In this connection the most important question was naturally whether any phenomenon could be found where particles of matter exhibited any of the behaviour characteristics of a wave motion, especially those of interference. Actually, some years before de Broglie advanced his theory as to the wave structure of matter, some American scientists, working under CLINTON JOSEPH DAVISSON [1881-1958], had already carried out experiments which could subsequently be interpreted in favour of de Broglie's basic assumption. These experiments involved a study of the scattering of a beam of electrons when reflected by the surface of a crystal, e.g. a nickel crystal. The irregular distribution of the reflected electrons, with maxima in certain definite directions, was very remarkable and difficult to explain. After de Broglie had published his theory, and further experiments had been carried out under more precise experimental conditions, Davisson was able to establish that his observations agreed well with the results which could be expected if the electrons were scattered in the same way as wave radiation incident on a crystal. The phenomenon is thus of exactly the same nature as that observed earlier in the case of reflection of X-rays by a crystal. The experiments also enabled Davisson to calculate the wave-length of a radiation with the same directions of maximum intensity for the reflected rays as the observed ones, and he found this wave-length to coincide with that postulated by de Broglie. The experiments of Davisson and his collaborators presented great technical difficulties, and it was therefore of the greatest importance to receive confirmation of the new wave-structure theory of matter from other quarters. GEORGE PAGET THOMSON [b.1892], the son of J. J. Thomson, the previously mentioned discoverer of the atomic structure of electricity, succeeded in demonstrating the reflection and diffraction of electrons in thin crystalline layers in a direct, simple and very obvious manner. While Davisson used electrons of relatively low velocities, Thomson carried out his experiments with very fast electrons capable of penetrating thin metal foils. As was the case in Friedrich's and Knipping's experiments described above [p.433], the electron radiation passing through the crystalline layer was registered on a photographic plate. After this had been developed, a number of rings appeared round the point where the direct ray had struck the plate. From the radii of these rings one could calculate the corresponding wave-lengths. In this manner convincing confirmation could be obtained of the formula given by de Broglie for the dependence of the wave-lengths on the velocity or on the momentum of the electron.

For these remarkable contributions to our knowledge of an entirely new aspect of the properties of matter the *1929* prize was awarded to DE BROGLIE 'for the discovery of the wave nature of electrons', and that for *1937* to DAVISSON and THOMSON jointly 'for the experimental discovery of the interference phenomenon in crystals irradiated by electrons'.

The discovery of the wave nature of the electron was not only of fundamental importance for our concepts of nature. It also gave research an extremely important and serviceable method for investigating the structure of matter, especially as it may be applied with ease even to extremely small quantities.

THE NEW QUANTUM THEORIES

De Broglie's doctoral dissertation naturally aroused an enormous interest in professional circles and also led to a new formulation of the quantum theory. In a discussion of de Broglie's theory, the Austrian physicist ERWIN SCHRÖDINGER [1887-1961], then Professor at the University of Zürich, took up the analogy between optical and mechanical phenomena, but in an essentially different form from that chosen by de Broglie. In his theory Schrödinger starts from the wave equation which in classical physics forms the basis for the description of the propagation of light. The difference between the two points of departure can be most easily characterized thus: de Broglie based his theory on the analogy with the optical laws which determine the path of a light ray, while Schrödinger proceeded from a more general equation which also accounts for the most characteristic properties of waves, e.g. the interference of light. In this equation Schrödinger introduced the connection postulated by de Broglie between the energy of a particle and its frequency, thus including Planck's constant in the theory. In this manner the most important result of experimental research relating to atomic processes, viz. a quantity characteristic of Nature and already exactly determined numerically, was taken into account in the initial formulation of the theory.

Schrödinger's famous papers, *Quantisierung als Eigenwertproblem* [1.-4. Mitteilung], were written during the first half of 1926. Since then 'Schrödinger's equation' has been extensively used in the interpretation and quantitative formulation of a large body of empirical data concerning various atomic processes with a minimum of initially postulated hypotheses. Among other things, the equation has been applied to the exchange of energy between electrons and light rays, the interpretation of the previously mentioned Zeeman and Stark effects, etc.

Even before Schrödinger had evolved his theory of wave mechanics, following up the analogy between optical and mechanical laws indicated by de Broglie, the twenty-four-year-old German physicist, WERNER HEISENBERG [b. 1901], had tried along entirely different lines to find a better foundation for a new quantum theory. Heisenberg's argument was of a very general nature: the theory ought to operate only with such physical elements as are capable of being observed. The implication of this postulate appears most simply from a discussion of the motion of the electrons in an atom, which, according to the older quantum theory, was determined by classical mechanics. Heisenberg points out that it is impossible to observe experimentally the motion of an electron in its orbit within the atom. For if one wishes to make an imaginary experiment, e.g. to observe an electron in its path with a microscope, light of a very short wave-length must be used. The ray which is to reach our eye by way of the microscope and thus give information about the motion of the electron will, however, completely change the orbit of the electron owing to the Compton effect. A single point in the path, at most, is observable. In following up this argument, Heisenberg was led to state a principle of wide applicability, *Heisenberg's uncertainty principle.* This principle gives limits for the accuracy with which, for example, the position of an electron and its simultaneous velocity can be measured and contains Planck's constant as the decisive factor.

In the mathematical formulation of his new *quantum mechanics*, Heisenberg thus started from the condition that the theory should include only such elements as, in principle, are observable. The electron orbits of the earlier theory are replaced in the new theory by the frequencies and intensities of the radiation emitted by the atoms. It was necessary to find a suitable calculus for these physical quantities and this should also take into account the quantized nature of atomic phenomena which experience had shown to exist, and of which Planck's constant is the most pregnant expression. Remarkably enough, the arsenal of the mathematicians had long included a calculus with so-called *matrices,* and this proved to be just what was needed. In the further development of this matrix mechanics, Born, Jordan and Dirac took an important part. Thus as a matter of principle this theory abandons the intuitive picture of atoms built up by electrons moving in definite orbits about a central body, the nucleus, which was a fundamental feature of the older theory of the atom. Instead, a theory was developed which accounted fully for the content of the older one insofar as the latter agreed with experience, and which, furthermore, was capable of interpreting observations beyond the scope of the classical theory.

Schrödinger's wave mechanics, on the one hand, and Heisenberg's matrix mechanics, on the other, represented two distinct approaches to such a theory, each of which was superior to the old one. Fortunately, Schrödinger was able to show that the two theories agreed with each other. It is therefore more a question of convenience which calculus should be employed in any individual case. Schrödinger's wave mechanics has the merit of employing a method in general use in mathematical physics and hence quite familiar to physicists.

Among the problems treated by Heisenberg, his theory for diatomic molecules should be mentioned. In the case of the hydrogen molecule he found that it ought to exist in two different forms, and he also computed the proportion between these two forms in ordinary hydrogen. Later experiments confirmed the correctness of Heisenberg's conclusions, and the proportion found between the two forms, nowadays called ortho-hydrogen and para-hydrogen, was in good agreement with the theory.

In the form which Schrödinger and Heisenberg have given to quantum mechanics, it covers in a logically satisfactory manner all phenomena where the effects anticipated by the theory of relativity do not show themselves. It proved to be far more difficult to formulate the theory in such a manner that relativistic phenomena are also accounted for. From very general assumptions, however, the British scientist, PAUL ADRIEN MAURICE DIRAC [b.1902], succeeded in developing a relativistic wave mechanics applicable to some of the simpler but still important special cases. Thus he was able to give a wave-mechanical discussion of the simplest of all one-body problems – namely that of the electron – in which the rotation of the electron, its so-called *spin,* is explained without supplementary hypotheses. The spin had earlier been introduced as an auxiliary hypothesis to explain a number of different observations concerning, among other things, the doublet structure of certain spectral lines, the magnetic properties of atoms, etc. The theory also furnished directly a numerical value for the magnetic moment of the electron. It was a special triumph for Dirac's theory when C. D. Anderson in 1932 discovered a particle, hitherto unknown, with the same mass as that of the electron but with a positive charge. As we shall see later, this particle, the *positron,* was discovered experimentally, but in Dirac's theory there was room for a particle having exactly those properties which the positron proved to have. In this manner Dirac's relativistic wave theory received effective support.

The new quantum or wave mechanics greatly influenced the subsequent development of physical theory. This fact led the Academy to award the *1932* prize to HEISENBERG 'for the creation of quantum mechanics, the application of which has, among other things, led to the discovery of the allotropic forms of hydrogen', and to divide the *1933* prize between SCHRÖDINGER and DIRAC 'for the discovery of new fruitful forms of atomic theory'.

In the development of the new quantum mechanics MAX BORN played a prominent role. Immediately after his pupil Heisenberg in 1925 had formulated the first laws of the new atomic theory, Born, in collaboration with Jordan and later on with Heisenberg, developed the mathematical formulation which adequately describes the new theory. Somewhat later, when Schrödinger put forward his wave equation, the physical interpretation of its solution in different cases was still rather obscure. Born then showed that the solution has a statistical meaning of physical significance. This interpretation of the wave equation has turned out to be of fundamental importance for the new atomic theory.

BORN received one-half of the *1954* prize 'for his fundamental research in quantum mechanics, especially for his statistical interpretation of the wave-function'.

At about the same time as the new quantum mechanics was developed, but on the basis of the earlier theory, the Austrian physicist WOLFGANG PAULI [1900–1958] put forward a very general principle which is usually called the 'exclusion principle'. It is to a certain extent supplementary to the quantum theory, but at the same time it occupies an independent position. In its original form the principle was built on the older quantum theory, which assumed fixed paths for the electrons in the atom. It stated that in every type of orbit determined by a definite combination of quantum numbers there can be only two electrons and that they must have opposite spins. This principle has proved to be of fundamental importance, not merely as an expression of the empirically discovered distribution of the electrons in the atom, but also for the interpretation of a number of other phenomena, such as the electric conductivity of metals and the properties of magnetic substances. It has been amply confirmed by its applications to the comprehensive observation material concerning the radiation of atoms and has become particularly valuable for the interpretation of the properties of atomic nuclei, as well as the primary particles, protons and neutrons, which make up the nucleus. After the formulation of the new quantum mechanics, Pauli's principle has been given a more general form, and its importance has become more and more obvious.

PAULI was awarded the *1945* prize 'for the discovery of the exclusion principle, also called the Pauli principle'.

MAGNETIC QUANTUM EFFECTS—QUANTUM ELECTRODYNAMICS

In both the older and the newer quantum theories the proper rotation or spin of the electron has played a decisive role, and it has been pointed out as a special merit of the Dirac theory that, automatically and without supplementary hypotheses, it affords an expression for the spin of the electron and for its magnetic moment. The existence of the magnetic moment of the atom was shown in a simple and clear manner by OTTO STERN [b. 1888] and W. Gerlach. At the same time their experiment gave direct confirmation of a related consequence of the quantum theory, namely that, owing to its own magnetic moment, an atom, when it is placed between the poles of a magnet, will orient itself in a few definite positions. For instance, according to this notion, the proton could only orient itself with its magnetic axis parallel to the direction of the magnetic field, where, however, half the protons would turn the north pole in one direction and the other half in the opposite direction. The experiment was carried out thus: a beam of the gaseous substance in question was allowed to pass between the poles of a magnet, after which it was intercepted in a suitable manner. If the poles are arranged so that the magnetic strength decreases to one side, the beam will be deflected, but the deflection of each particle will depend upon its orientation. By this experiment Stern showed that the beam of protons was split into two approximately equal beams, as would be expected from what has just been said. Subsequently he improved his method, thus obtaining a more accurate measurement of the magnitude of the deflection. This made it possible to determine the magnetic moment of atoms, one of their basic properties.

Even though this method was sufficiently exact to afford a general survey of the magnetic behaviour of atomic nuclei, it was still desirable to find a method leading to a higher degree of precision in the measurements. Stern's collaborator ISIDOR ISAAC RABI [b.1898] devised such a method based on resonance, which rendered possible a hundredfold increase in the accuracy of the measurements. Consequently, it could be employed with success in a great number of cases where it had previously not been possible to split the magnetic components.

STERN was awarded the *1943* prize 'for his contribution to the development of the molecular beam method and the discovery of the magnetic moment of the proton', and RABI that for *1944* for 'the resonance method employed by him for the registration of magnetic properties of atomic nuclei'.

A series of investigations on the magnetic behaviour of atoms were later taken up along new lines using the modern short-wave methods.

The Swiss physicist FELIX BLOCH [b. 1905], working at Stanford University and EDWARD MILLS PURCELL [b. 1912] at Harvard University, in 1946 independently of each other published experimental methods by which it was possible to measure with a very high degree of accuracy the magnetic properties of the atomic nuclei. A great advantage of these methods was that they could be used for objects in solid, fluid or gaseous states. Further, quite small quantities are needed for the measurements, which thus allow for the study of the magnetic properties of such isotopes of elements which are present only in very small proportions.

This resonance method also offers a new and highly exact method to determine the strength of magnetic fields and especially to show very small inhomogeneities in the field – all problems of great technical importance.

The nuclear magnetic resonance method has further given new possibilities to determine some of the fundamental physical constants.

A new kind of spectroscopy called nmr [nuclear magnetic resonance] has grown up from the discoveries in this field. At a given external magnetic field the condition for resonance absorption by particular nuclear constituents in a sample subject to a radiofrequency field from a surrounding coil is slightly dependent on the chemical environment around that nucleus in the molecule. The resonance line of a certain element, e.g. hydrogen, is therefore split up into a number of components, depending on the various positions of the element in the molecule studied. Because of the inherently high resolution of the nuclear resonance lines, very detailed information can be obtained concerning the chemical and other properties not only of particular liquids, but also of solids.

The *1952* prize was divided equally between BLOCH and PURCELL 'for their development of new methods for nuclear magnetic precision measurements and discoveries in connection therewith'.

In Rabi's laboratory at Columbia University WILLIS E. LAMB [b. 1913] and POLYKARP KUSCH [b.1911] in 1947, as leaders of two different research-groups, made some very important discoveries, which have had far-reaching consequences for the theory of our concepts on the interaction of electrons with an electromagnetic field.

Kusch and his group determined with advanced experimental methods of highest precision, the magnetic moment of the electron and found thereby that it was somewhat larger than was expected from the then generally accepted theory of Dirac. This lead to a reconsideration of the basic concepts of the theory. The discrepancies were then shown to be due to the interaction of the electron with the electro-magnetic field, an effect analogous to the influence of the waves of the air on the frequency with which a string vibrates in vacuum or in air.

Lamb's experiments deal in essence with the same problem, i.e. the interaction of the electron with an electromagnetic field. But Lamb studied another phenomenon, namely the optical radiation from hydrogen. The spectral lines sent out by a hydrogen atom are not so simple as they look in an ordinary prism-spectrometer. With instruments of very high resolving power they show a 'fine-structure'. That is also what could be expected if the Dirac theory is right. But in the finer details there seemed to be a small discordance between the calculations for this fine splitting of the spectral lines and the observed fine-structure. By applying in a most ingenious way the new resonance methods, Lamb succeeded in disentangling this extremely small splitting – results of fundamental value for a refinement of the theories. These investigations and the result he arrived at immediately started a discussion of the fundaments of the theory to find out in what way it would be possible to get the theory to fit the new facts. Obviously this would call for an essential refinement of quantum theory, as hitherto developed. Owing to works by Dirac, Heisenberg and Pauli, the original quantum theory had been broadened to apply not only to particles, but also to electromagnetic fields, a field of research which has been christened quantum electrodynamics. But this theory was fraught with serious difficulties. When, for instance, attempts were made to calculate the increased mass acquired by an electron through its interaction with the electromagnetic field, an infinitely large value was obtained. The new and exceedingly accurate experimental results obtained by Lamb and Kusch made it possible to look for an exact theory that could be accurately tested. A number of scientists, among them Hans Bethe, made important contributions; but not until the Japanese SIN-ITERO TOMONAGA [b. 1906] and the Americans JULIAN SCHWINGER [b. 1918] and RICHARD P. FEYNMAN [b. 1918] had made their thorough-going studies and presented their ideas, was it possible to establish a theory in all respects valid. This theory has been found to agree within margins of error of only a few hundred-thousandths and millionths, respectively, with Lamb's discovery of spectral line shifts and the anomalous part of the magnetic moment for the electron, accurately measured by Kusch and others. Further crucial applications have also been found in other aspects of elementary particle physics.

The *1955* prize was divided equally between LAMB for 'his discoveries concerning the fine structure of the hydrogen spectrum' and KUSCH for 'his precision determination of the magnetic moment of the electron'.

The *1965* prize was divided between TOMANAGA, SCHWINGER and FEYNMAN for their 'fundamental work in quantum electrodynamics, with deepploughing consequences for the physics of elementary particles'.

COSMIC RADIATION–ELEMENTARY PARTICLES

In connection with Dirac's theory, mention was made of C. D. Anderson's discovery of a new elementary particle, the positron, a positive counterpart of the electron. It may be asked why the discovery of the positive particle had not been made earlier, since the negative particle had long been so well known. The answer is that, in spite of having the same mass and the same charge, although of opposite signs, the two particles are quite different in their behaviour. In contrast to the electron, the positron has a very ephemeral existence. The experimenter must catch it during the fraction of a milliardth part of a second which is the span of its life. It was discovered in registrations of the radiation which constantly streams towards the earth from outer space, and is generally known as *cosmic radiation*. We know but little of the origin of this radiation, but in recent years important information has been gained as to its composition. The discovery of cosmic radiation resulted from a systematic investigation of radioactive radiation on the surface of the earth and in the atmosphere. Thanks to the experiments of the Austrian physicist VICTOR HESS [1883-1964] carried out in the course of balloon ascents up to a height of 5,000 metres during 1911-12, it became clear that a radiation from outer space was involved, since the radiation increased in strength above a height of 1,000 metres, so that at 5,000 metres it was twice as strong as at the surface of the earth. Later measurements at still greater heights indicated that at a height of 9,300 metres the radiation was about forty times stronger than at the surface of the earth. This radiation has a penetrating power many times greater than that of ordinary radioactive radiation. Hence cosmic radiation must be of quite a different nature and of a different origin from all previously known radiations.

With the object of ascertaining the nature of this radiation, all experimental methods evolved for the study of radioactive radiation have been used. As mentioned before, one of the best methods is that using the Wilson cloud chamber. When such a chamber is introduced between the poles of a powerful magnet, the paths of the electrically charged particles are deformed into circular arcs. The radius of the circle depends on the electric charge of the particle, its mass and its velocity. Additional information about the particle which gives rise to the track in question can be obtained from the density of the drop formation along its path.

In order to study the nature of cosmic radiation by this method, R. A. Millikan, who had devoted many years of research to the phenomenon, started investigations with a Wilson cloud chamber inserted between the poles of a large magnet. With this arrangement the tracks of occurring paths were registered photographically every fifteen seconds during both day and night. In 1932 CARL DAVID ANDERSON [b.1905], a young co-worker of Millikan's, while scrutinizing some thousands of such records, found tracks which did not seem to agree with any tracks characteristic of the then known electrically charged particles. Although they were bent in the same direction as the positively charged particles, the tracks did not exhibit the density typical of the latter. From further control experiments Anderson and Neddermeyer established the existence in cosmic radiation of a hitherto unknown positive particle with the same mass as the negative electron. The discovery was confirmed shortly afterwards by PATRICK MAYNARD STUART BLACKETT [b.1897] in England. In experiments with the Wilson cloud chamber carried out in co-operation with Occhialini, he used a brilliant method of exposing the registration plates in such a way that photographs were taken only when a cosmic ray was passing through the chamber. For this purpose two Geiger-Müller tubes, which give off an electric impulse when an electrically charged particle passes through both of them, were placed one above and one below the vertical Wilson chamber. The cloud chamber is brought into function only when the impulses from the two tubes coincide, and the track is then simultaneously photographed. Thanks to this automatic exposure, Blackett needed only a few plates to obtain the same results as had required thousands of exposures by ordinary procedures. He actually found a large number of tracks corresponding to a particle of the type indicated by Anderson.

Furthermore, Blackett pointed out that such a particle could be fitted into Dirac's theory, which has been mentioned above. After the new particle had been found in cosmic radiation, endeavours were naturally made to find it in connection with radioactive processes also, and several investigators, among them Anderson and Blackett, showed that gamma radiation of sufficiently high energy releases positrons. The plates showed that the positron track was also accompanied by an electron track, starting from the same point, a phenomenon usually called *pair production.* The magnetic field bends these two tracks in opposite directions. Measurements of the energy of the releasing gamma ray, on the one hand, and of the sum of the energies of the two particles, on the other, showed that the difference corresponds exactly to the mass of the electron and of the positron according to Einstein's formula for the conversion of mass into energy. Thus we have here a phenomenon where a gamma ray, a photon, is transformed into two material particles, a positron and an electron, plus a certain amount of kinetic energy. The latter accounts for the surplus energy of the photon above that required to generate the particles. The reverse process – a collision between a positron and an electron in which both are transformed into gamma radiation, so-called *annihilation radiation* – was also verified experimentally. Actually this phenomenon is very common in the nuclear processes studied nowadays in nuclear physics laboratories.

The *1936* prize was awarded jointly to HESS 'for the discovery of cosmic radiation' and to ANDERSON 'for the discovery of the positron'. BLACKETT received the *1948* prize 'for his development of the Wilson cloud chamber method, and his discoveries therewith in nuclear physics and concerning cosmic radiation'.

The first atomic disintegration had been achieved by Rutherford as early as 1919 by bombarding nitrogen with alpha particles from a radium preparation. His arrangements were very simple. In a cylindrical gas container, one wall of which was fitted with a window of extremely thin metal foil, the radioactive material was placed at an appropriate distance from the window. In front of the latter a zinc sulphide screen was placed, and the small flashes of light, so-called scintillations, resulting when alpha particles strike the screen, were observed by a magnifying glass or low-power microscope. With nitrogen in the container, scintillations were seen on the screen, even after an absorbing foil, impervious to the alpha particles from the radioactive material, was placed in front of it. A closer investigation showed that it was high-velocity protons which struck the scintillation screen, and that the nitrogen nucleus, after being hit by the alpha particle, was transformed into an oxygen nucleus. The proton, whose impact on the screen had been observed in the microscope, was emitted in this process. These pioneer investigations were pursued during the following years, nuclear reactions being studied for a number of other light elements.

These researches form the basis of an entirely new scientific discipline, *nuclear physics,* and they also led to one of the most important discoveries in physics, namely that of yet another nuclear particle, the *neutron.*

The history of the discovery of this particle, which has practically the same mass as the proton but no electric charge, is very remarkable. As early as 1920, Rutherford had assumed the existence of a neutral particle. He thought that such a particle might arise through an intimate combination of the two elementary particles then known, the positive proton and the negative electron. He pointed out that the existence of such a particle could not readily be proved spectroscopically, nor could it be enclosed in any container. In Rutherford's laboratory, and probably elsewhere, attempts were made – but in vain – to prove the existence of this particle. A large number of experiments were made by Rutherford's pupil and co-worker, JAMES CHADWICK [b.1891], in the Cavendish Laboratory at Cambridge. It was he who finally found the particle, but in a very surprising way, in which three stages can be distinguished. The first step was a remarkable observation made by Bothe and Becker in 1930 that a very penetrating radiation resulted when beryllium metal was bombarded with alpha particles. In accordance with the concepts then current, they considered this radiation to be made up of gamma rays. The next step in this development comprised some experiments which Irène Curie and her husband Frédéric Joliot undertook with a view to arriving at a better understanding of the 'beryllium radiation'. They placed a block of paraffin, or other substance rich in hydrogen, between the sheet of beryllium and the measuring apparatus and found that the registered effect was considerably greater with the paraffin inserted than without it. They also proved that this was due to the fact that a large number of protons were thrown out from the paraffin by the radiation. Their explanation of the phenomenon, based on current concepts of the effects of gamma rays, did not seem satisfactory, however. Then it occurred to Chadwick that perhaps the neutron he had so long been looking for might be involved in this process. After detailed investigations, employing various methods of registering rapid particles, Chadwick could furnish convincing proof that a *neutral* particle, with practically the same mass as the proton, had really been found. However, the particle observed did not quite correspond to Rutherford's hypothesis of a compound particle formed by a proton and an electron. On quantum-mechanical and other grounds, such a notion could not be accepted. Instead, it was necessary to assume that an entirely new elementary particle had been found, of the same fundamental character as the proton. According to Chadwick, it must be imagined that the atoms in the piece of beryllium, when they are hit by alpha particles, emit neutrons owing to a nuclear process. These particles in their turn eject protons from the paraffin, which is rich in hydrogen, and the protons are then caught up and registered in the measuring apparatus. Thus the neutrons form a not directly observable intermediary between the alpha particles striking the beryllium plate and the protons emitted from the paraffin. We now know that a so-called *nuclear reaction* takes place in which the alpha particle penetrates into the nucleus of the beryllium atom. Since the resulting complex nucleus is unstable, it disintegrates into a carbon atom and a neutron. In this splitting process the neutron attains a very great velocity.

The most important consequence of the discovery of the neutron was the resulting new picture of the composition of the atomic nucleus. Earlier concepts pictured the nucleus as composed of the two then known elementary particles, the positive proton and the negative electron. This concept seemed to be well documented, especially by the circumstance that when radioactive elements disintegrate, electrons [β-particles] are emitted which could not originate in the electron shells of the atom, but must be assumed to come from the nucleus. However, difficulties arose once a fairly reliable estimate of the dimensions of the nucleus – about one hundred-thousandth part of that of the atom – became available, chiefly thanks to the work of Rutherford. Finding enough room in such a minute space not merely for the protons but also for the unruly electrons – to a total of more than one hundred particles for the heaviest atoms – seemed perplexing. Instead it was now possible to assume the nucleus to be built up of *protons* to the number indicated by the positive charge of the nucleus or, what amounts to the same thing, equal to the number of electrons in the surrounding shells of the atom, and of *neutrons* to a number that, added to the number of protons, gives the atomic weight of the element in question. The first question which then presented itself was: whence come the electrons forming the beta radiation when atomic nuclei disintegrate? The proton and the neutron must be regarded as co-equal fundamental particles of the nucleus. Hence a new explanation has been developed in which one imagines that a neutron may be transformed into a proton by the emission of an electron and that, conversely, a proton may be transformed into a neutron by the emission of a positron. In the former case the beta radiation familiar from radioactivity arises without any need of assuming the existence of electrons in the nucleus; instead, the electrons are formed afresh in the transformation of the nuclear particles themselves. This is also the case with the positron radiation exhibited by artificially produced radioactive elements where a proton is transformed into a neutron with the emission of a positron. It may be mentioned in passing that, as pointed out by Pauli, in these neutron-proton transformations it appears to be necessary to postulate the existence of still another fundamental particle in order that the total spin [of the atomic nuclei and of the emitted particles] may be conserved in the process. The existence of such a hypothetical particle, called a *neutrino*, is generally assumed. This particle should not have any electric charge and, what is worse, practically no mass either. Its interaction with matter should also be extremely small. In spite of all this, serious attempts have been made in recent years to verify its existence experimentally. The experiments are highly complex and require large facilities. At present there exists, according to these experiments, quite positive evidence for the particle's existence.

CHADWICK was awarded the *1935* prize 'for the discovery of the neutron'.

The number of fundamental particles was increased still further through the discovery of the so-called *meson*. The history of this discovery is somewhat similar to that of the positron described above. In both cases the development of the wave-mechanical theory led to postulating the existence of a particle, not known experimentally, but later discovered independently of theory through the analysis of particle tracks obtained by the Wilson cloud chamber or by direct registration on photographic plates.

As has already been mentioned, atomic nuclei are now considered to be built up from protons and neutrons. In an attempt to find the laws for the forces holding these particles together, the Japanese physicist, HIDEKI YUKAWA [b. 1907], in 1935 presented a mathematical theory in which he assumed the existence of a field of force as the carrier of the nuclear forces and of certain particles belonging to this field. On this assumption and on the basis of available estimates of the nuclear forces, Yukawa was led to a value of the mass of the postulated particle of about 200 times that of the electron. This particle, the meson, would thus have a size between that of the electron and that of the previously known nuclear particles, the proton and the neutron, both of a mass of about 1840 times that of the electron.

When Yukawa propounded his theory, no particles of such a size had been observed in experiments, so the theory seemed to be unrealistic.

But early in 1937, Anderson and Neddermeyer in Pasadena, California, as well as Street and Stevenson at Harvard, when registering cosmic radiation with the Wilson cloud chamber, found some particle tracks indicating the existence of a previously unknown particle of a mass estimated roughly at about 130 times that of the electron. None of these workers associated this cosmic radiation particle with the meson postulated by Yukawa in his theory of nuclear forces. Continued investigations in various quarters for the study of the new particle and further development of Yukawa's theory suggested that the experiments in question had actually led to the identification of the particle which the theory postulated as existing in the nucleus of the atom. Yukawa had predicted that the meson could be liberated from the nucleus under certain circumstances, and in 1938 the Indian scientist Bhabha pointed out, as a further consequence of the theory, that free mesons could be expected to have a very brief span of life, only one-tenth to one-hundredth of a millionth of a second. This seemed to fit the particle of the experiments. However, the matter was not cleared up until 1946 when CECIL FRANK POWELL [b.1903], Bristol University and his co-workers Occhialini and Chilton of the Ilford Laboratories carried the method of photographic registration to a high degree of perfection by using specially made photographic plates. With this partly new technique, Powell and his collaborators definitely proved the existence of *two* different types of mesons. One of these, called the μ-meson, agrees in character with the particle previously found by the Wilson chamber method, and the new type, the π-meson, corresponds in nature and life span [10^{-8} seconds] to the particle postulated by Yukawa. Though in its present form Yukawa's theory may not be completely satisfactory, it has now received a contact with reality which was previously missing. For the investigation of the forces that are active in the nucleus, it has been of immense importance and it has also been of great value in interpreting experimental results.

YUKAWA was awarded the *1949* prize 'for his prediction of the existence of mesons on the basis of theoretical work on the nuclear forces', and POWELL the *1950* prize 'for his development of the photographic method of studying nuclear processes and his discoveries regarding mesons made with this method'.

Some of the laws of physics like those of energy, of momentum, and of angular momentum, had been given attractive formulation within the quantum theory based on *symmetry principles.* It seemed for many years rather obvious that this should be the case, because it meant that there is no distinction between right and left in the basic laws of Nature. A consequence of this was expressed in the so called *parity-laws.*

The experimental investigations of the spontaneous decays of newly discovered heavier mesons focussed the interest on these laws when in 1956 it became clear that the parent mesons in the so-called τ-decay [into three π-mesons] and θ-decay [into two π-mesons] had the same mass and lifetime. If parity shall be conserved this meant that there exist two particles in Nature with all properties alike differing only on parity. This situation challenged the Chinese scientists TSUNG DAO LEE [b. 1926] and CHEN NING YANG [b. 1922] both in the United States at the time to undertake a close study of the question of parity conservation. The strength of their work lies partly in the analyses of experiments showing that for the limited field of weak interactions no experiment had been performed capable to disclose parity violation – with the possible and notable exception of heavy meson decay. They further proposed that parity need not be conserved in some cases and suggested parity-sensitive experiments on decaying nuclei. A few months later some such experiments were carried out in several laboratories and the results showed unambiguously that parity was not conserved in the decays tested. The deviations in the results from those expected on basis of parity conservation were large. The new situation raised many important questions in the field of elementary particles.

The Academy decided to award the 1957 prize to LEE and YANG 'for their penetrating investigation of the so-called parity-laws, which have led to important discoveries regarding the elementary particles'.

The theoretical and experimental investigations just mentioned have been further developed with considerable success. It has been shown that there exist several types of mesons with great variations in masses. The mean lifetimes of the mesons also vary considerably. A great number of transitions among these mesons have also been discovered.

As mentioned above a particle with the same mass as the electron but with positive charge, called the positron, was discovered by C. D. Anderson in studies of the cosmic radiation. An interesting point in this discovery was the fact that the existence of such a particle had been postulated by the wave mechanical theory of Dirac. But from this same theory one could also expect a negative analogue to the proton, the positive nucleus of hydrogen. Some observations on the cosmic radiation seemed to indicate the presence of such a particle, the *antiproton*, but the data were not conclusive enough to give a definite evidence for its existence.

By theoretical considerations one could expect that with protons accelerated to at least 6.3 GeV [Ge V = 10^9 e V] it would be possible to generate antiprotons. With this in mind the big accelerator, the 'bevatron' at the Berkeley Radiation Laboratory was given such dimensions that the accelerated protons would attain the energies just mentioned. In 1955 a research team with O. CHAMBERLAIN [b. 1920], E. SEGRÉ [b. 1905], C. Wiegand and T. Ypsilantis working at the bevatron were able to give the first clear evidence of the antiproton and to show that the new particle had a negative charge equal to that of the electron and a mass equal to the proton. By an ingenious series of experiments and developing new methods of technique they further studied the stability of the new particle, its magnetic moment and other qualities which were to be expected on theoretical grounds. Later on the anti-neutron was discovered.

The *1959* prize was awarded to OWEN CHAMBERLAIN and EMILIO SEGRÈ for their discovery of the antiproton'.

In a series of experiments carried out by ROBERT HOFSTADTER [b.1915] and several coworkers at Stanford University some very interesting results have been obtained regarding the fundamental particles of the atomic nuclei: the proton and the neutron. The dimensions of these two particles [the *nucleons*] had been estimated to be some 100,000 times less than the size of the atoms. The method Hofstadter used in his attempts to study the structure of the nucleons was to send a beam of electrons with very high energies through suitable absorbers and then to register the scattering of the electrons by the atomic nuclei and especially by the nucleons. He found that the observed scattering of the electrons must be due to an extended distribution of the electrical charge within the proton, and also that the charge is concentrated to the central part of it. By these experiments also the most accurate scale of nuclear sizes was obtained for several of the lighter elements.

In his experiments Hofstadter used the giant linear electron accelerator at the University of Stanford which in the latest investigations produced beams of electrons having an energy of 1000 MeV [*M*illion *e*lectron *V*olts]. A new linear accelerator was later constructed at Stanford with considerably higher energy, 25 GeV.

HOFSTADTER was awarded one-half of the *1961* prize 'for his pioneering studies of electron scattering in atomic nuclei and for his thereby achieved discoveries concerning the structure of the nucleons'.

The development of the great particle accelerators can be regarded in many respects as a logical investment in Ernest Lawrence's original ideas, to which new technical suggestions had all the time been added. It was in this way that the conditions were established for creating new elementary particles of the most varied sorts in the laboratory. Many are of extraordinarily brief duration and require highly specialized experimental arrangements if they are to be demonstrated at all. A notably efficient aid for this purpose has been the so-called bubble chamber, invented by Glaser. Here it was LUIS W. ALVAREZ [b. 1911], at the Lawrence Radiation Laboratory at Berkeley, who notably speeded developments. He succeeded in constructing a considerably magnified version of the original bubble chamber, and this, when combined with specially developed recording techniques and data analysis systems, provided the right conditions for an effective study of the presence of new elementary particles. Together with his team of research workers at the Berkeley bevatron, Alvarez succeeded in discovering a great number of elementary particles, of a new sort – so-called resonance particles. One of the characteristics of these particles is their extremely brief duration, but they also possess others, which Alvarez was successful in determining systematically. Owing to these and other works based in many respects on the experimental techniques initiated by Alvarez, the number of elementary particles now known to science has gradually risen to more than one hundred fifty.

Parallel with this experimental work, intensive theoretical study has been devoted to attempts to discover the pattern behind this multitude of high-energy physical phenomena. Step by step, clarity has been reached. Of special importance have been the contributions of the American scientist, MURRAY GELL-MANN [b. 1929]. But also Yuvel Néeman from Israel, and such Japanese scientists as Kzuniko Nishijima and Yoichiro Nambu, and Abdus Salam from Pakistan, together with a number of others, have also made useful contributions. Their works have made it possible, for instance, to systematize these elementary particles in a relatively simple pattern in respect to such typical characteristics as their charge, spin and relation to other particles. The theory has been given a singularly elegant mathematical structure, known as the 'eightfold way'. Much still remains to be done in this subtle field of research. When, within a few years, even larger accelerators become available, this fascinating work in physics should become even better known to us.

The *1968* prize was awarded to ALVAREZ 'for his decisive contributions to elementary particle physics, in particular, the discovery of a large number of resonance states, made possible through his development of the technique of using hydrogen bubble chamber and data analysis'.

The *1969* prize was awarded to GELL-MANN 'for his contributions and discoveries concerning the classification of elementary particles and their interactions'.

NUCLEAR REACTIONS AND NUCLEAR STRUCTURE

One step in the research leading to the discovery of the neutron described earlier was represented by the experiments which M. and Mme Joliot-Curie carried out concerning the radiation produced when beryllium is bombarded with alpha particles. At the beginning of 1934 the Joliot-Curies announced a very sensational result from their further experiments. They found that if, for example, aluminium was bombarded with alpha particles, it continued for some time to emit a radiation of its own, even after the bombardment had ceased. The strength of the radiation decreased, however, and fell to one half in a few minutes. This successive decrease proved to follow the same law as holds for the disintegration of natural radioactive elements. Thus the Joliot-Curies had found the first method of producing radioactive forms of the ordinary elements, then called 'artificially' radioactive isotopes, the chemical properties of which are identical with those of the normal stable elements. They were awarded the Nobel Prize for Chemistry for this discovery, and hence their achievement is described more in detail elsewhere in this publication [see p. 382]. The discovery had to be mentioned here, however, since, together with that of the neutron, it formed the point of departure for another series of investigations of extreme importance for atomic research. Rutherford, it will be recalled, pointed out as a property of his postulated neutron that it could easily penetrate into an atomic nucleus, in contrast to protons and alpha particles, which, being positively charged, are strongly repelled by the atomic nuclei, which are also positively charged. It follows that the method of the Joliot-Curies for bringing about nuclear reactions by bombardment with high-speed alpha particles will work only for the lighter elements with relatively low positive charges. On the other hand, using *neutrons* from a tube containing beryllium and a radium preparation as the source of alpha particles, the Italian physicist ENRICO FERMI [1901-1954] showed that nuclear reactions may be produced with these particles, even in the case of the very heaviest elements. Of special importance was his discovery that in many cases the power of the neutrons of causing nuclear reactions could be considerably increased, up to a hundredfold, by first slowing them down before using them for bombardment purposes. The method of producing such *slow* neutrons is quite simple: the high-speed neutrons are allowed to pass through a substance with a high hydrogen content. Now the nucleus of the hydrogen atom is a proton, and thus of the same mass as the neutron, and in this large number of protons the neutrons will rapidly lose their velocity, owing to repeated collisions. Already after about twenty collisions, the speed of the neutrons is reduced to some millionth part of the original value. In the case of certain elements it was found that nuclear reactions could be started by neutrons of relatively low velocities, the minimal velocity in each case being characteristic of the reaction. Thanks to Fermi's discoveries, our knowledge of new radioactive isotopes was immensely increased at a single stroke. His experiments proved of fundamental importance for subsequent research and especially for the problem of releasing atomic energy.

FERMI was awarded the *1938* prize 'for his disclosure of new radioactive elements produced by neutron irradiation, and for his related discovery of nuclear reactions brought about by slow neutrons'.

Ever since the 1930's one of the most closely studied physical fields has been the structure of the nucleus of the atom and its nuclear reactions. One important factor, of course, was the invention of accelerators. Others were suitable nuclear particle detectors and spectrometers for various sorts of particles. Gradually, a considerable body of experimental material both on nuclear reactions, the scattering of particles against each other, and various excited states in atomic nuclei became available. At times it has been hard to say which scientists' research has done most to advance developments. Names such as Rutherford, Chadwick, Fermi and Lawrence are outstanding, but many others could be added. At various times the Nobel Committee has nevertheless found strong and special reasons to exist for rewarding certain of these scientists, among them EUGENE P. WIGNER [b. 1902], MARIA GOEPPERT-MAYER [b. 1906] and HANS D. JENSEN [b. 1907] together with HANS A. BETHE [b. 1906]. Wigner, who has made great general contributions to physics, early devoted himself to the interpretation of experiments then being made on the nature of nuclear forces. As early as 1933, Wigner found that the force between two nucleons remains very weak up to the point where the distance between them is very small; whereafter it suddenly grows immensely, indeed until it is millions of times stronger than anything previously known to physics, e.g. the electric force. Wigner was also able to determine other characteristics of nuclear forces. His theoretical conclusions have often been based on very generalized arguments and generally valid assumptions, as a consequence of symmetries in the laws of movement. The above-mentioned discoveries of Lee and Yang, and their revised interpretation of them, were in a high degree based on Wigner's earlier works, which were related also to the fundamental problem of differentiating between right and left. Wigner has also made crucial contributions to the general theory of nuclear reactions.

A major milestone along the road to our understanding of the construction of the nucleus of the atom and its structure was passed in 1948 by Goeppert-Mayer and, independently of her, by Jensen, the latter partly in collaboration with O. Haxel and H. Suess. By a systematic study of a large experimental material, these scientists demonstrated that atomic nuclei which were built up of nucleons in certain definite, so-called magic numbers, revealed special characteristics reminiscent of the noble gases in the periodic system of the elements. The 'magic' numbers were found to be 2, 8, 20, 28, 50, 82 and 126. They were also successful in finding a theoretical explanation of these numbers by assuming a coupling between the nucleon's own spin movement and the orbital movement in the nucleus of the atom. In this way they provided evidence for the fact that, like the atomic shells themselves, the nucleus, too, is constructed in various shells and, notwithstanding the enormous close-packing of the nucleons on the nucleus, it was possible to distinguish individual particle movements. These discoveries led to a new era in nuclear physics, to which the name nuclear spectroscopy can be given. Thus, rotation and vibration states have been found in the nuclear movement which can be linked to the movement of individual nucleons. *Ab initio* calculations of the nucleon pattern, based on the nature of the nuclear forces, are still fraught with great mathematical difficulties. As an alternative various simplified nuclear models have been constructed to describe, with varying degrees of approximation, different parts of the nuclei's periodic system. Particularly important contributions within this field have been made by A. Bohr and B. Mottelson in Copenhagen.

The *1963* prize was divided equally between, on the one hand, WIGNER, 'for his contributions to the theory of the atomic nucleus and the elementary particles, particularly through the discovery and application of fundamental symmetry principles', and the other half, also equally, between GOEPPERT-MAYER and JENSEN 'for their discoveries concerning nuclear shell structure'.

At an early stage Hans Bethe, like Wigner, made fundamental contributions to our understanding of nuclear reactions. In almost every field his influence has proved stimulating to research. An example of this was his calculations concerning the Lamb shift, immediately after it had been discovered experimentally. But of quite special interest was Bethe's fundamental and penetrating analysis of the generation of energy in the sun and stars. This problem had preoccupied many generations of scientists. As early as the mid-nineteenth century, Helmholtz in Germany and Lord Kelvin in Britain demonstrated that a far more effective mechanism generating energy in the sun than ordinary chemical reactions is the sun's own contraction by its own gravitational field, releasing stupendous quantities of energy. Yet this explanation, alone, is far from adequate. Later, it was assumed that ordinary radioactive disintegration within the sun might play a certain part; but for many reasons this theory, too, had to be abandoned. About the year 1930, a number of scientists, such as the Austrian, Houterman and the Englishman, Atkinson, as well as the German, von Wiezsäcker, had begun to discuss the possibilities that the most important source of energy in the sun might lie in the fusion of light nuclei, such as hydrogen, into heavier nuclei, e.g. helium. Bethe penetrated these questions with special profundity, his great knowledge of nuclear reactions proving to be of decisive significance. In great detail he was able to show the manner in which the energy cycle takes place and how hydrogen is successively built up to helium by a succession of reactions which keep the whole process and the generation of energy going at the right level. This is the famous hydrogen cycle. An alternative to it is the carbon cycle, which was also explored in detail. Here, too, it was finally found that, as energy is developed, protons are fused into helium. Which of these two processes is dominant in any given star will depend on the temperature in its interior. In the sun the first cycle predominates to some small extent, as it does in all cooler and lighter stars, while the carbon cycle dominates in heavier and brighter ones.

BETHE was awarded the *1967* prize 'for his contributions to the theory of nuclear reactions, especially his discoveries concerning the energy production in stars'.

EXPERIMENTAL METHODS IN NUCLEAR PHYSICS

The methods mentioned above of producing radioactive elements by nuclear reactions were based upon the use of naturally radioactive substances such as radium, either directly as a source of alpha particles, or indirectly for the production of neutrons with alpha particles. In view of the scanty supply of naturally radioactive substances, only extremely small quantities of active isotopes could be obtained by such methods. This led to a search for methods of inducing nuclear reactions without the use of radioactive material. In this respect too, Rutherford's laboratory produced the first positive result. Two members of the research group in the Cavendish Laboratory JOHN DOUGLAS COCKCROFT [1897-1967] and ERNEST THOMAS SINTON WALTON [b.1903] in 1930/32 constructed at the Cavendish Laboratory a high-tension apparatus producing 700,000 volts, with the aid of which they succeeded in accelerating protons to such a high velocity that they were able to penetrate into atomic nuclei of the light elements and start nuclear reactions. Of special interest, among other things, were the relations obtained in this manner between the energies of the incident protons and the energies of the created nuclear particles.

The fundamental discoveries of Cockcroft and Walton have had a great influence on the later development in the field of nuclear physics, and their methods to accelerate charged particles to produce nuclear reactions under well-defined conditions have been extensively used in a great number of laboratories all over the world.

A considerable technical advance was made when ERNEST ORLANDO LAWRENCE [1901-1958], of the University of California at Berkeley, a little later described an entirely new principle for accelerating electric particles, based on the idea of successively increasing the velocity of particles by means of repeated electric impulses. This can be effected in several ways. One method is that first indicated by the Swedish physicist G. Ising, i.e. the use of a device which in its modern technical form is known as a 'linear accelerator'. In the method invented by Lawrence, and developed by him in a brilliant manner, the particles are made to describe a spiral path between the poles of a large electromagnet where they are accelerated by means of an alternating electric field. An essential requirement is that the direction of the field shall change in step with the motion of the particle along its path. In this way one may attain an acceleration corresponding to 20 million volts or more with an alternating voltage amounting to only a couple of hundred thousand volts or even less. The technical development has continually raised the energy level to 100 MeV, 1,000 MeV (= 1 GeV), and 30 GeV. Accelerators are now being built for 400 GeV. The original apparatus, which Lawrence called the *cyclotron*, has become of epoch-making importance for the study of nuclear reactions. Its efficiency far surpasses the earlier methods of producing radioactive isotopes. Especially with the use of the nucleus of heavy hydrogen, the so-called *deuteron*, consisting of a proton and a neutron, as the accelerated particle, a number of most interesting nuclear reactions can be induced. With respect to multiplicity of uses for nuclear physical investigations, the cyclotron is superior to any other apparatus. It is true that when it comes to producing certain radioactive isotopes, the uranium pile developed in 1942 is far more efficient, but for a great number of important investigations in nuclear physics one still has to fall back on the cyclotron.

With the advent of this powerful aid all research on nuclear processes was raised to a hitherto undreamt-of plane. Lawrence and his many co-workers discovered a large number of new active isotopes and analysed their relations to the stable elements. Thanks to the possibilities which were opened up for the production in considerable quantities of active isotopes of practically every element, a method of analysis based on radioactivity could now be extensively used. Previously its use had been restricted to the naturally radioactive elements. A more detailed account of these researches, for which a Prize for Chemistry was awarded to G. de Hevesy, is given elsewhere in this publication [p.380].

LAWRENCE was awarded the *1939* prize 'for the invention of the cyclotron, its development and the results obtained with it, especially relating to artificial radioactive elements'.

COCKCROFT and WALTON were awarded the *1951* prize 'for their pioneer work on the transmutation of atomic nuclei by artificially accelerated atomic particles'.

The particles emitted in radioactive or other nuclear processes can be detected by means of different kinds of electrical counters, one of the most widely used being the Geiger-Müller tube. A particle which enters the tube ionizes the gas, and the electric charges, multiplied by an electron avalanche which takes place because of an electric field, are collected on a wire situated along the tube axis. The small electric pulses are then amplified and mechanically registered. In a great many cases more than one particle is emitted during a nuclear process. In order to study such events WALTHER

BOTHE [1891-1957] in 1925 invented an ingenious method in which two [or more] counters are connected to a common amplifier. Only when both counters were triggered simultaneously by nuclear particles could an electric pulse pass through the amplifier and be registered. He first applied this method, called the 'concidence method', to a problem of great principal interest. When a light quantum is scattered by an electron, it loses part of its energy by transfer to the electron [the Compton effect]. It had been questioned whether the energy and momentum were conserved in each such individual process or if it was only statistically so. Bothe showed the former to be the case. Bothe and others later on developed the coincidence method into a very powerful tool in nuclear and cosmic-ray physics. By putting a linear array of several counters in such a coincidence arrangement it was possible to study the *direction* of the radiation, for instance cosmic radiation.

BOTHE was awarded one-half of the *1954* prize 'for the coincidence method and his discoveries made therewith'.

A method which has been of great importance in studying the high energy particles from nuclear reactions is based on a new type of radiation discovered in 1934 by PAVEL ALEKSEVIČ ČERENKOV [b.1904]. When a γ-radiation enters a crystal or a fluid substance a blue very faint light is visible. This had been observed and reported many years before Čerenkov began his famous studies. Especially the French radiologist, L. Mallet had made experiments [1926-1929] to find out the character of this radiation. But it was not until Čerenkov, on suggestion of his teacher Vavilov, started a thorough experimental investigation of this radiation, that a real understanding of its nature was finally obtained. Most important in Čerenkov's experiments of the radiation in highly purified substances was his observation that it was polarized. In his continued systematic investigations of the radiation Čerenkov was able to show by magnetic deviation that the effect probably was caused by high-energy electrons. A theoretical explanation of the effect based on the observations of Čerenkov was given in 1937 by his compatriots ILJA MICHAJLOVIČ FRANK [b.1908] and IGOR JEVGENEVIČ TAMM [1895-1971] by applying the classical electromagnetic theory.

In principle the radiation is emitted when a charged particle passes a crystal or a fluid substance with a speed higher than the velocity of light [the so-called phase velocity]. The electromagnetic waves sent out by the moving particle have the shape of a cone with its top at the particle. The conic angle is dependent on the speed of the particle and its measurement therefore makes it possible to determine the speed or the energy of the particle. This relation as well as other specific properties of the radiation as given by the above-mentioned theory was in complete agreement with Čerenkov's experimental results. The theory was later worked out by Frank and Tamm on the basis of wave mechanics, which leads to the same conclusions as the former classical theory.

The 'Čerenkov-counter' has in the last years been an extremely valuable tool in high-energy nuclear physics and played an important role in the experiments which led to the discovery, for example, of the antiproton.

ČERENKOV, FRANK and TAMM were jointly awarded the *1958* prize 'for the discovery and the interpretation of the Čerenkov-effect'.

The methods by which it is possible to make the tracks of electrically charged particles visible have been of fundamental importance for the study of the nuclear phenomena. The earlier two methods using the photograhic-emulsion technique and the Wilson cloud chamber have been earlier mentioned in connection with the prizes given to C.F. Powell and C. T. R. Wilson, C. D. Anderson and P. M. S. Blackett respectively. Both these methods have their special fields of application.

For charged particles of the very high energy which it is now possible to produce in the big accelerators recently built for energies up to 20–30 GeV the two methods just mentioned were inadequate. It was therefore of the greatest importance that a new method for registration of particles in this energy region was invented just in time to be used in connection with the new big accelerators. The principle of the new method has some similarity with that of the cloud chamber, where the ions produced along the track of a particle in a supersaturated vapour constitute condensation centers for the formation of droplets, which may be seen or photographed. In the *bubble chamber* invented by DONALD A. GLASER [b.1926] in Ann Arbor, Mich., USA, the chamber encloses a suitable *superheated fluid*, e.g. liquid hydrogen, where *gas bubbles* are produced along the path of the electrically charged particle. The tracks may then be photographed just as they have been formed. The use of a liquid instead of a gas as medium means that the particles with very high energy can be followed from start to end in a chamber of reasonable dimensions. This is due to the fact that the path-length of the particle in a gas is about 1000 times as long as that in a fluid. A track in the latter medium of about 10 cm, which is the order of magnitude with high-energy particles, would need a cloud chamber of about 100 m in length.

Bubble chambers have been successively built with increasing dimensions up to 2 m. to allow the registration of very-high-energy particles from the biggest accelerators. To give information on the charge and mass of the particles the chamber is placed between the poles of an electromagnet of considerable size. For the bubble chamber of 180 cm in length used at the bevatron, the magnet has a field-strength up to 17000 Gauss and takes then 3000 kW. As the chamber contains liquid hydrogen an extensive low-temperature installation is also needed. Further it may be mentioned that the measurement of the particle tracks is automatized and that the data of the particles are obtained with an electronic computer. Of course every such bubble chamber of big size is the result of a teamwork with a great number of physicists and engineers.

GLASER was awarded the *1960* prize 'for the invention of the Bubble Chamber'.

In classical physics, resonance phenomena are well known. To mention just one example: the sound waves sent out from a vibrating string are taken up by another string which is tuned to the same frequency. There are several analogous phenomena in optics and other electromagnetical radiations. Also in nuclear physics some observations had shown that an incoming γ-radiation could be taken up by resonance in an atomic nucleus when the γ-radiation from that nucleus had the same natural frequency as the incoming one. The difficulties to observe this effect originated in the fact that the γ-radiation is usually strongly 'monochromatic', that is, the frequency is limited to a *very small frequency interval.* In a typical case this interval may be as small as one part in 10^{12}. This means that a condition for resonance absorption is that the frequency of the incoming ray may not deviate from that of the natural γ-radiation of the nucleons in question by more than this figure.

Now if the γ-radiation from a specific radioactive isotope hits the nucleus of another, identical isotope, one should expect a strong absorption of the radiation by the second atom. But in several earlier experiments only a very small effect was observed. The simple reason for this is that the emission of a γ-quantum from a free atom is accompanied by a recoil of the emitting nucleus which also means a change through the Doppler effect of the frequency of the γ-ray. Several methods had been tried experimentally to avoid this difficulty. But all these experiments gave very poor results.

Therefore a paper in 1958 by RUDOLF MÖSSBAUER, Munich, on this subject made a sensation by showing how a strong absorption of nuclear γ-radiation could be obtained. He used the γ-radiation sent out from an excited nucleus of iridium 191 in a *crystal* which was cooled down to the temperature of liquid air. Under these circumstances the recoil is taken up by the crystal lattice instead of by a single atom as the atoms here are strongly bound to each other. This reduced the recoil effect on the γ-quantum.

The 'Mössbauer Effect' as it is now called is nicely demonstrated if the γ-emitting substance is moved at a low speed in the direction of the absorber. Already with a speed of a few mm per second towards or away from the absorber the resonance is lost. The great sharpness of the resonance curve can easily be measured. The width of the curve gives quantitative information of the lifetime of the nuclear state and was the first result that Mössbauer presented from his effect. The extremely high precision obtainable with this method is rich in applications. It is, for example, possible with this method to measure atomic magnetic fields and to study other properties of solids. Another fascinating application is the possibilities which the Mössbauer effect opens for a direct verification of general relativity. Principally, this simply requires the emission of the γ-radiation vertically, say in the downward direction. Due to the gravitational field, the frequency of the radiation should then show a small increase which in suitable cases could be measured and compared with the estimate from the theory of relativity. Such experiments have been carried out with great precision.

MÖSSBAUER was awarded one-half of the *1961* prize 'for his researches concerning the resonance absorption of γ-radiation and his discovery in this connection of the effect which bears his name'.

MAGNETISM

Besides the electrical phenomena, the characteristics of magnetism in matter aroused tremendous interest at a very early stage in the history of physics. The coupling between electric currents and magnetism was described in a general way in Faraday-Maxwell's electro-magnetic theory. But to penetrate deeper into the magnetic characteristics of matter requires an atomic theory. Naturally, a complete description of these characteristics cannot be made without using quantum mechanics, but for each phenomenon a simple model can suffice. Diamagnetism, paramagnetism and ferromagnetism are the three main types, all of which have long been known. Diamagnetism, which is very weak, is induced by an external applied magnetic field and tries to counteract it at the atomic level in the same way as a magnetic field applied over a coil induces in the latter a current which counteracts the outer variation in the field. Paramagnetism is due to an alignment of permanent atomic magnetic dipoles, partially counteracted by thermal motion. The theory of this sort of magnetism was developed by the French physicist, P. Languevin at the start of the twentieth century. Ferromagnetism is strong and can be described in terms of a coordination of the magnetic dipoles of many atoms in magnetic domains, according to a theory of the French physicist P. Weiss, in 1907. Among other things, Pierre Curie demonstrated that various ferromagnetic phenomena suddenly lose their ferromagnetic character if the temperature is raised to the so-called Curie temperature, which varies for various ferromagnetic materials. In later developments in this field, LOUIS NÉEL [b. 1904] has made new and crucial contributions in magnetism, such as affect our theoretical view of the magnetic substructure of matter and its practical applications. In 1932, Néel discovered so-called anti-ferromagnetism. This is caused by two different ferromagnetic sub-lattices in a material having opposed magnetic contributions which, however strong each of them may be in itself, largely cancel out each other's affects. Néel also discovered another variant, so-called ferrimagnetism, and here too succeeded in providing a description of the phenomenon based on the electrons' spin in different atomic sites in the crystal lattice which have different valency. A series of synthetic materials, so-called ferrites, have resulted from this research, and are of great importance to electronics. For instance, these materials are nowadays used as memory units in modern computers.

Néel was awarded one-half the *1970* prize for 'fundamental contributions and discoveries concerning antiferromagnetism and ferrimagnetism which have resulted in important applications in solid state physics'.

CONCLUSION

According to the statutes governing the distribution of prizes, the Swedish Academy of Sciences is obliged to award a prize in each field every fifth year at least. One of the first years, when submitting his nominations to the Academy, a prominent French physicist expressed the opinion that it would be perfectly impossible to find a really worthy candidate every year. He based it on an examination of the number of physicists who during the past century had made discoveries of the importance prescribed in Nobel's will as a condition for award. He considered their number far too small to suffice for a yearly distribution of a prize with the stated requirements.

Does this mean that the Academy in making its awards has placed the requirements at a considerably lower level than what was contemplated by the physicist mentioned above in his retrospective survey of the discoveries in physics during the past century? Whoever wants to answer this question will have to pay attention to the following facts. Especially during the last decades, the civilized nations have shown much more interest in physical research than before, and its importance also for the material civilization is becoming more and more evident. Hence people everywhere have found it to be in the interest of society to support such research. A number of new laboratories have been created, older institutions have received improved facilities, and the number of research workers has increased many times. All this has taken place at a steadily accelerated rate. Naturally, the results of research have also increased correspondingly. There is no sign of any slowing down of this development. Physics as an essentially closed chapter of research was a possibility predicted in some quarters at the turn of the century, as mentioned in the introduction to this survey. Nothing could have been more unrealistic. Contrary to these prophecies more discoveries were made in physics during the past seventy years than during any corresponding period in the past.

Looking around the world to-day, one finds the physical research laboratories seething with activity. New, refined, and in some cases gigantic apparatus is created to facilitate a deeper penetration into the mysteries of matter. Indeed, there is good reason to believe that discoveries worthy of a Nobel Prize will occur with at least the present frequency during such parts of the future for which any forecast can be made.

THE NOBEL INSTITUTE OF THE ACADEMY OF SCIENCES

BY ARNE WESTGREN

Under the terms of the statutes of the Nobel Foundation, the Academy of Sciences was authorized to set up a Nobel Institute. The Institute was to help in the investigations necessary to the award of prizes and to promote the scientific purposes of the Foundation. It was planned to consist of two departments, one for physical and one for chemical research. As early as 1902, however, the Nobel Committees of the Academy proposed that a department of physical chemistry should be established. The development in this branch of science had been particularly rapid about the turn of the century, and it was considered desirable to afford one of its pioneers, Svante Arrhenius, a better opportunity of pursuing his researches.

In 1904, Arrhenius was offered the post of director of a research institute in Berlin of the same type as that set up for J. H. van 't Hoff. The Academy therefore asked the Government to authorize the establishment at the Nobel Institute of a department of physical chemistry, to be headed by Arrhenius, although the statutes of the Foundation contained no provision for such a department. The Government granted the request, and on October 1, 1905, this, the first department of the projected Nobel Institute to be set up, began its work.

At first it was housed in Stockholm in a modest rented flat consisting of three rooms and a kitchen. In the following year, however, the Academy purchased a site at Frescati, in the northern suburbs of the capital, where it planned to erect buildings for its own use. Here a special institute for physical chemistry was built, the costs being met by appropriations from the foundation funds of the chemistry- and physics-prize sections. The building was completed in the summer of 1909.

As Director of the new institute, Arrhenius continued his electrochemical researches with special reference to the application of his theory of electrolytic dissociation to problems of immunochemistry. His activities covered, however, a much wider field, and he made significant contributions to climatology, cosmology and biology. His institute also provided facilities for research students, and in the years that followed many young scientists from Sweden and foreign countries came there to work. Among them may be mentioned W. Öholm, E. H. Riesenfeld, H. S. Taylor, J. Kendall, O. Klein, and H. Bäckström.

After Arrhenius's death in 1927, the Academy decided to convert the department of physical chemistry, which remained the only one so far established, into a department of theoretical physics. Dr. C. W. Oseen,

Professor of Mathematical Physics at Uppsala University and a member of the Nobel Committee for Physics, was appointed its Director and he took up his duties on August 1, 1933. As has already been mentioned, one of the main functions of the Nobel Institute is to assist in making investigations preliminary to the award of the prizes, and it seemed desirable that Oseen should be able to devote himself to this task without being burdened by teaching duties. At that time progress in the branch of science he represented was particularly rapid. The Academy also decided to use some of the laboratory premises at the Institute for research, under the direction of Professor W. Palmaer, into the corrosion of metals.

At the Nobel Institute Oseen carried out research in different branches of physical theory. Besides purely mathematical investigations he worked on problems in classical mechanics and geometrical optics. He also made important contributions to the theory of anisotropic liquids and to modern atomic theory. Oseen was interested in the history of science and made a study of the development of physics and chemistry in Sweden during the eighteenth century, especially of the work of J. C. Wilcke, Torbern Bergman and Scheele.

On Palmaer's death in 1942, the Academy decided to place the laboratory premises used by him at the disposal of Professor B. Holmberg of the Stockholm Institute of Technology for his investigations into the chemistry of organic sulphur compounds and lignin. In 1944, a personal chair of organic chemistry was established for him at the Academy. When Oseen died at the end of the same year, his department again became a department of chemistry, this time organic chemistry, with Holmberg as its acting head. The financial and technical resources of this department were, however, comparatively small and its organization remained provisional.

In 1952 Professor Holmberg finished his work in the laboratory which had originally been developed by Arrhenius. He was later succeeded by Dr. Lars Melander who was appointed temporary head of chemical research of the Nobel Institute. The studies conducted there concentrated mainly on the problems of theoretical organic chemistry. Together with a great number of young coworkers, both Swedish and other nationals, Melander performed a series of investigations of very high quality in which he studied primarily the isotope effects on reaction rates. He left the Institute in 1964 to accept an appointment as Professor of Organic Chemistry at the University of Gothenburg.

In the same year the Nobel Foundation and the Academy made an agreement with the Swedish Government to transfer the ground and the building of the Nobel Institute to the State, which took over the management of research work being done at the Institute.

When the department of physical chemistry was established in 1905, it was anticipated that by 1922 the income from the funds would have increased so as to enable the Academy to set up the projected departments of physics and chemistry as well. However, the subsequent fall in the value of money and the increasing cost of laboratory equipment due to the rapid advance of science, upset these calculations, and it was not until 1935 that definite plans for the organization of these departments could be drawn up. It was then found that the income available would after all be insufficient for the purpose, and it was therefore decided to make a beginning with a department of physics only.

A request was accordingly submitted to the *Riksdag* to establish at the Academy a personal research professorship of experimental physics for Professor Manne Siegbahn of Uppsala. The Academy undertook to make the necessary appropriations from the foundation fund of the physics-prize section towards the erection of a building for the new department on the site of the Nobel Institute. Considerable grants for the purchase of instruments and equipment and for running expenses had been promised by the Knut and Alice Wallenberg Foundation. The *Riksdag* approved the request, and Siegbahn took up his duties as Director on July 1, 1937. In the course of the same year the building of the new institute was completed.

The principal item on its programme was nuclear research, and the construction of a cyclotron was therefore an urgent necessity. The expenses were met by a grant from the Wallenberg Foundation, and after a subterranean laboratory had been built and preliminary tests made, a cyclotron was constructed capable of accelerating deuterons of up to 5 to 6 million electron-volts. This apparatus, which was ready for use at the end of 1939, had subsequently been considerably improved. It has been of the greatest value, not only for the research carried out at the Institute but also for supplying radioactive isotopes to laboratories and hospitals throughout Sweden.

It soon became evident, however, that another cyclotron of greater capacity was required, both for research on nuclear processes and to meet the demand for radioactive material for various purposes. Liberal contributions from the Wallenberg and Rockefeller Foundations, and from other donors, as well as state subsidies have enabled a cyclotron for particle energies [deuterons] of 25 to 30 million electron-volts to be constructed recently.

A high-tension generator for 400,000 volts was built, as a provisional measure, during the war. It has recently been transformed into a plant for $1\frac{1}{2}$ million volts.

Research into the structure of atomic nuclei is mainly based on studies of the energy and radiation of the different radioactive isotopes. For this purpose an electromagnetic isotope separator has been constructed at the Institute, and several new types of nuclear spectrographs for various purposes have been designed and built.

With these technical resources, and after suitable methods, new in some respects, had been developed, a number of important projects for research were taken up. The radiation processes of unstable atomic nuclei and nuclear reactions of various kinds have been studied and exact measurements made of the magnetic properties of atomic nuclei. Other projects tackled by Siegbahn and his staff include the construction of an electron microscope of a new pattern and a ruling-engine for producing gratings, which are used for high-precision spectroscopic measurements.

THE PEACE PRIZE

BY AUGUST SCHOU

INTRODUCTION

Alfred Nobel's attitude to the peace question was from the very first influenced by his great interest in literature, not least by his youthful enthusiasm for Shelley. It was, however, not until later that his interest in peace crystallized into anything like a clear conception of what this problem really entailed and the most practical method of solving it.

Nobel's acquaintance with the Austrian writer, Bertha von Suttner, had a great bearing on this matter. They met for the first time in Paris in 1876 when she answered his advertisement for a private secretary. Their acquaintance was to prove somewhat fleeting, however, as the lady never took up the appointment, but got married instead. The next time they met was in 1887 when the von Suttners were staying in Paris, and the last time was in August 1892 when Nobel met her in Berne in order to get information about the IVth Universal Peace Congress held there. However, they carried on a fairly regular correspondence, and Bertha von Suttner declared later in her memoirs that her ideas were in every respect decisive for Nobel's view of the peace question and the drawing up of his bequest. Meanwhile a closer and more critical examination of Nobel's own letters has shown that this is not quite the case. Nobel certainly admired Bertha von Suttner both for her writings and for her propaganda work. But his versatile mind and his complicated attitude to social relations, especially where the peace question was concerned, made it difficult for him to accept the absolute ideas of the friends of peace on the subject of general disarmament and compulsory arbitration. In a letter to Bertha von Suttner on October 31, 1891, he gives a very detailed explanation of his point of view. If any practical results were to be achieved, he declared in this letter, it would be necessary to proceed gradually and carefully. Nobel alluded in this connection to a suggestion that the various governments should contract agreements on the peaceful settlement of disputes, and that the validity of such agreements should be limited to one year. Even the more cynical statesmen would, in the opinion of Nobel, have no real objections to committing themselves for such a short period of time, and once a start had been made this procedure could probably in time be crystallized into a system.

In 1892 Nobel appointed an unemployed Turkish diplomat, Aristarchi Bey, as an adviser on the peace problem. But they only worked together for a short time, as the diplomat in question was quite obviously not particularly keen on the task. Yet at the same time Nobel's letters show that Aristarchi's undoubted diplomatic prudence has played a considerable role in clarifying Nobel's own attitude to the peace problem. Especially remarkable was a plan for collective security which Nobel propounded to Bertha von Suttner in a letter written in 1892: by mutually binding military agreements between nations one might create an international atmosphere of security, which in its turn would facilitate gradual disarmament. In this connection Nobel alludes to the danger of the great social revolution: 'A new tyranny, that of the dregs of the population, is lurking in the shadows and one can almost hear its distant rumble.'

Apart from the gradual easing of tensions produced by agreements, Nobel hoped that the increased effectiveness of the means of war themselves would have a deterrent effect on powers with aggressive tendencies. According to Bertha von Suttner he formulated in 1892 his view on this matter thus: 'My factories may well put an end to war sooner than your congresses. The day when two army corps can annihilate one another in one second, all civilized nations, it is to be hoped, will recoil from war and discharge their troops.'

However, Nobel can hardly have had any real confidence in the automatic validity of this argument. For it was at this time that his idea of giving economic support to the peace movement by means of a bequest took shape. The actual circumstances attending the creation of this testament have already been mentioned elsewhere in this publication.* We shall merely repeat the formula as far as the Peace Prize is concerned, which is to be given to 'the person who shall have done the most or the best work for fraternity among nations, for the abolition or reduction of standing armies and for the holding and promotion of peace congresses'.

There is no reliable evidence to explain why Nobel gave the Norwegian Storting the right to choose the Peace Prize Committee. Some people have declared that Nobel's thought was that this in itself would bring about a relaxation of tension in the Swedish-Norwegian Union conflict which had just become acute at that time. There is, however, nothing to indicate that Nobel was particularly concerned with this conflict. Nor did the decision result in any immediate relaxation of tension, when it was made known. On the contrary, several Swedish newspapers were

* See pp. 26 ff.; cf. also Ragnvald Moe, *Le Prix Nobel de la Paix et l'Institut Nobel Norvégien*, Vol. I [Oslo 1932].

exceedingly indignant at the idea that the distribution of the Peace Prize should be entrusted to the 'separatist Norwegians'.

Another explanation which seems rather probable is that the regulation was a recognition of the Storting's positive attitude to international cooperation and especially to the question of arbitration; though here too there is no real proof. A third explanation involves that Nobel's stipulation with regard to the Peace Prize was based on his admiration for the great Norwegian poet Björnstjerne Björnson, who at that time played a prominent rôle in the peace movement.

The method of distributing the Peace Prize is briefly as follows: In order to be considered, proposals must be sent in prior to February 1 of the year in which the distribution is to take place. Those entitled to propose the name of a recipient are given warning in good time through circulars. The following are entitled to make proposals: Members and late members of the Nobel Committee of the Norwegian Parliament, as well as the advisers appointed at the Norwegian Nobel Institute; Members of Parliament and Members of Government of the different States, as well as Members of the Interparliamentary Union; Members of the International Arbitration Court at the Hague; Members of the Council of the International Peace Bureau; Members and Associates of the Institute of International Law; University professors of Political Science and of Law, of History and of Philosophy; and persons who have received the Nobel Peace Prize.

As a basis for judging the candidates who are found worthy of closer investigation, the Committee in its first years had statements worked out by the Secretary of the Committee. After 1904 this activity assumed more fixed forms when the Norwegian Nobel Institute was set up, with three advisers appointed, viz. in International Law, Political History, and Political Economy. Together with these three advisers the Secretary [1928 designated Director of the Norwegian Nobel Institute] works out the annual statements. To a large extent use is made of material in the library of the Institute, which on December 31, 1970, contained 90,580 volumes. Three librarians are attached to the library.

In addition the Nobel Institute has the task of disseminating information on international questions. For this purpose the reading room is regularly open to the public. The Institute has published eight volumes of *Publications de l'Institut Nobel Norvégien*. From 1923 onwards the Institute arranged lectures which were given by international scholars invited for the purpose.

In 1928 lectureships were established in International Law, Economics, and Political History. From 1947 courses have been held on international problems, especially for journalists and teachers. These courses have been arranged specially for people living outside Oslo, and the Committee has regularly made money grants for this purpose.

The fact that the Norwegian Storting chooses the Committee has often led to the supposition that it is the Storting as such which awards the prize. This is, however, not the case. The Norwegian Nobel Committee is completely sovereign in its decisions, and its members need not necessarily be representatives of the Storting. Another matter is that the composition of the Committee has throughout the years to a very large extent reflected the party political situation in the country, even though it would be impossible to claim that the Committee has taken any direct tactical considerations in making its dispositions. Thus one could rather speak of a definite fundamental viewpoint, viz. bourgeois-liberal. Only in more recent years have socialistic views been directly represented; in former days to a far more marked degree than is the case to-day, there was a considerable difference between the bourgeois and the socialist approach to pacifism. This state of affairs is also partly reflected in the awards of the prize. It was a long time before a Socialist was awarded the Peace Prize [La Fontaine, 1913]. On the other hand most of the prize-winners up to that time were not really anti-socialist in their attitude; on the contrary, many of them represented a fairly radical policy, and generally speaking most of them were opposed to the former conception of the peace movement as being organically bound up with the principles of free competition.

The Nobel Committee which awards the Peace Prize has, in contradistinction to the Swedish adjudicating institutions, seldom given any official reason for its decisions, and this has considerably increased the criticism which on many occasions has been levelled at its choice. An oft-repeated argument is that the Committee has acted against Nobel's decisions by setting aside peace workers in favour of political opportunists. Admittedly, if we follow the awards of the Peace Prize from year to year, we shall at first glance have some difficulty in tracing any line, let alone any development. But this may partly be due to the fact that the peace movement, taken all round, has not undergone any 'comprehensive development' as is the case with the various spheres of activity of the recipients of the science prizes, or the prizes for medicine. After all, this is characteristic of the fatal split in our culture. But if we try to arrange the prize-winners in groups, in botanical fashion, as it were, we shall nevertheless discover a clear continuity, and get the impression that the Committee has sought to further certain *tendencies* of the age, which have in many cases without any doubt resulted in a relaxation of international tension.

Another objection which has often been made is that the prize-winners are usually old people. Instead, it is pointed out, the Committee should have encouraged young and active people who, even though they might have made an important contribution, would nevertheless have many years of rich endeavour before them. The Peace Prize is undoubtedly the one which, of all the groups of prizes, has the highest average age for its recipients, viz. sixty-five years. For the period prior to 1914 there is a fairly obvious reason for this: in this period it was quite natural to award the prize principally to people who had carried out pioneer peace work, and these people had already reached a fairly advanced age by the time the Committee started its work. As far as later years are concerned, there is no such general explanation forthcoming. Many considerations and conditions may have contributed. But one would be well advised not to set any 'optimum age' for peace workers. People can just as well carry out a work of importance to peace at the age of thirty as they can at the age of seventy. And as far as the still older people are concerned, it may be that the ideas for which they fought have only at a later date proved their vitality and their efficacy in a certain situation. But some of them have without a doubt not received their reward until many years after their real great life's work was done. In such cases it would be natural to place them on the same footing as prize-winners from an earlier age. This is for example the case with Emily Greene Balch [1946], who is mentioned together with Jane Addams [1931], and John Mott [1946], who is described together with Nathan Söderblom [1930]. In other cases too it has been natural to make some alteration in the sequence, but this has as a rule been done within a certain period. For greater clarity the year of each award is added in italics wherever necessary. By 1970, 52 Peace Prizes had been awarded. Of these 14 have been divided between two prize-winners; in two cases this applied to institutions [The Friends' Service Council and the American Friends' Service Committee; The International Committee of the Red Cross and the League of the Red Cross societies]. Altogether 54 individuals have received the prize and 10 institutions, of which one, viz. the *Comité International de la Croix-Rouge* has been rewarded three times.

Table showing nationality of individual recipients

U.S.A., 15
France, 9
Gt. Britain, 7
Sweden, 4
Belgium, Germany, Switzerland, 3 each
Austria, Norway, 2 each
Argentina, Canada, Denmark, Italy, The Netherlands, South Africa, 1 each

PIONEER PEACE WORKERS

Dunant, Passy, Cremer, Moneta, Bertha von Suttner, Fried, Bajer, Arnoldson, Ducommun, Gobat, Bureau International Permanent de la Paix

On December 10, *1901*, the Peace Prize was awarde for the first time. The recipients were HENRI DUNANT [1828-1910] and FRÉDÉRIC PASSY [1822-1912]. Henri Dunant's remarkable and tragic career is so well-known to-day that it is unnecessary to go into details. Born and bred in Geneva, he was strongly influenced by the spirit which pervaded Calvin's town, with its blend of moral earnestness and a practical business outlook. At the same time he was a pronounced dreamer, and in money matters somewhat of a gambler. With his book *Un Souvenir de Solférino* [1862] and his indefatigable propaganda, it will be recalled, he evoked a new sense of responsibility in the civilized world, a feeling which found expression in the creation of the International Red Cross in 1864. Less generally known, perhaps, are the new international measures which Dunant tried to put into operation, even when economic disaster had brought him to poverty and misery in 1870. During the Franco-Prussian war, for example, he founded an association with international aims, the *Association de Prévoyance,* an association which in 1871 was renamed the *Alliance Universelle de l'Ordre et de la Civilisation.* It had branches in France, England, Belgium, Bavaria, and the United States of America. One of the principal aims of the Association was to work for the establishment of an international court of arbitration. In 1872 this Alliance held a meeting in Paris where Frédéric Passy delivered a lecture on arbitration. The French branch was, however, greatly handicapped by internal political conflicts. More positive work was done by the English branch, and during a stay in London from 1874 to 1877 Dunant carried out some important work there. Amongst other things he joined in the movement against the slave trade, which was still flourishing in many parts of the world, especially in Africa. He was also Secretary of a Committee working to solve 'The Eastern Problem' by means of peaceful European colonization in the Middle East, especially in Palestine.

His most important contribution, however, was his work for prisoners of war. Already in 1867, at the general meeting of the Red Cross held during the World Exhibition in Paris, he had proposed the principle of the inviolability of prisoners of war on the same lines as sick and wounded. The French and the British branches of the *Alliance Universelle* gave their warmest support to this idea, and in 1874, on the initiative of the Russian Czar, Alexander II, a conference was convened in Brussels with the object of drawing up a convention dealing with the rules of warfare generally, including also the question of the treatment of prisoners of war. The conference achieved no positive results, but Dunant's idea itself was later to have a decisive influence on international agreements in this field.

After the end of the 1870's, Dunant was gradually forgotten, and it was not until 1895 that he was, as it were, 'rediscovered' by a German journalist. In the following years he participated from time to time in peace-work propaganda, *inter alia* contributing articles to Bertha von Suttner's periodical *Die Waffen nieder*. In these years too there is clear evidence of Dunant's well-developed sense for the value of effective propaganda. One of the most typical examples of this is a letter which has been preserved in the archives of the Nobel Institute. The letter is dated March 14, 1898, and is addressed to Victor Hugo's daughter, Countess Wiznievski, who had founded a Women's Peace League in Paris. In this letter Dunant criticizes a member of the League for having described the movement, in a letter published in a newspaper, as numerically weak. 'That is always a nuisance,' writes Dunant, 'since the masses you appeal to love strength and numbers.' And he continues: 'If everybody were as good and well-disposed towards his neighbour as you yourself, Madam, and your friends, that would not matter, but we want to have with us in the League lots of people who do not possess those qualities, or at least only to a small degree, and who follow the fashion of the day or the great majority. For that reason we must not lower ourselves in their eyes. After joining out of sheer infatuation, these people will gradually learn to love peace and understand its value; thus it is from every point of view important that they should join. It's good propaganda that people have never considered what war costs! Once they are members they are bound to consider this great question.'

Both in 1901 and later on great surprise was caused by the fact that Dunant had to share the Peace Prize with Frédéric Passy. In that connection several people have wondered whether the Committee by their action wished to imply that the founding of the Red Cross was not really perfectly valid peace work. The Committee, as is its custom, issued no statement to explain the prize-awards, but it is most improbable that this was in fact the attitude of the Committee to the Red Cross or to Dunant's peace contribution. As far as the award of 1901 is concerned, it might perhaps be possible to explain it on these lines: first and foremost the Committee wished to make it clear that they considered Dunant's work to be the greatest individual contribution to 'fraternity among nations'; secondly, they wished to pay a tribute to a man whose work contributed directly to the organization of peace, and whose activity was an eminently positive combination of internationalism and patriotism. Dunant's undeniable Swiss patriotism was possibly more easily compatible with an international point of view, springing as it did from the neutral Swiss milieu. Frédéric Passy's activities, on the other hand, developed largely in the shadow of the conflict between France and Germany. His attitude to the peace movement had developed gradually, on a rational foundation and under the influence of the ideas of free trade. As a writer on economics he became an ardent champion of the theories of liberalism based on economic harmony achieved by freedom of enterprise; but at the same time he emphasized, more strongly than most, that *solidarity* must be the basis of all economic activity. At a comparatively early age Passy became acquainted with the ideas of the peace movement, but did not participate actively until 1856. The Crimean War was then entering its last phase, while at the same time the flooding of the Loire river had proved a great catastrophe. In this connection Passy drew attention to the contrast between the horror such natural catastrophes inspired in the masses, and the stoical calm so typical of the attitude towards the *artificial* catastrophes, for which man himself is responsible in war. From now on Passy devoted all his efforts to the peace movement, and he came into personal contact with the leading protagonists of free trade in England, Cobden and Bright.

He made an important contribution in 1867 with a peace appeal in *Le Temps*. It assisted greatly in allaying the war psychosis which seemed about to break out in connection with the Luxembourg conflict between France and Prussia. In the same year he assisted in founding the *Ligue Internationale et Permanente de la Paix*. He became Secretary of the organization and its driving force. The organization was broken up by the Franco-Prussian War of 1870, but was later restarted under the name of the *Société Française des Amis de la Paix*. Passy became its Secretary General, and in 1871 he published an appeal, *Revanche ou Relèvement*. In it he voiced a demand for a real peace settlement between France and Germany on the basis of voluntary arbitration and national sovereignty, with Alsace-Lorraine as an independent neutral area.

In 1881 Passy was elected a member of the Chambre des Députés, and thus entered practical politics. In the Chamber he succeeded in forming a group which worked to put into effect the ideas of the peace movement, especially the idea of voluntary arbitration. This instrument was used in a dispute with the Netherlands on the subject of Guiana. In 1889 he also managed to create a favourable atmosphere for a treaty of arbitration with the United States of America. But at the elections which took place before the matter was finally decided he lost his seat in the Chamber, so that his work in this respect had to be continued by others. At this point, however, Passy had helped to realize an idea which had been mooted by the British politician Randal Cremer, viz. the establishment of the Inter-Parliamentary Union. A start was made in 1888 at a meeting in Paris between French and British parliamentarians, and the next year the Union became an established fact with the holding of the first real International Conference [this too was in Paris, during the World Exhibition]. In all the exacting preliminary work, the drawing up of agenda, the printing and distribution of invitations, etc., Passy bore the brunt of the work.

Up to a ripe old age he was busy, organizing and agitating, encouraging and admonishing. Among his many lectures and pamphlets there are few which give such a clear impression of his intense preoccupation with the peace problem as a lecture on the future of Europe which was delivered in 1895. Here he describes the European situation as follows: 'I need hardly describe the present state of Europe to you. The entire able-bodied population are preparing to massacre one another; though no one, it is true, wants to attack, and everybody protests his love of peace and determination to maintain it, yet the whole world feels that it only requires some unforeseen incident, some unpreventable accident, for the spark to fall in a flash, as Lord Palmerston put it, on these heaps of inflammable material which are being foolishly piled up in the fields and on the highways, and blow all Europe sky-high.' At the same time he points out that peace between the nations is dependent on stable political conditions in the respective countries: 'Yes, there is error, there is vice, there is crime, if you will; but there is something else at the bottom of all this: it is easy to drag them into it. Beware! If you want the governments, be they monarchies or republics, to be calm and safe, try not to allow dangerous explosives to accumulate in what we might call the hidden depths of the community.'*

This connection between the policy of social reform and the peace question was still more strongly felt in the life work of Passy's friend and collaborator, WILLIAM RANDAL CREMER [1838-1908, *1903*]. While Dunant's social conscience had been moulded by the philanthropic tendencies of a puritan capitalist class, and Passy was conditioned by his position as an economically independent intellectual, Cremer's background was the working class and the sense of solidarity which was making itself felt within its ranks. He was born in Fareham in southern England, the child of poverty-stricken parents. He had to go to work at an early age, first as a pitch boy in a shipyard, later as a builder's carpenter in London. The building trade at that time played a leading role in the trade-union movement then in its infancy, and Cremer soon took a leading part in the organizing work. In 1858 a campaign was started for a nine-hour day, and Cremer was one of the leading spirits, both in his propaganda work and in the collection of funds.

Within the ranks of the British working class a strong feeling of international solidarity was evoked at an early stage, embracing not only the working classes themselves, but also just as much movements for national freedom. The nationalist movement in countries like Poland and Italy was followed with tense expectation, and during the American War between the States the British workers were given a practical opportunity of demonstrating what their love of freedom was worth. The blockade of the Southern ports inaugurated by the North had naturally resulted in a real shortage of cotton for the textile industry, and the employers were very largely on the side of the Southern States. But the workers, who were probably hardest hit by the results of the blockade, followed nevertheless

* *L'Avenir de l'Europe*, p. 16.

the Liberals in their sympathy for the cause of the Northern States, and at a meeting in 1863, led by John Bright, Cremer addressed the audience, together with other workers' leaders.

At this time the idea of an international organization of workers grew up. The initiative was taken by the joint body in London, and Cremer played an outstanding role when the First International was founded in 1864. Politically Cremer was, however, not really a Socialist, and he took strong exception to the revolutionary line represented by Karl Marx and many of the leaders from the continental countries. For Cremer and his friends practical social and political reforms implied primarily that the workers would have an opportunity of making their influence felt in the life of the nation, a development which in their opinion might proceed on the basis of the existing society. In practical politics therefore Cremer belonged to the radical section of the Liberal Party.

The reception of Garibaldi in London, in April 1864, which Cremer helped to organize, was the occasion of a strong democratic demonstration, and it was coupled with the agitation for an extension of the franchise. During the Franco-Prussian War in 1870, Cremer founded the *Workmen's Peace Association,* later renamed the *International Arbitration League.*

The first and foremost aim of this organization was to prevent Great Britain becoming embroiled in war. British war mentality at that time was undergoing two different phases. To start with it had its adherents mostly in aristocratic circles working for an alliance with Germany against France. On the other hand, after the fall of the Empire, certain democrats demanded that Britain should hasten to the aid of the new French Republic. Neither of these circles was, however, particularly influential. The situation was very different during the Russo-Turkish War of 1877-78. On this occasion 'Jingoism' coincided more naturally with Great Britain's traditional interests. The general excitement found expression in the flood of threats and abuse directed at Cremer and others who were striving to keep the country out of war. Later too Cremer was to have an opportunity of trying his strength with aggressive nationalism, not least during the Boer War.

At the same time he worked tirelessly to give practical form to the idea of arbitration, especially after he had been elected a member of the House of Commons in 1885. Here, like Passy, he had an opportunity of influencing leading politicians. As already mentioned, Cremer was the first to hit upon the idea of forming an international organization of parliamentarians. In 1888 he stayed in Paris in order to acquaint the French Foreign Minister, Goblet, with the progress of the idea of arbitration in Great Britain and the United States. At the same time he suggested to Frédéric Passy that he should arrange a meeting between French and British parliamentarians.

Cremer's most important contribution to the cause of international arbitration concerned an attempted agreement between Great Britain and the U.S.A. In 1885 he got 234 members of the House to sign an appeal to the American President and Congress on the subject of an Anglo-American treaty of arbitration. In 1893 the attempt was repeated with an even greater number of adherents, and Cremer made several trips to the U.S.A. in order to create a favourable atmosphere. American circles were favourable to the idea and President Cleveland gave it his personal support. His successor Mc Kinley shared the same views. The proposal for a treaty of arbitration also secured a majority in the Senate, though not large enough to effect its ratification. It was not till several years later that the matter was finally and successfully negotiated, but there never was any doubt but that Cremer had led the way.

While Cremer's political personality was the product of a social freedom movement, ERNESTO TEODORO MONETA [1833-1918, *1907*] bore all the marks of a struggle for national independence. The most far-reaching impressions of his early days he received in the fighting on the barricades in Milan during the revolution of 1848. His father, then a man of sixty, with a family of eleven children, joined in the fighting, and fifteen-year-old Ernesto helped to defend the house. During the years prior to the war of liberation of 1859-61, young Moneta was the leader of a secret society which maintained contact with the patriot hero Pallavicino. In 1859 he fought under Garibaldi in North Italy, and in the following year at Volturno in Calabria. Later he was an officer in the Italian army, but after the defeat at Custozza in 1866 he resigned his commission, and devoted himself wholly to publishing.

In 1867 Moneta became editor of *Il Secolo,* which under his leadership became the most widely read newspaper in Italy. To start with he wrote a number of articles on military questions, championing the idea of transforming the army into a militia. For, in common with so many champions of peace in those days, Moneta was no believer in the principle of non-violence in the face of aggression. He saw no incompatibility between defending the right of a nation to self-government and the work of promoting international understanding. In this respect too he was in agreement with the leaders of the Italian national movement, men like Mazzini and Garibaldi. In his Nobel lecture he quoted a manifesto which the Milanese revolutionaries published in 1848 after the Austrians had been expelled from the town: 'The day is probably not far distant when all nations will forget old quarrels and rally to the banner of international brotherhood, putting an end to all conflict and enjoying peace and friendship, strengthened by the bonds of commerce and industry. We look forward to that day. Italians! Free and independent we shall seal the peace of brotherhood with our own hands, not least with the nations which to-day constitute the Austrian Empire, if only they are willing.'*

Holding these views Moneta never became a militarist, and after he had taken up active peace work about 1870, he was to have frequent opportunities of proving that his feeling of international solidarity was proof against the nationalist fever which at intervals swept across the new Italy. Most important no doubt was his campaign directed against the Francophobia which flared up after the French occupation of Tunis in 1881. In the columns of *Il Secolo,* of which he remained editor-in-chief until 1896, through popular pamphlets and the periodical *Vita Internazionale,* and through his leadership of the peace league *Sociatà internazionale per la pace: Unione Lombarda,* which he had founded in 1887, he worked to calm strained tempers. The easing of tension in Franco-Italian relations which gradually ensued, and which was confirmed by the arbitration treaty of 1903, was undoubtedly due to definite factors in power politics. Yet there is no doubt that Moneta and his fellow workers to a very large extent contributed to create the atmosphere which facilitated an easing of tension. As far as Moneta himself was concerned, considerations of power politics played no role in this connection. This is most clearly demonstrated by his attitude to the 'Irredentist' movement, which aimed at winning Trentino and Trieste from Austria, if need be by force. In this case Moneta's attitude was always as follows: by right these two areas should belong to Italy, but a settlement could only be made on the basis of justice and in the spirit of goodwill. It was imperative not to exploit good relations with France or any other great power in order to press one's own claims.

The struggle against Irredentism, as Moneta himself often declared, en-

* Published [in French] in *Les Prix Nobel,* 1907.

tailed far greater psychological difficulties than 'Gallophobia'. In a pamphlet which he published in 1903, in connection with an attack on Italian students in Trieste, he expressed his views as follows: 'Gallophobia is characterized by base and ignoble sentiments: petty complaints, the feeling of slighted prestige or some injustice or other which the French people or their government may have done our nation, cause us to forget that Italy is largely indebted to France for her greatest benefit, namely her independence. In Irredentism, on the other hand, runs a strong vein of patriotism, a feeling of love and sympathy for brothers who are forced, by an ancient right of conquest, to live beneath a regime they detest. This emotion inspires the desire to work and toil for the day when they can be re-united with the common fatherland, which loves them and will never forget them.'*

BERTHA VON SUTTNER [1843-1914, *1905*] made a new and very real contribution to the peace movement. She was the first female peace worker of real stature, and through her novel *Die Waffen nieder* [1889] she gave the movement an effective slogan. These two factors helped to make her reputation almost legendary, and many people have credited her not only with decisively influencing Nobel's attitude to the peace question, but also Czar Nicolas II's initiative in convoking the Peace Conference at The Hague in 1899. But even if we set aside these purely legendary accretions, we shall still find a great life's work and a significant personality.

Bertha von Suttner had secured a solid ideological platform when in the middle of the 1880's she came into contact with the organized peace movement.

She was a member of an Austrian noble family, von Kinsky by name, and in 1876 she became the wife of Baron von Suttner. For a number of years after their marriage they lived in the Caucasus, making their living by all sorts of literary work. Von Suttner's family had been violently opposed to the match, and it was not till 1885 that a reconciliation was effected and they were able to enjoy easier circumstances.

During these years Bertha von Suttner had studied assiduously, especially the work of Buckle, Spencer and Darwin. She concluded from the doctrine of evolution that a new set of social standards was taking shape, a moral outlook which would gradually find expression in greater solidarity within the various nations and also in international relations. She embodied her ideas on these problems in a book, *Das Maschinenzeitalter,* which she pub-

* *Irredentismo e gallofobia,* p. 19.

lished anonymously in 1888. The book was written in the form of a series of imaginary lectures on her own age, given by a professor in about the year 3000 A.D. The writer makes her professor show, amongst other things, how 'atavistic' ideas about religion survived far into the age of science. In this connection she attacks the 'politically pious', 'the militarily pious', 'the respectably pious', and the 'spiritualistically pious' or those who officially pass for far-sighted philosophers but in reality support the most dogmatic religion.

The actual war mentality is in her opinion rooted primarily in the official attitude of hostility to life which permeates the community. 'Every effort was made to prevent school children getting to know anything at all about the forces in Nature which help to perpetuate Life, let alone anything about the attendant manifestations of pleasure. They could, however, not be told enough about the many ways in which Life is painfully destroyed, while in descriptions of past battles no sadistic detail was too gruesome to be excluded.' And further on we find this more forcibly expressed: 'The most honourable and enviable death is in your opinion the one found in 'homicidal struggle', and to your love-children you affix the label of 'illegitimate birth'. You praise death so highly that you deem it worthy of being suffered by your God Himself – in agony, bleeding, lamenting – on the cross, and the opposite of a lingering death, i.e. life perpetuated in delight, you have ascribed to the work of Satan.'*

The novel *Die Waffen nieder* which appeared the following year was designedly simpler in composition and contents. It described a young woman's war sufferings. In 1859 the chief character of the novel marries an officer who loses his life in the war in Italy. From that day she hates war. Later on she marries another officer who shares her views, but nevertheless out of a conventional sense of duty takes part in the wars of 1864 and 1866. Finally, however, he resigns his commission. During the Franco-Prussian War of 1870-71, the Austrian couple are staying in Paris. During the siege the man is arrested on suspicion of being a Prussian spy and is shot.

The book made a tremendous stir, and in the course of a short time it was translated into a great many foreign languages. Next to Harriet Beecher Stowe's *Uncle Tom's Cabin*, the novel *Die Waffen nieder* undoubtedly found a readier response than any other work of fiction in the nine-

* *Das Maschinenzeitalter*, pp. 54, 166.

teenth century. Both novels were written by women, and yet the personalities of the two authors were essentially different. They were both impelled by a strong and uncompromising feeling, but Bertha von Suttner was to a much greater extent an intellectual who aimed primarily at making people react against the *absurdity* of what she attacked. And believing as she did in the theory of evolution, she maintained that the very success of the book proved that the reaction against war was about to become a 'dominant idea' of the age. 'The lightning can only strike when the air is charged with electricity', as she expressed it. Now was the time to exploit this new spirit, canalize it, give it form. Immediately after her book had been published, she devoted her energies to the peace movement. In 1891 she founded the *Austrian Peace Organization* and in the same year she took part in the International Peace Congress in Rome. The establishment of an inter-parliamentary group in Austria was also largely due to her endeavours. Between 1892 and 1899 she was editor-in-chief of the periodical *Die Waffen nieder*, and at the same time she constantly extended her personal contacts, both by conferences and lecture tours. During the Peace Congress at The Hague in 1899 she kept a salon which was frequented by several of the most important delegates. Many optimists regarded this conference as the prelude to a new age. All the greater was their disappointment at the modest results achieved, at the defeat of the very idea of peace in the Boer War, and the barbaric suppression of the Boxer Rebellion shortly afterwards.

Bertha von Suttner, however, maintained that it was in just such a situation that the fight against war should be relentlessly pursued. Discussing the Boer War she declared that the imperialistic policy behind it was not the most dangerous thing, but the fact that the leaders were prepared, in order to back such a policy, to mobilize some of the noblest qualities of man – self-sacrifice, the belief that they were fighting for justice and culture, etc. Therefore it was necessary to try to direct these tendencies to other and loftier ideals. Then a favourable transformation of society could also take place. It is just here that Bertha von Suttner shows more clearly than most others the difference between the bourgeois and the socialistic conception of the peace problem. In an article written in 1896 she expressed it as follows: 'We do not say that this or that must happen, or this or that class come into power, and then war will certainly disappear or will disappear of its own accord, but we say: First the world must be released from the threat of world war and the armaments race, then the other social questions can be solved more easily and more justly.'*

Bertha von Suttner believed that the peace idea could be realized by personally influencing the ruling classes in the community. Her literary production appealed first and foremost to the upper middle classes, and here lay at the same time her strength and her limitations.

In her propaganda work Bertha von Suttner found an effective collaborator in her countryman ALFRED FRIED [1864-1921, *1911*]. Originally trained as a bookseller he later transferred to journalism, and in 1891 he started the periodical *Die Waffen nieder,* which he persuaded Bertha von Suttner to edit. In the autumn of 1892 he founded in Berlin the *Deutsche Friedensgesellschaft,* which was later moved to Stuttgart. Between 1894 and 1899 he published on behalf of this association the *Monatliche Friedenskorrespondenz*, and in 1899 he founded *Die Friedenswarte*. This periodical, from 1912 under the editorship of Professor Hans Wehberg, and from 1933 on with its headquàrters in Zurich enjoyed a very special position among peace publications. First and foremost the editors carefully observed absolute objectivity in their treatment of the peace question, and the periodical therefore included articles and book-reviews which were always highly instructive. Fried's primary aim was to deal with the peace question in such a way that it aroused interest in intellectual circles. In this way he was able to exercise a very considerable influence on German views on the problems of international law, which hitherto had chiefly been marked solely by the Prussian ideology of might.

In his fundamental attitude to the peace problem Fried was opposed to the idea of disarmament, maintaining that the antimilitarist conception of armaments and war as something primary was in fact quite mistaken. They were, he held, really only symptoms of the unhealthy state of international life. The real cause was to be found in the existing international anarchy and could only be removed by establishing an effective international organization. If this were done, disarmament would automatically follow. As far as the detailed plans for such an organization were concerned, Fried relied actually on the basis of the balance of power. But at the same time he maintained that such a balance of power did not necessarily imply national oppression, at any rate not in Europe itself. In this

* *Bertha von Suttner und der Kampf um die Vermeidung des Weltkrieges*, I, [Zurich 1917], pp. 419-20.

respect Pan-Americanism could serve as a model, and he suggested that the example of the New World should be followed, and a 'Pan-European Bureau' set up, which could act as a centre of information on all sorts of economic and cultural matters in the various countries. An information service of this nature would in itself contribute to furthering European unity.

Apart from these activities in the field of peace ideology, Fried was also actively pre-occupied with the problems of his own day. In connection with the first Hague Congress in 1899, for example, he wrote an article about the 'Philistine', who always turns up to mock the 'dreamers', i.e. all those people who by their contribution to science and human thought have constantly brought mankind a step further along the road. It was therefore not surprising that the Philistines should seek to discourage the international 'dreamers'. In this connection Fried utters a word of warning to the press: 'The priests of Philistinism, the newspaper editors, had the pleasant task of mocking and making ridiculous the work of the Hague Conference according to the spirit of their mandates. They performed that task...' And he continues with a few observations which are, alas, only too readily adaptable to our own times: 'The events at an international bicycle race are described in great detail and are eagerly swallowed by the readers, just as the least significant comedian on the local stage is better known to the public than the people who make world history, or the great events of historical importance.'*

In *1908* attention was focused on the peace problems in the Scandinavian countries by the joint award of the prize to the Dane FREDRIK BAJER [1837-1922] and the Swede KLAS PONTUS ARNOLDSON [1844-1916]. Bajer had been an officer, and had served during the German-Danish war of 1864. The following year, however, he had to resign his commission owing to the reductions which were being made in the armed forces. He turned to the study of languages, above all French, Swedish and Norwegian, and did a certain amount of teaching at schools, colleges, etc. The study of languages brought him into contact with the peace movement, and when Frédéric Passy founded his league in 1867, Bajer immediately wrote to him, offering his help in spreading information about the peace movement.

The other idea which absorbed much of his energy in the course of these

* *Unter der weissen Fahne* [Berlin 1901], pp. 190-191.

years was the work of effecting a *rapprochement* between the Scandinavian countries, first of all in the linguistic field and subsequently in the form of a federal agreement.

At an early stage, Bajer entered Danish political life, and in 1869 he assisted in founding the first Liberal association in Copenhagen. From 1872 to 1895 he was a member of the Folketing [one of the chambers in the Danish national assembly], where he proved an untiring advocate of the emancipation of women and the advancement of peace, and an ardent opponent of increased grants for national defence and the fortifications of Copenhagen. In a series of travel letters written in 1886 he ended every letter with this Catonian outburst: 'For the rest I am of the opinion that the fortifications of Copenhagen should be destroyed.' Bajer maintained that the problem of Danish security could not be solved by armaments, nor would a Nordic neutrality defence pact provide a solution. Real security could only be achieved by international recognition of Nordic neutrality. In an article written in 1875 he drew attention to the dangerous situation in which the Nordic countries would find themselves in the event of war breaking out between the North Sea powers and the Baltic powers. The belligerents would in this case do their utmost to win over to their side the states controlling the Sound and the Danish Belts. This danger could only be removed by an international agreement guaranteeing the permanent neutrality of the North, similar to the treaties already in existence for Switzerland and Belgium. Moreover, an arrangement of this kind would, in the opinion of Bajer, contribute greatly to a relaxation of international tension, and it is characteristic of the importance he attached to the matter that the first Danish peace league, which he helped to found in 1882, was given the name *Society for the Promotion of Danish Neutrality.* Bajer studied this question of neutrality very thoroughly, and at the Congress of Peace Societies held at Geneva in 1883 he put forward a concrete proposal. The congress also adopted a resolution in favour of his motion. At the same time he worked hard to promote the idea of arbitration. As an organizer Bajer probably made his greatest contribution when in 1890 he set to work to establish an international bureau of information for peace work. The following year saw the setting up of this office, the Permanent Peace Bureau, in Berne.

The Swedish prize-winner, K. P. Arnoldson, was to an even greater extent than Bajer a self-taught man in the world of international affairs. At the same time there was a great difference both in their personalities and the problems they tackled. Bajer was the prudent, persuasive advocate, Arnoldson the inspired and popular orator. While Bajer to a great extent had found his way to the peace movement via a matter-of-fact interest in languages, Arnoldson's connection with it was in part due to a personal conflict with all forms of strait-laced religious dogmatism. This, together with his violent reaction to the wars of the 1860's and 1870-71, made him a passionate advocate of pacifism. In 1881 he gave up his job as a clerk in the railways, and devoted himself entirely to work for peace and progress. The same year he was elected a member of the Swedish *Riksdag*. In 1883 he helped to found the *Swedish Peace and Arbitration League*.

Like Bajer, Arnoldson was also a champion of Nordic neutrality, though in Arnoldson's case the common Scandinavian problems were to play a far greater role; for after 1890 the problems of the Swedish-Norwegian union came to a head. As a political radical Arnoldson had with intense interest followed the rise of the Norwegian Liberal party, culminating in 1884 with the fall of the Conservative Government and the introduction of parliamentarism in Norway. On frequent journeys in both countries Arnoldson did his utmost to strengthen the friendship existing between Norwegians and Swedes, and it was on a lecture tour to Oslo in 1890 that he urged a number of representatives to pass a resolution in the Storting in favour of arbitration. When the union conflict became critical in 1895, Arnoldson did his utmost to make the Norwegian point of view known in Sweden, and he influenced public opinion in both countries in favour of a peaceful settlement. He continued this work right up to 1905 when the conflict entered on its final stages and resulted in a peaceful dissolution of the Norwegian-Swedish union. Arnoldson encountered fierce opposition in Swedish Conservative circles in this matter, and the award to him of the Peace Prize provoked considerable acrimony. On the other hand it was welcomed in Liberal and Social-Democrat circles, and it is characteristic that the proposal to give him the prize was sent in by thirty-four members of the Swedish *Riksdag*.

The prize-winners we have so far mentioned had one thing in common – with the exception of Dunant – viz. that they acted as pioneers of the organized peace movement in their respective countries, or – as in the case of Cremer – they built up organizations partly with the support of classes of the community which had not previously been brought into the movement. Gradually these national peace organizations established better mu-tual contact, and by 1889 peace congresses were held annually.

As we have already mentioned, it was Frederik Bajer who first conceived the idea of establishing a central bureau for peace work. At the congress in London in 1890 he got a committee organized, and in the following year at Rome the proposal to set up an information office, the *Bureau International Permanent de la Paix,* at Berne was agreed to. It commenced its activities on December 1, 1891. Its work consisted in collecting information about questions which concerned the propagation of, and the struggle to put into effect, their common ideas, in bringing together data about institu-tions, associations and individuals working for pacifism, and in improving contact all round. In addition the Bureau was to examine and prepare material for discussion at the International Peace Congresses, and likewise see to it that the resolutions passed at these meetings were implemented. Finally, the Bureau was supposed to keep itself informed about all sorts of peace publications and the most important events in international politics, especially cases of arbitration.

Thus the sphere of activity of the Bureau was fairly extensive, but the staff was not large enough to deal with the amount of work involved. In fact almost the entire work was carried out by one man, the Swiss ÉLIE DUCOMMUN [1833-1906, *1902*]. In daily life he had a high adminis-trative position with the Jura Railway, but he devoted all his spare time, weekdays and Sundays alike, to pacifism; and when he assumed the leadership of the Bureau, it was on the express condition that he should have no remuneration. The work carried out by Ducommun, both re-garding organization and mediation, was enough to occupy one man full time. For that reason he did not, like most of the other prize-winners, have a considerable literary production to his credit; but he undoubtedly had a lot to do with the appeals sent out by the International Peace Congresses, and in the pamphlets which were published in his name we find traces of considerable literary talent and striking acuity of thought. In a dialogue written in 1901, for example, he refutes the conception of the duration of a modern war which was current in the days before 1914. According to this conception, a war between the powers, with modern weapons involved, would admittedly be fearful in its immediate effects, but the damage done would, to a certain extent, be counterbalanced by the fact that the war would be of such short duration. To this conception Ducommun opposed the picture of a long drawn-out war of attrition with alternating advances and retreats, and with operations bound up with a system of trenches and strongpoints. As we all know this picture forecast with striking accuracy the First World War.

Even more of an administrator was the man who shared the Peace Prize with Ducommun, ALBERT GOBAT [1843-1914, *1902*].

He was a lawyer by profession and had held many important political posts. In 1882 he became a member of the Government in the Canton of Berne and for a time acted as its president. In 1884 he became a member of the Swiss *Diet*, and from 1890 on a member of the National Council. These positions enabled Gobat to come into contact with many leading politicians, both Swiss and foreign. While Ducommun's activities lay within the borders of the popular peace movement, Gobat was from the first connected with the Inter-Parliamentary Union. As already mentioned, this organization had been founded in 1888 by Randal Cremer, with Frédéric Passy as the driving force. The first Inter-Parliamentary Conference was held in Paris 1889, the second took place in London in 1890 and the third in Rome in 1891. These conferences were somewhat makeshift and private in appearance. However, the fourth conference in Berne in 1892 initiated a new phase. Even the meeting hall seemed unusual, for previous sessions had taken place in hotels, whereas at Berne they were held in the National Assembly, a custom which has always been followed since. Moreover, the Berne Conference passed a resolution to establish a permanent information office, the *Bureau Interparlementaire,* similar to the Peace Bureau. The object of this office was to list the various parliamentary groups in different countries, initiate the formation of groups where none as yet existed, act as a link between the national groups, and keep abreast of all questions concerning the peace movement and mediation. Gobat was elected General Secretary of this Bureau, and, like Ducommun, he worked without remuneration and almost unaided. After Ducommun's death in 1906, Gobat took over the direction of the BUREAU INTERNATIONAL PERMANENT DE LA PAIX, which was awarded the Peace Prize in *1910* in its capacity as an institution.

THE DEVELOPMENT OF INTERNATIONAL LAW

Institut de Droit International, Renault, Beernaert, Asser, La Fontaine, d'Estournelles de Constant

The work carried on by the pioneers of the peace movement usually embraced all aspects of pacifism, including the work for arbitration. The latter, however, undoubtedly demands, to a far greater extent than the other peace questions, special technical knowledge, at any rate as far as promoting the various aspects of it are concerned. The next group of prize-winners consists, in fact, of just this type of international-law expert. A start was made with the award of the prize in *1904* to the INSTITUT DE DROIT INTERNATIONAL. This institute was founded in 1873 as a private association of politicians and international jurists. The moving spirit in its foundation was Dr. Rolin-Jaquemyns who edited the *Revue de droit international* at Ghent. The aim of this institute was to investigate the guiding principles of international law, and to attempt its codification, to discuss urgent international problems and if possible suggest ways and means of solving them. In this connection the Institute emphasized the importance of clarifying the difficulties contingent on the differences in legal interpretation and practice prevailing in various countries. Finally it offered to give its opinion in disputed cases.

One of the first tasks undertaken by the Institute was to work out general rules for certain sections of private international law. At the annual meeting of the Institute at Oxford in 1880 a resolution was passed to invite the governments of the various countries to incorporate in their legislation rules formulated by the Institute. Several countries, such as Switzerland, Belgium, Spain and Germany, concurred with this suggestion in questions regarding the right of citizenship and the coming of age of foreign nationals. The law of exchange was in the Nordic countries based on a draft submitted to the Institute in 1885. Several rules were likewise adopted from the suggestions of the Institute and incorporated in the Norwegian-Swedish-Danish Maritime Law. In the sphere of criminal law the Institute worked out detailed rules for the extradition of criminals, and on the basis of these rules extradition treaties were gradually concluded between most of the civilized powers.

At the annual session in Geneva in 1874 the general principles for international judicial proceedings were laid down, and the next year the Institute formulated rules for the competency of the tribunals. The actual forms of procedure were dealt with in 1877, and in the next year rules were drawn up for the execution of judgements. This work was to be the foundation of an agreement about international proceedings which was adopted at an international conference at The Hague in 1894. This conference was the second in the series dealing with questions of private international law which the Dutch Government had initiated. A third conference in 1900 adopted an agreement dealing with a unified treatment of legal conflicts involving marriage, divorce and trusteeship.

As far as international public law was concerned, the Institute adopted in 1875 a proposal embodying detailed rules concerning the election of judges for arbitration courts, place and language for arbitration procedure, the communication of the verdict to the parties concerned, and the expenses incurred in arbitration cases. These rules were subsequently followed in several international arbitration trials.

In its attitude to war as a phenomenon, on the other hand, the reaction of the Institute was more or less one of resignation. When the Russo-Turkish War broke out in 1877, the Institute issued an appeal to the belligerents reminding them of the existence of the rules of warfare, and in 1880 it issued a detailed *Handbook of the rules and observances of warfare.* In the introduction the Institute expressed its main ideas as follows: 'War occupies a considerable place in the pages of history, and it is not reasonable to suppose that man will be capable of breaking away from it so soon, despite the protests it arouses and the disgust it inspires. For it proves to be the only possible solution to the conflicts which jeopardize the existence, the freedom, and the vital interests of nations. But the gradual raising of accepted standards and morals should be reflected in the way war is conducted. It is up to the civilized nations, as has so rightly been said, to try, 'to restrict the horrors of war while at the same time recognizing its inexorable demands'.' In this work 'to reduce the destruction of war', the Institute was of the opinion that it was of great importance to neutralize all areas vital to international communication. During the Russo-Turkish War it therefore set up a commission to examine the position of the Suez Canal in the event of war, and at a meeting in Brussels in 1879 a resolution was adopted appealing to the Powers to declare the canal neutral, and to place it under international protection. The proposal was accepted by the Powers, and a treaty was signed in Constantinople on October 21, 1885. Finally the Institute's proposal for the international protection of submarine cables was adopted in a treaty signed by 27 states in Paris on March 14, 1884.

The Institut de Droit International can, generally speaking, pride itself on quite a number of concrete results of its work, even though, as we have seen, it could not boast any great achievement as far as the struggle against war as a phenomenon was concerned. It is not possible to single out the individual members who in every case had deserved most for their contributions to the various causes. But we may assume that the various experts on international law who were subsequently awarded the prize have borne the brunt of the work. The first of these men was LOUIS RENAULT [1843-1918, *1907*]. From 1882 on he was professor of international law in Paris and from 1890 consultant to the French Foreign Office. He was elected delegate at all the legal conferences at which the French Government was represented, and was, together with Tobias Asser, very largely responsible for the positive results achieved at the Conferences of Private International Law at The Hague.

For it was Renault who above all others strove to produce positive results, and to prevent discussions on generalities and technical formulations from protracting proceedings. At the Hague Peace Conference in 1899 Renault likewise played a prominent role, not least by his efforts to extend the principles of the Geneva Convention to naval warfare. He was also largely responsible for the revised Red Cross Convention of 1906.

Quite naturally, Renault was an ardent advocate of the idea of arbitration, and he acted personally in the capacity of judge. His reputation for impartiality was so firmly established that during the so-called Savarkar Case between England and France in 1910 both parties to the dispute requested the services of Renault as a judge.

On the other hand, Renault was unable to share the disappointment felt at the fact that not *all* cases for arbitration were brought before the Permanent Arbitration Court at The Hague, which had been established by the Peace Conference of 1899. The main thing, in Renault's opinion, was that international disputes should as a general rule be submitted to juridical decisions. But it would frequently be unnecessary to set the whole of this machinery in motion; in fact, in some cases it might actually be an advantage to avoid the publicity which a submission of the case to the Hague tribunal would inevitably entail.

By discussing the various points at issue in a rational manner one would, in Renault's opinion, arrive at a 'jurisdiction de la vie internationale' which, in its turn, would create the atmosphere required for the growth of pacifism. In this connection he drew attention to the dangers involved in too absolute an insistence on 'international democracy'. The principle of equality between the nations should not, for example, be allowed to let Luxembourg's vote in a question of maritime law weigh equally with Great Britain's. This question, however, would not exactly prevent the small nations from playing a very important role. 'They most often represent justice, precisely because they are not able to impose injustice', as he expressed it in his Nobel lecture. Renault furthermore was of the opinion that in spite of all one should adhere to the rule of unanimity at international conferences. The disadvantages such an arrangement entailed were nevertheless preferable to a state being forced to accept something against its will. As we see, Renault here indicates what was to be one of the main problems for the League of Nations as well as for the United Nations.

Throughout the years Renault kept strictly to his own juridical sphere; thus he never took an active part in the political life of his country, as did the Belgian jurist AUGUSTE BEERNAERT [1829-1912, *1909*]. Originally a Liberal the latter was in 1873 a member of a clerical government. In 1884 he himself formed a government on the same party political basis, and continued as Prime Minister until the year 1894. In the years that followed he participated with great enthusiasm at the international conferences, where he strongly advocated arbitration and an effective reduction of armaments. As Belgium's first representative at the two Hague Conferences in 1899 and 1907 he had an opportunity of observing how negative were the debates dealing with the question of disarmament. At the same time he expressed his grave misgivings about the *de facto* recognition of the principle of military occupation, which was the outcome of the two conferences.

One of the problems that Beernaert tried to resolve was the treatment of enemy property in naval warfare. In this question Belgium voted in favour of an American proposal for full inviolability, except for contraband of war. As this proposal had no chance of being adopted, Beernaert broached the possibility of putting enemy property at sea under the same rules as on land. It could then be confiscated and held until the cessation of hostilities. In the event of its being destroyed by the enemy power concerned, compensation was to be made. The proposal had several adherents, but did not get a sufficient majority to persuade Beernaert to promote it further.

With regard to the question of arbitration, Beernaert found himself in 1907 in an awkward position. He had personally acted as spokesman for the principle of compulsory arbitration, but at the second Hague Conference the Belgian Government had adopted a new attitude to this question, seeking instead to obtain a more vague formulation, and closely following the German policy in this matter. The reason for this turn-about was evidently that King Leopold and his government were loth to apply the principle of arbitration in the case of the Congo dispute, and that in general they considered it advantageous to obtain the goodwill of Germany.

The results of Beernaert's activity in the international field were thus in many ways rather negative. His efforts were nevertheless not without their significance as a factor in 'creating atmosphere', not least in questions where the attitude of the smaller nations could have a positive influence on international relationships.

The work of the Dutch jurist TOBIAS ASSER [1838-1913, *1911*] was chiefly directed towards the development of private international law. In the field of international law he made his mark especially during the negotiations dealing with the neutralization of the Suez Canal. Among other things he managed to get Spain and Holland elected to the Suez Canal Commission as representatives of the smaller nations, side by side with the Great Powers and Turkey.

Asser's views on the subject of private international law were expressed in a thesis he wrote on the subject in 1880, in which he vigorously attacked the school of thought which, using the slogan 'Esprit d'internationalisme', aimed at juridical uniformity [dispensed by the national legislative bodies]. In Asser's opinion the most favourable solution would be for the nations at international conferences to agree as far as possible on common solutions of legal conflicts. This practice could be carried out without any violent breach in the legal development in the various countries; and in fact this became the general rule.

It was furthermore due to Asser's efforts that the Dutch Government took the step of summoning the International Conferences of Private Law at The Hague, where Asser presided.

The prize-winners so far dealt with who were experts on international law worked largely within the limits of their subjects, though they undoubtedly contributed at the same time to enlarging its scope. The Belgian HENRI LA FONTAINE [1854-1943, *1913*] went still further, participating actively in the organized popular peace movement; and after succeeding Frederik Bajer in 1907 as head of the Peace Bureau at Berne, he soon became the real leader of the movement. La Fontaine had previously made a very real contribution to the work of enlightenment by publishing exhaustive bibliographies of pacifist literature; and in a comprehensive work, *Pasicrisie internationale,* published in 1902, he supplied a very complete historical account of international arbitration cases from 1794 to 1900.

By political conviction La Fontaine was a Socialist, but at the same time he tried to bridge the gap between the bourgeois and socialist conceptions of the peace problem. He strove to arouse the interest of the workers' organizations in the peace movement, of which they had up to then been rather sceptical, while as an assiduous delegate to the Inter-Parliamentary Conference he also managed to win over many of his colleagues. Among the problems to which La Fontaine especially devoted his energies was that of rousing public opinion against the idea of aerial warfare. At the 19th Peace Congress in Geneva in 1912 he managed to get a resolution passed to this effect, while at the same time he got pacifists to pledge themselves to oppose a war of aggression undertaken by their respective countries.

As a Belgian La Fontaine deemed it especially desirable to work for friendlier relations between France and Germany, an aim for which the Frenchman PAUL D'ESTOURNELLES DE CONSTANT [1852-1924, *1909*] had also been working for many years. Within the international jurist group of Peace Prize winners prior to 1914 d'Estournelles was in every way the one who displayed the greatest *political* activity. Actually he did not belong to the legal experts in the real sense of the word. His starting-point was characteristic: trained as a diplomat he left the service in 1895, because a period of five years as Counsellor to the Embassy in London had convinced him that the methods of professional diplomacy were in themselves incapable of bringing about peaceful co-operation between the peoples of Europe.

He resolved to work for his ideals by active participation in French politics, and was elected a member of the Chambre des Députés for the Sarthe department, being curiously enough returned for the constituency which his celebrated grand-uncle Benjamin Constant had in his day represented. Later on he became a Senator. At both Hague conferences d'Estournelles participated as French delegate. At the first conference he succeeded in getting *inter alia* the agreement about compulsory arbitration recognized as being at any rate more vitally important than most countries had originally been willing to concede. The obligation was, however, only a moral one, and during the first few years the tribunal was systematically sabotaged by the Great Powers. d'Estournelles thereupon started to agitate in favour of the use of arbitration. In this connection a visit he paid to the United States in 1902 was of especial importance, for he managed to persuade President Theodore Roosevelt to refer a dispute with Mexico to the Hague Tribunal. At the same time Andrew Carnegie contributed a sum of money for the building of a 'Peace Palace'.

In d'Estournelles' eyes the idea of arbitration was an ideal to be applied equally in domestic politics, and he looked with favour upon the increased influence which the Socialists were acquiring in French politics. On the other hand, he consistently opposed the Nationalists. The nationalist disease, like certain other inflammations, has a tendency to work in more than one direction. Just as Moneta in Italy had to wrestle with Austrophobia as well as Francophobia, so d'Estournelles faced not only the feelings of revenge directed against Germany, but also the violent anti-English mood which was whipped up over the Fashoda incident in 1898. He worked zealously for a Franco-British *rapprochement,* and in 1903 he visited the British Parliament at the head of the French parliamentary group for voluntary arbitration. Later that year the British paid a return visit to Paris. This occurred shortly after a treaty of arbitration had been signed between the two countries. These activities undoubtedly helped to smooth the way for the Franco-British entente in 1904. But in d'Estournelles's opinion this agreement, like the Franco-Russian alliance of 1894, must not be used as a lever on Germany. The balance which these two agreements created should rather lead to a relaxation of tension, and d'Estournelles worked assiduously to further such a development. In 1903 he founded a Franco-German association in Munich, and the next year he was present at the regatta in Kiel, where King Edward was staying as Kaiser Wilhelm's guest. In 1909 he delivered a lecture in the Prussian House of Peers on 'The Franco-German *rapprochement* as a basis for world peace'. He maintained in his speech that what had happened could not be forgotten. But at the same time both countries must realize that peace was an absolute imperative. War, he declared, 'drives the republics into dictatorship, the monarchies into the grip of revolution'.

D'Estournelles worked with the aim of founding a European Union as a long-range objective. The rivalry between the European countries resulted in steadily increasing sums being spent on armaments, thus weakening Europe's position in world economy. The peculiar advantage of a European Union would be that it would not constitute a threat to any important non-European power, e.g. the U.S.A. On the contrary, declared d'Estournelles, many influential Americans were keen to see a greater measure of European co-operation. He expressed it thus: 'The Americans are businessmen, and they prefer well-organized and stable conditions to the armed peace which presents a constant menace to World Peace.'*

MEDIATION AND THE POLICY OF ARBITRATION

Theodore Roosevelt, Elihu Root

With the award of the prize to THEODORE ROOSEVELT [1858-1919, *1906*] a new element had been added to the principles governing the awarding of the prize; for the reward was in this case not made for continuous work in the service of peace, but as a mark of esteem for what might be called 'technical' conciliation, resulting in the peace treaty signed in Portsmouth [U.S.A.] in 1905 between Russia and Japan. In pacifist and especially in social-democrat quarters the award was strongly criticized, for Roosevelt was known almost as the very opposite of a pacifist. Nor had he ever tried to conceal this fact, by word or deed. His conception of the peace problem was determined by a definitely imperialistic philosophy. In his book, *The Strenuous Life* [1902], he put it like this: 'The growth of peacefulness between nations has been confined strictly to those who are civilized' [p. 31]. He expounded this thought later on in his autobiography when he dwelt on the typical pacifists. 'The trouble', he wrote, 'comes from the entire inability of these worthy people to understand that they are demanding things that are mutually incompatible when they demand peace at any price and also justice and righteousness.'**

With his imperialist outlook Roosevelt had, during his period of office as Assistant Secretary for the Navy from 1897 to 1898, done all in his power to increase the naval strength of the U.S.A. His constant concern

* Lecture on 'L'arbitrage', *Bulletin mensuel du Commerce et de l'Industrie*, September, 1903.

** Theodore Roosevelt, *An Autobiography* [New York 1913], p. 578.

was that the Americans, since the time of the War between the States, had asserted their fighting spirit solely in the economic field. The rise of monopolies based on private capital, which to a great extent had been the result of her conflicting economic interests, had accentuated class antagonism and sapped the nation's vitality. Its foreign policy consequently became vacillating, and according to Roosevelt the peculiar and dangerous situation arose that capitalists and pacifists – from widely differing motives – were opposed to the idea of building up an effective national defence force. For that reason the war against Spain in 1898 revealed some very obvious weaknesses. In his autobiography Roosevelt summed up his own experiences in the matter as follows: 'I suppose the United States will always be unready for war, and in consequence will always be exposed to great expense, and to the possibility of the greatest calamity when the nations go to war. This is no new thing. Americans learn only from catastrophes and not from experience.'*

Roosevelt served in the war against Spain as a colonel in a volunteer cavalry unit, 'The Rough Riders'. This greatly enhanced his popularity. In 1900 he was elected Vice-President under McKinley, and when the latter was murdered in September of the same year, Roosevelt became President. His immediate concern in foreign politics was the settling of relations with Cuba and the Philippines.

The next scene of action was in the Panama Canal Zone. In November 1903 a revolt broke out in Panama against Colombia, and the rebels were immediately recognized by the U.S. Government. Faced with a clear threat of war from the U.S.A., the Colombian Government deemed it prudent to yield and to recognize Panama as an independent state. The new republic immediately ceded a strip of land ten miles wide to the U.S.A., who thereupon constructed the Panama Canal under her suzerainty.

With the liquidation of the Spanish colonies [Cuba and the Philippines], the occupation of Hawaii and the construction of the Panama Canal, the U.S.A. had become a Pacific power in real earnest, with considerable interests in the Far East. This was the background for Roosevelt's act of mediation in the Russo-Japanese War. American policy in the years before the war had aimed at preventing increased Russian expansion in China which seriously threatened the principle of the 'open door'. For that reason Roosevelt considered that it would be advantageous if the war

* *Ibid.*, p. 223.

resulted in some extension of Japan's sphere of influence, as this would create a satisfactory balance of power. Characteristically the Secretary of State, John Hay, noted on January 1, 1905, after the fall of Port Arthur: 'The President is quite firm in his view that we cannot permit Japan to be robbed a second time of the fruits of her victory.'*

As far as the European powers were concerned, England had concluded an alliance with Japan, and Germany had everything to gain from Russia being committed as long as possible in the East, while France quite naturally strove to initiate negotiations aimed at bringing her Russian ally out of the war more or less unscathed. With this in view the French Foreign Minister Delcassé, in consultation with the Russian Government, put out peace feelers in Paris in April 1905, to which the Japanese proved not entirely unresponsive, though on the whole they seemed more inclined to support any move the Americans might make in this matter. At the end of May they made a formal application to President Roosevelt, requesting him to try to arrange direct negotiations.

Thus both parties had now made known their desire for negotiations, and at Roosevelt's invitation these were commenced in the seaside town of Portsmouth [New Hampshire] in August 1905. For tactical reasons Roosevelt kept in the background while the peace negotiations were going on. Nevertheless the result was satisfactory from an American point of view, first and foremost by preventing a partition of China.

The war in the East had had many consequences as far as European power politics were concerned. Among other things, Germany had taken advantage of it to stage the demonstration in Tangier. Roosevelt had a clear notion of the global implications of the balance of power. In 1911 he expressed it as follows: 'As long as England succeeds in keeping up the balance of power in Europe, not only on principle, but in reality, well and good; should she, however, for some reason or other fail in doing so, the U.S. would be obliged to step in, at least temporarily, in order to re-establish the balance of power in Europe, never mind against which country or group of countries our efforts may have to be directed. In fact, we ourselves are becoming, owing to our strength and geographical situation, more and more the balance of power of the whole globe.'** Neither Roosevelt's political career nor his act of mediation, therefore, had *per se* anything to do with the actual peace movement, and thus far the award

* Tyler Dennett, *Roosevelt and the Russo-Japanese War* [Baltimore 1924], p. 173.
** *Ibid.*, p. 1.

of the prize to him was open to criticism. And yet in this connection it is undoubtedly possible to attribute something positive to him. First of all, the very act of setting peace negotiations on foot was a useful one, even though its background was largely determined by considerations of power politics. Moreover, Roosevelt's personality contained certain elements capable of promoting international understanding – he was above all a man of integrity and at any rate neither unreasonable nor fanatical. His social outlook was markedly honest, as shown by the struggle he waged against the trusts and his work in favour of the trade unions. He pursued the principle of arbitration in labour conflicts and gave his Peace Prize money to a fund for the promotion of peace in labour relations. In international politics he also adopted a positive attitude to the idea of arbitration. We have already mentioned his accommodating conduct towards d'Estournelles de Constant.

This attitude was still more clearly in evidence in the case of the other Secretary of State in Roosevelt's government, ELIHU ROOT [1845-1937, *1912*]. Admittedly his background was likewise decidedly imperialistic in character. As Secretary of War from 1899 to 1905, he had helped to implement American imperialist policy, not only in the settlement which followed the war with Spain [especially the subjection of the Philippines] but also later on when pressure was brought to bear on Colombia. In a lecture delivered in February 1904 with the somewhat challenging title of 'The Ethics of the Panama Question', Root went so far in his statement of his case as to say that 'the people of Panama owned that part of the earth's surface [the Canal Zone] just as much as the State of New York owns the Erie Canal'.*

But at the same time Root realized more clearly than most people that the U.S.A. must enjoy the confidence of the Latin-American states. The Pan-American idea had been vigorously promoted by Secretary of State James G. Blaine from about 1880, and in 1890 the first Pan-American Conference was held in Washington; the second one was held in Mexico City in 1901. Nevertheless the Latin-American states looked with considerable suspicion at the U.S.A., nor was this feeling of distrust lessened after the Panama affair. All the more important was Root's effort to create a more favourable atmosphere. In conversations with a number of South American diplomats he proposed that the next Pan-American Conference should take place in Rio de Janeiro, and the idea was very well re-

* E. Root, *Addresses on International Subjects* [Cambridge, Mass. 1916], p. 200.

ceived. It was held in July and August 1906, and Root himself participated in the negotiations. Still more important, perhaps, was the fact that, in connection with the conference, he undertook an extensive good-will tour, visiting Uruguay, the Argentine, Chile, Peru, Panama and Colombia. In countless addresses and speeches he stressed the desire of the U.S.A. to co-operate on an equal basis. The most complicated question was quite naturally the relationship with Colombia, but in 1909 this was finally settled, after two years' negotiations. Another country whose relationship with the U.S.A. was the source of considerable difficulty – especially owing to the aggressive attitude of American capitalists – was Venezuela. However, Root managed towards the conclusion of his term of office as Secretary of State [he retired in January 1909] to lay the foundation for the settlement which William Buchanan was later able to conclude.

Root was also able to regularize the relationship with San Domingo, and he assisted in ironing out points at issue between the Central American republics. These negotiations resulted *inter alia* in the setting up of a permanent arbitration tribunal which was recognized by the countries concerned.

As far as relations with the European countries were concerned, the American Presidents from the time of Cleveland had become interested in treaties of arbitration, and Roosevelt and his Secretary of State Hay had in this respect shown increasing initiative, but now, just as formerly, the opposition of the Senate had proved an insurmountable obstacle. It was to Root's credit that he arrived at an approach which overcame the distrust, rooted in considerations of prestige, of the Senate; and in the course of less than a year [February 1908-January 1909] he had piloted 23 treaties of arbitration – with European and Latin-American countries as well as with Japan – to a successful conclusion. Relations with the last-mentioned country were at that very time especially difficult, because Japanese immigration to the Pacific coast had resulted in violent racial discrimination, which found expression, amongst other things, in Japanese children being refused admission to schools in California. President Roosevelt reacted strongly against this racial discrimination, not only as a matter of mere principle, but also owing to his liking for the Japanese. Japan at that time was a useful factor in the U.S.A.'s Far-East policy, and he personally admired the Japanese fighting spirit. But it was left to Root to solve this problem, which he did by discussing the whole question of immigration with the Japanese Government, and at the same time by persuading the

Californian authorities to see reason, achieving this in a sufficiently elastic way to prevent the whole matter getting bogged down in questions of mere prestige.

THE INTERNATIONAL IDEA DURING THE FIRST WORLD WAR

Comité International de la Croix-Rouge, Christian L. Lange

After the outbreak of the First World War in August 1914 the award of the Peace Prize was suspended for the subsequent three years. Pacifist circles have occasionally maintained that the peace idea should be kept alive by continued Peace Prize awards precisely in such times of open conflict. There might be champions of peace, it has been pointed out, in neutral states, or individuals opposing the war psychosis in the belligerent countries, men like MacDonald or Morel in England, or Liebknecht in Germany. [In fact none of these was actually proposed during the war years.]

The first and only prize awarded during the war fell, not to an individual peace worker or pacifist organization, but a humanitarian institution, the COMITÉ INTERNATIONAL DE LA CROIX-ROUGE [*1917*]. This Committee was a continuation of the *Société Genevoise d'Utilité Publique,* which in its time had formed the first organizational basis for Henri Dunant's idea of the international protection of the medical services in time of war. From that time the Committee set itself the task of implementing the Geneva Convention both in peace and in war, in addition stimulating the setting up of Red Cross organizations in every country, as well as supplementing the original provisions of the Geneva Convention. As an organization the International Red Cross Committee has retained its private and improvised character. Thus even to-day it has no definite international mandate and is still purely Swiss in composition. But its activity and initiative throughout the years have automatically given it a very real prestige and authority.

After the outbreak of war the Committee soon became an important centre for the various attempts which were made to establish the principles of humanity. But the Committee also took the initiative itself, first and foremost in protecting Red Cross organizations in the various belligerent countries. Among other things it managed to get the Turkish medical organization, the *Croissant Rouge Ottoman,* recognized by the signatory powers on the same footing as ordinary Red Cross organizations, and furthermore managed to have the Serbian Red Cross – at any rate officially – granted continued recognition, even after Serbia had been conquered.

Another point which the Geneva Committee raised was the right of medical personnel to be repatriated after being made prisoners of war. This right was recognized by England, France and Germany. As far as the treatment of prisoners of war in general was concerned, the Committee enforced the provisions of the Hague Convention, and early in 1915 succeeded in getting the French and German governments to introduce uniform rules for the exchange of correspondence from prisoners of war. In addition, it succeeded in enforcing the exchange of the seriously wounded via Switzerland, and the internment of seriously wounded officers. [The authorities in the belligerent countries were unwilling to exchange wounded officers, on the ground that their knowledge might still be used in the conduct of the war.] Altogether the Committee did its most important work in connection with prisoners of war. Its protests against cases of particularly inhumane acts of war, such as the German sinking of hospital ships or the Turkish massacres of the Armenians, were however ineffective.

The actual care of prisoners of war was originally outside the framework of the Geneva Convention, and for a long time was not one of the essential functions of the Red Cross, even though Henri Dunant and others – as already mentioned – had broached the idea already in the 1870's. It was not till the Red Cross Conference in Washington in 1912 that it was resolved to undertake this work. During the war the Geneva Committee set to work in real earnest, devoting all its energies to the information service. Many thousands of letters were dealt with every day, as well as countless money orders. The Committee itself dealt with the Western Front, while the Danish Red Cross took upon itself the Eastern Front, and the work was further supported by Red Cross associations in Petrograd, Vienna, Budapest, Constantinople and Rome.

The effects of the war on real, organized pacifism were, on the other hand, completely crippling. Organizations which had previously been awarded the Peace Prize, e.g. the *Institut de Droit International* and the *Bureau International de la Paix,* practically ceased their activities. The last-mentioned institution confined itself to work of a humanitarian nature.

The war had the same catastrophic consequences for the international organization which had attempted to translate some of the pacifist ideas into practical policy, viz. the Inter-Parliamentary Union. This organization had admittedly already been subject to severe strains, as in the case of the Boer War, the Russo-Japanese War and the Balkan Wars. But these had, after all, been isolated phenomena which were unable to shake the real foundation of the Union: the desire for understanding and co-operation of a personal nature. The World War, compared with previous upheavals, cut ruthlessly across all bonds of friendship in the belligerent countries. It made inexorable demands – for or against – of every individual. Only in the neutral countries was there a chance for the idea of universal brotherhood to survive. Yet here too initiative and courage were needed to meet this challenge. Of those who led the way the Norwegian CHRISTIAN L. LANGE [1869-1938, *1921*] was one of the foremost. After studying philology he had in 1899 worked as secretary for the organizing committee of the conference which the Inter-Parliamentary Union had held in Oslo that year. Lange proved on this occasion to be possessed of great administrative ability, and the Nobel Committee of the Norwegian Storting appointed him in the following year its first secretary. Apart from the very useful work he did for the Committee, Lange played an important part in organizing the library of the Norwegian Nobel Institute which was established in 1904. His knowledge of international problems was also soon utilized by the Norwegian Government, which appointed him as one of its technical delegates at the second Peace Congress at The Hague in 1907. Two years later Lange was made Secretary-General of the *Union Interparlementaire,* which under his guidance extended its activities and achieved a more rigid organization.

The Secretariat of the Union was located in Brussels, and it was one of the tragic consequences of the fresh outburst of international anarchy that engulfed the world in 1914, that Lange had to flee hurriedly after Belgium had become the victim of a flagrant breach of international law – an act which received the practically unanimous assent of Germany's parliamentarians.

Lange, however, did not abandon his work. From his home in Oslo he did his utmost to keep international contacts alive, and to bring the Union more or less intact out of the storm. He succeeded in keeping the Union going as an organization, with the assistance of Lord Weardale, the president of the organization. And at the meetings which the Nordic inter-parliamentarians held during the war, Lange contributed greatly to the shaping of the plans which were made for the revival of international co-operation. As far as the *Union Interparlementaire* itself was concerned, however, it was not until a year after the cessation of hostilities that a real conference could take place. A conference was finally held in Geneva in 1921, and from now on this city became the permanent seat of the organization. Neither Belgium nor France was represented at this conference.

Lange did not confine his activities to his own organization. In 1915 he took part in a congress at The Hague convoked by the recently founded Dutch peace organization, the *Anti Oorlog Raad.* This was attended by representatives from America, Austria, Belgium, Great Britain, Germany, Holland, Hungary, Norway, Sweden and Switzerland. In the agenda it was expressly stated that the congress had no intention of undertaking any course of action intended to procure an immediate conclusion of peace. Its aim was to discuss long-term policy with regard to peace. The *Organisation Centrale pour une Paix durable,* as it called itself, set up a number of committees to investigate the principles of non-annexation, the problem of nationality, the problem of armaments, etc. Lange was elected chairman of the committee which was examining plans for developing the international bodies that were in existence before the war.

Apart from these topical problems Lange worked during the war at a comprehensive task, the *Histoire de l'Internationalisme,* the first volume of which, going up as far as the Peace of Westphalia, was ready by 1919. It gives a critical and at the same time interesting account of the development of internationalist ideas from the earliest days. Lange himself always preferred the word 'internationalism' to the word 'pacifism'. In his Nobel lecture in 1921 he explained this very clearly: 'I speak of internationalism, not pacifism. The latter word has never appealed to me – it is a linguistic hybrid, and it leads one to think merely of the negative side of the peace movement, the struggle against war; and for this side of our efforts the term 'antimilitarism' is a more fitting name. Not that I disagree with pacifism or antimilitarism; these are necessary links in our struggle. But to my mind these words have the special significance – though not every one agrees about this – of a *moral* theory; by pacifism I mean the moral protest against the use of violence and war in international relations. A pacifist will usually – at any rate in our day – be an internationalist, and vice versa. But history shows us examples which prove that the pacifist need not think internationally. Jesus of Nazareth was a pacifist; yet all his sayings, in so far as they are preserved, prove that internationalism was quite foreign to him, for the very good reason that he did not think politically at all; he was a-political. If we were to place him in one of the categories of our age, we should have to call him an antimilitarist or an individualistic anarchist. Internationalism is a *social* and a *political* theory, a definite conception of how society should be organized, especially a conception as to how the nations should settle their mutual relations.'

This argument – as we see – agrees with the principle that had become the basis of the League of Nations, and Lange had undoubtedly made an important contribution both by participating in the work of ideological preparation for the League, and later on by giving the organization a firm foundation in practical politics and in the mind of the ordinary man. For many years he was a member of the Norwegian delegation to the League of Nations.

THE LEAGUE OF NATIONS AND ITS LEADING MEN

Wilson, Bourgeois, Lord Robert Cecil, Branting, Nansen

In 1920 the first post-war award of the Peace Prize was made. The reserved prize for the year *1919* was given on that occasion to WOODROW WILSON [1856-1924], and that for *1920* to LÉON BOURGEOIS [1851-1925]. Both in this and the following two years the prize distribution had a character all its own, as the recipients were people who played a leading part in the creation of the League of Nations. This also applies to Christian L. Lange who shared the prize with Branting in 1921, though, as already mentioned, the centre of gravity of his activities lies in the years before and during the war.

There can hardly be any doubt that Woodrow Wilson is the most *central* figure among all the prize-winners. Though it was not until late in his career that he devoted his energies to the actual problem of peace, few of the other prize-winners have experienced it so intensely, and none with such tremendous perspectives for the history of the world. In pro-German quarters it was ironically maintained that if yet another American President had to get the Peace Prize, it was most fitting that one should have been chosen who, like his predecessor, Theodore Roosevelt, had been so successful in war. Yet no one could doubt that Wilson's *vue d'ensemble* was essentially different from Roosevelt's, and that he regarded the U.S.A.'s participation in the war as a bitter necessity in order 'to make the world safe for democracy'. In fact, he regarded the establishment of a League of Nations as the central peace problem. The idea itself is very old, and at the two Hague conferences the phrase 'Société des Nations' was constantly used. During the war the idea was taken up by associations and individuals in various countries. But no one could give it the same potency as Woodrow Wilson, because as President of the U.S.A. he had the best chance of acting as an umpire in the bloody struggle.

Primarily he had aimed at maintaining the neutrality of the United States, and on that basis he was re-elected President in 1916. But at the same time he realized that the U.S.A. – not least in her own interests – was bound to make a serious attempt to arrive at a fair peace settlement. Wilson was in this at one with certain trends of American opinion, especially those who found an expression of their views in the founding of the *League to Enforce Peace* [June 17, 1915]. In the following year, on May 27, 1916, Wilson made a speech at a dinner arranged by the League. This speech was to prove significant, not only because in it the President of the U.S.A. emphasized the responsibility of his country for the fate of the world, but also because he declared that the U.S.A. was willing to take part in a peace settlement which would *inter alia* guarantee the freedom of the seas and effectively prevent breaches of treaties and acts of aggression. Thereby the idea of a League of Nations had received official American support, and Wilson's attitude undoubtedly contributed to the idea being mooted by the British Foreign Secretary, Sir Edward Grey [later Lord Grey], in his note of October 23, and by the German Chancellor von Bethmann-Hollweg in his declaration of November 9 the same year. Quite naturally, however, the points of view adopted by these two were marked by their position as belligerents, while Wilson's ideas were directly inspired by his position as a disinterested mediator.

Even after the U.S.A. had become a belligerent power, Wilson retained this basic idea in his attitude to the peace settlement. Peace would have to be established on a universal foundation and must ensure the right of every country to self-determination. These rights should also accrue to the German people, for the fault lay, in Wilson's opinion, not with the people but with the authoritarian state control which had led them astray. In a speech on July 4, 1918, he demanded therefore that autocratic forms of government should be overthrown or reduced to virtual impotence.

Wilson's concrete peace aims were enumerated in his Fourteen Points on January 8, 1918, with his demand for 'covenants of peace openly arrived at', the freedom of the seas, and national self-determination concretely expressed by the liberation of Belgium, the return of Alsace-Lorraine, the independence of Poland and of the minorities within the Habsburg monarchy. The last but most important of the points dealt with the setting up of a League of Nations. It was the most important, because according to Wilson it was in the long run the only means of maintaining a just peace.

For that reason he did his utmost to have the Covenant of the League of Nations incorporated in the Peace Treaty, in fact as the first condition for its other provisions. Wilson was criticized in many quarters for this. Several people were of the opinion that it would have been better first to negotiate a concrete peace agreement with Germany and her allies, and then later to found a League of Nations. But Wilson was working on the theory that it would be better to strike while the iron was hot. He wanted to exploit the great expectations for a lasting peace which were abroad, if need be use them to coerce cynical or vengeful statesmen. As he expressed it in his speech at Buckingham Palace on December 27, 1918: 'We have used great words, all of us, we have used the great words 'right' and 'justice', and now we are to prove whether or not we understand those words and how they are to be applied to the particular settlements which must conclude this war. And we must not only understand them, but we must have the courage to act upon our understanding. Yet after I have uttered the word 'courage', it comes into my mind that it would take more courage to resist the great moral tide now running in the world than to yield to it, than to obey it. There is a great tide running in the hearts of men...'*

With this conviction and with tireless energy he piloted the League of Nations Covenant safely through. The proposal was submitted on February 14 and finally approved on April 28, 1919. Wilson had been obliged to yield on certain points, but by and large he emerged from this round as the victor.

The subsequent tragic chapter in the story of his activities at the Peace Conference is well known: his bargaining with the principles of national self-determination, the influence brought to bear on the peace settlement by

* *The Public Papers of Woodrow Wilson. War and Peace,* I [New York & London 1927], pp. 337-338.

the secret treaties of the Entente Powers, etc., and finally his bitter defeat at home.

All this helped to create a new Wilson legend, quite different from that of the heavenly messenger of peace who had been acclaimed on his arrival in Europe in 1918. After all his rebuffs he was in many circles regarded as a doctrinaire school-teacher who, once faced with the inexorable demands of reality, cast his principles overboard and allowed himself to be led passively by astute political gamblers such as Clemenceau and Lloyd George.

That Wilson was doctrinaire is certain enough, and it is also true that his unshaken faith in the 'teachableness and reasonableness' of the masses caused him to make a fatal error of judgment with regard to the situation both in Europe and at home in the U.S.A. Furthermore, it is a fact that he reduced the chances of a ratification of the League Covenant and the Peace Treaty by making the role of the U.S.A. at the peace settlement a special concern of the Democratic party, and that he included no important Republican politicians in the peace delegation. After all, not all the Republican leaders were as isolationist in their attitude as Wilson's chief opponent, Henry Cabot Lodge. A place could easily have been found – as the American historian Thomas Bailey has stated – for such people as ex-President Taft, Charles Evans Hughes, or perhaps most of all Elihu Root.

It is also open to discussion whether Wilson might not, by showing a little more elasticity at the Peace Conference, have been in a better position to avoid the pitfalls of the peace settlement. On the other hand, it is a complete mistake to represent his efforts as being on the whole a failure. The terms of the Versailles Treaty would undoubtedly have been harder if Wilson had not been one of its sponsors. In addition, several recent publications have thrown a clearer light on the enormous difficulties he had to face, as well as on his capacity for surmounting them in many crucial instances. And even though his principal achievement, the League of Nations, deprived of American support, grew gradually less and less effective instead of gaining in strength, nevertheless Wilson's contribution was an outstanding mobilization of 'the international mind' both in America and throughout the rest of the world. The idea of an international system of justice founded on regular co-operation between the nations and on mutual responsibility had, despite all the disappointments, become a reality and a source of strength for the future.

In the actual working out of the Covenant of the League of Nations, Wilson received invaluable support from Lord ROBERT CECIL [1864-1958], and though the latter was not awarded the Peace Prize until many years later [*1937*], it seems appropriate to deal with this part of his activity here. Like Wilson, Cecil had not had any particular contact with organized pacifism, and it was not until a few years after the outbreak of war that he devoted his efforts to the creation of a League of Nations. Apart from him the idea had already at an early stage won support in England, not least among leading Liberals such as Asquith and Sir Edward Grey, and in 1915 a *League of Nations Society* was founded, probably the first organization which officially used the designation 'League of Nations'. It was not till 1916 that Cecil joined in this work, but from then on he adopted the idea as the guiding star of his policy. It was due more than anything else to his initiative that the British Government included the League of Nations in its peace aims, though Lloyd George and his circle regarded it as quite secondary compared to the winning of the war. In 1918 the Government appointed a commission to draw up a draft organization for the League. The chairman was Lord Phillimore, but Cecil was its driving force, and his ideas were decisive both in Wilson's and General Smuts's plans for a League of Nations.

Cecil's basic idea was that the League ought not to be a superstate, but a league comprising all nations. For that reason, in his capacity of British delegate to the Peace Conference, he maintained that Germany should be included from the start. The chief aim of the League – to prevent war – must be solved by establishing an effective apparatus aiming at the *postponement* and *discussion* of critical disputes, so that a solution might be arrived at in an atmosphere of cool deliberation. Furthermore Cecil drew up a plan for the League Secretariat, and he was the originator of the plan whereby the League, apart from being a political organ, was also to co-ordinate and lead the work of international co-operation in the humanitarian, social and economic field. Finally he managed to get a permanent international tribunal set up. In this case he encountered from the outset the stubborn resistance of Wilson, who was loth to have a too precisely defined judicial machinery for dealing with international conflicts. Otherwise the co-operation with Wilson went most smoothly, and Cecil presided over the commission while Wilson was in the U.S.A. For the realization of the League of Nations Wilson's personal initiative and authority were decisive, but where the actual building-up of the organization is concerned he must share the honours with Lord Robert Cecil and Jan Smuts.

LÉON BOURGEOIS, who won the Peace Prize for *1920,* could not, for very definite reasons, show as many positive results of his work with the League of Nations organization. The award of the prize to Bourgeois was more retrospective in character, as was the case with most of the pre-war prize-winners. Bourgeois represented first and foremost the *continuity* in the work for international co-operation, and politically he belonged to a type which is after all not so rare in France: the politician who is true to his principles, despite great tactical pliancy. This had been clearly shown during his work at the two Hague conferences as leader of the French delegation. On both occasions Bourgeois proclaimed stoutly the duty of the nations to submit to arbitration and to show loyalty in the solution of international conflicts. Despite the disappointments he suffered at the conferences he regarded the development optimistically. The essential thing was that the foundation had been laid for a juridical organization of peace, on which one might build. In a speech made in 1908 he ventured to say: 'The League of Nations is created. It is very much alive.'*

Even the World War could not shake Bourgeois's faith in an international community founded on justice; and, unlike so many others, he did not allow his instinctive rallying to the defence of his own country to cloud his international outlook. On the contrary, he believed that the problem of French security could only be solved on broad international lines. The old policy of alliances was no longer sufficient, for in the last resort it depended on the extent of material resources available, and in this respect France was outstripped by her rivals. In an article written in 1916 he put it as follows: 'We must see things as they are. We, in France, are not, from the point of view of birth rate and material strength, at the same stage of development as, for example, our enemies. Now the balance of power, however skilful diplomats may be, results in the triumph of the greatest number and the most brutal, and not in the triumph of the noblest, the proudest, the worthiest. It is another policy, therefore, the policy of justice, which alone can give France and the nations which do not seek to establish themselves by violence, peace and security. There will be no policy of justice if the League of Nations is not set up.'**

* Léon Bourgeois, *Pour la Société des Nations* [Paris 1910], p. 287.
** ——— *Le pacte de 1919 et la Société des Nations* [Paris 1919], pp. 18-19.

On the other hand, Bourgeois had no illusions about Germany. As long as German mentality remained unchanged, it was necessary to maintain the policy of alliances, while bearing constantly in mind that it was a temporary, alternative solution.

In the autumn of 1917, Bourgeois became the chairman of a commission which was to study the possibilities of the creation of a League of Nations and the conditions for its work. The principles laid down by this commission were later submitted to the Peace Conference by Bourgeois during the discussions about the League of Nations Covenant in January 1919.

The essential point in this French proposal was that it visualized the League of Nations as a juridical military organization. Its sole object was to be the preservation of peace, and it was only to function when a crisis arose. In Bourgeois's opinion the ideal international co-operation could be realized on the basis of the results of the two Hague Conferences of 1899 and 1907. The essential thing was to plug the two holes that still existed, viz. that arbitration had not been made obligatory and that the international apparatus of justice lacked sanctions for the enforcement of international agreement. Such sanctions should be of a diplomatic, juridical, economic and, if need be, of a military character. To secure the last-mentioned alternative there was no need for any permanent international army or navy. But an international commission [in reality a general staff] would be required, with plans ready at all times for military action.

In its actual form the French plan was therefore not so far-reaching as the Anglo-American one, but on the other hand it was more precise in the obligations it laid down, not least in the military sphere. During the negotiations these plans were rejected as impracticable by the U.S.A. and Great Britain. Nor did Bourgeois get any support for his suggestion that any disarmament that took place should take geographical considerations into account.

Thus, politically speaking, Bourgeois did not achieve very much during the negotiations, and there was not always any comprehensive reality beneath his fluent eloquence. With charming self-irony he confided to Lord Robert Cecil that once at a public meeting he had fallen asleep while he was speaking, and on waking up a few minutes later he realized that his audience had not noticed anything untoward.*

Despite the negative results of his work with the League of Nations Covenant, Bourgeois's activities were all the same of great significance.

* Viscount Cecil, *A Great Experiment* [London 1941], p. 65.

First and foremost he stood out as the influential spokesman of those circles in France who refused to allow themselves to be dazzled by victory into following blindly the power politics of Clemenceau and others. On the whole, Clemenceau regarded the League of Nations with scepticism and indifference. All the greater was the effect of Bourgeois's work in that direction, and not least the fact that he loyally accepted the resolutions which were adopted, even though in many cases they ran counter to his own proposals.

HJALMAR BRANTING [1860-1925, *1921*] was another prize-winner who, at the time he received the award, had no striking concrete results to show for his work in the League of Nations. While Bourgeois had to give up the idea of founding the League on a French-inspired system of military security, Branting encountered the greatest difficulties in his attempts to enforce international disarmament, and one of his bitterest opponents in this question was none other than Léon Bourgeois. The award made to Branting [as also to Lange] must primarily be regarded as an exhortation to continue the work despite the failures of the moment. But at the same time it was a mark of esteem bestowed on a life spent in the service of peace.

Few statesmen in the twentieth century could show such consistency in his development as Hjalmar Branting, and his views on the fundamental problems of domestic and foreign policy were from the very first so capacious that he never petrified into a doctrinaire, nor found himself obliged to resort to dialectic somersaults in order to maintain this continuity. With bourgeois radicalism as his starting-point he went over to socialism as a young man. From 1884 he had been on the editorial staff of K. P. Arnoldson's periodical *Tiden,* and when he became editor shortly afterwards the publication took a clear social-democratic line. In 1886 he became editor of *Social-Demokraten.* In 1897 he was elected to the Swedish *Riksdag,* and had already acquired considerable experience of politics, especially in defence questions and foreign affairs.

As far as national defence was concerned, Branting strongly opposed unduly large appropriations at the expense of the social services, and on every possible occasion he fought against the militaristic spirit in the state and in the community. But at the same time he dissociated himself quite clearly from 'defence nihilism'. In a speech made in 1892 he maintained that, just because social conditions were bad, people had 'neither right nor cause to lessen their children's chances of entering into better and completer possession of their heritage. However bad conditions may be here at home, if we should ever come under the domination of our all-powerful neighbour, shortsighted 'defence nihilists' would soon have to face the hard fact that things could become still worse. A nation's right to shape its own destiny, free from external pressure, should be as incontestable for all democrats as it should be worth a sacrifice to maintain.'* But this defence of freedom must not be organized in such a way as to increase class distinctions within the community. Our aim should rather be an equalization of political rights and economic benefits, otherwise even the most liberal military grants would be wasted. 'Should disaster befall us, and if in the hour of danger we could only muster an army the bulk of which nourished a doubt as to *what* they really had to defend in this native land, in which all they can hope for is work and toil in days of good health and the poorhouse in their old age, then our fate would be sealed, whether we had 90 days' military training or not.'** Therefore, in Branting's opinion, far-reaching social reforms implied not only the best domestic policy, but also the only possible defence policy.

On the basis of the socialist conception of national independence as an absolute condition for the liberation of the working classes, Branting supported the claims to independence of other countries, and his attitude to this question was clearly shown during the union conflict between Sweden and Norway. Branting was of the opinion that Sweden should grant Norway the separate foreign service which the Norwegians demanded, and during the crisis in 1895, in a speech made in May, he warned the activists sharply against the use of force. For this speech Branting was sentenced to three years' imprisonment, a monstrous sentence, even though the punishment was commuted to a fine.

During the final crisis in 1905, Branting once again threw all his influence into the scale in Norway's favour and for the sake of a peaceful outcome of the union conflict. Many Swedes share the honour of defeating activism on that occasion, not least K. P. Arnoldson, yet hardly any of them had such influence as Branting. He was really – as he was called – a champion of peace with an army behind him.

During the First World War Branting was once more fighting the activists, who on this occasion strove to make Sweden enter the war on the side of the Central Powers. Branting stuck unswervingly to neutrality,

* Hjalmar Branting, *Tal och skrifter* [Stockholm 1927], V, pp. 63-64.
** *Ibid.*, p. 63.

but in his case this did not imply isolationism. On the contrary, in his opinion Sweden should exploit her neutral position to work for a democratic peace. At the International Socialist Congress which met in Stockholm in 1917 this was the first item on the agenda, and Branting was the leader of the debate. The conference was, however, considerably weakened by the fact that the representatives of the Allied Powers were unable to attend, as the authorities had refused to grant them passports. This circumstance, however, did not change Branting's attitude to the belligerents. He never concealed the fact that his sympathies lay with the Allies. In this respect Branting and many other Swedish Social Democrats differed from some of the more influential of their political counterparts in Norway. This difference was partly rooted in the class situation: in Sweden the upper classes were largely pro-German, in Norway pro-Allied. But in Branting's case another factor, probably just as significant, played an important part. Despite everything, the Allied Powers represented in his eyes the cultural heritage of the West, with its liberal political institutions and extensive cultural freedom. For that reason Branting also maintained after the conclusion of the war that Sweden, despite the disappointments caused by the Versailles Treaty, should support the League of Nations, and do her best to make the League the instrument of democracy and international understanding which it was intended to be.

When Branting in 1920 appeared as the Swedish delegate at the first Assembly of the League of Nations, he soon became the leader of those who tried to work for these ends, especially in plans for an effective disarmament. However, it proved impossible to get the Powers to make even slight concessions in the limitation of armaments, and by a bitter irony of fate Léon Bourgeois's first public speech after he had received the Peace Prize turned out to be an attack on the limitation of armaments. Lord Robert Cecil was the only one of the representatives of the Great Powers who paid homage to Branting for his work in this cause.

The negative forces within the League of Nations which barred the way to Branting's disarmament plans were on the whole equally active in the case of the relief work conducted by FRIDTJOF NANSEN [1861-1930, *1922*]. Nansen's personal background and development were essentially different from Branting's. Branting's personality had matured during a long period of political activity at home, and his international repute had gradually assumed firm contours with his participation in the international workers' movement. Nansen's world fame was a direct result of his bold and epoch-making voyages of discovery. His relations to Norwegian politics were always rather sporadic; in this respect his greatest contribution was in 1905 and in the period immediately following, as Norway's first diplomatic representative in London. Politically he was firmly rooted in Liberalism, and with the years he grew almost conservative. And yet Branting and Nansen had much in common, not least a very real respect for human values, based on a scientific philosophy of life. In his attitude to the peace problem Nansen was a far more active supporter of military defence, yet both he and Branting, on different grounds, agreed nevertheless in the demand for the safeguarding of national independence. At the same time, Nansen always maintained a markedly international outlook, and his prestige – especially in the English-speaking world – was unique. For this reason he was employed as leader of a Norwegian delegation during negotiations for a trade agreement with the U.S.A. in 1917, a task which was more than usually complicated, as the States, after entering the war, were very strict in the demands they imposed on the neutrals. During the war years Nansen also worked energetically to achieve the setting-up of an international organization; he was an ardent spokesman for the idea of a League of Nations, and spent the first half of the year 1919 in Paris in order to bring his influence to bear on the leading statesmen, so as to ensure a constructive peace settlement. Later on he played an outstanding role in the sessions of the League of Nations in his capacity as a member of the Norwegian delegation.

He was given his first great humanitarian task in 1920, viz. to organize the return of the prisoners of war. The League Council approached Nansen in April, and he immediately laid aside his scientific work in order to tackle the job. He soon solved the many transport difficulties which were especially great in the case of the many prisoners of war held in Siberia. He also managed to solve the financial side of the problem, and in September 1921 he was able to report to the Assembly of the League of Nations that he had managed to send home 350,000 prisoners of war via the Baltic. From Vladivostok approximately 12,000 had been sent home, and from the Black Sea area approximately 5,000. All these transports had been effected at the very reasonable cost of £400,000. In his work Nansen had had invaluable support from such private associations as the American Red Cross and the *Comité International de la Croix-Rouge.* At the time when Nansen made his report, he had already undertaken a new, exacting post, that of League of Nations Commissioner for Refugees. It was above all the *émigrés* from the Russian revolution who were in dire need of help. Many of them had found their way to Constantinople, where they eked out a miserable existence. The refugees were by no means as numerous as the prisoners of war, but the work of placing them in a new country, in situations where they could hope to make a decent living, demanded the greatest patience, tact and energy. In order to make their admission less difficult, Nansen initiated an identity card, called the 'Nansen passport', which was recognized by fifty-two different governments. Still greater difficulties presented themselves when Nansen undertook yet another assignment, the task of alleviating the distress caused by the famine in Russia. As early as 1919 he had warned the Allied leaders that the 'Russian problem' must be solved, not by force of arms or blockade, but by negotiation and aid. Personally Nansen was violently opposed to the principles and methods of the Bolshevik Revolution, but at the same time he maintained that foreign pressure would merely strengthen the régime and create a series of crises for the Russian people, and this in turn would be a menace to Europe. However, anti-Bolshevik feelings were too strong for this line to be taken. In 1921 the great famine set in, largely as a result of drought in the Volga valley. In July Maxim Gorki appealed to Nansen who forthwith procured several hundred tons of salt fish for Leningrad. Immediately afterwards he consented to organize international aid, and at meetings of the League Assembly in September he made an urgent appeal to the governments to make a loan of 15 million pounds. 'We are running a race with the Russian winter,' he said in his speech on September 30, and he concluded with the words: 'Make haste to act before it is too late to repent.' But all sorts of scruples were raised and vociferously reiterated in reactionary quarters. Nansen then made his appeal to people the world over, and together with Hoover's American Relief he succeeded in saving millions of human lives.

Nansen continued his international work right up to his death. Not least famous is his organization of the transfer of populations which took place between Turkey and Greece. A Danish writer has paid a fitting tribute to Nansen's work to create peace and understanding between the nations: 'The Nobel Peace Prize has in the course of the years been given to many different sorts of men. It has surely never been awarded to anyone who in such a short time has carried out such far-reaching *practical* peace work as Nansen.'*

* Jens Marinus Jensen, *I Folkeforbundets Tjeneste* [Köbenhavn 1931], p. 101.

EASING OF INTERNATIONAL TENSION 1925-30

Dawes, Chamberlain, Briand, Stresemann, Buisson, Quidde, Butler, Kellogg

After the award made to Nansen in 1922 there was no further distribution of the prize until the year 1926. Once again the Nobel Committee were criticized for adopting a passive attitude, and on this occasion undoubtedly with more justification. It is at any rate somewhat remarkable that in the course of these years as many as four candidates were proposed who all received the prize at a later date, i.e. Lord Robert Cecil, Jane Addams, Ferdinand Buisson and Ludwig Quidde. These had without any doubt already at this stage done work which qualified them as recipients. And amongst the others who were suggested we find at any rate such names as Ramsay MacDonald and Carl Lindhagen.

Not till the easing of the European situation which took place after 1925 did the Committee make any further awards. In 1926 the prize for *1925* was shared between CHARLES DAWES [1865-1951] and Sir AUSTEN CHAMBERLAIN [1863-1937], while the prize for *1926* was shared between ARISTIDE BRIAND [1862-1932] and GUSTAV STRESEMANN [1878-1929]. Seldom has the award been bound up so closely with one definite achievement: in the case of the first-mentioned with the so-called Dawes Plan of 1924, and in the case of the other three with the Locarno Pact of 1925.

The background of General Dawes's work was the French occupation of the Ruhr in 1923 and the repercussions it had produced in the economic situation of Germany and most of the rest of Europe. It furthermore accentuated the inefficiency of the short-sighted and uncoordinated policy which the Allies had pursued since the Versailles Treaty.

The U.S.A. also felt the effects of the European economic anarchy. The States had enjoyed an enormous increase of prosperity after the war, but the isolationist policy which was followed in all spheres after the defeat of Wilson meant that in the long run Europe could not be regarded as a source of fresh revenue for the U.S.A. For that reason it was precisely in American quarters that demands for a rational solution to the European economic problems were voiced. As early as December 1922, Secretary of State Hughes had expressed these views in a speech at New Haven, in which he said, *inter alia:* 'Sentiment, however natural, must be disregarded, mutual recriminations are of no avail; reviews of the past, whether accurate or inaccurrate, promise nothing; assertions of blame on the one hand and excuses on the other, come to naught.'* Hughes concluded by recommending the setting up of a committee of experts and promised American support for it.

In the autumn of 1923 the French Government showed greater willingness to accept a plan of this nature, owing to the economic fiasco of the Ruhr occupation; and on November 30, 1923, the Allied Reparations Commission decided that a committee of experts should be appointed. As their representatives on this committee the American Government appointed Charles Dawes and Owen Young. Up till then the U.S.A. had only been represented on the actual Reparations Commission by an observer, Colonel Logan; but, as Dawes relates in his diary, he had done very useful work by clearing the way for views which were later incorporated in the report of the committee of experts.

Charles Dawes, a lawyer by training, had acquired extensive financial experience through long associations with private banking. During the war, he became head of the American Army Purchasing Office in Europe, a position which carried the rank and title of general. In January 1924 he was elected chairman of the first committee of experts. On April 9 the committee submitted its findings, the so-called Dawes Plan. The crux of the plan was to regulate Germany's payments of reparations according to the country's capacity, based on a stabilized monetary system and a balanced budget. The 'transfer problem', which had proved so difficult to solve, was to be tackled with a policy of extensive Allied capital investment in Germany. The plan assumed moreover that the Ruhr would once more be economically part and parcel of Germany. Reparations payments were to be guaranteed through mortgages on the German railways, industries, etc. It was assumed that the German concerns involved would be able to support a burden of this kind comparatively easily, as they had been able to pay off a considerable portion of their debts during the period of inflation.

The Dawes Plan was very largely a product of team-work, and Dawes himself has never concealed the great part played by his collaborators, not least the British representative, Sir Josiah Stamp [later Lord Stamp]. But there is little doubt that it was Dawes who co-ordinated their views, and that he was largely responsible for getting the French and the Germans to come together for discussion.

* Quoted in Charles Dawes, *A Journal of Reparations* [New York 1939], p. 243.

The inherent value of the Dawes Plan as a contribution to the work of peace is more debatable. It was noticeable that the plan greatly limited the economic self-determination of a sovereign power. But at the same time, as the subsequent German Chancellor, Heinrich Brüning, expressed it, it secured for Germany a breathing space in which she could create a new foundation for an independent foreign policy. In the light of later events one might naturally ask whether this in itself was of any benefit to the cause of peace. However, it is certain that at the time it was the only way of subduing the hatred which continued to smoulder after the war. The calmer atmosphere which the Dawes Plan created was at any rate a necessary condition for the policy which led to the evacuation of the Ruhr and the *Locarno Pact*.

The background for these agreements was that France's demands for security had not been satisfied, as the British-American guarantees had lapsed. In 1922 Aristide Briand, as head of the French Government, had tried to establish an agreement with England [at a meeting in Cannes], but his government was overthrown almost immediately afterwards by the Nationalist group in the Chamber. And the new and more detailed provisions dealing with collective security which the Geneva Protocol of 1924 laid down were not put into effect, as the British Government [Baldwin] refused to ratify the agreement.

On the other hand, the German Government had already at an early stage tried to satisfy the French demands. Thus at the end of 1922 the German Chancellor, Dr. Cuno, had via the American Secretary of State proposed as follows: the powers who had interests along the Rhine should – under a guarantee from the U.S.A. – bind themselves for a period of 30 years not to declare war on one another, unless such declaration of war had a basis in a previous plebiscite. This somewhat clumsy proposal was quite naturally sharply rejected by the French Government.

In May 1923 the German Government ventilated a new proposal for a Rhine pact, this time with chief emphasis on a treaty of arbitration. But neither this nor a general proposal in September from Stresemann, who was now Chancellor, had any results. In February 1925 the German Government once more took the initiative. At that time Dr. Luther was head of the government, with Stresemann as his Foreign Minister. In a memorandum issued by these two on February 9, they declared that Germany was willing to accept a pact which expressly guaranteed the Rhine frontiers. It went on to say: 'A pact of this nature can assume that the states interested in the Rhine will pledge themselves solemnly to respect the integrity of the existing possessions along the Rhine, and that both collectively and individually they guarantee the carrying out of this obligation, and that finally they will regard any act which is contrary to this obligation as a matter affecting them all. In this way the parties to this pact guarantee the fulfilment of the obligation to demilitarize the Rhineland to which Germany is pledged by Articles 42 and 43 of the Versailles Treaty. A pact of this nature could also be accompanied by arbitration treaties of the kind mentioned above between Germany and all the states which for their part are prepared to conclude them.'

The German memorandum had a somewhat varied reception in Paris. On the other hand, the British Government, with Austen Chamberlain as its Foreign Secretary, gave it a hearty welcome. The British Ambassador in Berlin, Lord d'Abernon, had actually been in contact with Stresemann ever since the autumn of 1924 and was on the whole very sympathetic towards Germany. As far as the Baldwin Government was concerned, the memorandum was in addition a very welcome argument for rejecting the Geneva Protocol. This occured on March 12.

The French Government [Herriot] was considerably more sceptical and refused at first to clarify its attitude to the proposal. It was not till a new government had come into power [Painlevé) with Briand as Foreign Minister, that an answer was forthcoming on June 16, 1925. It was couched in cordial terms, but nothing resulted from the exchange of notes which continued throughout that summer. Briand then suggested that verbal negotiations should be initiated. British, French and German jurists drew up in London a draft for a possible set of agreements. At the conclusion of the sixth Assembly of the League of Nations in September, Europe's leading statesmen met together in Locarno. France was represented by Briand, Great Britain by Chamberlain, and Luther and Stresemann appeared for Germany. Belgium, Italy, Poland and Czechoslovakia were also represented. The negotiations commenced on October 5 and terminated on October 16. The Rhine Agreement, which was concluded here between Germany, Belgium, France and Great Britain, laid down as follows: the parties guaranteed individually and collectively the boundaries between Germany and Belgium and between Germany and France. The other clause in the agreement dealt with the relations between Germany and Belgium and between Germany and France. These powers pledged themselves mutually not to attack or make war on one another except in the cases specifically mentioned and defined in the pact itself, viz. the right to defend themselves when the Rhine pact itself was violated, the right to defend themselves against a flagrant breach of Articles 42 and 43 of the Versailles Treaty, in the event of war as laid down in Article 16 of the League of Nations Covenant; and finally in defence against any power or powers which might attack them after the League Council, in accordance with Point 7 of Article 15 of the League of Nations Covenant, had declared that the conflict which had arisen came within the jurisdiction of the national law of one of the parties concerned. Simultaneously, the chief arbitration treaties were also concluded between Germany and Poland, and between Germany and Czechoslovakia.

The Locarno Treaty, which was signed in London on December 1, 1925, and which prepared the way for Germany's admission to the League of Nations the year afterwards, was greeted throughout the world as an epoch-making contribution to peace, and the award of the prize to its architects evoked a similar response. But at the same time, especially in bourgeois radical and socialist quarters, strong protests were made. It was maintained that the Locarno agreement merely marked a rather unusual episode in the political career of the three statesmen concerned. A Norwegian writer later on summed it up caustically as follows: 'Austen Chamberlain, who resembles his father, the imperialist, in everything except in intelligence, Stresemann, who would willingly belong to the German Nationalists if he were not too canny, and Briand who can belong to anything at all, if he believes that France and he himself stand to win by it.'*

In their political past the three prize-winners undoubtedly had little to commend them as champions of peace, and Briand and Stresemann had especially been ardent advocates of the policy of annexation during the war. When head of the government, for instance, Briand had in 1916 carried on secret negotiations with the Russian Government behind the backs of the British, the gist of which was that France would give Russia a free hand in the East on conditions that Russia guaranteed France's Rhine frontier. Stresemann had been a consistent spokesman of German annexation, covered in the West by the Flemings and in the East by the 'German Balts'. He subscribed fully to Friedrich Naumann's ideas of *Mitteleuropa,* and in a speech made on March 1, 1917, he indicated the means: 'The vital interests of the great powers cannot suffer the straight-jacket of legal paragraphs. If they are violated, these vital interests will

* A. O. Normann in *Bergens Tidende*, Nov. 5, 1928.

burst the bonds which are imposed by international agreements. This has been the situation as long as the world has lasted and thus it will remain.'

Amongst British politicians naturally enough such annexationist sentiments were not in evidence, nor was Chamberlain influenced by them. On the other hand he was blamed for not having taken heed of Keynes's advice during his chairmanship of the Supreme Economic Council at the peace negotiations in 1919, and in this way he was made chiefly responsible for the ineffective solution of the reparations problem. After the war both Briand and Stresemann had given up their annexationist proclivities. It was besides, especially in the case of Stresemann, a question of making a virtue of necessity. Briand, like Léon Bourgeois, placed more emphasis on solving France's security problem in a broad international context, and Stresemann for his part was desirous of establishing Germany's position of parity by pursuing a constructive foreign policy of reconciliation. Chamberlain was a man well fitted to act as arbitrator in any conflict between Germany and France. He followed – albeit somewhat reluctantly – his government's policy of *rapprochement* with Germany, but at the same time he enjoyed great confidence in France owing to his decidedly Francophile attitude.

Even at the time it was concluded there was little doubt that the Treaty of Locarno was the result of an interplay of power politics. The main thing for Germany was to regain her lost position of influence in Central Europe. The Western Powers for their part were interested in drawing Germany away from the *rapprochement* with Russia which was inaugurated by the Rapallo Agreement of 1922. Amongst those who criticized the award of the prize, the opinion was more or less general that, if this step had to be taken, Stresemann was after all the worthiest candidate. But this conception was undoubtedly due to the fact that first and foremost Stresemann represented beaten, disarmed Germany. In German domestic politics peaceful councils were not the only ones that were heard, and Stresemann made considerable concessions to nationalistic circles. He constantly maintained to the German public that the Pact did not imply any final recognition of the western frontiers, but merely a rejection of the use of force.* In a speech in Berlin on December 14, 1925, he declared amongst other things: 'It is obvious that it could never be a question of moral renunciation, but as every reasonable person would have to admit, it would simply be madness to toy with the idea of war with France to-day.'** Shortly

* Gustav Stresemann, *Vermächtnis*, II [Berlin], p. 212. ** *Ibid.*, p. 233.

before, he had asked Lord d'Abernon to persuade Chamberlain not to mention Alsace-Lorraine in his Guildhall speech, and if indeed Chamberlain had had any plan of so doing, Stresemann at any rate had his wish fulfilled. As far as Germany's eastern boundaries were concerned, Stresemann expressed himself even more plainly. In this respect the Locarno agreement had in his opinion the advantage that French aid to Poland had been made conditional on the League Council's *unanimous* recommendation of sanctions, in the event of Germany being declared the aggressor. There could no longer be any talk of unreserved French support.* Stresemann's reference to the Locarno representatives of Germany's Slavonic neighbours was in tone suspiciously like that Hitler was to employ later on: 'Messrs. Beneš and Skrzynski had to sit in the waiting-room until we let them in.'**

The pacifist assessment of the Locarno Pact must by and large lead one to the conclusion that France was the power which made the greatest sacrifice and that Briand despite everything was the most constructive pacifist of the three statesmen. That he was simply deceived – as some people have declared – is highly improbable. The most reasonable suggestion is that he believed the pact was the only means of securing for France at any rate a certain measure of support from England, and that he counted on a further development of the democratic forces in Germany, as a result of her economic and political stabilization.

In the eyes of the Nobel Committee and most friends of peace, the Locarno Pact was first and foremost a proof of a new and better relationship between France and Germany. And in this very connection the pact inspired a mood of confidence precisely because it was the outcome of discussions based on practical politics. As Fridtjof Nansen said in his speech at the prize distribution: 'What inspires our confidence is the fact that it was neither idealism nor altruism which compelled men to make this attempt; it was the feeling of necessity.'

Work to effect Franco-German reconciliation was also the basis of the awards which were made the next year, *1927,* when the prize was shared between FERDINAND BUISSON [1841-1932] and LUDWIG QUIDDE [1858-1941]. Ferdinand Buisson was the oldest of all the prize-winners, a noble representative of French nineteenth-century radical humanism, a man who by word and deed had fought against the régime of Napoleon III. But under the Third Republic too it was necessary to assert the ideas

* *Ibid.*, p.235. ** *Ibid.*, p.243.

of tolerance and especially perhaps to work for greater social solidarity. In a speech to the French Women's Red Cross Organization in 1897 he declared that the process of nationalization from the time of the French Revolution had made the demands on the individual greater than ever before. For example, where social-welfare work was concerned, one could no longer leave it passively to certain groups who had undertaken it on religious grounds; one must make one's own personal contribution. Buisson entered the French political arena at a comparatively late date. It happened at the time of the Dreyfus case, when in 1898 he helped to found the *Ligue des Droits de l'Homme,* which then and later fought to defend human rights. In 1902 he was elected a deputy for the Radical Socialist party.

Buisson had realized at an early age that work for human rights was organically bound up with pacifism; in 1867 he had taken part in the first congress of the *Ligue de la Paix.* He was, however, not an anti-militarist, and he supported France's defence during the First World War, because he was convinced that France had been unjustly attacked, and that only an Allied victory could continue to safeguard the idea of human rights. At an early stage he and others in the League worked to promote the establishment of a lasting peace, and in 1916 they expressed themselves in favour of a League of Nations. Buisson was profoundly disappointed by the Peace of Versailles, but he believed that the only way to offset its harmful effects was to fill the new international organization with a humanitarian spirit, first and foremost by working for Franco-German reconciliation. For that reason, though over 80 years old, he took up the cudgels against the French Ruhr policy and in 1924 he lectured in Germany, first in Mainz, and later on in Berlin. Characteristically enough, he encountered still greater opposition from the German nationalists than from the French.

This gives us some idea of the difficulties which German pacifists had to contend with. Ludwig Quidde was one of the most prominent of these, though he belonged possibly neither to the boldest nor the most consistent. His peace propaganda went right back to 1893, when [anonymously] he published a violent attack against German militarism. The next year he issued a pamphlet, *Caligula,* which had the form and appearance of a historical study but was in reality a caustic attack on Wilhelm II and his clique. Quidde was here following the example of David Friedrich Strauss's celebrated pamphlet against King Friedrich Wilhelm IV, *Der*

Romantiker auf dem Throne der Caesaren, and his writing aroused tremendous attention. In the same year, 1894, Quidde started a pacifist association in Munich. He was also an active participant at international peace congresses, and after being elected a member of the Bavarian Diet in 1907, he also participated in the Inter-Parliamentary Conferences. After the outbreak of the First World War, Quidde tried at an early stage to establish contact with pacifists in other belligerent and neutral countries, and he was a German delegate at the meeting at The Hague in 1915 arranged by the *Anti Oorlog Raad.*

In Germany itself he joined the campaign against the annexationists, and in a pamphlet entitled *Sollen wir annektieren?,* issued by the *Bund Neues Vaterland* in 1915, he pointed out how unreasonable and at the same time impracticable were the plans of the Greater Germany movement. The pamphlet was immediately confiscated; Quidde, however, issued another one which was likewise confiscated, but of which he managed in spite of all to distribute a few thousand copies.

In 1919 Quidde was elected a member of the German National Assembly where he made a violent speech against the acceptance of the Versailles Treaty; nor was he willing to recognize the clause dealing with Germany's sole responsibility for the War, as a few other German pacifists, amongst them Friedrich Wilhelm Foerster, were willing to do. On the other hand he devoted his energies to convincing people that Germany should try to be admitted to the League of Nations, and he was always aware of the danger which the continued growth of militarism within the Weimar Republic represented. On January 3, 1924, *Das Deutsche Friedenskartell,* a joint body of all German peace associations, forwarded an appeal to the Reich Chancellor, Dr. Marx, demanding an official investigation into the secret military training which was being carried out. The Chancellor rejected the request and went so far as to threaten legal proceedings. The threat was further emphasized in a letter from the Defence Minister, General von Seeckt. Thereupon the pacifists raised the matter in the press: first Walther Schücking in the *Berliner Volkszeitung,* and later on Quidde in Hellmuth von Gerlach's periodical, *Welt am Montag.* Quidde's main point was that to tolerate secret military training might provide France with a pretext for fresh punitive measures, while at the same time it undermined the prestige of the Republic. A few days after the publication of his article Quidde was arrested, accused of 'collaborating with the enemy'. Though he was only incarcerated for a week, the incident was nevertheless in itself a grim warning of what was in store and was to find expression not many years later in the legal persecution of another German pacifist, Carl von Ossietzky.

After the award of the prize to Buisson and Quidde there was once more an interval before the next nomination, in fact until 1930, when the prize for *1929* was given to FRANK BILLINGS KELLOGG and for *1930* to NATHAN SÖDERBLOM.

In Kellogg's case the award was due to a simple act, viz. the drawing up of the so-called Paris Pact or Briand-Kellogg Pact of 1928.

The preliminary work on this pact was carried out by Briand who wished to use the Locarno Agreement as a starting-point for a United Europe [Pan-Europa], and if possible to get the U.S.A. more permanently committed to the work of international co-operation, even though the States still remained outside the League of Nations. On April 6, 1927, he published an appeal, calling on France and the U.S.A. to renounce war as an instrument of policy in their mutual relations. The appeal was launched at a time when a certain aloofness existed between the two countries, owing to the question of outstanding debts. It was moreover an American, NICHOLAS MURRAY BUTLER [1862-1947, *1931*], who had given Briand the idea. After studying education and philosophy Butler in 1901 became President of Columbia University, which under his guidance made great headway. At an early date he became interested in international co-operation, and fully realized the part that education, in its widest implication, could play in this respect. Its object would be to create, not only a favourable opinion, but an active attitude, a truly 'international mind' in ever wider circles. In 1908 he drafted for Carnegie the principal lines of what was soon to emerge as the Carnegie Endowment for International Peace, in which he became Director of the Division of Intercourse and Education. From his early years Butler had many contacts in Europe, especially in Germany, France and England. After the First World War he took part in cultural reconstruction work. As early as 1917 he succeeded in establishing a fund for this purpose. The money thus collected was later on used to rebuild various cultural institutions in Yugoslavia, Belgium and France. Butler had contacts not only in university circles, but also among politicians. Proof of the confidence he inspired is the fact that Lloyd George in 1921 invited him to an Imperial Conference at Chequers, the conference which led to the creation of the modern British Commonwealth of Nations. Butler's talents were primarily those of an organizer and a negotiator. His comprehensive writings, on the other hand, do not reveal any special originality or clarity of conception. But they are marked by a positive optimism and a strong desire to sweep away prejudices in the international sphere.

His work with what was later to take shape as the *Kellogg Pact* originated in a meeting he had with Briand in June 1926. They talked about the Locarno Pact and the relaxation of tension in Franco-German relations. In answer to Briand's question as to what might be done to further the cause of peace, Butler cited Clausewitz's *Vom Kriege,* in which the author talks of 'war as an instrument of policy'. Butler considered that the time had now come for nations to renounce by voluntary agreement the use of such an instrument of policy.* Briand took up the idea and as already mentioned launched it on April 8, 1927. Briand's appeal, however, attracted hardly any attention in the U.S.A. It was Butler who, by campaigning eagerly for this idea and initiating his appeal by an open letter to the *New York Times* on April 25, 1927, really roused public opinion in favour of it. The actual idea of abolishing war as a juridical institution by means of treaties was in fact an American one, suggested by a Chicago lawyer, S. O. Levinson. Just as the 'League to Enforce Peace' had been a very real factor in establishing the League of Nations, so the subsequent Briand-Kellogg Pact was based on the ideas which Levinson's organization, with their slogan 'Outlawry of War', sought to promote. The aim of this movement was to abolish war as a juridical institution, just as in the civilized world duelling and slavery had been abolished. The adherents of the movement furthermore refused to recognize the usual distinction between a war of aggression and a defensive war, and consequently rejected the principles of the League of Nations in the sphere of 'security politics'. On the other hand, they maintained the right to self-defence, without giving any further definition of this conception. The general opinion among them was that disarmament would not become a fact until war as an institution was abolished. Peace would lead to disarmament, not vice versa.

These ideas had made their appearance in the American political arena as early as 1923, when the influential Senator Borah submitted a proposal that war should be outlawed as an institution.

Senator Borah belonged to the isolationist wing, and it may therefore appear remarkable that he, of all people, should devote himself to interna-

* Nicholas Murray Butler, *Across the Busy Years*, II, [New York 1940], p.202.

tional ideas of this kind. In reality there was nothing so very remarkable about this circumstance. Borah's proposal aimed at a multi-lateral agreement, based on purely general moral ideas, without any actual obligations. It was a means of capturing more internationally minded circles among the American people. The idea of a multi-lateral agreement was also to be the starting-point for the American Government when eventually, on December 28, 1927, it replied to the French proposal. Already in June [20th] Briand had handed the American Ambassador a draft of the proposed treaty. The French point of view was in this case – as expressed in Briand's speech on April 6 – that France and the U.S.A. should conclude an agreement which could serve as a pattern for treaties with other countries and between other countries. The Americans maintained on the other hand that the pact ought from the very start to embrace as many states as possible. It entailed a considerable amount of work and diplomatic skill to co-ordinate the various views, but success was finally achieved, and on August 27, 1928, the pact was signed in Paris.* Its two first principal articles ran as follows:

1. The high contracting parties solemnly declare in the names of their respective peoples that they condemn recourse to war for the solution of international controversies, and renounce it as an instrument of national policy in their relations with one another.
2. The high contracting parties agree that the settlement or solution of all disputes or conflicts of whatever nature or of whatever origin they may be, which may arise among them, shall never be sought except by pacific means.

FRANK BILLINGS KELLOGG [1856-1937, *1929*] is the prize-winner who is most closely bound up with the particular cause which formed the basis of this award. It is difficult to estimate his personal contribution to the work of piloting the Paris Pact safely through, but undoubtedly in his role of American Secretary of State from 1925 to 1929 he was to a large extent responsible for the positive result of the negotiations.

From the pacifist point of view the pact was first and foremost an expression of a more cordial state of international relations, despite the fact that disarmament had not made much progress. And the fact that the general desire among the nations for lasting peace now took shape in an

* The signatory powers were: U.S.A., Great Britain, France, Italy, Japan, Germany, Belgium, Poland and Czechoslovakia. The Pact was later on adhered to by practically all powers in the world.

international pact undoubtedly had important propagandistic repercussions. Yet the pact did not constitute a guarantee of peace. This was demonstrated only a few years later, when the 'vital interests' of some of the signatory states made themselves felt in earnest.

THE CHURCH AND PEACE

Söderblom, Mott, Society of Friends

In its conception of the problem of war and peace the Christian Church has never adopted a uniform attitude. 'The Church' is after all a very vague term, not only owing to the differences between the various creeds, but also because of the great variety of views prevailing within the different religious bodies on many questions of a non-dogmatic nature, including such a fundamental and comprehensive problem as the attitude to war and peace. During the First World War most Christians regarded their religion as a part of their nationalism. Others accepted war as a necessity 'for the sake of the hardness of men's hearts'. The consistent pacifists were very few in number.

In the neutral countries, quite naturally, church circles had an easier task in keeping alive the idea of world brotherhood, and among the churchmen who worked with this aim Sweden's Archbishop NATHAN SÖDERBLOM [1866-1931, *1930*] was undoubtedly one of the most outstanding. Even before the war, he had participated in the work of uniting the church communities of the world and thereby promoting international understanding. At a congress in Constance in 1914 he helped to found a 'General World Union of Churches for International Understanding'. The congress, however, had to close down on the outbreak of war. Söderblom nevertheless tried to continue this work, and in November 1914 – in co-operation with a Norwegian and a Danish bishop – he issued an appeal to this effect. In 1917, together with other churchmen from the Nordic and other neutral countries, he tried to arrange a general church congress, with representatives both from the belligerent and neutral countries. Many accepted the invitation, both in Germany, France, England and the U.S.A., as well as leading dignitaries of the Greek Orthodox Church. The congress never materialized, however, as the authorities refused to grant the delegates passports. The German Government was most favourably disposed, and this was also true of the Socialist Conference held in Stockholm the same year. In both cases this compliant attitude was probably due to a desire to strengthen pro-German sentiments in Sweden. When the plans for a truly international conference miscarried in this way, it was decided instead to hold a purely Nordic meeting in Uppsala from the 14th to 16th September, 1917. In the manifesto which was sent out afterwards attention was called to the bonds which unite all Christians, despite national and secterian divergencies. The manifesto also expressed the deep concern which all Christians must feel at the discrepancy between war and the will of Christ. Moreover, the Church, the manifesto went on, has all too often laid more stress on what divides rather than on what unites. It should instead emphasize Christian fellowship and strive with all its might to remove the causes of war. Christians should, moreover, always try to understand the background for other people's ideas and actions. Furthermore, the aim of the Church should be to train people to an ever increasing degree of self-government, and work for international understanding and the settling of disputes by mediation and arbitration. The Church should humbly admit its shortcomings in this respect, and strive with all its might to make up for them.

This manifesto was clearly inspired by Söderblom. While markedly High Church, he was at the same time a man of wide views. Though his religious beliefs made it impossible for him to accept the evolutionist theory of the perfectibility of human nature by purely rational influences, he never made Christian conversion a *sine qua non* for pacifism; and the Christian conception of war as a punishment from God must not prevent Christians from taking part in the work to remove the causes of war. It would be just as unreasonable as to adopt a passive attitude towards disease or other human sufferings.

Quite apart from the ethical values of Christianity, Söderblom believed that the Christian way of life was in itself of great value to pacifism. In a sermon in 1917 he emphasized two factors: first the Christian belief in the impossible and the fact that faith 'took the long view'. The *patience* of faith was perhaps the most important thing. The other factor was the ability of the Christian way of life to strengthen confidence in the community based on law. The early Christians had even recognized the heathen system of justice, and the anarchistic currents in Christianity had never played any outstanding role; nor should they do so, in the opinion of Söderblom. For, as he says, 'he who would abolish war and other misery by undermining the legally constituted state and the sanctity of the law, is only driving out devils with the help of Beelzebub, and is encouraging violence and the power of money and wealth.'*

On this basis he tried to rally the Christians to strike a blow for peace. The attempt failed in 1917 and again the following year. But in 1920 he managed to convoke a meeting in Geneva, at which the foundations were laid for an oecumenical conference in Stockholm. The conference – called 'The Universal Christian Conference on Life and Work' – was held in 1925 and was attended by more than 600 delegates from Protestant and Orthodox Church communities in 37 different countries. Of the major church communities the Roman Catholic Church was the only one not represented. At the conference the subject 'The Church and International Relations' was widely discussed, and it was largely due to Söderblom's personality that both this and subsequent oecumenical conferences were so internationally minded.

The other churchman among the prize-winners, JOHN MOTT [1865-1955, *1946*] was in many ways a very different type from Söderblom. The latter was markedly High Church, with a solid foundation of theological and ecclesiastical learning and an open mind in cultural and philosophical questions. Mott was a layman, who only enjoyed a brief university education, backed up by wide but somewhat desultory reading. But, in common with Söderblom, he had never allowed his particular religious faith [Methodism] to interfere with his efforts to rally people of divergent creeds. As a student at Cornell University he helped to organize a Christian Student Union, and in 1888 he became Secretary of the Inter-Collegiate Young Men's Christian Association. In this capacity he toured the universities of the U.S.A. and Canada, organizing new groups and renewing contact with old ones. At a meeting in Vadstena in Sweden in 1895 he founded an international Christian student organization, which was kept going during the First World War. At the same time he took part in mission work and became Chairman of the International Missionary Council.

During the First World War, Mott attempted to maintain international relations, and he played a leading part in the relief work which the Y.M.C.A. carried out among prisoners of war in various countries. This work was continued when the American forces were demobilized. Mott's practical grasp of things, and his ability to get in touch with all sorts and conditions of men, were the reason why President Wilson as early as 1913 asked him

* N. Söderblom, *Kyrkans uppgift i fredsarbetet* [Uppsala 1917], pp. 16-17.

to take over the position of Ambassador to the new Chinese Republic. Mott declined the offer, however, out of consideration for his religious organizational work. Nevertheless in 1916 he was a member of a commission which was to settle a number of delicate questions with the provisional Mexican government, and the next year he was a member of a special delegation to Russia led by Elihu Root. This journey of Mott's was strongly criticized by German students, because the aim of the delegation was believed to be an attempt to stimulate the Russian war effort. Mott was, however, able to convince them that *his* had been of a purely religious nature. At an early stage Mott had worked to get the Christian Young Men's Movement to support the organized work of peace, and not least the idea of voluntary arbitration. He also started a campaign against dangerous aggressive tendencies, particularly against racial prejudices. He always tried to maintain equal rights for Negroes and Asiatic people.

In the work of conciliation between nations and races no Christian community has made a contribution equal to that of the SOCIETY OF FRIENDS [Friends' Service Council, Great Britain, and American Friends' Service Committee, U.S.A., *1947*]. Ever since George Fox founded the sect in 1647, it has maintained its fundamental principles clearly and consistently: to combat war and militarism, and to work constructively for peace among the nations. The history of the Quakers is well known. Persecuted by the authorities in England a number of them emigrated to America, where William Penn founded the colony of Pennsylvania in 1682. Their work has nevertheless not always been given due recognition, as the Quakers have constantly worked unobtrusively. Numerically the sect is not large: even to-day it has not more than about 200,000 adherents, most of them in Great Britain and the U.S.A. Yet their activities are considerable. This is a natural result of their fundamental religious principle that in every human being there is an 'inner light'. By daily experience of this contact with the divine they believe that man will be able to establish the Kingdom of God on earth. For that reason they do not adopt a passive attitude to the problem of Evil, but at the same time they maintain that it can only be solved by the power of Good.

The attitude of the Quakers made it natural for them to be pioneers in modern pacifism. They had from the start refused to carry out military service, and about the year 1800 they founded the first peace societies in England and the U.S.A.

Otherwise they have worked primarily not by propaganda, but by force of example. This was clearly shown in the Crimean War, when they tried first of all to get the Czar to cease hostilities, and later sent a relief expedition to various places on the coast of Finland [at that time under Russia] after these had been bombarded by units of the British Navy. The same 'double-edged' humanitarian relief work was resumed during the First World War, when American Quakers worked extensively in war-damaged areas of France, only to go to the assistance of former enemy countries such as Germany and Austria as soon as the war was over. The Quakers also made a considerable contribution to Russian aid, and encountered in this work the same resistance from reactionary quarters as Nansen and others. But this only served to spur them on to greater efforts: precisely because the Russian régime in many respects represented the opposite of their own methods, the Quakers wished through their relief work to demonstrate the power of their humanitarian attitude. The Quakers subsequently encountered a similar resistance when in the 1930's they initiated in the U.S.A. a relief scheme for the benefit of the children of striking miners. They wished in this way to emphasize that, in order to establish peace among the nations, it was necessary to establish peace within the nations. Material assistance has in fact always been used as a means of promoting goodwill among men, and has not been provided by the Quakers to make converts to their own faith.

WOMEN AND PEACE

Jane Addams, Emily Greene Balch

Women as such cannot be said to have any special uniform attitude to pacifism any more than the various church communities. In this connection many people have pointed to such things as woman's fuller emotional life, her maternal instinct, etc., as a guarantee that women are always ready to work for peace. But characteristically enough the women who have hitherto received the Peace Prize have done their best to sweep away nebulous conceptions of this nature, and to present a true picture. They have all, each in her own way, shown how women often tend to be especially receptive to the spirit of militarism and nationalism, because they have for so long been suppressed and have submitted themselves passively to the prevailing conventions.

The three female prize-winners are really first and foremost intellectual in their outlook, without of course lacking the emotional element. Otherwise there is a noticeable difference between Bertha von Suttner on the one hand and Jane Addams and Emily Balch on the other. First there is a difference of time, Bertha von Suttner belonging entirely to the nineteenth century with its belief in progress based on science. Jane Addams and Emily Balch mark the transition to the twentieth century and transform the cultural optimism of the old world into a religious-minded philanthropy. It is social analysis and social responsibility which primarily makes them work for peace. Both of them became to a very marked extent women of action, organizers.

JANE ADDAMS [1860-1935, *1931*] was born in Cedarville, Illinois. Her father had been a man of some repute, a friend and colleague of Abraham Lincoln. Originally she had thought of becoming a doctor, but a chronic spinal affliction prevented the carrying out of this plan. After a protracted stay in hospital she went to Europe. In London she was considerably shaken by the conditions under which poor people lived in the East End. This made her take up social work, to which, being comfortably off, she was able to devote herself. On her return home she started together with a friend a philanthropic institution, Hull House, in Chicago, which became a centre of social-welfare work in the widest sense of the word. Personally Jane Addams was essentially religious in her moral outlook, but the institution never bore the usual hall-mark of charity, which so often goes hand in hand with moral bigotry and self-complacent godliness. Jane Addams in many ways asserted a Socratic view of man, and had a real horror of confining moral demands to certain definite strait-laced rules of conduct. During a visit to Tolstoy, for instance, she was horrified at the intolerance which characterized the ideas of the great Russian. Thus in her opinion even his absolute repugnance to physical violence might lead men into a new and possibly more dreadful tyranny. She says that Tolstoy drew 'too sharp a distinction between the use of physical force and the moral energy which just as ruthlessly can trample on other people's opinions and scruples'.

Jane Addams's idealism was above all practical by nature. Even though the struggle against injustice and misery must be uncompromising, the only way to achieve results was by the mental liberation of man. Not least her work with immigrants of various nationalities had taught her the importance of patience and a practical approach to all problems. It was precisely this activity which led her to pacifism.

When the First World War broke out, the Carnegie Foundation sent her out as one of its lecturers on pacifism. Work of this nature was highly desirable, for though the U.S.A. was far removed from the theatre of war, and people were by no means prepared to join in, yet the far-reaching effects of the great European conflicts were very noticeable, not least among the relatively 'fresh' immigrants. Therefore – in the opinion of Jane Addams and other pacifists – it was in the interest of the U.S.A. not only to subdue the warmongers in their midst, but also to make an active contribution to the setting up of a just and early peace. On this basis she founded in January 1915 the *Women's Peace Party*. In Europe too the voices of the pacifists could be heard, and, on the initiative of the Dutch, a Women's Peace Congress was held at The Hague from April 28 to May 1, 1915. At this congress Jane Addams presided; she was the moving spirit in framing resolutions against war and in the delegations which were afterwards sent out to statesmen in belligerent and neutral countries. The women's peace appeal made a considerable impression, not least with the handshake exchanged between the Belgian and the German representatives at the Congress. But in practice their action had no effect, nor could any success be claimed by an appeal for a conciliatory peace issued by a new Women's Congress in Zurich on May 12-17, 1919. But women had at any rate created an international organization which from this time received the name of the *Women's International League for Peace and Freedom*. Throughout its existence this organization has worked to create the international understanding which the peace settlement had failed to establish. Not only in Europe did pacifists have to combat a post-war atmosphere of great tension, but in the U.S.A. as well. Precisely because militarism had not previously had particularly deep roots in the American people, sentiment had been systematically whipped up so as to secure the maximum war effort. And after the war this wave of chauvinism rolled on with its own impetus. It was thus a difficult and exacting task to counter this mood with an appeal to moderation and humanity.

EMILY GREENE BALCH [1867-1961, *1946*] worked with Jane Addams, and after the latter's death she became the leader of the Women's Peace Movement. These two women are astonishingly alike, both in their social background and their development. They both sprang from an

American Puritan milieu, while both of them are closely connected with the Society of Friends and thus represent on the one hand a marked spirit of tolerance, on the other hand a firm attitude to oppression and violence, and a keen desire to improve social conditions. Emily Greene Balch was also roused to the work of active social reform by her personal impressions from the slum districts. Her path to pacifism too lay through social studies and philanthropic activity, *inter alia* with the founding of a social settlement in Boston. But there are also certain differences between them. First of all Emily Greene Balch represents to a greater extent the New England tradition. Secondly she had not suffered from any physical handicap, so that she was able to carry out research [in social economy] and later to become a professor in her subject. In her lectures she dealt with the immigration problem, and analysed it, not only with the help of documents and statistics, but also by actually living in typical immigration districts in the U.S.A. [especially among people of Slav origins], and visiting their homes in Europe. Politically speaking Emily Balch's attitude was more clearly defined than that of Jane Addams. The latter strove above all to find a middle way, even though she never hesitated to espouse the cause of the people who suffered injustice. Emily Balch, however, at an early stage sought direct contact with the American labour movement through the American Federation of Labor, and she was one of the founders of the Women's Trade Union League of America.

In all essentials, however, these two women pursued a common line, and with the outbreak of the First World War they devoted their entire energies to the struggle for peace. Emily Balch was also present at the meeting at The Hague, where she played a leading part. In 1916 she took part in a Neutral Conference on Continuous Mediation in Stockholm, which Henry Ford had financed. The comic aspect of the 'Peace Expedition' was not the fault of the leading American women pacifists, who had in advance deprecated the use of undue publicity. Jane Addams herself says in one of her books: 'Among other things which Mr. Ford had gained from his wide experience, was an overwhelming belief in the value of advertising; even derision was better than no 'story' at all.'*

Emily Balch represented moreover a useful rational element at the Congress in Stockholm, and the proposal she submitted for international colonial administration resembled in many respects the system of mandates which was later initiated by the Versailles peace treaties.

* Jane Addams, *Peace and Bread in Time of War* [New York 1922], p. 39.

On her return to the U.S.A. Emily Balch joined the campaign to prevent the entry of the States into the war, and this standpoint cost her her professorship when her contract came up for renewal in 1918. Apart from the undoubted moral value of her attitude, Emily Balch was here undeniably faced with the sort of dilemma which most consistent pacifists had to face: a victory for Prussian militarism would hardly under any circumstances smooth the way for a peace of conciliation. When, during the Second World War, with the menace of Nazism and Japanese imperialism, the problem assumed still clearer outlines, Emily Balch changed her point of view. From now on she believed that to defend the fundamental human rights, sword in hand, had become a bitter necessity.

In the inter-war years, like Jane Addams, she worked to establish and extend the Women's International League for Peace and Freedom, while at the same time she attacked all chauvinistic and imperialistic currents both at home and abroad. Together with the American Women's League she agitated in favour of the U.S.A. renouncing its claims to priority in its demands on Austria, and in 1926 she led a campaign to remove all American troops from Haiti and to establish a more satisfactory régime for the inhabitants of that island. This was later carried out.

Her struggle against isolationism was more difficult. Admittedly the demands for an American ratification of the Kellogg Pact had positive results; but the spirit which was to give the Pact reality was more difficult to create, and the U.S.A. continued to keep aloof from the League of Nations and the attempts to create a system of collective security.

ACTS OF AGGRESSION IN THE 1930'S AND RESISTANCE TO THEM

Sir Norman Angell, Arthur Henderson, Lord Robert Cecil, Carl von Ossietzky, Saavedra Lamas, Nansen Refugee Office

With the prize-award in 1931 the mood of optimism, which had prevailed ever since 1926, came to an end. There was no distribution of the prize in 1932, and the award for 1933 was postponed till the following year. The reason for this was probably the sudden deterioration in the international situation which followed in the wake of the economic crisis, and of which at the time the most drastic symptom was the Japanese occupation of Manchuria, completed in 1932.

In the circumstances the Nobel Committee quite obviously decided to await the outcome of events, but in 1934 the distribution was resumed. In this and the following years the prize went to people who more or less clearly represented the work for collective security and resistance to the powers of aggression.

Sir NORMAN ANGELL [1874-1968], who in 1934 received the prize for *1933*, was originally a journalist. In his youth he had spent several years in the United States, where he was struck by the animosity towards England which was fostered in many quarters. This forced him to put the following question to himself: when an atmosphere of this sort can be created in the case of nations which are closely related, how much easier and more dangerous must not similar activity be in the case of nations which are strangers to one another, and where concrete factors of power politics play their part? Norman Angell made it his aim from that moment to make public opinion, both in his own and other countries, more resistant to nationalistic influences by subjecting these phenomena to a clear analysis which would help people to consider these problems in a more commonsense way. His basic idea was in fact that it is not the phenomena themselves which are decisive, but people's opinions about them. From 1905 he worked in Paris as editor of the Continental edition of the *Daily Mail*, and in 1909 he published a pamphlet entitled *Europe's Optical Illusion*. The main ideas in this are further developed in his book *The Great Illusion*, which was published in 1910 and in a very short time ran through several editions, as well as being translated into a number of languages. In this book Norman Angell raised the question of what benefits war might bring. He took as a concrete example the possibility of a war between England and Germany. The object of such a war would, according to popular conception, be that one party would paralyse or destroy the other party economically. But this, Angell maintained, was an illusion. France, for example, recovered remarkably quickly after 1871, while victorious Germany, though receiving large reparations, shortly afterwards suffered a serious economic crisis. In the same way it would be impossible to ruin British trade, and even if this could be done, it would entail economic suicide for the victor. Despite all competitive factors it was actually in Germany's interest, just as much as in the interest of other countries, for British trade to flourish. Angell further investigated the question of direct annexation, and declared that, for example, a German conquest of The Netherlands would not entail any economic gain for Germany, for it would not be possible to kill all Dutch business people – in those days 'civilized' countries did not practice mass deportations or genocide – and these would continue to compete with the Germans, under the protection of the German custom barriers. Europe's 'optical illusion' was that a nation can increase its prosperity by expanding its territory.

Another illusion is the belief that human nature cannot be changed. What we call 'human nature' is in fact not a constant factor, but alters with the development of society and with changes in the ordinary conventions. As far as the peace problem is concerned, this is most clearly seen in the fact that acts of war based on religious motives are a thing of the past, or that such conventions as duelling or blood feuds have disappeared in civilized countries. Moreover, Angell regarded the increasing interdependence of nations as a significant factor in the prevention of war, as well as the fact that lines of cleavage in modern times follow *classes,* not nations. Nevertheless he has never denied the possibility or even the probability of war. It is, he says, not the probability of war which is a popular illusion, but the belief in its advantages.

In various quarters objections partly justified were raised against Angell's assertions. It was, for example, impossible to deny that Germany had had considerable economic advantages from Alsace-Lorraine, or that Germany's wars in the nineteenth century had on the whole increased the total economic strength of the country whatever might be said of the moral side.

Nor has Norman Angell always been infallible in his theories. It is above all as an agitator that he has been important, and the award of the Peace Prize was precisely due to the fact that many of his basic ideas proved to have surprising vitality and could be applied to a great number of the problems of the inter-war years. With these ideas as his starting point, Norman Angell in 1919 severely criticized the Versailles Treaty and made more or less the same forecast with regard to its economic clauses as did John Maynard Keynes. Furthermore, he continued his untiring work to sweep away prejudices in the international field – 'the unseen assassins' as he called them in a book written in 1932 – the belief that events in the world at large only concerned one when one's own national interests were directly menaced, and that real security could only be found in isolated defence. For that reason, he maintained, the aggressive tendencies which were so clearly shown by Japan and shortly afterwards by Nazi Germany, were primarily not dangerous in themselves, but in the fact that the pretext given – that a growing population needed *Lebensraum* – was so passively accepted in the democratic world and prevented the setting up of a system of collective security.

The Peace Prize for *1934* was given to another Englishman, ARTHUR HENDERSON [1863-1935]. With Branting he most clearly represents socialistic ideas amongst the prize-winners. Like MacDonald he sprang from the working class and had won his spurs in the trade-union movement. He was elected to Parliament as a Liberal in 1903, only to become Parliamentary leader of the Labour Party a few years later. During the first world conflict he supported England's entry into the war, in sharp contrast to MacDonald, and in 1915 he became a member of Lloyd George's Coalition Government. In 1917 he was sent to Russia to urge the new revolutionary government to continue the war. But at the same time Henderson was preoccupied with the constructive peace aims which a Socialist party would have to envisage, and his willingness to attend the Socialist Congress in Stockholm in 1917 led to a breach with Lloyd George. At the end of December in the same year he published a pamphlet, *The Aims of the Labour Party,* in which he forecast great revolutionary upheavals after the War, and appealed to the nations of the Western World to give democracy a sound foundation by means of far-reaching social reforms and by adhering to a system of international security.

Immediately after the war – during the reactionary period – Henderson associated himself with MacDonald's pacifist line of action, and when MacDonald formed his first government in 1924, Henderson took office as Home Secretary.

In MacDonald's second government, formed in 1929, Henderson was Foreign Secretary. In this position he strove to direct Great Britain's foreign policy according to the principles of the League of Nations. Though always a consistent Socialist, he did not hesitate to seek the help of Lord Cecil in questions concerning the League of Nations, and to appoint him a member of the British delegation to the League.

In 1931 Henderson was elected President of the Disarmament Conference due to assemble in Geneva. In the interim he became embroiled in a fresh conflict with MacDonald when the latter formed his National Coalition Government in the summer of 1931, an event which entailed Henderson's retirement from the government. Despite this he determined to carry on as President of the Disarmament Conference, which accordingly commenced its sessions at Geneva on February 2, 1932. The reason was that he interpreted his election to the office of president as a personal mark of trust, quite independent of his position as British Foreign Secretary. These circumstances were inevitably to have unfortunate consequences, as the British delegation worked quite independently of Henderson. Many of Henderson's adherents have in this connection asserted that the delegation, by its negative and arbitrary policy, must bear the main burden of responsibility for the collapse of the Conference. Indirectly this is true, in so far as the circles represented by the new British Foreign Secretary, Sir John Simon, always looked somewhat askance at the idea of real collective security and disarmament under international control. But in the circumstances then prevailing it is very doubtful whether Henderson's traditional disarmament programme could have produced any real results, as far as securing world peace was concerned. When the conference opened, one of the participating nations, Japan, was already committed to an act of war, and Henderson's willingness to accede to the German point of view [either all-round disarmament or the recognition of Germany's military equality], in itself logical enough, was based on a mistaken assessment of conditions in Germany. This was shown by the fact that he continued his attempts at mediation even after Hitler had come into power. As late as 1934 – after it had become obvious to everyone that the conference had failed – he said to Barthou, who wanted to establish a defensive front against Nazi Germany: 'The conference is a disarmament conference, a conference for the reduction and limitation of armaments; while security is important, it is important only as far as it leads to reduction.'* Arthur Henderson worked to counter the forces which promoted aggression: the vested interests of an uncontrolled armament industry, and the policy of unilateral national security. It was his tragic illusion and that of many other pacifists, that, by means of an international agreement which also included the 'dynamic states', one would be able to improve the international situation.

Henderson died in 1935, in the same autumn as Italy's attack on Ethiopia took place. The British statesman who took the lead in promoting a policy of broad collective security to check the aggressor, was Lord ROBERT CECIL [*1937*]. We have already dealt with the part he played in the setting-up of the League of Nations, and his work to establish the

* Mary Agnes Hamilton, *Arthur Henderson* [London 1938], p.438.

new organization on a solid foundation was no less important. As early as June 1919 he demanded at a public meeting that Germany and Russia should be admitted as members of the League. In the same year he became President of the League of Nations Union, and it was largely due to his personal initiative that the propaganda in favour of the League of Nations was most effective in the United Kingdom. A clear proof of the great confidence he enjoyed was that at the first three meetings of the League of Nations Assembly he served as delegate for the Union of South Africa, having been chosen by General Smuts as his personal representative. In the sessions of the League he played an outstanding role in the debates on all the important matters which came up for discussion, and he gave his unqualified support to Nansen in his humanitarian work.

In 1923 Cecil became a member of Baldwin's first government, and at the autumn assembly of the League of Nations he was present as British delegate. The most delicate international question at that time was the situation which had arisen after the brutal coup on the part of Fascist Italy directed against Greece [the Corfu incident]. On that occasion Lord Cecil was criticized, as later on other occasions, for not having asserted the fundamental principles of the League of Nations as rigidly as before. That he was to a very great extent compelled to conform to the main outlines laid down by the Government is reasonable enough. But even though the Corfu dispute was settled outside the League of Nations, Cecil had achieved a lot in this matter by asserting his principles of postponement and debate. He has, moreover, himself declared that, as a member of the Government, he had a greater opportunity of influencing its attitude to League of Nations matters. But gradually the differences became too great [Lord Cecil was a member of Baldwin's second government from 1924], and in 1927 he severed the official ties which bound him to the Conservative Party. In his book *A Great Experiment* [1941] he has made the following commentary on his development from 1914 on: 'Thenceforward the effort to abolish war seemed to me, and still seems to me, the only political object worth while. As time went on I became increasingly conscious that that view was not really accepted by most Conservative politicians and was indeed hotly and violently rejected by large numbers of the right wing of the party. Not only indeed did they reject in their hearts the League of Nations, but they did not propose to take any step for getting rid of war. Clearly, they and I could not honestly belong to the same party'.

With regard to the question of disarmament Lord Cecil had always held a realistic view. He had *inter alia* maintained that it was impossible to persuade countries whose position was strategically exposed, e.g. France, Poland and Czechoslovakia, to consent to immediate disarmament, unless they received a military guarantee. This guarantee had to be general in order to prevent the pre-war system of alliances and balance of power from being resurrected. But only countries which had actually disarmed would benefit from them. Until such a system of guarantees was set up, however, those agreements regarding mutual military aid which had already been concluded should, in Cecil's opinion, be temporarily recognized. For he believed it was more useful to have them thus under some sort of control by the League of Nations than to ignore them or try to prevent them.

Japan's attack on China and the growth of Nazi Germany further convinced him of the need for collective protection. Already in May 1933 Eduard Beneš had drawn his attention to the fact that 'Hitler's foreign policy was to absorb Austria and Czechoslovakia, to create an independent Ukraine as a counterpoise to Russia and Poland, to suppress the Danzig Corridor and reduce Poland to subservience'.* He was therefore horrified at the passiveness which the predominant Conservative element in MacDonald's Coalition Government exhibited towards aggressive tendencies. He had himself been League of Nations delegate for the Labour Government since 1929, and also for the Coalition Government from 1931, and had then been able to act far more freely than when he had represented Baldwin's governments. But the year 1932 marked Lord Cecil's last appearance as official delegate to the League Assembly. From now on he concentrated on influencing public opinion, and in contradiction to the usual statement that the League of Nations had proved a failure, he maintained that it was the *governments* which had failed. It was therefore necessary to mobilize public opinion so that it could force them to follow a different course. In 1934 he started the so-called Peace Ballot, which was vigorously supported by the Labour Party and the Liberals, but only by a few individual members of the Conservative Party. The Peace Ballot was based on questions affecting the League of Nations, disarmament, private control of the armament industry, and economic and military sanctions for the maintenance of collective security. The answers, sent in by 10 million people, showed an overwhelming majority in sup-

* *A Great Experiment*, p. 247.

port of the principles of international solidarity which Cecil represented; and it has been asserted, undoubtedly with truth, that this undertaking was to a large extent responsible for the demand for collective action against Italy in the following year receiving such a large measure of public support especially in Great Britain. All the greater was the disappointment caused by the subsequently vacillating policy of the Government. Cecil felt for a while as though his entire lifework had crumbled before his eyes. But soon afterwards he returned to the charge with a counter-attack, through the medium of a new international organization, the *Rassemblement Universel pour la Paix* [R.U.P.], which, on the broadest possible basis, sought to rally the forces of resistance against the increasing acts of aggression both in Europe and Asia. In Fascist and Isolationist-Conservative quarters the leaders of this movement were often decried as 'warmongers'. In the year that the organization held its first international meeting – in 1936 – similar charges were also levelled against the Norwegian Nobel Committee because of the award of the Peace Prize to CARL VON OSSIETZKY [1889-1938, *1935*].

Ossietzky had, from his youth on, always been an ardent pacifist, and on one occasion had incurred a court sentence for an attack on Prussian militarism. He was further confirmed in his pacifist convictions by his experiences as a front-line soldier in the German army during the First World War. Immediately after the war was over, he went in actively for the peace movement. In 1920 he was appointed secretary of the *Deutsche Friedensgesellschaft* by Ludwig Quidde. However, Ossietzky felt that his particular bent was not in the organizing sphere. It was as a writer that he was to make his mark. He was an outstanding stylist – trenchant, witty and elegant. In 1921 he became foreign editor of the *Volkszeitung*, in which capacity he became an ardent spokesman for the policy of conciliation. In 1924 he became joint editor of the radical periodical *Die Weltbühne*, and editor-in-chief from 1927 on. In the same year he published an article by Berthold Jacob, which attacked the authorities for shielding a number of military chiefs, who were in fact the real culprits, in their legal prosecution of the *Fehme*-murderers. Jacob and Ossietzky were sentenced, first to short periods of imprisonment, later to fines, which were, however, remitted under the terms of an act of amnesty.

The next time Ossietzky came into conflict with the authorities was in connection with his campaign against secret German rearmament. In the *Weltbühne* of March 12, 1929, he published an article by an aircraft technician, Walter Kreiser, which accused the Ministry of Transport of working, in the so-called 'Section M', to promote purely military ends, in contravention of the Constitution, which was committed to upholding the terms of the Versailles Treaty. Ossietzky himself was strongly in favour of a revision of the Peace Treaty, but this must, in his opinion, be done by open and frank discussions between the powers. Secret German rearmament would only strengthen the aggressive forces in Germany and other countries and bring fresh disasters to the people of Europe. Both Kreiser and Ossietzky were prosecuted on a charge, based on an Espionage Act of 1914, of disclosing military secrets. The case came before the Fourth Criminal Division of the Supreme Court in Leipzig, and proceedings were *in camera.* Sentence was passed on November 22, 1931. Both Kreiser and Ossietzky were found guilty and sentenced to eighteen months imprisonment. The sentence aroused tremendous bitterness in Liberal circles, and several protest meetings were held. Ossietzky's friends advised him to flee the country, but he preferred to go to prison so that he could continue to fight for his ideas in his native land. After seven months in prison he was released under the terms of an act of amnesty of December 22, 1932. He immediately resumed his work on the *Weltbühne,* and from now on he concentrated on the struggle against the rising tide of Nazism. Unlike so many others, Ossietzky had never underestimated Hitler and his movement, nor was he misled by the temporary setback which the Nazis suffered during the 1932 elections. He realized the strong appeal which the movement had for the German middle classes, which had always held aloof from real liberalism, and whose 'inner crudity, crass hostility to culture, and hard ambition' had been so clearly revealed during the economic crisis. With prophetic vision he had declared as early as 1931 [*Weltbühne*, April] that the semi-proletarian elements within the movement – the S.A. – would in a crisis be set aside under the influence of 'reactionary bourgeois politicians who would rather have the right to bloodshed monopolized by executioners and the armed forces'.

Politically speaking, Ossietzky stood apart from the various political parties. By temperament and attitude essentially an individualist, he nevertheless maintained that in the modern age the freedom of the individual could only be secured by an economic and social process of democratization, led by the working class. This view also determined his attitude to pacifism: individual anti-militarism had no chance of achieving anything. Only through the people's control of the means of production, including the armament industry, could one achieve a secure foundation for peace. It was necessary to proceed *offensively*. In an article published in January 1932 he declared that one could not 'defend oneself' against Fascism; it had to be attacked in its own social sphere. On this basis Ossietzky fought to the end, though he realized himself how small were the chances of victory, with a working class split between bureaucratic Socialism and sectarian Communism.

On February 3, 1933, Ossietzky was due to give a lecture on 'Cultural Barbarism' at the invitation of the German League for Human Rights. The Berlin Police Praesidium, however, banned the lecture, on the grounds that 'people of different views might take offence'. The lecture was given instead on February 26 to a closed meeting of German authors, in which he discussed the possibilities of a united front against Nazism. On February 27 the *Reichstag* fire took place; the same night Ossietzky was arrested and shortly afterwards taken to the Sonnenburg concentration camp, and later to Papenburg-Esterwegen. It is not difficult to imagine the physical and mental sufferings he had to undergo in these concentration camps. Not long after, the news trickled through that his health had broken down.

In 1934 the idea that Ossietzky should be proposed for the Peace Prize was mooted, though not until 1935 was a formal and valid proposal to this effect submitted. At that time the prize was reserved for the following year. In 1936 proposals were sent in by politicians and scholars from a number of European countries as well as the U.S.A., supported by a number of individual and collective recommendations. The action in favour of Ossietzky's candidature resulted in a significant change in the set-up of the Nobel Committee. One of the members, Halvdan Koht, was at the time Norwegian Foreign Minister, and it was obvious to all and sundry that the award of the prize to Ossietzky would imply a clear-cut demonstration against the Nazi regime. Politically Koht belonged to the Norwegian Labour Party, which supported Ossietzky's candidature. In the circumstances he decided that he could not participate in the deliberations of the Committee, and he was shortly afterwards followed by Johan Ludwig Mowinckel, who had held office both as Prime Minister and Foreign Minister. These two were replaced by substitutes, and the Storting later resolved [1937] 'that members of the Nobel Committee, upon becoming appointed to the Government, shall withdraw from the Committee'. On November 23, 1936, the Committee made its decision. Carl von Ossietzky was awarded the Peace Prize for *1935*.

The decision had tremendous repercussions in the press. In Radical and Socialist quarters it was greeted with enthusiasm, among Conservatives it aroused corresponding resentment and bitterness. Admittedly Fascism had few supporters in Norway, although several younger Conservatives were quite strongly influenced by authoritarian ideology. Already in the spring of 1933, for instance, the organ of the pro-Fascist association *Fedrelandslaget* [League of Patriots] had put forward Mussolini and Hitler as candidates for the Peace Prize [*A.B.C.*, 1933, No. 24]. Furthermore the idea of 'the strong man', who could stand up to Radicalism and Socialism, had not a few adherents among the big farmers and business people. Others, who did not exactly sympathize with Fascism, usually maintained that it was wrong to 'offend' Germany by interfering in her internal affairs. The reaction abroad was more or less the same as in Norway, with the same shades of opinion in evidence.

In Germany there was violent resentment, and on January 31, 1937, Hitler issued a decree forbidding German nationals in the future to accept any Nobel Prize. The Swedish explorer Sven Hedin suggested in this connection that Norway should be deprived of the right to award the Peace Prize, and that this function should be entrusted to Sweden.

Ossietzky himself had no chance of enjoying the pecuniary benefits which went with the prize. On the strength of a power of attorney the money was paid over in Oslo to the representative of a Berlin lawyer, who subsequently embezzled the bulk of the funds. Ossietzky continued to be kept in prison, and the treatment accorded him was constantly marked by the demoralizing mixture of hypocrisy and cynicism which the Nazi authorities had employed ever since the campaign in his favour had been started. [After the Second World War three Norwegian journalists came across the documents relating to this in the ruins of Berlin.] On May 4, 1938, Ossietzky died, after suffering for a long time from tuberculosis.

When the Peace Prize was awarded in 1936, Professor Fredrik Stang, then Chairman of the Nobel Committee, declared: 'A symbol may have its value; but Ossietzky is not only a symbol. He is something quite different and something more. He is a deed, and he is a man.' The actual award of the prize was also something more than a symbol. It was a deed, a brave deed at a time when leading circles in many countries smoothed the way for Fascism with their talk of a 'correct attitude', obviously without realizing what consequences such an attitude of mental neutrality to the enemies of democracy might entail.

At the same time as Ossietzky, the Argentinian Foreign Minister, CARLOS SAAVEDRA LAMAS [1878-1959], received the Peace Prize for *1936*. He represented a far more 'traditional' type, a mixture of the theoretician in matters of international law and the practical statesman working in the field of international agreements and active conciliation. The background of his activity was also very different from that of Ossietzky. In the case of the latter it was a question of a life and death struggle between democracy and dictatorship. The task of Lamas was the settlement of disputes in which the aggressive tendencies, not so one-sided as in the Fascist states of Europe, were rather an eruption of opposing interests of long standing. But with regard to the South American states we are concerned with here, Bolivia and Paraguay, the economic crisis also played a decisive part in bringing aggression to a head.

Lamas's work in the international sphere first bore fruit with the drafting of an anti-war pact, which was signed in Rio de Janeiro in October, 1933, by representatives of the Argentine, Brazil, Mexico, Chile, Uruguay and Paraguay. In June 1934 the pact had been signed by as many as fourteen Spanish American states, Brazil, the U.S.A. and Italy. The treaty was envisaged as a universal agreement, similar to the Kellogg Pact, and Argentinian diplomats worked with great energy to get the countries of Europe to join the pact. The peculiar feature of this South American pact was that, unlike the Kellogg Pact, it included a clause entailing the use of sanctions against an aggressor, even though it never went as far as the sanction provisions of the League of Nations. Another peculiar feature of the pact was that it also guaranteed international co-operation for the re-establishment of peace, while at the same time maintaining the principle of neutrality. Finally, the actual conclusion of the treaty took place at a time when one of the signatory powers, Paraguay, was embroiled in a war [with Bolivia]. Admittedly this country was, technically speaking, the victim of aggression, and the intention of the pact was undoubtedly to bring pressure to bear on Bolivia. Whether in fact the pact had the desired effect is difficult to decide; but it is improbable, at any rate as far as immediate results were concerned, since hostilities dragged on till June 1935. On the other hand it is quite clear that Saavedra Lamas played an important role as mediator. The subject of the dispute was the northern portion of the Gran Chaco country, where frontiers had not been properly fixed since the end of Spanish rule. For many years the dispute had threatened to break out, and in 1932 Bolivian troops marched to the attack. The reason for this action was the Bolivian desire to secure access to the lower reaches of the Paraguay River. This would facilitate an effective exploitation of the oil fields in East Bolivia which the Standard Oil Company had secured. In this way the Bolivian government hoped to be able to recoup some of the financial losses incurred in the economic crisis. The war, however, turned out to be a great disappointment. The Bolivian troops were unable to force their way through the difficult, swampy terrain, and were instead compelled to turn aside towards the adjacent mountains. Gradually a military deadlock set in, and this factor really opened the way to armistice negotiations. The appeals of the League of Nations had no effect.* Pressure from other American states was at any rate more effective. In May 1935 Saavedra Lamas got in touch with the diplomatic representatives of Brazil, Chile and Peru with a view to setting up a commission of mediation. The proposal was well received, and soon afterwards the U.S.A. and Uruguay also joined the commission. The belligerents agreed to accept mediation, and on June 12, 1935, the armistice protocol was signed. At the peace negotiations which were initiated shortly afterwards Saavedra Lamas played a leading role.

The last award before the oubreak of the Second World War was in *1938*, when the prize went to the OFFICE INTERNATIONAL NANSEN POUR LES RÉFUGIÉS. This office had in point of fact little direct bearing on what we have called 'resistance to aggression in the 1930's'. Most of the refugees with whom the office had to deal had actually lived in exile ever since the great upheavals during and immediately following the First World War. They were for the most part Russians and Armenians. But indirectly the Nansen Office was made to feel very keenly the mood of aggression which the economic crisis had created far and wide, and not only in Fascist countries. It had previously been difficult at the best of times to secure a decent livelihood for the refugees, but now it became almost impossible. Mass unemployment was acutely felt in every country, and hostility to 'foreign elements' was on the increase. The authorities were careful to see that unwanted people did not cross their borders, while the police were constantly on the look-out for people whose

* Lord Robert Cecil stated later however that a British move, in the form of an embargo on the delivery of arms to both sides, was of great importance. [*A Great Experiment*, p. 261].

papers were not in order. Imprisonment and expulsion from one country, further imprisonment and expulsion from another – this was often the bitter fate of the refugee. Those who strove to safeguard the interests of the refugee were compelled, more than ever before, to use their energy, patience and diplomatic ability to the full.

The *Office International Nansen pour les Réfugiés* had been set up by the League of Nations Assembly in the autumn of 1930. The aim of the office was to continue the work Nansen had carried out as High Commissioner for Refugees. Under the terms of the provisions agreed to by the League of Nations Council on January 19, 1931, the office was to have 'complete freedom of action [pleine capacité] in all matters concerning its administration and activities'. These activities were only binding on the office itself.

The most exacting of the tasks which faced the office was the settlement of the Armenian refugees. Nansen himself had devoted the last years of his life to the 'Armenian question' on a broad basis, but had achieved no satisfactory solution. The Nansen Office continued his work as far as possible, and by the end of 1935 it had settled approximately 10,000 in Erivan and 40,000 in Turkey. In 1935 the office had to deal with a special task which was directly related to developments in Nazi Germany, when 4,000 inhabitants of the Saar had to leave their homes, after the district once more became part of the German Reich. Political refugees from Germany were otherwise placed under the protection of the High Commissariat for Refugees from Germany, which had its seat in London and had been set up at the instigation of the League of Nations in the autumn of 1933. Apart from the actual settling of these national groups, the office had constantly to intervene on behalf of refugees in various countries, and protect them against bureaucratic unreasonableness and antagonism of various sorts, *inter alia* of a racial nature. The *Office International Nansen pour les Réfugiés* received the award of the Peace Prize at the conclusion of its span of activity. In 1939 the work was transferred to London and placed under a High Commissioner.

THE SECOND WORLD WAR AND AFTER

Comité International de la Croix-Rouge, Cordell Hull, George Marshall

The outbreak of the Second World War in 1939 put a stop to the distribution of the Peace Prize. No prizes were awarded until the end of the war. The Prize for 1939 was reserved for the following year. But then in conformity with the course adopted for the Swedish prizes the distribution of the Peace Prize for 1939-43 was suspended, and the amounts of the prizes were refunded. After April, 1940, two members of the Norwegian Committee had gone abroad. The other members, whose tenure of office expired in 1942, continued, at the request of the Nobel Foundation in Stockholm, to carry out such modest tasks as were possible; they withdrew in February 1944. After the end of the war, the reconstituted Nobel Committee of the Norwegian Parliament was finally able in 1945 to decide on the reserved Peace Prize for 1944 and the Prize for 1945. The Prize for *1944* was then given to the COMITÉ INTERNATIONAL DE LA CROIX-ROUGE, and that for *1945* to CORDELL HULL [1871-1955]. The work which the COMITÉ INTERNATIONAL DE LA CROIX-ROUGE had done during the First World War was restarted in the Second, only on a still larger scale. In some respects the work had become easier, especially work for prisoners of war. The Committee now had – apart from its own experiences – an official standing based on the Prisoner of War Convention of 1929, which had been recognized by all nations, with the exception of the Soviet Union and Japan. On the other hand, the work as a whole had been rendered more difficult by the fact that Fascist-Nazi ideology had to a large extent made warfare even more ferocious and rendered the German authorities still less responsive to humane arguments. At the same time the freedom of action of the Committee had been radically reduced by the fact that Switzerland was completely surrounded by the Axis Powers. One result of this state of affairs was that the Committee hesitated to initiate relief work on behalf of political prisoners in Germany; for the German authorities maintained that this was a political matter which was not covered by the Geneva Convention. From 1943, however, a regular parcel service was started, partly from Sweden. This Red Cross scheme saved many human lives, and acted as a very real encouragement to the relatives of the prisoners at home. The Committee also conducted a certain amount of legal and illegal relief work on behalf of Jews in Roumania, Hungary and Yugoslavia.

The Red Cross Committee was thus, on this occasion as well, awarded the Peace Prize for keeping alive the ideal of 'Fraternity among the nations' by its humanitarian work in the midst of war. Organized peace work was, however, dealt a far more crippling blow than on the previous occasion. First of all the Second World War was, to a far greater extent than the First, an ideological war. A peace of reconciliation with Nazism was unthinkable to anyone who would preserve freedom and humanity. For that reason, as we have seen, even such an out-and-out pacifist as Emily Balch did not on this occasion oppose the American entry into the war. Moreover, in the ranks of the Quakers absolute anti-militarism no longer held undisputed sway. Another reason was that the number of neutrals was now far smaller, and that those who were neutral at the opening of hostilities were nearly all swiftly drawn into the vortex. Actual peace work was in these circumstances confined to discussing, within each individual country, openly in the free democracies and covertly in the occupied countries, the possibility of a new international security organization. It was in this field that Cordell Hull made his supreme contribution.

By training Cordell Hull was a lawyer. In 1907 he became a member of the U. S. House of Representatives, a position he occupied – with one gap of two years – until 1931, when he became a Senator. During Wilson's presidency he played an outstanding role in the introduction of fiscal reforms in 1913 and 1916.

When Franklin Roosevelt was elected President in 1932, he appointed Cordell Hull his Secretary of State. In the first few years as president Roosevelt had such considerable domestic problems to solve that the conduct of foreign policy was largely left to Cordell Hull. On all essential points, however, he and the President agreed closely. One of the first tasks which faced Cordell Hull was to introduce Roosevelt's 'Good Neighbor policy'. In 1933 he called a Pan-American Conference, despite the fact that the time was not particularly auspicious, with war between Bolivia and Paraguay, and a serious state of tension between Colombia and Peru [the Leticia dispute]. Nevertheless he succeeded in convening a conference, which was opened in Montevideo in December, 1933. In order to emphasize its importance Cordell Hull personally led the North American delegation, and like Elihu Root he paid 'good-will visits' to the capitals of several countries on his way south. At the conference certain fundamental principles were agreed on. One of the most important and most characteristic was expressed in the clause that no state should have the right to interfere in the internal or external affairs of any other state. The following year the United States Government carried out this principle in its relations with Cuba, where formerly the right of intervention by the United States in certain specified circumstances had been fixed by treaty. At the same time, the last American troops were withdrawn from Haiti. The year 1934 also marked the granting of independence to the Philippines.

In the implementation of these policies involving fundamental principles, Roosevelt himself naturally played a large part, and in each particular instance it is not so easy to decide how great Cordell Hull's contribution was.

But in another important matter, tariff policy, Cordell Hull's personal initiative is quite obvious. He made it his aim to counteract the economic nationalism which made its influence so keenly felt throughout the world, not least in Europe. From 1934 onward he concluded a series of trade agreements with Canada and several Latin-American and European countries. In 1938 a particularly significant treaty was signed with Great Britain. All these treaties more or less bore the stamp of the free trade principle, and followed the pattern of the celebrated Cobden agreement of 1860 between Great Britain and France, with the bilateral system employed in the service of liberalism. A policy of this nature would, in Hull's opinion, help to ease the international situation; but at the same time he realized that these methods were not in themselves sufficient as far as the 'dynamic' great powers were concerned. In dealing with them he used tariff policy in certain cases as an economic punitive measure. After Hitler had occupied Czechoslovakia in 1939, for instance, the American Government put an extra duty on German goods, and on July 26, 1939, it repudiated the American-Japanese trade agreement of 1911. The American Government had already on several occasions attempted in vain to get the interested powers to assist in putting a stop to Japanese penetration into China. At the same time Roosevelt and Hull worked systematically to wean the American people from its isolationist attitude. The first step in this direction was achieved in 1937 with a certain mitigation of the neutrality laws – the proclamation of the 'cash and carry' principle.

After the outbreak of the Second World War, Roosevelt gradually became the dominant figure in foreign policy, especially after the attack on Pearl Harbor.

Hull's most important independent contribution during the war was that of laying the foundation for the new international organization, The United Nations. Immediately after the outbreak of war in 1939 he had assigned various experts to investigate the question and submit proposals. Shortly after the attack on Pearl Harbor these plans took shape, and were expressed in the Declaration by the United Nations, dated January, 1942. In his memoirs Hull has described how he continued to work on this project. As far as domestic policy was concerned, at an early stage he obtained guarantees from the Republicans to the effect that the projected world organization should be considered 'non-partisan policy'.

Furthermore, he relates how he managed to persuade Roosevelt and Churchill to abandon their original plans for regional agreements, with an international council as a controlling body. In this way Hull succeeded in preserving the universal character of the organization, while at the same time contributing greatly to the removal of outstanding differences between the Western Powers and the Soviet Union. There is every indication that Hull played a decisive rôle at the 1943 meeting of Foreign Ministers in Moscow. Hull was not, however, to participate in the actual setting-up of the organization; as early as January 1945 he had to withdraw from the post of Secretary of State, on grounds of ill-health.

After Cordell Hull had received the Peace Prize, it could be anticipated that several dominant political leaders within the structure of the United Nations would follow suit. So far these expectations have to a great extent been fruitless, and the reason for this is familiar to us all: it has not yet been possible to establish amicable relations between the Great Powers. The most important peace treaties, which were to provide a basis for effective work within the framework of the United Nations, have still not been concluded.

To a great extent the Great Powers' failure to cooperate hampered the reconstruction of war-devastated Europe. The so-called Marshall Plan, from 1948, however, served as a stimulus for eventual recovery.

In the person of GEORGE MARSHALL [1880-1959] an entirely new type of individual joined the ranks of Peace Prize winners. His life had been that of a soldier, and he had never been a member of any peace organization. For this reason the awarding of the prize to Marshall in *1953* aroused considerable criticism in pacifist quarters. Undeniably, it was a somewhat paradoxical choice. But on closer inspection the rationale for this choice is clear. In the first place, most responsible military leaders in the democratic countries have long been aware of the purely destructive effect of war; George Marshall was no exception, for as chief-of-staff of the Eighth American Army in France during the First World War, and subsequently as Chief of the General Staff in the Second World War, he had experienced war in all its horrible aspects. In his Nobel lecture in Oslo in 1953 he said: 'There has been considerable comment over the awarding of the Nobel Peace Prize to a soldier. I am afraid this does not seem as remarkable to me as it quite evidently appears to others... The cost of war in human lives is constantly spread before me, written neatly in many ledgers whose columns are grave-stones. I am deeply moved to find some means or method of avoiding another calamity of war.' It was precisely this aspect of his activities which justified the award of the Peace Prize to George Marshall.

After the Second World War, Marshall was entrusted with several important tasks of a political nature. In many ways he was excellently qualified to carry out such work. As a soldier he had shown outstanding qualities of leadership, unswerving loyalty, and an unprejudiced and humane attitude. And most important of all, he had always retained a correct concept of the borderline between military and civilian spheres of authority. This enabled his co-operation with President Roosevelt, and later with President Truman, to proceed with unusual smoothness. Marshall was entrusted with his first political task in the autumn of 1945, when Truman appointed him his personal envoy to China. Here Marshall worked to effect a reconciliation between Chiang Kai Shek and the Communists, but the plans he submitted for a solution were not accepted by either party.

In January 1947, Marshall was appointed Secretary of State. The first problem with which he had to cope was how to reduce the ever-increasing tension existing between the Western Powers and the Soviet Union, and the precarious economic situation in Europe. Failing to achieve any relaxation of tension in the relationship with the Soviet Union, Marshall after the abortive meeting of foreign ministers in Moscow in April 1947, realized that the United States would have to take the initiative if Europe was to be saved from an economic catastrophe, involving political anarchy. On June 5, 1947, in a speech at Harvard University, Marshall described the unstable economic conditions prevailing in Europe, and the lack of confidence and hope in the future. At the same time he pointed out how vitally important it was for the U.S.A. to take the lead in an economic reconstruction. There could be no political stability or secure basis for peace, he pointed out, in a world deprived of a normal economic life. 'Our policy', he stated, 'is directed not against any country or doctrine, but against hunger, poverty, desperation, and chaos.'

The constructive ideas expressed in Marshall's speech provided in outline form a new basis for the European economy fortified by large-scale American supplies of raw materials and machinery, essentially in the form of gifts. These supplies, however, were not to be doled out in a haphazard fashion; their distribution was based on a long-term policy now known as the Marshall Plan. One of the highlights of this plan was that European nations should co-operate to solve their own problems and to effect a gradual liberalization of their mutual trade.

The Soviet Union and the other countries in the Eastern bloc were also invited to participate in the Marshall Plan, however, after preliminary negotiations in Paris, the Soviet Union withdrew. Considerations for her relations with the Soviet Union also compelled Czechoslovakia to follow suit. Thus the Marshall Plan only comprised the countries of Western Europe, but the work of reconstruction which it ushered in undoubtedly had further international repercussions.

IN THE SERVICE OF THE UNITED NATIONS

Ralph Bunche, Lester Pearson, Dag Hammerskjöld, Lord Boyd Orr, Léon Jouhaux, I.L.O.

Although the United Nations did not develop into a universal security system, the organization has on some occasions been able to bring to an end 'local wars' and unrest, conflicts which otherwise might have threatened world peace. In such a context RALPH BUNCHE [1904-1971, *1950*] earned his award for the solution of a dispute which had come to a head: the Palestine conflict. The Palestine problem was one of those complicated questions which the United Nations faced at a very early stage in its existence. At a meeting of the General Assembly in the autumn of 1947, a plan had been adopted for partitioning Palestine between its Jewish and its Arab inhabitants. In the spring of 1948, however, this plan was abandoned. After the British had renounced their mandate in April and withdrawn from the country, and the Jews had proclaimed their own state of Israel, open warfare soon developed between the new state and its Arab neighbours. On May 20, the United Nations appointed a mediator to effect a settlement. For this exacting task the Swedish Count Folke Bernadotte, renowned for his Red Cross work and for organizing the repatriation of political prisoners from Germany before the end of hostilities in 1945, was chosen. After a series of difficult negotiations, Bernadotte succeeded, in the early part of July, 1948 – with the support of the Security Council – in effecting a cease-fire. On September 17, 1948, however, before a real truce could be arranged, Count Bernadotte was murdered by a Jewish terrorist whereupon the rôle of mediator devolved on Bernadotte's closest collaborator: the American, Ralph Bunche.

Bunche was in many ways eminently fitted to tackle this problem. As advisor to his government on African affairs during the war, and subsequently as director of the Division of Trusteeship of the United Nations, he had shown that he possessed sound political acumen. Bunche's personal background rendered him particularly competent to solve conflicts involving racial and religious issues, since he is a Negro by race and his grandmother was born a slave. From this remarkable woman he had learned to seek justice in an equitable manner. Undaunted by the extreme poverty of his early years and by ubiquitous racial prejudice, Bunche achieved a vision of interracial and international relationships based on a scientific approach.

The work of arbitration in the Palestine dispute demanded, above all, infinite patience. At first, it proved impossible to bring the parties to the conference table. Operating from his headquarters in neutral Rhodes, the mediator was, therefore, compelled to negotiate with each in turn. In the middle of October the truce was broken, and hostilities recommenced. At Bunche's suggestion the Security Council not only issued fresh orders for a cessation of hostilities, but also instructed the parties to conclude an armistice agreement. This was a bold move on Bunche's part. If the parties refused to accept the Security Council's orders, the prestige of the United Nations would be seriously jeopardized. However, Bunche's optimistic assessment of the possibilities turned out to be well-founded. After a meeting in Cairo he managed to persuade Egypt to negotiate. Finally, after protracted negotiations at Rhodes, an armistice was concluded between Israel and Egypt on February 24, 1949. Similar agreements between Israel and the other Arab states soon followed, the last agreement was signed on July 20, 1949.

As we know, the armistice in Palestine was not the prelude to lasting peace. On the contrary, during the last twenty years the situation has become critical. But this in no way detracts from the magnitude of Bunche's work. He was recognized as one of the most capable mediators on the world scene. The great confidence he inspired in the international field was emphasized by his appointment, in 1954, as one of the two Under-Secretaries of the United Nations.

The solution of a new crisis in the Middle East, in 1956, was the background for the Peace Prize awarded in *1957* to LESTER BOWLES PEARSON [b. 1897].

Pearson was born in Toronto, Canada. During the First World War he served in the University Medical Corps as a volunteer, and when the war was over resumed his historical studies, obtaining his B.A. in 1919. Later, he continued his studies at Oxford, and in 1923 took his Master of Arts degree. For some time he was a teacher, and then Assistant Professor of Modern History at the University of Toronto.

In 1928, Lester Pearson entered the service of the Canadian Department of External Affairs. This step brought his scholarly career to a close, and marked the beginning of his life as a civil servant. He was First-Secretary of the Department of External Affairs in Ottawa until 1935, when he was appointed Counsellor at the Office of the High Commissioner for Canada in London. In 1941 he returned to Ottowa as Assistant Undersecretary of State at the Department of External Affairs and in the following year was appointed Canadian Minister in Washington, where he stayed until 1946, for the last two years, as Ambassador. Then followed two years as Under-Secretary of State at home, until, in 1948, he became Secretary of State for External Affairs in the Canadian Government, a position he held until 1957, when the Liberal Party lost the elections.

From his work as a civil servant Lester Pearson had gained valuable experience in handling international problems, not least by attending important conferences in Europe. During the Second World War he achieved much in preparing international organizations to solve the grave problems certain to arise after the war had ended. After the Hot Springs conference of 1943, he was elected chairman of an 'interim commission for food and agriculture'–this commission being a preparation for the F.A.O. He also played a prominent part in organizing U.N.R.R.A. In the United Nations Lester Pearson soon became highly appreciated for his sound judgment and clear-cut argumentation in the debates concerning the veto-rules, as well as in such conflicts as the Palestine problem.

As president of the General Assembly in 1952 he presided over the very complicated discussions concerning the Korean problem. The year 1956 marked a summit in Lester Pearson's activity in the international field. At that time the United Nations faced one of the most dangerous of the post-war problems – the Suez conflict, which started with President Nasser's nationalization of the Suez Canal and came to a head with Israel's aggression against Egypt, on October 29, and the ensuing Franco-British military action.

The Security Council, which immediately requested the aggressors to cease hostilities, was made inoperative by the veto of Great Britain and France. The matter then came up before the General Assembly; and on November 2 a resolution was put to the vote, in which the aggressors were immediately required to stop fighting. To secure peace and order after the cessation of hostilities, many outstanding people in the United Nations among them the Secretary General, Dag Hammarskjöld worked hard to find a satisfactory solution. In this activity Lester Pearson took a leading part. On November 4 he submitted to the General Assembly a resolution in which the Secretary General was requested, within 48 hours, to place before the General Assembly a plan for an international United Nations force to be employed in the theatre of war to ensure and supervise the cessation of hostilities. This was actually carried out. Lester Pearson himself was quite aware of the fact that this arrangement did not mean a final solution to the Palestine conflict. Moreover, the Russian invasion of Hungary, which had started about the same time as the Suez conflict, clearly demonstrated that the United Nations Organization has no means of implementing its resolutions if a great power is not willing to accept them. Lester Pearson, however, is of the opinion that, in spite of everything, it must be possible to bring about an easing of tensions throughout the world.

As a Canadian representative to N.A.T.O. he has always stressed the importance of collaboration in the non-military field. At the same time he has warned against a 'tough' and dogmatic attitude towards Soviet Russia and other communist countries. In his Nobel lecture in Oslo he expressed his views in this way: 'The time has come for us to make a move, not only from strength, but from wisdom and from confidence in ourselves, to concentrate on the possibilities of agreement, rather than from disagreements and failures, evils or wrongs, from the past'.

In 1961, the Secretary General of the United Nations, who had led the organization through several years of serious international crises, DAG

HAMMARSKJÖLD [1905-1961] was awarded the Peace Prize posthumously, the first posthumous award in the history of the Prize. The procedure was authorized under the terms of §4 in the code of Statutes of the Nobel Foundation which at that time stated *inter alia*: 'The work of any person since deceased cannot be submitted for award; should, however, the death of the individual in question have occurred subsequent to a recommendation having been made in due course for his work to receive a prize, such a prize may be awarded'.

Dag Hammarskjöld was the son of the Swedish statesman and expert on international law, Hjalmar Hammarskjöld, who was prime minister of Sweden between 1914 and 1917, and for many years chairman of the board of the Nobel Foundation. As a young man, Dag Hammarskjöld studied law and economics; from 1936 to 1945 he worked as a secretary in the Swedish Ministry of Finance. In 1946, he entered the Foreign Ministry as a consultant on commercial policy, and in 1951 he was appointed a consultant minister of state. He participated in the Uniscan negotiations, and was Swedish delegate to, and for a time vice-chairman of, O.E.E.C.

In 1953, he was elected Secretary-General of the United Nations, a position which had been occupied by the Norwegian politician Trygve Lie during the seven first exacting years of the organization's existence. Unlike Trygve Lie, Dag Hammarskjöld had never been active in politics; but the development of events continued to present the Secretary-General with complicated problems, which could only be solved if he personally took the initiative in making decisions that were inevitably of a political nature. During the first few years, the Middle East, above all, posed a number of dangerous problems, first and foremost in the strained relations between Israel and the Arab states. In our account of Lester Pearson, we have already mentioned the important rôle played by Hammarskjöld in solving the 1956 Suez Crisis.

The next crisis in the Middle East arose in the summer of 1958, when Jordan and Lebanon, feeling that their security was threatened by infiltration from neighbouring Arab states, appealed respectively to Great Britain and the U.S.A. for military aid. Resolute and swift action on the part of Hammarskjöld made it possible to persuade the parties to this dispute to solve the conflict among themselves, so that foreign troops and United Nations observers could be withdrawn in the course of the autumn. In the summer of 1960 the United Nations faced a new, serious problem in connection with the liberation of the Belgian Congo, on June

30. It proved highly difficult for the new government, with Joseph Kasavubu as President and Patrice Lumumba as prime minister, to get the new state to function. The administration, which had been run by the Belgians, had disintegrated; the native troops were mutinying; and there were numerous attacks on white inhabitants, with the result that Belgian troops intervened. On July 11, the province of Katanga was proclaimed an independent state. These events prompted the new Congolese Government to turn to the United Nations with a request for civilian and military help. At a meeting in the Security Council on July 13 it was resolved to accede to this request. It was decided that the duty of the military contingent to be despatched to the Congo should be to ensure the maintenance of law and order, and to supervise the withdrawal of all other foreign troops still in the country. The U.N. contingent was composed of troops from the new African states, from India, and from non-committed states in Europe, such as Sweden and the Irish Republic. The task of the U.N. administration proved enormously difficult, partly because the evacuation of Belgian troops did not proceed as swiftly as expected, and partly because already, on July 14, Lumumba had despatched a cable to Khrushchev declaring that if the Western Powers did not terminate their 'aggression' he would ask the Soviet Union for aid, and finally because Katanga refused to be incorporated as part of the new independent Congolese state. In this situation Dag Hammarskjöld's fearless initiative, diplomatic skill, and unquestioned integrity proved invaluable.

But time passed without any solution to the Congolese riddle. There were a number of reasons for this: disintegration within the Congolese government, which made it impossible to maintain national unity; the request for a military intervention by the United Nations that would force the rebellious provinces – not least Katanga, where foreign influence was still dominant – to accept the authority of the central government; and, finally, the systematic Soviet smear campaign against the Secretary-General, which aimed at exposing him as an accomplice of 'western' interests. In a United Nations resolution of February 21, 1961, orders were given to the United Nations forces to do everything in their power to prevent civil war in the Congo, even, if necessary, by the use of force. The situation was particularly complicated in Katanga, where the separatist leader Moise Tshombe was supported by the international mining company *Union Minière*, which recruited foreign troops on a large scale. It was the United Nations' primary task to ensure the removal of all these foreign elements, and subsequently to arrange a reconciliation between Katanga and the central government. In the summer of 1961 Hammarskjöld viewed developments with a considerable measure of optimism; but soon the situation again deteriorated, with the result that United Nations troops were compelled to initiate military operations. In compliance with a request, Hammarskjöld himself set off for the Congo on September 12, and after discussions with the government in Leopoldville decided to make contact with Tshombe. On September 17, he set out for Katanga, but the plane in which he was a passenger never reached its destination. It crashed during the night, killing all its occupants.

Hammarskjöld's death was a serious blow to the United Nations and to all who work and hope for the establishment of an international system of justice. As one of the leaders of this great work, Dag Hammarskjöld had laboured to promote the independence of the post of Secretary-General, so that its incumbent could at all times take independent action on his own initiative. In a speech in 1957 he had emphasized that it was the duty of a Secretary-General 'to use his office and, indeed, the machinery of the Organization to its utmost capacity and to the full extent permitted at each stage by practical circumstances'. He believed, he continued, 'that it is in keeping with the philosophy of the Charter that the Secretary-General also should be expected to act without any guidance from the Assembly or the Security Council, should this appear to him necessary towards helping to fill any vacuum that may appear in the systems which the Charter and traditional diplomacy provide for the safeguarding of peace and security'.

Despite the criticism and hostility he often aroused among the former colonial powers and, to an even greater extent, within the Soviet bloc, Hammarskjöld consistently followed this approach. By exerting every effort, and finally by giving his life in an attempt to realize these lofty international ideals, he set a shining example, and still remains, even after his death, a powerful factor in the promotion of peace.

Whereas the activities of Ralph Bunche, Lester Pearson, and Dag Hammarskjöld were connected with grave international political problems, two other laureates–LORD BOYD ORR [1880-1971, *1949*], and LÉON JOUHAUX [1879-1954, *1951*], had played prominent roles in United Nations specialized agencies.

Boyd Orr was a Scot, born in Kilmaurs, Ayrshire. As a young man he studied medicine at Glasgow University, where he later took his doctor's degree. Over the years he had received many distinctions, both academic and others. In 1935 he was knighted, and in 1949 was raised to the peerage.

At an early age Boyd Orr started to study the physiology of nutrition; in 1914 he became Director of the Institute of Animal Nutrition in Aberdeen, and, in 1919, Director of the Rowett Research Institute in the same town. During the First World War he served in the Royal Army Medical Corps, and won a number of decorations.

Boyd Orr made his outstanding contribution to the nutrition problem in the 1930's. In 1932 he had been elected to a committee which was to examine nutrition in Great Britain. In many respects the findings of this committee came as a shock. It was found, for example, that the dole, given to the unemployed in those years of economic crisis, was quite insufficient to buy them enough food. In brief, the committee's conclusions – undoubtedly inspired by Boyd Orr – were that, if a balance were to be created between supply and demand in foodstuffs, the word 'demand' should be interpreted, not as the quantity which must be sold in order to maintain a definite price, but as the quantity necessary to cover the reasonable needs of all members of the community. To carry out a programme of this nature, the authorities, by means of state subsidies, would have to fix a price for agricultural produce which would stimulate production and enable the less well-to-do members of the community to buy it. Boyd Orr went even further in his investigations. In a provocative book, *Food, Health and Income*, published in 1936, he showed that nutrition was not only a problem among the unemployed, but also among people in the lower income groups generally. Boyd Orr's investigations and his urgent appeal to the authorities had decisive consequences for Britain's nutritional policy, and not least during the Second World War it was due to *his* work that the standard of nourishment for the population as a whole could, in spite of everything, be maintaine at a relatively high level, and in some respects even improved. Boyd Orr's ideas also proved important in the international field, for in 1936 the League of Nations set up a committee which was to investigate the relationship between nutrition, health, agriculture and economics. When this committee was appointed, two of its members, paraphrasing the famous words of two sixteenth century Protestant English martyrs, sent a telegram which ran as follows: 'Be of good courage, brother Orr, for we have today in Geneva lit such a candle as, with the help of God, shall never be put out.' The candle *was* put out; but in 1943, in the middle of the Second World War, it was re-lit, when the

F.A.O. [Food and Agriculture Organization] was founded. It was the first of the new U.N. agencies, and President Roosevelt had gone to considerable lengths to have it set up as early as possible, as it was to be an instrument in the securing of one of the four great peace aims – freedom from want. At the F.A.O.'s first conference in Quebec, in October 1945, Boyd Orr was unanimously elected the first Director-General of the organization. In this new office Boyd Orr worked as tirelessly as ever. He was always at hand with valuable advice, constructive proposals and stimulating criticism. Not all his proposals were accepted; he was especially disappointed that his plan for a 'World Food Council', with executive powers was not realized. Nevertheless, he looked with optimism on the future of the organization. When, in 1948, he was forced to retire on grounds of health, he gave a survey of the achievements of the F.A.O. during these first years of its existence. In it he said: 'I warned the F.A.O. conference in Quebec that it would be a miracle if the F.A.O. ever succeeded, but as we live in an age of miracles we must try, as there was no other hope for humanity. If the F.A.O. had achieved nothing else but warn governments and get the International Emergency Food Council started, it was well worth all the money that has been spent on it.' And he concluded: 'It is difficult to get nations to co-operate on a political level. The world is torn by political strife. But through the F.A.O. the nations are co-operating. Here at the Council table representatives of governments are not talking about war, not thinking about war. They are planning for the greatest movement that will make for peace – increased food production, the strengthening of agriculture, and food for the people of the world.'

Boyd Orr always regarded his work as a peace programme, as a means of creating harmony between classes and nations. He had consequently not been able to enjoy his leisure undisturbed after retiring from the F.A.O. He allowed himself to be elected President of the British Peace Council, and later President of the World Federalist Association and of the parent body of the World's Peace Associations. In this way the doctor and nutrition expert became a spokesman for peace, but one who in his testimony never abandoned the earthly – in the original sense of the word – foundation, which his research and his beliefs have created for him.

LÉON JOUHAUX first made his name as one of the leading personalities within the French trade-union movement. Himself a member of the working classes, from the age of thirteen he had helped to support his family, and at sixteen he was employed in a match factory. At an early age he entered the nascent French trade-union movement, and in 1909 became secretary of the C.G.T. [*Confédération Générale du Travail*], and as such contributed to a high degree in the work of improving the lot of the French working class.

In his attitude to the peace problem, Jouhaux, like most Social Democrats, was originally an out-and-out pacifist. But after the outbreak of the First World War as a result of his spontaneous reaction to German aggression and his firm desire to rally to defend the democratic tradition, he gave his whole-hearted support to the national defense.

After the war, during which he saw active service, Jouhaux resumed his work in the C.G.T. At the Peace Conference in Paris in 1919 he was appointed a member of the commission dealing with labour questions. Already, during the war Jouhaux had suggested an international organization capable of carrying out practical reforms in working conditions throughout the world. In this way Jouhaux became one of the pioneers of the International Labour Organization. When this was established in 1919, Jouhaux was elected a member of the Council, and continued to work on behalf of this organization right up to the time of his death.

Jouhaux's other claim to fame in the international sphere was his work during the 1920's to promote disarmament. In a book, *Le Désarmement*, he submitted *inter alia* proposals for the abolition of the private armaments industry, and international control of the armament trade.

In the 1930's, Jouhaux was one of the fiercest opponents of Fascism, and he became one of the leaders of the French Popular Front. In 1938, he tried to persuade Roosevelt to intervene in face of the threat of German aggression aimed at Czechoslovakia; and when the Second World War broke out in 1939 he threw all the weight of his influence – as he had done in 1914 – into the scales in favour of national defense.

After the defeat of France in 1940, Jouhaux was repeatedly asked to make his way to England in order to assist in the organization of the Free French Forces. But he considered that his place was in France, where he helped to organize an underground resistance within the trade-union movement. The Vichy Government had tried in vain to win him over to the policy of capitulation. From the end of 1941 he was under continuous police surveillance, and the following year he was arrested by the Germans and deported to Germany.

After the armistice, in May 1945, Jouhaux returned to France and resumed his work within the trade-union movement, where, as in the days of the Popular Front, Communists and Social Democrats joined forces. But, once again, their reconciliation was short-lived. Disagreement on several questions of principle – not least with regard to the acceptance or non-acceptance of the Marshall Plan – resulted, in 1947, in a schism. Under the leadership of Jouhaux, a new national organization, the C.G.T.-Force Ouvrière was formed. From 1946, he was president of the newly established state organ, *Le Conseil Économique*.

Jouhaux continued to play an outstanding rôle in the work of international co-operation. From 1946, he was a member of the French United Nations delegation. In 1949, at Churchill's suggestion, he was elected head of the European movement. But it was his old organization, the I.L.O., that claimed his chief attention. Just as Lord Boyd Orr hoped, through the medium of F.A.O., to be able to secure peace by an intensified production of food and its effective distribution, Léon Jouhaux saw in the I.L.O. an instrument capable of easing tension by a process of social levelling on an international scale. In 1948, he stated his programme as follows: 'It is the inequalities in working conditions that cause the social dumping between nations and create the economic background for war. By developing social legislation in more and more countries the I.L.O. will therefore be an instrument in the service of peace'.

In *1969*, the INTERNATIONAL LABOUR ORGANIZATION [I.L.O.] was awarded the Peace Prize. As already been mentioned, the object of the organization was to carry out reforms in working conditions in the different countries and thereby establish more stable social conditions. It was hoped that such an activity would also be an important contribution to world peace. 'Universal and lasting peace can be established only if it is based upon social justice', as was stated in the preamble to the I.L.O.'s constitution. Although I.L.O. was organized as a part of the League of Nations, its special status made it possible to admit as members states not adhering to the League. According to this principle, the organization from the very outstet could admit Germany and Austria. Moreover, the structure of I.L.O. is characterized by the fact that representatives to the meetings of the organization are nominated not only by governments, but also by trade unions and employers' organizations.

Until 1940, the head-quarters of I.L.O. was in Geneva. Then it was moved to Montreal, Canada. After the war, the organization's head-quarters were moved back to Geneva. With the International Court of

Justice, I.L.O. was the only League of Nations organization to survive the Second World War. This meant it could be immediately admitted as one of the special organizations of the United Nations Organization.

In later years, I.L.O., besides its activities in social reform, has also made important efforts in securing technical assistance for the developing countries.

PROBLEMS OF DISARMAMENT

Philip Noel-Baker, Linus Pauling

Like the Covenant of the League of Nations, the United Nations Charter contains a regulation concerning disarmament. As was the case during the years between the wars, however, all efforts to make the regulation a reality, have yielded only rather modest results. Yet the problem itself is still on the agenda, and among the individuals who, in spite of all difficulties, have campaigned untiringly for disarmament, PHILIP NOEL-BAKER [*1959* Peace Prize] occupies a prominent position.

He was born in 1889, the son of a business man whose family had been established in Canada ever since 1819, but had returned to England in 1879. The family were all members of the Society of Friends, or Quakers, and were thus convinced apostles of peace. For a number of years Noel-Baker's father sat in the House of Commons, where his vigorous denunciation of rearmament regularly aroused the attention of the House. The First World War,however, convinced him that pacificism alone was not enough. What was needed was the establishment of an international organization capable of ensuring the maintenance of peace in the world, yet capable, when necessary, of using force. Philip Noel-Baker elaborated and developed these ideas. At the outbreak of hostilities he had enlisted in the Royal Army Medical Corps, and served at the front, first in France and later in Italy. At the conclusion of the war, in his capacity as first secretary to Lord Robert Cecil, he took part in the peace negotiations in Paris, and also assisted in drafting the Covenant of the League of Nations. The wide experience he had gained in the sphere of international relations enabled him to play an important role in the administrative set-up of the League of Nations, particularly in its work on behalf of prisoners of war and refugees.

Noel-Baker not only persuaded Fridtjof Nansen to undertake this task, but, thanks to his own practical experience and fund of sound advice, proved an able second-in-command.

Among the great international problems during the period between the wars, Noel-Baker was primarily preoccupied with the question of disarmament. He was Arthur Henderson's adviser during the 1920's and subsequently at the great disarmament conference at Geneva, in the years 1931-33. He also elaborated his personal views on disarmament in several books. More especially he was a fierce critic of the private armament industry which, in his opinion, constituted the main stumbling-block to a satisfactory disarmament programme. Noel-Baker has, in fact, always maintained that the exorbitant cost of armament is not merely a consequence of rivalry and mutual distrust between nations, but that the armament race itself helps to increase international tension. Moreover, this tension can only with difficulty be reduced as long as armament production is in the hands of private vested interests. Unlike so many other pacifists, Noel-Baker does not regard armament manufacturers as an international gang.

If that were the case, it would probably have been easier to bring about the necessary reform. The influence exercised by those who control the armament industry is above all due to the fact that they are working hand-in-glove with the governments of the countries in question. Naturally every government would be interested in the existence of as efficient an armament industry as possible. To achieve this it would be necessary to ensure that the industry always had sufficient orders, and it is precisely for this reason that the export of arms to other countries is tolerated. In Noel-Baker's opinion the problem could only be solved by attacking the system itself, rather than by attacking the individual.

After the failure of the disarmament negotiations and the access to power of Hitler in 1933, Noel-Baker joined the ranks of those who demanded a more active policy on the part of the democracies in order to halt the aggression of the Fascists and Nazis.

During the Second World War, Noel-Baker was entrusted with several government missions, and was himself a member of the government when Attlee became prime minister in the summer of 1945. He played an important rôle in the creation of the United Nations and its specialized agencies, and as Minister of Commonwealth Relations was in charge of negotiations with India, Eire, and Newfoundland, when the status of these countries within the Commonwealth was decided.

After the Conservative victory in 1951 Noel-Baker returned to the Opposition. In the House of Commons he had figured prominently in the major debates on foreign policy, notably on the occasion of the 1956 Suez Crisis. At the same time he has continued his campaign in favour of disarmament. In 1958, he published a comprehensive work on this subject, in which he analyses the various stages of disarmament negotiations. He declares that in 1955 it would really have been possible to reach a solution, but that the opportunity was frittered away when the Western Powers went back on proposals that the Soviet Union at that time seemed disposed to accept. In examining the problem of disarmament, Noel-Baker declares emphatically that disarmament must be general. The primary aim, of course, must be to remove the menace of nuclear armaments; but at the same time one should be alive to the terrible danger represented by the possibility of chemical, bacteriological, and radiological warfare in the future. The only practical method of introducing disarmament must be to insist on a radical reduction in the first phase. In this connection, Noel-Baker often quotes Lloyd George's remark that 'an abyss cannot be crossed in *two* jumps'. He also envisages disarmament as taking place simultaneously and on a global scale. Unilateral disarmament on the part of certain countries, so far from removing international anarchy, would rather tend to increase the danger of war by encouraging aggression; while simultaneous disarmament would also involve a certain measure of risk, from the point of view of security policy. Noel-Baker, however, believes that this is a risk worth taking; it is, after all, a minor risk compared to the threat of total destruction represented by an unchecked armament race.

Whereas Noel-Baker's efforts to promote disarmament were connected with his activities as an internationally minded politician, the work of LINUS PAULING [b. 1901], recipient of the *1962* Nobel Peace Prize, represented a scientist's campaign against nuclear weapons. A serious warning had already been launched by Albert Einstein in 1945, just after the atomic bomb had fallen on Hiroshima and Nagasaki. This warning, however, did not create great sensation at that time. Much work had to be done in order to stir up public opinion in this area.

Linus Pauling was born in Portland, Oregon. His father was a druggist by profession. As a boy he became very interested in chemistry and as a result he received his B. Sc. in chemical engineering in 1922. In that same year, he became affiliated with the California Institute of Technology where from 1931 onwards he served as professor. In *1954* he was awarded the Nobel Prize for Chemistry 'for his research into the nature of the chemical bond and its application to the elucidation of the structure of complex substances'.

His activities in the field of peace problems started in 1946. At that time he became a member of a committee of which Albert Einstein was chairman. The task of this committee was to campaign against further development of nuclear weapons. It proved, however, extremely difficult to secure public support for this campaign in as much as the Cold War then set in, and more especially after the Soviet Union had exploded its first atomic bomb in 1949. The committee's efforts to stop the construction of the hydrogen bomb also proved futile. In 1952, the first hydrogen bomb was exploded in the United States. Just one year later, the Soviet Union did likewise.

In spite of these depressing events, the scientists persisted in their warnings, which were eventually formulated in the Mainau Declaration of 1955 – this declaration was signed by fifty-two Nobel Prize laureates, among them, Linus Pauling.

In May 1957, Pauling decided to start a campaign of his own against nuclear weapons. In a speech to students at Washington University, St. Louis, he dealt with the following question: What is known about the effect of radio-activity on human heredity factors? He said: 'I believe that no human being should be sacrificed to the project of perfecting nuclear weapons that could kill hundreds of millions of human beings and that could devastate this beautiful world in which we live'.

Pauling then decided to launch a mass campaign against nuclear weapons. To this end he drew up an appeal which was signed by more than 2,000 American scientists. During its subsequent circulation, it was signed by an additional 8,000 scientists from forty-nine countries. The appeal stressed the threat to humanity of radioactive fallout from nuclear tests, as well as the increased risks of atomic war. Pauling exhorted the 'atom powers' [at that time the United States, the Soviet Union and Great Britain] to stop the tests with nuclear weapons. In his opinion this might also serve as a significant step in the direction of general nuclear disarmament. In January 1958, Linus Pauling and his wife Ava Helen Pauling submitted the appeal, with its 11,021 signatures, to the Secretary-General of the United Nations Organization, Dag Hammerskjöld.

'The Pauling Appeal' caused a great sensation and was followed by vehement discussion. As to the threat represented by nuclear tests, there was in fact no disagreement among scientists. But several of them – among them Edward Teller – maintained that a definite renouncement of any use of nuclear weapons would imply too great a risk for the American defense system.

As for Pauling personally, his activity during these years had made him an object of suspicion in the eyes of the authorities. In order to purge himself of these suspicions [some of which involved the charge of being a communist], Pauling demanded an official interrogation, and the senator who presided over the commission said later that probably it was the communists who had been following Pauling's line, not vice versa.

A subsequent investigation in 1960 concentrated on the circumstances involved in the 1957 campaign. The sub-committee of the United States Senate regarded its main task as being the revelation of the manner in which the 11,000 signatures had been secured. Pauling explained the circumstances, but firmly declined to divulge the names of those who had assisted him in collecting the signatures by invoking the principle of 'freedom of petition'. The outcome was that the sub-committee abstained from its right to charge Pauling with 'Contempt of Congress'.

With regard to the problem of nuclear weapons in international politics, an important development took place between 1958 and 1963. In 1958, tests were stopped, first by the Soviet Union, later by the United States and Great Britain. However, in 1961, the Soviet Union resumed nuclear testing, and in the spring of 1962, the United States followed suit. At this point in time, it would seem as though all Pauling's admonitions were in vain. Nevertheless, the radio-active fallout had increased to such an alarming degree that even the politicians took fright.

Cumulative investigations resulted in the test-ban treaty of July 1963. The treaty had, as a matter of course, political overtones, but it can hardly be doubted that public opinion aroused by scientists, in particular Linus Pauling, had an important bearing on the conclusion of the treaty.

STRUGGLE FOR HUMAN RIGHTS

Albert John Lutuli, Martin Luther King, René Cassin

Among factors threatening world peace, the suppression of human rights has a rather sinister importance. A life-long struggle in quest of effective implementation of human rights was recognised by the *1960* Peace Prize to ALBERT JOHN LUTULI [1898-1967]. This award was remarkable in several respects: first and foremost, because for the first time a Nobel Prize was awarded to a Negro from the African continent; secondly, because it represented a decisive expression of opinion on the part of the Nobel Committee in a dispute between groups of people of different races.

Albert John Lutuli was born in 1898. His family belonged to a tribe of the Zulu people. Since the age of eight he had lived in Natal. Up to the age of sixteen he attended the local mission-school, and subsequently received his training as a teacher at various institutions run by American missionary societies. He became a teacher at one of these, Adams College, and continued on its staff for fifteen years. Through his education and subsequent activities Lutuli was greatly influenced by Christianity, above all by its doctrine of the equality of men and the Christian's duty to promote justice by peaceful means. In 1935 he was approached by the elders of his tribe with the request that he would assume the chieftainship. This was a difficult choice for Lutuli. It meant leaving his teaching post in an enlightened community and returning to the primitive existence of the native tribe. His loyalty to his fellow tribesmen, however, was strong, and the position of chief was a traditional one in his family: when he accepted the nomination he was the fourth successive member of his family to have done so. As a native chief he was called on to solve a great many problems – to arbitrate in disputes, collect fines, preside at tribal councils, play the chief part at festivals and ceremonies. He continued to occupy the chieftainship until he was deposed by the South African government in 1952. [Chiefs are chosen by their fellow tribesmen, but must be confirmed in their appointments by the Government.] The reason for his deposition was Lutuli's work within the African National Congress. This had been started in 1912 in order to promote the interests of the large non-white population in the new South African state. For it was quite clear that the white population would make every effort to maintain their privileged position, *inter alia* by radically limiting the franchise of non-whites, refusing them the right to enter parliament, and forbidding them to purchase land outside certain well-defined areas. The A.N.C. worked under very difficult conditions: the masses to whom they appealed were not only disunited but steeped in poverty, ignorance and fear. However, as pressure from the government increased, e.g. with the abolition of the vote for non-whites in the Cape Province in 1936, the organization received increasing support from people who had hitherto been loyal to the Government.

After the Second World War government intransigence hardened, finding expression in the slogan 'Apartheid'. Legislation which was now introduced deprived non-whites of all electoral rights, a special pass regulation even denied them the right to choose their own place of residence and place of employment, and facilities for schooling and education were rapidly reduced. Sexual relations between people of different races were forbidden, and heavy penalties for any infringements were imposed. This patent violation of human rights hardened the opposition, and in this movement Lutuli played a leading role. He had been a member of the African National Congress since 1944, serving in various official capacities, and in 1952 he was appointed chairman of the organization. The Government countered by deposing him from his role of chief,and placed all sorts of difficulties in his way during the next few years, including periodic restrictions on his liberty of movement and participation in meetings. After the so-called 'treason trial' in 1960 against a number of non-white leaders [which ended in a verdict of 'not guilty'] and the demonstrations against the Apartheid laws culminating in the massacre at Sharpeville, the A.N.C. was banned, and Lutuli was for all time forbidden to travel round the country or to take part in meetings. In his struggle for racial equality Lutuli had always preached the gospel of non-violence. In his opinion the use of violence will never achieve its goal, merely debasing both its protagonists and its victims. The aim must be, by a dignified attitude and an appeal to the sense of justice and reason, not only among whites in South Africa but among all the people, to establish a social order in which the rights of all people are secured. He has expressed it as follows: 'The African National Congress stands for a common society in our multi-racial country. This idea of a common society is consonant with a democratic outlook on life, whereas Apartheid is a negation of democracy. A common society implies the acceptance of a free society where individual liberties, so long as they do not endanger the interests of the state, are paramount, and human dignity is upheld.

Apartheid is so contrary to natural behaviour that it has to be enforced by numerous laws and regulations. Apartheid violates all standards of decency and humanity. It results in race antagonisms, and common loyalty to what should be a common country is never developed.'

After the announcement that Lutuli had been awarded the Peace Prize had been made public, the problem arose as to whether he would be able to make the journey to Oslo to receive it. The South African Government eventually granted him a travel permit, and permission to remain in Oslo one week. During his stay Lutuli was acclaimed for his notable contribution to the study of human rights, and although, as was only to be expected, in his address and his other speeches he dwelt primarily on the injustice that was being perpetrated in South Africa, he nevertheless impressed his listeners with his ability to see these problems in a more universal context. In this respect he recalled many of the great liberal national leaders of 19th century Europe. In essence the award of the prize to the great African leader was based on recognition of the fact that the struggle to maintain human rights is a universal one, and that the use of non-violent means to achieve this end will in itself help to promote world peace.

Whereas Lutuli had his origin in an African tribal society, MARTIN LUTHER KING [1928-1968], who was awarded the *1964* Peace Prize, had grown up in modern, industrialized America. Born in Atlanta, Georgia, the son of a baptist clergyman, he had studied theology at Harvard University, and later received a doctoral degree in philosophy at Boston University. Upon completion of this phase of his education he was faced with a choice: Should he pursue an academic career or should he work as a clergyman? In addition, he was indecisive as to where he should permanently reside – in the North, or in the South. Once resolved in the conviction shared with his young wife Coretta that the most fulfilling vocation would be the ministry and an opportune location would be the South in order to advance the cause of a totally equitable environment for his fellow Negroes, he was installed as minister of a baptist congregation in Montgomery, Alabama, in 1954. During the following year, this town witnessed some events that were to prove influential in King's future conduct. A synopsis of the events is as follows: On December 1, 1955, a Negro woman was arrested because she had refused to forfeit her seat on a bus to a white man. She was seated in a section at the rear of the bus that was reserved for Negroes – in this particular case the section designated 'for whites only' was fully occupied. As a direct result of this incident, a committee of Negroes of which Dr. King became an ardent member was formed to boycott the bus company. The boycott, which lasted for more than a year, proved totally effective, and although not all claims of the Negroes were realized, the action was a triumph for the 'civil rights movement'. Eventually, the Supreme Court rendered its verdict, declaring the bus segregation in Montgomery unconstitutional.

An important consequence of the bus boycott was that the entire structure of a civil rights effort could be implicitly entrusted to the aegis of one individual, Martin Luther King, who was elected, accordingly, president of the 'Southern Christian Leadership Conference' (S.C.L.C.).

In 1960 and 1961, several action groups, so-called 'sit-ins' and 'freedom rides' were formed. The expression 'sit-in' meant that young Negroes would enter 'segregated' restaurants and sit down, in spite of being refused any service. These young people were often reviled and molested by white fanatics, but their actions were acknowledged positively in most instances by the abolition of segregation. The 'freedom rides' were started in May, 1961. The participants in these action groups travelled by bus through specific districts in which the segregation system was particularly severe. The participants – Negroes as well as whites – were often victims of aggression and violence, but such experiences only intensified their campaign of non-violence.

In December, 1961, King acted as a leader of the 'Albany Movement', the first great collective action since the bus boycott in Montgomery. It was started as a demonstration in favour of some participants in 'freedom rides' who had been arrested. In connection with this demonstration, 700 Negroes – among them Dr. King – were arrested. After a while, by an agreement with the authorities, they were set free. The promises included in this agreement, however, were neglected by the said authorities.

On numerous occasions Dr. King was arrested. His arrest in connection with the 'Birmingham Action' in 1963 caused a special sensation. The aim of this action was to abolish race segregation and guarantee the Negro population the protection of the law. During this period, King published a book, 'Letter from the Prison in Alabama', in which he presented the principles of his 'non-violence' strategy. Against some prominent clergymen who had termed the Birmingham action as 'unwise' and 'untimely', King argued that the method of 'waiting on events' was indeed very ineffective in a reform campaign. 'Time', he said 'is in itself neutral, it has always been formed by human thoughts and human actions'. On this idea the non-violent strategy was founded, and its effectiveness had been clearly demonstrated by the Birmingham action. During the summer of 1963, most of the claims had been fulfilled; and although some difficulties arose in the implementation of the agreements, the action was a great triumph for King and his friends.

In order to give the centenary of the liberation of the slaves current appeal, a 'march to Washington' was arranged in August, 1963. At the Lincoln Memorial, King delivered a speech to an audience of 200,000 persons. In this speech he made a violent attack on race discrimination, but at the same time expressed the hope that the Negroes through non-violent methods might be able to obtain full human rights.

In 1964, President Kennedy's bill of civil rights was accepted by the Congress, albeit in a somewhat modified form. On July 2, 1964 the law was signed by President Johnson.

By his activities King had made many enemies, but also many friends. The Administration was very benevolent towards his organization. On numerous occasions Dr. King was awarded honorary degrees by universities, and as mentioned earlier, he was awarded the Nobel Peace Prize in 1964. For Dr. King these honours were an inducement to continue the struggle for human rights. In contrast to people of the younger generation in whose opinion violent methods were necessary, King went on emphasizing the importance and the effectiveness of non-violence. At the same time, he stressed the fact that necessary reforms had to be realized very soon, if civil war and chaos were to be avoided. He travelled all over the United States to stimulate action against social injustice. In the spring of 1968, he visited Memphis, Tennessee, to give his support to the claims of the city's sanitation workers, who were on strike. On April 5, 1968, he was shot down by an assassin.

The murder of Martin Luther King caused a wave of horror and anger throughout the world. In the United States it loosed violent unrest among the Negro population. This reaction, however understandable, was not in harmony with Dr. King's message.

His policy of non-violent campaigning is continued by his widow, Coretta King, and by Ralph Abernathy, who succeeded him as leader of the S.C.L.C.

The Peace Prize laureate for *1968*, RENÉ CASSIN [b. 1887] had also achieved much in the struggle for human rights. He is a rather different type of person than Lutuli and King. While these two laureates were primarily men of action, Cassin used his vast scientific knowledge for the promotion of the same ideals. However, Cassin had also experienced dramatic events. He was severely wounded in the First World War, and during the Second War, in June, 1940, he joined General de Gaulle in London, where he did very valuable work in securing independent status for the Free French Forces.

In the years between the wars, Cassin had played an important rôle on an international level, among other things as a prominent member of the International Veterans' Organization and as a French delegate to the League of Nations assemblies.

After the Second World War, Cassin, almost as a matter of course, was appointed a French delegate to the new world organization. In 1946, he became a member of a committee whose chairman was Eleanor Roosevelt and whose task was to elaborate a declaration of human rights. It was hoped that, through an international guarantee system, it might be possible to protect humanity against falling back into the terrible suppression of human rights it had experienced during the Second World War. The committee's deliberations showed, however, how difficult it was to formulate principles in such a way as to secure unanimous approval for such a declaration. Cassins's efforts to solve these problems were really decisive. In December 10, 1948, the declaration was approved, with no objections. It comprised political and juridical, as well as economic and social rights.

Though unanimously adopted, the United Nations' declaration lacked solidity in fact; the representatives of Eastern European countries and the Soviet Union having abstained.

Even in other ways the declaration might be characterized as a somewhat unsatisfactory expression of the real state of affairs prevailing in the world. Several of the states which voted in favour of it are governed by despotic régimes, and in some even slavery remains a legal institution. Even in democratic states, some fundamental human rights are as yet not fully realized.

The authors of the declaration, among them Cassin, were aware that the realization of the high principles thus formulated belongs to the future. Indeed, the two conventions by which the declaration was to acquire legal force were only approved after eighteen years had passed [1966].

The year 1968, proclaimed as Human Rights Year, saw new and terrifying acts of violence and oppression. It was not astonishing that some people wondered how a man like Cassin, the results of whose activities were apparently so modest, could be awarded the Peace Prize. Perhaps the question might be answered in this way: In his life-long fight for human rights, Cassin has never succumbed to adversity or defeat. He has continually stressed the fact that world peace can never be attained without a universal respect for human rights. Here the European Commission for Human Rights might be mentioned as an example. Various activities of this commission, such as its action against the dictatorship of the Greek colonels, have clearly demonstrated its efficiency in awakening public opinion against illegality and violence.

In European legal cooperation, too, Cassin has played a prominent part, among other things as a member and, from 1965 to 1968, as president of the European Court of Human Rights. His fundamental view has always been at once national, European and universal.

HUMANITARIAN ACTIVITIES

Albert Schweitzer, Office of the United Nations High Commissioner for Refugees, Father Pire, The International Red Cross, UNICEF, Norman Ernest Borlaug

In efforts to promote 'fraternity between nations' humanitarian activities have always been very important. This fact has been stressed by several Peace Prize awards, starting with Henry Dunant in 1901.

In 1953, one of the greatest humanitarians of our century, ALBERT SCHWEITZER [1878-1968] was awarded the *1952* Peace Prize.

Born in Kayserberg, Alsace, the son of a Protestant clergyman who moved shortly afterwards to the village of Günsbach, he studied theology, and wrote several works of a theological and religio-philosophical nature. As a theologian his leanings were markedly liberal.

Schweitzer was also a distinguished musician, and his interpretation of Bach's organ compositions won him a well-deserved reputation. In 1905, he published a large work on Bach, in which he propounded a great many new and stimulating views. But young Schweitzer cherished another and entirely different ambition: it was his earnest hope that he might undertake some great work for humanity, work that would engage his whole personality. In 1904, he had come across an article calling for the service of qualified people to assist in the work of the French Protestant Missionary Company in the Congo. The article made a tremendous impression on Schweitzer. Here was the opportunity to devote himself to humanitarian work, and in order to ensure that his own contribution should be as effective as possible, he decided to train as a doctor. In 1911, he took his medical degree, and 1913 became a doctor of medicine. The same year he set out, together with his wife, for Lambarene on the Ogow

River in French Equatorial Africa. Here, in the depths of the jungle, he set to work to build hospitals for the natives, and to cure them of a great many diseases – malaria, sleeping sickness, leprosy, cardiac complaints, hernia, and dysentery. Apart from occasional visits to Europe [during the First World War he was interned, as a German citizen], where Schweitzer spent most of his time collecting funds for his work, *inter alia* by giving organ recitals, he continued his medical work in Lambarene right up to his death in 1968.

There are undoubtedly many great philanthropists in various parts of the world who have devoted themselves just as whole heartedly to work of a similar nature. Schweitzer's peculiar distinction, however, is the cultural philosophy he developed, which greatly enhances the validity of the moral appeal radiated by his lifework. According to Schweitzer, all events in the life of mankind are rooted in one spiritual principle, a '*Weltanschauung*'. In essence, civilization consists in the strivings of individual and community to achieve perfection. Intellectual and material progress are undoubtedly important to the development of civilization. However, unless progress of this kind is based on some universal ethical principle, it will not advance civilization, but on the contrary, contribute to its dissolution. Schweitzer believed that this latter state of affairs had been reached in western civilization at the end of the nineteenth century.

As Schweitzer saw it, the question was as follows: Is dissolution an inevitable process, or is it possible to arrive at a universal ethical principle, which can once again animate our civilization, and create harmony between the actions and the thoughts of civilized man? Schweitzer has described how, in 1915, after years of pondering, he hit on the redeeming formula: 'respect for life'. What, he asked himself, does this respect for life mean and how does it arise in the individual? Schweitzer's answer was: If the individual is to understand himself and his relationship to the world, he must constantly and continuously look beyond all that knowledge and science have created in him, and penetrate to that which is elemental. A truly organic explanation of the problem of life is to be found in the elementary craving for life. This deepens, intensifies and heightens the will to live. On the basis of an absolute ethical principle, the individual will conceive the 'good' as the act of maintaining, promoting and ennobling all life that is capable of development and 'evil' as the destruction and suppression of life. Schweitzer considered that all ethical systems, which up to his own time had been built up, suffered from one decisive flaw – they confined themselves to the mutual relations between human beings, and failed to take into account all living things, *i.e.* plants and animals. Only an ethical system with a pantheistic basis of this nature would have a universal and binding character.

The chief significance of Schweitzer's cultural philosophy, formulated in the early 1920's, lies in the stimulus it gave to, and the expression taken by, his own strongly ethical personality. His philosophy of culture took shape in an age when intellectual circles in Germany and many other countries were very much under the influence of Oswald Spengler's philosophy of doom. To counteract Spengler's baneful doctrine of the specificity and limited life-span of each successive civilization, Schweitzer taught that, in essence, however much its forms may vary, civilization is always one and the same. Another important element in Schweitzer's view of life was that, unlike many other religious personalities, he always emphasized the primacy of reason. Last, but not least, the way in which his doctrine was embodied in his own lifework has exercised a strong and immediate ethical appeal.

A prominent aspect of humanitarian activities after the Second World War has been relief work for refugees. This was the background to the award, made in 1955, of the *1954* Peace Prize to the OFFICE OF THE UNITED NATIONS HIGH COMMISSIONER FOR REFUGEES. Ever since the First World War, refugees have been an endemic European problem, and one that was still unsolved at the outbreak of the Second World War. It was obvious from the start that the new war would still further complicate this problem. In order to relieve the general need which was bound to arise after the war, the Allies, in 1943, had set up a special organization: U.N.R.R.A. The first task of this organization was to assist those countries which had been occupied to restore their economies. Further, it would have to tackle the problem of helping to repatriate the many displaced persons, a field in which the organization, in the event, carried out work of great importance. U.N.R.R.A., however, was not intended to function as a long-term refugee organization. In 1947, this task was entrusted to a new organization, I.R.O. [The International Refugee Organization], which had been set up by the United Nations. Thanks to the generous funds placed at its disposal, notably by the U.S.A. and Great Britain, I.R.O. did valiant service. In 1950, it was in turn replaced by a fresh organization; the Office of the United Nations High Commissioner for Refugees, which started its functions in 1951. An unpolitical, social and humanitarian organ, this institution's essential task is to secure the rights of refugees, to find them employment, and, if necessary, assist them with loans.

Many and varied are the tasks confronting the Office of the U.N. High Commissioner for Refugees. Since the end of hostilities the stream of refugees has increased. Initially, it consisted of people driven from their homes; but to these have afterwards been added all those who have fled from the oppression of new totalitarian régimes.

The work of assisting all these enforced exiles demanded considerable sums of money. However, only the administrative expenses of the Office of the U.N. High Commissioner for Refugees are covered by the U.N.O. For the actual work of assisting refugees, the organization is forced to appeal for voluntary donations from governments and private individuals. Response to its appeals has not been particularly impressive; nor has there been much willingness to admit refugees or provide them with employment. But to the end of his days the High Commissioner, the Dutchman G. J. van Heuven Goedhart, who died in 1956, refused to be beaten by the many difficulties and disappointments of his task. He and his staff toiled indefatigably to do all that could possibly be done, at the same time ceaselessly endeavouring to rouse the consciences of governments and nations.

Refugee aid is obviously an important dimension in the work of promoting peace. In the first place, such a work is an attempt to heal the scars of war. Effective solution to the refugee problem, furthermore, will lead to greater political stability, thereby increasing the prospects of relaxing international tension. Finally, work for and among refugees looks beyond national frontiers, and fosters the idea of the fraternity of nations. It was considerations of this nature that had prompted the award of the Peace Prize to Fridtjof Nansen, in 1922, and to the Nansen Office, in 1938.

Relief work for refugees was also an essential dimension in the life-work of GEORGES PIRE [1910-1969, *1958*].

He was born at Dinant, in Belgium, in 1910. During the First World War his family lived as refugees in France. In 1927, Pire graduated and soon afterwards was admitted to the Dominican monastery of La Sarte-Huy, near Liège. After studying in Rome, he was ordained in 1934, and took his doctorate in 1936. Between 1937 and 1947 he lectured on moral philosophy and sociology in the monastery.

During the Second World War Pire took an active part in the resistance movement, both as a military chaplain and as an intelligence agent, receiving the Croix de Guerre and the Resistance Medal for his services. He also organized such social work as the setting-up of a children's camp to care for several hundred French youngsters during the immediate post-war period.

Father Pire's work for refugees began in 1949, after he had been inspired to devote himself to this task by a lecture on the problems of refugee camps delivered by an American U.N.R.R.A. official. From that moment Father Pire's activities may be grouped under three headings. The *first* was the so-called '*service de parrainage*' (sponsorship service), whereby inmates of refugee camps were put in touch with outside 'sponsors', the idea being to give them a new interest in life through the medium of personal contact beyond the precincts of their camp. This resulted in an exchange of letters, as well as gifts of money and parcels.

The *second* form of aid organized by him was the setting-up of homes for elderly refugees, clearly incapable of fending for themselves. The first of these homes was established in 1950 at Huy, Pater Pire's own home town. Others followed. Pater Pire's organization has undertaken to care for these old refugees for the remainder of their lives.

The *third* project he initiated was the 'European Villages', started in 1956. The first of these is situated in Aachen [Aix-la-Chapelle], the second in Bregenz in Austria, and the third in Augsburg. A fourth, named after Fridtjof Nansen, was commenced in 1958 at Berchem-Ste-Agathe near Brussels. Each of these 'villages' consists of twelve houses, each containing two flats. As the idea is to foster a sense of security among refugees and to give them an opportunity of fending for themselves – no easy task, since most of them belong to the category referred to as 'the hard core' – half the rent is paid by the occupants.

The basis of Pater Pire's activity is the organization called '*Aide aux personnes déplacées et ses villages européens*'. He has also instituted an association consisting of his closest co-workers, which he has named '*L'Europe du Cœur au Service du Monde*'. The title itself reveals the aim of Pater Pire's work; while re-habilitating the refugee's own belief in his worth as a human being, it aims to create in the minds of those engaged in this relief work a feeling of international solidarity and to bring a measure of warmth into human relations. We have not only an iron curtain in the East, declared Pater Pire; in the West too, there is a curtain of egoism, often just as impenetrable. Pater Pire was also aware that the struggle to promote a definite view of life often leads to an intolerance which in turn creates barriers between people. For this reason he especially emphasized that relief work must never be associated with any particular creed. In this connection he often quoted Newton's remark to the effect that men build too many walls and too few bridges. It is typical of Pater Pire's awareness on this point that, when one of his European villages was founded, the prayer of dedication was read jointly by four clergymen, all belonging to different denominations.

Although Father Pire's relief work, which was supported entirely by private funds, could of necessity only reach a minority of Europe's countless refugees, he hoped that the spirit in which this work is being carried out will help to promote a feeling of fellowship among the nations of Europe, and even the brotherhood of mankind.

In *1963*, on the centenary of the Red Cross, THE INTERNATIONAL RED CROSS COMMITTEE and THE LEAGUE OF RED CROSS SOCIETIES were awarded the Peace Prize. This was the third time the Committee had thus been honoured. As has already been mentioned, the first two awards had been made for humanitarian activities during the world wars. The third reflected a very similar activity. Although there have been no 'great wars' since 1945, many 'local' wars and conflicts have ravaged various parts of the world. The task of the Committee has therefore always been a double one. On one hand, it has had to carry out humanitarian tasks during conflicts; on the other, it must promote Red Cross activities in general.

Under the first head, the Committee made an important effort in connection with the Palestine conflict. Both during that war and its aftermath it did relief work among the Palestine refugees, work taken over by the United Nations in 1950.

The Committee's activities were also of great importance during the Korean War [1950-1953], as well as in connection with the 1956 uprising in Hungary. By agreement with the Hungarian government, the Committee undertook the control as well as the distribution of aid. As for the refugees, the relief work was coordinated with the League of Red Cross Societies, the aid in both cases being procured by the national Red Cross societies.

Among its other activities since 1945, one could mention the Committee's efforts to reunite families separated in wartime, and in obtaining damages for former prisoners of war in Japan, as well as for persons who had been the victims of the Nazis' monstrous medical experiments.

In 1959, the Committee administered the repatriation of Korean refugees in Japan. It also sought to be of use in connection with such civil strife as the conflicts between Hindus and Mahometans in India, as well as other conflicts in Latin America, Algeria, Vietnam and the Congo. In conflicts of this sort the main obstacle to relief actions is the lack of any international agreements – a shortcoming all too clearly exposed during the Nigeria-Biafra conflict.

In the development of Red Cross conventions, the 1949 diplomatic conference in Geneva marked an important step forward. Four conventions were made. The first drew up more efficient rules concerning the treatment of wounded in war on land. The second concerned victims of war at sea. The third dealt with the treatment of prisoners of war. And under the fourth, perhaps most important convention, civilian wartime internees were assured the same rights as military prisoners of war.

As has already been mentioned, the Committee has collaborated closely in its humanitarian activities with the League of Red Cross Societies. The main task of this organization, which had been founded in 1919 at Geneva, was to promote and coordinate the various Red Cross Societies' peacetime humanitarian activities. In 1963, the League comprised about 170 million members, organized in these societies.

The main difference between the tasks of the Committee and those of the League was originally that, while the League was supposed to run humanitarian activities in peacetime, the Committee would take over in event of war. However in the years immediately before and during the first year of The Second World War – the League in fact engaged itself in 'wartime tasks' by doing relief work for the benefit of refugees from Spain, Czechoslovakia, Poland and France.

In January, 1941, a common commission with representatives from the Committee and the League, was set up. In the collaboration thus established, the Committee, acting as an independent institution, made relief work possible during the war, while the League, with its many contacts within Red Cross societies, was able to procure the means for such work. This joint commission continued functioning until 1947.

Today, a mutual representation exists within the Committee and the League. In this way the two institutions together constitute what is called the International Red Cross. At the great international Red Cross conference, all governments adhering to the Geneva conventions are also represented.

In 1951, the Committee and the League made the following agreement: If the situation necessitates a neutral institution for relief work to be possible, the International Red Cross Committee shall step in.

The task of the League consists in organizing relief action by the national societies. In countries infested by war, occupation, civil war and other forms of unrest the activities shall be carried out in close collaboration with the Committee. They must never be made in such a way as to jeopardize the independent status of the Committee under the Geneva conventions.

In occupied or blockaded countries the Committee shall negotiate with the authorities concerned, in order to obtain permission for relief action. It is, moreover, the Committee's responsibility to control the delivery, as well as the distribution, of the means. Thereafter it is the League's task to stimulate the national societies to render all possible assistance.

When it is a question of relief action in connection with natural catastrophes, this task has regularly been carried out by the League alone. It has also achieved a great deal on behalf of refugees, both in Palestine and on behalf of refugees from Hungary in 1956. The League's activities during the Korean War are also well known.

In *1965*, the UNITED NATIONS CHILDREN'S FUND [*U.N.I.C.E.F.*] was awarded the Peace Prize. The organization had been set up by unanimous United Nations resolution of December 11, 1946. During its first years its main task had been the relief of children suffering from the effects of war, especially in Europe. Later, the organization's activities have been concentrated on the problems of developing countries.

In 1953, U.N.I.C.E.F. was made a permanent organization, founded on the following principles: Its work is limited to countries whose governments solicit its aid, and the countries receiving such aid are bound to make a contribution to the aid programmes not less than that of U.N.I.C.E.F. itself. The interest in U.N.I.C.E.F.'s aid programme for children has in fact been so great that on the average the contribution of the governments concerned has amounted to more than two dollars for every U.N.I.C.E.F. dollar. Authorities, as well as private persons, are entitled to participate in the relief work.

U.N.I.C.E.F. comes under the authority of the United Nations. However, several governments outside the organization, among them the German Federal Republic, Switzerland and Korea, are playing an active part in the relief work.

The various projects are prepared by the governments which apply for assistance. In the planning activity, however, U.N.I.C.E.F. experts take part. The organization is supposed to supervise the aid and ensure that it entails no expense for the recipients.

As for U.N.I.C.E.F.'s own finances, all contributions are voluntary. By far the larger part of the budget is covered by government contributions. The rest is procured by private subscriptions, e.g. from the sale of U.N.I.C.E.F. cards. In 1965, the organizations's budget represented about 30 million dollars, a small sum, indeed, compared with the enormous needs the organization is expected to meet. Its administration of such means as have been available has, however, been efficient.

The projects have usually been of the following sorts: assistance to mothers and children, campaigns against epidemics, general improvement of nutrition, relief work in connection with catastrophes.

The campaigns against epidemics have primarily been aimed against malaria, tuberculosis, 'yaws' [skin disease], eye diseases [especially trachoma], and leprosy. All these campaigns have been carried out in close collaboration with the World Health Organization [W.H.O.].

Against malnutrition, U.N.I.C.E.F. has supplied vast quantities of powdered milk and also proffered assistance by planning dairies and dried milk factories.

Relief work after natural catastrophes grew out of U.N.I.C.E.F.'s work for war victims.

The *1970* Peace Prize was awarded for a special sort of humanitarian contribution. Unlike the other individuals and institutions mentioned in this section, the prize-winner's motives had not been directly humanitarian: His achievement was the fruit of scientific research. But inasmuch as it has made a crucial contribution toward solving the world's hunger problem, the humanitarian results have also been epoch-making.

The prizewinner, NORMAN ERNEST BORLAUG, was born in 1914 at Cresco, Iowa, of Norwegian-American parents. They were farmers, and all his life Borlaug has kept in direct contact with the soil. After receiving his agricultural education at the University of Minnesota, he did experimental work in Massachusetts and Idaho. In 1942, he took his doctor's degree in plant pathology at the University of Minnesota.

In 1944, after a short period of employment with the E. I. du Pont de Nemours, he was attached to the Rockefeller Foundation as a geneticist. A couple of years earlier this institution, in cooperation with the Mexican government, had initiated an agricultural project in Mexico. It had been planned by the well-known plant pathologist Elvin C. Stakman, who had also been Borlaug's teacher. In 1943, one of Stakman's pupils, Prof. J. George Harrar – later president of the Rockefeller Foundation – was appointed project leader. The objective was to arrive at methods for increasing wheat yield. And it was here that Borlaug, as project leader, was to make his central contribution. As his starting point he made studies of soil fertility and the possibility of improving it by adding artificial fertilizers and water. The next stage was to arrive at varieties of wheat capable of yielding more than the existing varieties. Borlaug made a great number of crossings, and produced a number of new varieties. These he sowed in two different areas in Mexico, with different growing seasons. In this way two crops could be grown each year, thus halving the time taken to develop a new variety.

His next problem was to develop varieties of wheat resistant to various sorts of rust. Because the rust mildew develops in such a way that varieties of wheat earlier resistant are open to attack by new types of rust, he had to continually replace the wheat varieties. Here Dr. Borlaug, in his fight against rust, hit on the idea of sowing mixed corn, i.e. varieties of wheat resistant to different sorts of rust. In this way it became possible to prevent a whole field from falling prey to a single attack.

The Mexican wheat programme's final success came with the introduction of short-stemmed, so-called semi-dwarf wheat. True, the wheat varieties previously used by the project had produced heavy yields; but it had been realised at an early stage that there must be limits to this sort of increase in efficiency. If the plants were given more than a certain quantity of nitrogen, the stems broke. And that was why it was so important to obtain a new, short-stemmed variety. Such a variety had been produced experimentally by the American agriculturalist Dr. Orville Vogel.

In 1953, the first exciting crossing experiments were begun in Mexico. But the results were negative. Now patience was the order of the day. At last, after two years' intense work, these efforts were crowned with success, and further experimental crossing work led to the development of a whole series of dwarf types obviously possessing the necessary qualities to raise the yield to a hitherto unknown level.

Essential to the project's breakthrough, of course, was a positive attitude in the peasantry. Peasants tend to be conservative; they do not easily allow themselves to be talked into investing in new methods of uncertain outcome. But in the case of the new brands of wheat, the results were so convincing that it did not take long for them to come into general use in Mexican agriculture. From 1955 to 1964 the yield rose to far above twice its previous level. Mexico became self-supporting in wheat and in recent years has even had a slight export surplus.

Experiences from Mexico soon spread to other countries. Borlaug was asked to act as adviser to the governments of Pakistan and India. There, too, the results have been encouraging. The new varieties of wheat have also been used in Turkey, Afghanistan, Tunisia, Morocco and Argentina.

Parallel with the effectivization of wheat production there has been a similar development in recent years in rice production, stimulated by the activity of the International Rice Research Institute in the Filippines established on the initiative of the Rockefeller Foundation, in collaboration with the Ford Foundation. This expansion in agriculture, which also includes maize production, has rightly been called 'The Green Revolution'.

It gives the populations of the developing countries well-founded hopes of better living conditions. Both Borlaug and his collaborators, however, are well aware that this revolution, alone, cannot secure harmonious social conditions. The outcome is also in a high degree dependent upon political conditions in those countries. First and foremost, the State must ensure that not only well-to-do peasants shall derive advantage from the new methods. Further, Borlaug has time and again emphasized that, if not followed up by great efforts to halt the population explosion, 'The Green Revolution' may well prove to be no more than a deferment of the ultimate catastrophe of world-wide famine. In this field the nations must cooperate with the same efficacy as they have done in bringing about 'The Green Revolution'.

Looking back over the Peace Prize awards of the last seventy years, what judgment can we pass upon them? The problem is complex. One standing criticism is that the Prize has never been awarded to 'real' pacifists. But if we run through the list of all those pacifists who have been proposed, only one name really seems to justify this objection: namely, that of Mahatma Gandhi. Other doubtful cases are MacDonald [in the 1920's], and, possibly, Carl Lindhagen. It might, of course, be maintained that too few individuals and institutions have the right to submit proposals. Yet this right is by no means so exclusive as to bar the way to many well-founded suggestions. Members of parliament and governments, together with professors in various fields, compose a very mixed body, and really worthwhile proposals are not altogether likely to escape their notice.

Another objection, which is in fact contained in the first, that 'non-pacifist politicians have been rewarded', is more concrete; and we have tried to analyse these instances as objectively as possible.

With regard to the more 'universal' champions of peace, public opinion has been pretty well unanimous. As a rule, no one has questioned their lofty moral standard or international outlook. How far they have been able to influence events or improve the prospects of peace is another question. Today, the discrepancy between the overwhelming movement and magnitude of events and the efforts of any individual seems insuperable. But no one can doubt that *without* this outlook, *without* this urge to achieve something, there can never be peace on earth.

One final consideration: What type of person do these advocates of peace represent? Are any common traits, deeper than a mere conformity of basic ideas, to be discerned in them? Here, the first outstanding fact is that, although the various individuals disagree in their philosophies of life, they do share a clearly defined fellowship of values. In this way, the prize winners belie the assertion that pacifism must be closely allied with religion. We do find religious minds among them – people such as Henri Dunant, Nathan Söderblom, Jane Addams and the Quakers. We also find such free-thinkers as Bertha von Suttner, Hjalmar Branting, Fridtjof Nansen and Carl von Ossietzky. Admittedly the latter, too, have to a significant degree inherited their social sense of duty from Puritanism. However, both groups managed to rise above a stringent puritanical ethic, and thus they were free to perform their tasks with a marked tolerance of individuals, nations, and races. When reading the biographies of these people, we get a clear impression that their dissatisfaction with the prevailing condition of the world is born not out of a neurotic reaction toward their immediate surroundings, but out of a superabundance of innate compassion – an urge to *give* of oneself in the broadest definition of the word. We may, therefore, claim that these individuals are exemplary Victorians.

The main problem of our century is to extend this feeling of security in everyone so that it will encompass the masses, and thus simultaneously preserve individual integrity.

As the young Norwegian poet, Nordahl Grieg, who was killed in the Second World War while on a bombing raid over Berlin, once expressed the idea: 'In creating human worth, we are creating peace'.

ADMINISTRATION AND FINANCES OF THE NOBEL FOUNDATION

BY NILS K. STÅHLE

The Nobel Foundation was established under the terms of the will of Alfred Nobel, dated November 27, 1895, about one year before his death on December 10, 1896. The statutes governing the Foundation and the prize-awarding institutions were promulgated by the King-in-Council on June 29, 1900, the latest amendments being dated 1970. The Foundation thus came into being about three and one-half years after Alfred Nobel's death.

The bodies governed by the statutes are:

1. Four *Prize-Awarding Institutions*, viz. the Royal Swedish Academy of Sciences, The Royal Caroline Institute, and The Swedish Academy, all in Stockholm, Sweden; and the Nobel Committee of the Norwegian Storting [Parliament] in Oslo, Norway.
2. Five *Nobel Committees* [including the above-mentioned committee of the Norwegian Storting, which is in itself a prize-awarding institution] – one for each prize section.
3. Four *Nobel Institutes* – one for each prize-awarding body.
4. The *Nobel Foundation* with its *Trustees* and *Board of Directors*.

The *Prize-Awarding Institutions* each represent one prize section, except the Royal Academy of Sciences, which represents two. Thus there are five prize sections. Each year the adjudicating bodies decide on the award of the prizes. Candidates' nominations must have reached the prize-awarding institutions before February 1 each year and be made by individuals [not institutions or governments] qualified, under the special regulations of the relevant prize-awarding body, to make such nominations. The awards are usually decided between October 1 and November 15. The deliberations are secret, but the decisions are published immediately. They are not subject to confirmation by any other authority, and are not subject to appeal; nor may they be contested.

The presentation of the prize money, the Nobel gold medals and the diplomas takes place at ceremonies held in Stockholm and Oslo on December 10, the anniversary of the death of Alfred Nobel.

Each of the five *Nobel Committees* consists of between three and five members, appointed by the respective prize-awarding body. Each committee may call in experts to take part in its deliberations and to make recommendations. Members and experts may also be chosen from outside the prize-awarding institutions, without regard to nationality. The committees' function is to do the preparatory work and advise the relevant prize-awarding institution.

Nobel Institutes may be set up by each prize-awarding body in order to assist in such investigations as may be necessary for making the awards and in other matters germaine to the Foundation's purposes. The institutes are [year of establishment in brackets]:

The *Nobel Institute of the Academy of Sciences* [1905]; since 1966, jointly for physics and chemistry.
The *Nobel Institute of the Caroline Institute*, with a
Department of Biochemistry [1937]
Department of Neurophysiology [1945]
Department of Cell Research and Genetics [1945]
The Nobel Institute of the Swedish Academy, with its *Nobel Library of modern literature* [1901]
The *Norwegian Nobel Institute*, with its *Library of works on the preservation of international peace and on international relations* [1902].

The heads and employees of the Nobel Institutes are chosen by the relevant prize-awarding body. Appointments may be made irrespective of nationality.

The activities and organization of the Nobel Institutes are adapted to the needs of each prize-awarding institution; likewise to changing times, conditions and resources. In recent years, there has been less emphasis on research and more on symposia and other activities designed to spread knowledge under the Nobel aegis.

The *Trustees* of the Nobel Foundation are fifteen in number, three for each prize section. They are appointed by the prize-awarding institutions. The Trustees elect all the members of the Board of Directors of the Foundation, except the Chairman and his Deputy, who are appointed by the King of Sweden. The other principal task of the Trustees is to examine the annual accounts of the Board and the reports of the auditors, and to decide whether or not the Board shall be absolved from further responsibility for the year under report.

The *Board* of the Foundation consists of five members with three deputies. From their own number they elect an Executive Director.

The *Executive Director* is the administrative head of the Foundation. It rests with him to draw up the principal lines of the investment policy of the Foundation; to make suggestions to the Board regarding investments, personnel, public relations, publications, etc.; to administer the property of the Foundation; and to handle legal matters. It is also his responsibility to arrange for the ceremonies in connection with the solemn prize presentation in Stockholm.

The most notable of the Executive Directors has been Ragnar Sohlman, a personal friend and collaborator of Alfred Nobel and one of the executors of his will. In this capacity Mr. Sohlman, who served the Foundation in different ways from its inception until his death in 1948, can be said to have embodied the spirit of Alfred Nobel. In fact, the Foundation largely owes its existence to his sober enthusiasm and devoted work in executing the will. With his death the last personal link between the Foundation and the donor was broken.

The *Staff* has remained practically unchanged in number since 1901. This has only been made possible by adapting the organization to meet an ever-increasing and more complicated burden of work. Administration costs represent about 7 per cent of revenue.

Since 1926 the Foundation has had its offices in its own building in Stockholm – the Nobel House.

The money received from the estate of Alfred Nobel was well over 31 million Swedish kronor and formed the *Fund Capital*. In accordance with stipulations in the statutes, the bulk of the money formed the *Main Fund* [*Prize Fund*], while smaller amounts were set aside for a *Building Fund* [the administration building and the hall for the annual prize-giving ceremonies] and for *Organization Funds*, each one to cover the costs of organizing the five prize sections' respective Nobel Institutes; and, finally, for other stipulated purposes.

The *Main Fund* grows by annual addition to the capital of one-tenth of its net proceeds for the year, by interest on prize money for the current year and – since 1970 – by the whole capital of undistributed prize money. Each year the net proceeds of the Main Fund, minus the above-mentioned one-tenth, are divided into five equal parts and placed at the disposal of the prize-awarding bodies. One-fourth of each part is withheld to meet the expenses in connection with the prize-adjudication work and for the Nobel Institutes. The remainder constitutes the prize money.

Besides the *Organization Funds*, the various prize sections also have at their disposal *Special Funds*, accumulated over the years, mainly from prize money which, either as a whole or in part, has not been distributed. This arrangement, however, has recently been changed, in 1970, by statutory amendment. Instead, the Special Funds now grow by adding 10 per cent of their annual interest to the capital. From 1970, the rest of the total residue is divided equally, in the same fashion as the interest on the Organization Funds, between the five prize groups, to be used for the prize adjudication and the Nobel Institutes. The fund capital of the Special, Organization, Saving and Building Funds may also be utilized. Savings for future needs may be accumulated, but from 1970 without interest.

All funds and buildings are owned and administered by the Nobel Foundation.

To sum up, the proceeds of the Main Fund – minus 32.5 per cent [i.e. 10 per cent to the capital plus 25 per cent of the remaining 90 per cent to cover the expenses of the prize sections] – are divided up into five equal parts and, as has already been mentioned, constitute the yearly sum available for the *Nobel Prize money*. The first prizes, distributed in 1901, amounted to about 150,800 Swedish kronor each. The nominal value of the prizes is now [1970] about 170 per cent higher, but of course its real value is considerably lower. In 1946 the Foundation was exempted from all Swedish taxation, except local real estate tax, both on its property and on the revenue arising from it. In some foreign countries, too, where money has been invested, the Foundation is exempt from tax. As far as is known, the prize money has in most cases been exempted, either de lege or de facto, from income tax in the recipient's country.

The Foundation's *investment policy* is naturally of paramount importance to the preservation and increment of the funds, and thus also of the prize money. In his will, Nobel directed the executors to invest the residue of the estate in 'safe securities', which were to form the Nobel Funds. In the original 1901 investment rules for the Board, the term 'safe securities' was interpreted, in the spirit of that time, as meaning gilt-edged bonds or loans against such securities or against mortgages on real property – principally of Swedish or Norwegian origin. But two World Wars and their economic and financial aftermath have required the term 'safe securities' to be reinterpreted in the light of prevailing economic conditions and trends. Thus, at the Foundation Board's request, the original restrictions on investments have gradually been liberalized. Since 1958, the Foundation has in principle been free to invest not only in bonds and secured loans, but also in real estate and in certain types of stocks. Certain restrictions, however, still apply, notably on investment in foreign stocks. The purpose of these changes has been as far as possible to safeguard the capital and revenue – and thereby also the prizes – against the falling value of money; and also, without impairing the capital, to counter a falling interest rate on the loan market. The Foundation has chiefly invested its fund capital in Sweden, but to some extent also in foreign countries.

The Nobel Foundation has received two money awards: one from the Swiss-Italian 'Fondation Internationale Balzan', in 1961, for promoting 'la paix, l'humanité, la fraternité des peuples', and the other 'the Empress Menen Award', in 1964, for 'services to humanity', from the Ethiopian 'Haile Selassie I Prize Trust'.

In 1966 it also received a donation of the Nobel Peace Prize posthumously awarded to Dag Hammarskjöld, from his brother and legatee.

At its 150th Anniversary in 1967, the New York Academy of Sciences solemnly acknowledged the Nobel Foundation by presenting it with its first 'Distinguished Service Award' diploma for contributions to science and other related areas.

By a donation of Sveriges Riksbank [The Central Bank of Sweden] at its tercentenary in 1968, the Nobel Foundation undertook through the Royal Academy of Sciences to award an annual *Prize in Economic Science in Memory of Alfred Nobel.* This memorial prize is equal in value to a Nobel Prize, and is adjudicated in the same way. It is also presented in Stockholm at the same time as the Nobel Prizes, on December 10 each year. This memorial prize was awarded for the first time in *1969*.

STATUTES

STATUTES OF THE NOBEL FOUNDATION

*Given at the Royal Palace, Stockholm, on the 29th day of June, 1900**

OBJECTS OF THE FOUNDATION

§ 1. The Nobel Foundation is established under the terms of the will of Dr. Alfred Bernhard Nobel, drawn up on November 27, 1895, which in its relevant parts runs as follows:

'The whole of my remaining realizable estate shall be dealt with in the following way: The capital shall be invested by my executors in safe securities and shall constitute a fund, the interest on which shall be annually distributed in the form of prizes to those who, during the preceding year, shall have conferred the greatest benefit on mankind. The said interest shall be divided into five equal parts, which shall be apportioned as follows: one part to the person who shall have made the most important discovery or invention within the field of physics; one part to the person who shall have made the most important chemical discovery or improvement; one part to the person who shall have made the most important discovery within the domain of physiology or medicine; one part to the person who shall have produced in the field of literature the most outstanding work of an idealistic tendency; and one part to the person who shall have done the most or the best work for fraternity among nations, for the abolition or reduction of standing armies and for the holding and promotion of peace congresses. The prizes for physics and chemistry shall be awarded by the Swedish Academy of Sciences; that for physiological or medical works by the Caroline Institute in Stockholm; that for literature by the Academy in Stockholm; and that for champions of peace by a committee of five persons to be elected by the Norwegian Storting. It is my express wish that in awarding the prizes no consideration whatever shall be given to the nationality of the candidates, so that the most worthy shall receive the prize, whether he be a Scandinavian or not.'

The terms of the will as set forth above shall be observed by the Foundation with the elucidations and more detailed provisions embodied in these statutes and in a settlement arrived at with certain of the testator's heirs on June 5, 1898, in which, after an agreement had been reached in respect of a minor part of Dr. Nobel's estate, they declared that they 'hereby acknowledge Dr. Nobel's will and renounce unconditionally, for themselves and their heirs, all further claims on Dr. Nobel's estate and all claims to take part in its administration, and similarly every right to protest against the elucidations of, or additions to, the will as well as any other provisions as to its carrying into effect and the uses to which the proceeds shall be put, which, now or in the future, shall be enjoined by the Crown or whomsoever it may concern; subject, however, to the following express reservations:

a] That the basic statutes, common to the prize-awarding bodies, dealing with the manner of, and the conditions for, the award of prizes as prescribed in the will,

* Later changes in the different statutes have been included

shall be drawn up in consultation with a representative nominated by the family of Robert Nobel and submitted to the approval of the Crown; and

b] that there shall be no departure from the following main principles, viz. that each of the annual prizes established by the will shall be awarded at least once during each five-year period from, and including, the year immediately following that in which the Nobel Foundation commences its activities,

and that the amount of a prize thus awarded shall under no circumstances be less than sixty [60] per cent of the part of the annual yield of the fund available for each prize, nor shall it be divided into more than three [3] prizes at most.'

§ 2. By the 'Academy in Stockholm', mentioned in the will, shall be meant the Swedish Academy.

Under the term 'literature' shall be comprised, not only belles-lettres, but also other writings which, by virtue of their form and method of presentation, possess literary value.

The provision in the will that the annual award of prizes shall refer to works 'during the preceding year' shall be understood in the sense that the awards shall be made for the most recent achievements in the fields of culture referred to in the will and for older works only if their significance has not become apparent until recently.

§ 3. To be eligible for consideration for the award of a prize, a written work must have appeared in print.

§ 4. A prize may be equally divided between two works each of which may be considered to merit a prize.

If two or more persons have together produced a work which is rewarded, the prize may be awarded to them jointly.

Work produced by a person since deceased cannot be rewarded with a prize; if, however, his death occurred subsequently to a proposal having been submitted, in the manner stipulated, that the work should be rewarded, then a prize may be awarded.

Each prize-awarding body shall be competent to decide whether the prize it is entitled to award may be awarded to an institution or association.

§ 5. No work shall be awarded a prize unless it has been found by experience or expert scrutiny to be of such outstanding importance as is manifestly intended by the will.

If it is deemed that none of the works that have come under consideration are of the character here indicated, the amount of the prize shall be reserved until the following year. If the prize cannot be awarded even then, the amount shall be added to the main fund; however, two-thirds of the amount of the prize may instead be placed in a special fund for that prize section, provided that four-fifths of those taking part in the decision are agreed.

Such a special fund shall be administered in conjunction with the main fund, and the yield on it may, at the discretion of the awarding body, be used, otherwise than for the award of prizes, to promote the purposes ultimately intended by the testator.

§ 6. For each Swedish prize section the prize-awarding body shall appoint a 'Nobel Committee', consisting of three, four or five persons, to pronounce an opinion in the matter of the award of prizes. The scrutiny requisite for the award of the Peace Prize shall be carried out by the committee of the Norwegian Storting referred to in the will.

It shall not be a necessary qualification for election to membership of a Nobel Committee that a person should be a Swedish subject or a member of the adjudicating institution. Persons other than Norwegians may be members of the Norwegian committee.

For the work involved by his task a member of the Nobel Committee may receive reasonable remuneration, the amount to be determined by the adjudicating body.

In special cases, where it shall be deemed necessary, the prize-awarding body shall be entitled to appoint an expert to take part, as a member, in the deliberations and decisions of the Nobel Committee.

§ 7. To come under consideration for the award of a prize it is necessary that a person shall be recommended in writing by someone with the competence therefore. Personal applications for the award of a prize shall not be considered.

Competence to submit proposals shall be enjoyed by representative persons, both native and foreign, within the particular fields of culture concerned, in conformity with the detailed regulations issued by the prize-awarding body.

Each year the prize adjudication shall embrace such proposals as have been submitted during the preceding twelve months up to the first of February. If, in addition to the prize for the current year, the prize-awarding body has at its disposal prize money reserved under § 5, the question of the award of the first-mentioned prize shall be decided before a decision is taken as to the amount reserved from the preceding year.

§ 8. Evidence shall be adduced in support of each proposal, which shall be accompanied by the writings and other documents referred to.

If a proposal is not made in one of the Scandinavian languages, or in English, French, German, or Latin, or if, for the full appraisement of a work proposed, the prize-awarding body is under the necessity of making itself acquanted with the contents of a writing in some language which cannot be translated without very considerable trouble or expense, then the prize-awarding body shall not be under obligation to give the proposal further consideration.

§ 9. On the Commemoration Day of the Foundation, which is the tenth of December, the anniversary of the death of the testator, the prize awarders shall present to each prize-winner an assignment for the amount of the prize, a diploma, and a gold medal bearing the image of the testator and an appropriate inscription.

Should it happen that a prize-winner declines the prize or should he fail, before the first of October in the calendar year immediately following, to draw the amount of the prize in the manner laid down by the Board, then the amount of the prize shall be added to the main fund; but at the meeting for the adjudication of the Nobel Prize for the last-mentioned year, four-fifths of the members of the prize-awarding body taking part in the decision may decide that two-thirds of the amount of the prize shall instead be paid into a special fund for the section, as laid down in § 5.

It shall be incumbent on a prize-winner, whenever this is possible, to give a public lecture on a subject connected with the work for which the prize has been awarded, such lecture to be given, within six months of Commemoration Day, in Stockholm, or in the case of the Peace Prize, in Christiania [Oslo].

§ 10. No protest shall lie against the award of an adjudicating body. If conflicts of opinion have arisen, they shall not be recorded in the minutes or otherwise revealed.

§ 11. For assistance with the scrutiny necessary for the prize adjudication and for the promotion in other ways of the purposes of the Foundation, the prize-awarding bodies shall be empowered to set up scientific institutions and other establishments.

These institutions and establishments belonging to the Foundation shall be called 'Nobel Institutes'.

§ 12. Each Nobel Institute shall be under the direction of the prize-awarding body that has established it.

With regard to their organization and finance the institutes shall be independent. Therefore their assets may not be used to defray the expenses of the awarding bodies' own establishments or those of other institutions. Nor may a scientist who has a permanent paid appointment at a Swedish Nobel Institute at the same time hold a similar appointment at another institution, unless the Crown accords permission in that special case.

Provided that the awarding bodies find it appropriate, the Nobel Institutes shall be set up on one common site and uniformly organized.

Men and women of foreign nationality may also be engaged by the Nobel Institutes.

§ 13. Of that part of the revenues from the main fund which is annually at the disposal of each prize section one quarter shall be witheld from distribution. When the immediate expenses of the prize distribution have been defrayed, the remainder of the amount withheld shall be used to defray the expenses of each section for the maintenance of its Nobel Institute. What is not required for the year's expenses shall be reserved for the future needs of the Institute.

ADMINISTRATION OF THE FOUNDATION

§ 14. The Foundation shall be represented by a Board, which shall have its seat in Stockholm and consist of five Swedish men, one of whom, who shall be the Chairman of the Board, shall be nominated by the Crown, and the remainder shall be appointed by the trustees elected by the prize-awarding bodies. The Board shall choose one of their own number as Executive Director.

One deputy shall be appointed for the member nominated by the Crown and two deputies for the other members.

The members of the Board elected by the trustees and their deputies shall be appointed for two years, as from the first of May.

§ 15. The Board shall administer the funds and other resources of the Foundation and also other property, provided that it is common to the prize-awarding bodies.

It devolves upon the Board to effect payment to a prize-winner of the prize awarded to him in accordance with these statutes and also, after due requisition, to effect the necessary disbursements for prize distributions, Nobel Institutes or other purposes. If requested, the Board shall also afford assistance to such persons as have to do with the Foundation in matters affecting the Foundation which are not of a scientific nature.

The Board shall be authorized to appoint a representative to institute legal proceedings on behalf of the Foundation, to appear in its defence, or otherwise plead its cause. The Board shall also engage such assistants as are necessary for its administration and fix the rates of salaries and pensions.

§ 16. The prize-awarding bodies shall appoint, for two calendar years at a time, fifteen trustees, six of whom shall be chosen by the Academy of Sciences, and three by each of the other prize-awarding bodies. Deputies shall be appointed to serve in place of trustees in case of need, namely four by the Academy of Sciences and two each by the other prize-awarding bodies.

The trustees shall elect a chairman from among their number, and they shall be called together for such election by the oldest in years among the trustees of the Academy of Sciences.

A quorum of at least nine trustees must be present for a decision to be taken. If any prize-awarding body neglects to appoints trustees, that shall not prevent decisions being taken by the other trustees on matters dealt with.

If a delegate is resident in some place other than that where the meeting is held, he shall be entitled to receive reasonable reimbursement for the expenses involved by his attendance.

§ 17. The administration and accounts of the Board for each calendar year shall be scrutinized by five auditors, of whom each prize-awarding body shall appoint one before the expiry of that year, and the Crown shall nominate one, who shall also be the chairman of the auditors.

Before the expiry of the month of February, a report on the administration of the Board shall be handed to the chairman of the auditors, after which it shall be incumbent on the auditors to complete their scrutiny before the first of April and thereafter deliver their report to the trustees of the prize-awarding bodies.

In the auditors' report, which shall be published in the public press, there shall be given a survey of the uses to which the revenues from the special funds have been put.

If a prize-awarding body neglects to appoint an auditor, or an auditor fails to attend after he has been summoned to a meeting, this shall not prevent the remaining auditors from carrying out their scrutiny.

§ 18. An auditor shall enjoy free access at all times to all the books, accounts and other documents of the Foundation; and any information which he may call for concerning the administration may not be refused by the Board. All the Foundation's securities shall be examined and scrutinized by the auditors at least once a year.

The Minister of Public Education and Worship, or such deputy as he may nominate, shall also enjoy right of access to all the documents of the Foundation.

§ 19. On the basis of the auditors' report the trustees of the prize-awarding bodies shall have the authority to absolve the Board from further financial responsibility for the year under review or to take such measures against the Board or any member thereof as may be called for. If no action is taken within a year and a day from the day when the Board's report was handed to the auditors, then the acts and measures of the Board shall be deemed to have been approved.

§ 20. The Crown shall determine the emoluments of the Executive Director and reasonable remuneration for the members of the Board and for the auditors.

Instructions in respect of the administration beyond what is laid down in these statutes shall be given in special regulations issued by the Crown.

§ 21. One tenth part of the annual revenues derived from the main fund shall be added to the capital. To the same fund shall also be added the interest accruing from the amounts of the prizes up to the time these are paid over the prize-winners, or are carried over to the main fund or special funds, as laid down in § 5.

CHANGES IN THE STATUTES

§ 22. Questions as to changes in these statutes may be raised by any prize-awarding body, by the trustees of the prize-awarding bodies, or by the Board. In respect of proposals advanced by a prize-awarding body or by the Board, an opinion shall be given by the trustees.

The prize-awarding bodies and the Board shall take part in the proceedings for arriving at a decision on a proposal that has been advanced, the Academy of Sciences exercising two votes and the other prize-awarding bodies and the Board one vote each. If the proposal does not secure at least four votes, or, when the change affects the rights and authority of only one prize-awarding body, that body does not approve the proposal, then the proposal shall fall. In other cases the proposal shall be submitted by the Board for the consideration of the Crown.

If, within four months of receiving notice thereof, any party fails to express its opinion as to a proposal that has been advanced, this shall not prevent a decision being arrived at on the proposal.

PROVISIONAL STATUTES

1. Immediately after the Crown has ratified the statutes of the Foundation, the prize-awarding bodies shall nominate, for the period expiring on December 31, 1901, the prescribed number of trustees, who, as soon as may be, shall meet in Stockholm for the purpose of electing the members of the Board of the Foundations.

In calculating the term of service of those members of the Board who are appointed for the first time, it shall be observed, firstly, that to the prescribed term of service, which shall be reckoned from May 1, 1901, shall be added the period between the election and the said day, and, secondly, that it shall be decided by lot which two members shall retire after one year, reckoned from the said day.

2. From the beginning of the year 1901, the Board of the Foundation shall take over the assets of the Foundation; but, insofar as the executors of the will deem it necessary, the remaining measures for the winding up of the estate may be effected by them during the course of the said year.

3. If possible, the first distribution of prizes for all sections shall take place in the year 1901.

4. From the Foundation's assets shall be taken: firstly, an amount of 300,000 kronor for each prize section, making an aggregate of 1,500,000 kronor, which, together with the interest from January 1, 1900, shall be appropriated, as required, to defray the expenses of organizing the Nobel Institutes; and secondly, such amount as the Board, after consultation with the trustees, shall deem necessary to procure for the Foundation its own premises for administration and an assembly hall.

A prize-awarding body shall be empowered to decide that the said 300,000 kronor and the interest thereon, or any part thereof, shall be added to the special fund of that section.

Whereto all whom it may concern are required to conform, in faith whereof We have attached Our signature and Royal Seal. Given at the Royal Palace, Stockholm, on the twenty-ninth day of June in the year of grace nineteen hundred.

[L.S.] OSCAR
Nils Claëson.

STATUTES

COMPRISING SPECIAL REGULATIONS FOR THE AWARD BY THE ROYAL ACADEMY OF SCIENCES OF PRIZES FROM THE NOBEL FOUNDATION, ETC.

Given by His Gracious Majesty at the Royal Palace, Stockholm, on the 29th day of June, 1900

AWARD OF PRIZES

§ 1. Competence to submit proposals for the award of prizes, as laid down in § 7 of the statutes of the Nobel Foundation, shall be enjoyed by:

1. Swedish and foreign members of the Royal Academy of Sciences;
2. Members of the Nobel Committees for Physics and Chemistry;
3. Scientists who have been awarded the Nobel Prize by the Academy of Sciences;
4. Permanent and acting professors in the sciences of physics and chemistry at the universities of Uppsala, Lund, Christiania, Copenhagen, and Helsingfors, the Caroline Medico-Chirurgical Institute, and the Royal Institute of Technology, as well as teachers of these sciences holding permanent posts at the University of Stockholm;
5. Holders of corresponding chairs in at least six universities or corresponding institutions selected by the Academy of Sciences with a view to ensuring the appropriate distribution of the commission over the different countries and their seats of learning; and
6. Other scientists from whom the Academy may see fit to invite proposals.

Decisions as to the selection of the teachers and scientists referred to in sections 5 and 6 shall be taken each year before the end of the month of September.

§ 2. As prescribed in § 6 of the statutes of the Nobel Foundation, for each of the sections for Physics and Chemistry, the Nobel Committee shall consist of three, four or five persons, one by virtue of his office, namely the head of the corresponding department of the Nobel Institute referred to in § 14 of these statutes, and the remainder elected by the Academy. The members of a Nobel Committee may not, however, be less than five in number unless an opinion on the question has been obtained, first from the two Nobel Committees jointly and then from the third and fourth classes of the Academy jointly.

Members shall be elected for a period of two, three or four calendar years, according as the number of members is three, four or five. A retiring member shall be eligible for re-election.

If a member retires before the expiry of his term of office, another shall be nominated in his stead for the remaining part of that term.

§ 3. Before the election of a member of a Nobel Committee takes place, proposals shall be put forward by the third class of the Academy in the case of the Committee for Physics, and by the fourth class of the Academy in the case of the Committee for Chemistry. Such proposals shall be submitted to the Academy before the end of the month of November.

If the class which shall submit the said proposals deems it necessary, it may co-opt a specially qualified member from another class of the Academy.

§ 4. From the elected members of a Nobel Committee the Academy shall nominate, for one year at a time, one member to be chairman of the Committee. In the absence of the chairman, the chair shall be taken by the oldest in years among the elected members present.

If the two committees meet jointly, the chair shall be taken by the chairman who is older in years.

§ 5. A Nobel Committee shall not be competent to take a decision unless at least three of its members, elected as prescribed in § 2, are present.

Voting shall be by open ballot. In the event of the voting on both sides being equal, the Chairman shall have the casting vote.

§ 6. Every year, during the month of September, the Nobel Committee shall send out to such persons as, under the regulations in § 1, are competent to put forward proposals for the award of prizes, invitations to submit their proposals before the first of February in the following year, such proposals to be accompanied by evidence in support of them.

§ 7. Before the end of September the Nobel Committee shall submit to the Academy its opinion and proposals for the award of prizes.

Subsequently, and before the end of October at the latest, that class of the Academy which is concerned shall submit to the Academy its comments and observations in the matter. If the class in question deems it necessary for that purpose, it may co-opt a specially qualified member from another class of the Academy.

The Academy shall take up the matter for a final decision before the middle of the following November.

§ 8. The deliberations, opinions and proposals of the Nobel Committees in connection with the award of prizes may not be made public or otherwise revealed.

§ 9. The remuneration which, under § 6 of the statutes of the Nobel Foundation, shall be granted to a member of a Nobel Committee shall be decided after the joint opinion of the third and fourth classes has been obtained.

The amount of the remuneration which shall be enjoyed by anyone who, under § 6 of the statutes of the Nobel Foundation, has been co-opted as an expert member of a Nobel Committee shall be decided by the Academy after the opinion of the class concerned has been obtained.

§ 10. To each member of the Academy who takes part in a meeting at which, under § 7, section 2 or 3, a class gives its final opinion or the Academy arrives at a decision on the award of a prize, and also to the keeper of the minutes, shall be given a Nobel medal in gold for each occasion.

§ 11. The Academy shall deal with all questions concerning the Nobel Foundation at special meetings. The minutes of such special meetings shall be kept separate from those kept at the other meetings of the Academy. All expenses incurred in connection with such special meetings shall be defrayed by the Nobel Foundation.

THE NOBEL INSTITUTE

§ 12. The chief task of the Nobel Institute which, in conformity with § 11 of the statutes of the Nobel Foundation, the Academy of Sciences is authorized to establish, shall, in cases where the Nobel Committee concerned deems it necessary, be to effect a scientific investigation of the discoveries in the fields of physics and chemistry which have been proposed for the award of a Nobel Prize.

Furthermore, insofar as its resources permit, the Institute shall promote such investigations within the fields of the said sciences as give promise of outstanding usefulness.

§ 13. The Nobel Institute shall have two departments, one for physical and one for chemical research.

The necessary buildings for these departments shall be erected on one and the same site. There shall be a session room common to the two Nobel Committees, and also archive and library accommodation, etc.

§ 14. The Nobel Institute shall be under the supervision of an inspector appointed by the Crown.

As head of each of the two departments of the Nobel Institute the Academy of Sciences shall, on the proposal of the class concerned, appoint a Swedish or foreign scientist who has an established reputation as a research worker and a wide knowledge of the science which the department is to promote.

The head of a department shall have the title of professor.

The conditions on which the head of a department is appointed shall be decided by the Academy, after it has requested and received proposals from the class concerned.

§ 15. The head of a department shall devote the whole of his time to matters connected with his department. He shall exercise supervision over the officials and other staff, the premises and the collections, and have immediate charge of the finances of the department.

The head of a department shall cause to be carried out at the Institute the work of investigation referred to in § 12. Should the subject of the investigation fall within the field of his own researches, it shall be incumbent on him to carry out the investigation himself.

Further regulations which it is incumbent on the head of a department to observe shall be brought to his notice in the form of special instructions.

§ 16. If, for the carrying out of some particular investigation, it should be necessary to call on the services of a specially qualified scientist, the Nobel Committee concerned shall make representations in the matter to the Academy. Remuneration for such work shall be fixed by the Academy on the proposal of the Committee, but subject to what is laid down in § 17 below.

§ 17. If, in cases where, under the statutes of the Nobel Foundation, the Academy has not the sole right of decision, it is decided to accord remuneration to a member of the Academy, such decision shall be submitted to the Crown for consideration and sanction.

§ 18. On conditions laid down by the Academy, after it has obtained proposals from the two Nobel Committees jointly, there shall be appointed, for the two departments of the Nobel Institute in common, a secretary, who shall also keep the minutes of the meetings of the Nobel Committees, and a librarian. The post of librarian may be combined with that of secretary or of an assistant at the Institute.

Such assistants, instrument-makers, attendants and others as are required by a Nobel Institute shall be appointed and dismissed by the Nobel Committee concerned.

§ 19. Permission for persons other than members of the Institute's own scientific staff to carry out investigations at the Institute may be granted by the Nobel Committee concerned, but only in cases where the object of such investigations is to prepare the ground for a scientific discovery or for an invention.

SPECIAL FUNDS

§ 20. When, in conformity with § 5 of the statutes of the Nobel Foundation, special funds have been established, the Academy shall be entitled to employ the annual revenues accruing from such funds, in order to promote the purposes ultimately intended by the testator, in support of such work within the fields of physics and chemistry as is considered to be of scientific or practical importance.

Such support shall be afforded preferably to persons who have already attained results in their work within the sciences mentioned, the further development of which is considered to merit support from the Nobel Foundation.

Proposals for support shall be drawn up by the Nobel Committee concerned and submitted to the Academy, which, after having obtained the opinion of the class concerned, shall make its decision in the matter.

The revenues from a special fund may also be used for the requirements of the Nobel Institute.

CHANGES IN THE STATUTES

§ 21. Proposals for changes in these statutes may be put forward by a member of the Academy or of a Nobel Committee. Before the Academy takes up such a proposal for consideration, an opinion thereon shall be obtained, first from the two Nobel Committees jointly and then from the third and fourth classes of the Academy jointly. Any proposal for a change which has been approved by the Academy shall be submitted to the Crown for consideration and sanction.

PROVISIONAL STATUTES

When the election of members to the Nobel Committees takes place for the first time, the Academy shall appoint, for the time being, a secretary for these committees.

Before temporary or permanent heads of the departments of the Nobel Institute have been appointed, the Academy shall elect from its members acting heads of departments, who shall retire as soon as temporary or permanent heads have been appointed.

In calculating the term of service of the four other members who are appointed for the first time, it shall be observed, firstly, that to the prescribed term of service shall be added the period between the election and the beginning of the year 1901, and, secondly, that it shall be decided by lot at the time of the election which member shall retire at the end of each of the years 1901, 1902 and 1903, respectively.

The heads of the departments of the Institute shall be appointed provisionally, after the Academy has decided on taking measures for the establishment of the Institute.

The permanent appointment of the heads of departments and the secretary shall not be made until the Institute has been finally established.

Before the Nobel Institute has been established and fully organized, the Nobel Committees shall obtain such relevant information as they consider necessary for the award of the prizes from the reports of prominent experts, and they shall be empowered, if necessary, to have experimental investigations and tests made at a Swedish or foreign institution. The remuneration for such work shall be decided in each particular case by the Academy, after it has obtained proposals from the Nobel Committee concerned, but subject to what is laid down in § 17.

Whereto all whom it may concern are required to conform, in faith whereof We have attached Our signature and Royal Seal. Given at the Royal Palace, Stockholm, on the twenty-ninth day of June in the year of grace nineteen hundred.

[L.S.] OSCAR
Nils Claëson.

STATUTES

COMPRISING SPECIAL REGULATIONS FOR THE AWARD BY THE CAROLINE MEDICO-CHIRURGICAL INSTITUTE OF PRIZES FROM THE NOBEL FOUNDATIONS, ETC.

Given by His Gracious Majesty at the Royal Palace, Stockholm, on the 29th day of June, 1900

AWARD OF PRIZES

§ 1. Questions concerning the award of prizes shall be prepared by the Nobel Committee, as constituted under the statutes of the Nobel Foundation, and decided by the teaching body, that is, the permanent professors of the Caroline Institute.

§ 2. 1. The Nobel Committee consists of five members, who are elected by the teaching body, it being understood that the Rector of the Institute should be a member of the Committee.

A Rector may be elected a member until further notice for the duration of his appointment as Rector. Otherwise, a member is elected for not more than three calendar years, and he shall be eligible for re-election, though he may not remain a member for a longer consecutive period than two election periods. The election periods shall be so adjusted that not more than two members are due to retire at the same time.

2. The teaching body shall nominate from among the members of the Committee a Chairman and a Vice Chairman for one year at a time. Such an appointment may not be held for a longer consecutive period than three years.

3. The teaching body is entitled, if necessary, to appoint one or more experts to take part in the Committee's deliberations and decisions as co-opted members.

§ 3. The Nobel Committee shall not be competent to take decisions unless at least half the number of the members of the Committee are present.

In the event of the voting on both sides being equal, the chairman shall have the casting vote.

§ 4. Every year, during the month of September, the Nobel Committee shall send out to such persons as, in accordance with the regulations set forth below, are competent to put forward proposals for the award of prizes, invitations to submit their proposals before the first of February in the following year, such proposals to be accompanied by evidence in support of them.

§ 5. Competence to submit proposals for the award of prizes shall be enjoyed by:

1. Members of the teaching body of the Caroline Institute;
2. Members of the medical class of the Royal Academy of Sciences;
3. Previous recipients of the Nobel Prize for Physiology or Medicine;
4. Members of the medical faculties of the universities of Uppsala, Lund, Christiania, Copenhagen, and Helsingfors;

5. Members of at least six medical faculties selected by the teaching body with a view to ensuring the appropriate distribution of the commission over the different countries and their seats of learning; and
6. Other scientists from whom the teaching body may see fit to invite proposals.

Decisions as to the selection of the teachers and scientists referred to in sections 5 and 6 shall be taken after proposals have been made by the Nobel Committee each year within the first half of September.

§ 6. The proposals submitted by duly competent persons during one year, reckoned from and including the first of February up to the following February, shall be arranged by the Nobel Committee and, together with a memorandum, submitted to the teaching body within the first half of February.

§ 7. The Nobel Committee shall decide which among the works proposed shall be submitted to a special investigation and make arrangements for such a special investigation, for which purpose it shall have the power to call in any necessary assistance.

When the Committee's decision has been communicated to the teaching body during the month of April, then, at its first meeting in May, that body shall decide whether, in addition to works already referred by the Nobel Committee to special investigation, any other work shall be submitted to such investigation.

A proposal that a prize should be awarded for a certain work shall fall if the work is not referred to a special investigation.

§ 8. During the month of September the Nobel Committee shall submit to the teaching body its opinion and proposals for the award of the prize.

§ 9. The teaching body shall make its decision as to the award of the prize during the month of October, on a day appointed at an earlier meeting.

§ 10. A member of the Nobel Committee who is not a member of the teaching body shall have the right to take part in the discussions, but not in the decisions, of the teaching body concerning the award of prizes.

Only permanent members of the teaching body shall be entitled to take part in the discussions and decisions concerning the award of prizes.

Voting in respect of prize awards shall be by secret ballot. When necessary, lots shall be drawn.

Every member of the teaching body who takes part in the final decision on the award, as well as the secretary and the members of the Nobel Committee, shall receive a gold medal struck especially for the purpose.

§ 11. The Nobel Committee shall be entitled to make application to the Finance Committee of the Caroline Institute for the means to defray its expenses. If the Finance Committee approves the application, it shall be entitled to authorize the payment of the amount from the Nobel Foundation. If the Finance Committee does not approve the application, or for any other reason, it shall refer the question to the decision of the teaching body.

After consultation with the Finance Committee, the teaching body shall have the right to decide on the disbursement of means to defray other expenses incurred in connection with the award of prizes.

If, in cases where, under the statutes of the Nobel Foundation, the teaching body has not the sole right of decision, it is decided to accord remuneration to a member of the teaching body, such decision shall be submitted to the Crown for consideration and sanction.

Printed publications which accompany proposals for prizes, or which are purchased in connection with the prize adjudication, shall be kept in the library of the Caroline Institute, but no responsibility shall be borne by the State.

Instruments and other similar appliances procured for use in the investigation necessary for the prize adjudication, shall be the property of the Nobel Foundation. They shall be kept, without responsibility on the part of the State, in such departments of the Caroline Institute as the teaching body decides, and may be used there until they can be transferred to the future Nobel Medical Institute. An inventory of this property of the Nobel Foundation shall be handed in every calendar year to the Board of the Foundation by those who have such property in their care.

THE NOBEL MEDICAL INSTITUTE

§ 12. The Nobel Medical Institute, which shall be under the supervision of the Chancellor of the Universities of the Kingdom, shall be established and organized in accordance with the decision of the teaching body, as soon as that body considers that the necessary means are available.

Proposals for the establishment of the Institute can be put forward by members of the teaching body or of the Nobel Committee. Such proposals shall be examined by the Nobel Committe before they are submitted to the teaching body.

Before activities are begun at this Nobel Institute, more detailed regulations concerning it shall be submitted for consideration and sanction by the Crown.

THE SPECIAL FUND OF THE MEDICAL PRIZE SECTION

§ 13. The yield on this fund shall be used, in other ways than by the award of prizes, to promote medical research and the utilization of its results for the purposes ultimately intended by the testator.

The yield on the fund may not be used for paying the salary of any person engaged at the Caroline Institute.

§ 14. Proposals for the use of the yield on the fund may be put forward by members of the teaching body or of the Nobel Committee.

Such proposals shall be examined and decided upon by the teaching body, after the Finance Committee has given its opinion on the subject.

§ 15. If the available yield for the year is not expended, the teaching body shall decide whether the balance shall be added to the capital of the fund or reserved until a future year.

PROVISIONAL STATUTES

In calculating the term of service of the three members of the Nobel Committee who are appointed for the first time by the teaching body, it shall be observed, firstly, that to the prescribed term of service shall be added the period between the election and the beginning of the year 1901, and, secondly, that it shall be decided by lot at the time of the election which member shall retire at the end of the year 1901 and which at the end of the year 1902.

Whereto all whom it may concern are required to conform, in faith whereof We have attached Our signature and Royal Seal. Given at the Royal Palace, Stockholm, on the twenty-ninth day of June in the year of grace nineteen hundred.

[L.S.] OSCAR
Nils Claëson.

STATUTES OF THE NOBEL MEDICAL INSTITUTE

Given at the Royal Palace, Stockholm, on the 30th day of October, 1936.

§ 1. The Nobel Medical Institute, established by the teaching body of the Caroline Medico-Chirurgical Institute, in accordance with § 11 and § 12 of the statutes of the Nobel Foundation, shall have as its purpose to assist, when the Nobel Committee for Medicine deems it necessary, in the investigations necessary for the prize adjudication and to carry out and promote such researches within the field of physiology or medicine as give promise of outstanding usefulness.

§ 2. The activities of the Nobel Institute shall be carried on in separate departments for different branches of physiology and medicine, and also by individual research workers engaged by the Institute.

The requisite buildings for the departments shall be erected or rented.

§ 3. The departments of the Nobel Institute shall be established by a decision taken by the teaching body on the proposal of a member of that body.

§ 4. The Nobel Institute shall be under the supervision of the Chancellor of the Universities of the Kingdom.

The financial estimates of the Nobel Institute and the decisions of the teaching body concerning the establishment of departments at the Nobel Institute, its choice of directors of departments and its decisions as to their conditions of employment, shall be submitted to the Chancellor for consideration and sanction.

§ 5. The teaching body shall issue regulations for the activities of the Nobel Institute, make decisions as to the estimated expenditure of the Institute, and engage the staff for its departments.

Decisions concerning the appointment of assistants, attendants, and other staff required at the Institute, as well as their conditions of employment shall be made by the teaching body on the proposal of the heads of the departments concerned.

§ 6. The Nobel Committee shall exercise the immediate supervision of the activities of the Nobel Institute. It shall prepare all matters concerning the Nobel Institute, and before the end of February each year shall submit to the teaching body a report on the activities of the Institute during the year immediately preceding.

§ 7. On the proposal of one of its members, the teaching body shall appoint as head of a department at the Nobel Institute a Swedish or foreign scientist who has an established reputation as a research worker and a wide knowledge of his science.

What has been said above about the head of a department shall also apply to individual research workers, as referred to in § 2.

The conditions on which the heads of departments and individual research workers are appointed shall be decided by the teaching body.

§ 8. The head of a department shall have the title of professor. He shall devote the whole of this time to the work of the department, with the obligation nevertheless, when requested by the Nobel Committee, to take part in the work of investigation for the award of prizes even if such work does not normally devolve upon his department. When the head of a department is charged with such investigation work for the award of prizes as makes great demands on his time, he may receive special remuneration for it, under § 11 of the special regulations concerning the award of prizes from the Nobel Foundation by the Caroline Medico-Chirurgical Institute, etc.

The head of a department shall direct the activities of that department, shall exercise supervision over the officials engaged in the department and have immediate charge of the finances of the department. He shall have the right within the limits of the grant to certify accounts for payment from the funds of the Nobel Foundation.

It shall be incumbent on the head of a department, before the end of the month of January each year, to submit to the Nobel Committee a report on the activities of the department during the year immediately preceding.

§ 9. The head of a department shall have the right to take part in the discussions of the teaching body, but not in its decisions, when matters concerning his department or such activities of the Nobel Institute as fall within the field of research of his department are under consideration.

§ 10. If there is more than one department at the Nobel Institute, the teaching body shall have the right to appoint one of the heads of the departments to deal, insofar as it is found necessary, with matters common to the various departments.

STATUTES

COMPRISING SPECIAL REGULATIONS FOR THE AWARD BY THE SWEDISH ACADEMY OF PRIZES FROM THE NOBEL FOUNDATION, ETC.

Given by His Gracious Majesty at the Royal Palace, Stockholm, on the 29th day of June, 1900

§ 1. The right to nominate candidates for the prize shall be enjoyed by members of the Swedish Academy and of other academies, institutions and societies similar to it in membership and aims, by professors of the history of literature or of languages at universities and university colleges, by previous winners of the Nobel Prize for Literature, and by presidents of authors' organizations which are representative of the literary activities of their respective countries.

§ 2. At its Nobel Institute, with which shall be associated a considerable library containing mainly modern literature, the Academy shall appoint a librarian and one or more assistants, and, if necessary, officials and assistants with a literary training, some permanent and some temporary, who shall prepare matters referring to prizes, give reports on recently published literary works abroad and arrange for the necessary translations of foreign publications.

The Nobel Institute of the Swedish Academy shall be under the supervision of an inspector appointed by the Crown and under the immediate management of the member of the Academy who shall be appointed by that body.

§ 3. The Academy shall have the right to use the yield of the special fund to promote, for the purposes ultimately intended by the testator, such literary activities as, whether carried on in Sweden or abroad, may be considered of cultural importance, especially in the field to which the Academy should devote attention and care.

§ 4. Those members of the Academy who are resident in the provinces are entitled, if they cannot attend in person, to send in voting papers for the election of trustees which it is incumbent on the Academy to hold in accordance with the statutes of the Nobel Foundation.

When decisions are to be made on questions referring to the award of prizes, the reservation of prizes, or the placing of reserved money in special funds, the members resident in the provinces who wish to take part in the decisions are entitled to reimbursement for travelling expenses, the amount of which shall be determined by the Academy.

§ 5. If, in cases where, under the statutes of the Nobel Foundation, the Academy has not the sole right of decision, it is decided to accord remuneration to a member of the Academy, other than such reimbursements for travelling expenses or attendance as stated above in § 4 and in § 16 of the statutes of the Nobel Foundation, such decision shall be submitted to the Crown for consideration and sanction.

Whereto all whom it may concern are required to conform, in faith whereof We have attached Our signature and Royal Seal. Given at the Royal Palace, Stockholm, on the twenty-ninth day of June in the year of grace nineteen hundred.

[L.S.] OSCAR

Nils Claëson.

STATUTES

SPECIAL REGULATIONS

FOR THE AWARD OF THE NOBEL PEACE PRIZE AND THE NORWEGIAN NOBEL INSTITUTE, ETC.

Adopted by the Nobel Committee of the Norwegian Storting on the 10th day of April in the year 1905

THE NOBEL COMMITTEE OF THE NORWEGIAN STORTING

§ 1. On the 5th August, 1897, the Storting came of the following decision concerning the election of the Nobel Committee of the Norwegian Storting:

'On the nomination of the selection committee, the five persons who are to undertake the award of the prize shall be elected every third year. After three years, two of those chosen shall retire, and subsequently every third year three and two alternately. In addition three deputies shall be elected every third year. The retiring members shall be eligible for re-election.'

On the 1st April, 1903, the Storting decided that the appointments should date from the following 1st day of January.

§ 2. For each calendar year the Nobel Committee shall elect a chairman and a vice-chairman. The chairman shall prepare the matters to be submitted to the Committee and summon members to meetings. He shall sanction payments and decide matters of an administrative nature, a report of which shall be submitted at the following meeting of the Committee.

A secretary shall be appointed to assist the chairman, with six months' notice of termination on either side, who shall also be the accountant of the Committee. The chairman shall engage further clerical assistance, provided that means are granted for that purpose.

THE NOBEL PEACE PRIZE

§ 3. In order to be considered for the award of the year, nominations for the Nobel Peace Prize shall be sent in to the Nobel Committee of the Norwegian Storting in Christiania before the 1st day of February of the same year.

The right to submit proposals for the award of the Nobel Peace Prize shall be enjoyed by:

1. Active and former members of the Nobel Committee of the Norwegian Storting and the advisers appointed by the Norwegian Nobel Institute;
2. Members of the national assemblies and governments of the different states and members of the Inter-parliamentary Union;
3. Members of the International Court of Arbitration at The Hague;
4. Members of the Commission of the Permanent International Peace Bureau;
5. Members and associate members of the Institute de Droit International;

6. University professors of political science and jurisprudence, history and philosophy;
7. Persons who have been awarded the Nobel Peace Prize.

§ 4. The Nobel Peace Prize may also be awarded to institutions and associations.

THE NORWEGIAN NOBEL INSTITUTE

§ 5. The Nobel Institute shall be established by, and be under the management of, the Nobel Committee of the Norwegian Storting in conformity with the statutes of the Nobel Foundation.

§ 6. The object of the Institute shall be to follow the development of international relations, especially the work for their peaceful adjustment, and thereby to guide the Committee in the matter of the award of the prize.

It shall also work for mutual knowledge and respect, for peaceful intercourse, justice and fellowship between nations.

§ 7. The Institute shall have a library, a selection of periodicals and a reading-room. With these shall be associated scholarly activities and popular educational work.

The Institute may support from its revenue other similar work at home and abroad.

§ 8. The Nobel Committee shall determine the expenditure of the Institute and engage its staff. An annual report shall be submitted to the Storting.

LIST OF THE NOBEL PRIZE WINNERS

	Physics	*Chemistry*	*Physiology or Medicine*
1901	W. C. Röntgen, *Germany*	J. H. van 't Hoff, *Netherlands*	E. A. von Behring *Germany*
1902	A. H. Lorentz, *Netherlands* P. Zeeman, *Netherlands*	H. E. Fischer, *Germany*	R. Ross, *Gt. Britain*
1903	H. A. Becquerel, *France* P. Curie, *France* Marie S. Curie, *France*	S. A. Arrhenius, *Sweden*	N. R. Finsen, *Denmark*
1904	Lord Rayleigh, *Gt. Britain*	W. Ramsay, *Gt. Britain*	I. P. Pavlov, *Russia*
1905	P. E. A. Lenard, *Germany*	J. F. W. A. v. Baeyer, *Germany*	R. Koch, *Germany*
1906	J. J. Thomson, *Gt. Britain*	H. Moissan, *France*	C. Golgi, *Italy* S. Ramón y Cajal, *Spain*
1907	A. A. Michelson, *U.S.A.*	E. Buchner, *Germany*	C. L. A. Laveran, *France*
1908	G. Lippmann, *France*	E. Rutherford, *Gt. Britain*	P. Ehrlich, *Germany* I. I. Metchnikoff, *Russia*
1909	G. Marconi, *Italy* C. F. Braun, *Germany*	W. Ostwald, *Germany*	E. T. Kocher, *Switzerland*
1910	J. D. van der Waals, *Netherlands*	O. Wallach, *Germany*	A. Kossel, *Germany*
1911	W. Wien, *Germany*	Marie S. Curie, *France*	A. Gullstrand, *Sweden*
1912	N. G. Dalén, *Sweden*	V. Grignard, *France* P. Sabatier, *France*	A. Carrel, *U.S.A.*
1913	H. Kamerlingh-Onnes, *Netherlands*	A. Werner, *Switzerland*	C. R. Richet, *France*
1914	M. von Laue, *Germany*	T. W. Richards, *U.S.A.*	R. Bárány, *Austria*
1915	W. H. Bragg, *Gt. Britain* W. L. Bragg, *Gt. Britain*	R. M. Willstätter, *Germany*	No award
1916	No award	No award	No award
1917	C. G. Barkla, *Gt. Britain*	No award	No award
1918	M. K. E. L. Planck, *Germany*	F. Haber, *Germany*	No award
1919	J. Stark, *Germany*	No award	J. Bordet, *Belgium*
1920	C. É. Guillaume, *France*	W. H. Nernst, *Germany*	S. A. S. Krogh, *Denmark*

Literature	Peace	
R. F. A. Sully-Prudhomme, *France*	J. H. Dunant, *Switzerland* F. Passy, *France*	1901
M. T. Mommsen *Germany*,	É. Ducommun, *Switzerland* C. A. Gobat, *Switzerland*	1902
B. M. Björnson, *Norway*	W. R. Cremer, *Gt. Britain*	1903
F. Mistral, *France* J. Echegaray, *Spain*	Institut de Droit International	1904
H. Sienkiewicz, *Poland*	Bertha S. F. von Suttner, *Austria*	1905
G. Carducci, *Italy*	T. Roosevelt, *U.S.A.*	1906
R. Kipling, *Gt. Britain*	E. T. Moneta, *Italy* L. Renault, *France*	1907
R. C. Eucken, *Germany*	K. P. Arnoldson, *Sweden* F. Bajer, *Denmark*	1908
Selma O. L. Lagerlöf, *Sweden*	A. M. F. Beernaert, *Belgium* P. H. B. B. d'Estournelles de Constant, *France*	1909
P. J. L. Heyse, *Germany*	Bureau International Permanent de la Paix	1910
M. P. M. B. Maeterlinck, *Belgium*	T. M. C. Asser, *Netherlands* A. H. Fried, *Austria*	1911
G. J. R. Hauptmann, *Germany*	E. Root, *U.S.A.*	1912
R. Tagore, *India*	H. La Fontaine, *Belgium*	1913
No award	No award	1914
R. Rolland, *France*	No award	1915
C. G. V. von Heidenstam, *Sweden*	No award	1916
K. A. Gjellerup, *Denmark* H. Pontoppidan, *Denmark*	Comité International de la Croix-Rouge	1917
No award	No award	1918
C. F. G. Spitteler, *Switzerland*	T. W. Wilson, *U.S.A.*	1919
K. P. Hamsun, *Norway*	L. V. A. Bourgeois, *France*	1920

LIST OF THE NOBEL PRIZE WINNERS [CONT.]

	Physics	*Chemistry*	*Physiology or Medicine*
1921	A. Einstein, *Germany*	F. Soddy, *Gt. Britain*	No award
1922	N. Bohr, *Denmark*	F. W. Aston, *Gt. Britain*	A. V. Hill, *Gt. Britain* O. F. Meyerhof, *Germany*
1923	R. A. Millikan, *U.S.A.*	F. Pregl, *Austria*	F. G. Banting, *Canada* J. J. R. Macleod, *Canada*
1924	K. M. G. Siegbahn, *Sweden*	No award	W. Einthoven, *Netherlands*
1925	J. Franck, *Germany* G. Hertz, *Germany*	R. A. Zsigmondy, *Germany*	No award
1926	J. B. Perrin, *France*	T. Svedberg, *Sweden*	J. A. G. Fibiger, *Denmark*
1927	A. H. Compton, *U.S.A.* C. T. R. Wilson, *Gt. Britain*	H. O. Wieland, *Germany*	J. Wagner-Jauregg, *Austria*
1928	O. W. Richardson, *Gt. Britain*	A. O. R. Windaus, *Germany*	C. J. H. Nicolle, *France*
1929	L.-V. de Broglie, *France*	A. Harden, *Gt. Britain* H. K. A. S. von Euler-Chelpin, *Sweden*	C. Eijkman, *Netherlands* F. G. Hopkins, *Gt. Britain*
1930	C. V. Raman, *India*	H. Fischer, *Germany*	K. Landsteiner, *Austria*
1931	No award	C. Bosch, *Germany* F. Bergius, *Germany*	O. H. Warburg, *Germany*
1932	W. Heisenberg, *Germany*	I. Langmuir, *U.S.A.*	C. S. Sherrington, *Gt. Britain* E. D. Adrian, *Gt. Britain*
1933	E. Schrödinger, *Austria* P. A. M. Dirac, *Gt. Britain*	No award	T. H. Morgan, *U.S.A.*
1934	No award	H. C. Urey, *U.S.A.*	G. H. Whipple, *U.S.A.* G. R. Minot, *U.S.A.* W. P. Murphy, *U.S.A.*
1935	J. Chadwick, *Gt. Britain*	F. Joliot, *France* Irène Joliot-Curie, *France*	H. Spemann, *Germany*
1936	V. F. Hess, *Austria* C. D. Anderson, *U.S.A.*	P. J. W. *Debye, Netherlands*	H. H. Dale, *Gt. Britain* O. Loewi, *Austria*
1937	C. J. Davisson, *U.S.A.* G. P. Thomson, *Gt. Britain*	W. N. Haworth, *Gt. Britain* P. Karrer, *Switzerland*	A. Szent-Györgyi, *Hungary*
1938	E. Fermi, *Italy*	R. Kuhn, *Germany*	C. J. F. Heymans, *Belgium*

Literature	Peace	
A. France, *France*	K. H. Branting, *Sweden* C. L. Lange, *Norway*	1921
J. Benavente, *Spain*	F. Nansen, *Norway*	1922
W. B. Yeats, *Ireland*	No award	1923
W. S. Reymont, *Poland*	No award	1924
G. B. Shaw, *Gt. Britain*	A. J. Chamberlain, *Gr. Britain* C. G. Dawes, *U.S.A.*	1925
Grazia Deledda, *Italy*	A. Briand, *France* G. Stresemann, *Germany*	1926
H. Bergson, *France*	F. Buisson, *France* L. Quidde, *Germany*	1927
Sigrid Undset, *Norway*	No award	1928
T. Mann, *Germany*	F. B. Kellogg, *U.S.A.*	1929
S. Lewis, *U.S.A.*	L. O. J. Söderblom, *Sweden*	1930
E. A. Karlfeldt, *Sweden*	Jane Addams, *U.S.A.* N. M. Butler, *U.S.A.*	1931
J. Galsworthy, *Gt. Britain*	No award	1932
I. A. Bunin, *Russia*	N. Angell, *Gt. Britain*	1933
L. Pirandello, *Italy*	A. Henderson, *Gt. Britain*	1934
No award	C. von Ossietzky, *Germany*	1935
E. G. O'Neill, *U.S.A.*	C. Saavedra Lamas, *Argentine*	1936
R. Martin du Gard, *France*	Viscount Cecil of Chelwood, *Gt. Britain*	1937
Pearl S. Buck, *U.S.A.*	Office International Nansen pour les Réfugiés	1938

LIST OF THE NOBEL PRIZE WINNERS [CONT.]

	Physics	*Chemistry*	*Physiology or Medicine*
1939	E. O. Lawrence, *U.S.A.*	A. F. J. Butenandt, *Germany* L. Ružicka, *Switzerland*	G. Domagk, *Germany*
1940	No award	No award	No award
1941	No award	No award	No award
1942	No award	No award	No award
1943	O. Stern, *U.S.A.*	G. de Hevesy, *Hungary*	H. C. P. Dam, *Denmark* E. A. Doisy, *U.S.A.*
1944	I. I. Rabi, *U.S.A.*	O. Hahn, *Germany*	E. J. Erlanger, *U.S.A.* H. S. Gasser, *U.S.A.*
1945	W. Pauli, *Austria*	A. I. Virtanen, *Finland*	A. Fleming, *Gt. Britain* E. B. Chain, *Gt. Britain* H. W. Florey, *Gt. Britain*
1946	P. W. Bridgman, *U.S.A.*	J. B. Sumner, *U.S.A.* J. H. Northrop, *U.S.A.* W. M. Stanley, *U.S.A.*	H. J. Muller, *U.S.A.*
1947	E. V. Appleton, *Gt. Britain*	R. Robinson, *Gt. Britain*	C. F. Cori, *U.S.A.* Gerty T. Cori, *U.S.A.* B. A. Houssay, *Argentine*
1948	P. M. S. Blackett, *Gt. Britain*	A. W. K. Tiselius, *Sweden*	P. H. Müller, *Switzerland*
1949	H. Yukawa, *Japan*	W. F. Giauque, *U.S.A.*	W. R. Hess, *Switzerland* E. A. Moniz, *Portugal*
1950	C. F. Powell, *Gt. Britain*	O. P. H. Diels, *Germany* K. Alder, *Germany*	E. C. Kendall, *U.S.A.* T. Reichstein, *Switzerland* P. S. Hench, *U.S.A.*
1951	J. D. Cockcroft, *Gt. Britain* E. T. S. Walton, *Ireland*	E. M. McMillan, *U.S.A.* G. T. Seaborg, *U.S.A.*	M. Theiler, *Union of S. Africa*
1952	F. Bloch, *U.S.A.* E. M. Purcell, *U.S.A.*	A. J. P. Martin, *Gt. Britain* R. L. M. Synge, *Gt. Britain*	S. A. Waksman, *U.S.A.*
1953	F. Zernike, *Netherlands*	H. Staudinger, *Germany*	H. A. Krebs, *Gt. Britain* F. A. Lipmann, *U.S.A.*
1954	M. Born, *Gt. Britain* W. Bothe, *Germany*	L. C. Pauling, *U.S.A.*	J. F. Enders, *U.S.A.* T. H. Weller, *U.S.A.* F. C. Robbins, *U.S.A.*
1955	W. E. Lamb, *U.S.A.* P. Kusch, *U.S.A.*	V. du Vigneaud, *U.S.A.*	A. H. T. Theorell, *Sweden*

Literature	Peace	
F. E. Sillanpää, *Finland*	No award	1939
No award	No award	1940
No award	No award	1941
No award	No award	1942
No award	No award	1943
J. V. Jensen, *Denmark*	Comité International de la Croix-Rouge	1944
Gabriela Mistral, *Chile*	C. Hull, *U.S.A.*	1945
H. Hesse, *Switzerland*	Emily G. Balch, *U.S.A.* J. R. Mott, *U.S.A.*	1946
A. P. G. Gide, *France*	The Friends' Service Council The American Friends' Service Committee	1947
T. S. Eliot, *Gt. Britain*	No award	1948
W. Faulkner, *U.S.A.*	Lord Boyd Orr of Brechin, *Gt. Britain*	1949
Earl Russell, *Gt. Britain*	R. Bunche, *U.S.A.*	1950
P. F. Lagerkvist, *Sweden*	L. Jouhaux, *France*	1951
F. Mauriac, *France*	A. Schweitzer, *France*	1952
W. L. S. Churchill, *Gt. Britain*	G. C. Marshall, *U.S.A.*	1953
E. M. Hemingway, *U.S.A.*	Office of the United Nations High Commissioner for Refugees	1954
H. K. Laxness, *Iceland*	No award	1955

LIST OF THE NOBEL PRIZE WINNERS [CONT.]

	Physics	*Chemistry*	*Physiology or Medicine*
1956	W. Shockley, *U.S.A.* J. Bardeen, *U.S.A.* W. H. Brattain, *U.S.A.*	C. N. Hinshelwood, *Gt. Britain* N. N. Semenov, *U.S.S.R.*	A. F. Cournand, *U.S.A* W. Forssmann, *Germany* D. W. Richards, *U.S.A.*
1957	C. N. Yang, *China* T. D. Lee, *China*	A. R. Todd, *Gt. Britain*	D. Bovet, *Italy*
1958	P. A. Čerenkov, *U.S.S.R.* I. M. Frank, *U.S.S.R.* I. J. Tamm, *U.S.S.R.*	F. Sanger, *Gt. Britain*	G. W. Beadle, *U.S.A.* E. L. Tatum, *U.S.A.* J. Lederberg, *U.S.A.*
1959	E. G. Segrè, *U.S.A.* O. Chamberlain, *U.S.A.*	J. Heyrovský, *Czechoslov.*	S. Ochoa, *U.S.A.* A. Kornberg, *U.S.A.*
1960	D. A. Glaser, *U.S.A.*	W. F. Libby, *U.S.A.*	F. M. Burnet, *Australia* P. B. Medawar, *Gt. Britain*
1961	R. Hofstadter, *U.S.A.* R. L. Mössbauer, *Germany*	M. Calvin, *U.S.A.*	G. von Békésy, *U.S.A.*
1962	L. D. Landau, *U.S.S.R.*	M. F. Perutz, *Gt. Britain* J. C. Kendrew, *Gt. Britain*	F. H. C. Crick, *Gt. Britain* J. D. Watson, *U.S.A.* M. H. F. Wilkins, *Gt. Britain*
1963	E. P. Wigner, *U.S.A.* M. Goeppert-Mayer, *U.S.A.* J. H. D. Jensen, *Germany*	K. Ziegler, *Germany* G. Natta, *Italy*	J. C. Eccles, *Australia* A. L. Hodgkin, *Gt. Britain* A. F. Huxley, *Gt. Britain*
1964	C. H. Townes, *U.S.A.* N. G. Basov, *U.S.S.R.* A. M. Prochorov, *U.S.S.R.*	H. Crowfoot, *Gt. Britain*	K. Bloch, *U.S.A.* F. Lynen, *Germany*
1965	S.-I. Tomonaga, *Japan* J. Schwinger, *U.S.A.* R. P. Feymnan, *U.S.A.*	R. B. Woodward, *U.S.A.*	F. Jacob, *France* A. Lwoff, *France* J. Monod, *France*
1966	A. Kastler, *France*	R. S. Mulliken, *U.S.A.*	P. Rous, *U.S.A.* C. B. Huggins, *U.S.A.*
1967	H. A. Bethe, *U.S.A.*	M. Eigen, *Germany* R. G. W. Norrish, *Gt. Britain* G. Porter, *Gt. Britain*	R. Granit, *Sweden* H. K. Hartline, *U.S.A.* G. Wald, *U.S.A.*
1968	L. W. Alvarez, *U.S.A.*	L. Onsager, *U.S.A.*	R. W. Holley, *U.S.A.* H. G. Khorana, *U.S.A.* M. W. Nirenberg, *U.S.A.*
1969	M. Gell-Mann, *U.S.A.*	D. H. R. Barton, *Gt. Britain* O. Hassel, *Norway*	M. Delbrück, *U.S.A.* A. D. Hershey, *U.S.A.* S. E. Luria, *U.S.A.*
1970	H. Alfvén, *Sweden* L. Néel, *France*	L. F. Leloir, *Argentina*	B. Katz, *Gt. Britain* U. von Euler, *Sweden* J. Axelrod, *U.S.A.*

Literature	Peace	
J. R. Jiménez, *Spain*	No award	1956
A. Camus, *France*	L. B. Pearson, *Canada*	1957
B. L. Pasternak, *U.S.S.R.*	G. Pire, *Belgium*	1958
S. Quasimodo, *Italy*	P. J. Noel-Baker, *Gt. Britain*	1959
Saint-John Perse, *France*	A. J. Lutuli, *Union of S. Africa*	1960
I. Andrić, *Yougoslavia*	D. Hammarskjöld, *Sweden*	1961
J. Steinbeck, *U.S.A.*	L. C. Pauling, *U.S.A.*	1962
G. Seferis, *Greece*	International Committee of the Red Cross League of Red Cross Societies	1963
J.-P. Sartre, *France*	M. L. King, *U.S.A.*	1964
M. A. Solochov, *U.S.S.R.*	United Nations Children's Fund	1965
S. Y. Agnon, *Israel* N. Sachs, *Germany*	No award	1966
M. A. Asturias, *Guatemala*	No award	1967
Y. Kawabata, *Japan*	R. Cassin, *France*	1968
S. Beckett, *Ireland*	International Labour Organization	1969
A. Solzhenitsyn, *U.S.S.R.*	N. Borlaug, *U.S.A.*	1970

TABLE II

SHOWING THE DISTRIBUTION OF PRIZES BETWEEN DIFFERENT NATIONALITIES

Nationality	*Phys.*	*Chem.*	*Med.*	*Lit.*	*Peace*	*Total*
The Argentine	—	1	1	—	1	3
Australia	—	—	2	—	—	2
Austria	3	1	3	—	2	9
Belgium	—	—	2	1	3	6
Canada	—	—	2	—	1	3
Chile	—	—	—	1	—	1
China	2	—	—	—	—	2
Czechoslovakia	—	1	—	—	—	1
Denmark	1	—	4	3	1	9
Finland	—	1	—	1	—	2
France	9[1]	6[1]	6	11	9	41
Germany	14	22	10	6[2]	3	55
Gt. Britain	15	18	16	6	7	62
Greece	—	—	—	1	—	1
Guatemala	—	—	—	1	—	1
Hungary	—	1	2[3]	—	—	3
Iceland	—	—	—	1	—	1
India	1	—	—	1	—	2
Ireland	1	—	—	2	—	3
Israel	—	—	—	1	—	1
Italy	2	1	2	4	1	10
Japan	2	—	—	1	—	3
The Netherlands	5	2	2	—	1	10
Norway	—	1	—	3	2	6
Poland	—	—	—	2	—	2
Portugal	—	—	1	—	—	1
Russia [later U.S.S.R.]	6	1	2	4[4]	—	13
Spain	—	—	1	3	—	4
Sweden	3	4	4	4	4	19
Switzerland	—	3	4	2	3	12
Union of S. Africa	—	—	1[5]	—	1	2
U.S.A.	28	16	39	6	15	104
Yugoslavia	—	—	—	1	—	1
Institutions	—	—	—	—	10[6]	10
						405

[1] Marie Curie is then being counted twice, as she received half of the Physics Prize jointly with her husband Pierre Curie in 1903 and, later, the whole Chemistry Prize in 1911. [2] One of them Sachs, born in Germany and writing in German although domiciled in Sweden. [3] One of them Bárány, b. in Vienna, of Hungarian family. [4] One of them, Bunin, born a Russian. [5] Theiler, citizen both of Switzerland [whence his family originated] and of South Africa; scientific work achieved in the U.S.A. [6] The International Committee of the Red Cross is counted as one institution, although it has received a prize three times once in 1917 and again in 1944 and in 1963.

INDEX

Page numbers in italics indicate that the passage referring to the work for which the prizes were awarded appear on that page.

Abbe, E., 441
Abel, F., 23, 24
Abel, J.J., 225
Abelson, P.H., 322
Abernathy, R., 594
Acheson, E.G., 304
Addams, Jane, 489, 535, *551*, *552*, 553, 554, 607
Addison, T., 226, 227
Adrian, E.D., *247*, 253, *254*, 255, 263
Agnon, S., *132*
Agramonte, A., 179
Åkerman, A.R., 71
Alder, K., 351, *352*
Alexander II, 491
Alfvén, H.G., *419*
Almquist, E., 71
Almquist, H.J., 231
Alvarez, L.W., 462, *463*, 464
Ampère, A.M., 392
Andersag, H., 369
Andersen, V., 104
Anderson, C.D., 317, 449, 454, *455*, 460, 471
Andreé, S.A., 34, 36
Andrewes, C.H., 178
Andrić, I., 127, *128*
Angell, N., 555, 556, 557
Ångström, A.J., 392
Appleton, E.V., *416*
Arnoldson, K.P., 490, *502*, 503, 504, 530
Arrhenius, S., 62, 169, 288, 289, 290, 291, 292, 293, 294, 295, 306, 341, 345, 397, 479
Arthus, M., 176
Aschan, O., 356
Asquith, H.H., 526
Asser, T., 507, 504, *511*
Aston, F.W., *311*, 312, 313, 314, 315
Asturias, M.A., 132, *135*
Atkinson, 467
Attlee, Cl., 586
Aurivillius, C., 71
Avery, O.T., 199, 201
Avogadro, A., 285, 290
Axelrod, J., 250, *251*, 259

Bach, J.S., 596
Bäckström, H., 479
Bacq, Z.M., 250
Baeyer, A.J.F.W. von, 288, 289, *295*, 297, 298, 355, 356, 362
Bailey, T., 526
Bajer, F., 490, 502, 503, 504, 505
Bakhuis Roozeboom, H.W., 286
Balch, Emily G., 489, 551, 552, *553*, 554, 555
Baldwin, S., 538, 561
Balmer, J.J., 392
Balzan, E., 615
Bang, O., 178, 189
Banga, I., 212
Banting, F.G., 224, *225*
Bárány, R., *268*, 269
Barbe, P., 21, 22
Bardeen, J., *417*
Barger, G., 224, 250
Barkla, C.G., 435, 436
Barlow, T., 230
Barthou, P., 559
Barton, D.H.R., 354, *355*
Basov, N.G., 418, *419*
Bastianelli, G., 162
Bataillon, O., 195
Battelli, F., 211
Bauer, J.H., 179
Bayliss, W.M., 223
Beadle, G.W., *198*, 199
Becker, H., 457
Beckett, G.H., 30
Beckett, S., *134*
Becquerel, A.H., 305, 396, 398, 399, *400*
Becquerel, E., 305, 398, *400*

INDEX

Becquerel, H., 398
Beernaert, A., 507, *510*, 511
Behring, E. von, 159, *160*, 168, 175
Beijerinck, M., 177
Békésy, G. von, 267, *268*
Bell, C., 247
Bell, J., 247
Bémont, G., 399
Benavente, J., 88, *107*
Beneš, E., 540, 541, 561
Bergius, F., 277, 329, *330*
Bergman, T., 480
Bergson, H., *110, 136*
Bernadotte, F., 575
Bernal, J.D., 380
Berner, C., 71
Bernhard, C.G., IX, 139
Bernstein, J., 253, 256
Bertheim, A., 182
Berthelot, M., 287-, 289
Berthelot, P., 91
Berzelius, J.J., 294, 312, 331, 355, 359, 373
Best, C.H., 224, 225
Bethe, H.A., 453, *466, 467*
Bethmann-Hollweg, T. von, 524
Bey, A., 485
Bhabba, H.J., 460
Biasotti, A., 226
Bignami, A., 162
Bijvoet, M., 382
Bildt, C., 96
Billing, G., 87, 94
Billingham, R.E., 175
Biot, J.B., 392
Birge, R.T., 313, 315
Bishop, K.S., 231
Björnson, B.M., 487
Blackett, P.M.S., 316, *455*, 471
Blaine, J.G., 517
Blehr, O.A., 68, 71
Bloch, F., *451*
Bloch, K., *217*
Bodenstein, M., 341, 342
Bohr, N., 321, 323, 339, 430,*431*
Boll, F., 265
Boltzmann, L., 427
Bõõk, F., 113
Borah, W.E., 545, 546
Bordet, J., 171, *172*
Borlaug, N.E., 596, 604, 605
Born, M., *448*
Bosch, C., 328, 329, *330*
Boström, C.J., 97
Boström, E.G., 72
Bothe, W., 457, *470*
Bouckaert, J.P., 242
Bourgeois, L.V.A., 523, *528*, 529, 530, 540
Bourget, P., 96
Bouté, Dr., 21
Bovery, T., 191
Bovet, D., 183, 260, *261*
Boyd Orr of Brechin, Lord, 574, *579*, 580, 581, 584
Bragg, W.H., 434, 435, 436
Bragg, W.L., 201, 380, *434*, 435, 436
Brandes, G., 96, 105
Branly É., 413
Branting, H., 43, 85, 523, 530, 531, 532, 533, 607
Brattain, W.H., *417*
Braun, C.F., 253, 396, *413, 414*
Breit, G., 416
Brent, L., 175
Briand, A., 535, 537, 539, 540, 544, 545
Bridges, C.B., 192, 194
Bridgman, P.W., *426*
Bright, J., 492, 495
Brisson, A., 47
Brock, L.G., 257
Brogger, W.C., 45
Broglie, L.V. de, 338, 444, 445, 446
Broglie, M. de, 436
Bronk, D., 254
Brossel, J., 418
Brown, R., 331, 332, 425
Bruce, D., 168
Brüning, H., 537
Buchanan, W., 518
Buchner, E., 373, *374*
Buck, Pearl, 115
Buckle, H.T., 498
Bugie, E., 185
Buisson, F., 535, *541*, 542
Bunche, R., 574, 575
Bunin, I.A., *113*
Bunsen, R.W., 391
Burckhardt, J., 105
Burke, E., 122
Burnet, F.M., 174, 175, 178, 206
Burr, G.O., 231

Butenandt, A.F.J., *357*, *369*, 370
Butler, N.M., 535, *544*, 545

Cajal, see, Ramón y Cajal
Calmette, A., 168, 176
Calvin, M., 362, 363, *364*
Campbell, W.W., 396
Camus, A., *125*
Cannizzaro, S., 285, 286, 301, 302
Cannon, W.B., 249, 250
Carducci, G., *96*
Carnegie, A., 513, 544
Carnot, N.L.S., 390
Carrel, A., 240, *241*
Carroll, J., 179
Caspersson, T., 200, 275, 276
Cassin, R., 589, *594*, 595
Castellani, A., 163
Cavendish, H., 299, 300, 316, 400
Cecil, R., Lord, 523, 527, 528, 529, 532, 555, 562, 585, 535, 558, *559*, 560, 561, 567 foot-note
Cederblom, J.E., 71
Čerenkov, P.A., 469, 470, *471*
Chadwick, J., 313, 457, *458*, 459
Chagall, M., 132
Chain, E.B., 184, *185*
Chamberlain, A.J., 535, 538, 540
Chamberlain, O., 462
Chargaff, E., 201, 202
Chase, M., 201, 208
Chauveau, A., 237
Chekhov, A.P., 113
Chevreul, M.E., 216
Chiang Kai Shek 573
Chilton, L.V., 460
Christian, W., 210, 368, 369
Christiansen, J.A., 341
Chrusjtjev, N., *see* Khrushchev
Churchill, W.L.S., *121*, 122, 572, 584
Cierer, A., 201
Clausewitz, C. von, 545
Clemenceau, G., 526, 530
Cleve, P.T., 292, 293
Cleveland, G., 496
Cobden, R., 492, 571
Cockcroft, J.D., 468, *469*
Cohen, S.S., 206
Colding, L.A., 390
Cole, K.C., 256
Collip J.B., 225
Compton, A.H., *438*, 470
Constant, P., 507, *512*, 513
Coombs, J.S., 257
Cori, C.F., 221, 222, 226, 278
Cori, Gerty T., 221, *222*, *226*, 378
Cornforth, J.W., 217
Correns, K., 191
Coulet, P., 45, 46, 48, 53, 54, 58, 59
Cournand, A.F., 238, *239*
Cremer, W.R., 490, *493*, 494, 495, 504
Crick, J.F.C., 201, 202, 204, 208, 380
Crookes, W., 300, 394, 403
Crowfoot-Hodgkin, Dorothy, 233, 372, 381, 382, *383*
Cuno, W., 537
Curie, Marie, 305, 306, 307, 397, 399, *400*, 401
Curie, P., 278, 305, 306, 397, 399, *400*, 401, 474
Cushing, H.W., 262

D'Abernon, Lord, 541
Daguerre, L.J.M., 391
Dahmen, F., 177
Dale, H.H., 248, *249*, 250, 258
Dalén, N.G., *441*
Dam, H.G.P., 231, *232*
Darwin, C., 498
Dautrebande, L., 242
Davis, M., 229
Davisson, C.J., 277, 445, *446*
Dawes, C.G., *535*, 536, 537
Debierne, A., 306, 307
Debye, P.J.W., *337*
Decastello, A. von, 173
de Laval, G.P., 33
Delbrück, M., 206, 207, *208*
Delcassé, T., 516
Deledda, Grazia, 109
Dennett, T., 516 foot-note
Denny-Brown, D., 246
Dewar, J., 23, 24, 423
D'Herelle, F., 206
Dickinson, W.L., 248
Diels, O., 351, *352*
Dirac, P.A.M., *448*, 449, 452, 453, 454, 462
Disraeli, B., 122
Doisy, E.A., 231, *232*, 369
Domagk, G., 156, *157*, 158, *183*, 184, 186

Doppler, C., 408, 472
Drachmann, H., 96
Dreiser, T., 112
Dreyfus, A., 542
Drude, P., 411
Du Bois Reymond, E., 253, 256
Ducommun, É., 490, *505*, 506
Due, F.G.K., 45
Dulong, P.L., 285
Dunant, J.H., *490*, 491, 492, 504, 520, 607
Dungern, E. von, 173
Durham, E., 171

Eccles, J.C., 246, 257, *258*
Echegaray, J., 88, *95*
Edward VII, 513
Ehrenborg, S., 31
Ehrenheim, P.J. von, 71
Ehrlich, P., 166, 168, 169, *170*, 172, 173, 181, 182, 183
Eigen, M., 343, *344*
Eijkman, C., 228, *229*, 230
Einbeck, H., 211
Einstein, A., 331, 409, 410, 417, 425, 429, *428*, 456, 588
Einthoven, W., 236, *237*
Eliot, T.S., *119*, 136
Ellermann, V., 178, 189
Elliott, T.R., 248
Ellis, E., 207
Embden, G., 219, 220, 221
Emmerling, A., 297
Enders, J.F., 180, *181*
Engelhardt, W.A., 221
Ericsson, J., 33
Erlanger, J., 254, 255, *256*
Ernst, P., 113
d'Estournelles de Constant, P., 507, *512*, 513, 517
Eucken, R.C., 88, *97*, 103
Euler-Chelpin, H. von, 367, 375, *376*
Euler-Chelpen, U.S. von, 242, 250, *251*, 259
Evans, G.H., 163
Evans, H.M. 228, 231
Ewald, P.P., 433

Faguet, E., 101
Fajans, K., 311
Faraday, M., 331, 392, 394, 403, 423
Faulkner, W., *119*, 120
Feldberg, W., 249
Feldman, W.H., 185
Fenner, F., 174
Fermat, P., 445
Fermi, E., 318, *465*
Ferrero, G., 108
Feynman, R.P., *453*
Fibiger, J.A.G., *188*, 189
Fick, A., 237
Fieser, L.F., 231
Finlay, C.J., 178
Finsen, N.R., 160, 186, *187*
Fischer, E.H., 288, 289, 295, *296*, 297, 355, 366, 378
Fischer, H., *360*, 361, 364
Fleming, A., 184, *185*
Fletcher, W.M., 218
Florey, H.W., 184, *185*
Foerster, F.W., 543
Fogazzarro, A., 96
Folkers, K.A., 217, 233
Ford, H., 554
Forssell, H., 56, 57, 58, 71, 80
Forssmann, W., 238, *239*
Fourneau, E., 260
Fox, G., 549
Fraenkel-Conrat, H., 201
France, A., 105, *106*, 136
Franck, J., 429, *430*
Frank, I.M., 469, 470, *471*
Frankland, E., 300
Fraunhofer, J., 391
Fredericia, L.S., 265
Fresnel, A.J., 391
Freud, S., 114
Freycinet, C. de, 21
Fried, A., 490, *501*, 502
Friedrich, W., 433, 435, 446
Friedrich Wilhelm IV,542
Frisch, O.R., 321
Fritsch, G., 252
Fröding, G., 99
Frólich, T., 230
Frosch, P., 177
Fujimaki, A.Y., 188
Fulton, J.F., 262

Gaddum, J.H., 249
Gadolin, J., 323
Galdôs, P., 88, 103

Galsworthy, J., 83, 105, *113*
Galvani, L., 253
Gandhi, M.K., 606
Garibaldi, G., 495, 496, 497
Gasser, H.S., 254, *256*
Gaulle, C. de, 594
Gell-Mann, M., 462, 463, *464*
Gengou, O., 171, 172
Gerard, R., 256
Gerlach, H. von, 543
Gerlach, W., 450
Getz, B., 71
Giauque, W.F., 313, 325, *326*, 336
Gibbon, E., 93
Gibbs, J.W., 286, 287, 324, 326, 335, 389
Gibson, G.E., 325
Gide, A.P.G., 118, *119*, 136
Giesel, F., 308
Gjellerup, K.A., *104*
Glaser, D.A., 462, 463, 471, *472*
Gobat, C.A., 490, *506*
Goblet, R., 496
Goeppert-Mayer, Maria, 465, *466*
Goethe, J.W. von, 99
Goldberger, J., 230
Goldstein, E., 403
Golgi, C., 161, 243, 244, *245*
Goncharov, I.A., 113
Goodwin, T.W., 265
Gorgas, W.C., 179
Gorki, M., 110, 534
Gōzsy, B., 213
Granit, R., *265*, 266, 275
Granny, Mrs., 77
Grassi, G.B., 162
Grey, E., 524, 527
Grieg, N., 607
Grignard, V., 349, *351*, 358
Grijns, G., 229
Gruber, M., 171
Guérin, C., 168
Guillaume, C.É., 441, *442*
Guldberg, C., 290
Gullberg, H., 117
Gullstrand, A., 264, 265
Gustav III, 80

Haber, F., 328, *329*
Haffkine, W., 161
Hagedorn, H.C., 225
Hagelin, E., 59
Hahn, O., 310, 321, *322*
Haile Selassie I, 615
Haldane, J.S., 209, 241
Haller, A., 356
Hallström, P., 85, 105, 107, 108, 109, 112
Halpern, B., 260
Hamilton, H., 36
Hamilton, M.A., 559 foot-note
Hamilton, W.R., 389
Hammarskjöld, D., 574, *577*, 578, 579, 615
Hammarskjöld, H., 578
Hammarsten, O., 346
Hampson, W., 423
Hamsun, K.P., 83, *105*, 108, 136
Hansemann, D. von, 160
Hansen, A., 168
Hanson, J., 221
Harden, A., 374, 375, *376*
Hardy, T., 90, 107, 108
Harington, C.R., 224
Harley, 300
Harnack, A., 97
Harrar, J.G., 605
Harrison, R.G., 197
Hartline, K., *265*, 266, 267
Hartman, F.A., 226
Hassel, O., 354, 355
Hasselberg, B., 67
Hata, S., 170
Hauptmann, G.J.R., *100*, 103, 136
Haworth, W.N., *366*, 367
Haxel, O., 466
Hay, J., 516, 518
Haeviside, O., 415, 416
Hedin, S., 565
Heidenstam, C.G.V. von, 101, *104*
Heisenberg, W., 447, *448*, 453
Heitler, W., 339
Helmholtz, H. von, 253, 264, 266, 268, 389, 467
Hemingway, E., *123*, 128
Hench, P.S., 227, *228*
Henderson, A., 555, 558, 586
Henderson, Y., 241
Herriot, É., 538
Hermann, L., 253
Hershey, A.D., 201, 206, 207, *208*
Hertz, G., 429, *430*

Hertz, H., 393, 403, 412, 414
Hess, A.F., 230
Hess, V., 454, 456
Hess, W.R., 251, 252
Hesse, H., *117*, *118*, 136
Heumann, K., 297
Heuven Goedhart, G.J., van, 599
Hevesy, G. de, 315, *316*, 318, 362, 370, 469
Heymans, C.J.F., 241, *242*
Heyrovský, J., 347, 348, *349*
Heyse, P.J.L., 98, *99*
Hill, A.V., *218*
Hillarp, N.A., 250
Hinshaw, H.C., 185
Hinshelwood, C.N., *341*, 342
Hirst, E.L., 367
Hirst, G.K., 178
Hirszfeld, L., 173
Hitler, A., 153, 157, 158, 284, 559, 561, 563, 571, 565, 586
Hittorf, J.W., 394
Hitzig, R.E., 252
Hjärne, H., 96, 97, 100, 101, 102, 103, 105, 107
Hoagland, M., 205
Hodgkin, A.L., 256, 257, *258*
Hodgkin, D., 233, 372, 381, 382, *383*
Hoffmann, E., 168, 182
Hoffmann, E.T.A., 118
Hofstadter, R., 462, *463*
Hofsten, S. von, 141
Holley, R., 205, *206*
Holm, E., 265
Holmberg, B., 480
Holst, A., 230
Hoover, H., 534
Hopkins, F.G., 218, *229*
Horsley, V., 261
Horst, H.J., 71
Houssay, B.A., *226*
Hubbard, R., 265
Hudson, N.P., 179
Hückel, E., 336
Hughes, C.E., 526, 536, 535
Huggins, C.B., *190*
Hugo, V., 491
Huldschinsky, K., 230, 231
Hull, C., 569, 570, 571
Hume, D., 120
Hund, F., 340
Hunt, R., 261
Huxley, A.F., 221, 256, 257, 258
Huxley, H.E., 221
Hvass, L., 31, 49

Ibsen, H., 90, 94
Ichikawa, K., 189
Irvine, J., 367
Ising, G., 468

Jacob, B., 562
Jacob, F., *203*, *204*
Janssen, P.J.C., 300
Jensen, H.D., 465, *466*
Jensen, J.V., 116, *117*
Jimenez, J.R., *124*
Johannsen, W., 191
Johansson, J.E., 141, 142, 247
Johnson, L.B., 594
Johnson, W.A., 214
Johnston, H.L., 313
Joliot, F., 317, *318*, 321, 464
Joliot-Curie, Irène, 317, *318*, 321, 457, 464
Jordan, P., 448
Jouhaux, L., 574, 580, 582, 583
Joule, J.P., 390, 423

Kalckar, H.M., 222
Kamerlingh-Onnes, H., *423*, 424
Kapitza, P., 424
Karlfeldt, E.A., 107, *112*, *113*
Karrer, P., 231, *366*, 367, 368
Kasavubu, J., *579*
Kastler, A., *418*, 419
Katz, B., *251*, 256, 258, 259
Kawabata, Y., *133*, 134
Kay, E.E., 23
Kayser, H., 392
Keilin, D., 210
Kekulé, F.A., 298
Kellogg, F.B., 535, 544, 545, 546, 566
Kelvin, Lord, 390, 396, 423, 467
Kendal, E.C., 224, 227, *228*
Kendall, J., 479
Kendrew, J.C., *380*, 381
Kennedy, J.F., 594
Kennelly, A.F., 415, 416
Kerr, J., 407
Key, A., 56, 57
Keynes, J.M., 537, 557

Keynes, R.D., 256
Khorana, H.G., 205, 206
Khrushchev, N.S., 579
Kilbourne, F.L., 163
King, Coretta, 594
King, H., 216, 261
King, M.L., 589, *592*, 593, 594
Kinsky, Bertha, von Chinic und Tettau 25, 26, 27, 498
Kipling, R., 86, 96, *97*, 103, 136
Kirchhoff, G., 391
Kitasato, S., 160
Klarer, J., 183
Klein, O., 479
Knipping, P., 433, 434, 446
Knoop, F., 214
Koch, R., 166, 167, *168*, 187
Kocher, E.T., *223*, 224
Koht, H., 564
Kolle, W., 161
Komppa, G., 356
Kornberg, A., 202, 203
Kossel, A., 199, *200*
Kramers, H.A., 341
Krebs, H.A., 214, 215, 230
Kreiser, W., 563
Krishnan, K.S., 440
Krogh, S.A.S., 239, *240*
Kuhn, R., 368, *369*
Kühne, W., 265
Kusch, P., 451, *452*

Labitte, M., 45
La Fontaine, H., 488, 507, *511*, 512
Lagerkvist, P., 120, *121*
Lagerlöf, Selma O.L., 88, 96, 97, *98*
Lagrange, J.L., 389
Laidlaw, P.P., 178
Lamartine, A. de, 95
Lamas, S., *566*, 567
Lamb, W.E., *452*, 467
Lamm, P., 47
Landau, L.D., 424, *425*
Landsteiner, K., 173, 174
Lange, C.L., 519, *521*, 522, 523
Langerhans, P., 224
Langley, J.N., 248
Langmuir, I., 277, *335*
Languevin, P., 474
Lapicque, L., 255
Laqueur, F., 370
Larmor, J., 407
Laue, M. von, 284, 432, *433*, 434
Läuger, P., 164
Laveran, A., 161, 162, *164*
Lawrence, E.O., 322, 363, 463, 468, *469*
Laxness, H.K., 123, *124*
Lazear, J., 179
Le Bel, 353, 355
Lederberg, J., 198, *199*
Lee, T.D., *461*, 466
Léger, A., see Perse, St.-J.
Lehmann, J., 186
Leloir, L.F., 222, *377*, 378
Leman, P., 58
Lenard, P.E.A. von, 253, 394, 404
Lennmalm, F., 274
Leopold II, 511
Levaditi, C., 182
Levene, P.A., *200*
Levertin, O., 85
Levine, P., 174
Levinson, S.O., 545
Lewis, G.N., 286, 314, 325, 339, 345
Lewis, S., *111*, 112, 128
Lewis, T., 237
Li, C.H., 228
Libby, W.F., 319, *320*, 363
Liddell, E.G.T., 246
Lie. T., 578
Liebig, J. von, 362, 373
Liebknecht, K., 519
Liebman, P.A., 266
Liedbeck, A., 8, 9
Liljestrand, G., IX, 229
Lilljeqvist, R., 38, 39, 40, 41, 43, 45, 48, 50, 58, 59
Lincoln, A., 552
Lindboe, J., 68
Linde, K. von, 423
Lindhagen, C., 41, 43, 45, 46, 47, 48, 49, 55, 56, 58, 59, 60, 61, 62, 65, 67, 68, 535, 606
Ling, G., 256
Lipmann, F.A., 215, *216*
Lippmann, G., 396, 442
Lister, J., 166
Ljubimova, M.N., 221
Lloyd, D.P.C., 257
Lloyd George, D., 526, 527, 544, 558, 587
Locke, J., 120

Lockyer, N., 300
Lodge, H.C., 526
Loeb, J., 194, 195
Löffler, F.A., 159, 168, 177
Löwenstein, C.E., 169
Loewi, O., 248, *249*
Logan, Caldvel, 536
London, F., 339
Lope de Vega, 107
Lorente de Nó, 257
Lorentz, H.A., 397, *407*, 411, 432
Lumumba, P., 579
Lundegård, A., 85
Lundsgaard, E., 220
Luria, S.E., 206, 207, *208*
Luther, H., 537
Lutuli, A.J., 589, *590*, 591, 592
Lwoff, A., *203*, *204*, 206
Lynen, F., 214, 215, *217*

MacCarthy, M., 201
McCollum, E.V., 229, 230
MacDonald, R., 519, 535, 558, 606
Machado, A.L., 215
McKinley, W., 496,515
MacLeod, C.M., 201
Macleod, J.J.R., 224, *225*
McMillan, E.M., 322, *323*
MacMunn, C.A., 209, 210
MacNichol, E., 266
Madsen, T., 169
Maeterlinck, M.P.M.B., *99*, *100*, 103, 136
Mallet, L., 470
Malmström, C.G., 80
Mann, T., 83, *111*, 136
Manson, P., 162
Marconi, G., 253, 396, 397, 413, *414*
Marey, E., 237
Marie, P., 226
Marlborough, Duke of, 122
Marshall, G., *572*, 573, 574, 583
Martin, A.J.P., 201, *334*, 335, 362
Martin du Gard, R., 83, 114, *115*
Martius, C., 214
Marx, K., 495
Marx, W., 543
Matteucci, C., 256
Matthei, J.H., 205
Maupertuis, P.L.M., 445
Mauriac, F., *121*, 122
Maxwell, J.C., 392, 411, 432, 472
Mayer, R., 390
Mazzini, G., 497
Medawar, P.B., *175*
Meitner, Lise, 321
Melander, Lars, Dr., 480
Mellanby, E., 229, 230
Mendel, J.G., 173, 191, 192
Mendeleev, D., 301, 302, 303
Menzel, R.E., 313, 315
Mering, J. von, 224
Metchnikoff, E.J.J., *170*
Meyer, E. 108
Meyer, L., 291, 301, 302
Meyer, S., 400
Meyerhof, O.F., *219*, 220
Michelson, A.A., 409, *410*
Mietzsch, F., 183
Millikan, R.A., 406, 429, 455
Minkowski, O., 224
Minot, G.R., *233*
Mischer, F., 199, 200
Mistral, F., 87, *95*
Mistral, Gabriela, *117*
Moe, R., 485 foot-note
Mörike, E., 118
Mörner, K.A.H., 57, 61, 71
Mössbauer, R.L., *473*
Moissan, H., 288, 289, 302, *303*, 304, 305
Moltke, H., von 65
Mommsen, M.T., 83, 86, 87, *93*
Moneta, E.T., 490, *496*, 497, 512
Moniz, E.A., *261*, 262
Monod, J., *203*, *204*
Moore, T.S., 100
Morel, E.D., 519
Morgan, T.H., 192, *193*, 194
Morgenroth, J., 172, 173
Morley, E.W., 409
Morley, J., 96, 122
Morton, R.A., 265
Moseley, H.G.J., 436, 437
Mott, J.R., 489, 547, 549
Mowinckel, J.L., 564
Müller, E., 274
Müller, P.H., 164, 165
Muller, H.J., 192, 193, *194*
Mulliken, R.S., 339, *340*
Murphy, W.P., *233*
Mussolini, B., 565

Myrbäck, K., 375

Nachmansohn, D., 215
Nambu, Y., 463
Nansen, F., 523, *532*, 533, 534, 535, 541, 567, 568, 586, 607
Napoleon III, 583
Nasser, G.A., 577
Nátta, G., *358*, 359
Naumann, F., 539
Navratil, E., 249
Neddermeyer, S.H., 460
Neél, L., *474*
Neéman, Y., 463
Nencki, M., 142
Nernst, W.H., 324, *325*, 328
Newton, I., 411, 601
Nicolas II, 498
Nicolle, C.J.H., *164*
Nielsen, S., 45
Nilson, L.F., 61, 67
Nilsson, R., 375
Nirenberg, M., 205, *206*
Nishijima, K., 463
Nitti, J., 183
Nobel, Alfred B., 3–11, 17–50, 52–55, 59–62, 64, 66, 72, 75–85, 88, 94, 102, 106, 110, 120, 124, 137, 141–146, 151, 156, 160, 224, 276, 277, 278, 281, 323, 385, 485–487, 497, 611, 612–614, 615
Nobel, Andriette, 8, 24, 134
Nobel, Emanuel, 22, 32, 37, 38, 39, 40, 47, 61, 62, 63, 64, 65, 66, 68, 69
Nobel, Emil, 6, 20
Nobel, Hjalmar, 27, 32, 37, 38, 48, 51, 52, 53, 59
Nobel, Immanuel, 4, 5, 6, 39
Nobel, Ingeborg, see Ridderstolpe
Nobel, Ludvig jr., 27, 28, 32, 48, 51, 52, 59
Nobel, Ludvig sr., 5, 19, 20, 24, 33, 37, 64
Nobel, Pauline, 59
Nobel, Robert, 5, 27, 37, 48, 49, 51, 59, 64, 67
Nobelius, P.O., 3
Noel-Baker, P.J., *585*, 586, 587
Nordenfelt, T., 31
Nordenskiöld, A.E., 36, 396
Nordling, G., 45, 46, 47, 48, 51, 52, 54, 55
Norrish, R.G.W., 343, *344*
Norström, V., 97
Northorp, J.H., *178*, 212, 376, *377*
Nyblom, C.R., 82

Occhialini, G.P.S., 455, 460
Ochoa, S., 202, *203*, 214
Odhner, C. Th., 83
Öholm, W., 479
Örsted, H.C., 392
Österling, A., IX, 73
Ohm, G.S., 402
Olitzky, P.K., 180
Olszewski, K.S., 423
O'Neill, E.G., *114*, 136
Onsager, L., 326, 327
Orzesko, Eliza, 88, 96
Oscar II, 36, 37, 50, 65, 97
Oseen, C.W., 479, 480
Ossietzky, C. von, 544, 555, *562*, 563, 564, 565, 566, 607
Ostwald, W., 256, 277, 288, 290, 292, *294*, 295, 331, *341*
Overton, E., 256

Painlevé, P., 538
Pallavicino, G., 495
Palmaer, W., 480
Palamas, C., 110, 129
Palmerston, Lord, 494
Paracelsus, P.T.B., 331
Parrot, J.C., 260
Paschen, E., 177
Passy, F., *490*, 492, 493, 494, 495, 501, 506
Pasternak, B., 125, *126*
Pasteur, L., 160, 166, 170
Pauli, W., 449, *450*, 459
Pauling, Ava Helen, 588, 589
Pauling, L.C., 202, 338, 339, 381, 585, *587*, 588
Pavlov, I.P., 142, 160, 234, 235
Payr, E., 240
Pearson, L.B., 574, *576*, 577, 580
Pedro of Brazil, 7
Peltier, J.C.A., 327
Perrin, J.B., 330, 425, *426*
Perse, St.-J., *126*, 127
Perutz, M.F., *380*, 381
Petit, A.T., 285
Pettersson, O., 61, 62, 290, 292

INDEX

Pfeiffer, R., 161, 171
Pfiffner, J.J., 226
Philipp, M.A., 7, 59
Phillimore, Lord, 527
Pirandello, L., *113*, 114, 136
Pire, G., 596, *599*, 600
Pirquet, C. von, 177
Planck, M.K.E.L., 324, 325, 408, *428*, 429, 430, 438, 443, 444, 445, 446, 447
Plücker, J., 403
Poincaré, H., 398
Polley, H.F., 227
Pontoppidan, H., *104*
Popjak, G., 217
Popov, A.S., 413
Porter, G., 343, *344*
Powell, C.F., 460, *471*
Pregl, F., *346*, 347
Priestley, J.G., 241
Prochorov, A.M., *418*
Prout, W., 312, 313, 421
Purcell, E.M., 451, *452*
Purdie, T., 367

Quasimodo, S., *126*
Quiddle, L., 535, *541*, 542, 543, 562

Rabi, I.I., *451*
Raman, C.V., 440
Ramon y Cajal, S., 169, *245*
Ramsay, W., 288, 289, 299, 301, 422
Ranges, 238
Raoult, F.M., 290
Rayleigh, Lord, 288, 299, 301, 421, 428, 440
Reed, W., 179
Regnault, H.V., 421
Reichstein, T., 227, *228*, 367
Renault, L., 507, *509*, 510
Renshaw, B., 257
Retzius, M.G., 56, 268
Reverdin, J.L., 223
Reymont, W.S., 83, *108*
Richards, D.W., 238, *239*
Richards, T.W., *344*, 346
Richardson, O.W., *411*
Richet, C.R., *176*
Ridderstolpe, C.G., 51, 52, 59
Ridderstolpe, Ingeborg, born Nobel, 51, 59
Riecke, E., 411
Riesenfeld, E.H., 479
Righi, A., 413
Rilke, R.M., 90
Robbins, F.C., 180, *181*
Robert, A.E., 182
Robinson, R., 217, *361*, 362, 375
Röntgen, W.C., 394, *395*, 396, 397 401, 432
Rolin-Jaequemyns, G., 507
Rolland, R., *103*, 114
Roosevelt, Eleanor, 594
Roosevelt, F.D., 570, 571, 582, 583
Roosevelt, T., 514, 515, 516, 517, 518, 523
Root, E., 514, *517*, 518, 526, 570
Rosa, V., 413
Rosenheim, O., 216, 231
Ross, R., 160, 162, *163*
Rous, P., 178, 189, *190*
Roux, E., 159
Roux, W., 195, 196
Rowland, H.A., 392, 407
Royds, T., 308
Rudbeck, O., 3
Rudbeck, Vendela, 3
Ruhmkorff, H.D., 394
Runge, C., 392
Rushton, W.A.H., 266
Russell, A.S., 311
Russell, B.A.W., *120*
Rutherford, E., 307, 308 *309*, 310, 315, 316, 380, 400, 402, 430, 456, 457, 464, 468
Ružicka, L., 356, *357*, 369, 370
Rydberg, J.R., 392
Rydberg, V., 78, 92, 93, 430, 431

Saavedra Lamás, C., 555, 566
Sabatier, P., 350, *351*
Sabin, A.B., 180
Sachs, Nelly, *132*
Salam, A., 463
Sanger, F., 225, 335, *379*, 380, 381
Santesson, H., 56, 68, 71, 72
Sarrau, E., 21
Sartre, J.-P., *130*
Sauton, B., 182
Savart, F., 392
Sazerac, R., 182
Scharlach, J., 54, 58
Schatz, A., 185

Schaudinn, F., 168, 182
Scheele, C.W., 214, 297, 303, 355, 480
Schelling, F. von, 110
Schmidt, G.C., 399
Schönheyder, F., 232
Schou, A, IX, 483
Schramm, G., 201
Schrödinger, E., 446, 447, *448*
Schück, H., IX, 1, 87, 105, 106, 108, 116, 278
Schücking, W., 543
Schweidler, E. von, 400
Schweigaard, C.H., 68
Schweitzer, A., 596, 597, 598
Schwinger, J., 453
Seaborg, G.T., 322, *323*
Seeckt, H. von, 543
Seferis, G., 129, 130
Segrè, E.G., 462
Seligmann, J., 51, 52, 59
Semenov, N.N., *341*, 342
Senderens, J.B., 350
Shaw, G.B., 77, *109*, 136
Shelly, P.B., 9, 11, 12, 75, 76, 78, 484
Sherrington, C.S., 243, 245, 246, *247*, *254*, 257, 258
Shields, J., 300
Shockley, W., *417*
Sholokhov, M., 130, *131*
Shope, E.R., 178, 189
Sidenbladh, E., 71
Siedentopf, H., 330
Siegbahn, K., also on page IX, 386
Siegbahn, M., also on page IX, 338 foot-note, 386, *437*, 438, 481, 482
Sienkiewicz, H., 88, *95*, 96
Sikelianos, A., 129
Sillanpää, F.E., *115*, 116
Simon, J., 539
Skrzynski, A., 541
Slater, J.C., 339
Slocumb, C.H., 227
Smith, J.L., 209
Smith, L., 233
Smith, T., 163, 168
Smith, W., 178
Smitt, F.A., 56
Smitt, J.V., 28
Smoluckowski, M. von, 331
Smuts, J., 527, 528, 560
Snoilsky, C., 83, 85
Sobolev, L.V., 224
Sobrero, A., 5
Soddy, F., 307, 310, *311*, 402
Söderblom, N., 10, 38, 99, 488, 489, *547*, *548*, 549, 607
Sohlman, H., 41
Sohlman, R., IX, 15, 50, 62, 71, 613
Solshenitsyn, A., *134*, 135
Sommerfeld, A., 431
Spemann, H., 196, *197*
Spencer, H., 87, 498
Spengler, O., 598
Spitteler, C.F.G., 83, 102, *104*, 105
Ståhle, N., IX, 608
Stakman, E.C., 605
Stamp, J., 536
Stang, E., 68
Stang, F., 565
Stanley, W.M., *178*, *377*
Stark, J., 408, 432, 447
Starling, E.H., 223
Stas, J.S., 312
Staudinger, H., 357, *358*
Steen, J., 68
Steenbock, H., 230, 231
Stefan, J., 426, 427
Steinbeck, J., 128, *129*
Stern, L., 211
Stern, O., *450*, 451
Stevenson, A.F., 460
Stifter, A., 118
Stokes, A., 179
Storm, T., 93
Stowe, Harriet Beecher, 499
Strassmann, F., 321
Strauss, D.F., 542
Street, J.C., 460
Strehlenert, R.V., 31, 49
Stresemann, G., 535, 537, 539, 540, 541
Strindberg, A., 35, 77, 90, 99, 109
Strömholm, D., 310
Strutt, J.W., *421*
Sturli, A., 173
Sturtevant, A.H., 192, 194
Suess, H., 466
Sully Prudhomme, R.F.A., *91*, 92, *93*
Sumner, J.B., 212, 376, *377*
Suttner, Arthur von, 25, 26, 498
Suttner, Bertha S.F. von, 7, 12, 36, 485, 490, 498, 500, 501, 607
Sutton, W., 191

Svaetichin, G., 266
Svedberg, T., 310, *330*, 331, 332, 376
Svirbely, J.L., 230
Swinburne, C., 88, 96, 97
Swingle, W.W., 226
Synge, R.L.M., 201, *334*, 335, 362
Szent-Györgyi, A. von, 212, *213*, 221, 230, 367, 368

Taft, W.H., 526
Tagore, R., 100, 101, *102*
Tamm, I.J., 470, *471*
Tatum, E.L., *198*, 199
Taveau, R. de M., 261
Taylor, H.S., 479
Tegnér, E., 83, 101
Teller, E., 589
Theiler, M., 179, *180*
Theorell, H., 211, *212*, 275, 276
Thomsen, J., 287, 290, 390
Thomson, G.P., *445*, *446*
Thomson, J.J., 396, 400, *404*, *405*, 411, 432, 445
Thomson, W., 390
Thunberg, T., 210, 211, 214
Tiselius, A.W.K., 332, *333*, *334*
Todd, A.R., 200, *371*, 372
Törnebladh, R., 71
Törnebohm, A.E., 71
Tolstoy, L.N., 90, 91, 92, 95, 113, 552
Tomonaga, S., 453
Townes, C.H., 417, *418*
Trefouël, J., 183
Truman, H.S., 573
Tschermak, E. von, 191
Tschombe, M., 579
Tsutsui, H., 189
Tswett, M., 333
Turgenev, L., 113
Tuve, M.A., 416
Twort, F.W., 206

Uhlenhurt, P., 172, 182
Ullman, V., 68
Undset, Sigrid, *110*
Ungar, G., 260
Urey, H.C., 313, *314*

Valéry, P., 88, 90
Van der Waals, J.D., 396, *422*
Van't Hoff, J.H., 287, 288, *289*, 290, 291, 293, 294, 295, 324, 341, 353, 355, 479
Varley, C.F., 403
Vavilov, 470
Vieille, P.M.E., 21
Vigneaud, V. du, 370, *371*
Villard, P., 401
Vincent, H., 161
Virtanen, A.I., 383, *384*
Vogel, O., 605
Vries, H. de, 191, 193

Waage, P., 290
Waern, C., 49
Waern, J., 71
Wagner-Jauregg, J., *187*
Waksman, S.A., 185, *186*
Wald, G., *265*, 266
Waldeck-Roussau, P., 54
Waldeyer, W., 245
Wallach, O., 355, *356*
Walton, E.T.S., 468, *469*
Warburg, O.H., 208, 209, *210*, 211, 368, 369
Warren, T., 48, 58, 59
Washburn, E.W., 314
Wassermann, A. von, 171, 172
Watson, J.D., 201, *202*,
Weardale, Lord, 521
Webster, T.A., 231
Wehberg, H., 501
Weiner, A.S., 174
Weiss, P., 474
Weizäcker, C.F. v., 467
Weller, T.H., 180, *181*
Wells, H.G., 113
Wendt, H., 369
Werkman, C.H., 216
Werner, A., *344*, 345
Westgren, A., IX, 279, 476
Westphal, K., 58, 59, 369
Whipple, G.H., 232, *233*
Widal, F., 171
Widman, O., 298
Widmark, J., 186, 187
Wiechert, E., 407
Wiegand, C., 462
Wieland, H.O., 210, 211, 216, 217, *364*, 365
Wien, W., *427*, 428
Wiener, O., 442

Wigner, E.P., 465, 466
Wilcke, J.C., 480
Wilhelm II, 513, 542
Wilkins, M., 201, *202*, 380
Willstätter, R.M., *360*, 361, 362, 376
Wilson, C.T.R., 316, 405, *439*, 454, 460, 471
Wilson, Woodrow, 523, 524, 525, 526, 527
Windaus, A.O.R., 216, 231, *364*, 365, 366
Wirsén, C.D., 56, 61, 71, 80, 83, 85, 87, 88, 91, 92, 94, 98, 99, 100
Wiznievski, Countess, 491
Wood, H.G., 216
Woodward, R.B., 352, *353*
Wright, A., 161
Wroblewski, S.F., 423

Yamagiwa, K., 189
Yang, C.N., 461, 466
Yeats, W.B., 88, *107*, 136
Yersin, A., 159, 168
Young, O., 536
Young, T., 266
Young, W.J. 374
Ypsilantis, T., 462
Yukawa, H., *459*

Zeeman, P., 397, *407*, 408, 418, 432, 447
Zernike, F., 442, *443*
Zeromski, S., 108
Ziegler, K., *358*, 359
Zinin, N., 5
Zinzendorf, L. von, 101
Zola, É., 91, 106
Zotterman, Y., 253
Zsigmondy, R.A., *330*, 331, 332

Wright, B. F. [illegible]
Wilson, C. 430
Wilson, H. [illegible]
Wilkins, M. [illegible]
[illegible]
Wilson, C. T. R. [illegible]
[illegible]
Wright, W. [illegible]

Williams, [illegible]
[illegible]
Wilson, [illegible]
[illegible]
[illegible]
Wood, [illegible]
Woodward, [illegible]
Wright, [illegible]
[illegible]

Yamakawa, K., 384
Yens, C. N., [illegible]
Yeh, W. H., [illegible]
[illegible], A., [illegible]
Young, C. [illegible]
Young, T. [illegible]
Young, W. J. [illegible]
[illegible]
[illegible]

[illegible]
[illegible]
[illegible]
[illegible]
[illegible]
[illegible]
[illegible]
[illegible]